Speech

Learning, Development, and Conceptual Change
Lila Gleitman, Susan Carey, Elissa Newport, and Elizabeth Spelke, editors

Names for Things: A Study in Human Learning, John Macnamara, 1982

Conceptual Change in Childhood, Susan Carey, 1985

"Gavagai!" or the Future History of the Animal Language Controversy, David Premack, 1986

System That Learn: An Introduction to Learning Theory for Cognitive and Computer Scientists, Daniel N. Osherson, 1986

From Simple Input to Complex Grammar, James L. Morgan, 1986

Concepts, Kinds, and Cognitive Development, Frank C. Keil, 1989

Learnability and Cognition: The Acquisition of Argument Structure, Steven Pinker, 1989

Mind Bugs: The Origins of Procedural Misconception, Kurt VanLehn, 1990

Categorization and Naming in Children: Problems of Induction, Ellen M. Markman, 1990

The Child's Theory of Mind, Henry M. Wellman, 1990

The Organization of Learning, Charles R. Gallistel, 1990

Understanding the Representational Mind, Josef Perner, 1991

An Odyssey in Learning and Perception, Eleanor J. Gibson, 1991

Beyond Modularity: A Developmental Perspective on Cognitive Science, Annette Karmiloff-Smith, 1992

Mindblindness: An Essay on Autism and "Theory of Mind," Simon Baron-Cohen, 1995

Speech: A Special Code, Alvin M. Liberman, 1996

Speech: A Special Code

Alvin M. Liberman

A Bradford Book
The MIT Press
Cambridge, Massachusetts
London, England

© 1996 Massachusetts Institute of Technology

All rights reserved. No part of this book may be reproduced in any form by any electronic or mechanical means (including photocopying, recording, or information storage and retrieval) without permission in writing from the publisher.

This book was set in Palatino by Asco Trade Typesetting Ltd., Hong Kong and was printed and bound in the United States of America.

Library of Congress Cataloging-in-Publication Data

Liberman, Alvin M. (Alvin Meyer)
  Speech : a special code / Alvin M. Liberman.
    p.   cm.—(Learning, development, and conceptual change)
  "A Bradford book."
  Includes bibliographical references and index.
  ISBN 0-262-12192-1 (alk. paper)
  1. Speech perception. I. Title. II. Series.
BF463.S64L52   1995
153.7—dc20   95-30668
                                                  CIP

For Isabelle, Mark, Charles, and Sarah

Contents

Series Forward   xi
Acknowledgments   xiii

Chapter 1
Introduction: Some Assumptions about Speech and How They Changed   1

PART I
On the Spectrogram as a Visible Display of Speech

Introduction   47

Chapter 2
The Interconversion of Audible and Visible Patterns as a Basis for Research in the Perception of Speech (1951)   49

PART II
Finding the Cues

Introduction   57

Chapter 3
The Role of Selected Stimulus-Variables in the Perception of the Unvoiced Stop Consonants (1952)   59

Chapter 4
The Role of Consonant-Vowel Transitions in the Perception of the Stop and Nasal Consonants (1954)   75

Chapter 5
Acoustic Loci and Transitional Cues for Consonants (1955)   89

Chapter 6
Tempo of Frequency Change as a Cue for Distinguishing Classes of Speech Sounds (1956)   99

Chapter 7
Effect of Third-Formant Transitions on the Perception of the Voiced Stop Consonants (1958)   111

Chapter 8
Some Cues for the Distinction between Voiced and Voiceless Stops in Initial Position (1958)   121

Chapter 9
Minimal Rules for Synthesizing Speech (1959)   133

PART III
Categorical Perception

Introduction   151

Chapter 10
The Discrimination of Speech Sounds within and across Phoneme Boundaries (1957)   153

Chapter 11
An Effect of Learning on Speech Perception: The Discrimination of Durations of Silence with and without Phonemic Significance (1961)   165

PART IV
An Early Attempt to Put It All Together

Introduction   185

Chapter 12
Some Results of Research on Speech Perception (1957)   187

PART V
A Mid-Course Correction

Introduction   201

Chapter 13
Perception of the Speech Code (1967)   203

PART VI
The Revised Motor Theory

Introduction   235

Chapter 14
The Motor Theory of Speech Perception Revised (1985)   237

PART VII
Some Properties of the Phonetic Module

Introduction   269

Chapter 15
Specialized Perceiving Systems for Speech and Other Biologically Significant Sounds (1988)   271

PART VIII
More about the Function and Properties of the Phonetic Module

Introduction   291

Chapter 16
A Specialization for Speech Perception (1989)   293

PART IX
Auditory vs. Phonetic Modes

Introduction   307

Chapter 17
An Effect of Linguistic Experience: The Discrimination of [r] and [l] by Native Speakers of Japanese and English (1975)   309

Chapter 18
Some Experiments on the Sound of Silence in Phonetic Perception (1979)   325

Chapter 19
Perceptual Integration of Acoustic Cues for Stop, Fricative, and Affricate Manner (1978)   351

Chapter 20
Perceptual Equivalence of Two Acoustic Cues for Stop-Consonant Manner (1980)   371

Chapter 21
Duplex Perception of Cues for Stop Consonants: Evidence for a Phonetic Mode (1981)   385

Chapter 22
Some Differences between Phonetic and Auditory Modes of Perception (1983)   403

Chapter 23
Speech Perception Takes Precedence over Nonspeech Perception (1987)   423

PART X
Reading/Writing Are Hard Just Because Speaking/Listening Are Easy

Introduction   431

Chapter 24
The Relation of Speech to Reading and Writing (1992)   433

Index   447

Series Foreword

This series in learning, development, and conceptual change will include state-of-the-art reference works, seminal book-length monographs, and texts on the development of concepts and mental structures. It will span learning in all domains of knowledge, from syntax to geometry to the social world, and will be concerned with all phases of development, from infancy through adulthood.

The series intends to engage such fundamental questions as

The nature and limits of learning and maturation: the influence of the environment, of initial structures, and of maturational changes in the nervous system on human development; learnability theory; the problem of induction; domain-specific constraints on development.

The nature of conceptual change: conceptual organization and conceptual change in child development, in the acquisition of expertise, and in the history of science.

Lila Gleitman
Susan Carey
Elissa Newport
Elizabeth Spelke

Acknowledgments

The many colleagues to whom I am indebted are named at various points in this introduction and as co-authors of the chapters that follow. Others who have offered helpful comments include Ruth Millikan, Kenneth Wilson, Milton Stern, Julius Elias, Elizabeth Spelke, Lila Gleitman, Mark Liberman, Cynthia McLemore, Randy Diehl, and Keith Kluender. I would also like to thank Amy Pierce and Kathleen Caruso, both of The MIT Press.

The research that underlies all the chapters of this book has been supported by the National Institute of Child Health and Human Development under Grant HD 01994. I am moved here to offer special thanks to the agency for its long-continued help, and to Dr. James Kavanagh, a member of its staff, for the kind and wise counsel that he has, for so many years, given me. I am indebted to Alice Dadourian for her invaluable assistance with virtually everything that appears in this book.

Chapter 1

Introduction: Some Assumptions about Speech and How They Changed

Reprinted in this book are papers that sample the progress, as I saw it, of research on speech at the Haskins Laboratories. That progress was slow and not always steady, partly because we spent so much time developing appropriate methods, but mostly because we were so ill prepared for what we found. In getting from where we started to where I think we are now, we therefore left a long trail of assumptions. I aim in this introduction to describe the development of those assumptions, hewing as closely as I can to the order in which they were made, and then either modified or abandoned. The resulting essay is intended to stand on its own feet, and also to provide a framework for the collection of papers that follows.

My account is necessarily inaccurate, not just because I must rely in part on memory about my state of mind almost fifty years ago when, in the earliest stages of our work, we did not always make our underlying assumptions explicit, but, even more, for reasons that put a proper account beyond the reach of any recall, however true. The chief difficulty is in the relation between the theoretical assumptions and the research they were supposed to rationalize. Thus, it happened only once, as I see it now, that the assumptions changed promptly in response to the results of a particular experiment; in all other cases, they lagged behind, as reinterpretations of data that had accumulated over a considerable period of time. Moreover, theory was influenced not only by our empirical findings, but equally, if even more belatedly, by general considerations of plausibility that arose when, stimulated by colleagues and by the gradual broadening of my own outlook, I began to give proper consideration to the special requirements of phonological communication and to all that is entailed by the fact that speech is a species-typical product of biological evolution. The consequence for development of theory was that, with the one exception just noted, I never changed my mind abruptly, but rather segued from each earlier position to each later one, leaving behind no clear sign to mark the time, the extent of the change, or the reason for making it. Faced now with having to describe a theory that was in almost constant flux, I can only offer what I must, in retrospect, make to seem a progress through distinct stages.

My account is also necessarily presumptuous, because I will sometimes say "we" when I probably should have said "I," and vice versa. In so doing, I am not trying to avoid blame for bad ideas that were entirely mine, nor to claim credit for good ideas that I had no part in hatching. It is, rather, that everything I have done or thought in research on speech has been profoundly influenced by my colleagues at the Laboratories. In most cases, however, I can't say with certainty just how or by whom. A consequence is that, of all the words I use in this chronicle, the most ambiguous by far are "I" and "we."

"I" began to be confused with "we" on a day in June 1944, when I was offered a job at the Laboratories to work with Frank Cooper on the development of a reading machine for the blind, a device that would convert printed letters into intelligible sounds. Of course, we appreciated from the outset that the ideal machine would render the print as speech that the blind user had already mastered. Though that is done quite routinely now, it was, in 1944, far beyond the science and technology that was available to us. There were no optical character readers to identify the letters, and no rules for synthesis that would have enabled us to produce speech from their outputs. But, reassured by our assumptions about the relation of speech to language, of which more later, we did not think it critical that the machine should speak. Rather, we supposed that it had only to produce distinctive sounds of some kind that the blind would then learn to associate with the consonants and vowels of the language, much as we supposed they had done at an earlier stage of their lives with the sounds of speech. Thus conceived, our enterprise lay in the domains of auditory perception and discrimination learning, two subjects I had presumably mastered as a graduate student at Yale University. Indeed, my dissertation had been based on experiments about discrimination learning to acoustic stimuli, and I was thoroughly familiar with the neobehaviorist, stimulus-response theory that was thought by my professors and me to account for the results. In the course of my education in psychology, I had learned nothing about speech, but I didn't think that mattered, because the theory I had absorbed was supposed, like most other theories in psychology, to apply to everything. I was, therefore, enthusiastic about the job, confident that I knew exactly how to make the reading machine serve its intended purpose, and so put the theory to practical use. In the event, the theory—and, indeed, virtually everything else I had learned—proved to be, at best, irrelevant and, at worst, misleading. I think it unlikely that I would ever have discovered that had it not been for two fortunate, as they proved to be, circumstances. One was the collaboration, from the outset with Frank Cooper, whose gentle but nonetheless insistent prodding helped me accept that the theory might be wrong, and see what might be more nearly right. The other was that speech lay constantly before me, providing an existence proof that language could be conveyed efficiently by sound, and thus setting the high standard by which I was bound to evaluate the performance of the acoustic substitutes for speech that our early assumptions led us to contrive. But for Frank Coooper on the one hand and speech on the other, I might still be massaging those substitutes and modifying the conditions of learning, satisfied to achieve trivial improvements in systems that were, by comparison with speech, hopelessly inadequate. As it was, experience in trying to find an alternative set of sounds brought Frank and, ultimately, me to the conclusion that speech is uniquely effective as an acoustic vehicle for language. It remained only to find out why.

But I get ahead of the story. To set out from the proper beginning, I should say why we initially believed there was nothing special about speech or its underlying processes, and where that belief led us, not only in the several stages of the reading machine enterprise, but also in the development of, and early work with, a research synthesizer we called the Pattern Playback.

The assumptions about speech that have been made by us and others differ in many details. As I see it now, however, there is one question that stands above those details, dividing theories neatly into two categories: Does speech recruit motor and perceptual processes of a general sort, processes that cut horizontally across a wide variety of behaviors; or does it belong to a special phonetic mode, a distinct kind of action and perception comprising a vertical arrangement of structures and mechanisms specifically and exclusively adapted for linguistic communication? I will use this issue as the basis for organizing my account of the assumptions we made, calling them "horizontal" or "vertical" according to the side of the divide on which they fall. (For references to papers that offer these views, see the lists at the end of this introduction.)

The Horizontal View of Speech and the Design of Reading Machines

As it pertains to the perceptual side of the speech process, the horizontal view, which is how we saw speech at the outset, rests on three assumptions: (1) The constituents of speech are sounds. (2) Perception of these sounds is managed by processes of a general auditory sort, processes that evoke percepts no different in kind from those produced in response to other sounds. (3) The percepts evoked by the sounds of speech, being inherently auditory, must be invested with phonetic significance, and that can be done only by means of a cognitive translation. Accordingly, the horizontal view assumes a second stage, beyond perception, where the purely auditory percepts are given phonetic names, measured against phonetic prototypes, or associated with "distinctive feature." Seen this way, perceiving speech is no different in principle from reading script; listener and reader alike perceive one thing and learn to call it something else.

These assumptions were—and, perhaps, still are—so much a part of the received view that we could hardly imagine an alternative; it simply did not occur to us to question them, or even to make them explicit. At all events, it was surely these conventional assumptions that gave us confidence in our assumption that nonspeech sounds could be made to work as well as speech, for what they clearly implied was that the processes by which blind users would learn to "read" our sounds would differ in no important way from those by which they had presumably learned to perceive speech. Our task, then, was simply to contrive sounds of sufficient distinctiveness, and then design the procedures by which the blind would learn to associate them with language.

Auditory Discriminability Is All It Takes
As for distinctiveness, I was, at the outset, firmly in the grip of the notion that it was just so much psychophysical discriminability, almost as if it were to be had simply by separating the stimuli one from another by a sufficient number of just-noticeable-differences. This notion fit all too nicely with our ability, even then, to engineer a print-to-sound machine that would meet the discriminability requirement, for such a machine had only to control selected parameters of its acoustic output according to what was seen by a photocell positioned behind a narrow scanning slit. Provided, then, that we chose wisely among the many possible ways in which the sound could be made to reflect what the photocell saw, the auditory results would be discriminable, hence learnable.

In all these machines the sound would be controlled directly by the amount or vertical position of the print under the scanning slit. We therefore called them "direct translators" to distinguish them from an imaginable kind we called "recognition machines," having in mind a device that might one day be available to identify each letter, as present-day optical character readers do, and produce in response a preset sound of any conceivable type. Since we were in no position to build a recognition machine, we set our sights initially on a direct translator.

We were aware that a reading machine of the direct-translation kind had been constructed and tested in England just after World War I. This machine, called the Optophone, scanned the print with five beams of light, each modulated at a different audio frequency. When a beam encountered print, a tone was made to sound at a frequency (hence, pitch) equal to the frequency at which that beam was modulated. Thus, as the scanning slit and its beams were moved across the print, the user heard a continuously changing musical chord, the composition of which depended, instant by instant, on the modulation frequencies of the beams that struck print. The user's task, of course, was to learn to interpret the changing chords as letters and words. I recall not ever knowing what tests, if any, had been carried out to determine just how useful the machine was, only that a blind woman in Scotland had been able to make her way through simple newspaper text. We did know that the machine was not in use anywhere in 1944, so we could only assume that it had been found wanting. At all events, the lesson I took from the Optophone was not that an acoustic alphabet is no substitute for speech, but that the particular alphabet produced by the Optophone was not a good one. Moreover, it seemed likely, given the early date at which the machine had been made, that the signal was less than ideally clear. I, perhaps more than Frank, was sure we could do better. (Indeed, I think that Frank, even at this early stage, had reservations about any machine that read letter by letter, but he shared my belief that we could design a letter-reading machine good enough to be of some use.)

Doing better, as we conceived it then, simply meant producing more learnable sounds. Unfortunately, there was nothing in the literature on auditory perception to tell us how to do that, so we set out to explore various possibilities. For that purpose, Frank built a device with which we could simulate the performance of almost any direct translator, with the one limitation that the subjects of our experiments were not free to choose the texts or to control the rate of scan. (This was because the print had to be scanned by passing a film negative of the text across a fixed slit.) Otherwise, the simulator was quite adequate for producing the outputs we would want to screen before settling on those that deserved further testing.

For much of the initial screening, Frank and I made the evaluations ourselves after determining roughly how well we could discriminate the sounds for a selected set of letters and words. On this basis, we quickly came to the conclusion that there was, perhaps, some promise in a system that used the print to modulate the frequency of the output signal. (Certainly, this was very much better than modulating the amplitude, which had been tried first.) Having made this early decision, we experimented with different orientations and widths of the slit, the shape of the sound wave, and the range of modulation, selecting, finally, a vertical orientation of a slit that was somewhat narrower than, say, the vertical bar of a lowercase *t*, and a sine wave with a modulation range of 100 to 4,000 Hz.

Further informal tests with this frequency-modulation (FM) system showed that it failed to provide a basis for discriminating certain letters (for example, *n* and *u*), which led us to conclude that it would likely prove in more thorough tests to be not good enough. This conclusion did not discourage me, however, for I reckoned that the difficulty was only that the signal variation, being one-dimensional, was not sufficiently complex. Make the signals more complexly multidimensional, I reasoned, so that somewhere in the complexity the listeners would find what they needed as the basis for associating that signal with the letter it represented. I recall that here, too, Frank was skeptical, but, open-minded as always, he agreed to try more elaborate arrangements. In one, the Dual FM, the slit was divided into an upper and lower half (each with its own photocell), so that two tones, one in the upper part of the 4,000-Hz range, the other in the lower, would be independently modulated. In another (Super FM), the slit was divided into thirds (each with its own photocell), and the difference between the output of the middle cell and the sum of the upper and lower cells controlled the (relatively slow) frequency modulations of a base tone, while the sum of all three cells controlled an audio frequency at which the base tone was itself frequency modulated. The effect of this latter modulation was to create side bands on the base frequency at intervals equal to the modulation frequency, and thus cause frequent, sudden, and usually gross changes in timbre and pitch as a consequence of the amount and position of the print under the slit. At all events, the signals of the Super FM seemed to me to vary in wonderfully complex ways, and so to provide a fair test of my assumption about the necessary condition for distinctiveness and learnability. We also simulated the Optophone, together with a variant on it in which, in a crude attempt to create consonant-like effects, we had the risers and descenders of the print produce various hisses and clicks. We even tried an arrangement in which the print controlled the frequency positions of two formantlike bands, giving an impression of constantly changing vowel color.

We tested all of these systems, together with three or four others of similar type, by finding how readily subjects could learn to associate the sounds with eight of the most common four-letter words. To determine how well these systems did in relation to speech, we applied the same test to an artificial language that we spoke simply by transposing phonological segments. Thus, vowels were converted into vowels, stops into stops, fricatives into fricatives, etc., so that the syllable structure remained unchanged, hence easy for our human reading machine to pronounce. We called this new language "Wuhzi," in honor of one of the transposed words.

The results of the learning test were simple enough: of all the nonspeech signals tested, the original, simple FM and the original Optophone were the most nearly learnable; all others trailed far behind. Worst of all, and by a considerable margin, were the extremely complex signals of the Super FM, the system for which I had entertained such high hopes. As for Wuhzi, the transposed speech, it was in a class of its own. It was mastered (for the purposes of the test) in about fifteen trials, in contrast to the nonspeech sounds, on which subjects were, after twenty-four trials, performing at a level of only 60 percent with the simple FM and Optophone signals, and at 50 percent or lower for the others, and all seemed at, or close to, their asymptotes. More troubling was the fact that learnability of the nonspeech signals went down appreciably as the rate of scan was increased, even at modest levels of rate. What should have been most troubling, however, were the indications that learning would be rate specific. Though we did not pursue the point, it seemed clear in my own experience with the FM system that what I had learned to "read" at a rate of, say, ten words per minute, did not transfer to a rate of fifty. My impression, as I remember it now, was not that things sounded much the same, only speeded up, but rather that the percept had changed entirely, with the result that I could no longer recognize whatever I had learned to respond to at the slower speed. To the extent that this observation was correct, users would have had to learn a different nonspeech "language" for every significantly different rate of reading, and that alone would have made the system impractical. It also became clear that at rates above fifty or so words per minute, listeners could identify the words only on the basis of some overall impression—I am reluctant to call it a pattern—in which the individual components were not readily retrievable. The consequence of this, though we did not take proper account of it at the time, was that perception of the nonspeech signals would have been, at best, logophonic, as it were, not phonologic, so users would have had to learn to identify as many sounds are there were words to be read, and would not have been able to fall back on their phonologic resources in order to cope with new words.

At this point it had become evident that, as Frank had been saying for some time, perception of the acoustic alphabet produced by any letter-reading machine would be severely limited by the temporal resolving power of the ear—that is, by its poor ability to segregate and properly order acoustic events that are presented briefly and in rapid succession. Taking account of the number of discrete frequency peaks in each alphabetic sound and the average number of alphabetic characters per word, we estimated the maximum rate to be around fifty words per minute, which I now believe to have been very much on the high side of what might have been achieved. Still, fifty words per minute would be quite useful for many purposes, and we had a considerable investment in the letter-reading direct-translator kind of system, so we felt obliged to see how far a subject could go, given control of the scanning rate, a great variety of printed material, and much practice. Frank therefore built a working model of a direct-translating FM reading machine, and we set several subjects to work trying to master it. After ninety hours of practice, our best subject was able to manage a fifth-grade reader (without correction) at an average speed of about four words per minute. Moreover, the subject seemed to have reached her peak performance during the first forty-five hours. Comparing performance at the end of that period with performance after ninety hours, we found no increase in rate and no decrease in errors. Tests of the same system conducted by John Flynn at the Naval Medical Research Laboratory yielded results that gave no more grounds for optimism.

I must not omit from this account a reference to our experience with a sighted subject named (dare I say, appropriately?) Eve, who, having first produced a properly shaped learning curve, attained a reading speed of over one hundred words per minute, and convincingly demonstrated her skill before the distinguished scientists who were sponsoring our research. In that demonstration, as in all of her work with the machine, she wore blacked-out welder's goggles so she would not suffer the discomfort of having to keep her eyes shut tight. We all remember the day when one of our number, acting on what seemed an ungentlemanly impulse, put an opaque screen between her and the print she was "reading," at which point she bounded from her chair and fled the lab, confessing later to the young man who had been monitoring her practice sessions that, by leaning her cheek against her fist, she had, from the very beginning, been raising the bottom of the goggles and so seeing the print. In designing the training and testing procedures, I had controlled for every possibility except that one. Obviously, I was the wrong kind of psychologist.

Having concluded at last that, given the properties of the auditory system, letter-by-letter reading machines were destined to be unsatisfactory, we experimented briefly with a system in which the sound was controlled by information that had been integrated across several letters. This was intended to reduce the rate at which discrete acoustic events were delivered to the ear, and so circumvent the limitation imposed by its temporal resolving power. I cannot now imagine what we thought about the consequences of having to associate holistically different sounds with linguistically arbitrary conjunctions of letters. But whatever it was that we did or did not have in mind, this integrating type of reading machine failed every test and was quickly abandoned.

One other scheme we tested deserves mention if only because it now seems incredible that we should ever have considered it. I suppose we felt obliged to look forward to the time when optical character readers would be available, and so to test some presumably appropriate output of the "recognition" machine that would then be possible. Prerecorded "phonemes" seemed an obvious choice. After all, the acoustic manifestations of phonemes were known to be distinctive, and people had, on the horizontal view, already learned to connect them to language. As for difficulty with rate, we must have supposed that these sounds carried within them the seeds of their own integration into larger wholes. At all events, we recorded various phonemes on film—'duh' for /d/, 'luh' for /l/, etc.—and then carefully spliced the pieces of film together into words and sentences. The result was wholly unintelligible, even at moderate rates, and gave every indication of forever remaining so.

Perhaps Auditory Patterning Is the Answer
From all this experience with nonspeech we drew two conclusions, one right, one wrong. The right conclusion was that an acoustic alphabet is no way to convey language. Of course, it was humbling for me to realize that I might have reached that conclusion without all the work on the reading machines, simply by measuring the known temporal-resolving characteristics of the ear against the rate at which the discrete sounds would have to be perceived. As I have already suggested, Frank must have thought this through, though he might not have been sufficiently pessimistic about the limits, and that would account for his early opinion that an acoustic alphabet might be at least marginally useful. I, on the other hand, took the point only after seeing our early results and having my nose rubbed in them.

The wrong conclusion—wrong because it was still uncompromisingly horizontal in outlook—was that what we needed was not discriminability but proper auditory patterning. Speech succeeds, we decided, because its sounds conform to certain gestalt-like principles that yield perceptually distinctive patterns, and cause the phonetic elements to be integrated into the larger wholes of syllables and words. Apparently, it did not occur to me that phonological communication would be impossible if the discrete and commutable elements it requires were to be absorbed into indissoluble gestalten. Nor did I bother to wonder how speakers might have managed their articulators so as to force all of the many covarying but not-independently-controllable aspects of the acoustic signal to collaborate in such a way as to produce just those sounds that would form distinctive wholes.

In any case, nobody knew what the principles of auditory pattern perception were. Research in audition, unlike the corresponding effort in vision, had been quite narrowly psychophysical, having been carried out with experimental stimuli that were not sufficiently complex to reveal such pattern perception as there might be. So if, for the purposes of the reading machine, we were going to make its sounds conform to the principles that underlie good auditory patterns, we had first to find the principles. We therefore decided to turn away from the reading machine work until we should have succeeded in that search. We were the more motivated to undertake it, because the outcome would not only advance the construction of a reading machine, but also count, more generally, as a valuable contribution to the science of auditory perception.

The Pattern Playback: Making the Right Move for the Wrong Reason

It is exactly true, and important for understanding how horizontal our attitude remained, to say that our aim at this stage was to study the perception of patterned sounds in general, not speech in particular. As for the reading machine, we did not suppose we would use our results to make it speak, only that we would have it produce sounds that would be as good as speech because they would conform to the same principles of auditory perception. These would be sounds that, except for the accidents of language development, might as well have been speech. Obviously, we would look to speech for examples of demonstrably well patterned sounds. Indeed, we would be especially attentive to speech, but only because we did not know where else to search for clues. At this stage, however, our interest lay in auditory perception.

Since we barely knew where to begin, we expected to rely, especially at the outset, on trial and error. Accordingly, we had to have some easy way to produce and modify a large number and wide variety of acoustic patterns. The sound spectrograph and the spectrograms it produced were no longer a wartime secret, and, like many others, we were impressed with the extent to which spectrograms made sense to the eye. (Figure 1.1 is a spectrogram of a speech sample, with labels that identify the various parts.) Beyond a doubt, they provided an excellent basis for examining speech; it seemed to us a small step to suppose that they would serve equally well for the purpose of experimenting with it. The experimenter would have immediately available

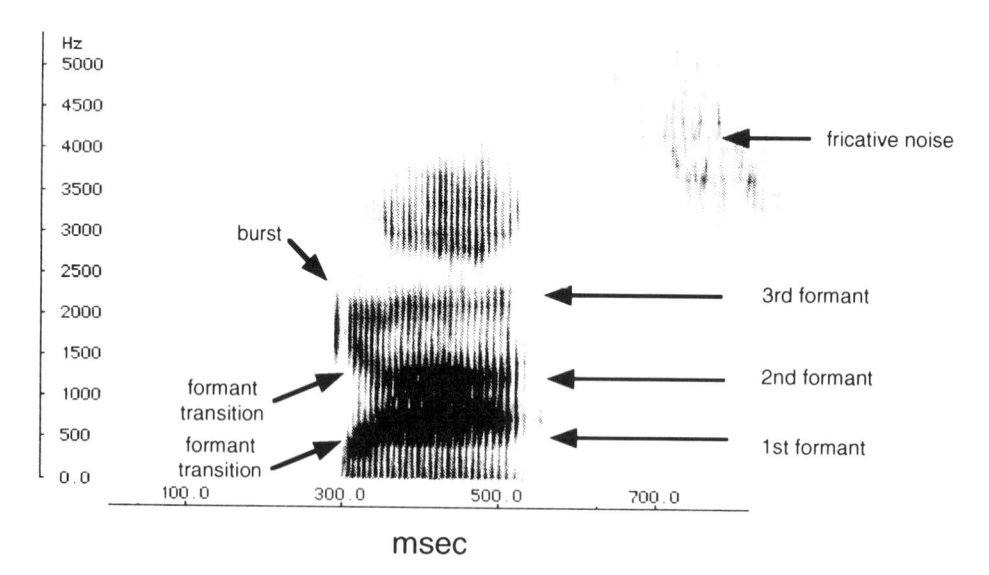

Figure 1.1
Spectrogram of the syllable /gas/, showing the phonetically important parts of the pattern.

the patterned essence of the sound, and thus easily grasp the parameters that deserved his attention. These would be changed to suit his aims, and he would then have only to observe the effects of the experimental changes on the sound as heard. But that required a complement to the spectrograph—that is, a device that would convert spectrograms, as well as the changes made on them, into sound.

It was in response to these aims and needs that the Pattern Playback was designed and, in the case of its most important components, actually built by Frank Cooper. My role was simply to offer occasional words of encouragement, and, as the device took shape, to appreciate it as a triumph of design, a successful realization of Frank's determination to provide experimental and conceptual convenience to the researcher. The need for that convenience is, I think, hard to appreciate fully, except as one has lived through the early stages of our speech research, when little was known about acoustic phonetics, and progress depended critically, therefore, on the ability to test guesses at the rate of dozens per day.

Seven years elapsed between the start of our enterprise and the publication of the first paper for which we could claim significance. I would therefore here record that the support of the Haskins Laboratories and the Carnegie Corporation of New York was a notable and, to Frank and me, essential exercise of faith and patience. Few universities or granting agencies would then have been, or would now be, similarly supportive of two young investigators who were trying for such a long time to develop an unproved method to investigate a question—what is special about speech that it works so well?—that was not otherwise being asked. I managed to survive in academe by changing universities frequently, thus confusing the promotion-tenure committees, and also by loudly trumpeting two rat-learning studies that I published as extensions of my thesis research.

There were many reasons it took so long to get from aim to goal. One was the failure, after two years of work, of the first model of the device that was to serve as our primary research tool. It was the second and very different model (hereafter the Pattern Playback or simply the Playback) that was, for our purposes, a success. In the form in which it was used for so many years, this device captured the information on the spectrogram by using it to control the fate of frequency-modulated light beams. Arrayed horizontally so as to correspond to the frequency scale of the spectrogram, there were fifty such modulated beams, comprising the first fifty harmonics of a 120-Hz fundamental. Those beams that were selected by the pattern of the spectrogram were led to a phototube, the resulting variations of which were amplified and transduced to sound. In effect, the device was, as someone once said, an optical player piano.

When the Pattern Playback was conceived, we thought that we might not be able to work from hand-painted copies of spectrograms, but only from real ones. Therefore, we needed spectrograms on film so that, given photographic negatives, the phototube would see the beams that passed through the film. (When operating from hand-painted patterns, the phototube would receive the beams that were reflected from the paint.) For convenience in manipulating the patterns, we also wanted the frequency and time scales to be of generous dimensions. Moreover, we thought at this stage that we would need spectrograms with a large dynamic range. None of these needs was fully met by the spectrograph that had been built originally at the Bell Telephone Laboratories, and it was not available for sale in any case, so Frank set about to design and build our own. Unfortunately for the progress of our research, that took time. As for the Playback itself, it was, as our insurance inspector remarked when first he saw it, "homemade." And, indeed it was. Only the raw materials were store-bought. Everything else was designed and fashioned at the Laboratories, including, especially, the tone wheel, the huge circular film with fifty concentric rings of variable density used to produce the light beams that played on the spectrograms.

Once the special-purpose spectrograph and the Playback were, at last, in working order, we had to determine that speech could survive the rigors of the transformations wrought first by the one machine and then by the other. I well remember the relief I felt—Frank probably had more faith and therefore experienced correspondingly less relief—when, operating from a negative of a spectrogram, the Playback produced, on its first try, a highly intelligible sentence.

But that was only to pass the first test. For using these "real" spectrograms as a basis for experimenting with speech would have been awkward in the extreme, since it would have been very hard to make changes on the film. We therefore began immediately to develop the ability to use hand-painted spectrograms to control the sound. For that purpose, we had first to find a paint that would wet the acetate tape (i.e., not bead up), be easily erased (without leaving scars), and dry quickly. (The last requirement became nearly irrelevant when, quite early in the work, we acquired a hair-dryer.) Unable to find a commercially available paint that met our specifications, we became paint manufacturers, making our way by trial and error to a satisfactory product. That much we had to do. But there was time spent in other preliminaries that proved to be quite unnecessary. Thus, overestimating the degree of fidelity to the original spectrogram we would need, we assumed that we would have to control the relative intensities of the several parts of the pattern, and so devoted considerable effort to preparing and calibrating paints of various reflectances. We also supposed that we would have to produce gradations of a kind that could best be done with an airbrush, so we fiddled for a time with that.

But then, having decided that the price of fidelity was too high, we simply began, with an artist's brush and our most highly reflecting paint, to make copies of spectrographic representations of sentences, using for this purpose a set of twenty that had been developed at Harvard University for work on speech intelligibility. Taking pains with our first copies to preserve as much detail as possible, we succeeded in producing patterns that yielded what seemed to us a level of intelligibility high enough to make the method useful for research. We were then further encouraged about the prospects of the method when, after much trial and error, we discovered that we could achieve even greater intelligibility—about, 85 percent for the twenty sentences—with still simpler and more highly schematized patterns. (An example can be seen in figure 2.2.)

Having got this far, we ran a few preliminary experiments no different in principle from those, very common at the time, in which intelligibility was measured as a function of the filtering that the speech signal had been subjected to. But instead of filtering, we presented the formants one at a time and in all combinations. The grossly statistical result seemed of no great interest, even then, so we did not pursue it. There was, however, one unintended and unhappy result of our interest in the relative contributions of the several formants. In the course of giving a talk about the Playback at a meeting of the Acoustical Society of America, Frank played several copy-synthetic sentences, first with each formant separately, and then with the formants in various combinations. It was plain from the reaction of the audience that everyone was greatly surprised each time Frank read out the correct sentence. Apparently, people had formed wrong hypotheses as they tried to make sense of the speech produced by the individual formants, and subsequently had trouble correcting those hypotheses when presented with the full pattern. So the sentences got nowhere near the 85 percent intelligibility they deserved, and Frank got little recognition on that occasion for a promising research method.

An Excursion into Nonspeech and the Infinitely Horizontal Hypothesis

We were, at this stage, strongly attracted to the notion that spectrograms of speech were highly readable because, as tranformations of well-patterned acoustic signals, they managed still to conform to basic principles of pattern perception. Implicit in this notion was the assumption that principles of pattern perception were so general as to hold across modalities, provided proper account was taken of the way coordinates were to be transformed in moving from the one modality to the other. As applied to the relation between vision and audition, this assumption could be tested by the extent to which patterns that looked alike could be so transformed as to make them sound alike. To apply this test to the spectrographic transform, we varied the size and orientation of certain easily identifiable geometric forms, such as circles, squares, triangles, and the like, converted them to sound on the Playback, and then asked whether listeners would categorize the sounds as they had the visual patterns. Under certain tightly constrained circumstances, the answer was yes, they would; otherwise, it was no, they would not. At all events, we were so bold as to publish the idea, together with a description of the Playback, in the *Proceedings of the National Academy of Sciences.* (See chapter 2.) Fortunately for us, that journal is not widely read in our field, so our brief affair with the mother of all horizontal views has remained till now a well-kept secret.

We also experimented briefly with a phenomenon that would today be considered an instance of "streaming," though I thought of it then as the auditory equivalent of the phi phenomenon that had for so long occupied a prominent place in the study of visual patterns. Using painted lines so thin that each one activated only a single harmonic, we observed that when they alternated between a lower and a higher frequency, the listener heard the alternation only if the resulting sinusoids were sufficiently close in frequency and sufficiently long in duration; otherwise, the impression was of two streams of tones that bore no clear temporal relation to each other. In pursuing this effect, we looked for that threshold of frequency separation and duration at which the subject could not distinguish a physically alternating pattern from one in which the two streams of tones came on and went off in perfect synchrony. We did, in fact, succeed in finding such thresholds and in observing that they were sensitive to frequency separation and duration, as our hypothesis predicted, but, after exhibiting a certain threshold for a while, the typical subject would quite suddenly begin to hear the difference and to settle down, if only temporarily again, at a new threshold. Discouraged by this apparent lability, we abandoned the project and began to put our whole effort into speech.

Early (and Still Horizontally Oriented) Research on Speech

It was at about this point that Pierre Delattre came to the lab to visit for a day and, fortunately for us, stayed for ten years. Initially, his interest was in discovering the acoustic basis for nasality in French vowels, but once he found what the Playback was capable of, his ambition broadened to include any and all elements of phonetic structure. So, while continuing to work on nasality, Pierre applied himself (and us) to producing two-formant steady-state approximations to the cardinal vowels of Daniel Jones. (Pierre supplied the criterial ear.) The result was published in *Le Maitre Phonetique*, written in French and in a phonetic transcription. Thus, in our second paper, we continued the habit that had been established in the first of publishing so as to guarantee that few among our colleagues would read what we wrote.

Meanwhile, we had begun to put our attention once again on the copy-synthetic sentences, but now, instead of inquiring into the contribution of each formant to overall intelligibility, we sought, more narrowly, to find the acoustic bases—the cues—for the perception of individual phones. I recall working first on the word 'kill' as it appeared in simplified copy we had made from a spectrogram of the utterance 'Never kill a snake with your bare hands.' Looking for the phone [l], we held the pattern stationary at closely spaced temporal intervals, thus creating at each resting point a steady-state signal controlled by the static positions of the formants at that instant. The result, to our ears, was a succession of vowel-like sounds, but nothing we would have called an [l]. Yet, running the tape through at normal speed, and thus capturing the movement of the formant, produced a reasonable approximation to that phone. I don't remember what we made of this (to me) first indication of the importance of the dynamic aspects of the signal, but we did not immediately pursue it, turning instead to the [k] at the beginning of the same word.

Context-Conditioned Variability and the Horizontal Version of the Motor Theory
The advantage of [k] from our point of view as experimenters was that it appeared, in the copy-synthetic word 'kill', to be carried by a clearly identifiable and nicely delimited cue: a brief burst of sound that stood apart from the formants. Since we knew that [k] was a voiceless stop, in the same class as [p] and [t], we reckoned that all three stops might depend on such a burst, according to its position on the frequency scale. So, after a little trial and error, we carried out what must be counted our first proper experiment. (See chapter 3.) Bursts (about 360 Hz in height, 15 msec in duration at their widest, and of a shape that caused Pierre to call them "blimps") were centered at each of twelve frequencies covering the full range of our spectrograms. Each burst was placed in front of seven of Pierre's steady-state cardinal vowels, and the resulting stimuli were randomized for presentation to listeners who would be asked to identify the consonant in each case as [p], [t], or [k].

Of all the synthetic patterns ever used, these burst-plus-steady-state-vowel "syllables" were undoubtedly the farthest from readily recognizable speech. Indeed, they so grossly offended Pierre's phonetic sensibilities that he agreed only reluctantly to join Frank and me as a subject in the experiment. After discharging my own duty as a subject, I thought, as did Frank, that Pierre's reservations were well taken, and that our responses would reveal little about stop consonants or, indeed, anything else. We were therefore surprised and pleased when, on tabulating the results, we saw a reasonably clear and systematic pattern, and then equally surprised and pleased when a group of undergraduates, known for technical purposes as "phonetically naive subject," did much as we had done, if just a little more variably. For us and for them, the modal [k] response was for bursts at or slightly above the second formant of the vowel, wherever that was; [t] was assigned most often to bursts centering at frequencies above the highest of the [k] bursts; and a [p] response was given to most of the bursts not identified as [t] or [k].

This experiment was, for me, an epiphany. It is the one, referred to earlier, that changed my thinking within hours or days after its results were in. What caused the change was the finding that the effect of an acoustic cue depended to such a very large extent on the context in which it appeared, and, more to the point, that perception accorded better with articulatory gesture than with sound.

The effect of context was especially apparent in the fact that the burst most frequently perceived as [k] was the one lying at or slightly above the second formant of the following vowel, even though that formant sampled a range that extended from 3,000 Hz (for [i]) at the one end, to 700 Hz (for [u]), at the other. Moreover, this evidence that the same phonetic percept was cued by stimuli that were acoustically very different was but one side of the coin, for the results also showed that, given the right context, different percepts could be evoked by stimuli that were acoustically identical. This was the case with the burst at 1,440 Hz, which was perceived predominantly as [p] before [i], as [k] before [a], and then again as [p], though weakly, before [u].

As an empirical matter, then, this first, very crude experiment demonstrated a kind and degree of context-conditioned variability in the acoustic cues that subsequent research has shown to be pervasive in speech. As for its relevance to our earlier work on reading machines, it helped to rationalize one of the conclusions we had been brought to, which was that speech cannot be an acoustic alphabet; for what the context effects showed was that the commutable *acoustic* unit is not a phone, but rather something more like a syllable.

From a theoretical point of view, the results revealed the need to find, somewhere in the perceptual process, an invariant to correspond to the invariant phonetic unit, and they strongly suggested that the invariant is in the articulation of the phone. Thus, in the case of the [k] burst we noted that it was the articulatory movement—raising and lowering the tongue body at the velum—that remained reasonably constant, regardless of the vowel, and, further, that coarticulation of the constant consonant with the variable vowels accounted for the extreme variability in the acoustic signal. As for the other side of the coin—the very different perception of the burst before different vowels—which resulted, it should be noted, from a fortuitous combination of circumstances probably unique to this experiment, we supposed that, in order to produce something like a burst at 1,440 Hz in front of [i] or [u], one had to close and open at the lips, while in front of [a], closing and opening at the velum was required.

Taking all this into account, we adopted a notion—the Early Motor Theory—that I now believe to have been partly right and partly wrong. It was right, I think, in assuming that the object of perception in phonetic communication is to be found in the processes of articulation. It was wrong, or at least short of being thoroughly right, because it implied a continuing adherence to the horizontal view. As earlier indicated, that view assumes a two-stage process: first an auditory representation no different in kind from any other in that modality, followed, then, by linkage to something phonetic, presumably as a result of long experience and associative learning. The phonetic thing the auditory representation becomes associated with is, in the conventional view, a name, prototype, or distinctive feature. As we described the Early Motor Theory in our first papers, we made no such explicit separation into two stages, but only because our concern was rather to emphasize that perception was more closely associated with articulatory processes than with sound, and then to infer that this was because the listener was responding to the sensory feedback from the movements of the articulators. However, we offered no hint that phonetic perception takes place in a distinct modality, thus omitting to make explicit the assumption that is, as will be seen, the heart of the vertical view. Indeed, we implied, to the contrary, that the effects we were concerned with were, potentially at least, perfectly general, and so would presumably occur for any perceptual response to a physical stimulus, given long association between the stimulus and some particular muscular movement, together with its sensory feedback. What was special about speech was only that it provided the par excellence example of the opportunity for precisely that association to be formed.

In any case, my own view, as I remember it now, did comprehend two more or less distinct stages: an initial auditory representation that, as a result of associative learning, ultimately gave way to the sensory consequences of the articulatory gesture that had always been coincident with it. I had, I must now suppose, not spent much time wondering exactly what "gave way" might mean. Had I been challenged on this point, I think I should have said that in the early stages of learning there surely was a proper auditory percept, no different in kind from the response to any other acoustic stimulus and equally available to consciousness, but that later, when the bond with articulation was secure, this representation would simply have ceased to be part of the perceptual process. But however I might have responded, the Early Motor Theory was different from the standard two-stage view in a way that had an important effect on the way we thought about speech, and also on the direction of our research. It mattered greatly that we took the object of perception, and the ultimate constituent of phonetic structure, to be an articulatory gesture, not a sound (or its auditory result), for this began a line of thinking that would in time be seen to eliminate the need for the horizontalists' second stage, and so permit us to exorcise the linguistic ghosts—the phonetic names or other cognitive entities—that haunted it. As for the direction of our research, the Early Motor Theory caused us to turn our attention to speech production, and so to initiate the inquiry into that process that has occupied an ever larger and more important place in our enterprise.

Some Mildly Interesting Assumptions that Underlay the Methods We Used
Given the extreme unnaturalness of the stimuli in many of our experiments, and the difficulty subjects reported in hearing them as speech, we had to assume that there would be no important interaction between the degree of approximation to natural speech quality and the way listeners perceive the phonetic information. I therefore note here that this assumption has proved to be correct: no matter how unconvincing our experimental stimuli as examples of speech, those listeners who were nevertheless able to hear them as speech provided results that have held up remarkably well when the experiments were carried out subsequently with stimuli that were closer approximations to the real thing. This was the first indication we had of the theoretically important fact that accurate information about the relevant articulator movements, as conveyed, however unnaturally, by the acoustic signal, is sufficient for veridical phonetic perception, provided only that the listener is not too put off by the absence of an overall speechlike quality.

We also had to assume that the validity of our results would be little affected by a practice, followed throughout our search for the cues, of investigating, in any one experiment, only a single phonetic feature in a single phonetic class, and instructing the subjects to limit their responses to the phones in that class. Obviously, this procedure left open the possibility that cues sufficient to distinguish phones along, say, the dimension of place in some particular condition of voicing or manner would not work when voicing or manner was changed, or when the set of stimuli and corresponding response choices was enlarged. In fact, the results obtained in the limited contexts of our experiments were not overturned in later research when, for whatever reason, those limits were relaxed. I take this to be testimony to the independence in perception of the standard feature dimensions.

Finally, given early indications that there were several cues for each phonetic element, and given that, to make our experiments manageable, at least in the early stages, we typically investigated one at a time, we had to assume the absence of strong interactions among the cues. In fact, as we later discovered, there are such interactions—specifically, the trading relations that bespeak a perceptual equivalence among the various cues for the same phone and that are, therefore of some theoretical interest, as I will say later—but these occur only within fairly narrow limits, and they only change the setting of a cue that is optimal for the phone; they do not otherwise affect it. Therefore, working on only one cue at a time did not cause us to be seriously misled.

More Context-Conditioned Variability and the Dynamic Aspects of the Speech Signal
The most cursory examination of a spectrogram of running speech reveals nothing so clearly as the almost continuous movement of the formants; even the band-limited noises that characterize the fricatives seem more often than not to be dynamically shaped. Indeed, Potter, Kopp, and Green, in their book, *Visible Speech*, had remarked these movements, but they considered the effect to proceed from (constant) consonant to (variable) vowel, at least in the case of stop consonant-vowel syllables; and since their interest was primarily in how these transitional influences might help people to "read" spectrograms, they simply called attention to the direction of the movement, up or down, and did not speculate about the role of these movements in speech perception. Martin Joos, on the other hand, wrote explicitly about the consonant-vowel transitions, as well as their context-conditioned variability, and showed, by cutting out properly selected parts of magnetic-tape recordings, that these transitions conveyed information about the consonants. He also made the important observation that there was, therefore, no direct correspondence between the segmentation of the acoustic signal and the segmentation of the phonetic structure. But Joos could not vary the transition for experimental purposes, so his conclusions could not be further refined. We therefore thought it a reasonable next step to make those variations, and so learn more about the role of the transitions in perception, choosing first to study place of production among stop and nasal consonants. (See chapter 4.)

Our research to that point had prepared us to deal only with two-formant patterns, and since inspection of spectrograms indicated that transitions of the first formant did not vary with place, we chose to experiment with transitions of the second. To that end, we varied the starting point, hence the direction and extent, of these transitions by starting them at each of a number of frequencies above and below the steady state of the following vowel. In one condition, the first formant had a fixed transition that rose to the steady state from the very lowest frequency (120 Hz); the resulting patterns were intended to represent voiced stops, and it was our judgment that they did that reasonably well. In a second condition, the first formant had a zero transition—that is, it was straight. We hoped that these patterns would sound voiceless, but, in fact, they did not. They were used nevertheless. The stimuli in each of these conditions were presented for identification as [b], [d], [g] to one group of listeners and as [p], [t], [k] to another. The results showed clearly that the transitions do provide important information about the place dimension of the voiced and voiceless stops, and, also, that this information is independent of voicing. Indeed, it mattered little whether the listeners were identifying a particular set of synthetic stops as voiced or voiceless; the same transitions were associated with the same place, and there was, at most, only slightly less variability in the condition with the rising first formant, where the stimuli sounded voiced to us and the subjects were asked to judge them so. In a third condition, we strove, fairly successfully we thought, for nasal consonants by using a straight first formant, together with what we considered at the time to be an appropriate (fixed) nasal resonance. Here, too, the second-formant transitions provided information about place, and that information was in no way affected by the change in manner, even though we had reversed the patterns so as to make the nasals syllable-final, and so to take account of the fact that the velar nasal never appears initially in the syllable in English. As for context effects, they were large and systematic. Thus, the best transition for [d] (or [t] or [n]) fell from a point considerably above the steady state of the vowel with [u], but with [i] it rose from a point below the vowel's steady state, and similar effects were evident with the transitions for other phones. We thought it supportive of a motor theory that the highly variable transitions for the same consonant were produced by a reasonably constant articulatory gesture as it was merged with the gesture appropriate for the following vowel. Equally supportive, in our view, was the fact that mirror-image transitions in syllable-initial and syllable-final positions nevertheless yielded the same consonantal percept, for surely these would sound very different in any well behaved auditory system. From an articulatory point of view, however, these transitions are seen as the acoustic consequences of the opening and closing phases of the same gesture. As with the bursts, then, perception cued by the transitions accorded better with an articulatory process than with sound. (See chapter 12 for an account of the early experiments, together with an interpretation according to the Early Motor Theory.)

Despite the demonstration, by us and others, of the extreme context sensitivity of the acoustic cues, some researchers have been concerned for many years to show that there are, nevertheless, invariant acoustic cues, implying, then, that no special theoretical exertions are necessary in order to account for invariant phonetic percepts. My own view of this matter has always been that, whatever the outcome of the seemingly never-ending search for acoustic invariants, the theoretical issue will remain largely untouched; for there is surely no question that the highly context-sensitive transitions *do* supply important information for phonetic perception—they can, indeed, be shown to be quite sufficient in many circumstances—and that incontrovertible fact must be accounted for.

A Brief Flirtation with Binary Decisions
In our first attempt to interpret the significance of the burst and transition results, we took seriously, if only for a short time, the possibility that the two kinds of cues collaborated in such a way that two binary decisions resolved all perceptual ambiguity. Our data had shown that the bursts were identified as [t], if they were high in fre-

quency and as [p] or [k], if low; the second-formant transitions evoked [t] or [k], if they were falling, and [p], if rising. So a low burst and a rising transition would be an unambiguous [p]; a high burst and falling transition would be [t]; and a low burst coupled with a falling transition would be [k]. We were, of course, influenced to this conclusion not just by our data but also, if only indirectly, by the then prevailing fashion for binary arrangements. At all events, we made no attempt to link our notion about binary decisions with the Early Motor Theory, perhaps because that would have been hard to do.

Acoustic Loci: Rationalizing the Transitions and Their Role in Perception
It required only a little further reflection, combined with an examination of the results of our experiments on the second-formant transitions, to see that perception was sensitive to something more than whether the transition was rising or falling. Since those transitions reflect the cavity changes that occur as the articulators move from the consonant position to the vowel, and, since the place of production for each consonant is more or less fixed, we saw that we should expect to find a correspondingly fixed position—or "locus," as we chose to call it—for its second formant. More careful examination of the results of our experiments suggested that, for each position on the dimension of place, the transition might, indeed, have originated at some particular frequency, and then made its way to the steady state of the vowel, wherever that was. To refine this notion, we carried out a two-step experiment. (See chapter 5.) In the first, we put steady-state second formants at each of a number of frequency levels, from 3,600 Hz to 720 Hz, and paired each with one of a number of first formants in the range 720 Hz to 2,400 Hz. The first formants had rising transitions designed to evoke the effect of a voiced stop consonant. Careful listening revealed that [d] was heard when the second formant was at 1,800 Hz, [b] at 720 Hz, and [g] at 3,000 Hz, so we settled on these frequencies as the loci for the places of production of the three stops.

The second step was to prepare two-formant patterns in which the second formant started at each of these loci, and then rose or fell to the steady state of the vowel, wherever that was. With these patterns, the consonant appropriate to the locus was not evoked clearly. For [d], indeed, starting the transitions at the locus produced, for some steady states, [b] and [g]. To get good consonants, we had in all cases to "erase" the first half of the transition so as to create a silent interval between the locus and the actual start of the transition. We noted, further, that in the case of [g], this maneuver worked only with second-formant steady states from 3,000 Hz to about 1,200 Hz, which is approximately where the vowel shifts from spread to rounded; below 1,200 Hz, no approximation to [g] could be heard.

The concept of the locus, together with the experimental results that defined it, made simple sense of the transitions. It also tempted me to temper the emphasis on context-conditioned variability by assuming that the perceptual machinery—by which I might have meant the *auditory* machinery—"extrapolated" backward from the start of the transition to the locus, and so arrived at a "virtual" acoustic invariant. Fortunately, I yielded to this temptation only briefly, and there is, I think, no written record of my lapse. In any case, we began early to take the opposite tack, using the locus data to strengthen our conclusions about the role of context by emphasising the untoward consequences of actually starting the transitions at the locus, and by pointing to the sudden shift in the [g] locus when the vowel crosses the boundary from spread to rounded.

Stop vs. Semivowel, or Once More into the Auditory Breach
It was apparent on the basis of articulatory considerations, and also by inspection of spectrograms, that an acoustic correlate of the stop-semivowel distinction was the duration or rate of the appropriate transitions. To find out how this variable actually affected perception, we carried out the obvious experiment. (See chapter 6.) We particularly wanted to know whether it was rate or duration, and also where on the rate or duration continuum the phonetic boundary was. By varying the positions of the vowel formants, and hence the extent of the transition, we were able to separate the two variables and find that duration seemed to be doing all the work. We also found that the boundary was at about 50 msec.

I recall thinking that 50 msec might be critical for some kind of auditory integration. As I have already said, it seemed reasonable to me at the time to suppose that phonetic distinctions had accommodated themselves to the properties of the auditory system as revealed at the level of psychophysical relations, since the (implicit) motor activity that was ultimately perceived was itself *initially* evoked by some kind of first-stage auditory representation. I was therefore naturally attracted to the possibility that transition excursions of less than 50 msec duration were, perhaps, integrated by the auditory system so as to produce a unitary impression like that of a stop consonant, while transitions with excursions longer than that would evoke the impression of gradual change that characterizes the semivowels. I well remember the excitement I felt when, having decided that a 50-msec duration might well be the auditory key, I appreciated how easy it would be to find out if indeed it was. The experimental test required only that I draw on the Playback a series of rising and falling isolated transitions in which the duration was varied over a wide range. What I expected and hoped to find was that a duration of 50 msec would provide a boundary between perception of a unitary stoplike burst of sound on the one side, and a semivowel kind of glide on the other. So far as I could tell, however, there appeared to be no such boundary at 50 msec and thus no evidence of an auditory basis for the results of our experiment on the distinction between stop and semivowel. I was disappointed, but not enough to abandon my horizontal attitude about the role of auditory representations in the ontogenetic development of phonetic perception.

Categorical Perception: The Right Prediction from the Wrong Theories
According to just those aspects of the Early Motor Theory that I now believe to be mistaken, the auditory percept originally evoked by the speech signal was supposed to give way to the sensory consequences of the articulatory gesture, and it was just those consequences that were ultimately perceived. In arriving at this theory, I had, of course, been much influenced by the behaviorist stimulus-response tradition in which I had been reared. It was virtually inevitable, then, that I should take the next step and consider the consequences of two processes—"acquired distinctiveness" and "acquired similarity"—that were part of the same tradition. The point was simple enough: if two stimuli become connected, through long association, to very different responses, then the feedback from those responses, having become the end states of the perceptual process, will cause the stimuli to be more discriminable than they had originally been; conversely, if these stimuli become connected to the same response,

then, for the same reason, they will be less discriminable. In fact, there was not then, and is not now, any evidence that such an effect occurs. But that did not trouble me, for I supposed that investigators had not thought to look in the right place, and I could not imagine a better place than speech perception. Neither was I troubled by what seems to me now the patently implausible assumption, basic to the concepts of acquired distinctiveness and acquired similarity, that the normal auditory representation of a suprathreshold acoustic stimulus could be wholly supplanted, or even significantly affected, by the perceptual consequences of some motor response just because the acoustic stimulus and the motor response had become strongly associated. It was for me compelling that listeners had for many years been making different articulatory responses to stimuli that happened to lie on either side of a phonetic boundary, so, by the terms of the Early Motor Theory and the theory of acquired distinctiveness, that difference should have become more discriminable. On the other hand, those listeners had been making the same articulatory response to equally different stimuli that happened to lie within the phonetic class, so, by the same theories, those stimuli should have been rendered less discriminable.

To test the theories, I thought it necessary only to get appropriate measures of acoustic-cue discriminability. As I know now, one can easily get the effect I sought simply by listening to voiced stops, for example, as the second-formant transition is changed in relatively small and equal steps, for what one hears is, first, several consonants that are almost identical [b]'s, then a rather sudden shift to [d], followed by several almost identical [d]'s, and then, again, a sudden shift, this time to [g]. Though we had the means to make this simple and quite convincing test, we did not think to try it. Instead, I put together two wrong theories and produced what my professors had taught me to strive for as one of the highest forms of scientific achievement: a real prediction.

The test of the prediction was initially undertaken by one of our graduate students, Belver Griffith, who, with my enthusiastic approval, elected to do the critical experiment on steady-state vowels. We know now that the effect we were looking for does not occur to any significant extent with such vowels, so it was fortunate that Griffith, by nature very fussy about the materials of his experiments, was unsuccessful in producing vowels he was willing to use. The happy consequence was that he, together with the rest of us, decided to move ahead, in parallel, with stop consonants. (See chapters 10 and 11.)

It was not our purpose to obtain discrimination thresholds, but only to measure discriminability of a constant physical difference at various points on the continuum of second-formant transitions. To that end, we synthesized a series of fourteen syllables in which the starting point of the second formant was varied in steps of 120 Hz, from a point 840 Hz below the steady state of the following vowel to a point 720 Hz above it. We then paired stimuli that were one, two, and three steps apart on the continuum, and for each such pair measured discriminability by the ABX method (A and B were members of the pair, X was one or the other, and the subject's task was to match X with A or B). The result was that there were peaks in the discrimination functions at positions on the continuum that corresponded to the phonetic boundaries as earlier determined by the way the subjects had identified the stimuli as [b], [d], or [g] when they were presented singly and in random order. This is to say that, other things equal, discrimination was better between stimuli to which the subjects habitually gave different articulatory responses than it was between stimuli to which the responses were the same. Thus, the prediction was apparently confirmed by this instance of what we chose to call "categorical perception."

In the published paper, we included a method, worked out by Katherine Harris, for computing from the absolute identification functions what the discrimination function would have been if, indeed, perception had been perfectly categorical—that is, if listeners had been able to perceive differences only if they had assigned the stimuli to different phonetic categories. Applying this calculation to our results, we found that, in this experiment at least, perception was rather strongly categorical, but not perfectly so.

To this point in our research, psychologists, including even those interested in language, had paid us little attention. Requests for reprints, and such other tokens of interest as we had received, had come mostly from communication engineers and phoneticians, and there were few references to our work in the already considerable literature of psycholinguistics, a field that had been established, seemingly by fiat, by a committee of psychologists and linguists who had met for a summer work session at Cornell University. The result of their deliberations was a briefly famous monograph in which they defined the new discipline, constructed its theoretical framework, and posed the questions that remained to be answered. That done, they officially launched the field at a symposium held during the next national convention of the American Psychological Association. At the end of the symposium, I asked a question that provoked one of the founding fathers to inform me, icily, that speech had nothing to do with psycholinguistics. He did not say why, but then, as one of the inventors of the discipline, he was entitled to speak ex cathedra. It is, however, easy to appreciate that in looking at speech horizontally, as he and the other members of the committee surely did, one sees nothing that is linguistically interesting, only a set of unexceptional noises and equally unexceptional auditory percepts that just happen to convey the more invitingly abstract structures where those who would think deeply about language ought properly to put their attention.

The categorical perception paper seemed, however, to touch a psycholinguistic nerve. Perhaps this was because, if taken seriously, it showed that the phonetic units were categorical, not only in their communicative role, but also as immediately perceived; and this nice fit of perceptual form to linguistic function must have seemed at odds with the conventional horizontal assumption that the auditory percepts assume linguistic significance only after a cognitive translation, not before. Our results could be taken to imply that no such translation was necessary, and that there might, therefore, be something psycholinguistically interesting and important about the precognitive—that is, purely perceptual—processes by which listeners apprehend phonetic structures.

Most psychologists seemed unwilling to accept that implication, though not all for the same reason. Some argued that categorical perception, as we had found it, was of no consequence because it was merely an artifact of our method. This criticism boiled down to an assertion, perfectly consistent with the standard horizontal view, that the memory load imposed by the ABX procedure made it impossible for the subject to compare the initial auditory representations, forcing him to rely, instead, on the categorical phonetic names he assigned to the rapidly fading auditory echoes as they were removed from the ever changing sensory world and elevated, for safer keeping, into short-term memory. It is, of course, true that reducing the time interval between the stimuli to be compared does raise the troughs that appear in the within-category parts of the discrimination function, and thus reduces the approximation to categorical perception. But the Early Motor Theory did not require that the articulatory responses within a phonetic category be identical, so it did not predict that perception had to be perfectly categorical. (The degree to which the articulatory responses within a category are similar presumably varies according to the category and the speaker; it is, therefore, a matter for empirical determination.) Neither did the theory in any way preclude the possibility that perceptual responses would be easier to discriminate when fresh than when stale. In any case, it surely was relevant that the peaks one finds with various measures of discrimination merely confirm the quantal shifts a listener perceives as the stimuli are moved along the physical continuum so rapidly as to make the memory load negligible.

The other criticism, which seemed almost opposite to the one just considered, was that categorical perception is not relevant to psycholinguistics because it is so common, and, more particularly, because those boundaries that the discrimination peaks mark are simply properties of the general auditory system, hence not to be taken as support for the view that speech perception is interesting, except, perhaps, within the domain of auditory psychophysics. As for the criticism that categorical perception is common, it seemed to have been based on the misapprehension that we had claimed categorical perception to be unique to speech, but in fact we had not, having merely observed (correctly) that, given stimuli that lie on some definable physical continuum, observers commonly discriminate many more than they can identify absolutely. Our claim about phonetic perception was only that there is a significant, if nevertheless incomplete, tendency for that commonly observed disparity to be reduced. On the other hand, the claim by our critics that the boundaries are generally auditory, not specifically phonetic, was important and deserved to be taken seriously. It has led to many experiments on perception of nonspeech control stimuli and on perception of speech by nonhuman animals, leaving us and the other interested parties with an issue that is still vexed. In fact, I think the weight of evidence, taken together with arguments of plausibility, overwhelmingly favors the conclusion that the boundaries are specific to the phonetic system, but I reserve the justification for that conclusion for the last section of this introduction.

There was yet another seemingly widespread misapprehension about categorical perception, which was that it had served us as the primary basis for the Early Motor Theory. In fact, we (or, at least, I) have long believed that the facts about this phenomenon are consistent with the theory, but they do not by any means provide its most important support; indeed, they were not available until at least five years after we had been persuaded to the theory, as I earlier indicated, by the very first results of our search for the acoustic cues.

Finally, in the matter of categorical perception, I will guess that consonant perception is likely, when properly tested, to prove more nearly categorical than experiments have so far shown it to be. The problem with those experiments is that they have used acoustic synthesis, so it has been prohibitively difficult in any single experiment to make proper variations in more than one of the many aspects of the signal that are perceptually relevant. But when only one cue is varied, as in the experiments so far done, then, as it is changed from the form appropriate for one phone to the form appropriate for the next, it leaves all the other relevant information behind, as it were, creating a situation in which the listener is discriminating, not just the phonetic structure, but also increasingly unnatural departures from it. I suspect that, with proper articulatory synthesis, when the acoustic signal will change in all relevant aspects—at least for the cases that are produced by articulations that can be said to vary continuously—the discrimination functions will come much closer to being perfectly categorical.

The Concept of "Cue" as a Theoretically Relevant Entity
At the very least, "cue" is a term of convenience, useful for the purpose of referring to any piece of signal that has been found by experiment to have an effect on perception. We have used the word in that sense, and continue to do so. But there was a time when the word cue had, at least in my mind, a more exalted status. I supposed that there was, for each phone, some specifiable number of particulate cues that combined according to a scientifically important principle to evoke the correct response. It was this understanding of cues that was implicit in the "binary" account of their effects that I referred to earlier. The same understanding was more explicit in a dissertation on cue combination that I had urged on Howard Hoffman (chapter 10 coauthor). Finally, and perhaps most egregiously, it became the centerpiece of our interpretation of an experiment on the effects of third-formant transitions on perception of place among the stops. (See chapter 7.) Having found there that, in enhancing the perception of one stop, any particular transition does not do so equally at the expense of the other two, we concluded that a cue not only tells a listener what a speech sound is, but also which of the remaining possibilities it is not. It was almost as if we were supposing that the third-formant transition had been designed, by nature or by the speaker, just to resolve an ambiguity that the more important second-formant transition had overlooked. At all events, we went on to speculate that the response alternatives exist in a multidimensional phonetic space, and, though we were not perfectly explicit about this in the published paper, that a cue has a magnitude and a direction, just like a vector, with the result that the final position of the percept in the phonetic space is determined by the sum of the vectors. Such a conception is, of course, at odds with all the data now available that indicate how exquisitely sensitive the listener is to *all* the acoustic consequences of phonetically significant gestures, for what those data mean is that any definition of an acoustic cue is always to some extent arbitrary. Surely, it makes little sense to wonder about the rules by which arbitrarily defined cues combine to produce a perceptual result.

The Voicing Distinction; an Exercise in Not Seeing That which Is Most Visible
We discovered very early how to produce stops that were convincingly voiced, but we had been frustrated for five years or more while seeking the key to synthesis of their voiceless counterparts. In our quest, we had examined spectrograms, sought advice from colleagues in other laboratories, and, by trial and error on the Playback, tried every trick we could think of. We varied the strength of the burst relative to the vocalic section of the syllable, drew every conceivable kind of first-formant transition, and substituted various intensities of noise for the harmonics through varying lengths of the initial parts of the formant transitions.

In fact, there was no noise source in the Pattern Playback, only harmonics of a 120-Hz fundamental, but we had been able in research on the fricatives to make do by placing small dots of paint where noise was supposed to be. In isolation, patches of such dots sounded like a twittering of birds, but in syllabic context they produced fricatives so acceptable that, when we used them in experiments, we got results virtually identical to those obtained later when, with a new synthesizer called Voback, we were able to deploy real noise. In our attempts at voiceless stops, before Voback was available, we had to rely on the trick that had worked for the fricatives. When it did not help, we concluded that, unlike the fricatives, the voiceless stops needed true noise and, accordingly, that our inability to synthesize them was to be attributed to the noise-producing limitations of the Playback.

That we were wrong to blame the Playback became apparent one day as a consequence of a discovery by Andre Malecot, one of Pierre Delattre's graduate students. While working to synthesize the syllable-final releases of stops, he omitted the first formant of the short-duration syllable that constituted the release. I believe that he did this inadvertently. But whether by inadvertence or by design, he produced a dramatic effect: we all heard a stop that was quite clearly voiceless. Encouraged by this finding, we adapted it to stops in syllable-initial position, and carried out several related experiments. (See chapter 8.) In each, we varied one potential cue for the voicing contrast for all three stops, paired with each of the vowels [i], [æ], and [u]. Our principal finding was that, with all else equal, simply delaying the onset of the first formant relative to the second and third was sufficient to cause naive listeners to shift their responses smartly between voiced and voiceless. Then, recognizing that in so delaying the onset of the first formant we were, at the same time, starting it at a higher frequency, we reconfirmed the observation we had made in our earlier experiments, which was that starting the first formant at a very low frequency was important in creating the impression of a voiced stop, but that starting it higher, at the steady state of that formant, did not, by itself, make much of a contribution to voicelessness. On the other hand, delaying the onset of the first formant without at the same time raising its starting frequency did prove to be a very potent cue. Indeed, it appeared from the responses of our listeners to be about as potent as the original combination of delay and raised starting point. (For the purpose of this experiment, we varied the delay alone by contriving a synthetic approximation to the vowel [o] in which the first formant was placed as low on the pattern as it could go; it was, then, just this straight formant that was delayed.) Next, we took advantage of the newly available synthesizer, Voback, which, as I earlier said, had a proper noise source, to experiment with the effect of noise in place of harmonics during the transitions. What we found was that substituting noise in all three formants was, by itself, ineffective, but that substituting it for harmonics in the second and third formants for the duration of the delay in first-formant onset did somewhat strengthen the impression of voicelessness. In connection with this last conclusion, we noted that when, in an attempt to produce an initial [h], which is, of course, the essence of aspiration, we replaced the harmonics of all the formants with noise for the first 50 or 100 msec, we did not get [h], but rather the impression of a vowel that changed from whispered to fully voiced; to get [h], we had to omit the first formant. To explain all this, we advanced a suggestion, made to us by Gunnar Fant, that the vocal cords were open during the period of aspiration, and that it was this circumstance that reduced the intensity of the first formant, thus effectively delaying its onset. We emphasized, then, that all the acoustically diverse cues were consequences of the same articulatory event, and therefore led, in accordance with the Motor Theory, to a percept that was perfectly coherent.

This early work on the voicing distinction was subsequently refined and considerably extended by Arthur Abramson and Leigh Lisker. In particular, it was they who established how the acoustic boundaries for the voicing distinction vary with different languages, and thus provided the basis for the great volume of later research by other investigators who exploited these differences in pursuit of their interests in the ontogenesis of speech. And it was Abramson and Lisker who accurately characterized the relevant variable as voice-onset-time (VOT), defined as the duration of the interval between the consonant opening (in the oral part of the tract) and the onset of voicing at the larynx. Unfortunately, some of the researchers who later used the voicing distinction for their own purposes ignored the fact that the VOT variable is articulatory, not acoustic, and therefore failed to take into account in their theoretical interpretations that its acoustic manifestations are complexly heterogeneous.

As for our initial discovery of the acoustic cues for the voicing distinction, I note an irony in the long search that preceded it, for once one knows where to look in the spectrogram, the delay in the first-formant onset can be measured more easily, and with greater precision, than almost any of the other consonant cues we had found. Consider, for example, how important to perception is the frequency at which a formant transition starts, and then how hard it is to specify that frequency precisely from an inspection of its appearance on a spectrogram. Yet our tireless examination of spectrograms had, in the case of the voicing distinction, availed us nothing; we simply had not seen what we now know to be so plainly there.

Synthesis by Rule and a Reading Machine that Speaks
In this very personal chronicle of our early research, I have chosen to write of just those experiments that best illustrate certain underlying assumptions I now find interesting. I have said nothing about the many other experiments that were carried out during roughly the same period of time. I would now partly repair that omission by recognizing the existence of those others, and by emphasizing that they provided a collection of data sufficient as a basis for synthesizing speech from a phonetic transcription, without the need to copy from a spectrogram. Unfortunately, all the relevant data had been brought together only in Pierre Delattre's head. Relying only on the experience he had gained from participation in our published research, and also from the countless unpublished experiments he had carried out in his unflagging effort to refine and extend, Pierre could "paint" speech to order, as it were. But the knowledge that Pierre had in his head was, by its nature, not so public as science demands.

We therefore recommended to Frances Ingemann, when she came to spend some time at the Laboratories, that she write a set of rules for synthesis, making everything so explicit that someone totally innocent of knowledge about acoustic phonetics could, simply by following the rules, draw a spectrogram that would produce any desired phonetic structure. Accepting this challenge, she decided to rely entirely on the papers we had published in journals or in lab reports; she did not use the synthesizer to test and improve as she went along, nor did she attempt to formalize what Pierre and other members of the staff might know but had never written down. She nevertheless succeeded very well, I think, in producing what must count as the first rules for synthesis. I don't recall that we ever formally assessed the intelligibility of the speech produced by these rules, but I know that we found it reasonably intelligible. At all events, an outline of the rule system was published in 1959 under the title, "Minimal Rules for Synthesizing Speech." (See chapter 9.) The word "minimal" was appropriate because the rules were written at the level of features, the presumed "atoms" of phonetic structure, not at the level of the more numerous segments or "molecules." I should note, too, that we took explicit notice in the paper of our belief that the rules for synthesis had better be written in articulatory terms, for then *all* the relevant acoustic information would be provided to the listener. There was, however, no alternative to the acoustically based rules we offered, because there was not enough known about articulation, but also because there was, in any case, no satisfactory articulatory synthesizer. Articulatory synthesis would therefore have to wait.

Meanwhile, we had, by 1966, a computing facility, and had constructed a computer-controlled, terminal-analog formant synthesizer. It was then that Ignatius Mattingly joined the staff and undertook to program the computer to produce speech by rule. For this purpose, he drew on the work he had done previously with Holmes and Shearme in England, and also on all that had been learned about the cues and rules for synthesis at the Laboratories. By 1968 the job was done. Accepting an input of a phonetic string, the system would speak. The intelligibility of the speech was tested on several occasions and in several different ways. Thus, it was tested informally by having blind veterans listen, for example, to rather long passages from Dickens and Steinbeck. It was evident that they understood the speech, even at rates of 225 words per minute, but we had no measure of exactly how hard they found it to do so, and they did complain, not without reason we thought, of what they called the machine's "accent." In more formal tests, the rule-generated synthetic speech came off quite well by comparison with "real" speech, but, not unexpectedly, there were signs of a price exacted by the extra cognitive effort that was required to overcome its evident imperfections, a price that had to be paid, presumably, by the processes of comprehension.

At that point, we had in hand a principal component of a reading machine that would convert text to speech, and thus avoid all the problems we had encountered in our earlier work with nonspeech substitutes. What was needed, in addition, was an optical character reader to convert the letters into machine-readable form, and also, of course, some way of translating spelled English into a phonetic transcription appropriate to the synthesizer. Given our history, it was inevitable that we should have been impatient to acquire these other components and see (or, more properly, hear) what a fully automatic system could do. So, Frank Cooper, Patrick Nye, and others cobbled together just such a system, using an optical character reader we bought with money given us for the purpose by the Seeing Eye Foundation, a phonetic dictionary made available by the Speech Communications Research Laboratory of Santa Barbara, and, of course, our own computer-controlled synthesizer. Tests revealed that the speech produced in this fully automatic way was almost as good as that for which the phonetic transcription had been hand-edited. But we were concerned about the evidence we had earlier collected concerning the probable consequences for ease of comprehension that arose out of the shortcomings of the speech. We therefore put together a plan to evaluate the machine with blind college students who would use it to read their assignments; having found its weaknesses, we would then try to correct them. I assumed that various federal agencies would compete to see which one could persuade us to accept their support for this undertaking. We could, after all, show that a reading machine for the blind was not pie-in-the-sky, but a doable thing that stood in need of just the kinds of improvement that further research would surely bring. Yet, though we tried very hard with several agencies, and for several years, we failed utterly to get support, and were forced finally to abandon our plans. Still, we had the satisfaction of having proved to ourselves that a reading machine for the blind was close to being a reality. The basic research was largely complete; what remained was just the need for proper development.

On Becoming Vertical, or How I Righted Myself

To this point, my concern has been to describe the various forms of the horizontal view that my colleagues and I held during our work on nonspeech reading machines and in the early stages of the research on speech to which it led. Now I mean to offer a more detailed account of the important differences between that view and the vertical view I now hold. In so doing, I draw freely, and without specific attribution, on a number of theoretically oriented papers that were written in close collaboration with various of my colleagues. Among the most relevant of these are several reviews by Ignatius Mattingly and me in which we hammered out the vertical view as I (we) see it now. (See chapters 13, 14, 15, and 16.)

All these theoretically oriented papers deal, at least implicitly, with questions about speech to which the horizontal and vertical views give different, sometimes diametrically opposed, answers. Such questions serve well, therefore, to define the two positions, and to explain how I came to abandon the one for the other; for those reasons, I will organize this section of the paper around them.

The issue that unites the questions pertains to the place of speech in the biological scheme of things. That I should have come to regard that issue as central is odd, given the habits of mind I had brought to the research, for, as I earlier implied, my education in psychology had been unremittingly abiological. I had, to be sure, studied a little physiology, narrowly conceived, and it cannot have escaped my notice that in the physiological domain things were not of a piece, having been formed, rather, into distinct systems for correspondingly distinct functions. At the level of behavior, however, I saw only an overarching sameness, a reflection of my attachment to principles so general as to apply equally to a process as natural as learning to speak and as arbitrary as memorizing a list of nonsense syllables.

I think I was moved first, and most generally, to a different approach by scientists who work, not on speech, but on other forms of species-typical behavior. Thus, it was largely under the influence of people like Peter Marler, Nobuo Suga, Mark Konishi, and Fernando Nottebohm that I came to see myself as an ethologist, very much like them, and to appreciate that I would be well advised to begin to think like one. They helped me understand that speech is to the human being as echolocation is to the bat or song is to the bird—to see, that is, that all these behaviors depend on biologically coherent faculties that were specifically adapted in evolution to function appropriately in connection with events that are of particular ecological significance to the animal. To the horizontalist that I once was, this was heresy; but to the verticalist I was in process of becoming, it was the beginning of wisdom.

Meanwhile, back at the Laboratories there were biological stirrings on the part of Michael Studdert-Kennedy, who is nevertheless not a committed verticalist, and Ignatius Mattingly, who is. Michael has been a constructive critic in regard to virtually every biologically relevant notion I have dared to entertain. As for the biological slant of the vertical view (including the Revised Motor Theory), that is as much Ignatius's contribution as mine. Indeed, the view itself is the result of a joint effort, though, of course, he bears no responsibility for what I say about it here.

Among the influences of a somewhat different sort, there was the growing realization that my early horizontal view did not sit comfortably even with the results of the early research it was designed to explain. That will have been seen in what I have already said about my attempts to account for those results, and, especially, about the patch on the horizontal view that I have here called the Early Motor Theory. Heavily loaded as it was with untested and wholly implausible assumptions—for example, that auditory percepts could, as a result of learning, be replaced by sensations of movement—it had begun to fall of its own weight.

Contributing further to the collapse of the Early Motor Theory was the research, pioneered by Peter Eimas and his associates, in which it was found that prelinguistic infants had a far greater capacity for phonetic perception than a literal reading of the theory would allow.

My faith was further weakened by the work of Katherine Harris and Peter MacNeilage, who, as the first of the Laboratories' staff to work on speech production, were busily finding a great deal of context-conditioned variability in the peripheral articulatory movements (as reflected in electromyographic measures), and thus disproving one of the assumptions of the Early Motor Theory, which was that the articulatory invariant was in the final-common-path commands to the muscles.

At the same time, Michael Turvey was pointing the way to an appropriate revision by showing how, given context-conditioned variability at the level of movement, it is nevertheless possible, indeed necessary, to find invariance in the more remote motor entities that Michael called "coordinative structures." In any case, Michael Turvey and Carol Fowler were strongly encouraging me to persevere in the aspect of the Early Motor Theory that took gestures to be the objects of speech perception, while simultaneously heaping scorn on the idea that perception was a second-order translation of a sensory representation, as the horizontal version of the theory required. I began, therefore, to take more seriously the possibility that there is no mediating auditory percept, only the immediately perceived gestures as provided by a system—the phonetic module—that is specialized for the ecologically important function of representing them.

Not that Michael and Carol or, indeed, any of the other "ecological" psychologists in the Laboratories, are verticalists. They most certainly are not, because they do not accept (yet) that there is a distinct phonetic mode, preferring, rather, to take speech perception as simply one instance of the way all perception is tuned to perceive the distal objects; in the case of speech, these just happen to be the articulatory gestures of the speaker. Thus, I have been in the happy position of taking advantage of the best of what my ecological friends have had to offer, while freely rejecting the rest, and, as an important bonus, being stimulated by our continuing disagreements to correct weaknesses and repair omissions in my own view.

It was also relevant to the development of my thinking that Isabelle Liberman, Donald Shankweiler, and Ignatius Mattingly—followed later by such younger colleagues as Benita Blachman, Susan Brady, Anne Fowler, Hyla Rubin, and Virginia Mann—had begun to see in our research how to account for the fact that speech is so much more natural (hence easier) than reading and writing, and thus to be explicit about what is required of the would-be reader/writer that mastery of speech will not have taught him. As I will say later, their insights and the results of their empirical work illuminated aspects of the vertical view that I would otherwise not have seen.

I was affected, too, by the results of experiments on duplex perception, trading relations, and integration of cues—experiments that went beyond those, referred to earlier—that merely isolated the cues and looked for discontinuities in the discrimination functions. (See chapters 17, 18, 19, 20, 21, 22, and 23.) These later experiments, done (variously) in close collaboration with a number of colleagues (few of whom are admitted verticalists) provided data that spoke more clearly than the earlier findings to some of the shortcomings of the horizontal position, and therefore inclined me ever more strongly to the vertical alternative.

Finally, I should acknowledge the profound effect of Fodor's provocative monograph, *The Modularity of Mind*, which, in the early stages of my conversion, enlightened and stimulated me by its arguments in favor of the most general aspects of the vertical view.

That I should finally have asked the following questions, and answered them as I do, reflects the influences I have just described, and fairly represents the theoretical position to which they moved me.

In the Development of Phonological Communication, What Evolved?
Defined as the production and perception of consonants and vowels, speech, as well as the phonological communication it underlies, is plainly a species-typical product of biological evolution. All neurologically normal human beings communicate phonologically; no other creatures do. The biologically important function of phonologic communication derives from the way it exploits the combinatorial principle to generate vocabularies that are large and open, in contrast to the vocabularies of nonhuman, nonphonologic systems, which are small and closed. Thus, phonological processes are unique to language and to the human beings who command them. It follows that anyone who would understand how speech works must answer the question: what evolved? Not when, or why, or how, or by what progression from earlier appearing stages. The first question is simply: what?

The answer given by the horizontal view is clear: at the level of action and perception, nothing evolved; language simply appropriated for its own purposes the plain-vanilla ways of acting and perceiving that had developed independently of any linguistic function. Thus, those horizontalists who put their attention rather narrowly on the perceptual side of the process argue that the categories of phonetic perception simply reflect the way speech articulation has accommodated itself to the production of sounds that conform to the properties of the auditory system, a claim that I will evaluate in some detail later. A recent and broader, but still horizontal, take on the same issue distributes the emphasis more evenly between production and perception, arguing that phonetic gestures were selected by language on the basis of constraints that were generally motor, as well as generally auditory, However, the important point in this, as in the narrower view, is that the constraints are independent of a phonetic function, hence in no way specific to speech. Put forth as an explicit challenge to the vertical assumption, the broader view has it that there is no reason to assume a special mode for the production and perception of speech, if, with the proper horizontal orientation, one can see that the units of speech are optimized with respect to motor and perceptual constraints that are biologically general.

But the question is not whether language somehow developed out of the biology that was already there; surely, it could hardly have done otherwise. The question, to put it yet again, asks, rather, what did that development produce as the basis for a unique mode of communication? When the horizontalists say that the development of this mode was accomplished merely by a process of selection from among the possibilities offered by general faculties that are independent of language, they are giving an account that applies as well to the development of, say, a cursive writing system. Was not the selection of the cursive gestures similarly determined by motor and perceptual constraints that are independent of language? Yet, what that selection produced were not the biologically primary units of speech, but only a set of optical artifacts that had then to be connected to speech in a wholly arbitrary way. Of course, this is merely to say the obvious about the relation between speech and a writing system, which is that the evolution of the one was biological, the other, not. That is surely a critical difference, but one that the horizontal view must have difficulty comprehending.

If pressed further to answer the question about the product of evolution, the horizontalists would presumably have to say that, while nothing evolved at the level of perception and action, there must have been relevant developments at a higher cognitive level. Thus, it would have been evolution that produced the phonetic entities of a cognitive type to which the nonphonetic acts and percepts of speech must, on the horizontal view, be associated. Being neither acts nor percepts, these cognitive entities—or ideas, as they might be—would presumably be acceptable within the horizontal framework as genetically determined adaptations for language, hence special in a way that speech is not allowed to be. In itself, this seems an unparsimonious, not to say biologically implausible, assumption. And it can be seen to be the more unparsimonious and implausible once the horizontalist tries to explain how the phonetically neutral acts and percepts got connected to the specialized cognitive entities in the first place. In the case of a script, to wring one more point out of that tired example, the obviously nonphonetic motor and visual representations of the writer and reader were connected to language by agreement among the interested parties. Can we seriously propose a similar account for speech?

If the horizontalists should reject the notion that phonetic ideas were the evolutionary bases for speech, there remains to them the most thoroughly horizontal view of all, which is that what evolved was a large brain. In that case, they might suppose either that phonological communication was an inevitable by-product of the cognitive power that such a brain provides, which seems unlikely, or that phonological communication was an invention, created by large-brained people who were smart enough to have appreciated the immense advantages for communication of the combinatorial principle, which seems absurd.

The vertical view is different on all counts. What evolved, on this view, was the phonetic module, a distinct system that uses its own kind of signal processing and its own primitives to form a specifically phonetic way of acting and perceiving. It is, then, this module that makes possible the phonological mode of communication.

The primitives of the module are gestures of the articulatory organs. These are the ultimate constituents of language, the units that must be exchanged between speaker and listener if linguistic communication is to occur. Standing apart as a class from the nonphonetic activities of the same organs—for example, chewing, swallowing, moving food around in the mouth, and licking the lips—these gestures serve a phonetic function and no other. Hence they are marked by their very nature as exclusively phonetic in character; there is no need to make them so by connecting them to linguistic entities at the cognitive level. As part of the larger specialization for language, they are, moreover, uniquely appropriate to other linguistic processes. Thus, the syntactic component is adapted to operate on the specifically phonetic representations of the gestures, not on representations of an auditory kind. Indeed, it is precisely this harmony among the several components of the language specialization that makes the epithet "vertical" particularly apposite for the view I am here promoting.

Of course, the gestures constitute only the phonetic structures that the perceptual process extracts from the speech signal. Such aspects of the percept as, for example, those that contribute to the perceived quality of the speaker's voice are not part of the phonetic system. Indeed, these are presumably auditory in the ordinary sense, except as they may figure in speaker identification, for which there may be a separate specialization.

It is not only the gestures themselves that are specifically phonetic, but also, presumably, their control and coordination. Surely, there is in speech production, as in all kinds of action, the need to cope with the many-to-one relations between means and ends, and also to reduce degrees of freedom to manageable proportions. In these respects, then, the management of speech and nonspeech movements should be subject to the same principles. But there is, in addition, something that seems specific to speech: the grossly overlapped and smoothly merged movements at the periphery are controlled by, and must preserve information about, relatively long strings of the invariant, categorical units that speech cares about but other motor systems do not. And, certainly, it is relevant to the claim about a specialized mode of production that speech, in the very narrowest sense, is species specific: given every incentive and opportunity to learn, chimpanzees are nevertheless unable to manage the production of simple CVC syllables. (The fact that the dimensions of their vocal tracts presumably do not allow a full repertory of vowels should not, in itself, preclude the articulation of syllables with whatever vowels their anatomy permits.)

As for the evolution of the phonetic gestures, I should think an important selection factor was not so much the ease with which they could be articulated, or the auditory salience of the resulting sound, but rather how well they lent themselves to being coarticulated. For it is coarticulation that, as I will have occasion to say later, makes phonological communication possible.

But it is also this very coarticulation that, as we saw earlier, frustrates the attempt to find the phonetic invariant in the acoustic signal or in the peripheral movements of the articulators. Still, such motor invariants must exist, not just for the aspect of the Motor Theory that explains how phonetic segments are perceived, but for just any theory that presumes to explain how they are produced; after all, speech does transmit strings of invariant phonological structures, so these invariants must be represented in some way and at some place in the production process. But how are they to be characterized, and where are they to be found? Having accepted the evidence that they are not in the peripheral movements, as the Early Motor Theory assumed, Mattingly and I proposed in the Revised Motor Theory that attention be paid instead to the configurations of the vocal tract as they change over time and are compared with other configurations produced by the same gesture in different contexts. As for the invariant causes of these configurations, they are presumably to be found in the more remote motor entities—something like Turvey's coordinative structures—that control the various articulator movements so as to accomplish the appropriate vocal-tract configurations. It is, I now think, structures of this kind that represent the phonetic primitives, providing the physiological basis for the phonetic intentions of the speaker and the phonetic percepts of the listener. Unfortunately for the Motor Theory, we do not yet know the exact characteristics of these motor invariants, nor can we adequately describe the processes by which they control the movements of the articulators. My colleagues, including especially Cathe Browman, Louis Goldstein, Elliot Saltzman, and Philip Rubin, are currently in search of those invariants and processes, and I am confident that they will, in time, succeed in finding them. Meanwhile, I will, for all the reasons set forth in this introduction, remain confident that motor invariants do exist, and that they are the ultimate constituents of speech, as produced and as perceived.

According to the Revised Motor Theory, then, there is a phonetic module, part of the larger specialization for language, that is biologically adapted for two complementary processes: one controls the overlapping and merging of the gestures that constitute the phonetic primitives; the other processes the resulting acoustic signal so as to recover, in perception, those same primitives. On this view, one sees a distinctly linguistic way of doing things down among the nuts and bolts of action and perception, for it is there, not in the remote recesses of the cognitive machinery, that the specifically linguistic constituents make their first appearance. Thus, the Revised Motor Theory is very different from its early ancestor; the two remain as one only in supposing that the object of perception is the invariant gesture, not the context-sensitive sound.

How Is the Requirement for Parity Met?
In all communication, whether linguistic or not, sender and receiver must be bound by a common understanding about what counts: what counts for the sender must count for the receiver, else communication does not occur. In the case of speech, speaker and listener must perceive, or otherwise know, that, out of all possible signals, only a particular few have linguistic significance. Moreover, the processes of production and perception must somehow be linked; their representations must, at some point, be the same. Though basic, this requirement tends to pass unnoticed by those who look at speech horizontally, and, especially, by those whose preoccupation with perception leaves production out of account. However, vertical motor theorists like Ignatius Mattingly and me are bound to think the requirement important, so we have given it a name—"parity"—and asked how, in the case of speech communication, it was established and how maintained.

Horizontalists must, I think, find the question very hard. For if, as their view would have it, the acts of the speaker are generally motor and the percepts of the listener generally auditory, then act and percept have in common only that neither has anything to do with language. The horizontalist is therefore required to assume that these representations are linked to language and to each other only insofar as speaker and listener have somehow selected them for linguistic use from the indefinitely large set of similarly nonphonetic alternatives, and then connected them at a cognitive level to the same phonetic name or other linguistic entity. Altogether, a roundabout way for a natural mode of communication to work.

For the verticalists, on the other hand, the question is easy. On their view, it was specifically phonetic gestures that evolved, together with the specialized processes for producing and perceiving them, and it is just these gestures that provide the common currency with which speaker and listener conduct their linguistic business. Parity is thus guaranteed, having been built by evolution into the very bones of the system; there is no need to arrive at agreements about which signals are relevant and how they are to be connected to units of the language.

How Is Speech Related to Other Natural Modes of Communication?
I noted earlier that human beings communicate phonologically but other creatures do not, and, further, that this difference is important, because it determines whether the inventory of "words" is open or closed. Now, in the interest of parsimony, I ask whether either view of speech allows that there is, nevertheless, something common to two modes of communication that are equally natural.

On the horizontal view, the two modes must be seen as different in every important respect. Nonhuman animals, the horizontalists would presumably agree, communicate as they do because of their underlying specializations for producing and perceiving the appropriate signals. I doubt that anyone would seriously claim that these require to be translated before they can take on communicative significance. For the human, however, the horizontal position, as we have seen, is that the specialization, if any, is not at the level of the signal, but only at some cognitive remove. I find it hard to imagine what might have been gained for human beings by this evolutionary leap to an exclusively cognitive representation of the communicative elements, except, perhaps, the smug satisfaction they might take in believing that they communicate phonologically, and the nonhuman animals do not, because they have an intellectual power the other creatures lack, and that even in the most basic aspects of communication they can count themselves broad generalists, while the others must be seen as narrow specialists.

On the vertical view, human and nonhuman communication alike depend on a specialization at the level of the signal. Of course, these specializations differ one from another, as do the vehicles—acoustic, optical, chemical, or electrical—that they use. And, surely, the phonetic specialization differs from all the others in a way that is, as we know, critical to the openness or generativity of language. Still, the vertical view permits us to see that phonetic communication is not completely off the biological scale, since it is, like the other natural forms of communication, a specialization all the way down to its roots.

What Are the (Special) Requirements of Phonological Communication, and How Are They Met?
If phonology is to use the combinatorial principle, and so serve its critically important function of building a large and open vocabulary out of a small number of elements, then it must meet at least two requirements. The more obvious is that the phonological segments be commutable, which is to say discrete, invariant, and categorical. The other requirement, which is only slightly less obvious, concerns rate. For if all utterances are to be formed by stringing together an exiguous set of commutable elements, then, inevitably, the strings must run to great lengths. There is, therefore, a high premium on rapid communication of the elements, not only in the interest of getting the job done in good time, but also in order to make things reasonably easy, or even feasible, for those other processes that have got to organize the phonetic segments into words and sentences.

Consider how these requirements would be met if, as the horizontal view would have it, the elements were sounds and the auditory percepts they evoke. If it were these that had to be commutable, then surely it would have been possible to make them so, but only at the expense of rate. For sounds and the corresponding auditory percepts to be discrete, invariant, and categorical would require that the segmentation be apparent at the surface of the signal and in the most peripheral aspects of the articulation. How else, on the horizontal view, could commutability be achieved, except as each discrete sound and associated auditory percept were produced by a correspondingly discrete articulatory maneuver? Of course, the sounds and the percepts might be joined, as are the segments of cursive writing, and that might speed things up a bit, but, exactly as in cursive writing, the segmentation would nevertheless have to be patent. The consequence would be that, to say a monosyllabic word like 'bag', the speaker would have to articulate the segments discretely, and that would produce, not the monosyllable 'bag', but the trisyllable [bə] [æ] [gə]. To articulate the syllable that way is not to speak, but to spell, and spelling would be an impossibly slow and tedious way to communicate language.

One might imagine that if production had been the only problem in the matter of rate, nature might have solved it by abandoning the vocal tract, providing her human creatures, instead, with acoustic devices specifically adapted to producing rapid-fire sequences of sound. That would have taken care of the production problem, while, at the same time, defeating the ear. The problem is that, at normal rates, speech produces from eight to ten segments per second, and, for short stretches, at least double that number. But if each of those were a unit sound, then rates that high would strain the temporal resolving power of the ear, and, of particular importance to phonetic communication, also exceed its abililty to perceive the order in which the segments had been laid down. Indeed, the problem would be exactly the one we encountered when, in the early work on reading machines, we presented acoustic alphabets at high rates.

According to the vertical view, nature solved the rate problem by avoiding the acoustic-auditory (horizontal) strategy that would have caused it. What evolved as the phonetic constituents were the special gestures I spoke of earlier. These serve well as the elements of language, because, if properly chosen and properly controlled, they can be coarticulated, so strings of them can be produced at high rates. In any case, all speakers of all languages do, in fact, coarticulate, and it is only by this means that they are able to communicate phonologically as rapidly as they do.

Coarticulation had happy consequences for perception, too. For coarticulation folds information about several successive segments into the same stretch of sound, thereby achieving a parallel transmission of information that considerably relaxes the constraint imposed by the temporal resolving properties of the ear. But this gain came at the price of a relation between acoustic signal and phonetic message that is complex in a specifically phonetic way. One such complication is the context-conditioned variability in the acoustic signal that I identified as the primary motivation for the Early Motor Theory, presenting it then as if it were an obstacle that the processes postulated by the theory had to overcome. Now, on the Revised Motor Theory, we can see that same variability as a blessing, a rich source of information about phonetic structure, and, especially, about order. Consider, again, the difficulty the auditory system has in perceiving accurately the ordering of discrete and brief sounds that are presented sequentially. Coarticulation effectively gets around that difficulty by permitting the listener to apprehend order in quite another way. For, given coarticulation, the production of any single segment affects the acoustic realization of neighboring segments, thereby providing, in the context-conditioned variation that results, accurate information about which gesture came first, which second, and so on. Hence, the order of the segments is conveyed largely by the shape of the acoustic signal, not by the way pieces of sound are sequenced in it. For example, in otherwise comparable consonant-vowel and vowel-consonant syllables, the listener is not likely to mistake the order, however brief the syllables, because the transitions for prevocalic and postvocalic consonants are mirror images. But these will have the proper perceptual consequence only if the phonetic system is specialized to represent the strongly contrasting acoustic signals, not as similarly contrasting auditory percepts, but as the opening and closing phases of the same phonetic gesture. Accordingly, order is given for free by processes that are specialized to deal with the acoustic consequences of coarticulated phonetic gestures. Thus, we see that a critical function of the phonetic module is not so much to take advantage of the properties of the general motor and auditory systems—a matter that was briefly examined earlier—as it is to find a way around their limitations.

Could the Assignment of the Stimulus Information to Phonetic Categories Plausibly Be Auditory?
Many of the empirically based arguments about the two theories of speech, including, especially, most of those that have been advanced against the vertical position, come from experiments, much like those described in the first section of this introduction, that were designed very simply to identify the information that leads to perception of phonetic segments. The results of these experiments have proved to be reliable, so there is quite general agreement about the nature of the relevant information. Disagreement arises only, but nonetheless fundamentally, about the nature of the event that the information is informing about. Is it the sound, as a proper auditory (and horizontal) view would have it, or the articulatory gesture, which is the choice of the vertically oriented Motor Theory.

The Multiplicity of Acoustic-Phonetic Boundaries and Cues Research of the kind just referred to has succeeded in isolating many acoustic variables important to perception of the various phonetic segments, and in finding for each the location of the boundary that separates the one segment from some alternative—for example, [ba] from [da]. The horizontalists take satisfaction in further experiments on some of these boundaries in which it has been found that they are exhibited by nonhuman animals, or by human observers when presented with nonspeech analogs of speech, for these findings are, of course, consistent with the assumption that the boundaries are auditory in nature. In response, the verticalists point to experiments in which it has been found that the boundaries differ between human and nonhuman subjects, and, in humans, between speech and nonspeech analogs, arguing, in their turn, that these findings support the view that the boundaries are specifically phonetic. Indeed, for some parties to the debate it has been in the interpretation of these boundaries that the difference between the two views has come into sharpest focus. The issue therefore deserves to be further ventilated.

It is now widely accepted that the location of the acoustic-phonetic boundary on every relevant cue dimension varies greatly as a function of phonetic context, position in the syllable, and vocal-tract dimensions. It is now also known, and accepted, that some vary with differences in language type, linguistic stress, and rate of articulation. For at least one of these—rate of articulation—the variation is possibly continuous. From all this it follows that the number of acoustic-phonetic boundaries is indefinitely large, far too large, surely, to make reasonable the assumption that they are properties of the auditory system. How would these uncountably many boundaries have been selected for as that system evolved? Surely, not just against the possibility that language would come along and find them useful. Indeed, as auditory properties, they would presumably be dysfunctional, since they are perceptual discontinuities of a sort, and would, therefore, cause continuously varying acoustic events to be perceived discontinuously, thereby frustrating veridical perception.

The matter is the worse confounded for the auditory theory when proper account is taken of the fact that, for every phonetic segment, there are multiple cues, and that phonetic perception uses all of them. For if, in accounting for the perception of certain consonantal segments, we attribute an auditory basis to all the context-variable boundaries on, say, the second-formant transitions—already a dubious assumption, as we've seen—then what do we do about the third-formant transitions and the bursts (or fricative noises)? These various information-bearing aspects of the signal are not independently controllable in speech production, so one must wonder about the probability that a gesture so managed as to have just the "right" acoustic consequences for the second-formant transition would happen, also, to have just the right consequences in all cases for the other, acoustically very different cues. On its face, that probability would seem to be vanishingly small.

Nor does it help the horizontal position to suggest, as some have, that the acoustic-phonetic boundaries exhibited by nonhuman animals served merely as the auditory starting points—the protoboundaries, as it were—to which all the others were somehow added. For this is to suppose that, out of the many conditions known to affect the acoustic manifestation of each phonetic segment, some one is canonical. But is it plausible to suppose that there really are canonical forms for vocal-tract size, rate of articulation, condition of stress, language type, and all the other conditions that affect the speech signal? And what of the further implications? What, for example, is the status of the countless other boundaries that had then to be added in order to accommodate the noncanonical forms? Did they infect the general auditory system, or were they set apart in a distinct phonetic mode? If the former, then why does everything not sound very much like speech? If the latter, then are we to suppose that the listener shifts back and forth between auditory and phonetic modes depending on whether or not it is the canonical form that is to be perceived?

None of this is to say that natural boundaries or discontinuities do not exist in the auditory system—I believe there is evidence that they do—but rather to argue that they are irrelevant to phonetic perception.

All of the foregoing considerations are simply grist for the Motor Theory mill. For on that theory, the phonetic module uses the speech stimulus as information about the gestures, which are the true and immediate objects of phonetic perception, and so finds the acoustic-phonetic boundaries where the articulatory apparatus happened, for its own very good reasons, to put them. The auditory system is then free to respond to all other acoustic stimuli in a way that does not inappropriately conform their perception to a phonetic mold.

Integrating Cues that Are Acoustically Heterogeneous, Widely Distributed in Time, and Shared by Disparate Segments   Having already noted that there are typically many cues for a phonetic distinction, I take note of the well-known fact that these many cues are, more often than not, acoustically heterogeneous. Yet, in the several cases so far investigated, they can, within limits, be traded, one for the other, without any change in the immediate percept. That is, with other cues neutralized, the phonetic distinction can be produced by any one of the acoustically heterogeneous cues, with perceptual results that are not discriminably different. Since these perceptual equivalences presumably exist among all the cues for each such contrast, the number of equivalences must be very great, indeed. But how are these many equivalences to be explained? From an acoustic or auditory-processing standpoint, what do such acoustically diverse, but perceptually equivalent, cues have in common? Or, in the absence of that commonality, how plausible is it to suppose that they might nevertheless have evolved in the auditory system in connection with its nonspeech functions? In that regard, one asks the same questions I raised about the claim concerning the auditory basis of the boundary positions. What general auditory function would have selected for these equivalences? Would they not, in almost every case, be dysfunctional, since they would make very different acoustic events sound the same? And, finally, what is the probability that speakers could so govern their articulatory gestures as to produce for each particular phonetic segment exactly the right combination of perceptually equivalent cues?

The Revised Motor Theory has no difficulty dealing with the foregoing facts about stimulus equivalence. It notes simply that the acoustically heterogeneous cues have in common that they are products of the same phonetically significant gesture. Since it is the gesture that is perceived, the perceptual equivalence necessarily follows.

Also relevant to the argument is the fact that phonetic perception integrates into a coherent phonetic segment a numerous variety of cues that are, because of coarticulation, widely dispersed through the signal and used simultaneously to provide information for other segments in the string, including not only their position, as earlier noted, but also their phonetic identity. The simplest examples of such dispersal were among the very earliest findings of our speech research, as described in the first half of this introduction. Since then, the examples have been multiplied to include cases in which the spread of the cues for a single segment is found to be much broader than originally supposed, extending, in some utterances, from one end of a complex syllable to the other; yet, even in these cases, the phonetic system integrates the information appropriately for each of the constituent segments. I have great difficulty imagining what function such integration would serve in a system that is adapted to the perception of nonspeech events. Indeed, I should suppose that it would sometimes distort the representation of events that were discrete and closely sequenced.

Again, the Revised Motor Theory has a ready, if by now expected, explanation: the widely dispersed cues are brought together, as it were, into a single and perceptually coherent segment because they are, again, the common products of the relevant articulatory gesture.

Integrating Acoustic and Optical Information   It is by now well known that, as Harry McGurk demonstrated some years ago, observers form phonetic percepts under conditions in which some of the information is acoustic and some optical, provided the optical information is about articulatory gestures. Thus, when observers are presented with acoustic [ba], but see a face saying [de], they will, under many conditions of intensity and clarity of the signal, perceive [da], having taken the consonant from what they saw and the vowel from what they heard. Though the perceptual effect is normally quite compelling, the result is typically experienced as slightly imperfect by comparison with the normal case in which acoustic and optical stimuli are in agreement. But the observers can't tell what the nature of the imperfection is. That is, they can't say that it is to be attributed to the fact that they heard one thing but saw another. Left standing, therefore, is the conclusion that the McGurk effect provides strong evidence for the equivalence in phonetic perception of two very different kinds of physical information, acoustic and optical.

For those who believe that speech perception is auditory, the explanation of the McGurk effect must be that the unitary percept is the result of a learned association between hearing a phonetic structure and seeing it produced. As an explanation of the phenomenon, however, such an account seems manifestly improbable, since it requires us to believe, contrary to all experience, that a convincing auditory percept can be elicited by an optical stimulus, or that an auditory percept and a visual percept become indistinguishable as a consequence of frequent association. Indeed, we are required to believe, even more implausibly, that the seemingly auditory percept elicited by the optical stimulus is so strong as to prevail over the normal (and different) auditory response to a suprathreshold *acoustic* stimulus that is presented concurrently. If there were such drastic perceptual consequences of association in the general case, then the world would sometimes be misrepresented to observers as they gained experience with percepts in different modalities that happened often to be contiguous in time. Fortunately for our relation to the world, there is no reason to suppose that such modality shifts, and the consequent distortions of reality, ever occur. As for the implications of the horizontal account for the McGurk effect specifically, we should expect that the phenomenon would be obtained between the sounds of speech and print, given the vast experience that literate adults have had in associating the one with the other. Yet the effect does not occur with print. It also weighs against the same account that prelinguistic infants have been shown to be sensitive to the correspondence between speech sounds and seen articulatory movements, which is, of course, the basis of the McGurk effect.

On the vertical view, the McGurk phenomenon is exactly what one would expect, since the acoustic and optical stimuli are providing information about the same phonetic gesture, and it is, as I have said so relentlessly, precisely the gesture that is perceived.

Just How "Special" Is Speech Perception?
The claim that speech perception is special has been criticized most broadly, perhaps, on the ground that it is manifestly unparsimonious and lacking in generality. Unparsimonious, because a "special" mechanism is necessarily an additional mechanism; and lacking in generality, because that which is special is, by definition, not general.

As for parsimony, I have already suggested that the shoe is on the other foot. For the price of denying a distinctly phonetic mode at the level of perception is having to make the still less parsimonious assumption that such a mode begins at a higher cognitive level, or wherever it is that the auditory percepts of the horizontal view are converted to the postperceptual phonetic shapes they must assume if they are to serve as the vehicles of linguistic communication.

But generality is another matter. Here, the horizontal view might appear to have the advantage, since it sees the perception of speech as a wholly unexceptional example of the workings of an auditory modality that deals with speech just as it does with all the other sounds to which the ear is sensitive. In so doing, however, this view sacrifices what is, I think, a more important kind of generality, since it makes speech perception a mere adjunct to language, having a connection to it no less arbitrary than that which characterizes the relation of language to the visually perceived shapes of an alphabet. The vertical view, on the other hand, shows the connection to language to be truly organic, permitting us to see speech perception as special in much the same way that other components of language perception are special. I have already pointed out in this connection that the output of the specialized speech module is a representation that is, by its nature, specifically appropriate for further processing by the syntactic component. Now I would add that the processes of phonetic and syntactic perception have in common that the distinctly linguistic representations they produce are not given directly by the superficial properties of the signal. Consider, in this connection, how a perceiving system might go about deciding whether or not an acoustic signal contains phonetic information. Though there are, to be sure, certain general acoustic characteristics of natural speech, experience with synthetic speech has shown that none of them necessarily signals the presence of phonetic structure. Having already noted that this was one of the theoretically interesting conclusions of the earliest work with the the highly schematized drawings used on the Pattern Playback, I add now that more convincing evidence of the same kind has come from later research that carried the schematization of the synthetic patterns to an extreme by reducing them to three sine waves that merely follow the center frequencies of the first three formants. These bare bones have nevertheless proved sufficient to evoke phonetic percepts, even though they have no common fundamental, no common fate, nor, indeed, any other kind of acoustic commonality that might provide auditory coherence and mark the sinusoids acoustically as speech. What the sinusoids do offer the listener—indeed, all they offer—is information about the trajectories of the formants, which is to say movements of the articulators. If those movements can be seen by the phonetic module as appropriate to linguistically significant gestures, then the module, being properly engaged, integrates them into a coherent phonetic structure; otherwise, not. There are, then, no purely acoustic properties, no acoustic stigmata, on the basis of which the presence of phonetic structure can, under all circumstances, be reliably apprehended. But is it not so with syntax, too? If a perceiving system is to determine whether or not a string of words is a sentence, it surely cannot rely on some list of surface properties; rather it must determine if the string can be parsed—that is, if a grammatical derivation can be found. Thus, the specializations for phonetic and syntactic perception have in common that their products are deeply linguistic, and are arrived at by procedures that are similarly synthetic.

As for specializations that are adapted for functions other than communication, Mattingly and I have claimed for speech perception that, as I earlier hinted, it bears significant resemblances to a number of biologically coherent adaptations. Being specialized for different functions, each of these is necessarily different from every other one, but they nevertheless have certain properties in common. Thus, they all qualify as modules, in Fodor's sense of that term, and therefore share something like the properties he assigns to such devices. I choose not to review those here, but rather to identify, though only briefly, several other common properties that such modules, including the phonetic, seem to have.

To see what some of those properties might be, Mattingly and I have found it useful to distinguish broadly between two classes of modules. One comprises, in the auditory modality, the specializations for pitch, loudness, timbre, and the like. These underlie the common auditory dimensions that, in their various combinations, form the indefinitely numerous percepts by which people identify a correspondingly numerous variety of acoustic events, including, of course, many that are produced by artifacts of one sort or another, and that are, therefore, less than perfectly natural. We have thought it fitting to call this class "open." It is appropriate to the all-purpose character of these modules that its representations be commensurate with the relevant dimensions of the physical stimulus. Thus, pitch maps onto frequency, loudness onto amplitude, and timbre onto spectral shape; hence, we have called these representations "homomorphic." It is also appropriate to their all-purpose function that these homomorphic representations not be permanently changed as a result of long experience with some acoustic event. Otherwise, acquired skill in using the sound of automobile engines for diagnostic purposes, for example, would render the relevant modules maladapted for every one of the many other events for which they must be used.

Members of the other class—the one that includes speech—are more narrowly specialized for particular acoustic events or stimulus relationships that are, as particular events or relationships, of particular biological importance to the animal. We have, therefore, called this class "closed." It includes specializations like sound localization, stereopsis, and echolocation (in the bat) that I mentioned earlier. Unlike the representations of the open class, those produced by the closed modules are incommensurate with the dimensions of the stimulus; we have therefore called them "heteromorphic." Thus, the sound-localizing module represents interaural differences of time and intensity, not homomorphically as time or loudness, but heteromorphically as location; the module for stereopsis represents binocular disparities, not homomorphically as double images, but heteromorphically as depth. The echolocating module of the bat presumably represents echo time, not homomorphically as an echoing (bat) cry, but heteromorphically as distance. In a similar way, the phonetic module respresents the continuously changing formants, not homomorphically as smoothly varying timbres, but heteromorphically as a sequence of discrete and categorical phonetic segments.

Unlike the open modules, those of the closed class depend on very particular kinds of environmental stimulation, not only for their development, but for their proper calibration. Moreover, they remain plastic—that is, open to calibration—for some considerable time. Consider, in this connection, how the sound-localizing module must be continuously recalibrated for its response to interaural differences as the distance between the ears increases with the growth of the child's head. The similarly plastic phonetic module is calibrated over a period of years by the particular phonetic environment to which it is exposed. Significantly, the calibration of these modules in no way affects any of the specializations of the open class, even though their representations figure importantly in the final percept, as in the paraphonetic aspects of speech, for example. This is to say that the closed modules must learn by experience, as the phonetic module most surely does, but the learning is of an entirely precognitive sort, requiring only neurological normality and exposure (at the right time) to the particular kinds of stimuli in which the module is exclusively interested.

As implied above, the two classes have their own characteristically different ways of representing the same dimension of the stimulus. Why, then, does the listener not get both representations—heteromorphic and homomorphic—at the same time? Given binocularly disparate stimuli, why does the viewer not see double images in addition to depth? Or, given two syllables [da] and [ga] that are distinguished only by the direction of the third-formant transition, why does the listener not hear, in addition to the discrete consonant and vowel, the continuously changing timbre that the most nearly equivalent nonspeech pattern would produce, and to which the two transitions would presumably make their distinctively different, but equally nonphonetic, contributions.

Mattingly and I once proposed that the competition between the modules is normally resolved in favor of those in the closed class by virtue of their ability to preempt the information, and thus, in effect, to remove it from the flow. However, further research and reflection has shown that to be a rather extravagant characterization. It seems better to suppose that the modules of the closed class simply have an extraordinary sensitivity to the information that is ecologically appropriate to the heteromorphic percepts they are specialized to represent. As for what is ecologically appropriate, the closed modules have an elasticity that permits them to take a rather broad view. Thus, the module for stereopsis represents depth for binocular disparities considerably greater than would ever be produced by even the most widely separated eyes. The phonetic module will, in its turn, tolerate rather large departures from what is ecologically plausible. Imagine, for example, two synthetic syllables, [da] and [ga], distinguished only by the direction of a third-formant transition that, as I indicated earlier, sounds in isolation like a nonspeech chirp. If the syllables are now divided into two parts—one, the critical transition cue; the other, the remainder of the pattern (the "base") that, by itself, is ambiguously [da] or [ga]—then, the phonetic system will integrate them into a coherent [da] or [ga] syllable even when the two parts have, by various means, been made to come from perceptibly different sources. (Mattingly has a different interpretation of this particular phenomenon, so I must take full responsibility for the one I offer here.) In what is, perhaps, the most dramatic demonstration of this kind of integration, the isolated transition cue is presented at a location opposite one ear, the ambiguous base at a location opposite the other. Under these ecologically implausible circumstances, the listener nevertheless perceives a perfectly coherent [da] or [ga], and, more to the point, confidently localizes it to the side where only the ambiguous base was presented. (This happens, indeed, even when both the base and the critical transition cue are made of frequency-modulated sinusoids, which is a most severe test, since the differently located sinusoids would, as I pointed out earlier, seem to lack any kind of acoustic coherence that might cause them to be integrated on some auditory basis.) But there are limits to this elasticity, and seemingly similar effects occur in phonetic perception and in stereopsis when those limits are exceeded. Thus, in the speech case, as the stimulus is made to provide progressively more evidence for separate sources—for example, by increasing the relative intensity of the isolated transition on the one side—listeners begin to hear both the integrated syllable *and* the nonspeech chirp. In other words, the heteromorphic and homomorphic percepts are simultaneously represented. In the speech case, this has been called "duplex perception." Appropriate (and necessary) tests for the claim that the duplex percepts are representations of truly different types, and not simply a cognitive reinterpretation of a single type, are in the demonstration that listeners cannot accurately identify the chirps as [da] and [ga], and that they hear only the integrated syllable and the chirp, not those and also the ambiguous base. It is also relevant to the claim that the discrimination functions obtained for the percepts on the two sides of the percept are radically different, for that shows that the listeners cannot hear the one in the other, even when, under the conditions of the discrimination procedure, they try. (Unfortunately, these tests have not been applied to the cases of nonspeech auditory perception that some have claimed to be duplex.)

In the case of stereopsis, the elasticity of the module is strained by progressively increasing the binocular disparity. Beyond a certain point, the viewer begins to perceive not only heteromorpic depth, but also homomorphic double images. This seems quite analogous to duplex perception, though it has not been called that.

In both speech and stereopsis, providing further evidence of ecological implausibility causes the heteromorphic percept (phonetic structure or depth) to weaken as its homomorphic counterpart (nonphonetic chirp or double images) strengthens, until, finally, the closed module fails utterly, and only the homomorphic percept of the open modules is represented. Thus, the information in the stimulus can seemingly be variously divided between the two kinds of representation, and, since either gains at the expense of the other, it is as if there were a kind of conservation of information.

Putting the matter most generally, then, I should say that speech is special, to be sure, but neither more nor less so than many other biologically coherent adaptations, including, of course, language itself.

How Do Speaking and Listening Differ from Writing and Reading?
Among the most obvious, and obviously consequential, facts about language is the immense difference in biological status, hence naturalness, between speech, on the one hand, and writing/reading, on the other. The phonetic units of speech are the vehicles of every language on earth, and are commanded by every neurologically normal human being. On the other hand, many, perhaps most, languages do not even have a written form, and, among those that do, some competent speakers find it all but impossible to master. Having been thus reminded once again that speech is the biologically primary form of the phonological behavior that typifies our species, we readily appreciate that alphabetic writing is not really the primary behavior itself, but only a fair description of it. Since what is being described is species typical, alphabetic writing is a piece of ethological science, in which case a writer/reader is fairly regarded as an accomplished ethologist. It weighs heavily against the horizontal view, therefore, that, as I have already said and will say again below, it cannot comprehend the difference between speaking/listening and writing/reading, for in that respect it is like a theory of bird song that does not distinguish the behavior of the bird from that of the ethologist who describes it. (See chapter 24.)

To see the problem created by the horizontal view, we need first to appreciate, once again, that writing-reading did not evolve as part of the language faculty, so the relevant acts and percepts cannot be specifically linguistic. The important consequence, of course, is that they require to be made so, and, as I have said so many times, that can be done only by some kind of cognitive translation. Now I would emphasize that it is primarily in respect of this requirement that writing and reading differ biologically from speech. Indeed, it is precisely in the need to meet this requirement that writing-reading are intellectual achievements in a way that speech is not. But the horizontal view of speech does not permit us to see that essential difference. Rather, it misleads us into the belief that the primary processes of the two modes of linguistic communication are equally general, hence equally nonphonetic. That being so, we must suppose that the relevant representations are equally in need of a cognitive connection to the language, and so have the same status from a biological point of view. We are, of course, permitted to see the obvious and superficial differences, but, for each one of those, the horizontal view would seem, paradoxically, to give the advantage to writing/reading, leading us to expect that writing-reading, not speaking-listening, would be the easier and more natural. For, surely, the printed characters offer a much better signal-to-noise ratio than the phonetically relevant parts of the speech sound; the fingers and the hand are vastly more versatile than the tongue; the eye provides far greater possibilities for the transmission of information than the ear; and, for all the vagaries of some spelling systems, the alphabetic characters bear a more nearly transparent relation to the phonological units of the language than the context-variable and elaborately overlapped cues of the acoustic signal.

The vertical view, on the other hand, is appropriately revealing. Given the phonetic module, speakers do not have to know how to spell a word in order to produce it. Indeed, they do not even have to know that it has a spelling. Speakers have only to access the word, however that is done; the module then spells it for them, automatically selecting and coordinating the appropriate gestures. Listeners are in similar case. To perceive the word, they need not puzzle out the complex and peculiarly phonetic relation between signal and the phonological message it conveys; they need only listen, again leaving all the hard work to the phonetic module. Being modular, these processes of production and perception are not available to conscious analysis, so the speakers and listeners cannot be aware of how they do what they do. Though the representations themselves *are* available to consciousness—indeed, if they were not, use of an alphabetic script would be impossible—they are already phonological in nature, hence appropriate for further linguistic processing, so the reader need not even notice them, as he would have to if, as in the case of alphabetic characters, some arbitrary connection to language had to be formed. Hence, the processes of speech, whether in production or perception, are not calculated to put the speaker's attention on the phonological units that those processes are specialized to manage.

On the basis of considerations very like those, Isabelle Liberman, Donald Shankweiler, and Ignatius Mattingly saw, more than twenty years ago, that, while awareness of phonological structure is obviously necessary for anyone who would make proper use of an alphabetic script, such awareness would not normally be a consequence of having learned to speak. Isabelle and Donald proceeded, then, to test this hypothesis with preliterate children, finding that such children do, indeed, not know how to break a word into its constituent phonemes. That finding has now been replicated many times. Moreover, researchers at the Laboratories and elsewhere have found that the degree to which would-be readers are phonologically aware may be the best single predictor of their success in learning to read, and that training in phonological awareness has generally happy consequences for the progress in reading of those children who receive it. There is also reason to believe that, other things equal, an important cause of reading disability may be a weakness in the phonetic module. That weakness would make the phonological representations less clear than they would otherwise be, hence that much harder to bring to awareness. Indeed, there is at least a little evidence that reading-disabled chilren do have, in addition to their problems with phonological awareness, some of the other characteristics that a weak phonetic module might be expected to produce. Thus, by comparison with normals, they seem to be poorer in several kinds of phonologically related performances: short-term memory for phonological structures, but not for items of a nonlinguistic kind; perception of speech, but not of nonspeech sounds, in noise; naming of objects—that is, retrieving the appropriate phonological structures—even when they know what the objects are and what they do; and, finally, production of tongue twisters.

The vertical view was not developed to explain the writing-reading process or the ills that so frequently attend it, but rather for all the reasons given in earlier sections of this introduction. That it nevertheless offers a plausible account, while the horizontal view does not, is surely to be counted strongly in its favor.

Are There Acoustic Substitutes for Speech?

When Frank Cooper and I set out to build a reading machine for the blind, we accepted that the answer to that question was not just "yes," but "yes, of course." As I see it now, the reason for our blithe confidence was that, being unable to imagine an alternative, we could only think in what I have here described as horizontal terms. We therefore thought it obvious that speech sounds evoked normal auditory percepts, and that these were then named in honor of the various consonants and vowels so they could be used for linguistic purposes.

On the basis of our early experience with the nonspeech sounds of our reading machines, we learned the hard way that things were different from what we had thought. But it was not until we were well into the research on speech that we began to see just how different and why. Now, drawing on all that research, we would say that the answer to the question about acoustic substitutes is "no," or, in the more emphatic modern form, "no way." The sounds produced by a reading machine for the blind will serve as well as speech only if they are of a kind that might have been made by the organs of articulation as they figure in gestures of a specifically phonetic sort. If the sounds meet that requirement, then they will engage the specialization for speech, and so qualify as proper vehicles for linguistic structures; otherwise, they will encounter all the difficulties that fatally afflicted the nonspeech sounds we worked with so many years ago.

References

For representative expressions of the horizontal view, see:

Cole, R. A., and B. Scott. 1974a. The phantom in the phoneme: Invariant cues for stop consonants. *Perception and Psychophysics* 15:101–107.

———. 1974b. Toward a theory of speech perception. *Psychological Review* 81:348–374.

Crowder, R. G. 1983. The purity of auditory memory. *Philosophical Transactions of the Royal Society, Section B*, 302:251–265.

Crowder, R. G., and J. Morton. 1969. Pre-categorical acoustic storage (PAS). *Perception and Psychophysics* 5:365–373.

Diehl, R., and K. Kluender. 1986. On the objects of speech perception. *Ecological Psychology.*

Fujisaki, H., and T. Kawashima. 1970. Some experiments on speech perception and a model for the perceptual mechanism. *Annual Report of the Engineering Research Institute* (Faculty of Engineering, University of Tokyo) 29:207–214.

Hillenbrand, J. 1984. Perception of sine-wave analogs of voice onset time stimuli. *Journal of the Acoustical Society of America* 75:231–240.

Kuhl, P. K. 1981. Discrimination of speech by nonhuman animals: Basic auditory sensitivities conducive to the perception of speech-sound categories. *Journal of the Acoustical Society of America* 70:340–349.

Lindlom, B. 1991. The status of phonetic gestures. In I. G. Mattingly and M. Studdert-Kennedy (eds.), *Modularity and the motor theory of speech perception.* Hillsdale, NJ: Lawrence Erlbaum Associates.

Massaro, D. W. 1987. *Speech perception by ear and eye: A paradigm for psychological enquiry.* Hillsdale, NJ: Lawrence Erlbaum Associates.

Miller, J. D. 1977. Perception of speech sounds in animals: Evidence for speech processing by mammalian auditory mechanisms. In T. H. Bullock (ed.), *Recognition of complex acoustic signals* 49 (Life Sciences Research Report 5). Berlin: Dahlem Konferenzen.

Oden, G. C., and D. W. Massaro. 1978. Integration of featural information in speech perception *Psychological Review* 85:172–191.

Pisoni, D. B. 1973. Auditory and phonetic memory codes in the discrimination of consonants and vowels. *Perception and Psychophysics* 13:253–260.

Samuel, A. G. 1977. The effect of discrimination training on speech perception: Noncategorical perception. *Perception and Psychophysics* 22:321–330.

Stevens, K. N., and S. E. Blumstein. 1978. Invariant cues for place of articulation in stop consonants. *Journal of the Acoustical Society of America* 64:1358–1368.

Stevens, K. N., and S. Hawkins. 1982. Acoustic and perceptual correlates of nasal vowels. *Journal of the Acoustical Society of America* 71:S76(A).

Sussman, H. 1989. Neural coding of relational invariance in speech: Human language analogs to the barn owl. *Psychological Review* 96:631–642.

———. 1991. The representation of stop consonants in three-dimensional acoustic space. *Phonetica* 48:18–31.

Sussman, H., H. McCaffrey, and S. Matthews. 1991. An investigation of locus equations as a source of relational invariance for stop place categorization. *Journal of the Acoustical Society of America* 90:1309–1325.

van Hessen, and M. E. H. Schouten. 1992. Modeling phoneme perception. II: A model of stop consonant discrimination. *Journal of the Acoustical Society of America* 92:1956–1968.

For representative expressions of the vertical view, see:

Liberman, A. M. 1992. The relation of speech to reading and writing. In L. Katz and R. Frost (eds.), *Orthography, phonology, morphology, and meaning,* 167–178. Amsterdam: Elsevier Science Publlshers.

Liberman, A. M., and I. G. Mattingly. 1985. The motor theory of speech perception revised. *Cognition* 21:1–36.

———. 1989. A specialization for speech perception. *Science* 243:489–494.

Mann, V. A., and A. M. Liberman. 1983. Some differences between phonetic and auditory modes of perception. *Cognition* 14:211–235.

Mattingly, I. G. 1991. In defense of the motor theory. *Perilus* 14:167–172. Stockholm: Institute of Linguistics, University of Stockholm.

Mattingly, I. G., and A. M. Liberman. 1984. Verticality unparalleled. *Haskins Laboratories Status Report on Speech Research* SR-79/80:241–245.

———. 1990. Speech and other auditory modules. In G. M. Edelman, W. E. Gall, and W. M. Cowan (eds.), *Signal and sense: Local and global order in perception maps.* New York: Wiley.

Remez, R. E., P. E. Rubin, S. M. Berns, J. S. Pardo, and J. M. Lang. 1994. On the perceptual organization of speech. *Psychological Review* 101(1):129–156.

Whalen, D., and A. M. Liberman. 1987. Speech perception takes precedence over nonspeech. *Science* 237:169–171.

PART I

On the Spectrogram as a Visible Display of Speech

Introduction to Part I

When we wrote this article, we were rightly impressed with the advantages of the spectrogram as a way to display speech to the eye, and wrongly inclined to assume that those advantages had something to do with principles of pattern perception so general as to hold across modalities. We were also inclined, wrongly again, to attribute the distinctiveness of speech sounds to principles of auditory pattern perception to which they had somehow come, in their development, to conform. To these two mistakes, we added yet another by supposing that the spectrogram was a good display because it transformed the stimulus coordinates in the right way, thus preserving good patterns across the transform, and so permitting the cross-modal generality of the underlying principle to manifest itself.

I long ago abandoned the notion that there are speech-relevant principles of pattern perception that hold across hearing and seeing. Nor do I believe any longer that the distinctiveness of speech sounds has anything to do with perception of good auditory patterns. Indeed, I don't think it has all that much to do with auditory patterns of any kind, whether good or bad, believing now, as I said in chapter 1, that speech perception occurs in a distinct phonetic mode, where it finds correspondingly distinct processes and primitives that were specifically adapted in evolution to the special requirements of phonological communication. As for spectrograms, they are relatively good displays of speech, not for their ability to convert distinctive auditory patterns into equally distinctive visual patterns, but because they represent the dynamic spectral properties of the sounds, which is where the production processes of the phonetic mode happen to put most of the phonetically important information.

We were right, I think, to see the potential of the spectrographic display as a basis for experimenting with the speech signal, and I would not now retract what we said in that connection. There was, however, yet another application that we had in mind, though we made only a passing reference to it in the paper. Given our assumptions about the nature of speech, cross-modality generality, and the goodness of the spectrographic transform, we, along with many others, supposed that spectrograms of speech could, with practice, become as intelligible to the eye as the sounds are to the ear. We therefore nursed the hope that our research would provide a basis for making the spectrogram a more nearly perfect transform, while also showing exactly how its patterns were to be interpreted as language. Hence, we saw, among the practical consequences of our work, that it would not only enable the blind to hear print, which was our initial objective, but also make it easier for the deaf to read speech.

In the end, our research did help make print available to the blind, though not in the way we had initially thought. Unfortunately for the deaf, however, reading spectrograms is forever doomed to be, at best, a slow and laborious procedure. As research on speech has shown, the difficulty lies in the special, and especially thorny, complications that characterize the relation between the sounds that the spectrograms represent and the phonetic messages they convey. Those complications, which result largely from the specialized coarticulatory mechanisms that make speech communication possible, are described in various parts of this book. They present no problem for the listener, of course, but only because he or she has access to a biological specialization specifically adapted to dealing with them; there is no reason to think that experience can ever attach that specialization, together with its entirely automatic processes, to the eye.

Chapter 2

The Interconversion of Audible and Visible Patterns as a Basis for Research in the Perception of Speech

In investigating the acoustic aspects of speech it has long been the practice to convert these extremely complex sounds into a visible display, and so to enlist vision as an aid in dealing with a problem which lies largely in the area of auditory perception. Of the various displays which have been used, perhaps the most effective is provided by the sound spectrograph, which has come to be recognized as a valuable research tool for the study of the acoustic correlates of perceived speech.[1] By examining numerous spectrograms of the same sounds, spoken by many persons and in a variety of contexts, an investigator can arrive at a description of the acoustic features common to all of the samples, and in this way make progress toward defining the so-called invariants of speech, that is, the essential information-bearing sound elements on which the listener's identifications critically depend. The investigator can also take account of the variations among spectrograms, and by correlating these with the observed variations in pronunciation, he can begin to sort out the several acoustic features in relation to the several aspects of the perception.

There are, however, many questions about the relation between acoustic stimulus and auditory perception which cannot be answered merely by an inspection of spectrograms, no matter how numerous and varied these may be. For any given unit characteristic of the auditory perception, such as the simple identification of a phoneme, the spectrogram will very often exhibit several features which are distinctive to the eye, and the information which can be obtained from the spectrogram is, accordingly, ambiguous. Even when only one feature or pattern is strikingly evident, one cannot be certain about its auditory significance, unless he assumes that those aspects of the spectrogram which appear most prominently on visual examination are, in fact, of greatest importance to the ear. That assumption, as we shall try to point out later in this paper, is itself extremely interesting, but it has not been directly tested, nor, indeed, has it always been made fully explicit.

To validate conclusions drawn from visual examination of spectrograms, or, more generally, to determine the stimulus correlates of perceived speech, it will often be necessary to make controlled modifications in the spectrogram, and then to evaluate the effects of those modifications on the sound as heard. For these purposes, we have constructed an instrument, called a pattern playback, which reconverts spectrograms into sound, either in their original form or after modification.

The basic operating principle[2] is quite simple (figure 2.1). The playback scans a spectrogram from left to right along the time axis, using a line of light modulated by

Originally published in *Proceedings of the National Academy of Sciences* 37, 5 (May 1951): 318–325, with Franklin S. Cooper and John M. Borst. Reprinted with permission.

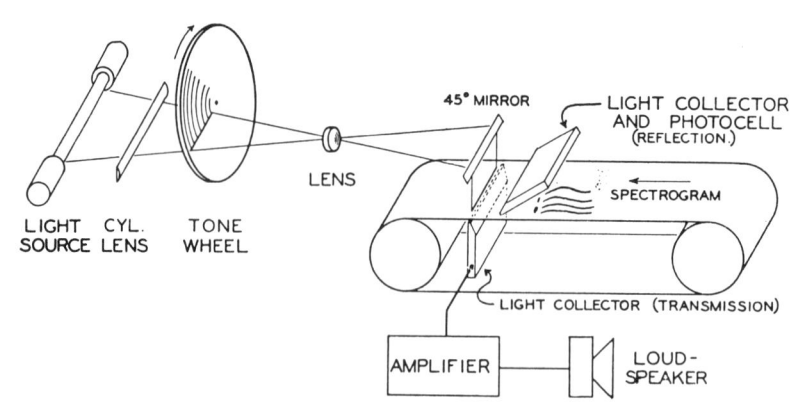

Figure 2.1
Operating principle of the pattern playback.

a tone wheel at some fifty harmonically-related frequencies which match approximately the frequency scale of the spectrogram. Those portions of the modulated light which are selected by the spectrogram—by transmission through a film transparency or by diffuse reflection from a painted design—are collected by an optical system and led to a phototube. Thus the photocurrent, amplified and fed into a loudspeaker, produces sounds which have, at every instant, approximately the frequency components shown on the spectrogram.

For convenience in research the playback is designed to operate from either of two kinds of spectrograms (figure 2.2). In the one case, the spectrogram is a film transparency, and the sound is produced by the light which is transmitted through the relatively transparent portions of the film. These transmission spectrograms, so called, are photographic copies (on film) of an original produced from recorded sound by a spectrograph designed specifically for this purpose. The transmission spectrograms are most useful if one wishes to recreate the original sound as accurately as possible, or to make minor changes (especially deletions) in some detail of the spectrogram. In the other case, the playback operates from spectrograms which are drawn with white paint on a transparent plastic base, and the playback uses only the light which is reflected from the painted portions. The drawing is done by brush or pen, and the spectrograms can be prepared or modified in a variety of ways. These spectrograms are most appropriate, then, if one wishes to make drastic changes in the sound, or, in the extreme case, to employ entirely synthetic patterns.

In general, the playback appears to be a most useful tool in research involving the experimental manipulation of speech sounds. By comparison with more conventional instruments for modifying the speech stream, the playback method is extremely flexible and convenient, and has the particular advantage that it allows considerable freedom in dealing with the dynamic or constantly varying aspects of speech. This was, indeed, the specific function for which it was designed. It is of course obvious that such a playback will be useful as a research tool only to the extent that it is able to produce intelligible speech which may then be degraded or dissected in various ways.

We have measured the intelligibility of the playback speech produced from transmission spectrograms, using for this purpose twenty standard test sentences, and have found it to be approximately 95 percent. The intelligibility of reflection spectrograms

Interconversion of Audible and Visible Patterns 51

Figure 2.2
(a) Transmission spectrogram copied photographically from an original spectrogram without modification. (b) Reflection spectrogram drawn by hand as a simplified version of the original spectrogram. (c) Text of the sentence.

will obviously depend on how they are drawn. In drawing these spectrograms we have attempted, in a preliminary way, to determine the extent to which they could be simplified without serious loss of intelligibility. The procedure was, first, to copy from an actual spectrogram the features which were most prominent visually, and then, largely on a trial-and-error basis, to make such further changes as were required for reasonable intelligibility. For the degree of schematization shown in figure 2.2, the median intelligibility is about 85 percent, as determined with twenty test sentences. The experimental procedures and the nature of the simplifications will be reported in detail elsewhere.[3] For present purposes it is important merely to note that the simplified spectrograms are, in general, a reduction of the originals to their most obvious visual patterns. Although the first rough paintings were modified in many details in order to produce these highly simplified spectrograms, the modifications have not destroyed the over-all visual resemblance to the originals. To the extent that these similarities remain, and also to the extent that the simplified spectrograms are intelligible, these results provide a partial validation of the assumption, referred to earlier, that the spectrogram displays most prominently to the eye those acoustic features which are of greatest importance in auditory perception. If this were not the case, the spectrograph would not be so useful a tool in describing the sounds of speech, and, more significantly for our purposes, the playback would have no special advantage as a means of manipulating speech.

That the playback does have special advantages is indicated by our experience with it, and this fact seems, moreover, to have theoretical implications which deserve examination. It does not appear that the advantage is solely one of stopping time, that is, of converting a transitory sound into a stationary visible display which can be modified and then reconverted into sound for aural evaluation. This is an obvious advantage and an important one in experimenting with speech, but it is neither unique nor quite sufficient. For example, sounds can be represented to the eye by means of an oscillograph, and the oscillogram can be reconverted into sound by a device somewhat like a phonograph, yet the oscillographic representation is virtually useless as a basis for experimenting with the sounds of speech. The critical requirement, and the one which is not adequately met by the oscillogram, is that the display must provide for the eye information which is organized into patterns corresponding to the acoustic patterns on which auditory identifications depend; that is, the conversion must be from patterned acoustic information to patterned visual information. When this is so, the significant aspects of the acoustic pattern become comprehensible to the eye, and the display will have conceptual and also experimental utility in manipulating the sounds of speech. We believe that a reasonable approximation to the required conversion is represented by the spectrograph-playback combination, which interconverts the x and y coordinates of visual space with time and frequency in the acoustic domain (preserving intensity as a parameter in both cases), and that this accounts for the special utility of these instruments as practical research tools.

On the theoretical side it would seem that the existence of this particular intersensory conversion, with its special advantages, may have interesting implications for the perceptual processes operating in vision and audition. Perhaps the most general implication is that there is an important similarity between visual and auditory perception, sufficient to permit an interconversion at the stimulus level such that patterns in the one sensory modality may, after conversion, be perceived as patterns in the other modality. The term pattern, as used here, implies an organization of stimuli which has the property of retaining its perceptual integrity in spite of gross and diverse changes in the absolute values of the several stimulus components. In vision, for example, a triangle will continue to be perceived as a triangle despite wide changes in size, position, etc. Similarly, in an auditory case, the perception of speech is to a certain extent independent of any fixed and isolated stimulus values, inasmuch as the sounds of speech can be considerably stretched or compressed in time, frequency and intensity without serious damage to intelligibility. These patterns of information, on which visual and auditory perception so largely depend, may then be defined operationally in terms of the particular alterations in stimulus which do and do not impair perceptual identification. By this definition, and according to our assumption about the general nature of the similarity between visual and auditory perception, it should be possible so to convert from vision to audition that varying the visual stimulus will affect the visual and the auditory identifications about equally, i.e., that stimulus changes which do or do not destroy the pattern in the one modality will, correspondingly, destroy it or not in the other. More simply, and only somewhat less precisely, stimuli which look alike can be made to sound alike, and stimuli which look different should then sound different.

It is most unlikely that visual and auditory patterns can be interconverted in complete detail and in all respects, and hence one must expect that the best of audio-visual transforms will be rather less than perfect. For all its inadequacies, however, such a transform will be of practical interest for its bearing on the problems of sensory prosthesis,[4] and for its application, as in the case of the playback, to investigations of the perception of a wide variety of sound patterns, including speech as a special and obviously important case.[5]

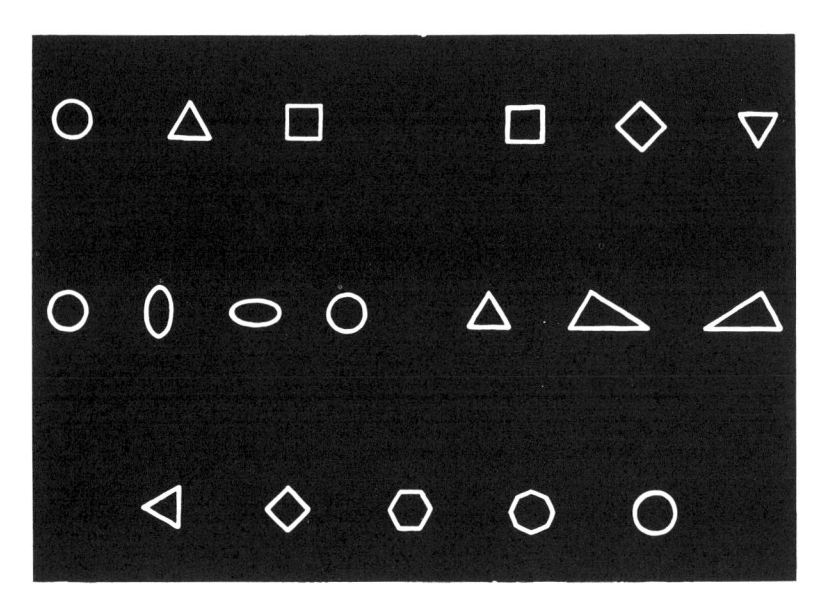

Interconversion of Audible and Visible Patterns 53

Figure 2.3
Three sequences of geometric figures used in testing the audo-visual transform.

It appears, from a theoretical point of view, that the fact of intersensory pattern conversion implies functional similarities between vision and audition at a presumably high level of perception. Moreover, the specific nature of the similarities will be indicated by the precise way in which the best possible conversion is to be made. The transform concept also implies some degree of intersensory generality for certain perceptual laws, since one may suppose that patterns will be interconvertible between vision and audition only to the extent that common principles determine the way in which visual and auditory stimuli are organized in perception. The further development and extensive testing of the transform concept, according to the criteria implicit in our assumptions, may therefore serve to reveal certain principles which are so basic as to have a special importance for theories about perceptual mechanisms in general.

We have taken a first and very tentative step toward testing the transform concept with materials other than speech sounds. In studying speech, we have been dealing with patterns which were quire obviously more familiar to the ear than to the eye. What will be heard when the playback is used to transform patterns which are familiar to the eye but not to the ear? The tests that we have so far made employed common geometrical forms such as circles, ellipses, triangles and squares (figure 2.3). As represented on the playback tape, each figure was varied in size and position, drawn in outline and in solid form, variously distorted in shape, and rotated about axes perpendicular to the tape. When these figures are converted by the playback, a listener hears sound which he rather readily puts into categories corresponding to the grouping of the figures in visual perception. All of the triangles, for example, sound somewhat alike, regardless of variations in size and position on the tape, and these sounds are quite distinctively different from the sounds corresponding to squares or circles. The one apparent exception is that rotation of many of the figures causes very large changes in the sound, and the listener tends not to put rotated forms of a rectangle, for example, into the same category. This may represent a limitation of the transform, though it must be remembered that the identifications of visual figures sometimes change when the figures are rotated, a familiar example being that of square and diamond.

These studies were intended to be exploratory and the results are most incomplete; there is not, of course, any special significance in the choice of geometric figures as test patterns. The experiments are described here because they illustrate how the playback transform can be tested according to our criterion of pattern interconvertibility, and because the results indicate in a general way the extent to which the playback transform, with its present imperfections, meets that test.

In summary, we have found it useful to assume, as a working hypothesis, that the perceptual processes in vision and audition exhibit important similarities in operating upon patterned information. A consequence of this hypothesis, put more explicitly and in operational terms, is that information which is perceived as a pattern when displayed to the eye can be so converted into sound for presentation to the ear that the pattern characteristics will be preserved, that is, that the sounds will be perceived as patterned information in audition. Conversely, patterned acoustic information can, by the reverse transformation, be displayed as visual patterns. The sound spectrograph and pattern playback are appropriate even though imperfect instrumental means of effecting such an interconversion, which in this case is that the x and y dimensions of the visual array are changed to the time and frequency dimensions of sound, with intensity remaining a parameter in both cases. Stated symbolically, the audio-visual transform then becomes $F_v(x, y, I) \rightleftarrows F_a(f, t, I)$.

This conceptualization of a particular relationship between vision and audition, quite aside from its theoretical interest, provides a basis for understanding the demonstrated utility of the sound spectrograph in displaying the sounds of speech for visual study, and of the pattern playback as a tool for the manipulation and synthesis of speech.

Notes

The research reported here was made possible by funds granted by the Carnegie Corporation of New York. The paper, as read before the Academy on October 10, 1950, employed recordings to illustrate various points in the discussion. Some revision of the text has therefore been necessary.

1. Potter, R. K., and Steinberg, J. C., *J. Acous. Soc. Am.*, 22, 803–823 (1950). Joos, Martin, *Acoustic Phonetics* (Language Monograph No. 23), Linguistic Society of America, 1948. Potter, R. K., Kopp, G. A., and Green, Harriet C., *Visible Speech*, D. van Nostrand, 1947.
2. Potter, R. K., U. S. Patent No. 2,432,123 (1947). Cooper, F. S., Liberman, A. M., and Borst, J. M., *J. Acous. Soc. Am.*, 21, 461 (1949). Vilbig, F., Ibid., 22, 754–761 (1950).
3. Cooper, F. S., Borst, J. M., and Liberman, A. M., "Pattern Playback and Sound Spectrograph: Tools for Research in the Perception of Speech and Other Complex Sounds" (in preparation).
4. Zahl, P. A., Ed., *Blindness: Modern Approaches to the Unseen Environment*, Princeton University Press, 1950. Potter, R. K., Kopp, G. A., and Green, Harriet, C., *Visible Speech*, D. van Nostrand, 1947. Cooper, F. S., *Physics Today*, 3, 6–14 (1950).
5. Delattre, Pierre, *J. Acous. Soc. Am.*, 22, 678 (1950). Cooper, F. S., Liberman, A. M., and Borst, J. M., Ibid., 22, 678 (1950). Cooper, F. S., Ibid., 22, 761–762 (1950).

PART II

Finding the Cues

Introduction to Part II

In this section are articles that describe some of the experiments we carried out in our early and relatively straightforward search for the acoustic cues. It was these papers, together with others of similar stripe, that provided the basis for the early conclusions and speculations that appeared in the first part of chapter 1.

The variables we chose to test in these experiments had not sprung full blown from an understanding of acoustic phonetics. They were, rather, the results of hundreds of trial-and-error probes designed simply to identify the promising stimulus dimensions and explore their limits. Given the great convenience of the Playback as an experimental tool, plus faith in our own phonetic judgments, we were able to do these numerous and unrecorded experiments at a very rapid rate. Thus, we counted it progress when, at the end of a day at the Playback, we had, perhaps, made one hundred trials, but only ninety-nine errors. After we had, by this means, found and appropriately "polished" some part of the acoustic signal that showed promise of being phonetically significant, we prepared and "ran off" with phonetically naive listeners the experiments reported here.

Chapter 3
The Role of Selected Stimulus-Variables in the Perception of the Unvoiced Stop Consonants

In earlier reports we have described a method for investigating the perception of speech and other complex sounds.[1] This method uses a spectrographic display as a basis for controlling the acoustic stimuli, and depends on an instrument, called a "pattern playback," which converts spectrograms into sound and thus makes it possible to evaluate by ear the effects of a wide variety of experimental modifications in the acoustic (spectrographic) pattern. As part of the development of the playback method, and in a preliminary attempt to strip the speech stream down to its phonemic essentials, we undertook to simplify the spectrographic pattern and yet preserve the intelligibility of the message.[2]

The first step in the simplifiction procedure was to copy from spectrograms of connected speech those patterns which appeared most prominently on visual inspection. These patterns, painted by hand on a clear cellulose acetate base, were converted into sound and then, on a trial-and-error basis, they were altered in various details in order to restore intelligibility and gain still greater simplicity. The result was a set of highly simplified and somewhat schematized spectrograms, corresponding to twenty test-sentences, which yielded a median intelligibility of about 85 percent when converted into sound by the playback and presented to naïve listeners. Figure 3.1 shows a sample of the kind and degree of simplification that was achieved, and, for comparison, a spectrogram of the sounds as they appear in their original, spoken form.[3] In preparing the schematized spectrograms we attempted merely to find an intelligible version of simplified speech, rather than to explore the effects of systematic variations; hence, the spectrogram of figure 3.1 and the others like it represent only a first approximation to the stimulus-essentials of phoneme communication, and, at best, the results obtained suggest the directions which more intensive and specific investigations might reasonably take. One result which has seemed to us to deserve more careful study relates to the stimuli for the perception of p, t, and k; the experiment reported here is concerned with that problem.

Perceptually, acoustically, and also in terms of the articulatory movements which produce them, the unvoiced stop consonants comprise a distinct class of speech sounds. That they form a class in the perception of speech is indicated by the results of Wiener and Miller, who asked Ss to identify nonsense syllables spoken against a background of noise, and found that the unvoiced stops were confused most frequently with other unvoiced stops; in only a small percentage of cases were the unvoiced stops identified as sounds belonging to any other class of phoneme.[4]

Originally published in *The American Journal of Psychology* 65 (October 1952): 497–516, with Pierre Delattre and Franklin S. Cooper. Reprinted with permission.

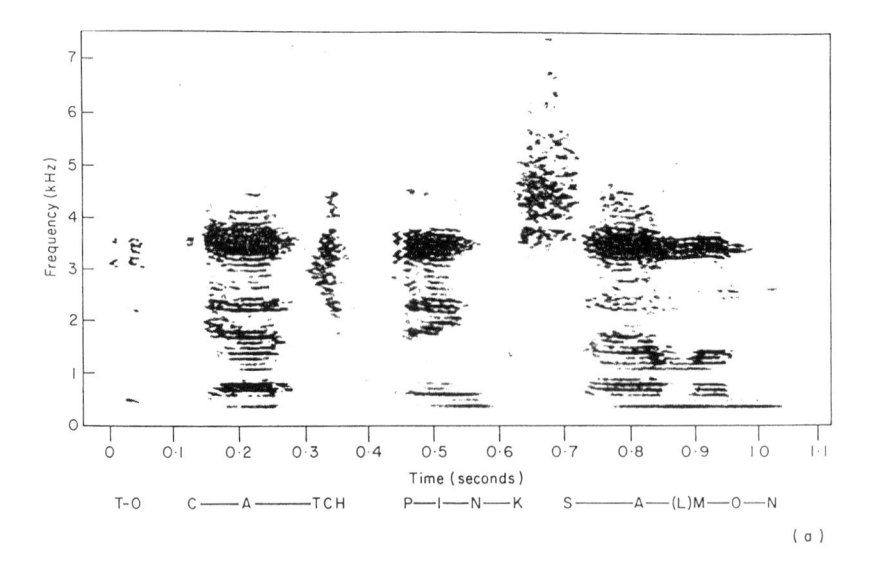

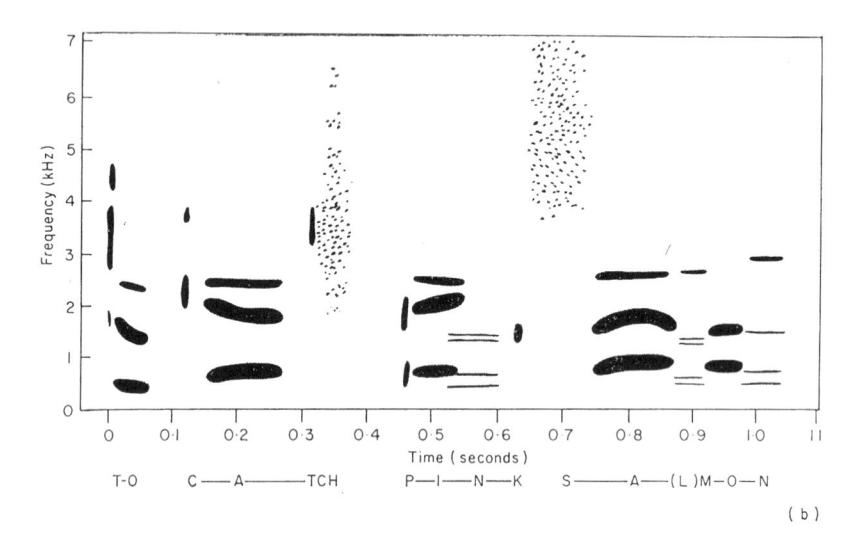

Figure 3.1
Showing spectrogram (a) and simplified version (b) of a spoken phrase.

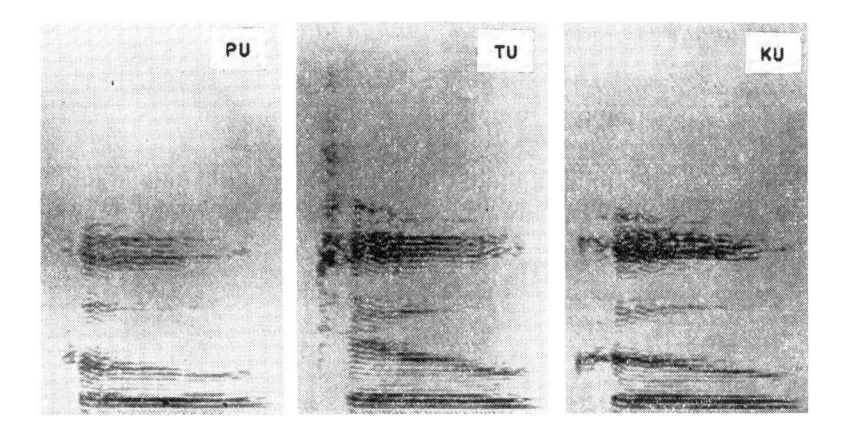

Figure 3.2
Spectrographic representations of unvoiced stop consonants before vowels.

Acoustically, the stops are similar to each other and different from the other categories of speech sounds in that they are relatively short bursts of comparatively low energy, including most often a rather wide range of frequencies. The unvoiced stops (*p*, *t*, and *k*) are presumably distinguished from their voiced cognates (*b*, *d*, and *g*) on the basis that the voiced stops, like all voiced sounds, have acoustic energy at the fundamental frequency of the voice, whereas the unvoiced stops do not.[5] From the standpoint of articulatory movements, the three unvoiced stops are produced in common by the relatively quick opening of the oral tract with the consequent release of the interrupted breath steam. (For *p* the interruption is produced by joining the upper and lower lips, for *t* by raising the tongue tip against the upper teeth or the alveols, and for *k* by raising the back of the tongue against the velum or soft palate.) The vocal cords do not vibrate during the phonation of *p*, *t*, and *k*, which accounts for the absence of acoustic energy at the fundamental frequency of the voice.

Some of the acoustic features which presumably distinguish one stop from another can be seen in figure 3.2. The energy in any one of the stops is usually spread over a rather wide range of frequencies, but the range is typically less than the total frequency-scale of the spectrogram, and a characteristic difference among the stops appears to lie in the frequency at which the energy centers. Without attempting to specify the actual frequencies, Potter, Kopp, and Green have noted that the energy of *p* is concentrated at a relatively low frequency position, that of *t* centers at a high value, while that of *k* is at a high frequency for the front vowels (e.g., *i* as in *eat*), at a middle frequency for the mid-vowels (e.g., as in *up*), and at a low frequency for the back vowels (e.g., *u* as in *moot*).[6] These investigators have also seen that an initial stop normally affects the frequency-positions of the formants[7] at the start of the vowel which follows, the magnitude and direction of the effect being somewhat different for each of the three stop sounds. There may be other characteristic differences among the stop sounds, as, for example, in intensity and in the time-interval between explosion and voicing, but these differences are less obvious from an examination of spectrograms than the differences in frequency-position or the effects on the following vowel. In general, the acoustic features which differentiate *p*, *t*, and *k*, can be defined only in the broadest terms on the basis of the spectrographic evidence now available. That evidence is quite sufficient, however, to enable us to select the acoustic variables which should be manipulated in our experiments, and there is enough evidence to indicate that experimental manipulation will, in fact, be necessary if we are to find the essential stimulus-correlates for the perception of the unvoiced stops, inasmuch as it appears that for each of these phonemes there are several distinctive acoustic features which do not vary independently in a collection of speech samples.

The experience gained in producing "synthetic" speech from simplified spectrograms permits several very tentative conclusions in regard to the acoustic stimuli for *p*, *t*, and *k*, and forms the basis for the present extension of that experimental approach to the problem. It was found in working with the simplified spectrograms that stops as a class could be approximated satisfactorily by representing the sounds as vertical bars (see figure 3.1), and it was reasonably clear that the position of the bar on the frequency scale was a most important factor, though not necessarily the only one, in determining whether the stop would be heard as *p*, *t*, or *k*. With the possible exception of *t*, however, there appeared to be no fixed and single frequency-position which characterized the stop. Adjustments in the frequency-position of the bar had to be made according to the nature of the vowel which followed, the need for this adjustment having been shown most clearly by one case in which a particular bar (in one frequency-position) was heard as *k* before one vowel and as *p* before another. If confirmed this result would mean that the identification of the stop depends, in the case of *p* and *k* at least, not on the acoustic characteristics of the hand-drawn stop (bar) itself, but rather on the stop in relation to the following vowel. In the present experiment we shall attempt to extend and refine these preliminary observations. For that purpose we shall adopt a bar-like figure as a schematized representation of the unvoiced stop consonant, systematically vary its position on the frequency-scale before each of seven cardinal vowels, and determine the effect of these variations on the auditory identification of the stop as *p*, *t*, or *k*.

Apparatus and Procedure

Apparatus
The sounds used in this study were produced by the pattern-playback, an instrument shown in schematic form in figure 3.3. A variable density tone-wheel modulates a thin sheet of light and produces a 120 ∼ fundamental together with its first 50 harmonics, the tones being arranged across the sheet on a scale which matches the frequency scale of the spectrogram. As a painted spectrogram moves through the light, those modulated beams which correspond in position (and hence in frequency) to the painted portions of the spectrogram are reflected into an optical system and led to a phototube, whose current is then amplified and supplied to a loud-speaker.[8] In this way the playback produces sounds which have approximately the frequency-, time-, and intensity-characteristics of the spectrographic picture. (Intensity is controlled by varying the reflectance of the paint or the width of the lines.)

The playback provides an attenuation of approximately 6 db. per octave, which corresponds roughly to the distribution of energy in normal speech.

Total harmonic distortion in the individual tones produced by the playback does not exceed 3 percent; most of this is second harmonic.

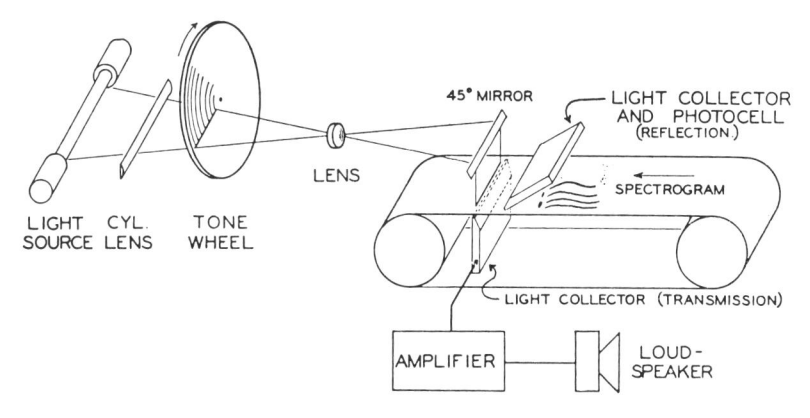

Figure 3.3
Operating principle of the pattern-playback.

Stimuli
The purpose of this experiment required that a schematic stop be presented for auditory identification (as *p*, *t*, or *k*) at various frequency positions before each of several vowels. On the basis of spectrographic evidence and our earlier experience with the simplified spectrograms, we decided that an adequate sample of frequency positions could be had by placing the schematic stop at intervals of 360 ∼ within the range 360 to 4320 ∼. Seven schematic vowels were used, representing a comprehensive and rather systematic selection from the so-called vowel triangle.

In figure 3.4A we see the 12 frequency-positions of the schematic stops and in figure 3.4B the positions of the vowel formants. The 12 frequency-positions of the schematic stop before each of seven vowels made a total of 84 consonant-vowel syllables to be presented to the Ss. One of these syllables is shown in figure 3.4C.

The schematic stop produces a reasonably adequate and indifferent stop-like sound, and was selected after trial-and-error exploratory work. It has a height equal to five contiguous harmonics of the 120 ∼ fundamental, a maximal width of 15 m.sec., and is drawn as an ellipse to reduce transients.

For all the schematic vowels, except *u*, the formants have the shape and dimensions of those shown in figure 3.4C. To produce the *u* sound it was necessary to reduce the width of the second formant by approximately two-thirds.

The schematic vowels are taken from the results of an earlier study, the purpose of which had been to synthesize the cardinal vowels by the use of two formants only.[9] When converted into sound by the playback, these schematic vowels rather closely approximate normal vowel color, and, with a group of students in phonetics as Ss, they had been found to be very highly identifiable.

It should, perhaps, be noted that the sounds produced by the schematic vowels differ slightly from the nearest American English equivalents given at the bottom of figure 3.4. As can be seen in the figure, the schematic vowels maintain a steady state, which is to say they are pure and without diphthongization. In American English speech, on the other hand, at least two of our seven vowels, namely *e* and *o*, are quite noticeably diphthongized. Also, the acoustic differentiations between and among the schematic vowels are probably somewhat greater than those which are produced by an average American speaker.

64   Chapter 3

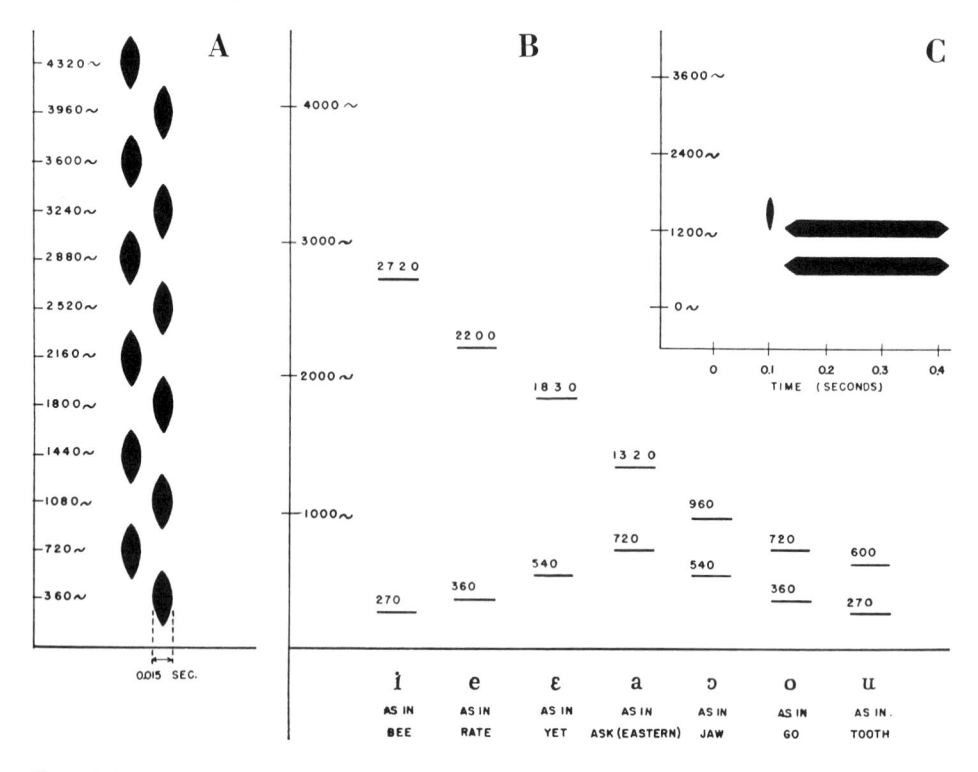

Figure 3.4
Showing frequency-positions (A) of the schematic stops; (B) of the vowel-formants; and (C) one of the schematic syllables.

To increase the intensity of the schematic stop relative to the vowel, we added a small amount of black pigment to the paint used in drawing the vowel formants, thereby reducing the reflectance of that paint to a level equivalent to 3 db. below the flat white with which the schematic stops were drawn.

Each of the syllables was converted into sound by the playback and was recorded on magnetic tape.

Presentation of Stimuli
The syllables were arranged for presentation in a "random" order, subject to the following restrictions: (1) within each successive block of seven stimuli each vowel appears once, and (2) within each successive block of 12 stimuli each stop position appears once. There was, of course, the general restriction that each combination of stop position and vowel appear only once in the entire series of 84 stimuli.

The recorded syllables were spliced into a master magnetic tape according to the random order described above. To facilitate judgment by S, a second recording of each syllable was made and spliced in at such a distance from its twin that each syllable would be presented and then repeated after 0.2 sec. Successive pairs of syllables were separated by $4\frac{1}{2}$ sec. of blank tape; thus S had $4\frac{1}{2}$ sec. in which to make his identification of one syllable before being presented with the next.

Disk recordings were made from the magnetic tape master, and all the judgments secured in this experiment were made in regard to sounds reproduced phonographically from the disks.

For every S the entire list of 84 syllables was presented twice. The order of presentation of the syllables was reversed for the second series of judgments.

S was instructed to listen to each of the syllables and to identify the initial stop consonant as *p*, *t*, or *k*. He was strongly urged to make such an identification for every syllable heard, even though in some cases the judgment might represent no more than a guess, and he was asked, also, to qualify every judgment by indicating on a four-point scale the degree of confidence he felt in his judgment. An analysis of the results showed a very close relation between the mean of the confidence ratings assigned to any particular identification and the number of Ss who agreed in making the identification. That relation was, indeed, so very high that the rating data did not reveal anything which cannot be seen in the frequency distributions of the *p*, *t*, and *k* judgments; therefore, the ratings will not be dealt with further in this report.

To simplify S's task we asked him to identify and record only the initial stop consonant. He was specifically instructed not to try to identify the vowel, or, at least, not to bother to record his identification.

Subjects

Judgments regarding stimuli were secured from 30 Ss, who were obtained in two groups: 18 from the University of Connecticut, all of whom were students in an undergraduate course in psychology; and 12 from the University of Pennsylvania, 9 of whom were students in an undergraduate course in phonetics and 3 of whom were advanced students in phonetics.

Results

Figure 3.5 shows how the judgments of *p*, *t*, and *k* vary according to the frequency-position of the schematic stop in relation to the schematic vowel with which it was paired. This is essentially a three-dimensional plot, showing the 12 frequency-positions of the schematic stops along the y-axis, the vowels along the x-axis (arranged in order of their front-to-back positions of articulation), and the number of judgments of *p*, *t*, and *k* for each consonant-vowel combination on auxiliary scales parallel to the x-axis (i.e., z-axis scales folded into the x,y-plane). There is a total of 60 judgments for each syllable, each of 30 Ss having been given the stimulus-series twice.

Looking first at the distribution of *k* judgments, we find in the case of the vowel *u* that the schematic stop at 720 ∼ was called *k* 56 times out of 60, and that the number of *k* judgments falls sharply on either side of that mode, levelling off, on the high frequency-side, at 10 judgments out of 60 when the schematic stop reaches 1440 ∼. By comparison with *k* before *u*, the other distributions of *k* judgments are somewhat less sharply peaked and the modes do not represent quite so high a percentage of the total number of judgments. Except in the case of *i*, however, all of the *k* distributions show definite humps or peaks which rise above the levels of the *p* and *t* judgments and reflect considerable agreement among the subjects that schematic stops in certain frequency positions sounded more like *k* than like *p* or *t*.

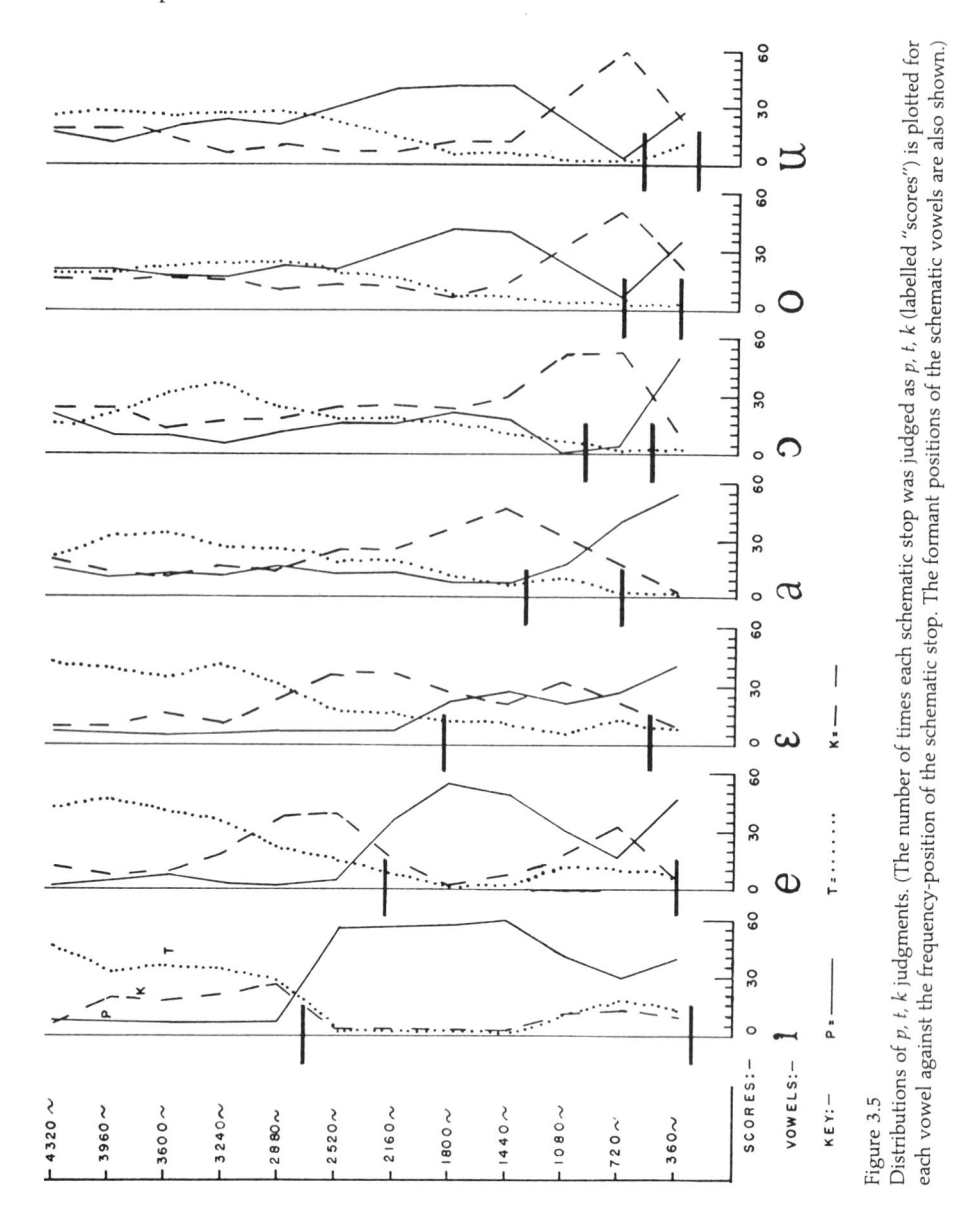

Figure 3.5
Distributions of *p*, *t*, *k* judgments. (The number of times each schematic stop was judged as *p*, *t*, *k* (labelled "scores") is plotted for each vowel against the frequency-position of the schematic stop. The formant positions of the schematic vowels are also shown.)

It is possible that there would have been less agreement in the identification of the schematic stops if the Ss had been presented with a wider variety of stimuli and required to select their judgments from among a correspondingly greater number of phonemes. In that connection, however, it is worth noting again the finding of Wiener and Miller that listeners seldom confused an unvoiced stop with a sound belonging to some other class of phonemes;[10] an unvoiced stop, if heard at all, was most often identified as one of the unvoiced stop sounds, even though, within the limits of that category, the specific identification as *p*, *t*, or *k* might have been incorrect. It is also relevant to recall here that schematized stops similar to those of the present experiment were used previously in the simplified spectrograms of sentences (described earlier in this paper), and were found there to be quite highly identifiable. On the basis of these considerations we should suppose that the identifications made in the present experiment will not be radically changed when the schematic stops are presented for judgment among all the other phonemes of American speech, either in the context of meaningful sentences or as parts of nonsense syllables.

Perhaps the most obvious and notable fact about the distributions of k judgments is the movement of the mode or peak upward on the frequency scale in the vowel series from u to i. This movement rather clearly follows the second formant of the vowel as it moves up in frequency, and it would appear that the schematic stop which sounds most like k is the one which lies at a frequency slightly above (or, perhaps, in a few cases on a level with) the frequency of the second formant of the vowel which follows.

In the distributions of k judgments before e and ϵ there is quite clearly a second mode at a point slightly above the first formant. A suggestion of that mode appears also in i, but it does not rise above the p or t judgments and would not be noted here if it did not fit the pattern set by the vowels which precede it in the series.

The presence of two modes at e and ϵ suggests that the k impression might be strengthened if we were to place schematic stops at the frequency positions corresponding to each of the two modes. We have tried this, in a preliminary way, and have found no dramatic improvement in the k. Whether there is any improvement at all can be determined only by more extensive and systematic observations.

The fact that the distribution of k judgments tends to be bimodal for the front vowels (i, e, and ϵ) and unimodal for the back vowels (u, o, and $\mathrm{ɔ}$) may be related to some evidence we have regarding the number of formants necessary to produce these two classes of vowel sounds. With the back vowels, in which the first and second formants are normally close together in frequency, a reasonable approximation to the vowel sound can be produced by a single formant placed at a frequency intermediate between the frequency positions of the first and second formants; in the front vowels, on the other hand, where the two formants are widely separated in frequency, a single intermediate formant will not produce the vowel sound. A tentative rule, then, might be that the schematic stop is heard as k when the acoustic energy is just above (or at) the frequency positions of those formants (whether one or two) which are essential for the identification of the vowel.

In addition to the shift in frequency position of the k mode through the vowel series, there is a tendency for the height of the mode to decrease from u to i. The amount of decrease is not very great in the series u through a, nor is it precisely regular; in ϵ and e the apparent decrease might be accounted for by the splitting into two modes; but in i it is clear that the schematic stops did not sound very much like k.

The difference in the number of k judgments between u and i may mean that additional cues are necessary for the identification of k when it precedes an extreme front vowel such as i. We cannot define these cues with confidence, but, on the basis of what is known about the articulatory movements required to produce ki as against ku, we can suspect the presence of at least one peculiar feature in the normal utterance of ki. To articulate k, a speaker places the back of his tongue at a point relatively far back on the roof of the mouth and then quickly lowers the tongue to produce the k explosion. A back vowel, such as u, is also formed with the back of the tongue arched toward the back of the palate. In contrast to these movements, the articulation of an extreme front vowel, such as i, consists normally is raising the front of the tongue toward the front of the mouth. Phoneticians have established that the difference in tongue position between k and i affects the articulation of k before i, causing the point of tongue-palate contact for *k* to move forward in the mouth; with *u*, on the other hand, there is no such effect. One might suppose, conversely, that an initial *k* would influence an *i* which follows it, at least to the extent of producing some transition between the *k* explosion and the steady state of the vowel, and that this effect would be considerably less, or even absent, when the vowel is *u*. In this connection, Potter, Kopp, and Green have pointed out that an initial *k* causes a "rounding together" of the second and third formants (sometimes the third and fourth formants), and they have suggested that this rounding is more apparent in the front vowels than in the back vowels.[11] If *k* does, in fact, have some effect on the vowel formants of *i*, but not on *u*, this effect might be an important cue to the identity of *k* when it precedes *i*, and the complete absence of this cue in our schematized syllables would then account for the fact that the schematic stop before *i* was not often heard as *k*.

Another possibility, of course, is that the *ki* syllable is simply less identifiable than *ku*, even when all the significant cues are present. Such a difference in identifiability, if it does exist, should not be assumed to result from the subjects' having had less experience with the one combination than with the other, inasmuch as Dewey's phonetic count of English shows *k* before the front vowels, *i*, *e*, and *ɛ* to be at least as frequent in occurrence as *k* before the back vowels, *u*, *o*, and *ɔ*.[12]

It may be relevant to our obtained difference between *ki* and *ku* that in the evolution of several languages, including English in the case of words coming from the Latin by way of Old French, the *k* sound has been unstable before the front vowels—e.g., Latin *centum* [kɛntum] becomes English *cent* [sɛnt], while it survives as *k* when it precedes the back vowels—e.g., Latin *cortem* [kɔrtɛm] becomes English *court* [kɔrt]. (The fact, pointed out in the preceding paragraph, that the *k* sound seems to occur in English with equal frequency before the front the back vowels is to be attributed to the presence in the language of a relatively large number of borrowed words and words of Germanic origin). The instability of *k* when it introduces a front vowel can be attributed to purely articulatory, that is motor, factors which cause *k* to shift toward consonants which are somewhat closer to the front vowels, or it can be assumed to be caused by an inherent difficulty in identifying *k* when it is followed by a front vowel.

The distributions of *p* judgments are to a large extent the inverse of the distributions for *k* (in the range 300 to 3000 ∼). In *i*, *e*, *ɛ*, and perhaps, *a*, the second (higher) formant of the vowel sets an upper limit to the frequency position of the schematic stop which will sound like *p*. Then, beginning with *a* and becoming increasingly apparent in the back vowel series (*a* through *u*), a mode appears in the *p* distribution somewhere above the second formant of the vowel, reaching its highest point at *u*. In this *latter* series the second formant of the vowel becomes a lower limit to the *p* sound.

For all the vowels the judgment *p* predominates as the response to the lowest stop position (360 ∼). The number of *p* judgments for this lowest position appears to increase regularly in the *i* through *a* series, with one slight inversion at *e*, and then to decrease in very orderly fashion in the series *a* to *u*. Although the lowest stop position attracts more judgments of *p* than of *k* or *t*, it is the most preferred position for *p* in only three of the seven vowels (*ɛ*, *a*, and *ɔ*); therefore the critical aspect of the stimulus for *p* is not simply its low position on the frequency scale.

The distributions of *t* judgments are quite broad and flat, without any obvious peaks or modes, and it is difficult to define a *t* point or region beyond the statement

Perception of the Unvoiced Stop Consonants 69

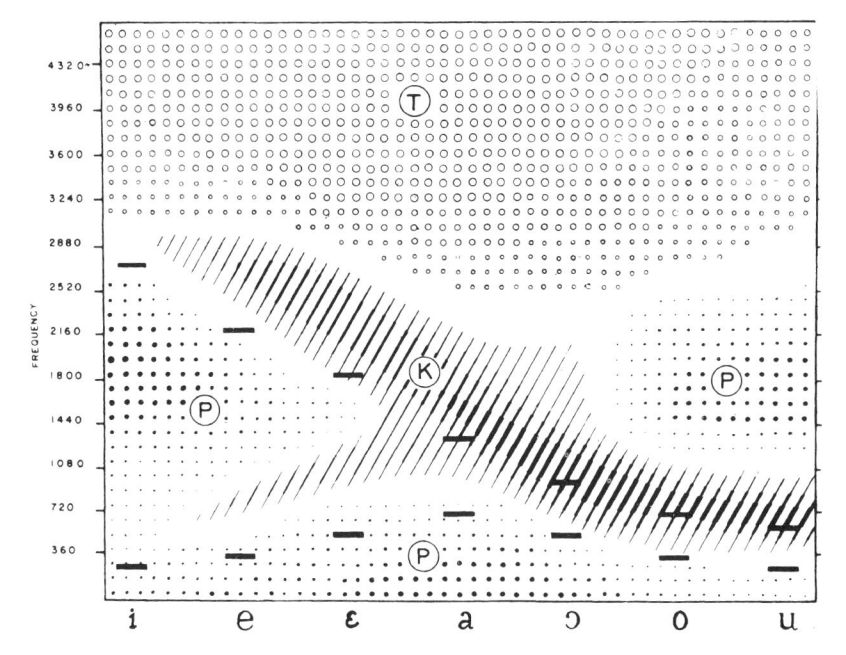

Figure 3.6
Map of the areas in which the judgment p, t, or k predominates.

that *t* occupies the frequency range lying above the stop positions which are judged to be *p* or *k*. There is little else to be seen in the *t* distributions except, perhaps, that the Ss had a greater disposition to judge the stop as *t* when it preceded the front vowels (i, e, and ε) than when it preceded the back vowels (u, o, and ɔ).

In figure 3.6 we have attempted to represent the results of this experiment in rather general form. The zones of the figure correspond to those areas (cf. figure 3.5) in which one of the judgments (p, t, k) occurred more often than the other two; within each zone, the thickness of the line or the size of the dot or circle indicates roughly the extent to which that judgment was preferred.

The reproducibility of the data can be seen by comparing the curves of figures 3.7 and 3.8. In these figures the data are plotted separately for our two groups of Ss, the one being relatively naïve in regard to phonetics and the other relatively sophisticated. The two sets of curves are obviously very similar.

As a further test of reliability, we have compared the curves corresponding to the judgments made on the first and second times through the series of syllables. These curves, which are not shown here, resemble each other quite as much as do the curves for the two groups of subjects in figures 3.7 and 3.8.

The results of this experiment show clearly the influence of the following vowel on the perception of the schematic stops *p* and *k*.[13] The modes of the *p* and *k* distributions shift in frequency position according to the frequencies of the formants in the vowel which follows, and these shifts are so great, relatively, that the *k* mode crosses over the *p* mode in the vowel series *i* through *u*. Perhaps the clearest single example of this effect is seen (figure 3.5) in the judgments of the schematic stop at 1440 ∼. Before *i* this schematic stop was called *p* 59 times out of 60; in the series *i* to *a* there was a progressive decrease in the number of *p* judgments, and a correspondingly

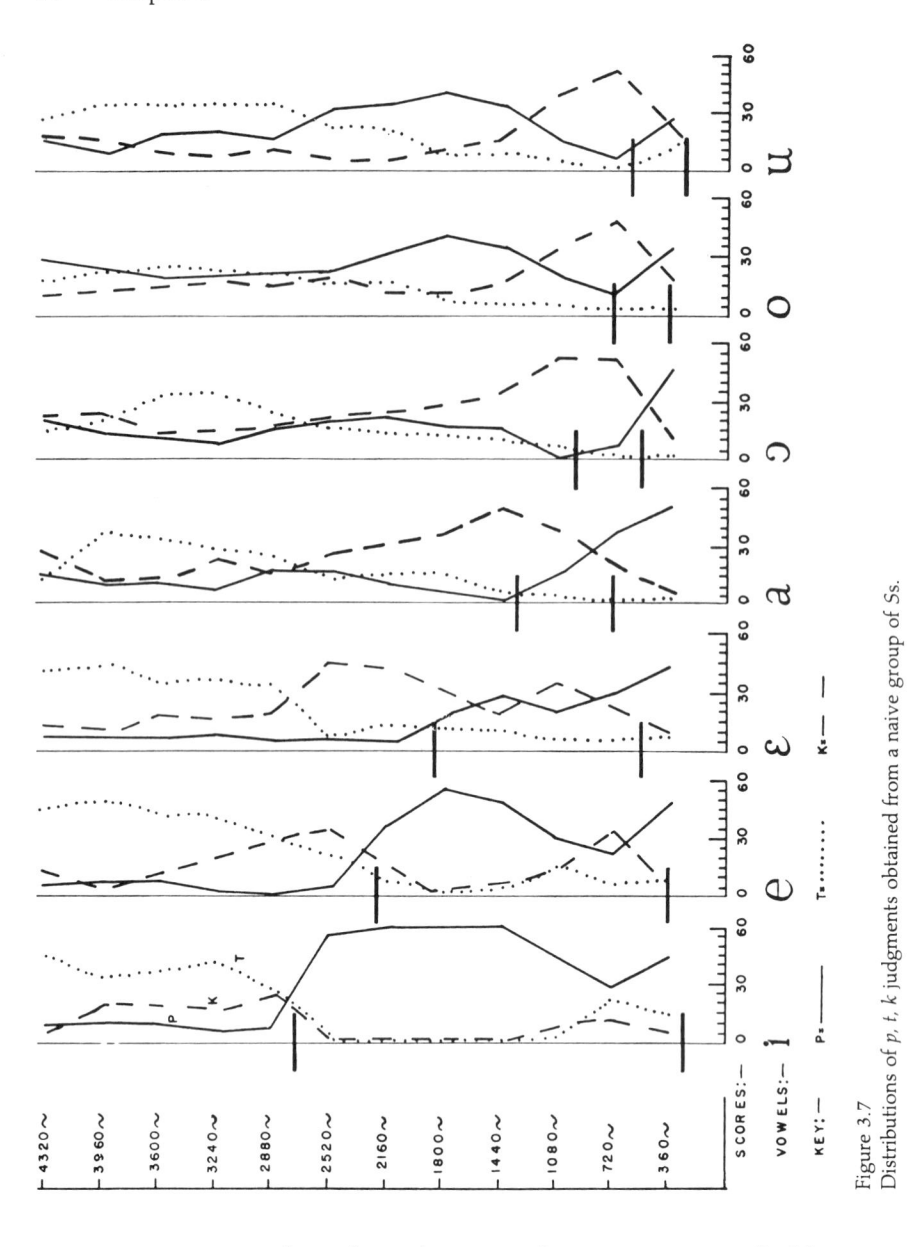

Figure 3.7
Distributions of p, t, k judgments obtained from a naive group of Ss.

progressive increase in *k*, until at *a* this same schematic stop was called *k* 47 times out of 60; then from *a* to *u* the number of *k* judgments decreased, as *p* increased, and at *u* this stop was called *p* 42 times out of 60. In brief, the identity of the *same* schematic stop was judged in a large majority of cases to be *p* when paired with *i* and *u*, but to be *k* when paired with *a*. If these results with schematized syllables truly represent the situation as it is in the perception of actual speech, then it must be concluded that the vowel plays a critical part in the auditory perception of *p* and *k*, and in that event the irreducible acoustic correlate for *p* and *k* is the sound pattern corresponding to the consonant-vowel syllable.

It may be of interest, also, that our results relate to the assumption that the perception of speech depends ultimately on the proprioceptive return from the articulatory

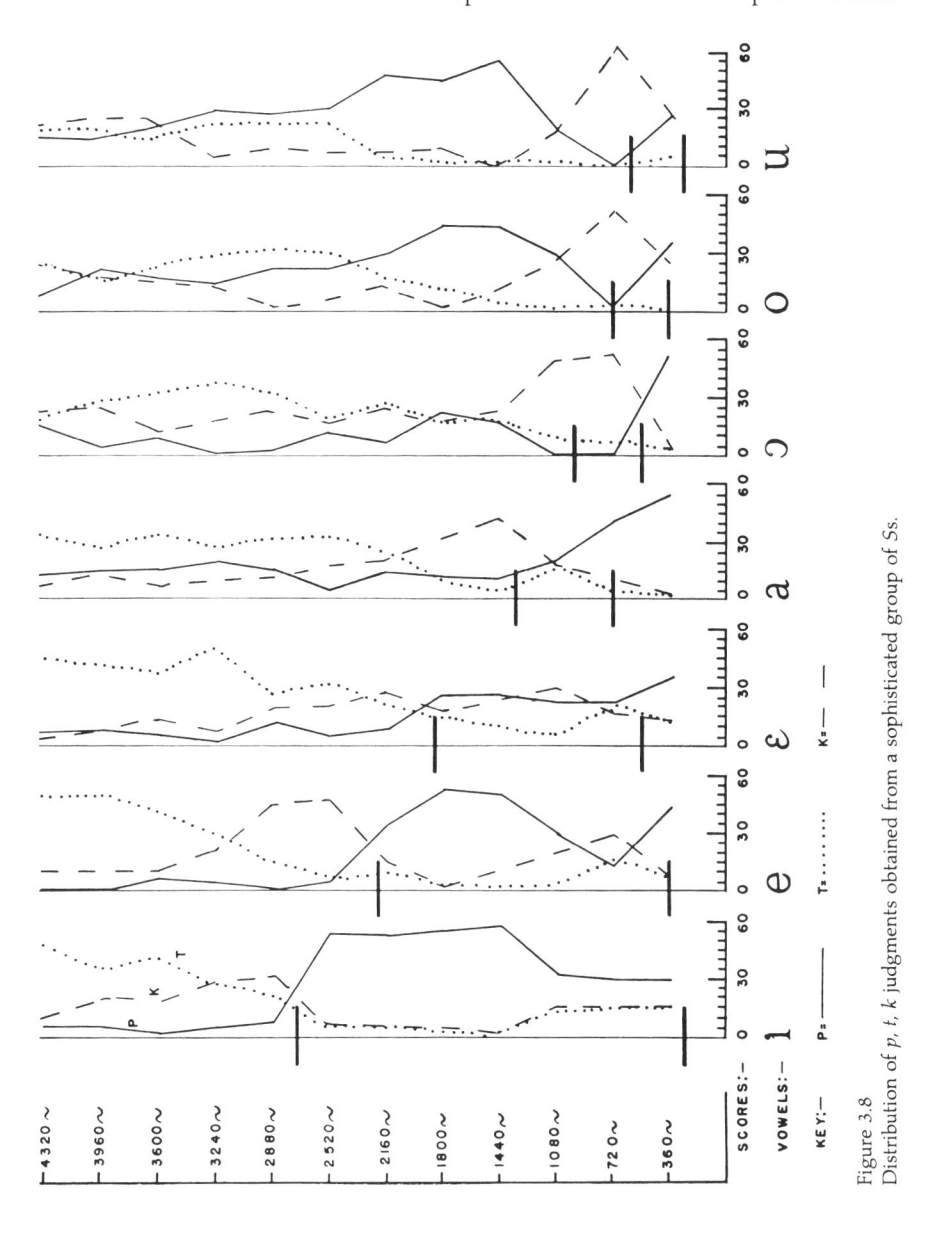

Figure 3.8
Distribution of p, t, k judgments obtained from a sophisticated group of Ss.

movements which are made in speaking. One test of this assumption depends on, and is suggested by, the fact that the relation between the articulatory and acoustic events is a rather complex one, i.e., that relatively large changes in articulation can, under certain conditions, produce relatively small acoustic differences, and vice versa. Given this kind of relation between articulation and the acoustic result, and given the assumption that the ultimate cues for the perception of speech arise from the movements of articulation, we should expect that the relation between perception and articulation will be considerably simpler (more nearly direct) than the relation between perception and acoustic stimulus, or, to put it another way, that for any group of speech sounds the perceived similarities (and differences) will correspond more closely to the articulatory than to the acoustic similarities among the sounds.

It will, of course, be very difficult to test this expectation with all the sounds of a language, since we cannot readily arrange the sounds along comparable scales of similarity in the acoustic, articulatory, and perceptual domains. We can, however, look for extreme cases in which the question of similarity is reduced to a categorical matter of identity or difference; in the results of our experiment we find several cases which reach, or very closely approximate, those extremes. One such case (the schematic stop at 1440 ∼) was described in the preceding paragraph, where it was seen that acoustically identical schematic stops before *i*, *a*, and *u* can add to these vowels initial sounds which, as perceived, are as distinctively different as the *p* of *pi* and *pu* and the *k* of *ka*.[14] On the basis of what is known about the acoustic and articulatory aspects of this particular situation, it is altogether reasonable to assume that these acoustically identical schematic stops could be most closely approximated in the act of speaking only by very different kinds of articulatory movements, and we should suppose that the proprioceptive stimuli which will result from these movements would also be very different. With the mouth set to articulate *i* or *u*, a speaker would presumably use a movement of the lips to produce a sound having roughly the same acoustic characteristics as our schematic stop at 1440 ∼; for the vowel *a*, the same acoustic result would be most closely approximated by lowering the back of the tongue from a point of contact with the roof of the mouth. (Our schematic stops are considerably simpler acoustically than the sounds produced in actual speech, and it is likely, also, that the acoustic identity which we have been able to impose on the schematic stops is only approximated in speaking.) We assume, then, that the sound patterns corresponding to the syllables *pi* (or *pu*) and *ka* set off the appropriate movements in the listener (that is, the articulatory movements which the listener would make in attempting to reproduce these acoustic patterns) or perhaps only the short-circuited neural equivalents of these movements, with the result that the initial schematic phonemes *p* and *k*, which can be entirely identical as acoustic stimuli, become clearly differentiated in proprioceptive terms and are therefore finally perceived as distinctively different sounds. Thus we have, at the one extreme, a case in which there is complete identity of acoustic stimuli (in the consonant part of the syllable), considerable difference in movement and proprioception, and, in accordance with the proprioceptive rather than the acoustic stimuli, considerable difference in perception. At the other extreme, one would look for a case in which there is (again in the consonant part of the syllable) a large acoustic difference, no articulatory difference, and no perceived difference. In its extreme form that case is not to be found in our data, but we have a reasonable approximation to it in the schematic stops which sounded most like *k*. As can be seen in figure 3.5 or figure 3.6, the frequency position of the "best" *k* is quite different for *u*, *o*, ɔ, *a*, ɛ, and *e*, and these differences are large enough to cover a very significant part of our total frequency range. The nearest spoken equivalents to these schematic *k*'s will be produced by articulatory movements which are not precisely identical (the point of tongue contact is toward the back of the mouth for the back vowels and moves forward when the *k* precedes a front vowel), but the differences in articulation are certainly very small by comparison with the articulatory differences between *k* and *p*. We may say, then, in regard to the schematic stops which were heard as *k* that the perception reflects the basic similarity in the articulatory patterns rather than the relatively gross differences among the acoustic stimuli; though this is not the extreme case that we should have liked ideally to find, it does come sufficiently close to provide some additional support for the assumption that the perception of speech depends, in any final analysis, on the proprioceptive stimuli which arise from the movements of articulation.

Summary

Earlier work on the perception of speech yielded a method by which an investigator makes experimental modifications of spectrographic displays and then, with an appropriate playback instrument, converts the spectrograms into sound for aural evaluation. Exploratory research with this method produced reasonably intelligible sentences from highly simplified spectrograms, and provided a basis for more intensive research into the stimulus-essentials for the perception of individual phoneme, syllable, or word units.

The present study is an intensive investigation of this kind into the effect of one acoustic variable on the perception of unvoiced stop consonants which introduce a consonant-vowel syllable. For that purpose a schematized, spectrographic representation of the unvoiced stop consonants was placed at each of 12 frequency-positions before each of seven schematized vowels. The schematic stop was 600 ∼ high and 15 m.sec. wide, as it appeared on the spectrogram, and the 12 positions of the stop sampled the range 360 to 4320 ∼ at interval of 360 ∼; the schematic vowels were composed of two formants, and were so chosen as to represent a systematic sampling of the vowel triangle. These spectrographic patterns, each one corresponding to a consonant-vowel syllable, were converted into sound by a playback and presented in random order to 30 Ss with instructions to identify the initial stop-like sound as *p*, *t*, or *k*.

The Ss' responses indicate that the identification of *p* and *k* did not depend solely on the frequency position of the schematic stop, but rather on this position in relation to the schematic vowel which followed. Thus, for each of the vowels, the distribution of *k* judgments showed a pronounced mode (that is, a strong preference for the *k* identification) at the schematic stop which lay slightly above the second formant of the vowel; this mode moved upward along the frequency-scale with the rise in frequency of the second vowel-formant in the back-to-front vowel series, *u*, *o*, *ɔ*, *a*, *ɛ*, *e*, and *i*. For *ɛ*, *e*, and perhaps *i* in which the two formants of the vowel are far apart in frequency, there was a second mode in the *k* distribution at a point just above the first vowel-formant. The height of the *k* mode tended to vary with the vowel, but if we exclude *i*, where none of the schematic stops was identified very often as *k*, the amount of variation was not great. In the frequency range 300 to 3000 ∼, within which the *k* and *p* modes lie, the distributions of *p* judgments were in large part the inverse of the *k* distributions.

Above 3000 ∼ the schematic stops were judged most often to be *t*. There was very little effect of the schematic vowel on the identification of *t*.

The judgments made in regard to one schematic stop (at 1440 ∼) exhibit most clearly the influence of the schematic vowel on the perception of the schematic stop. At the one end of the vowel series, before *u*, this stop was called *p* 70 percent of the time; from *u* through *o* and *ɔ* the number of *p* judgments steadily decreased as *k* increased, until at *a* 78 percent of the judgments were to the effect that the stop was *k*; this trend was then reversed from *a* through *ɛ* and *e*, and finally, at *i* the stop was once again identified as *p*, this time in 98 percent of the responses. This and the other results of the experiment demonstrate that in the perception of the schematic p and k before schematic vowels, and perhaps for their equivalents in normal speech also, the irreducible acoustic stimulus is the sound pattern corresponding to the consonant-vowel syllable.

Notes

This research was made possible by funds granted by the Carnegie Corporation of New York and the University of Pennsylvania Faculty Research Fund.

1. F. S. Cooper, Reading machines, in *Research on Guidance Devices and Reading Machines for the Blind, Committee on Sensory Devices*, Nat. Acad. Sci., 1947, 38–41, also Appendix F; Spectrum analysis, *J. Acoust. Soc. Amer.*, 22, 1950, 761–762; F. S. Cooper, A. M. Liberman, and J. M. Borst, The interconversion of audible and visible patterns as a basis for research in the perception of speech, *Proc. Nat. Acad. Sci.*, 37, 1951, 318–325.
2. We shall deal here only with those acoustic stimuli which determine phoneme, syllable, or word identification, leaving aside the various other kinds of information (e.g., the identity and mood of the speaker) which are presumably carried in the speech wave.
3. This spectrogram and those of figure 3.2 were produced by a spectrograph similar in principle, but considerably different in detail, from the one developed originally at the Bell Telephone Laboratories. (For a description of the original sound spectrograph see a series of articles by members of the Bell Telephone Laboratories in *J. Acoust. Soc. Amer.*, 18, 1946.) The spectrograph from which our spectrograms were made was designed specifically for use with the pattern playback. It yields film transparencies which record relative sound intensities over a range of approximately 40 db.
4. F. M. Wiener and G. A. Miller, Some characteristics of human speech, in *Summary Technical Report of Division 17, NDRC, Vol. 3, Transmission and Reception of Sounds under Combat Conditions*, 66–67.
5. There may be other acoustic differences between voiced and unvoiced stops, but they are less apparent than the presence or absence of voicing..
6. R. K. Potter, G. A. Kopp, and H. C. Green, *Visible Speech*, 1947, 79–103.
7. The term "formant," as applied to vowels and to the so-called resonant consonants (l, m, n, r, etc.), refers to a frequency region in which there is a relatively high concentration of acoustic energy.
8. The playback speaks either from photographic copies of actual spectrograms, using the modulated light which is *transmitted* through the relatively transparent portions of the film, or from spectrograms which are painted on a clear base of cellulose acetate, in which case the sound is controlled by the light *reflected* from the painted areas. In this experiment only the painted spectrograms have been used.
9. Pierre Delattre, Liberman, and Cooper, Voyelles synthétique à deux formantes, et voyelles cardinales, Le Maître Phonétique, December 1951 (in press).
10. Op. cit., 66–67.
11. Op. cit., 97–103.
12. G. Dewey, *Relative Frequency of English Speech Sounds*, 1923, 66.
13. We have made some preliminary tests to determine how the 12 schematic stops are judged when they are presented without the schematic vowels. For the three lowest stopped positions, at 360, 720, and 1080 ∼, the judgments of k predominate, and show a rather high mode at the last-named position. The three next higher positions, at 1440, 1800, and 2160 ∼, are called p, t, and k almost equally, with t being very slightly favored over p and k. Above 2160 ∼ the frequency of judgments of t increases somewhat, largely at the expense of k, while p remains as it was.

    We expect, in a later publication, to present these results in more nearly complete form, and to discuss their relation to the results obtained with the schematic syllables. In the present paper we can only suggest that the Ss' identifications of the isolated schematic stops do not appear to be inconsistent with our conclusion that the vowel plays an important part in the perception of a p or k which precedes it.
14. The quality of p or k cannot be assumed to be given by the schematic vowel alone, since a listener does not hear an initial p or k when any one of the schematic vowels is presented without the schematic stop. It should be noted that this is true only of steady-state vowels. We have some very preliminary indications that when the vowel formants are appropriately "bent" an initial p or k can, perhaps, be heard even though the schematic stop has been entirely omitted.

Chapter 4

The Role of Consonant-Vowel Transitions in the Perception of the Stop and Nasal Consonants

In spectrograms of stop consonant-plus-vowel syllables one commonly sees several acoustic variables that might conceivably be important in the auditory identification of the stop consonant phones. One such variable is a short burst of noise, found near the beginning of the syllable, as in figure 4.1, and presumed to be the acoustic counterpart of the articulatory explosion. By preparing hand-drawn spectrographic patterns of burst-plus-vowel and then converting these patterns into sound, we found in an earlier experiment (Liberman, Delattre, and Cooper 1952) that the frequency position of the burst could serve as a cue, though not necessarily as a completely adequate one, for distinguishing among *p*, *t*, and *k*.

Bursts above 3,000 cps were, in general, judged to be *t*. Below that level, the perception of the burst was determined by its frequency position in relation to the vowel with which it was paired: the burst was heard as *k* when it lay at or slightly above the second formant of the following vowel; otherwise, it was identified as *p*. The effect of the vowel on the perception of the burst was shown most strikingly in the case of one burst, centered at 1,440 cps, which was heard as *p* before *i* and *u*, but as *k* before *a*.

A second possible cue to the perception of the stops lies in the transition between consonant and vowel, seen in figure 4.1 as a curvature of the formants[1] during the vowel onset. Such shifts in the frequencies of the vowel formants presumably reflect the articulatory movements that are made in going from one position to another; one expects, then, to find these shifts in the region where two phones join.[2]

In their discussion of the cues that might be used in "reading" speech spectrograms, Potter, Kopp, and Green (1947, 81–103) have noted the transitions between stop consonant and vowel, especially in the second formant, and have described in general terms the forms that these transitions seem characteristically to take. According to these authors, the movement of the second formant is typically upward when the vowel follows *p* or *b*; after *t* or *d* the second formant of the vowel starts at a position "near the middle of the pattern," with the result that this formant will then rise or fall depending on whether its normal, steady-state position in the vowel is higher or lower than the *t-d* starting point; after *k* or *g* the second formant starts at a position slightly above its steady-state position in the vowel, wherever that may be, and the transition is always, therefore, a relatively small shift downward. Joos (1948, 121–125), also, has noted that the transitions are characteristically different for the various syllabic combinations of stop and vowel, and, in addition, has made explicit

---

Originally published in *Psychological Monographs: General and Applied* 68, 8 (1954): 1–13, with Pierre C. Delattre, Franklin S. Cooper, and Louis J. Gerstman. Reprinted with permission.

76   Chapter 4

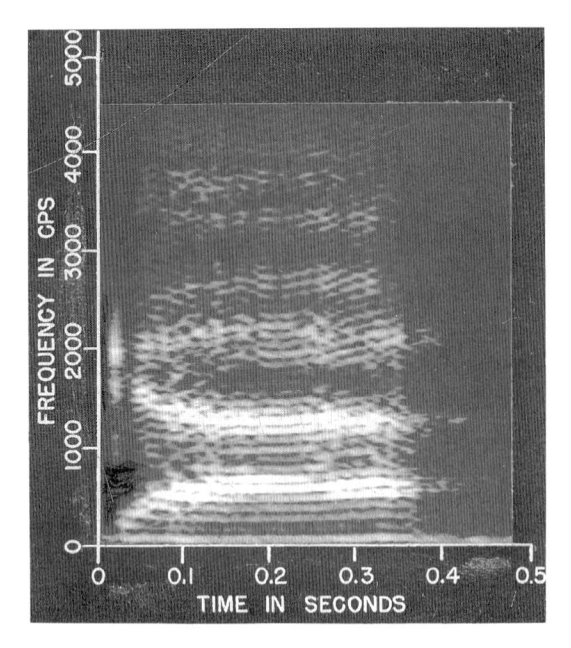

Figure 4.1
Spectrogram of the syllable *ga*, showing a burst and a transition.

the assumption that the transitions may well be important cues for the perception of the stops. Without this latter assumption, he points out, one may have difficulty in explaining how listeners distinguish among the stop sounds, since the explosive portions are sometimes of very low intensity.

Further analysis of spectrograms may result in a more nearly precise description of the typical patterns of transition for the various combinations of stop consonant and vowel. It will be no less necessary, however, to isolate the transitions experimentally if we are to determine whether they are perceptual cues or nulls, since the transitional movements do not occur independently of other possible cues in spectrograms of actual speech. To find whether or not the transitions can, in fact, enable a listener to distinguish among the stop consonants, we have, in the first experiment to be reported here, varied the direction and extent of second-formant transitions in highly simplified synthetic syllables and presented the resulting sounds to a group of listeners for identification as *b*, *d*, or *g* and, separately, as *p*, *t*, or *k*.

Since the nasal consonants *m*, *n*, and ŋ are closely related in articulatory terms to the voiced and unvoiced stops—*f-b-m* are all articulated by the lips, *t-d-n* by the tip of the tongue against the alveols, and *k-g-*ŋ by the hump of the tongue against the velum—we might guess that the transitional cues for *p-t-k* or *b-d-g* would also serve to distinguish among *m-n-*ŋ. A second experiment was carried out, then, to determine whether the variable second-formant transitions of the first experiment could function as cues for the perception of the nasal consonants. For that purpose we added to the patterns of vowel-plus-transition a certain neutral and constant resonance that had been found to impart to these patterns, as heard, the color or character of nasal consonants as a class. The sounds produced from these patterns were presented to subjects for judgment as *m*, *n*, or ŋ.

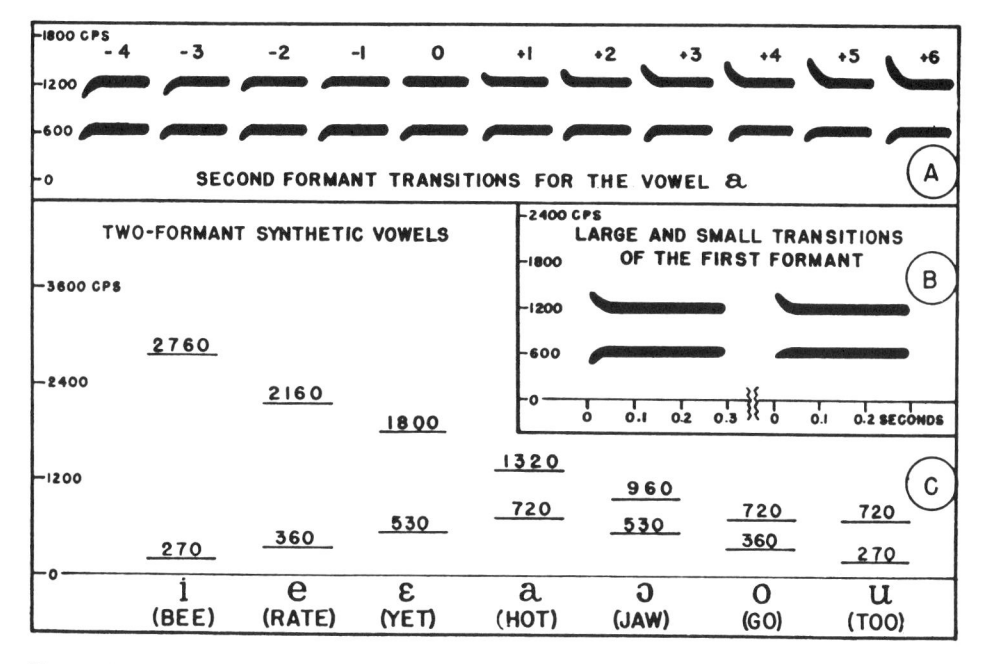

Figure 4.2
The stimuli of Experiment I.

Experiment I: Stop Consonants

Apparatus
All the stimuli of this experiment were produced by using a special purpose playback to convert hand-painted spectrograms into sound. This playback, which has been described in earlier papers (Cooper 1950; Cooper, Liberman, and Borst 1951), produces 50 bands of light modulated at harmonically related frequencies that range from a fundamental of 120 cps through the fiftieth harmonic at 6,000 cps. The modulated light beams are arranged to match the frequency scale of the spectrogram. Thus, when a spectrogram, painted in white on a transparent base, is passed under the lights, the painted portions reflect to a phototube those beams whose modulation frequencies correspond to the position of the paint on the vertical (frequency) axis of the spectrogram.

Stimuli
As shown in figure 4.2, the second-formant transitions, which constituted the experimental variable of this study, differed in direction and extent. From the frequency at which the second formant begins to the frequency at which it levels off, the transitions vary in steps of one harmonic (120 cps) from a point four harmonics (480 cps) below the center of the steady-state portion of the second formant to a point six harmonics (720 cps) above the second formant. This range of transitions was judged, on the basis of exploratory work, to be sufficient. For two of the synthetic vowels, *o* and *u*, the close proximity of first (lower) and second (higher) formants made it impossible to extend the transition as much as 480 cps below the second formant; in these cases

the transitions that rise from points below the second formant were varied in four half-harmonic steps.

For convenience in reference, the direction and extent of second-formant transitions will be indicated as in section A of figure 4.2. Transitions that go through a frequency range lying below the steady-state formant of the synthetic vowel will be called "minus" (−); those that cover a range of frequencies above the steady-state formant will be called "plus" (+). The extent of a transition will be given by the number of harmonics (of the 120-cps fundamental) through which the formant moves before arriving at its steady-state position. A transition of −3, for example, is one that goes through the first three harmonics below the steady state of the vowel.

In determining the curvature of the transitions, we tried simply to approximate the transitions we have seen in spectrograms of actual speech. The duration of the transition, i.e., the time interval between the beginning and end of the frequency shift, varied linearly with the size of the transition, from 0.04 sec. for a transition of +1 or −1, to 0.08 sec. for a transition of +6. This made it possible to keep the shape of the transition (as judged by eye) roughly constant. We have found in exploratory work that variations in the duration of the transition or in curvature do not cause the sound to change from one stop consonant to another.

The two-formant synthetic vowels used in this study, and arranged in section C of figure 4.2 along an articulatory continuum of front-to-back tongue positions, represent a rather systematic sampling of the vowel triangle. They have been adapted from a set of synthetic vowels that had been found in an earlier study (Delattre et al. 1952) to approximate rather closely the color of the corresponding cardinal vowels as spoken; with the exception of *u*, the vowels of the present experiment are substantially identical with those used in an earlier experiment (Liberman, Delattre, and Cooper 1952) on bursts as cues for the stop consonants. The frequency extent of each formant is three harmonics of the 120-cps fundamental. The value that is to be found just above each formant in section C of figure 4.2 gives the frequency that corresponds approximately to the center of the formant.[3] Each pattern of transition-plus-vowel has a total duration of 0.3 sec.

In our essentially exploratory attempts to produce acceptable stop consonants with nothing more than a transition and a schematic vowel, we had adopted for the first formant the constant minus transition seen in section A of figure 4.2.[4] This first-formant transition seemed to increase the realism and identifiability of the sounds, but it imparted to all of them a rather strong voiced quality; that is, it made them sound much more like *b-d-g* than *p-t-k*. Although we were not concerned in this study to isolate the cues that distinguish the voiced stops from their voiceless counterparts, we did wish to investigate the role of second-formant transitions in both classes of sounds, and, on the assumption that phonetically native listeners might have difficulty in trying to identify the voiced sounds as voiceless, we thought it wise to try to "unvoice" the sounds before presenting them for judgment as *p-t-k*. The closest approximation we could achieve, without adding the burst of noise that appears to characterize *p-t-k*, was obtained by considerably reducing the transition of the first formant.[5] This reduces somewhat the impression of voicing; it makes the stops resemble the unaspirated voiceless stops used, for example, by a native speaker of French, but it does not succeed in producing the clearly unvoiced quality typical of aspirated *p-t-k* in an American pronunciation. The "unvoiced" and "voiced" types of first-formant transition are illustrated in section B of figure 4.2.

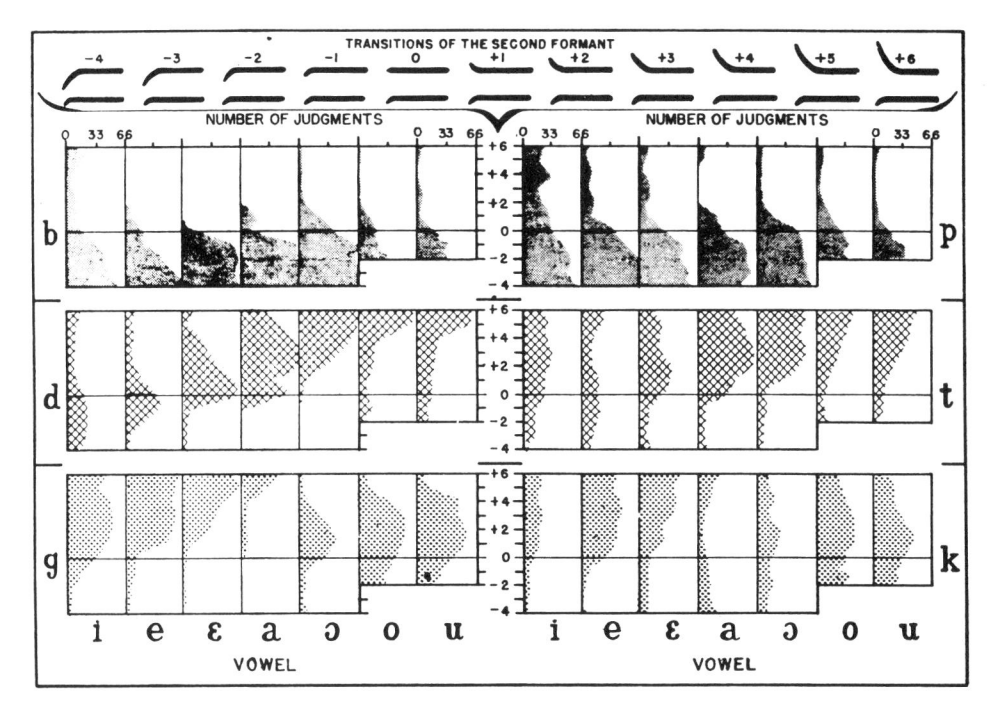

Figure 4.3
Responses to the variable transitions of the second formant obtained with large transitions of the first formant. Within each small rectangle, the number of times a stimulus was judged as *b*, *d*, or *g* (or as *p*, *t*, or *k*) is plotted on the horizontal axis as a function of the direction and extent of the second-formant transition (shown on the vertical axis and illustrated at the top of the figure). The data were obtained from two groups of 33 Ss each. One group judged the stimuli as *b*, *d*, or *g*, the other as *p*, *t*, or *k*. Each S made two judgments of each stimulus. The vowels with which the second-formant transitions were paired are arranged along an articulatory continuum of tongue position from front to back. Because of the close proximity of the first and second formants of *o* and *u*, the minus transitions for these vowels were not extended beyond a value of two.

There were, then, two sets of stimuli that were identical in all respects, except that in one set the minus transition of the first formant was relatively large and in the other very small.

Presentation of Stimuli
A total of 77 stimuli (11 transitions times 7 schematic vowels) was used for each of the two sets of test patterns (voiced and unvoiced). These 77 stimuli were recorded from the playback onto magnetic tape, and then spliced into a random order, subject to the restrictions that in each successive group of 11 sounds each transition appear once and only once, and that each vowel appear at least once in each group but never more than twice and never in immediate succession.

In the final test tape the sound stimuli were arranged in such a way that each stimulus would be presented and then repeated after an interval of 0.9 sec., with an interval of 6 sec. between successive pairs of identical stimuli. The latter interval provided sufficient time for S to make and record his judgment of one stimulus before being presented with the next. A rest period of 15 sec. was interpolated between successive groups of 11 stimuli.

The "voiced" patterns (i.e., those with large transitions of the first formant) were presented to one group of 33 Ss for judgment as *b*, *d*, or *g*; the "unvoiced" patterns (i.e., those with small transitions of the first formant) were presented to a second group of 33 Ss for judgment as *p*, *t*, or *k*. Then, to exhaust all combinations of the two kinds of first-formant transition and the two kinds of judgment, we recruited two additional groups of 33 Ss each and asked one of these groups to judge the patterns with the large first-formant transitions as *p*, *t*, or *k*, and the other to judge the patterns with the small transitions of the first formant as *b*, *d*, or *g*.

In all cases S was asked to make an identification of each stimulus, even when he felt that his judgment was only a guess. The range of identifications permitted was limited to *p*, *t*, or *k* for two groups of Ss, and to *b*, *d*, or *g* for the other two groups.

The entire stimulus series was presented twice for each S. Thus, each S made a total of 154 judgments.

Before Ss began to record their judgments, they were asked to listen to the first group of 11 stimuli in order that they might become somewhat acquainted with the nature of the sounds and the format of the experiment. For all Ss the opportunity to hear these 11 stimuli constituted the sum of their experience with the sounds produced by the pattern playback prior to their participation in this experiment.

Subjects

A total of 132 Ss (33 in each of the four conditions) served in the experiment. All were volunteers from undergraduate and graduate courses at the University of Connecticut.

Results

Before considering the particular responses that were made to the various second-formant transitions, we ought, first, to note in figures 4.3 and 4.4 the similarities and differences in the general pattern of responses obtained with the two types of first formant (large and small minus transitions) and the two types of judgment (voiced and unvoiced). By comparing figures 4.3 and 4.4, we see that the amount of agreement among Ss is somewhat greater when the first formant has the larger minus transition. It will be remembered in this connection that we had adopted the relatively straight first formant in an attempt to reduce the impression of voicing; that is, to make the synthetic stops sound less like *b-d-g* and somewhat more like *p-t-k*. Clearly, we did not succeed by this means in increasing the amount of agreement among Ss who tried to identify these stimuli as *p-t-k*.

We have noted earlier that it was not the purpose of this study to find the cues that distinguish voiced from unvoiced stops, and it should be emphasized here that we have not yet investigated this matter, except cursorily and in a few isolated cases. On the basis of such evidence as is now available, however, we believe that the voiced-voiceless distinction is more easily made if one is free, as we were not in this particular experiment, to use both burst and transition. The proper combination of burst and transition tends to produce an impression of the general class of unvoiced stops, the particular identity of the stop (i.e., *p*, *t*, or *k*) being determined both by the frequency position of the burst and the nature of the transition. It will presumably be possible, then, to obtain the voiced counterparts by making certain constant changes in the pattern, as, for example, by varying the time interval between burst and transition, or by adding constant "markers," such as a "voice bar" (a tone of 120 or 240

Consonant-Vowel Transitions 81

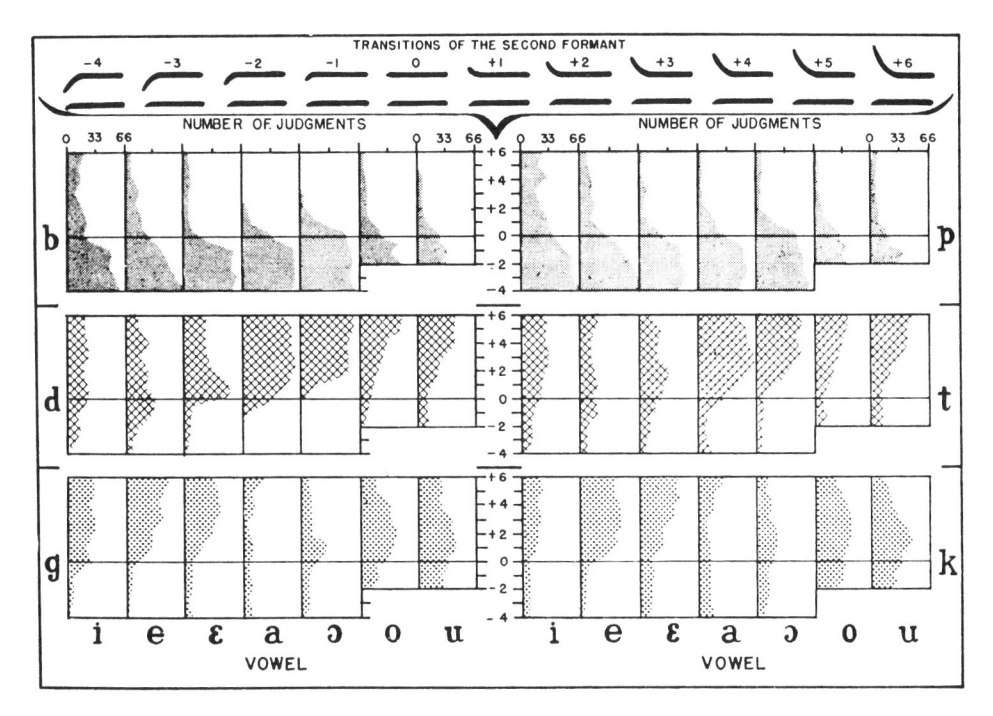

Figure 4.4
Responses to the variable transitions of the second formant obtained with small transitions of the first formant. The data are displayed as in figure 4.2.

cps sounding simultaneously with the burst). Thus, a particular combination of burst and second-formant transition would, with any given vowel, be used for the synthesis of either *p* or *b*, a second such combination would be used for *t* or *d*, and a third for *k* or *g*; one could expect to shift back and forth between the voiced and voiceless stops without making significant changes in the frequency position of the burst or in the direction and extent of the second-formant transition.

With large or with small transitions of the first formant (figures 4.3 or 4.4) we see that the amount of agreement is, in general, slightly greater when Ss are trying to identify the sounds as *b-d-g*. (This is not surprising, perhaps, in view of the fact that all of the stimuli sounded quite voiced.) It is nonetheless clear that the various second-formant transitions produce the same general pattern of responses, whether the stimuli that contain them are judged as *b-d-g* or as *p-t-k*. For the purposes of this paper, then, we shall consider that the second-formant transitions have essentially the same effect within each of the two classes (voiced and unvoiced) of stop consonants, and we shall treat the results as if each of the pairs, *p-b*, *t-d*, and *k-g*, were a single sound.

The response distributions of figures 4.3 and 4.4 show, in general, that *b* (or *p*) was heard when the second formants of the vowels had minus transitions (i.e., transitions that extend into a frequency region lower than the frequency of the steady-state portion of the formant). When these minus transitions were presented with the vowels *i*, *e*, *ɛ*, *a* and *ɔ*, there was considerable, and in some cases complete, agreement among Ss in identifying the sounds as *b-p*. With the vowels *o* and *u*, on the other hand, these same transitions elicited few responses of b-p (in relation to g-k and d-t), but there is, nevertheless, a significant similarity in the pattern of judgments as between o-u and i-e-ɛ-a-ɔ in that the bulk of b-p judgments occurs, for all these vowels, within the range of minus transitions.

The distributions of d-t judgments center at different positions on the scale of transitions, depending on the vowel with which the transition was paired. In the case of i the d-t distributions are rather flat and low; indeed, there is for this vowel no value of transition at which the d-t response was dominant. For the remaining vowels, however, there is a rather strong preference for identifying d (or t) within some relatively narrow range of transitions, starting in the vicinity of a zero transition for the vowels e and ɛ, and progressing to larger plus transitions through the vowel series a-ɔ-o-u.

The distributions of g-k judgments would appear, for all plus transitions at least, to be the inverse of the d-t distributions; that is, the g-k judgments occur wherever the d-t judgments do not. Considered in their own right, the distributions of g-k responses show that the extreme plus transitions were heard as g-k in the vowel series i to a. The smaller plus transitions were also heard as g-k with i and e, but a ɛ only the transitions of +4, +5, and +6 were judged very often as g or k, and at a such g-k responses as did occur were made, for the most part, to the extreme transition of +6. With ɔ, the g-k responses center at the small positive transitions and the distribution of g-k responses seems then simply to grow in height and width through o and u.

With the vowels e and ɛ relatively good d's and t's were produced by transitions of zero, or near zero, extent. This suggests that d and t have a characteristic second-formant position, or locus, somewhere near the level of the second formant of e or ɛ, from which point transitions might be expected to fall or rise to the second formants of other vowels.[6] This possibility is consistent with our finding that the d-t responses occurred primarily to progressively larger plus transitions as the frequency level of the second formant of the vowel became lower in the series a through u. We have evidence from experiments now in progress that adds support to the assumption or fixed consonant loci for d-t, and suggests that there may be comparable loci for b-p and for g-k, also. The establishment of these consonant loci would, of course, provide the basis for a greatly simplified description of the data of the present experiment.

It may be noted here that a consonant will be heard with the second formant at zero transition only when the first formant has some degree of minus transition. When both formants are straight, one hears nothing but the vowel.

Figure 4.5, which is intended to be a broader and less detailed representation of the results, is derived form the data in the left half of figure 4.3 (stimulus patterns with the large transitions of the first formant, judged as b-d-g). For the purposes of figure 4.5, a particular response was taken as "dominant" when (for any stimulus) the difference in the number of judgments between the most numerous and the next most numerous response exceeded 20 percent of the sum of all responses. This constitutes the lowest degree of dominance, and is indicated in the figure by the lightest shading. The three darker shadings of figure 4.5 correspond to increasing degrees of dominance (40, 60, and 80 percent, respectively).

The results of this experiment show that the direction and degree of second-formant transitions can serve as cues for the aurally perceived distinctions among the stop consonants.[7] In judging some of the stimuli all, or almost all, Ss made the same identifications. In other cases, the amount of agreement was considerably less than complete, but still sufficient to indicate that the second-formant transition has consid-

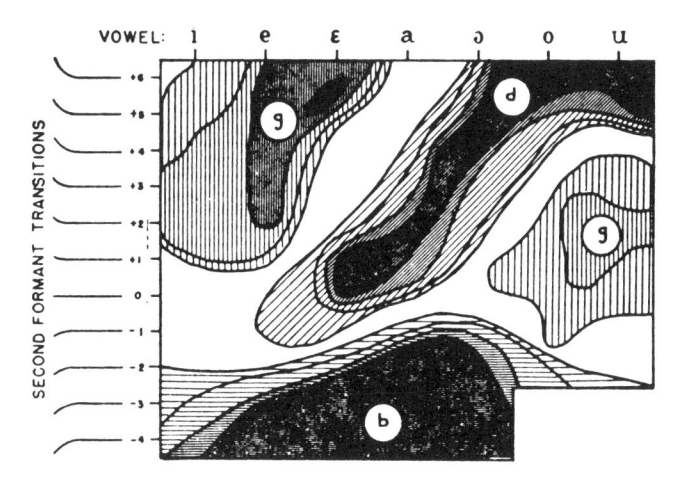

Figure 4.5
Map of the regions in which the judgments *b*, *d*, or *g* were dominant.

erable cue value. However, certain cases remain in which the second-formant transition does not appear to provide an adequate basis for identifying the stop: with *i*, for example, we do not get, with any transition, a clearly dominant *t* or *d* response.

There is evidence from preliminary investigations that an increase in the identifiability of the synthetic stops will result from the inclusion of appropriate transitions of the *third* formant. It is quite clear, however, that the third-formant transitions are, in general, considerably less important for the perception of the stop consonant than are transitions of the second formant.

We have prepared and listened to a series of patterns in which, for each of the seven schematic vowels (*i*, *e*, *ɛ*, *a*, *ɔ*, *o*, and *u*), third-formant transitions of −3, *o*, and +3 were added to each of nine second-formant transitions (from −4, through *o*, to +4). When −3 transitions of the third formant are added to minus transitions of the second formant, *b* is heard with all vowels. The addition of the −3 transition in the third formant seems in these cases to improve the *b*, particularly with the back vowels *o* and *u*, where, according to the data of figures 4.3 and 4.4, the *b* produced without third-formant transition is relatively poor. Adding a −3 transition of the third formant to plus transitions of the second formant produces, in general, a *g* impression, and in the cases of those plus transitions of the second formant that were heard as *g* in the two-formant patterns, the identifiability of the *g* is somewhat improved. As might be expected, the addition of a third formant with zero transition does not appreciably change the sound; one hears essentially what was heard with the two-formant version. The addition of a +3 transition of the third formant tends in general to produce an impression of *d*. Combining this third-formant transition with the appropriate second-formant transition creates a *d* that seems significantly better than the best that could be produced with first- and second-formant transitions alone.

Reference to the results of the earlier study on bursts will show that bursts are often effective just where the second-formant transitions alone fail. We should expect, then, that adding an appropriate burst to the transitions will further reduce the number of cases in which the response is equivocal.

84 Chapter 4

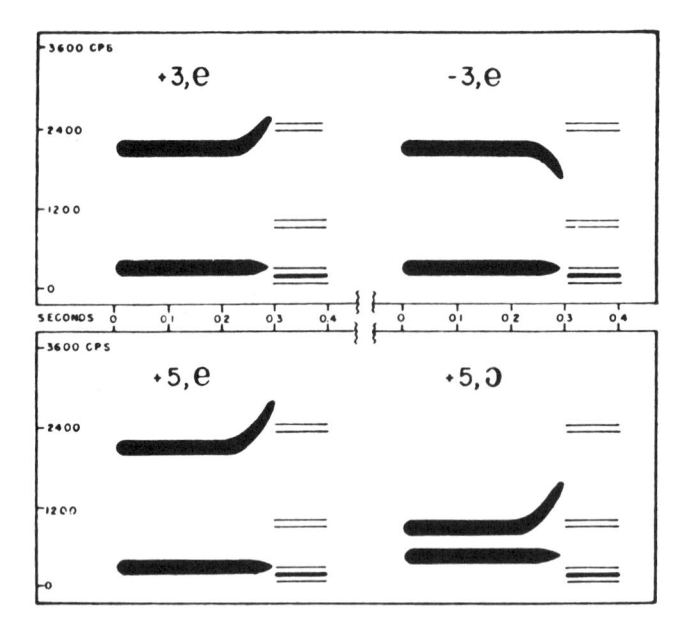

Figure 4.6
Examples of the stimuli used in Experiment II.

Experiment II: Nasal Consonants

Procedure
The stimuli of Experiment II were identical with those of Experiment I, except that (a) the transitions were placed at the ends of the syllables rather than at the beginnings, (b) neutral, constant resonances were added after the transitions, and (c) the first formants had no transitions, instead of the constant minus transitions of Experiment I. It was considered advisable to put the nasal consonants (*m*, *n*, ŋ) at the ends of the syllables because ŋ does not occur in the initial position in English. The purpose of the neutral resonance was to add to all the sounds the nasal quality characteristic of *m*, *n*, ŋ as a class. A straight first formant was used throughout because it had seemed in exploratory work that the best nasal consonants were produced in this way.

It will be seen in the patterns of figure 4.6 that the nasal resonance consists of three formants, centered at 240 cps, 1,020 cps, and 2,460 cps, and, also, that the formants of the nasal resonance are somewhat less intense than those used to produce the synthetic vowels. The particular frequency positions and intensities of these nasal "markers" were selected on the basis of exploratory experimentation, and were judged by the authors to produce rather indifferently the nasality of *m*, *n*, or ŋ.[8]

The procedure for presenting the stimuli was identical with that of Experiment I. The instructions to *S*s were also exactly as they were in Experiment I, except, of course, the *S*s were asked in Experiment II to identify the sounds as *m*, *n*, or ŋ.

Subjects
A total of 33 undergraduate and graduate students at the University of Connecticut judged the stimulus patterns. All *S*s were without prior experience in judging or listening to the synthetic speech sounds produced by the playback.

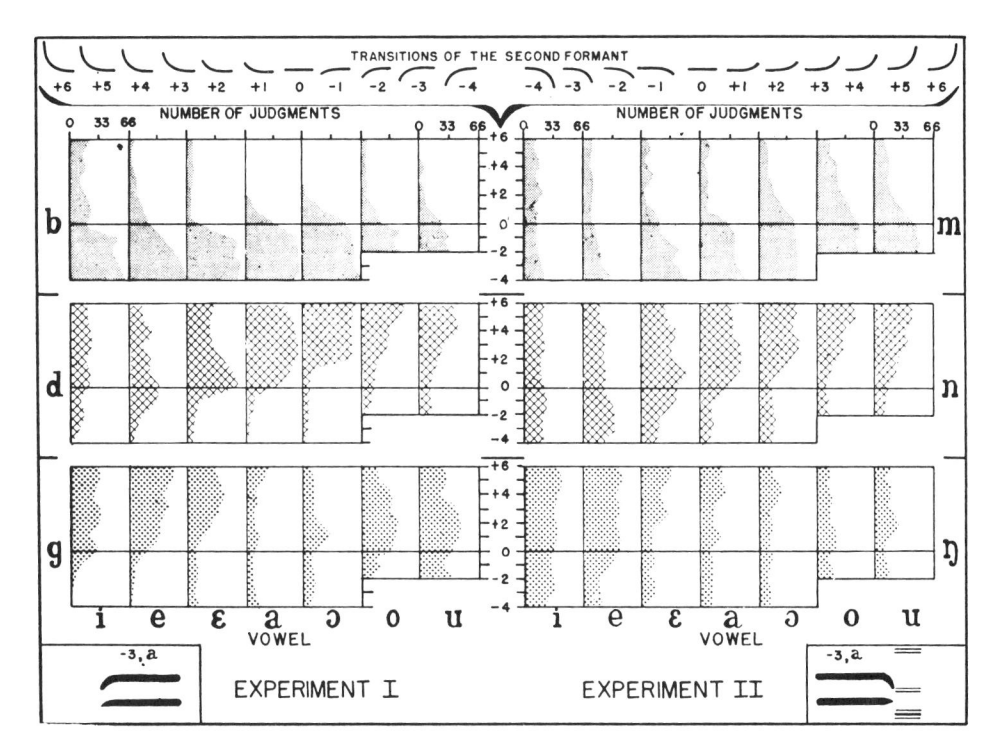

Figure 4.7
Distributions of *m*, *n*, and ŋ judgments (Experiment II) and *b*, *d*, *g* judgments (Experiment I). The data are displayed as in figure 4.2.

Results
The response distributions of figure 4.7 show how the stimulus patterns of Experiment II, which contained the second-formant transitions of Experiment I plus a nasal resonance, were identified as *m*, *n*, or ŋ. To provide a ready comparison between the results of Experiments I and II we have reproduced in figure 4.7 the left half of figure 4.4, showing how the *b-d-g* judgments varied as a function of variations in the second-formant transitions (when the first formants had the small minus transitions that most closely approximate the straight first formants of Experiment II).

The minus transitions that were heard in the first experiment as *p* (or *b*) are heard here as *m*. The major difference between the stop and nasal consonants as cued by these minus transitions of the second formant would appear to be that the response to the stops is relatively strong (i.e., there is considerable agreement among Ss in identifying the minus transitions as *p-b*) for the vowels *i*, *e*, ɛ, *a*, ɔ, and relatively weak for *o* and *u*, while for the nasals the *m* response is relatively weak with *i*, *e*, and strong with ɛ, *a*, ɔ, *o*, and *u*.

The distributions of *n* responses are quite flat for *i* and *e*; for the remaining vowels, the *n* responses clearly fall in the region of plus transitions an the bulk of the *n* responses tends to move toward higher values of plus transition from ɛ through *u*. As can be seen by comparison with the results of Experiment I, the distributions of *n* responses are very similar to those obtained for *d* (or *t*).

The distributions of ŋ responses are relatively flat and low for all the vowels—it is only with *i* and *e* that any transition is judged more often as ŋ than as *m* or *n*—but one sees nevertheless that the ŋ responses correspond to the k-g responses of Experiment I in that they occur primarily in the region of plus transitions. One can also see, perhaps, that there is a tendency, roughly comparable to that seen in the k-g distributions, for the bulk of the ŋ responses to be displaced progressively toward the higher plus transitions for the vowels from i through a; beyond a the number of ŋ responses is too few and the distributions are too nearly rectangular to permit detailed comparisons with k-g.

It is clear that the variable second-formant transitions can be cues for the perceived distinctions among m, n, and ŋ. A comparison with the results of Experiment I, however, shows that the second-formant transitions were probably somewhat less effective as cues for the nasals than they were in providing a basis for distinguishing among the stops.

We do not conclude from the superiority of the stimuli of Experiment I that the transitions are necessarily less important for the perception of the nasals than for the stops. It is at least possible that changes in certain constant aspects of the stimulus patterns, such as the frequency positions of the formants that comprise the nasal resonance, might raise the amount of agreement in the m-n-ŋ judgments, and it may be that the nasals are simply less identifiable than the stops in actual speech. One must consider also that the transitions were presented in the initial position in the syllable when they were judged as b-d-g, but in the terminal position for judgment as m-n-ŋ. By reversing the magnetic tape recordings that contain the stimuli for the first experiment (on the perception of b-d-g) we have been able to determine how the second-formant transitions are identified when the transitions (and hence the stops) are in the terminal position in the syllable. Under this condition we obtain response distributions that have patterns very similar to those of Experiments I and II, but the amount of agreement among Ss is lower even than that which we have found for m-n-ŋ.[9] One might suppose, then, that greater agreement would have been obtained in the m-n-ŋ experiment had the transitions been presented at the beginning of the syllables. We have obtained judgments under this condition (by reversing the magnetic tape of Experiment II), but in this case we find no very large difference in the responses, either in regard to pattern or to amount of agreement. (The interpretation of this result is, of course, somewhat complicated by the fact that English-speaking Ss are not accustomed to hearing ŋ in the initial position.)

For the purposes of this study the difference in the amount of agreement among Ss between Experiments I and II is less important, perhaps, than the very apparent similarities in the patterns of the response distributions. One finds in these distributions that a single second-formant transition can serve for p, b, and m, another for t, d, and n, and a third for k, g, and ŋ. Thus, three transitions are sufficient to classify nine speech sounds into three categories of three sounds each, and to enable a listener, with some degree of reliability, to distinguish among the categories. This arrangement of the sounds corresponds to a commonly accepted linguistic classification according to the place of articulation, in term of which p-b-m are bilabial, t-d-n are linguoalveolar, and k-g-ŋ are linguovelar.

If a listener is to identify each of the nine sounds uniquely, he will need, in addition to the cues for place of articulation, some basis for determining whether a given sound belongs in the class of unvoiced stops (p-t-k), voiced stops (b-d-g), or nasal consonants (m-n-ŋ). It is possible that the distinctions among these three classes are effectively cued by a limited number of acoustic markers, such as voice bar and nasal resonance, each of which is constant within its class and characteristic of a manner, rather than a place, of articulation. The experiments reported here were not designed to test this possibility.

Summary

Spectrograms of stop consonant-plus-vowel syllables characteristically show rapid transitional movements (frequency shifts) of the formants at the vowel onset. To determine whether the transitions (particularly those of the second formant) are cues for the perceived distinctions among the stop consonants, two series of simplified, hand-painted spectrograms of transition-plus-vowel were prepared, then converted into sound by a special purpose playback and presented to naive listeners for judgment as *b*, *d*, or *g* and, separately, as *p*, *t*, or *k*. In terms of the extent of frequency shift, from the beginning of the syllable to the steady-state level of the second formant of the vowel, the transitions were varied in steps of 120 cps from a point 480 cps below the second formant ("minus" transitions) to a point 720 cps above that formant ("plus" transitions).

Minus transitions were, in general, heard as *p* or *b*. Plus transitions were heard as *t-d* or *g-k*, depending on the size of the transition and the vowel with which it was paired. The amount of agreement among Ss indicated that the second-formant transitions can be important cues for distinguishing among either the voiceless stops (*p-t-k*) or the voiced stops (*b-d-g*).

A second experiment was performed to determine whether or not these same transitions of the second formant would serve to distinguish among the nasal consonants (*m-n-ŋ*), which are related to the stops in that the buccal occlusion is bilabial for *m-p-b*, linguoalveolar for *n-t-d*, and linguovelar for *ŋ-k-g*. The stimulus patterns of the second experiment were identical in all important respects to those of the first, except that a constant nasal resonance was added to each pattern and that the transitions were placed at the ends of the syllables.

There was in general somewhat less agreement among Ss in the second experiment than there had been in the first. Otherwise the results of the two experiments were quite similar: the transitions that had served for *p* and *b* were heard as *m*, those for *t* and *d* were heard as *n*, and those for *k* and *g* were heard as *ŋ*.

Notes

This research was supported in part by the Carnegie Corporation of New York and in part by the Department of Defense in connection with Contract DA49-170-sc-773. The first of the two experiments reported here was described at the 1952 meeting of the American Psychological Association; also, it was summarized in a discussion of related research at the 1952 Conference on Speech Analysis (Cooper et al. 1952).

1. Formant: A relatively high concentration of acoustic energy within a restricted frequency region. In spectrograms the formants appear as dark bands whose general orientation is parallel to the horizontal (time) axis of the graph. Typically, three or more formants are seen, as, for example, in figure 4.1; these several formants are conventionally referred to by number, formant one being the lowest in frequency and in position on the spectrogram, formant two the next higher, and so on.
2. We do not mean to imply that frequency shifts occur only between regions of steady-state resonance. It is, in fact, not unusual, especially in spectrograms of connected speech, to find that the formants are in almost constant movement. We shall deal here, however, with consonant-vowel syllables in which the vowel does assume a steady state following the transitional movement at the vowel onset.
3. Although the tones produced by the playback are spaced 120 cps apart, an auditory impression of finer gradations of formant pitch can be obtained by varying the relative intensities of the three contiguous

harmonics (of the 120-cps fundamental) that comprise the formant. In this study the intensities of the two outlying harmonics of a formant were sometimes intentionally unbalanced in an attempt to produce closer approximations to correct vowel color. The unbalancing is accomplished by varying the extent to which the white paint covers the "channel" corresponding to a particular harmonic. Wherever this procedure has been used, we have estimated the equivalent center frequency of the formant by the relative widths of the painted lines.

4. With the vowels ϵ, a, and $ɔ$, the first-formant transitions started at a point 360 cps below the steady-state level of the first formant. For i, e, o, and u, the transitions of the first formant were necessarily smaller, since the steady-state levels of the first formants of these vowels are all less than 360 cps above the lowest frequency (120 cps) produced by the playback; in these cases the first-formant transitions started at 240 cps below the steady-state level for e and o, and at 120 cps below the steady state for i and u.

5. We did not wish to add the burst because it not only produces an impression of the class of unvoiced stops, but, as was shown in an earlier experiment (6), it also serves, by its position on the frequency scale, to differentiate the stops within that class. We should note here that the frequency position of the burst can probably be used as a cue for distinguishing among the voiced stops also. This will, of course, require the addition of certain "voicing" constants.

6. Potter, Kopp, and Green (1947, 81–103) have inferred from spectrograms the existence of a "hub," or second formant, for each of the stop consonants. They assume that the frequency position of this hub is fixed for p and t, being always at a relatively low frequency for p and a relatively high frequency for t. The hub of k is assumed to vary according to the following vowel.

7. It appears that the duration of transition is also a cue for distinguishing among speech sounds, not within the class of stop consonants, but between this class and others. Thus, increasing the transition time beyond the largest value (0.08 sec.) used in the present experiment causes some of the stop consonants to be transformed first into semivowels and then, with further increases in duration of transition, into vowels of changing color. In the case of a +6 transition with ϵ, for example, the sound will be heard as $g\epsilon$, then $j\epsilon$, and, finally, as $i\epsilon$, as the duration of the transition is progressively lengthened. If the transition time is reduced below the lowest value used in the present experiment (0.04 sec.), a point is reached, eventually, at which the perception begins to change in various and complex ways; these changes are probably attributable to the fact that at very short durations the transitions are so abrupt as to be, in effect, bursts.

8. It is possible that the frequency positions of the "nasal" formants are, in actual speech, characteristically different for m, n, and $ŋ$; if so, the synthetic sounds will presumably be improved when these differences are included in the patterns. We have tried here simply to find a particular position of the formants that would produce a general nasal quality without strongly biasing the sound toward any one of the three nasal phones.

9. It may be noted that the effect of reversing the magnetic tape recordings of the stimuli is to convert a rising transition in initial position to a falling transition in terminal position, although both are minus transitions in the terminology of this paper and both are identified (with more or less agreement) as the same consonant.

We have not yet explored the possibility that the terminal transitions must be somewhat different from initials, in intensity or rate of change, for example, if they are to be maximally effective.

References

Cooper, F. S. Spectrum analysis. *J. Acoust. Soc. Amer.*, 1950, 22, 761–762.

Cooper, F. S., Delattre, P., Liberman, A. M., Borst, J. M., and Gerstman, L. J. Some experiments on the perception of synthetic speech sounds. *J. Acoust. Soc. Amer.*, 1932, 24, 597–606.

Cooper, F. S., Liberman, A. M., and Borst, J. M. The interconversion of audible and visible patterns as a basis for research in the perception of speech. *Proc. Nat. Acad. Sci.*, 1951. 37, 318–325.

Delattre, P., Liberman, A. M., Cooper, F. S., and Gerstman, L. J. An experimental study of the acoustic determinants of vowel color; observations on one- and two-formant vowels synthesized from spectrographic patterns. *Word*, 1952, 8, 195–210.

Joos, M. Acoustic phonetics. *Language*, Suppl., 1948, 24, 1–136.

Liberman, A. M., Delattre, P., and Cooper, F. S. The role of selected stimulus-variables in the perception of the unvoiced stop consonants. *Amer. J. Psychol.*, 1952, 65, 497–516.

Potter, R. K., Kopp, g. A., and Green, H. C. *Visible speech*. New York: Van Nostrand, 1947.

Chapter 5

Acoustic Loci and Transitional Cues for Consonants

In an earlier experiment[1,2] we undertook to find out whether the transitions (frequency shifts) of the second formant—often seen in spectrograms in the region where consonant and vowel join—can be cues for the identification of the voiced stop consonants. For that purpose we prepared a series of simplified, hand-painted spectrograms of transition-plus-vowel, then converted these patterns into sound and played the recordings to naive listeners for judgments as *b*, *d*, or *g*. The agreement among the listeners was, in general, sufficient to show that transitions of the second formant can serve as cues for the identification of the stops and, also, to enable us to select, for each vowel, the particular transitions that best produced each of the stop consonant phones. These transitions are shown in figure 5.1.

We found in further experiments[2] that these same second-formant transitions can serve as cues for the unvoiced stops (*p–t–k*) and the nasal consonants (*m–n–*ŋ), provided, of course, that the synthetic patterns are otherwise changed to contain appropriate acoustic cues for the voiceless and nasal manners of production. Moreover, and more important for the purposes of this paper, the results of these experiments plainly indicated a relationship between second-formant transition and articulatory place of production. Thus, the same second-formant transitions that had been found to produce *b* proved to be appropriate also for the synthesis of *p* and *m*, which, like *b*, are articulated at the lips; the second-formant transitions that produced *d* produced the consonants *t* and *n*, which have in common with *d* an articulatory place of production at the alveols; and, similarly, the second-formant transitions were found to be essentially the same for *g*, *k*, and ŋ, which are all produced at the velum.

It is an obvious assumption that the transitions seen in spectrograms reflect the changes in cavity size and shape caused by the movements of the articulators, and if we further assume that the relation between articulation and sound is not too complex, we should suppose, on the basis of the evidence of the preceding paragraph, that the second-formant transitions rather directly represent the articulatory movements *from* the place of production of the consonant *to* the position for the following vowel. Since the articulatory place of production of each consonant is, for the most part, fixed, we might expect to find that there is correspondingly a fixed frequency position—or "locus"—for its second formant; we could then rather simply describe the various second-formant transitions as movements from this acoustic locus to the steady-state level of the vowel, wherever that might be.[3] As may be seen in figure

Originally published in *The Journal of the Acoustical Society of America* 27, 4 (July 1955): 769–773, with Pierre C. Delattre and Franklin S. Cooper. Reprinted with permission.

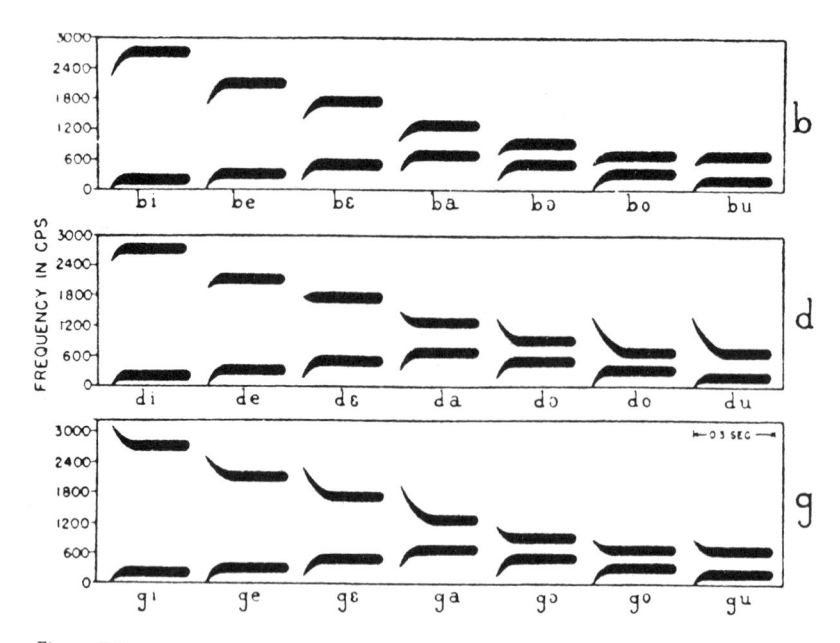

Figure 5.1
Synthetic spectrograms showing second-formant transitions that produce the voiced stops before various vowels.

5.1, the various transitions that produce the best *d* with each of the seven vowels do, in fact, appear to be coming from the same general region, and on the assumption that the first part of the acoustic transition is somehow missing, one may suppose that the transitions originate from precisely the same point. Clearly, *d* is the best case. For *b* the transitions all appear to be coming from some point low on the frequency scale, but an exact position for the *b* locus is not evident. In the case of *g*, there would appear to be a single high-frequency locus for the front vowels *i, e, ɛ,* and the mid-vowel *a;* but for the back vowels *ɔ, o,* and *u* the acoustic pattern breaks sharply, and it is obvious that the same *g* locus cannot serve for all vowels. In this connection it is known that the articulatory place of production of *g* is displaced somewhat according to the vowel that follows it, but there is no evidence that there is in this displacement the kind of discontinuity that occurs at the acoustic level in the sudden and large shift of the *g* transition. It would appear, then, that in this particular instance the relationship between place of production and sound has become rather complex, and a simple correspondence between this articulatory variable and a second-formant acoustic locus is not found.

In the series of experiments to be reported here we have, first, undertaken to collect additional evidence concerning the existence and position of the second-formant loci for *b, d,* and *g,* and, in particular, to determine whether these loci are independent of vowel color as, indeed, they must be if the concept is to have any utility; second, we have tried to determine whether, in the case of the stops, the locus can be the actual starting point for the transition, or whether, alternatively, the locus is a place to which the transition may only point; and, third, we have collected evidence concerning a first-formant locus.

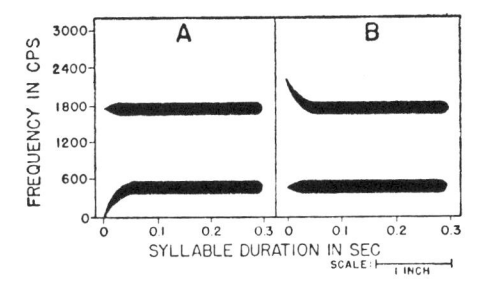

Figure 5.2
Scale drawings of sample two-formant patterns used in this study. (A) A rising transition in the first formant and a straight transition in the second. (B) A straight transition in the first formant and a falling transition in the second.

Apparatus and General Procedure

All the acoustic stimuli used in this study were produced by converting hand-painted spectrograms into sound. The special-purpose playback that accomplishes this conversion has been described in earlier papers.[4,5] It produces 50 beams of light, separately modulated at each of the first 50 harmonics of a 120-cycle fundamental, and spreads them across the hand-painted spectrogram in such manner that the frequency of the modulated light at any point corresponds approximately to the frequency level of the place at which it strikes the spectrogram. The painted portions of the spectrogram reflect the appropriately modulated beams of light to a phototube whose current is amplified and fed to a loudspeaker.

As shown in figure 5.2, the hand-painted patterns consisted of two formants, each of which included three contiguous harmonics of the 120-cycle fundamental. The intensity of the central harmonic of the formant was 6 db more than the two outlying ones; the frequency of that harmonic is used in specifying the frequency position of the formant. All transitions of either formant were always painted and heard in initial position in the syllable. A transition is called "rising" or "falling" according to whether it originates at a frequency lower than (rising) or higher than (falling) the steady state of the corresponding formant of the vowel.

Second-Formant Loci

The purposes of this part of the investigation were to find the positions of the second-formant loci of the stop consonants, and to test whether their existence and position are independent of vowel color and, also, of the extent of first-formant transition. Accordingly, we prepared the series of patterns shown schematically in figure 5.3, and converted them to sound for evaluation by ear.

As shown in the figure, each stimulus pattern had a straight transition of the second formant and some degree of rising transition of the first formant. This arrangement was dictated by two considerations: first, the possibility that the initial part of the transition is not sounded, in which case we should suppose that only a straight second formant can "point" precisely to the frequency position of the locus;[6] and, second, the fact that with zero transition of the second formant, a consonant will be heard, if at all, only when the first formant is curved.

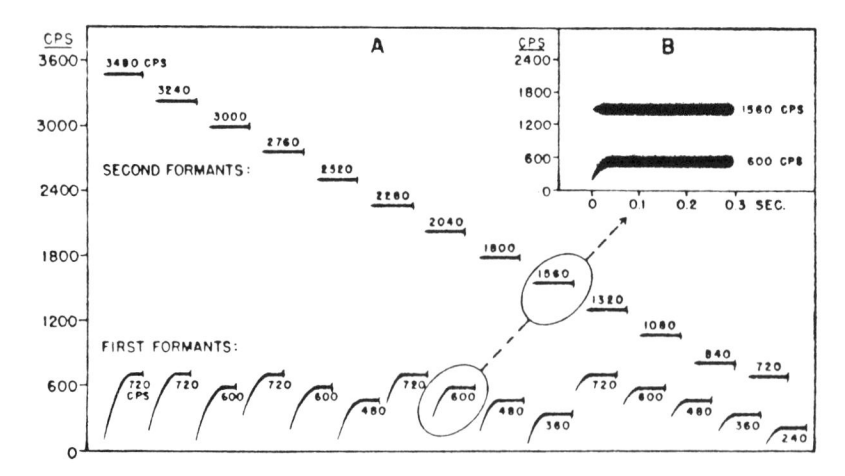

Figure 5.3
Schematic display of the stimuli used in finding the second-formant loci of b, d, and g. (A) Frequency positions of the straight second formants and the various first formants with which each was paired. When first and second formants were less than 240 cps apart they were permitted to overlap. (B) A typical test pattern, made up of the first and second formants circled in (A).

When the first and second formants of figure 5.3 are paired in all combinations, 65 vowels are produced, comprising a wide variety of colors and including many that do not correspond to known speech sounds. The extent of first-formant transitions was varied as shown in the figure. Each of the two-formant patterns was converted into sound and listened to carefully by the authors of this paper, who identified and evaluated each sound as b, d, or g. When the judgments thus obtained are appropriately tabulated, the following conclusions emerge:

(1) Rather clear stop consonants are heard at particular positions of the second formant. The best g is produced by a second formant at 3000 cps, the best d at 1800 cps, and the best b at 720 cps.[7,8] We shall suppose that these three frequencies represent the acoustic loci of g, d, and b, respectively. At other frequency levels of the straight second formant a stop-like sound is heard, the identity of which is more or less clear depending on its nearness to one of the three frequencies given above. At about 1320 cps the sound is indifferently b, d, or g.

(2) The steady-state level of the first formant has essentially no effect on either the strength or identity of the consonant impression, with the exception that when the straight second formant is about midway between the g locus (at 3000 cps) and the d locus (at 1800 cps), raising or lowering the level of the first formant tends to push the sound toward d or g. Otherwise, it appears that the second-formant loci are independent of the changes in vowel color that are produced by varying the position of the first formant.

(3) The extent of the first-formant transition has little or no effect on the identity of the stop consonant. Such variations do, however, affect the strength of the consonant impression. As was pointed out earlier, the first formant must have some degree of rising transition if a consonant is to be heard at all when the second formant is straight. Our observations in this experiment point additionally to the conclusion that in the case of the voiced stops the consonant impression is stronger as the first-

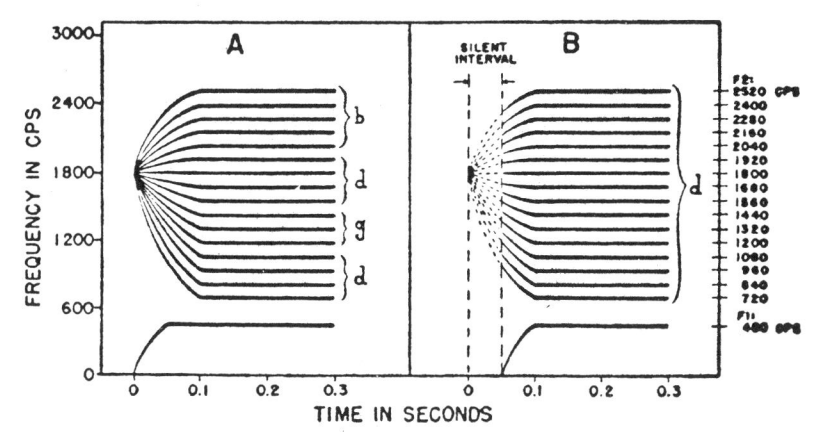

Figure 5.4
Stimulus patterns (shown schematically) and identifications with and without a silent interval between the second-formant locus and the onset of the transition. (A) Second-formant transitions that originate at the *d* locus and go to various steady-state levels, together with the first formant with which each was paired. (B) The same patterns, except that a silent interval of 50 msec has been introduced between the locus and the start of the transition. Note that there is no silent interval in the first formant, but that it has been displaced along the time scale so that its onset is, as in (A), simultaneous with that of the second formant. Similar adjustments in time of onset were made for all the silent intervals tested in this experiment. The introduction of a silent interval into the first formant always weakened the consonant, but did not affect its identity.

formant transition is larger. The strongest stop is obtained when the first formant starts at the lowest frequency (120 cps) and rises from that point to the steady-state level appropriate for the following vowel.

The Locus and the Start of the Transition

This part of the investigation was designed to determine whether the transitions can start from the locus and move to the steady-state level of the vowel, or whether the transitions must only point to this locus, as they appeared to do in figure 5.1. For that purpose we used the locus values that had been found in the first part of this investigation, and, making the assumption that the transition can actually originate at the locus, we prepared a series of patterns like those shown schematically in A of figure 5.4. There we have, with a fixed lower formant, a choice of second formants which all originate at the *d* locus, i.e., 1800 cps, and move from that point to their respective steady-state positions. When these patterns are sounded—the fixed first formant with each of the second formants in turn—we do not hear *d* in every case. Rather, we hear *b* when the steady state of the second formant is in the range 2520 cps through 2040 cps, then *d* from 1920 cps through 1560 cps. With second-formant levels from 1440 cps through 1200 cps, *g* is heard, and then *d* again when the second-formant level goes below about 1200 cps.

We find, however, that if we erase the first 50 msec of the transition, creating a silent interval between the locus and the start of the transition, as shown in B of the figure, then reasonably good *d*'s are heard in all cases. A silent interval less than 50 msec does not produce *d* at all steady-state levels of the second formant, and intervals greater than 50 msec also fail, at least at some second-formant levels, to give *d*. As we pointed out earlier in this paper, the second-formant locus of a consonant presumably reflects the articulatory place of production, and the transition can be assumed to show the movement from that place to the articulatory position appropriate for the following vowel. The fact that the transition serves best if it does not begin at the locus might be taken as an indication that no appreciable sound is produced until at least part of the articulatory movement has been completed.

In all the patterns of figure 5.4, the time interval between the locus and the steady state of the second formant was 100 msec. We should suppose that this corresponds to some particular rate of articulation. To find out what might happen at other articulatory rates we have repeated the procedures described above with sets of patterns in which the total interval between locus and steady state of the vowel was 40, 60, 80, and 120 msec; that is, for these additional total intervals we prepared and listened to patterns in which the transition went all the way to the locus, and also to patterns in which various amounts of the initial part of the transition had been erased. For total intervals of 80 and 120 msec the results are almost identical with those that were obtained with a total interval of 100 msec, except that the "best" silent intervals (that is, the ones at which *d* is most clearly heard at all steady-state levels of the second formant) are about 40 and 60 msec, respectively. From these values (together with that of 50 msec which was best for a total interval of 100 msec) it would appear that the best silent interval is approximately half the total interval. When the total interval is 60 msec or less, we do not get good *d*'s at any silent intervals.

We have repeated these procedures with the *b* locus (at 720 cps) and with the *g* locus (at 3000 cps). It is reasonably clear in these cases, as it was with *d*, that the transition cannot start at the locus and go all the way to the steady state. The length of the silent interval that gives the best results seems to depend on the total duration of the interval (from locus to steady state), the best silent interval, as with *d*, is approximately half the total interval. With *b* and *g* the best results are obtained (with the appropriate silent intervals) when the total interval is 80 or 100 msec. Both these sounds are relatively poor (at all silent intervals) with a total duration of 120 msec; at total durations of 60 and 40 msec, *g* suffers rather more loss in clarity than *b*.

The results obtained with *b* and *g* are in certain other respects different from those that were found with *d*, and they are also, perhaps, somewhat less definite. When the transition started at the *d* locus, consonants having other than the *d* (alveolar) place of production were clearly heard at some levels of the second-formant steady state. (Thus, as shown in A of figure 5.4, *b* was heard at relatively high levels of the second formant, and *g* was heard when the steady-state level of the second formant was in the range 1440 cps to 1200 cps.) When the transition starts at the *b* locus, however, we hear *bw* (which has the same place of production as *b*) for steady-state levels from 2520 cps through 1440 cps, and then from 1220 cps through 960 cps we hear something that sounds very vaguely like *gw*. The alveolar consonant (*d*) is not heard at all in the *b* series, and the *g* in the *gw* cluster is very weak. Thus, the impossibility of starting the transition at the locus is less strikingly demonstrated for *b* than it was for *d*, and the improvement in the *b* which results from the introduction of a silent interval is, accordingly, less dramatic than the effects that are produced when a silent interval precedes the *d* transitions.

The results obtained with the *g* locus were different from those with *b* and *d* in that there is, apparently, no silent interval that will produce *g* at all steady-state levels of

Acoustic Loci and Transitional Cues   95

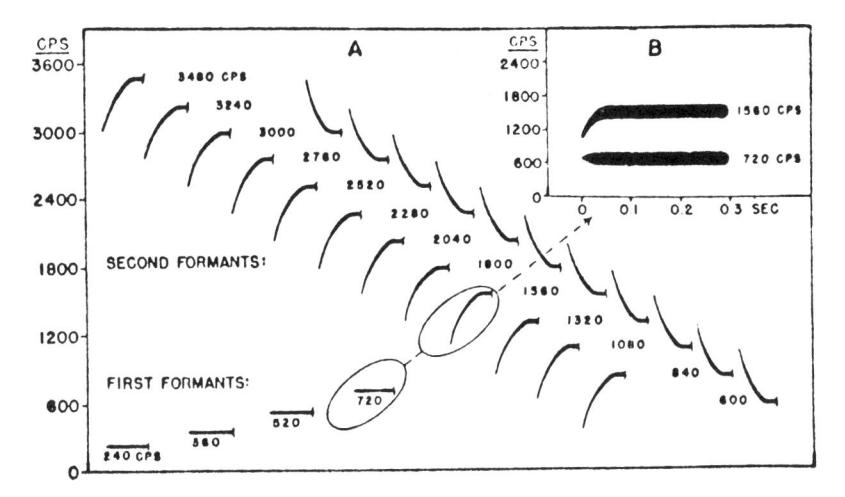

Figure 5.5
Schematic display of the stimuli used in finding the first-formant locus of *b*, *d*, and *g*. (A) Frequency positions of the straight first formants and the various second formants with which they were paired. All combinations of first and second formants were used, except for eight cases in which the two formants were so close together as to overlap. The formant shown at 520 cps is composed, in slightly unequal parts, of the fourth harmonic at 480 cps and the fifth harmonic at 600 cps; 520 cps is an estimate of its equivalent frequency.

the second formant. In the best case—that is, with the best silent interval—one hears *g* from a steady state of 2520 to one of approximately 1200 cps. Below the latter value we hear *d*. This result is not surprising, since it was quite clear from our earlier data on transitions as cues that the same *g* locus could hardly apply to all vowels.

First-Formant Locus

In the first part of this investigation, which was concerned primarily with finding the second-formant loci, it appeared that the best stop consonants were produced when the curved first formant started at the lowest possible frequency. The purpose of the third part of the study was to explore further the problem of the first formant, using straight first formants and curved second formants. The straight first formant will presumably serve here, as the straight second formant did in the first part of the investigation, to avoid the problems introduced by the possibility that the transition does not reach all the way to the locus; the transition in the second formant will be necessary, as was the first-formant transition of the earlier experiment, to produce a consonant effect.

The experimental patterns are shown schematically in figure 5.5. Four first formants were used having frequencies appropriate for the first formants of the cardinal vowels *i*, *e*, *ε*, and *a*. These were paired with various second formants as shown in the figure and explained in the legend. The second formants always had transitions that rose or fell through four harmonics (of the 120-cycle fundamental). These patterns were converted into sound by the playback and judged by the authors of this paper.

As we should have expected from the results we had previously obtained in our work on second-formant transitions, the listeners heard *g* or *d* when the transition of the second formant was falling, and *b* when it was rising. (With falling transitions of the second formant, *g* was heard for steady-state levels from 3000 to 2280 cps; between 2280 and 1320 cps the sound could be identified either as *g* or *d*; and below about 1320 cps it was clearly *d*.) It will be remembered, however, that our primary interest was not in the second formant, but rather in the first, and, more particularly, in the effects of its frequency level. In this connection we found that the stop consonant—whether *b*, *d*, or *g*—was best when the first formant was at the lowest position (240 cps). When the first formant was raised from 240 cps, there was, apart from the change in vowel color, a weakening of the stop consonant; however, the identification of the stop as *b*, *d*, or *g* was not affected by the frequency level of the first formant. It would appear, then, that the locus of the first formant is at 240 cps for all the voiced stops, but inasmuch as we did not, and, indeed, with our playback could not, center the first formant much lower than 240 cps, we should rather conclude that the first-formant locus is somewhere between that value and zero.

Discussion

The experiments reported here were concerned only with the voiced stops, *b*, *d*, and *g*. We know, however, that the same second-formant transition that produces *b*, for example, will also produce other consonants, such as *p* and *n*, which have the same articulatory place of production. From some experiments now in progress it appears, further, that with an appropriate lengthening of its duration, this same transition will produce the semivowel *w*. We should suppose, then, that *b*, *p*, *m*, and *w* might have the same second-formant locus, which would correspond, as it were, to their common place of production, and that we might generalize the results of this study by assuming that the second-formant loci we found here are appropriate not only for *b*, *d*, and *g*, but, more broadly, for the three places of production (bilabial, alveolar, and velar) that these stop consonants represent.

Although we expect that consonants with the same place of production will be found to have the same second-formant locus, we do not think that they will necessarily have the same best silent interval. In the case of the stops it is clear that approximately the first half of the total interval from locus to steady state must be silent. With a semivowel like *w*, on the other hand, it appears on the basis of exploratory work that the second-formant transition can be made to go all the way from the locus to the steady state of the vowel without adversely affecting the identifiability of the sound—indeed, it may well be that the best semivowel is made in this way.

The results of these experiments indicate that the locus of the first formant is not different for *b*, *d*, and *g*. We might guess, then, that the first-formant locus has little or nothing to do with *place* of production. Evidence from experiments now in progress suggests rather that it is closely related to the articulatory dimensions of *manner*.

We know from earlier experiments that third-formant transitions are cues for the identification of the stop consonants according to place of production, and we might expect, therefore, that there would be a third-formant locus for each of the stops. We have been trying to find these loci by procedures analogous to those used in the present study, that is, by varying the frequency position of a straight third formant. These procedures have yielded some evidence that the third-formant loci do exist.

The results are less clear than for the second-formant loci, however, and it appears that additional and more sensitive techniques will be required.

Notes

This work was supported, in part, by the Carnegie Corporation of New York and, in part, by Department of Defense Contract. Some of the results of this research were reported in a paper read before the Acoustical Society of America on October 15, 1953.

1. Cooper, Delattre, Liberman, Borst, and Gerstman, J. Acoust. Soc. Am. 24, 597–606 (1952).
2. Liberman, Delattre, Cooper, and Gerstman, Psychol. Monogr. 68, No. 8, 1–13 (1954).
3. We do not wish to restrict the concept of locus to the second formant, nor do we mean to relate it exclusively, on the articulatory side, to place of production. By "locus" we mean simply a place on the frequency scale at which a transition begins or to which it may be assumed to "point." We have found this to be a useful concept, since, for first and second formants, there appear to be many fewer loci than there are transitions.

    The locus is in certain respects similar to the concept of the "hub" as developed by Potter, Kopp, and Green. See Potter, Kopp, and Green, *Visible Speech* (D. Van Nostrand Company, Inc., New York, 1947), pp. 39–51.
4. F. S. Cooper, J. Acoust. Soc. Am. 22, 761–762 (1950).
5. Cooper, Liberman, and Borst, Proc. Natl. Acad. Sci. 37, 318–325 (1951).
6. Potter, Kopp, and Green (pp 81–103 of reference given in note 3) located the "hub" of each of the stop consonants by a technique which obviously takes account of the same consideration. They made spectrograms of each of the stops paired with a variety of vowels and then looked for those patterns in which the second formant was straight. The syllables *d*æ (as in "dad") and *b*ʊ (as in "book") yielded straight second formants, and they concluded that the hub of *d* is in the same position as the hub of æ and that, in similar fashion, *b* goes with ʊ. The hub of *g* was found to be variable.
7. One would infer from the graphs of figure 5.1, that the locus of *b* must be somewhere below the second formant or *u* (720 cps), since the best *bu*, as indicated by the amount of agreement among our naive listeners in the earlier transition study, was formed when the second formant had a rising transition. We believe that the discrepancy between that result and the present one is to be attributed to differences of detail in the patterns used in the two studies.
8. As is indicated in figure 5.3, the straight second formants were spaced at intervals of 240 cps. After it had begun to appear that the stop consonant loci were in the vicinity of 3000, 1800, and 720 cps, we experimented, on an exploratory basis, with straight second formants 120 cps on either side of each of these three values, and found that none of the stops was significantly improved by these adjustments.

    Of the three stops that are produced when the straight second formants are at the loci, the *d* (at 1800 cps) is the most compelling, the *b* (at 720 cps) is slightly less so, and *g* (at 3000 cps) is, perhaps, the least satisfying.

Chapter 6

Tempo of Frequency Change as a Cue for Distinguishing Classes of Speech Sounds

In recent experiments with synthetic speech (Cooper et al. 1952; Delattre, Liberman, and Cooper 1955; Liberman, Delattre, and Cooper 1952; Liberman et al. 1954) we have isolated many of the acoustic cues by which a listener identifies various consonants of American English. Some of the cues that we have found to be important for the voiced stops (b, d, g), the voiceless stops (p, t, k), and the nasal consonants ($m, n, ŋ$) are illustrated in the hand-painted spectrograms of figure 6.1. These spectrographic patterns are very highly simplified and schematized by comparison with spectrograms of real speech, yet capable of producing fair approximations to the intended consonant-vowel syllables when converted into sound by an appropriate playback instrument. The vowel, which is a in all cases, is given by the two concentrations of acoustic energy, or "formants" as they are called, the one centering at about 720 cps and the other at 1320 cps. The consonant cues, with which we will be more concerned, begin at the left-hand side of each pattern and extend to the point at which the formants assume the steady state that characterizes the vowel.

As can be seen in the hand-painted spectrograms, the acoustic cues that distinguish the columns of the figure (i.e., b–p–m from d–t–n from g–k–$ŋ$) are the direction and extent of the relatively rapid shifts in the frequency position of the second (higher) formant. These frequency shifts, or "transitions," are typically found in spectrograms of real speech at the junction of consonant and vowel.[1] By converting patterns like those of figure 6.1 into sound, we have found that the second-formant transitions can, in fact, be cues for the perceived distinctions among the three classes, b–p–m, d–t–n, and g–k–$ŋ$. There are other acoustic cues for these same classes—we have discovered that appropriate transitions of the third formant, for example, contribute to the identification of these sounds—but our results indicate that the second-formant transitions are very nearly sufficient.

We know rather less about the cues that distinguish the patterns that form the rows (i.e., b–d–g, p–t–k, m–n–$ŋ$). Though we have isolated several cues for the distinction between the voiced (b–d–g) and voiceless (p–t–k) stops, we have not yet investigated the problem carefully enough to know which of these are most important. That omission need not concern us here, however, since for this paper the most relevant consideration is the evidence that each of these cues is essentially constant within a row (of figure 6.1) and more or less capable of distinguishing that row from others. As shown in the figure, one cue that marks the voiced stops (b–d–g) as a class is the low-frequency voice bar that immediately precedes the transitions. The voiceless stops probably depend in part on the presence of aspiration (i.e., noise) in place of harmonics in the first part of the transition. For the distinction between the nasal

---

Originally published in *Journal of Experimental Psychology* 52, 2 (August 1956): 127–137, with Pierre C. Delattre, Louis J. Gerstman, and Franklin S. Cooper. Reprinted with permission.

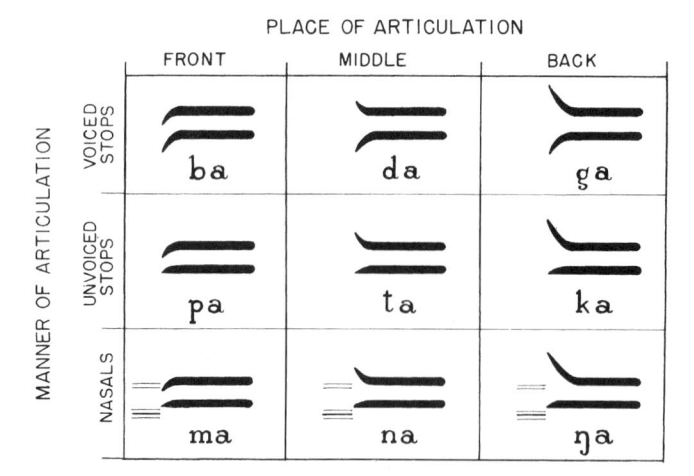

Figure 6.1
Hand-painted spectrograms of nine consonant-vowel syllables, showing some of the principal acoustic cues for the perception of the stop and nasal consonants.

consonants (m–n–ŋ) and stops (b–d–g, p–t–k) the short, steady-state resonance seen at the beginning of each of the nasal consonants in the bottom row is quite adequate.

The patterns of figure 6.1 provide the basis for a table of acoustic elements out of which many of the sounds of speech can be made.[2] The table is interesting, we think, because it indicates that a small number of cues on one acoustic dimension (second-formant transition) combine in all possible pairs with various acoustic markers (the constant resonance of the nasal consonants, for example) to produce some of the highly distinctive sounds of speech. Thus, highly identifiable stimuli are created out of the wholly unpatterned combination of simple and discrete elements. We expect that the table of figure 6.1 will ultimately be expanded to include all the consonant sounds. It is one of the purposes of this study to take a step in that direction.[3]

Exploratory work suggested that we might convert the patterns of figure 6.1 into different speech sounds by varying only the tempo of the transitions, thus pointing to time as another of the stimulus dimensions which may be important in the perception of the individual phones of speech. As the transitions are progressively slowed, the pattern for the stop consonant *b* plus the vowel *a* (as in *bottle*) begins to be heard as the semivowel *w* plus *a* (as in *wobble*), and then as a vowel which changes color from *u* to *a* (as in *too odd*). Similarly *ga* (as in *goggle*) goes to *ja* (as in *yacht*), and then to *ia* (as in *theology*). The remaining stop, *d*, goes through comparable transformations, producing (with the vowel *a*) the semivowel ɥ (as in French *nuage*) and then the vowel-of-changing-color *ya* (as in French *cru a*).[4]

The experiments to be reported here were designed to extend our exploratory observations concerning transition tempo as a cue for the perceived distinctions among stop consonants, semivowels, and vowels of changing color.

Experiment I

In this part of the study we have tried to determine whether changing the tempo of first- and second-formant transitions is sufficient to convert the syllables *bɛ* and *gɛ* (stop consonant plus vowel) into wɛ and jɛ (semivowel plus vowel) and, in the extreme, into uɛ and iɛ (vowels of changing color). The semivowel (plus vowel) ɥɛ and vowel-of-changing-color yɛ, which presumably result from a slowing of the *d* transition, are not familiar to our American listeners and were for that reason excluded from the experiment.

The vowels of changing color are very different linguistically (and perceptually) from stops and semivowels in that they are not single linguistic units and occur only in situations in which one of the vowels belongs to one syllable and the other to the next. We thought it appropriate, therefore, to deal separately with the two-category distinction between stop and semivowel and the three-category choice among stop, semivowel, and vowel of changing color.

Method

General Aspects of Procedure and Apparatus   In these experiments hand-painted spectrograms have been used as a basis for creating and controlling speech-like sounds. To convert the spectrograms into sound—an obviously necessary step in this method—we take advantage of a special-purpose instrument called a pattern playback. Descriptions of this instrument, together with discussions of our method are to be found in earlier papers (Cooper 1950, 1953; Cooper, Liberman, and Borst 1951).

The playback employs a variable-density tone wheel to modulate the light from a mercury arc, producing a fundamental of 120 cps and all its harmonics through the fiftieth at 6000 cps. The modulated light beams are imaged on the spectrogram, and are so spread across it as to match its frequency scale. As the hand-painted spectrogram is moved through the light, the white paint reflects beams whose modulation frequencies correspond to the position of the paint on the frequency scale of the spectrogram. The reflected beams are led by plastic light guides to a phototube, the current of which is amplified and converted to sound.

Stimuli   To vary the tempo of the transitions, we prepared (for conversion into sound) spectrographic patterns like those shown in figure 6.2. The series of patterns illustrated in the top and bottom rows were designed to produce bɛ, wɛ, uɛ, and gɛ, jɛ, iɛ, respectively. In each series the duration of first- and second-formant transitions was varied from 10 msec. to 300 msec. in steps of 10 msec. When we vary the duration of the transition we are also, of course, varying the rate of transition (that is to say, the frequency shift per unit time) so long as the frequency extent of the transition remains constant. For convenience, we will present specific values in terms of duration; however, we will continue to speak of this variable generally as tempo.

As can be seen in figure 6.2 the first- and second-formant transitions were varied together, the durations of the two being always equal in any one sound. This approximates what would seem, on the basis of an inspection of spectrograms, to happen in real speech.

The steady-state portion of the pattern has a duration of 300 msec. in all cases, and its formants are so placed as to produce an approximation to the vowel ɛ. By using this vowel, it has been possible to make the frequency shifts for the bɛ–wɛ–uɛ series exactly equal in extent to those that produce gɛ–jɛ–iɛ. The *b* transition begins 720 cps below, and the *g* transition 720 cps above, the steady state of the second formant of the vowel (1800 cps). The first-formant transition begins at 120 cps and rises to the steady state of the first formant at 480 cps.

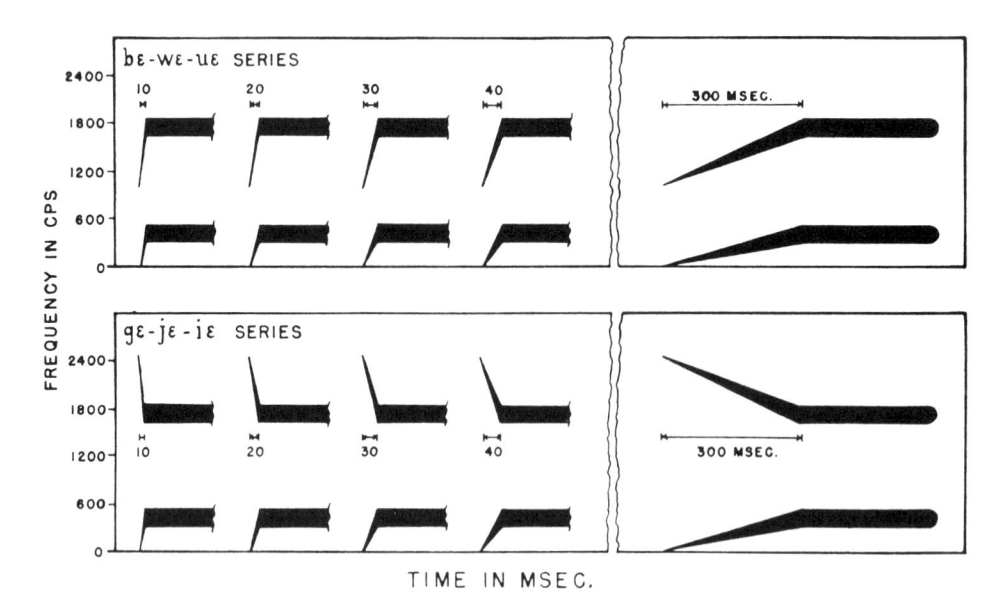

Figure 6.2
Illustrations of the spectrographic patterns used to produce the stimuli of Experiment I. The first four patterns in each row show how the tempo of the transitions was varied. At the extreme right of each row is a complete stimulus pattern, i.e., transition plus steady-state vowel, for the longest duration of transition tested.

The transitions of actual speech are not, of course, so angular as those shown in figure 6.2. We have found, however, that drawing the transitions as we have in that figure does not adversely affect the synthetic speech, and it does, for obvious reasons, enable us to control transition durations more precisely. Each formant consisted of a central strong harmonic and two flanking harmonies of lower intensity.

Presentation of Stimuli As was pointed out in the introduction to Exp. I, we had thought it desirable to experiment separately with the two-category distinction between stop and semivowel and the three-category choice among stop, semivowel, and vowel of changing color. To investigate the distinction between stop and semivowel we assembled two sets of test stimuli. One, which we will call Test B–W, included 12 patterns from the series illustrated in the top row of figure 6.2 (rising second-formant transitions). The transition durations of these 12 patterns ranged from 10 to 120 msec. in steps of 10 msec., and had seemed on the basis of exploratory work to cover quite adequately the range from *bɛ* through *wɛ*. The other set of stimuli, which we will call Test G–J, included the 12 corresponding patterns from the bottom row of figure 6.2 (falling second-formant transitions). These had appeared in exploratory work to produce sounds that ranged from *gɛ* through *jɛ*.

For the three-category choice among *bɛ*, *wɛ*, and *uɛ*, we used all the patterns of the series illustrated in the top row to make up a set of stimuli that we will refer to as Test B–W–U. The series in the bottom row was used in connection with the distinctions among *gɛ*, *jɛ*, and *iɛ*, and will be referred to as Test G–J–I. For each of these two tests there was a total of 30 stimuli with transition durations that ranged from 10 to 300 msec. in steps of 10 msec.

The spectrographic patterns in each of the four tests were converted into sound and recorded on magnetic tape. By cutting and splicing the magnetic tape we assembled two random orders of stimulus presentation for each test. The signals were arranged on the magnetic tape in such a way that each stimulus would be presented and then repeated after an interval of 1 sec. There was an interval of 6 sec. between successive pairs of stimuli (i.e., a sound and its repetition). This interval provided time for S to make and record his judgment. The Ss heard and identified each stimulus only once in Tests B–W and G–J. Half the Ss heard the stimuli in one random order, and half in the other. The Ss who identified the stimuli of Tests B–W–U and G–J–I made two judgments of each stimulus, each of these tests having been given to the Ss once in each random order.

The Ss were told that each stimulus would be a synthetically produced syllable consisting of an initial speech sound followed in all cases by the vowel ε. They were asked to identify only the initial sound, and to limit their responses to the choices offered by E. For tests B–W, G–J, B–W–U, and G–J–I these choices were b or w, g or j, b, w, or u, and g, j, or i, respectively. Examples of these sounds, in syllabic contexts with the vowel ε, were given. The Ss were urged to make an identification of every stimulus, even though their judgments might in some cases be guesses. Before Ss made judgments in any test they were asked to listen to the first four stimuli of the series in order that they might become familiar with the nature of the sounds and the general method of presentation.

The four tests were variously interspersed among other tests involving synthetic speech (for example, groups of stimuli set up to study the fricative and nasal consonants), and sometimes two tests of the present experiment were given to the same group of Ss at the same session. The only restriction was that Test B–W was never paired with Test B–W–U, and, similarly, that Test G–J was never paired with Test G–J–I in the same session. An analysis of the results showed essentially no effect of the context in which a particular test was given (or of the random order used), so in reporting the results we have combined all the judgments for each test.

Subjects A total of 168 paid volunteers, all of them undergraduate students at the University of Connecticut, served as Ss. Of this group, 59 took Tests B–W and 60 took Test G–J. The stimuli of Tests B–W–U and G–J–I were presented to groups of 41 and 49 listeners, respectively. Of the 41 listeners for Test B–W–U, 19 had previously heard and identified the stimuli of Test G–J; 22 of the 49 listeners for Test G–J–I had previously saved in Test B–W. Prior to serving in this experiment none of the Ss had had experience in identifying the synthetic speech sounds produced by the pattern playback.

Results
Figure 6.3 shows that our listeners were able to use the tempo of first- and second-formant transitions as a cue for distinguishing between stop consonant and semi-vowel. The change from b to w occurred when the duration of the transitions reached 40 msec., while g changed to j in the neighborhood of 50–60 msec. It is apparent from both curves that the very shortest duration of transition did not produce the best stop consonant.

Figure 6.4 shows the judgments we obtained when the range of transition tempos was increased and a third judgment category ($u\varepsilon$ or $i\varepsilon$) was added. Apparently, our Ss

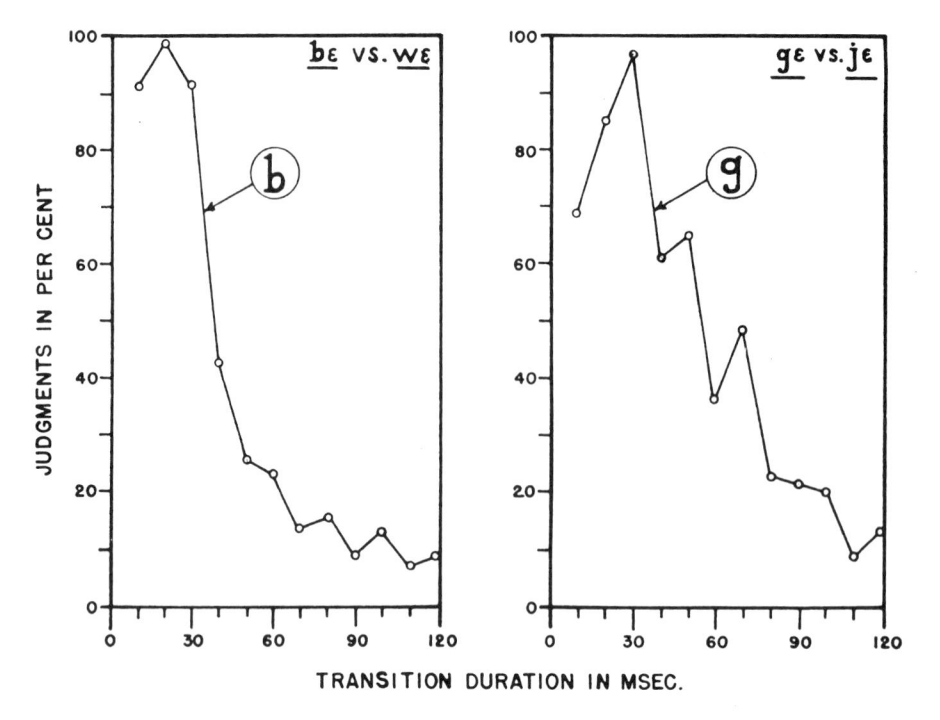

Figure 6.3
The distinction between stop consonant and semivowel as a function of the tempo of transition. These curves show the percentage of stop consonant responses, and are based on the judgments of separate groups of 59 and 60 listeners for the *b–w* and *g–j* distinctions, respectively. Tempo is here expressed in terms of duration.

can reliably discriminate the three categories, stop, semivowel, and vowel of changing color on the basis of tempo of transition alone. It is also apparent, however, that the amount of agreement among our subjects was not so great in the three-category as in the two-category situations (cf. figure 6.3). The expansion of the stimulus range and the inclusion of the third judgment category obviously had the least effect on the responses to the stimuli at the short-duration end of the scale.

Experiment II

All the results of Experiment I, which indicated that transition tempo can distinguish stop consonant from semivowel from vowel of changing color, were obtained with the vowel ε following the initial transition. In Experiment II we have tried to find out how listeners respond to variations in transition tempo when vowels other than ε constitute the second part of the syllable. This experiment was concerned only with the distinction between the stop consonant *b* and the semivowel *w*. We have omitted the *g–j* distinction because to produce *g* with a variety of vowels requires a radical shift in the frequency level at which the second-formant transition begins, and introduces complications which are largely irrelevant to our present purposes.

In Experiment I rate and duration of transition were varied together. This was unavoidable, of course, because the extent of the transition—that is to say, the fre-

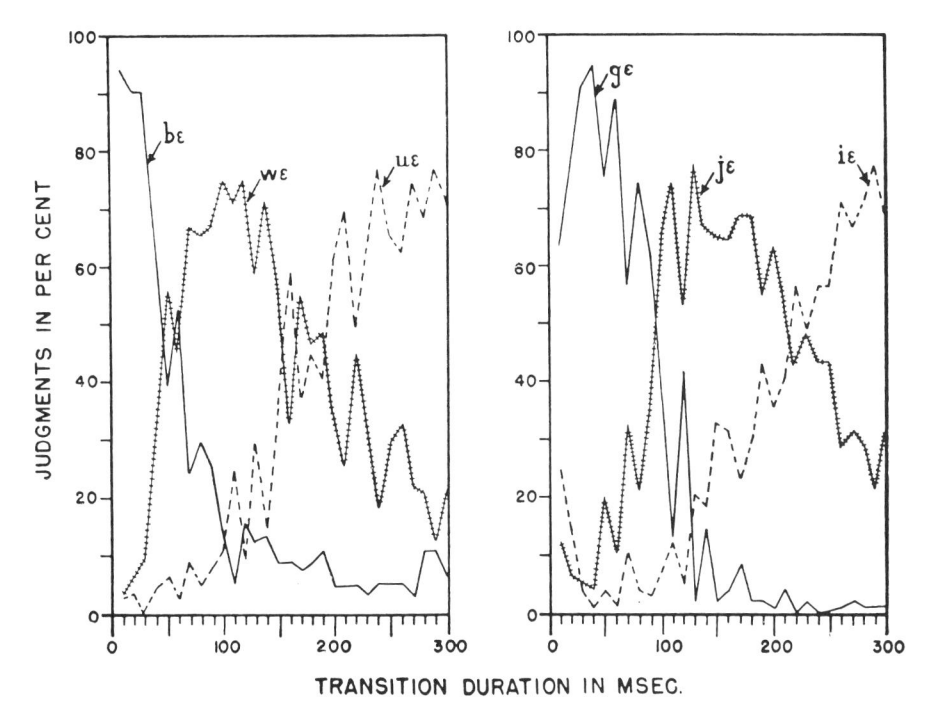

Figure 6.4
The distinctions among stop consonant, semivowel, and vowel of changing color as functions of the tempo of transition. The curves representing the bε–wε–uε and gε–jε–iε responses are based on the judgments of separate groups of 41 and 49 listeners, respectively. Two judgments of all stimuli were obtained from each listener. As in figure 6.3, tempo is expressed in terms of duration.

quency range through which the formant moved—remained constant. To produce the various vowels that have been used in Experiment II we have had, necessarily, to put the steady-state formants at several different frequency levels. By starting the transitions from the same point for all these vowels, as can be done with b, we have been able to vary the extent of the transitions (from vowel to vowel) and thus to separate the rate and duration aspects of transition tempo. The results of this experiment should, therefore, help to determine which of these variables—rate or duration—is the controlling cue.

Method

Stimuli In figure 6.5 are samples of the spectrographic patterns that were used to produce the stimuli of this experiment. These patterns are the same as those of the B–W test of Experiment I except in three respects. The principal difference concerns the steady-state vowel. In Experiment I the first and second formants of the steady-state portion of the syllable were always set at frequency levels that would produce synthetic approximations to the vowel ε. (See figure 6.2.) In Experiment II there are six different steady-state levels of the formants, these levels being appropriate to the vowels i, e ε, a, ɔ, and o. The second difference is in the frequency at which the second-formant transitions begin—1080 cps in Experiment I and 600 cps in Experiment II. It was necessary in Experiment II to lower the starting point of the second-formant

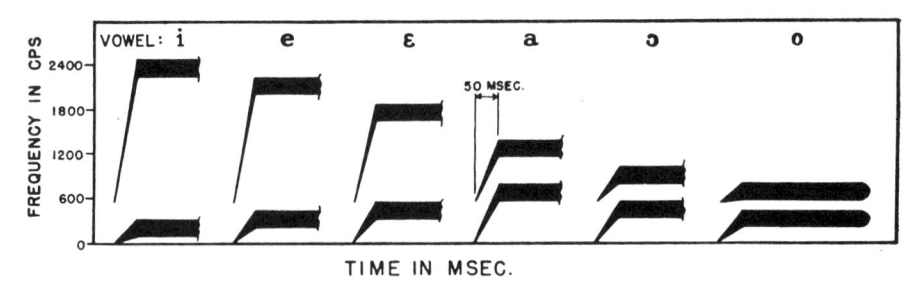

Figure 6.5
Illustrations of the spectrographic patterns used to produce the stimuli of Experiment II. One only of the 15 transition durations, viz., 50 msec., is shown with each of the vowels. A complete stimulus pattern is shown at the extreme right.

transition in order to produce *b* and *w* with vowels whose second-formant frequencies are as low as those of ɔ and *o*. For syllables that contain the other vowels, *i, e, ɛ*, and *a*, it is not necessary to start the second formant at so low a frequency, but, as we pointed out above, it is possible to do so.[5] We thought in this case that it would be desirable to start all the second-formant transitions at the same low frequency because in so doing we produced the greatest variation in extent of transition from vowel to vowel and thus obtained the greatest separation of rate and duration. The third difference between the patterns of Experiment I and those of Experiment II concerns the particular transition durations we chose to test. The results of Experiment I (see figure 6.3) had suggested that it would be most appropriate to sample the range 10 to 160 msec., using smaller steps at the short end and larger steps at the long end. Accordingly, we selected for use in Experiment II the following 15 values of transition duration for each vowel: 10, 15, 20, 25, 30, 40, 50, 60, 70, 80, 90, 100, 120, 140, and 160 msec.

Presentation of Stimuli The 90 stimuli of Experiment II (15 transition durations times six vowels) were converted into sound on the pattern playback and recorded on magnetic tape. By cutting and splicing the magnetic tape we prepared two random orders of these sounds. The presentation of the stimuli was exactly as it had been in the B–W test of Experiment I, except that each S heard and judged the stimuli once in each random order. Thus two judgments of each stimulus were obtained from each S.

Subjects There were 38 Ss, all of whom were paid volunteer undergraduates at the University of Connecticut. None of the Ss had previously served in Experiment I or had any other opportunity to hear the synthetic speech sounds produced by the pattern playback.

Results
We see in figure 6.6 that transition tempo is sufficient to distinguish the stop consonant *b* from the semivowel *w* with each of a wide variety of vowels. A comparison of the curves of figure 6.6 with those obtained for the vowel ɛ alone (see figure 6.3 in Experiment I) shows no very great difference.

When our listeners' judgments are plotted against transition duration, as in figure 6.6, the curves for the various vowels are very nearly superimposed. We may rea-

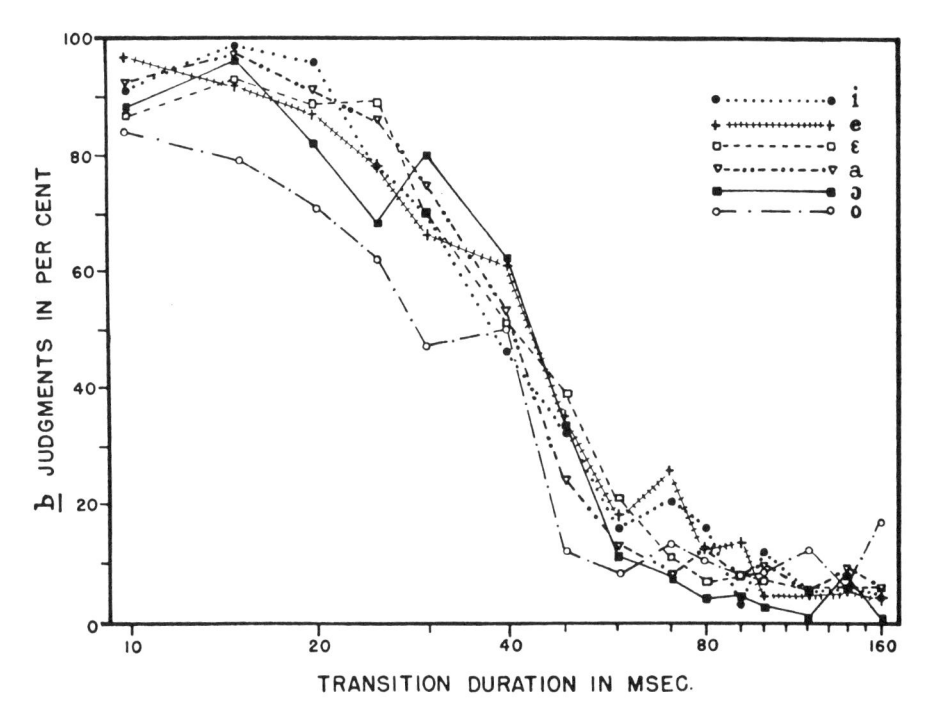

Figure 6.6
The distinction between *b* and *w* with various vowels. These curves show the percentage of *b* judgments as a function of transition tempo when tempo is expressed as duration of transition. Each of 38 listeners judged all stimuli twice. Duration is scaled logarithmically to make these curves more directly comparable with those of figures 6.7. and 6.8.

sonably wonder what these curves will look like when the judgments are plotted against rate of transition, since, as we pointed out earlier, rate and duration can be separated in this experiment. Such plots are shown, separately for second and first formants, in figures 6.7 and 6.8.

It will be remembered that our stimulus patterns were so drawn as to make the duration of first- and second-formant transitions always equal in any one pattern. Transition rates, on the other hand, are different for first and second formants inasmuch as the transition extents differ. In considering the responses as a function of rate, we must, therefore, deal with first and second formants separately.

We should note in regard to figure 6.8 that duration and rate of first-formant transition covary for the vowels *e-o* and, also, for *ɛ-ɔ*, since, as can be seen in the stimulus patterns of figure 6.5, the extent of first-formant transition is the same within each of these two pairs. It follows, then, that if the data for *e* and *o*, or for *ɛ* and *ɔ*, should yield similar curves when plotted against duration, they would necessarily produce similar curves against rate of first-formant transition.

Clearly the curves for the various vowels are not so nearly coincident for either of the rate plots as they are when the abscissa is laid out in terms of duration. This result would appear to support an assumption that duration of transition is the essential component of what we have been calling "tempo"—that is to say, that duration rather than rate is the controlling cue.

108 Chapter 6

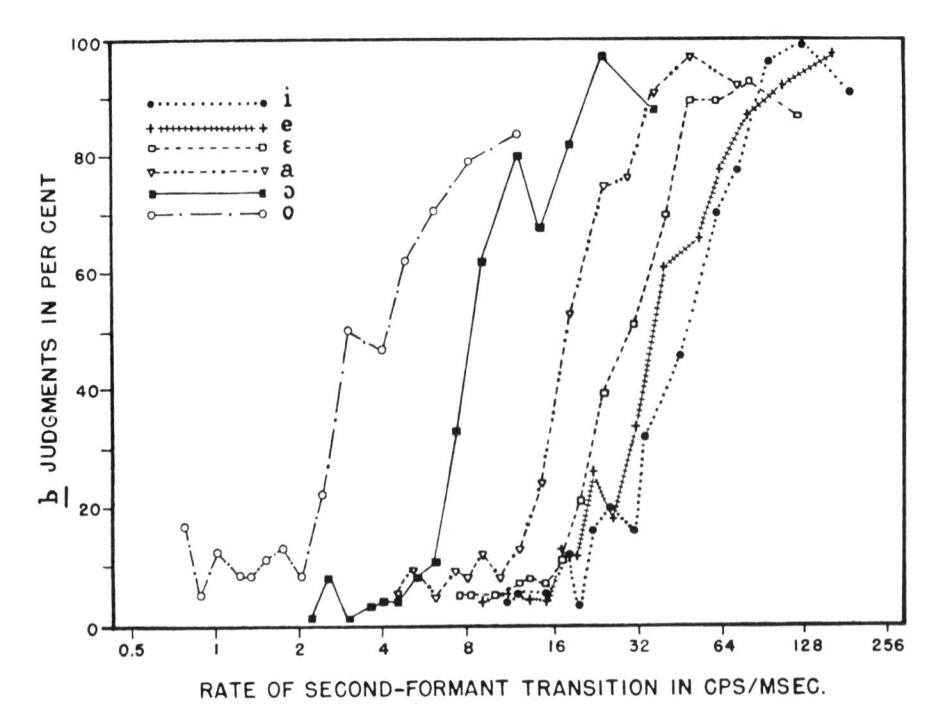

Figure 6.7
The same data as shown in figure 6.6, here plotted against rate of second-formant transition. Scaling the rates logarithmically serves to equate the distance on the abscissa occupied by the range of rates for each of the vowels.

In assessing the relative importance of duration and rate we should take account of the fact that the rates of first- and second-formant transitions move in opposite directions in the vowel series from *i* through *a*. (The extent of the second-formant transition decreases from 1800 cps for *i* to 720 cps for *a*, while, for the same change in vowel, the extent of the first-formant transition increases from 120 cps to 600 cps. Hence, for a given duration of transition, the rate of the second-formant transition decreases and the rate of the first-formant transition increases as the vowel is changed from *i* through *e* and *ɛ* to *a*.) It is possible, if unlikely, that the rate cues produce effects which cancel each other in such a way as to generate curves that appear to be invariant with duration.

For the vowels *a*, *ɔ*, and *o*, the extents (and hence the rates) of first- and second-formant transitions vary in the same direction, so we ought with these vowels to be able to make a less ambiguous comparison of the roles of duration and rate. If we look at the results for these three vowels, we see that the curves appear to be more closely bunched when plotted against duration than when plotted against rate, though in these cases the relatively small change in frequency extent of transition provides something less than an ideal basis for comparison.

Obviously, the clearest separation of rate and duration could be made if we were to hold the transition of one formant constant in all respects while varying the rate, duration, and extent of the other. A series of exploratory studies made it clear that for distinguishing stop and semivowel the tempo of the second-formant transition is

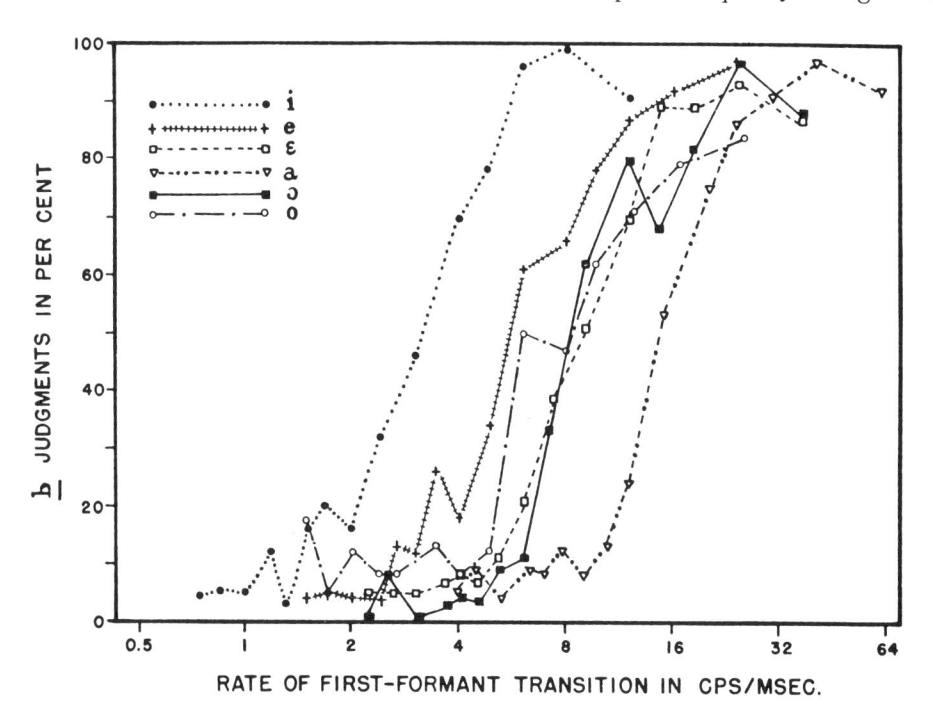

Figure 6.8
The same data as shown in figures 6.6 and 6.7, here plotted against rate of first-formant transition.

considerably more important than that of the first. Nevertheless, we failed to produce a highly realistic series from stop to semivowel with one transition fixed, and we have therefore been unable by this means to obtain direct evidence in regard to rate vs. duration.

We have found in exploratory work that the conversion of the stop consonant *b* to the semivowel *w* is most effectively accomplished if, in addition to slowing the transitions, we also make other changes in the spectrographic pattern. The accurate specification of these other cues and an evaluation of their relative contributions have yet to be made. At the present time we can only say that we have so far found no cue that promises to be more important than the time cue we have isolated in the present experiment. In any event, it is clear from the data reported here that the tempo or, more specifically, the duration of transition is a sufficient cue for distinguishing stop from semivowel from vowel of changing color. Thus, duration is to be added to the list of dimensions that are important for the discrimination and identification of individual speech sounds.

Notes

This research was supported in part by the Carnegie Corporation of New York and in part by the Department of Defense in connection with Contract DA49-179-sc-1642.
1. The transitions presumably reflect the changes in the oral cavities that necessarily occur as the articulators move from the position of the consonant to that of the vowel.
2. The 3 × 3 table of figure 6.1, in which the patterns are arranged in terms of the acoustic cues, parallels a commonly accepted phonetic classification according to the articulatory dimensions of *place* and *manner* of articulation. The three columns correspond to three places of production (i.e., points along the oral

tract at which the consonant closure is made), *p–b–m* being produced at the lips, *t–d–n* at the alveolar ridge, and *k–g–ŋ* at the velum. Manner of production refers to the particular articulatory features (for example, the presence or absence of voicing or nasality) that are common to the sounds in any given row.

3. Students of language have long found it useful to describe each consonant as an articulatory event in which one of a small number of places of production is combined with one manner. The specification of place and manner is, then, sufficient to describe a consonant uniquely. To the extent that the relation between articulation and sound is not too complex, we should expect that the categories of place and manner might be equally appropriate for a classification of the acoustic characteristics. That such a classification has utility for a study of speech perception has recently been shown in an important experiment by Miller and Nicely (1955). They took account of the confusions that occur when English consonants are heard against progressively increasing amounts of noise and found, for example, that a listener will continue to identify a sound correctly as being a member of a certain manner class even though he does not hear it accurately in regard to its place of production. In general, their results indicated that the place and manner cues, whatever their nature, may be perceived quite independently of each other.

4. In articulatory terms *b* and *w* have a common place of production at the lips; *d* and *y* are both produced at the alveols. The semivowel *j* is normally articulated at a point slightly forward of the velar *g*; however, there is in English no semivowel whose place of articulation is closer to *g*.

5. To produce the very best *b*'s we must start the second-formant transition at levels higher than 600 cps, especially when the *b* is followed by a front vowel such as *i*, *e*, or *ɛ*. When we start this transition from a point as low as 600 cps, we not only produce a somewhat inferior *b*, but we tend in some cases to add at least a suggestion of *bw*. This is to say that starting the second-formant transition at or near the *b–w* locus is itself a cue for the semivowel *w*. For a discussion of "locus" see Cooper, Liberman, and Borst (1952).

The addition of a small amount of *w* is counterbalanced, perhaps, by the fact that starting the first formant at 120 cps, as we do in all the patterns of this experiment, provides a cue for the stop consonant *b* as opposed to the semivowel *w*. The synthesize the best semivowel we must start the first formant at a somewhat higher frequency.

References

Cooper, F. S. Spectrum analysis. *J. acoust. Soc. Amer.*, 1950, 22, 761–762.

Cooper, F. S. Some instrumental aids to research on speech. In *Report of the fourth annual round table meeting on linguistics and language teaching*. Washington, D.C.: Institute of Languages and Linguistics, Georgetown University. 1953. Pp. 46–53.

Cooper, F. S., Delattre, P. C., Liberman, A. M., Borst, J. M., and Gerstman, L. J. Some experiments on the perception of synthetic speech sounds. *J. acoust. Soc. Amer.*, 1952, 24, 597–606.

Cooper, F. S., Liberman, A. M., and Borst, J. M. The interconversion of audible and visible patterns as a basis for research in the perception of speech. *Proc. Nat. Acad. Sci.*, 1951, 37, 318–325.

Delattre, P. C., Liberman, A. M., and Cooper, F. S. Acoustic loci and transitional cues for consonants. *J. acoust. Soc. Amer.*, 1955, 27, 769–773.

Liberman, A. M., Delattre, P. C., and Cooper, F. S. The role of selected stimulus-variables in the perception of the unvoiced stop consonants. *Amer. J. Psychol.*, 1952, 65, 497–516.

Liberman, A. M., Delattre, P. C., Cooper, F. S., and Gerstman, L. J. The role of consonant-vowel transitions in the perception of the stop and nasal consonants. *Psychol. Monogr.*, 1954, 68, No. 8 (Whole No. 379).

Miller, G. A., and Nicely, P. E. An analysis of perceptual confusions among some English consonants. *J. acoust. Soc. Amer.*, 1955, 27, 338–352.

Chapter 7
Effect of Third-Formant Transitions on the Perception of the Voiced Stop Consonants

We have found in earlier studies with synthetic speech that formant transitions are cues for the identification of various consonants. Transitions of the third formant, with which this paper will be primarily concerned, have been investigated intensively in two studies[1,2] of the cues for /w,j,r,l/, where it was found that a listener must depend to a large extent on the third-formant transition in order to distinguish /r/ from /l/. Apart from the investigation of /w,j,r,l/, however, transitions of the third formant have received relatively little attention. In an earlier paper[3] that dealt with second-formant transitions as cues for the stop consonants, we described parenthetically the effects of adding three rather arbitrarily selected third-formant transitions. Our conclusion at that time was that transitions of the third formant did affect the perception of the consonant, though their effects were less important than those of the second-formant transitions. The purpose of the present paper, then, is to report the results of a more thorough investigation into the role of third-formant transitions in the perception of the voiced stops /b,d,g/.

Special Problems in Experimenting with Third-Formant Transitions

When we undertake to find the effects of third-formant transitions, we encounter several special difficulties that affect the procedure of this experiment and limit the nature of the conclusions we can expect to draw. The first of these concerns the question: where—that is, at what frequency level—shall we put the third formant of the following vowel? This was never a problem in studying transitions of the second formant, since the frequency level at which one places this formant is rather precisely determined by the vowel being synthesized. Within rather broad limits the steady-state level of the third formant, on the other hand, has little or no effect on the phonemic identity or color of the vowel, with the result that an experimenter has considerable latitude in deciding where it shall go. Unfortunately for the generality of that experimenter's results, however, the steady-state level of the third formant *does* affect the way in which various third-formant transitions are heard. Thus with certain synthetic patterns that consist of formant transitions followed by steady-state formants, one can move the entire third formant, with its transition, up and down on the frequency scale and observe that the phonemic identity of the consonant changes, though that of the vowel does not. In the present experiment, we have used third-formant levels that had been found by Peterson and Barney[4] to be fairly typical of

Originally published in *The Journal of the Acoustical Society of America* 30, 2 (February 1958): 122–126, with Katherine Safford Harris, Howard S. Hoffman, Pierre C. Delattre, and Franklin S. Cooper. Reprinted with permission.

the particular American English vowels chosen for this experiment. This procedure gives us reasonable assurance that the results will have some generality, though we must of course be careful to describe the effects of the variable transitions with reference to the particular steady-state formants to which they are attached.

A better statement of the results will be possible when, and if, the consonant loci of the third formant are found. Consonant loci, which have so far been specified only for the first and second formants,[5] are the more-or-less fixed frequency positions, each characteristic of a particular consonant, at which the transitions begin or to which they may be assumed to point. To the extent that these loci are independent of the steady-state frequency of the formant, they would permit one to describe the transition cues of the third formant in general terms, and without regard to the frequency level of the third formant of the vowel. It is not the primary purpose of this experiment to find the third-formant loci, and in this connection we have previously noted that they are very difficult to pin down,[6] but the results will possibly throw some light on their existence and positions.

A second problem, less serious and more obvious than the first, concerns the difficulty of isolating the third-formant transition so as to obtain a direct measure of the effect of this cue alone. The difficulty arises from the fact that the third formant cannot be presented without the first and second. The first formant presents no problem here, since its transitions do not affect the distinctions among /b,d,g/. However, transitions of the second formant are potent cues for distinguishing among these sounds, and their effects are not readily neutralized. Even when straight, the second formant will contribute appreciably to the perception of /b,d,g/ so long as the first formant has the rising transition that characterizes the voiced stops as a class. We find it necessary, therefore, to combine each of the third-formant transitions with a variety of second-formant transitions. This not only increases greatly the number of stimuli to be tested, but also makes it difficult to know as directly and as exactly as we might wish just how much of a contribution the third formant is making relative to the second.

Method

Apparatus
All the stimuli of this experiment were produced with a pattern playback, a device which converts hand-painted spectrograms into sound. Descriptions of this instrument, together with accounts of certain general aspects of our procedure, are to be found in earlier papers.[7,8,9]

Stimuli
In (A) and (C) of figure 7.1 are examples of the hand-painted spectrograms from which the stimuli of this experiment were made. Each spectrogram was intended to synthesize a stop consonant-vowel syllable, the cues for the consonant being contained in the transitions of the various formants, while the differences in vowel color are given by the frequency positions of the formants in the steady-state parts of the pattern. Only two vowels were used: /æ/, as shown in the upper half of figure 7.1, and /i/, as shown at the bottom.

For convenience in description, the various formants will be designated by F (for formant) and a numeral (1, 2, or 3) to indicate whether it is the first, second, or third formant.

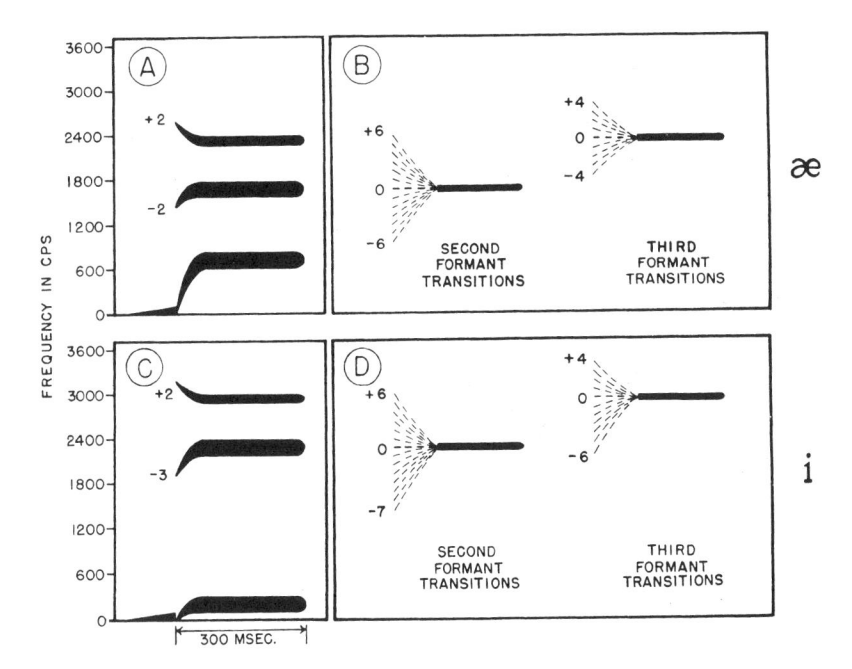

Figure 7.1
The stimuli of the experiment. Parts (A) and (C) show scale drawings of sample patterns for the vowels /æ/ and /i/, respectively. Parts (B) and (D) show schematically the ranges of second- and third-formant transitions which were used for each of the vowels.

The F1 transition was constant in all the patterns. It always began at the lowest frequency the playback produces (120 cps) and proceeded from there to the steady state to F1. It has been found previously that such a transition serves primarily as a marker for the class of voiced stops; it appears to have essentially no effect on the perceived distinctions within the class. Another constant feature of the patterns is the low-frequency voice bar that immediately precedes the onset of the F1 transition. This, too, is a marker for the class of voiced stops.

The F2 transitions, which are represented in (B) and (D) of figure 7.1, were selected on the basis of previous research and constitute, for each of the two vowels, a sampling of the range from /b/ through /d/ to /g/. The direction of the transition will be indicated by "plus" for all transitions which begin above the steady state and by "minus" for those that begin below the steady state. The extent of the transition will be specified by the number of 120-cy steps (i.e., harmonics of the fundamental frequency) which separate its point of origin from the steady state. Thus a transition of "−2" is one that begins two channels (240 cps) below the steady-state frequency of the formant.

As shown in figure 7.1, the transitions leading into /æ/ were varied through 13 steps (of 120 cps each) from −6 to +6. With the vowel, /i/ the range of F2 transitions was the same as with /æ/, except that there was, with /i/, and additional F2 transition of −7.

To provide a baseline for evaluating the effects of F3 transitions, we prepared for each of the two vowels a series of two-formant patterns that contained only the fixed F1 and the various F2 transitions.

As we noted in the introduction, it is not possible to neutralize the effects of F2 transitions on the perceived distinctions among /b,d,g/; hence, to find the effects of

F3 transitions, we have combined each of them with each of the F2 transitions described above. The range of F3 transitions was set on the basis of exploratory work. With the vowel /æ/ there were nine transitions of F3, as shown in (B) of figure 7.1. These transitions varied in steps of 120 cps from 480 cps below the steady state of F3 to 480 cps above this level, that is, from −4 to +4. With the vowel, /i/, we had found in exploratory work that the third-formant transition had to rise by as much as 720 cps to the steady state if we were to have a range of stimuli that would include all the possible effects of F3 transitions. Accordingly, as shown in (D) of figure 7.1, we have added transitions of −5 and −6.

There were, then, for the vowel, /æ/, 9 F3 transitions combined with 13 transitions of F2, or 117 three-formant patterns; there were, in addition, 13 two-formant patterns, making a total of 130 stimulus patterns. For /i/, 11 F3 transitions were combined with 14 F2 transitions. When added to the 14 two-formant patterns, this gave a total of 168 patterns.

We wished the synthetic vowels to approximate American English /i/, as in *beet*, and /æ/, as in *bat*. To produce these vowels we started with the values of formant frequency that Peterson and Barney[10] had obtained by measuring a large sample of utterances. These values were then adjusted slightly in order to make the vowels, as produced by the playback, sound right to our ears. The F1 and F2 frequencies which were used in the experiment were 780 cps and 1740 cps for /æ/, and 240 cps and 2400 cps for /i/.

The frequency levels of F3 were set as close to the Peterson and Barney values as the frequency resolution of the playback permitted. These were 2400 cps for /æ/ and 3000 cps for /i/.

We should have liked to include one of the back vowels, /ɔ/, /o/, or /u/, and so obtain a more representative sample of the vowel triangle. It is well known, however, that the third formant is typically very weak with the back vowels—the data of Peterson and Barney show that in the case of /ɔ/, for example, F3 is 34 db down relative to F1. We have done a rather large amount of exploratory work on F3 transitions with the back vowels, but at this point the only conclusion we are willing to venture is that the effects of F3 transitions are considerably smaller and more variable with the back vowels than with the front. We have, therefore, chosen to omit the back vowels from this particular experiment.

Presentation of Stimuli
All the spectrographic patterns described in the preceding section were converted into sound with the playback and recorded on magnetic tape. By cutting and splicing the magnetic tape we arranged the stimuli in a random order for presentation to the listeners.

The listeners were 101 undergraduate students at the University of Connecticut. One group of 50 judged the stimuli that included the F2 and F3 variations with the vowel, /æ/. A second group of 51 judged the stimuli with the vowel, /i/. All listeners were asked to identify each stimulus as /b/, /d/, or /g/, and to guess if necessary.

Results

In the topmost row of figure 7.2 are the response distributions that show the effects on perception of various F2 transitions before the vowel, /æ/. There data, which were

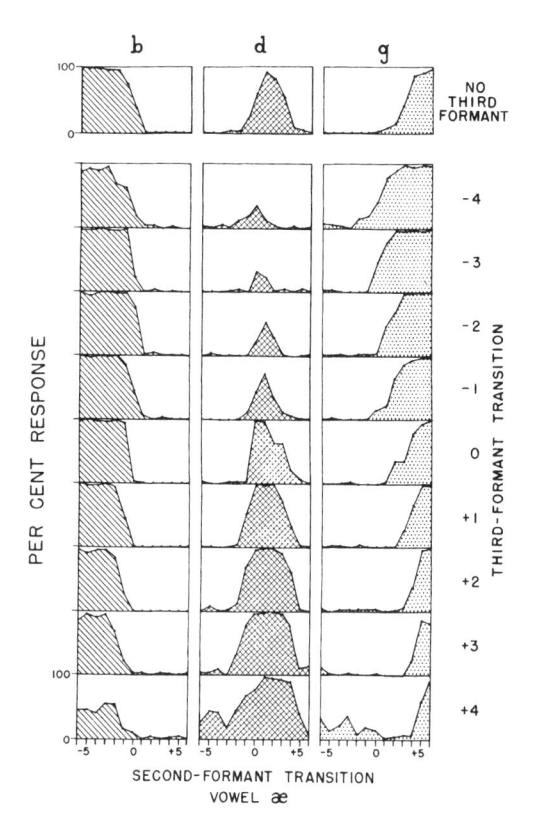

Figure 7.2
Responses to patterns with variable second- and third-formant transitions leading into the vowel /æ/. Within each small rectangle, the percentage of responses /b/, /d/, or /g/ is plotted as a function of the value of the second-formant transition. The rows represent the various third-formant conditions. These data are based on the judgments of 50 subjects.

obtained from patterns without third formants, provide a baseline against which to compare the results for various added transitions of F3. We see that the F2 transitions from −6 to −2 were judged by almost all listeners as /b/. The /d/ curve has its peak at a transition of +1. From there to the higher values of plus transition, the /g/ responses increase and reach a very high maximum at the most extreme "falling" transition, +6. These results are in general very similar to those obtained and reported in an earlier investigation of F2 transitions as cues for the stop consonants.[11]

Of the three stops, only /d/ failed to achieve unanimous agreement among the listeners at some value of F2 transition. Except in the case of /d/, therefore, F3 transitions cannot produce an increase in identifiability as measured by the amount of agreement among the subjects. We can, however, reasonably hope to see the effects of F3 transitions in terms of changes in the shapes, sizes, and positions of the response distributions.

In the remaining response distributions of figure 7.2, F3 transitions are shown as the parameters. It is seen that plus transitions raise the /d/ peak to 100 percent agreement and, furthermore, increase the range of F2 transitions that are heard predominantly as /d/. A straight F3 also improves /d/ slightly, while minus transitions of F3

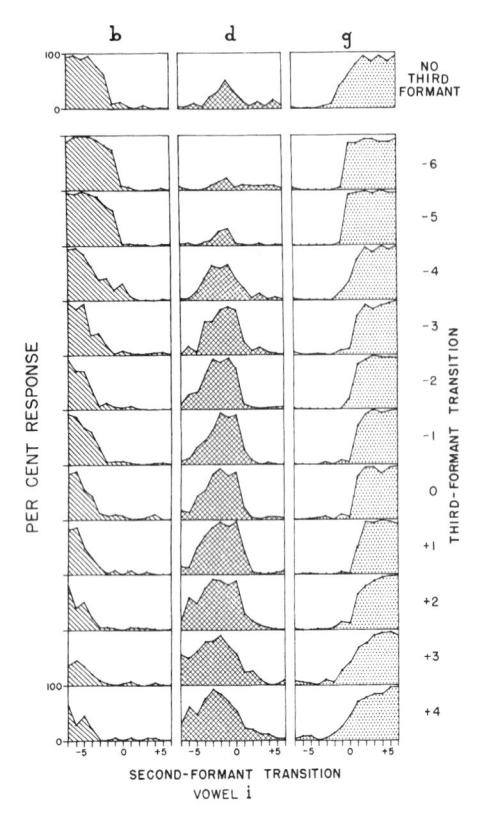

Figure 7.3
Responses to patterns with various second- and third-formant transitions leading into the vowel /i/. Each point is based on the judgments of 51 subjects. The data are displayed as in figure 7.2.

clearly harm this consonant, the effect being greater as the extent of the minus transition is larger. Minus transitions of F3 tend to increase the range of both /b/ and /g/ responses, but a close examination of the curves shows that a −2 transitions of F3 increases the /b/ area most, and that −4 produces the largest area of /g/ responses. In general, however, the effect of the F3 transitions is greater on /g/ than on /b/.

Figure 7.3 shows the responses that were obtained with the patterns in which the various F2 and F3 transitions led into the vowel, /i/. As in the earlier figure, the topmost row shows the results that were obtained with patterns that included F1 and F2 only. There we see that F2 transitions of −7 to −4 yielded strong /b/ responses. The greater number of /d/ responses occurred with an F2 transition of −1, but, at best, the /d/ response was weak. Transitions of +1 or more were heard by almost all of the listeners as /g/. These data, like those for /æ/ described above, are very similar to results obtained in earlier experiments on F2 transitions.[12] The effects of added F3 transitions seem to be limited to /b/ and /d/; there is little effect on /g/ responses. As F3 transition is varied from minus to plus, the /d/ judgments increase and the /b/ judgments decrease. Third formant transitions from −3 to +4 increase the number of /d/ responses.

Comparing the results obtained with the two vowels, we see that /d/ is favored in both cases by plus transitions of F3. There is a difference between the two sets of data, however, in that /d/ begins to improve at 0 transition for /æ/ but at −3 in the case of /i/. When we recall that the F3 steady state was 600 cy higher with /i/ than with /æ/, we see that the results obtained with the two vowels can be reconciled on the assumption that there is an F3 locus for /d/ somewhere between the F3 steady-state levels used for /i/ and /æ/—that is, between 3000 and 2400 cps. By this assumption, transitions from a /d/ locus would fall to the F3 of /æ/, but would rise to that of /i/. In any event the difference in steady-state levels and the possible existence of an F3 locus must be taken into account in any consideration of the difference between the results obtained with the two vowels. Indeed, we have preliminary evidence that when we raise the frequency of the /æ/ F3 to the level of the /i/ F3, we get results with /æ/ that begin to approximate those obtained with /i/.

We have performed a number of additional experiments in which we have moved F3 (and its transition) up and down on the frequency scale. These shifts usually affect the perception of the consonant—that is, the consonant produced by a particular F3 transition (other things equal) changes as the steady-state level of F3, and consequently the starting point of the transition, is moved up and down on the frequency scale. The reinforces and extends the observations already noted and provides more general evidence for the assumption that there are F3 loci analogous to those we have already found for F2. Although the results suggest that these loci exist, especially for /d/, the data are not yet sufficient to permit specification of their positions.

The results obtained in this study cannot throw very much light on the mechanism of cue addition, partly because, as we pointed out in the introduction, we cannot measure the effects of F3 independently, and partly because we obtained such a high measure of agreement among listeners with patterns containing only F1 and F2 that it becomes somewhat difficult to detect the effects of adding the F3 transitions. It is nevertheless possible to see, especially in the case of /d/, that the effects of F2 and F3 transitions must be combining in some relatively simple way. We note in particular that the F2 transition that produces the best /d/ in a two-formant pattern continues to produce the best /d/ regardless of which F3 transition is added to it. Whether the effect of a particular F3 transition is to raise or to lower the peak of the /d/ response curve, the *position* of the peak on the F2 transition scale tends to remain relatively fixed.

To determine whether the cues are similarly independent for /b/ and /g/, we cannot profitably examine the peaks of the distributions, since, as one can see in figures 7.2 and 7.3, the /b/ and /g/ distributions are flat and extend to the ends of the stimulus scale. One can, however, suppose that if the cues are independent, then combining them in various ways will have no effect other than to change the positions of the boundaries between response distributions. This can be seen qualitatively by an examination of figure 7.2 and 7.3. A more precise test, for the data shown in figure 7.2, is described below.

If we assume that the only effect of adding a given F3 is to shift boundaries, then the amount of shift should be predictable from the change in the total number of /b/, /d/, and /g/ judgments when any given F3 transition is added to all the F2's. An example from the data may make this clear.

When an F3 transition of −3 was added to each of the two-formant patterns for the vowel /æ/, there was no change in the number of /b/ judgments, while the number of /g/ judgments was increased by 132, and the number of /d/ judgments was decreased by 132. Assuming that the only effect of adding F3 was at the boundary,

Chapter 7

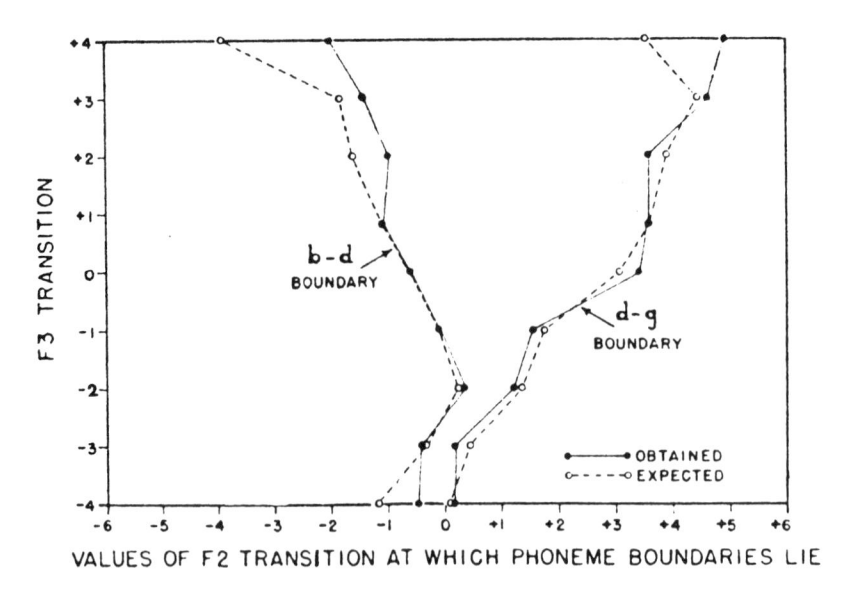

Figure 7.4
Location of phoneme boundaries under various conditions of third-formant transition. The open circles show the location of the boundaries that are to be expected on the assumption that a shift in the boundary is the only effect of adding a third-formant transition. The filled circles show the boundary values that were actually obtained.

we should expect that the /d-g/ boundary would have moved on the F2 continuum so as to decrease /d/ judgments by 132 and increase /g/ judgments by 132. Before F3 was added, the /d-g/ boundary, which we shall define as that point on the F2 transition continuum which is judged as /g/ 50 percent of the time, was at −2.1. To obtain the amount by which the boundary should have moved along the abscissa as a result of adding −3 F3, we divide 132 (the number of judgments added to /g/) by 50 (the number of subjects in the experiment), and obtain 2.6. Thus, on the boundary shift hypothesis, we should expect to find the /d-g/ boundary displaced 2.6 abscissa units in a direction such as to increase the /g/ area and decrease the /d/ area. This displacement would locate the expected /d-g/ boundary at +0.5 on the abscissa (the scale of F2 transitions); the actual position of this boundary, obtained from the data by linear interpolation, is +0.15 F2.

The positions of the expected and observed phoneme boundaries were calculated for each F3 condition by the procedure described in the example above. The results are shown in figure 7.4. It can be seen that the "expected" and "obtained" functions lie close together in most cases. The type of analysis described above for the vowel /æ/ has also been made for the /i/ data shown in figure 7.3. The "expected" and "obtained" functions, which are not shown in this paper, were again found to be quite similar. Apparently, then, the effect of combining cues is indeed simply to change boundary positions. In this sense the effects of F2 and F3 transitions are independent.

The display of the data shown in figure 7.4 enables us to examine further a point which we made in our initial discussion of the data for the two vowels. We noted then that adding a third formant did not have equal effects on all three phonemes. For the vowel /æ/, the effects of added F3 transitions were somewhat greater on /d/ and

/g/ than on /b/. In terms of the present discussion, this means that there are large changes in the F2 position of the /d-g/ boundary as F3 is varied, while changes in the /b-d/ boundary are smaller. It can be seen in figure 7.4 that the /d-g/ boundary moves from about 0 to +5 (on the F2 axis) as F3 is varied, while the /b-d/ boundary moves from about +0.5 to −2.0; the displacement of the /b-d/ boundary is only about half as great as that of the /d-g/ boundary. The boundary effects of a given F3 transition can be considered as a measure of its cue value—that is, an F3 which moves a /d/ boundary in a direction such that the number of /d/ judgments is increased, is a /d/ cue. The fact that F3 transitions typically have unequal effects at the two boundaries means that a cue which enhances one response does not necessarily do so equally at the expense of the other response alternatives. Such a cue may be said not only to indicate to a listener what a speech sound *is*, but also to tell him what it is *not*. The latter information may be important in reducing equivocation when two cues are combined. If one conceives the various response alternatives as existing in some kind of multidimensional stimulus space, he may then assume that each cue element has components in more than one direction.

Notes

This research was supported in part by the Carnegie Corporation of New York and in part by the Department of Defense in connection with Contract DA49-170-sc-2159. The experiments reported were summarized in a paper read before a meeting of the Acoustical Society of America on May 24, 1957.

1. O'Connor, Gerstman, Liberman, Delattre, and Cooper, Word 13, 24–43 (1957).
2. L. Lisker, "Minimal cues for separating /w,r,l,y/, in intervocalic positions," Word (to be published).
3. Liberman, Delattre, Cooper, and Gerstman, Psychol. Monogr. 68, No. 8, 1–13 (1954).
4. G. E. Peterson and H. L. Barney, J. Acoust. Soc. Am. 24, 175–184 (1952).
5. Delattre, Liberman, and Cooper, J. Acoust. Soc. Am. 27, 769–773 (1955).
6. See note 5.
7. F. S. Cooper, J. Acoust. Soc. Am. 22, 761–762 (1950).
8. Cooper, Liberman, and Borst, Proc. Natl. Acad. Sci. U. S. 37, 318–325 (1951).
9. F. S. Cooper, "Some instrumental aids to research on speech," in *Report of the Fourth Annual Round Table Meeting on Linguistics and Language Teaching* (Institute of Languages and Linguistics, Georgetown University, Washington, D. C., 1953), pp. 46–53.
10. See note 4.
11. See note 3.
12. See note 3.

Chapter 8
Some Cues for the Distinction between Voiced and Voiceless Stops in Initial Position

Phonetic observations and the results of spectrographic analysis point to several acoustic features that may underlie the discrimination of voiced and voiceless stops in initial position. Of these, the presence or absence of vocal cord vibration ought, perhaps, to be considered first, since it is the nominal basis for the designation of the two classes as "voiced" and "voiceless." On spectrograms this feature should be visible, and often is, as a line in the low-frequency region, appearing relatively earlier for the voiced than for the voiceless stops. Although this "voice bar" may be adequate as a phonetic basis for distinguishing the two classes of sounds, there is no reason to believe that it is necessarily of overriding importance in perception.[1]

In the case of English, phoneticians agree about a second characteristic, aspiration, which is presumed to be present in initial stops uttered in the voiceless manner and absent in their voiced counterparts. It is difficult to guess what all the acoustic correlates of aspiration are likely to be, but it is reasonable to suppose that one of its acoustic manifestations will be the presence of noise rather than harmonics in the beginning parts of the formant transitions.[2] Observation of spectrograms indicates that this might be the case, but the details are often unclear.

Experimental work with synthetic speech suggests other possible cues. Thus there have been persistent indications that an important aspect of voicing is somewhere to be found in the first formant. In this connection, we have known for some time that we could produce a strong voiced stop only by starting the first formant very low on the frequency scale (Delattre, Liberman and Cooper 1955). Starting the first formant anywhere else weakens the voicing impression, though it cannot be said to produce a strong impression of voicelessness. In the case of released stops in *final* position, Malécot has found some indication that he could convert voiced stops into voiceless ones by reducing the intensity of the first formant of the release, or by omitting it entirely.[3] Exploratory work by the authors of this paper indicated that Malécot's manœuvre seemed to produce essentially the same effect when applied to stops in *initial* position; this is not at all surprising, since the release of the final stop is, in effect, the beginning part of a new syllable, albeit a short one.

The experiments to be described in this paper were intended primarily to investigate further this last-mentioned feature—the elimination of a portion of the first-formant transition—as a cue for the distinction between voiced and voiceless stops in initial position.[4,5,6] Investigation of the effects of the other two features described above, viz., vocal cord vibration and noise in the transitions, have also been undertaken, and their results will be presented.

Originally published in *Language and Speech* 1 (July–September 1958, Part 3): 153–167, with P. C. Delattre and F. S. Cooper. Reprinted with permission.

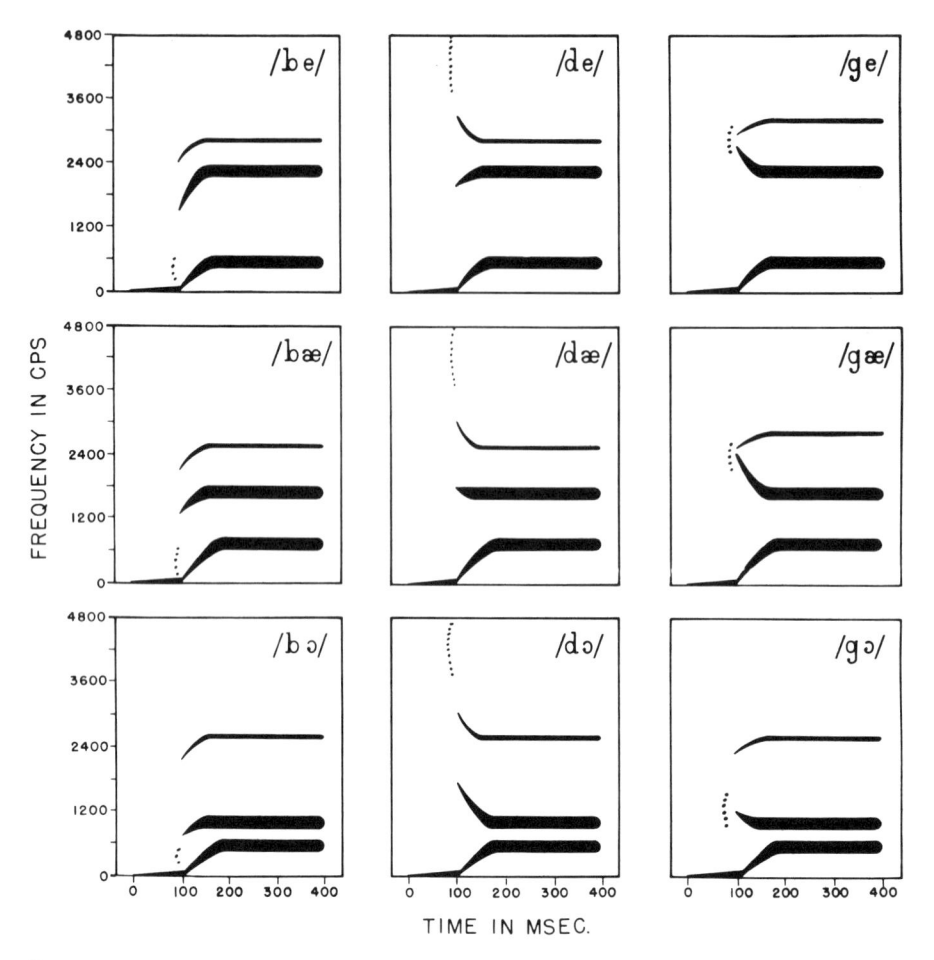

Figure 8.1
Hand-painted spectrographic patterns used to produce the most extremely voiced stops (plus vowels).

First-Formant Cutback

In this experiment we studied the effects of progressively eliminating the transition of the first formant. For that purpose we first prepared hand-painted spectrographic patterns like those shown in figure 8.1. These patterns were made in accordance with the results of several experiments (Liberman, Delattre, and Cooper 1952; Delattre, Liberman, and Cooper 1955; Harris, Hoffman, Liberman, Delattre, and Cooper 1958) on the acoustic cues for the stop consonants and were intended to synthesize stop consonant-plus-vowel syllables, the bursts, transitions, and steady states being appropriate for /b/, /d/, and /g/ before /e/, /æ/, and /ɔ/. Since the intensity of the burst is itself a cue for the voiced-voiceless distinction, great care had to be exercised to make this feature essentially neutral. This was accomplished, separately for each pattern, on a trial-and-error basis.

The patterns of figure 8.1 have the fully rising first formant which is presumed to produce the strongest voiced effect. Each of these patterns was then altered in the

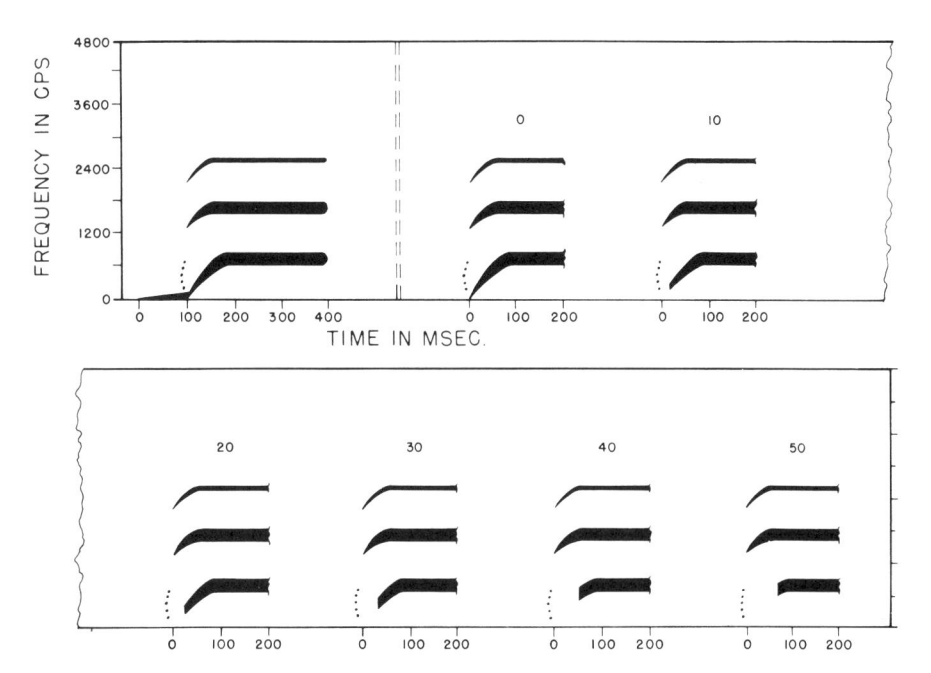

Figure 8.2
Spectrographic patterns illustrating the way in which the voice bar was removed and the first formant was cut back to produce one stimulus series. The patterns shown are appropriate for /b,p/ with /æ/. The numbers above the patterns show the amount of first-formant cutback in msec.

manner illustrated (for /b,p/ with /æ/) in figure 8.2. The first step was to remove the voice bar and so produce the pattern labelled "O." Successive cutbacks of the first formant in steps of 10 msec. produced the stimuli labelled "10" to "50."

It should be emphasized here that the duration of cutback in the first formant corresponds to the period of aspiration, during which the vocal cords are open. Any energy in the second and third formants during this period must, therefore, consist of noise rather than harmonics. In the first set of experiments, the second and third formants were nevertheless filled with harmonics. The effects of replacing the harmonics with noise will be dealt with in the third part of this paper.

Cutbacks of the first formant analogous to those described above were made on the other synthetic stop-plus-vowel patterns. In this way nine series (three stops times three vowels), each consisting of seven stimulus patterns (the six cutback conditions plus the zero cutback with the voice bar) were produced. These patterns were converted into sound by the playback, recorded on magnetic tape, and spliced into a random order. The resulting tape was played for 28 listeners who were instructed to judge each sound as /b/, /d/, /g/, /p/, /t/, or /k/ and to guess if necessary. Of the 28 listeners, 20 were phonetically naive students at the University of Connecticut, five were workers at the Haskins Laboratories who had no special linguistic training, and three were trained linguists.

Before considering the major results of the experiment, we should note that in making their responses the listeners had to choose from among six alternatives. In effect, they had not only to determine whether the sound was voiced or voiceless, but also to identify its place of production (i.e., to decide whether it was a labial,

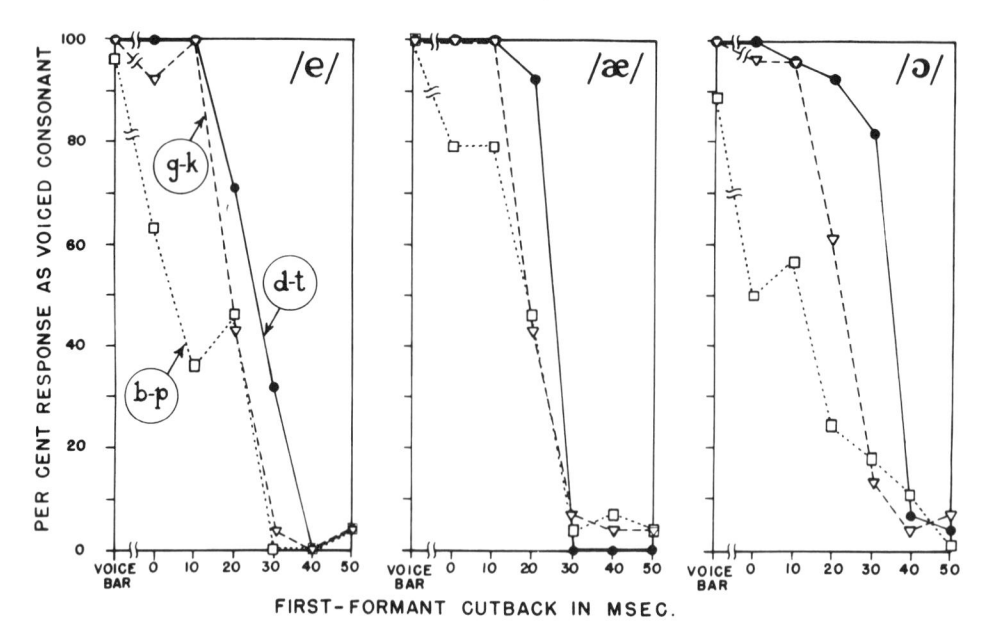

Figure 8.3
Responses of 28 phonetically naive listeners as a function of amount of cutback of the first formant. The data are shown as the percentage of listeners who identified each pattern as a voiced stop. For the stimulus condition in which the voice bar preceded the patterns, the responses are shown on the separate ordinate at the left of each graph. The graphs are arranged in groups according to the vowels /e, æ, ɔ/ with which the consonant transitions were paired.

alveolar, or velar stop). Out of a total of 1,764 judgments made, only 15 represented "place" error—that is, less than one per cent of the sounds were identified by the listeners as having a place of production other than that intended by the experimenters. This aspect of the data has, therefore, been ignored and in figure 8.3 the judgments for each "place" category have been plotted separately in such a way as to show how the identification as voiced or voiceless varied as a function of the changes in the stimulus variable.

It is seen from figure 8.3 that the first-formant cutback effectively converted voiced stops into voiceless. The alveolar stop /d,t/ required the greatest amount of cutback to be heard as voiceless, and the velars /g,k/ only slightly less, while the labials /b,p/ changed to voiceless with relatively small amounts of the first formant removed. Indeed, in the case of the labials many listeners judged them as voiceless when the voice bar had been taken away and before any part of the first-formant transition had been eliminated. This is the only case in which the effect of the voice bar can be seen, since all the alveolar and velar stops were heard as voiced by all the listeners whether the voice bar was in or out.

The effect of the first-formant cutback appears to be largely independent of the vowel for /b,p/ and /g,k/; in the case of /d,t/, however, there is a tendency for the shift to the voiceless member to occur at progressively larger cutbacks through the series /e, æ, ɔ/.

Although each stimulus was judged only once by each listener, it is nevertheless possible to assess the consistency of the individual subject's responses. For this pur-

Table 8.1
Percentages of 28 listeners who sorted the stimuli perfectly.

	STOP /b,p/	/d,t/	/g,k/
/e/	64	86	82
/æ/	86	100	96
/ɔ/	71	89	86

(VOWEL on vertical axis)

pose we tabulated the responses of each subject separately against the various values of the stimulus variable. Since the stimuli were presented in random order, we can take it as an indication that the subject was self-consistent if it is possible to locate a dividing line on the stimulus series such that all responses on one side of the line are voiced and on the other side unvoiced—that is, if the subject has sorted perfectly across one step of the stimulus scale. The results of this kind of analysis are presented in table 8.1, where we see, for each stop paired with each vowel, the percentage of listeners who sorted the stimuli perfectly. (For the purpose of this analysis the voice-bar condition has been treated as if it were the first step on the stimulus continuum.)

It can be seen that individual self-consistency is highest for /d,t/, slightly lower for /g,k/, and, relatively, quite a bit lower for /b,p/. Although it is difficult to define standards for a situation like this, it would appear in general that the self-consistency is remarkably high. In the case of /d,t/ with /æ/, all subjects sorted perfectly.

In addition to questions about self-consistency or variability of the individual, we can ask about variability between individuals. It is clear from the plots of group data in figure 8.3 that the inter-subject agreement must be quite high for /d,t/ and /g,k/, especially with /æ/. Indeed, for /d,t/ with /æ/, one can see from the group data that 26 of the 28 listeners, changed their judgments from /d/ to /t/ at the same point on the abscissa (30 msec.); the remaining two listeners changed at a point one step removed (20 msec.). In the case of /b,p/, there is, as we have seen, considerably more intra-subject variability, and it becomes difficult to compare individuals. It is possible, however, to find enough listeners who were sufficiently consistent with their own judgments to permit conclusions concerning differences between individuals (as distinct from random variability). By examining the responses of these listeners, we find that individual differences are indeed relatively greater for /b,p/ than for /d,t/ or /g,k/.

To provide a further test of these conclusions about intra- and inter-subject variability, we arranged several additional random orders of the stimuli and presented each order a number of times to each of 11 phonetically naive subjects. In this way we built up a sufficient number of responses to enable us to plot, separately for each subject, functions similar to those of figure 8.3. These plots, which are not shown here, fully support the conclusions reached on the basis of the group data. Both intra- and inter-individual differences are very small for /d,t/ and /g,k/ and relatively larger for /b,p/.

These facts about intra- and inter-individual differences may mean that the first-formant cutback is less important for /b,p/ than for /d,t/ or /g,k/. On the other hand it is possible that these results will prove to be peculiar to the types of patterns used or to the general methods of synthesis. Thus, it may be that the synthetic labial stops are less realistic than the others and this produces the relatively greater variability we observed. Similar considerations must, of course, be taken into account in interpreting the fact that the labial, alveolar, and velar stops changed from voiced to voiceless at different amounts of first-formant cutback. Certain constant aspects of the patterns (such as the relative strength of the burst) may have contributed to voicing or voicelessness. If this were the case, the shift from voiced to voiceless might well occur at different first-formant cutbacks in different experiments, depending on the particular balance of cues. In exploratory work with quite a wide variety of patterns, however, we have obtained results that are, in general, much like those reported for the particular patterns of this experiment, and we think, therefore, that those aspects of the results being discussed here do have considerable generality.

Comparisons among the stops in regard to the relative importance of the first-formant cutback or the amount of cutback required do not in any event affect the major conclusion of this part of the study: namely, that the presence or absence of a "cutback" in the first formant is a sufficient cue, and very likely an important one, for distinguishing voiced and voiceless stops in initial position.

Experimental Separation of Time and Frequency Changes Involved in the First-Formant Cutback

In the patterns of the first series of experiments, the cutback of the first-formant produced two correlated changes in the stimulus: (1) a progressively greater elevation in the starting frequency, and (2) a progressively greater delay in the time at which the first formant began. In the second series, we carried out a number of studies in an attempt to separate these two variables and to determine the role of each in the effects just described. In general we have found that both factors are important: a rising first formant is a cue for the class of voiced stops, and a time delay in the first formant, without the rising transition, is a cue for the voiceless stops. Thus, a continuum of patterns from voiced to voiceless can, in general, be produced only by raising the first-formant starting frequency and also delaying its onset. This is what we did in the first experiments, and this is presumably what occurs in nature.

In a few special cases, however, it is possible to go from voiced to voiceless by making only one change. We were motivated to try to find such a set of stimuli by the desire to know whether the high degree of accuracy with which listeners identified the stimuli in the first experiment could be maintained when the physical difference was reduced to a single acoustic dimension—in this case, time of onset of the first formant.

One of the special cases in which time of onset of the first formant is the only variable is shown in figure 8.4. When the stop is in front of /o/, as in this case, the

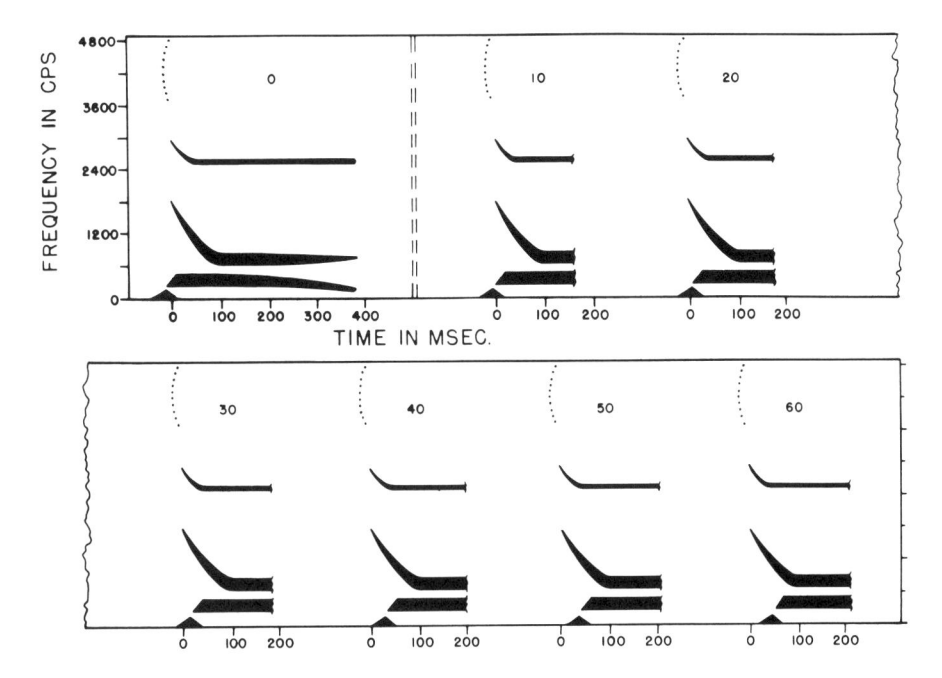

Figure 8.4
Illustrations of the patterns used to study the effects of the first-formant time of onset on the perceived distinction between /d/ and /t/. The numbers above the patterns show the extent of cutback in msec.

first formant does not have far to rise, and, given a large second-formant transition, a reasonably compelling voiced stop can be produced with a first formant like that shown.[7] The various patterns in the figure show successive delays of 10 msec. in the onset of the first formant. These patterns were recorded on magnetic tape and assembled into three random orders, each stimulus pattern being represented twice in each order. All of these stimuli were then presented to a group of 27 phonetically naive listeners for judgment as /d/ or /t/. The judgments of these listeners, plotted in figure 8.5, make it clear that the delay in first-formant onset is sufficient to cue the distinction between /d/ and /t/. More interesting, perhaps, is the fact that quite a few listeners sorted these randomly presented stimuli perfectly across a stimulus difference equal to only 10 msec. of delay in the first formant. Out of the total group of 27 subjects, 7 sorted perfectly on the first random order, 12 on the second, and 15 on the third. (It should be remembered in this connection that going through a single random order means going through the stimulus set twice.) In effect, these listeners were applying phoneme labels with perfect consistency to stimuli which differed by 10 msec. of first-formant delay. Given the appropriate non-speech controls, it should be possible in future research to determine whether this represents, as we think it does, an exceptionally great sensitivity brought about by long experience with the language.

Noise in Place of Harmonics in the Formant Transitions

As was pointed out earlier in this paper, it is to be presumed that the first-formant cutback corresponds to the period of aspiration. If so, the second and third formant

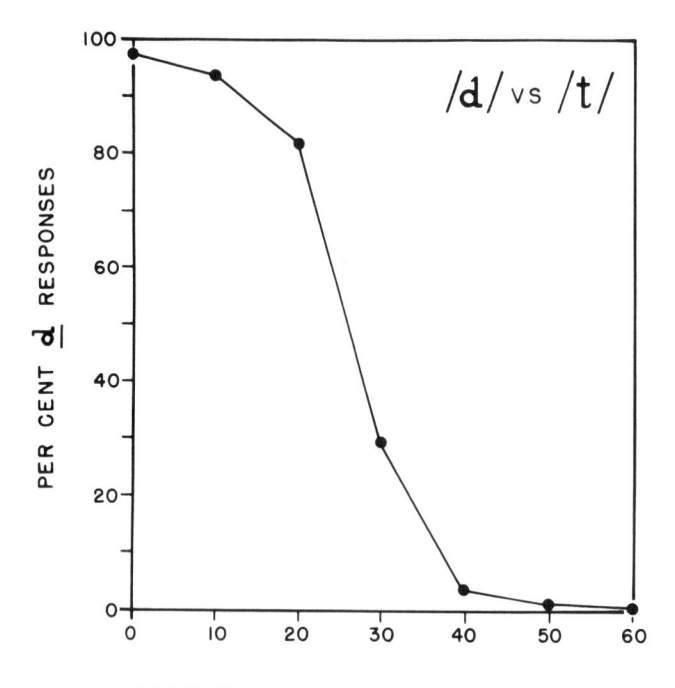

[Figure 8.5 — graph: /d/ vs /t/; x-axis "FIRST-FORMANT TIME DELAY IN MSEC." 0–60; y-axis "PER CENT /d/ RESPONSES" 0–100]

Figure 8.5
Responses of 27 phonetically naive listeners to the patterns in which time of onset of the first formant was varied (see figure 8.4). Each listener judged each stimulus six times, making a total of 162 judgments per stimulus. The data are shown as the percentage of times each stimulus was heard as /d/.

should, of course, contain noise rather than harmonics for the duration of the first-formant cutback. This noise might be expected to be a cue for voicelessness, either by itself or in combination with the cutback. In this part of the study we have undertaken to measure the effect of combining noise in the second and third formants with first-formant cutback, and to compare this effect with that produced by first-formant cutback alone (harmonics rather than noise in the transitions of the second and third formants, as in the first experiment) and by noise alone (noise in all three transitions, without cutback of the first formant). For this purpose we used the Voback, a relatively new synthesizer (Borst and Cooper 1957). Like the Pattern Playback used in the first two parts of this study, the Voback converts hand-painted spectrograms into sound; indeed, the same spectrogram can be used with either instrument. There are many differences between these synthesizers, but for the present study the most relevant one is that with the Pattern Playback the experimenter cam use only an harmonic series of tones as a source, while with the Voback he can use either an harmonic series or noise (though not both at the same time), as he wishes. It may prove to be of some consequence for this experiment that the Voback is significantly superior to the Pattern Playback in signal-to-noise ratio.

Taking advantage, then, of the possibility of putting noise rather than harmonics into the formant transitions, we experimented with the types of stimulus conditions illustrated in figure 8.6. The pattern at the left, which is very similar to the zero cutback pattern of figure 8.2; is a starting point from which the changes illustrated in the

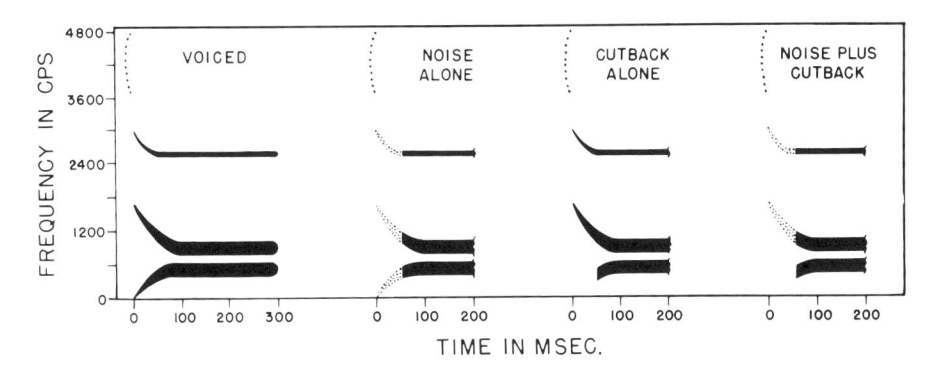

Figure 8.6
Patterns illustrating the stimulus conditions designed to evaluate the effects of noise in the formants.

other patterns are made. It has the fully rising first formant previously found to be a voicing cue combined, in this case, with place cues (burst and transitions of first and second formants) appropriate for /d/ before /ɔ/. The next pattern to the right, labelled "noise alone," differs only in that noise has been substituted for harmonics in all three formants.[8] Third from the left is the "cutback alone" condition, which essentially duplicates the cutback patterns of the first experiment. The "noise plus cutback" at the extreme right differs from "cutback alone" only in that noise has replaced harmonics in the first and second formants for the duration of the cutback of the first formant. In all case the stimuli were changed in steps of 10 msec.; the patterns shown in figure 8.6 illustrate the extreme, or 50 msec., condition. The stimulus conditions described here were arranged for /b,p/, /d,t/, and /g,k/ paired in all combinations with /e/, /æ/, and /ɔ/, a total of 54 stimuli. (As was pointed out above, the patterns shown in figure 8.6 are for /d,t/ before /ɔ/.)

Exploratory work with these various patterns made it clear that the use of noise alone (i.e., substitution of noise for harmonics in all three formants) produces essentially no voicelessness. This conclusion was based on the judgments of phonetically naive listeners. We proceeded, then, to look into the possibility that the rising first formant in the "noise alone" pattern (see figure 8.6) was such a potent voicing cue as to override any impression of voicelessness contributed by the noise in the formants. For these experiments we straightened the first formant in patterns that were otherwise like the one labelled "noise alone." Listening to these patterns made it clear that while this manœuvre may have reduced the effect of voicing, it did not produce voiceless consonants.

The conclusion that voicelessness in stops is not produced by filling all the transitions with noise (without cutting back the first formant) is strengthened by suggestions that have come from some as yet incomplete studies on /h/. Here we find that steady-state ("straight") formants which are filled with noise for the first 50 msec. and then with harmonics for the remainder of the sound produce an impression of a brief whispered vowel followed by a longer voiced vowel. If, with this same pattern, we remove the first formant for the duration of the initial noise section, we hear something more closely approximating /h/ followed by a voiced vowel. To see these results in relation to those obtained in the attempt to produce voiceless aspirated stops, one need only take account of the common assumption that aspiration is to be equated, at least roughly, with /h/.

The exploratory work with the patterns of figure 8.6 confirmed that, while putting noise into the formants does not convert voiced stops into voiceless ones, cutting back the first formant is quite effective for this purpose, as it was in the first experiments. Further exploratory work indicated that substituting noise in the second and third formants seemed to produce a greater impression of voicelessness than can be obtained with first-formant cutback alone. To permit a better comparison of the effects of "cutback alone" and "cutback plus noise," we obtained judgments from 32 phonetically naive listeners. The stimuli they judged were those illustrated by the two patterns at the right in figure 8.6 and described earlier in this section of the paper; the "noise alone" condition was omitted. Thus, for each stop-vowel combination there were six patterns of first-formant cutback alone (from 0 cutback through 50 msec. in steps of 10 msec.) and six patterns of noise plus cutback (again from 0 cutback through 50 msec. in steps of 10 msec.). These conditions were arranged for each of the three stops paired with each of three vowels, /e/, /æ/, and /ɔ/.

As in the earlier experiment, the listener had to identify each sound according to place and voicing. Out of a total of 3,456 judgments made, only 87 (or 2.5%), were in error as to place. We have, therefore, ignored this aspect of the subjects' judgments, and, as in the first part of the paper, have dealt only with the judgments of the sounds as voiced or voiceless. In figure 8.7 the judgments are plotted against the experimental variables: for the data plotted in the top row the variable was first-formant cutback alone; in the bottom row the variable was first-formant cutback with noise in the second and third formants for the duration of the cutback.

Clearly, cutting back the first formant on Voback produced a significant shift toward voicelessness. In the graphs of the bottom row it is seen that a further contribution to voicelessness was made by substituting noise in the second and third formants for the duration of the cutback in the first formant.

The condition of cutback alone essentially duplicates with Voback the experiment previously done on the Pattern Playback and reported in the first part of the paper. A comparison of the results obtained in the two studies shows that the first-formant cutback was somewhat less effective in the present experiment than in the earlier one. There is, however, a very close correspondence in all respects between the results obtained in the earlier experiment and those obtained with the Voback in the condition of first-formant cutback plus noise. Bearing in mind that there is considerably less background noise in the Voback than in the Pattern Playback, we can assume that the absence of noise in the transitions is more noticeable in sounds produced by the former machine than in sounds produced by the latter. Given the noise background in the sounds produced by the Pattern Playback the listener might well have "filled in" with noise wherever appropriate, and it would, then, have made less difference whether we had put noise into the transitions or not. On this basis we should suppose that the data obtained with the Voback show a clearer separation of effects, and we should conclude that, while cutting back the first formant is a most effective cue to voicelessness, it is perhaps, somewhat less effective than we might have been led to suppose from looking at the data obtained with the Pattern Playback. We should conclude, further, that the addition of noise to the second and third formants for the duration of cutback in the first formant increases voicelessness, even though the addition of noise alone (without cutback) is not at all effective for the this purpose.

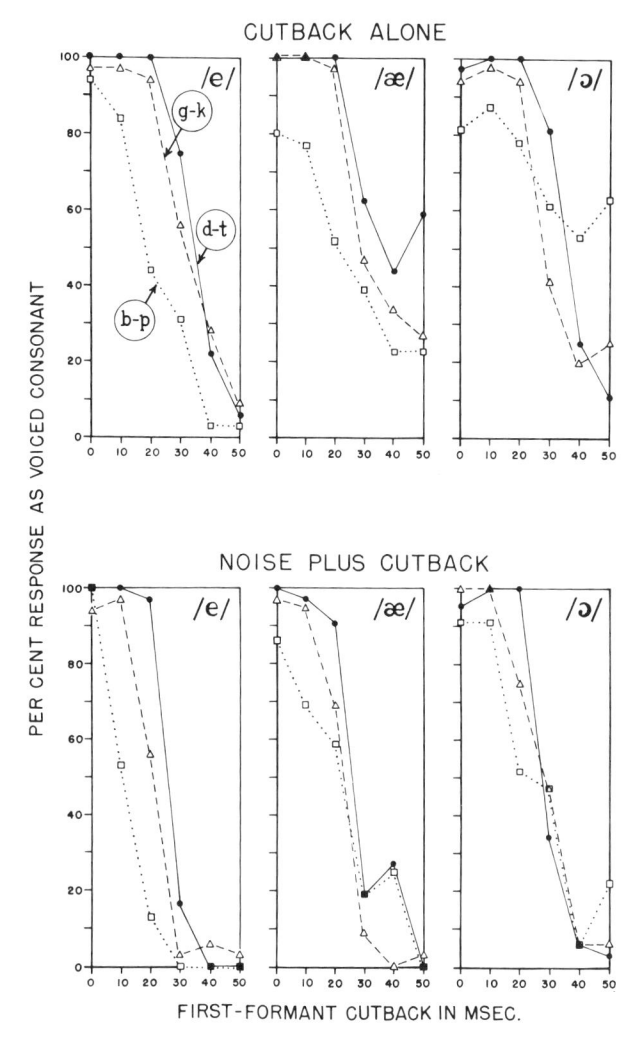

Figure 8.7
Responses by 32 phonetically naive listeners to patterns designed to compare the effects of cutback alone and noise plus cutback (see figure 8.5). The data are shown as the percentage of listeners who identified each of the patterns as a voiced stop. The graphs are arranged in the rows according to the experimental conditions and in the columns according to the vowel with which the consonant transitions were paired.

Notes

This work was supported in part by the Carnegie Corporation of New York and in part by the Department of Defense in connection with Contract No. DA49-170-sc-2564. A portion of this paper was presented at a meeting of the Acoustical Society of American in Ann Arbor, Michigan on October 24, 1957.

1. The distinction between voiced and voiceless stops (in initial position) is quite perceptible in whispered speech. In itself, this must mean that the presence or absence of vocal cord vibration cannot be the only cue.
2. Dr. Fischer-Jørgensen (1954) has presented a lengthy discussion of this and related matters.
3. Personal communication from Dr. André Malécot.
4. Our interest in this cue was heightened as a result of a conversation with Dr. Gunnar Fant in which he informed us that he had observed this effect in spectrograms, and suggested that there were reasons for supposing that it would occur. Since this article was written Dr. Fant has published these and related observations. See especially: G. Fant, Acoustic Theory of Speech Production. Royal Institute of Technology (Division of Telegraphy-Telephony) Report No. 10, 1958, Stockholm; and G. Fant, Modern instruments and methods for acoustic studies of speech. Acta Polytechnica Scandinavia, Ph. Series No. 1, 1958.
5. It is not appropriate in this paper to attempt a detailed explanation of the first-formant intensity change in terms of articulatory-acoustic considerations, and, indeed, we are not at this point fully prepared to do so. In general, however, such an explanation is possible on the basis of several factors which singly or in combination might produce the effect. One consideration, suggested to us by Dr. K. N. Stevens, is that the noise source of affrication may be weak in the low frequencies. A second suggestion, for which we are indebted to Dr. G. Fant, is that in English speech the vocal cords are open during the articulation of the aspirated portion of the voiceless stop, and that, in consequence, the lower resonance may be effectively "lost" in a large back cavity that extends beyond the open cords into the bronchial tubes. Also, there is at least a possibility that the noise source is not in such a position as to excite the entire tract.
6. Mlle. Durand (1956) has found that increasing the rate of first formant-transition contributes some voicelessness to the stop consonants. We have not ourselves investigated this cue systematically, nor have we carefully compared its effects with those produced by reducing the intensity of the first-formant transition. It is our impression, however, that in the case of English the latter change has by far the larger and more realistic effect.
7. The triangular patch just below and to the left of the first formant was added because it was found, in this special case, to increase the realism of the sound. It may function as a voice bar or possibly, in combination with the first formant, as a transition. In either event its position is constant in relation to the first formant, and the only difference among the patterns is in the time of onset of the first formant-plus-triangular-patch.
8. In this case, and in all others in which noise was substituted for harmonics, the noise was 2 db down from the harmonics. These measurements were made with a VU meter, the noise and harmonics being in essentially steady state during the measurement.

References

Borst, J. M., and Cooper, F. S. (1957). Speech research devices based on a channel vocoder. *J. acoust. Soc. Amer.*, 29, 777 (Abstract).

Delattre, P. C., Liberman, A. M., and Cooper, F. S. (1955). Acoustic loci and transitional cues for consonants. *J. acoust. Soc. Amer.*, 27, 769.

Durand, M. (1956). De la perception des consonnes occlusives; questions de sonorité. *Word*, 12, 12.

Fischer-Jørgensen, E. (1954). Acoustic analysis of stop consonants. *Miscellanea Phonetica*, 2, 42.

Harris, K. S., Hoffman, H. S., Liberman, A. M., Delattre, P. C., and Copper, F. S. (1958). Effect of third-formant transitions in the perception of the voiced stop consonants. *J. acoust. Soc. Amer.*, 30, 122.

Liberman, A. M., Delattre, P. C., and Cooper, F. S. (1952). The role of selected stimulus variables in the perception of the unvoiced stop consonants. *Amer. J. Psychol.*, 65, 497.

Chapter 9
Minimal Rules for Synthesizing Speech

Introduction

During the past ten years a series of studies has been carried out at Haskins Laboratories in an attempt to uncover the acoustic cues that underlie the perception of speech. Many different aspects of the problem have been investigated. Some of the results have been published in acoustical, linguistic, and psychological journals, and some time have been quietly entombed in the files of the Laboratory. A few members of the staff have been close to all stages of the work, and so, with all the published and unpublished information quite literally at their fingertips, they have been able for some time to paint spectrographic patterns appropriate for the synthesis of almost any utterance. That is, they can paint to order, as it were, simple, schematized spectrograms which, when run through the Pattern Playback or the Voback,[1] produce speech at rather respectable levels of intelligibility. These spectrograms are prepared largely on the basis of research results and without looking at a real speech spectrogram of the utterance being synthesized. To that extent we have for a rather long time now been synthesizing speech by rule. At least in a sense. But not in the sense that the phrase "rules for synthesizing speech" is used in the title of this paper. In the ideal case, and that is what we want to talk about here, the rules would be together in one place, written down for all to see, and they would be perfectly explicit in all particulars, so that a person with no knowledge of speech or spectrograms could, by reference to the rules, synthesize speech as well as anyone else.

Recently, one of the authors of this paper, Frances Ingemann, undertook to prepare just such a set of rules. For this purpose she combed, winnowed, refined, and distilled the material in our files. Her first set of rules for synthesis was described to this Society at the Ann Arbor meeting in 1957,[2] and recorded samples of the results were played.

We do not propose in this paper to set forth all of the rules in detail or to consider the improvements that have been made since Dr. Ingemann's earlier report to the Society. Rather, we intend to talk about rules for synthesis in relation to some general aspects of the processes of speech production and perception. We shall try, then, to organize some relatively familiar data and concepts in terms of their relevance to a somewhat less familiar problem.

It may help in setting the problem to think in terms of a machine that will process a discrete phonemic input in such a way as to produce a speech output. We shall

Originally published in *The Journal of the Acoustical Society of America* 31,11 (November 1959): 1490–1499, with Frances Ingemann, Leigh Lisker, Pierre Delattre, and F. S. Cooper. Reprinted with permission.

suppose that the information available at the input is in the form of a succession of phonemes such as would result from an analysis of a series of utterances by a competent linguist. Fortunately, we need not be concerned here with the precise nature of the phonemic system that was assumed in making this analysis. For our present purposes it is sufficient to know that these phonemes represent discrete elements of the kind everyone knows as consonants and vowels. So far as the output is concerned, we ask simply that it be easily intelligible at normal rates of production.

This exercise may be considered to have any one or all of several purposes. On the one hand it may be practical. One thinks, for example, of the synthesizer end of a speech-recognizer band width compression system or, perhaps, of a reading machine for the blind. On the other hand, the aim may be quite academic, and, in a rather specific sense, not too different from that which motivates the linguist. Given that we know something about the acoustic cues for the various phonemes, we should like to systematize the data by deriving from them an orderly set of rules for synthesis, and, ideally, we should like to produce rules that are few in number, simple in structure, and susceptible of mechanization.

Synthesis from Prerecorded Elements

For the purpose of this paper it will be helpful to begin by assuming that we know nothing about the acoustic patterns that underlie language, and that we are going to try nevertheless to convert a phonemic input to speech. In that case we are likely to consider, as the simplest solution, a system in which an inventory of prerecorded sounds is assigned in one-to-one fashion to the phonemic signals at the input end. In this system the incoming phonemes simply key the prerecorded sounds. If we instrument such an arrangement, we will almost surely find it quite unsatisfactory. Of all the various difficulties that one will ultimately experience with this system, the most immediately obvious will be a noticeable bumpiness and roughness in the output. One thinks, then, of setting up various smoothing operations, and, indeed, it is surely possible to improve the output by such means. But no amount of smoothing will solve what is here a very fundamental, and, by now, familiar problem. One has only to look at spectrograms to see that speech tends to vary more or less continuously over stretches of greater than phonemic length. The patterns rarely break at what might be considered to be phoneme boundaries, and those who have tried to find the acoustic limits of the phoneme have come to know this as the problem of segmentation.

Now none of this should be taken to deny the existence of the phoneme, either as a convenient linguistic abstraction or as a perceptual unit. It indicates merely that the perceptually and linguistically discrete phonemes are often combined and, indeed, in some case encoded, into units that are more than one phoneme in length. They are not strung together like beads on a string. It is for this reason that one encounters difficulties when he tries to snip phonemes out of a magnetic tape recording, or when, conversely, he tries to synthesize speech from prerecorded phonemic elements.[3]

If one insists, nevertheless, on trying to produce speech from prerecorded phonemes, he is likely to be forced into one of two undesirable courses. One possibility is to employ different recordings, or allophonic variants, of most of the phonemes for most of the combinations in which they occur. This obviously requires a formidable inventory of prerecorded elements. The number of elements can be reduced by creating classes of variants, each class being represented by a single typical form. But this reduction in the number of items is only to be had by severely compromising the quality of the output; in short, the rougher the approximation to proper junctions, the rougher and less intelligible the speech.

An alternative is to try to record, or recover, the speech sounds in very brief form as, for example, in a rapid recitation of the alphabet (plus a baker's dozen of additional sounds). The difficulty, of course, is that the phonemes have now become syllables and the intended synthetic speech has become a kind of "spelling bee." Nor is this difficulty avoidable: a shift from spelling to phonetic pronunciation only shortens and centralizes the vowel that clings to almost every consonant; indeed, it it difficult to imagine how a voiced stop, for example, could possibly be produced or heard without some vowel-like sound preceding or following it. Thus, we see that alternative does violence to the speech process; moreover, it has but limited practical utility, since the spelling-bee output will not be so readily or rapidly comprehended as ordinary speech with its phonemes in syllabic combination.

What has been said so far does not mean that one cannot work from prerecorded elements. Rather, it suggests that if one wants by this technique to produce speech rather than spelling, and if he prefers not to deal with allophonic variants, then he has got to include among the prerecorded elements a number of units which exceed one phoneme in length. An inevitable result is that the inventory must be very large (as it was found, above, to be for the method of allophonic variants when high-quality speech was desired). Thus, in a recent attempt to synthesize speech from discrete segments, Peterson, Wang, and Sivertsen[4] have used what they call "dyads," a dyad being a segment which contains "parts of two phones with their mutual influence in the middle of the segment." To produce one idiolect by this technique Peterson, Wang, and Sivertsen estimate that some 8000 dyads are necessary. (It should be noted that this number includes provision for three levels of intonation for many of the dyads.) For some purposes such a system may well represent a practical solution. It is not the only solution, however, and from one standpoint not the most interesting. We have in mind here that one may quite properly regard a set of rules for synthesis as a description of the acoustic basis for the perception of language.[5] If so, it must be concluded that discrete segments provide an uneconomical description, since, as has been seen, the number of segments or entries in the system is extremely large.[6]

Synthesis by Phonemic Rules

Although it is very difficult to produce speech from prerecorded phonemic segments, it is nevertheless possible to generate speech from discrete phonemic instructions. That is, rules for synthesis *can* be written which make it possible to go from phonemic units to speech, and thus reduce by a very large factor the total number of rules needed.[7] This can be done by taking advantage of what is known about the cues for speech perception.

The patterns of figure 9.1 illustrate some of these cues and also point to one of the reasons why it is so very difficult to cut and re-assemble phonemic segments. When converted into sound by the Pattern Playback, the hand-drawn spectrograms seen in the figure produce reasonably close approximations to the consonant-vowel syllables indicated. All that we can say about these particular spectrograms that is relevant to

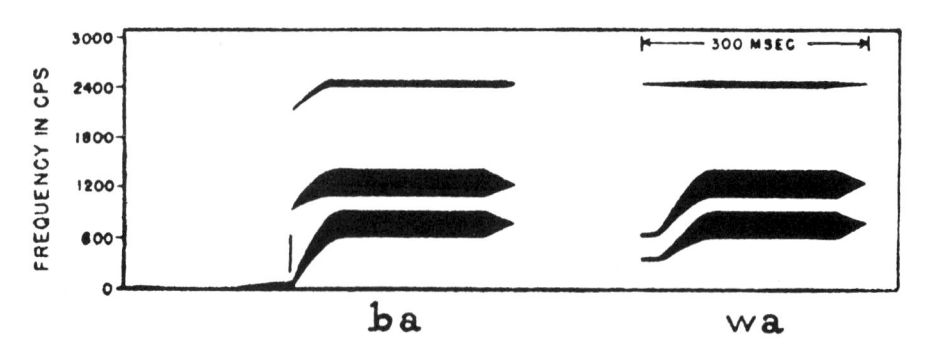

Figure 9.1
Hand-drawn spectrographic patterns illustrating some of the acoustic cues for the stop consonant /b/ and the semivowel /w/.

the present discussion has been said at other times in talks before this Society and in published papers.[8] Therefore, we ask the indulgence of the reader and, in return, promise to be brief.

Research with patterns such as those shown in figure 9.1 has shown that a primary cue for the perception of these and certain other consonants is the relatively rapid shift in the formants frequencies seen at the left of each pattern. These shifts have been named "transitions," which is unfortunate because this designation implies that they are mere incidents in the process of going from phoneme to phoneme. Far from being incidental links between phonemes, these transitions are themselves among the most important cues to the perception of many of the consonants. It cannot be too strongly emphasized that the perceptual function of the transitions is not to avoid clicks and thumps, but rather to provide important and sometimes essential information for phoneme identification. This is to say that the essential perceptual cue is sometimes given by information concerning the change from one frequency position to another. For the consonant phonemes of figure 9.1 and for others too, it is unqualifiedly true that there is no position in the pattern that will be perceived as the intended consonant, or, indeed, as any consonant, when it is in steady state. Sounding the initial steady-state portion of /w/ will cause the listener to hear the vowel /u/. Every point on the transition leading into the steady-state vowel will, if prolonged, produce a vowel-like sound.[9,10] The listener will perceive /w/ only if he is given information about where the formant begins, where it ends, and how long it takes to move from the one frequency to the other. Normally, this information is conveyed continuously by the transitions. It is always possible, of course, to degrade the patterns to some degree, as for example by erasing parts of the transitions, without utterly destroying the phoneme as perceived. Indeed, in the case of /w/ one can synthesize it reasonably well by moving from the initial steady state to the steady state of the vowel without actually sounding the transition at all, provided the normal time relationships are preserved.[11] This is a rather extreme case—one cannot remove nearly so much of the transition for the /b/ of figure 9.1 or, indeed, for any of the stop or nasal consonants—and even so it is clear that some indication of the /w/ transitions, as given by the abrupt shift from the initial steady state to the vowel, is a necessary condition for the perception of the /w/ phoneme. These considerations lead us to disagree with an assumption that Peterson, Wang, and Sivertsen took as basic

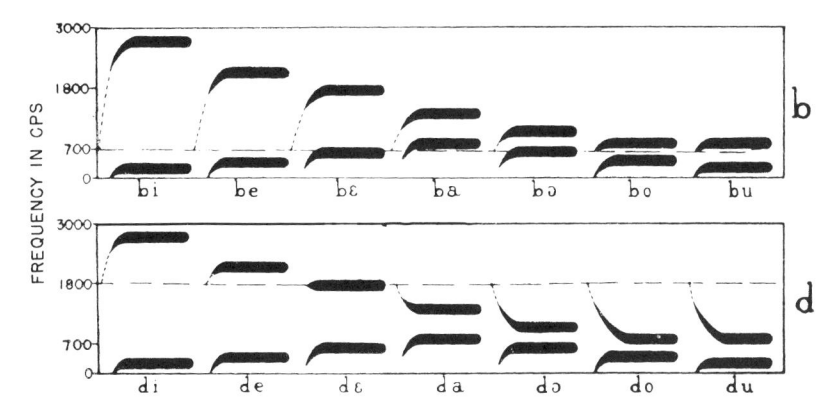

Figure 9.2
Second-formant transitions appropriate for /b/ and /d/ before various vowels.

to their segmentation technique, namely, that "the intelligibility of speech is carried by the more sustained or target positions of the vowels, consonants, and other phonetic features."[12] We would rather say that for many of the consonants an important and sometimes necessary condition for intelligibility is that the listener be provided with information concerning the direction, extent, and duration of formant "movement." When we consider that this information is normally present in formant transitions, and that it cannot really be dispensed with, we see one of the reasons why it is so difficult, starting with recorded utterances, to isolate and recombine phonemic segments.

Now to arrive at "phonemic" rules for the generation of syllables like those of figure 9.1, we begin by taking into account that all the transitions for a given consonant have a common feature. This is illustrated in figure 9.2, where we see in the bottom row that, although the extent and direction of the transitions are different for /d/ before different vowels, it is nevertheless clear that the transitions have originated from approximately the same place. This common origin has been called the locus,[13] and it has been possible to define characteristic loci for essentially all the consonants.

Knowing the first-, second-, and third-formant loci for all the consonants is the key that unlocks the syllable and makes it feasible to write rules at the phoneme level. For example, we may say of /d/ that its second formant should start at about 1800 cps and proceed then at a certain rate to the steady-state level appropriate for the second formant of the following vowel. If, alternatively, we want to synthesize a syllable consisting of /b/ plus vowel, we see from the patterns in the top row of the figure that we should start the second formant at about 700 cps and proceed to the vowel level from there. In fact, the situation is somewhat more complicated than this in several ways. For example, the stops must not actually start at the loci—rather, they should only "point" to them. In the patterns of the figure the dashed lines represent nonexplicit portions of the complete transition specified by the locus hypothesis. This characteristic of the locus is one of the class markers for the stops,[14] as it is also for the nasals. For these and other classes of consonants it is, of course, necessary to add other acoustic cues, such as the noises that occur with stops, affricates, and fricatives,[15] and the relatively brief steady-state resonances that mark the nasals, liquids, and semivowels.[16]

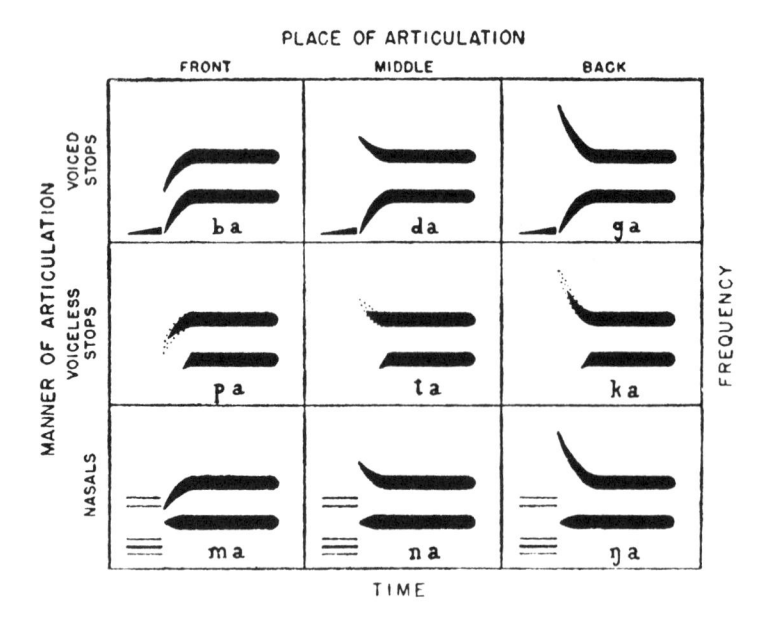

Figure 9.3
Patterns illustrating some of the acoustic cues for the stop and nasal consonants.

At a different level of complication it is, as we have already implied, necessary that the application of a phoneme rule be made in relation to the phonemes on either side. Thus, in the example used, the second-formant transition for /d/ led to the second-formant level appropriate for the next vowel, wherever that might have been. This means that contextual information must be used in *applying* the rules for successive phonemes, but only to the extent that one must know—as he must in any case—the appropriate formant levels for the next phoneme so that the transition may be properly connected. Given that the situation is even approximately this simple, we can see how, in principle, the number of rules can approximate the number of phonemes.

Synthesis by Subphonemic Rules

But if economy in terms of number of rules is our aim—and it would appear to be a reasonable one—we can go further by setting up the rules in terms of subphonemic dimensions. Figure 9.3 contains hand-drawn spectrographic patterns that illustrate how this can be done. Here we see hand-painted spectrograms that will produce reasonable approximations to the syllables /ba, da, ga, pa, ta, ka, ma, na, ŋa/. All the sounds having the same place of articulation—that is, all the sounds in a given column—have the same second-formant transition. Similarly, all the sounds having the same manner of articulation—that is, those in a given row—have the same first-formant transition, and, in some cases, additional markers, as for the nasality of /m, n, ŋ/. Thus, it is possible to set up a rule for a front place of articulation, a middle place of articulation, and a back place of articulation. Similarly, there is a rule for the class of voiced stops, one for the voiceless stops, and one for nasality. In this way we obtain nine phonemes with six rules.

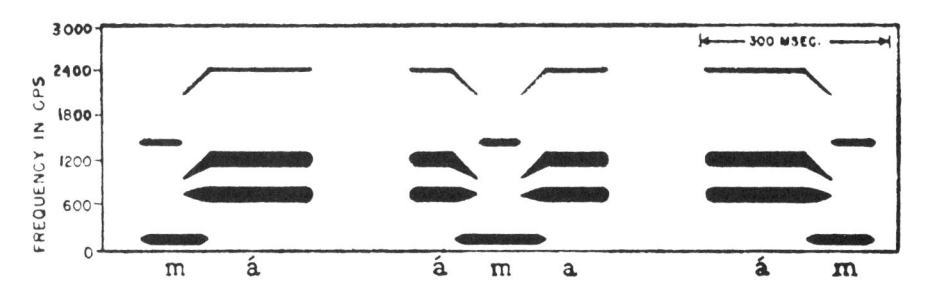

Figure 9.4
Patterns illustrating some of the cues for /m/ in different positions.

It should be noted here that when the rules are written at a subphonemic level, arrangements must be made for simultaneous (as well as sequential) combination. Thus, for the consonant phoneme of a syllable, for example, we must put together, at the very least, the appropriate rule for place of articulation and the appropriate rule for manner; these, in turn, must be "meshed" with the rules for the vowel or other consonants of the syllable.

As we have seen, the number of rules is considerably reduced by operating at a subphonemic level. In the ideal case we would, of course, have only as many rules as there are subphonemic features, and this would be in the neighborhood of ten. However, for reasons which will be given below, it is not possible to achieve this ideal.

Additional Rules for Position

One complication at either the phonemic or subphonemic level is that we must sometimes make special provision for positional variations. The few simple examples so far have been of consonants in initial position. Now in most cases it is possible to produce patterns suitable for other positions from the same basic rules.[17] That is, it is usually possible to frame a basic rule for a phoneme or a subphonemic dimension and then derive the particular patterns for each of several positions. As an example, let us take the patterns for the nasal labial consonant /m/ in initial intervocalic, and final positions, as shown in figure 9.4. The basic rules for /m/ require that there be steady-state formants of specified duration, intensities, and frequencies. Furthermore, they require that any adjacent formants have transitions of a specified duration which are discontinuous with the nasal formants and which point to certain locus frequencies. As we see from figure 9.4, the differences among the initial, intervocalic, and final pattern for /m/ involve only the presence or absence of transitions on either side of the nasal formants. Whether or not a transition is to be drawn depends on whether adjacent formants are specified, and that depends, of course, on the rules appropriate for the immediate neighbors of /m/ in the sequence of input phonemes. In other words, before we can have a transition we must have, at the input, two contiguous phonemes both of whose rules call for this acoustic feature.

The preceding example illustrates the most common type of positional variation that must be accommodated by our rules of synthesis. As we have elected to handle them, such positional variations follow from the different ways in which rules for adjacent phonemes "mesh" to specify the transitional portions of our patterns; therefore, additional "connection" rules are not necessary.

140 Chapter 9

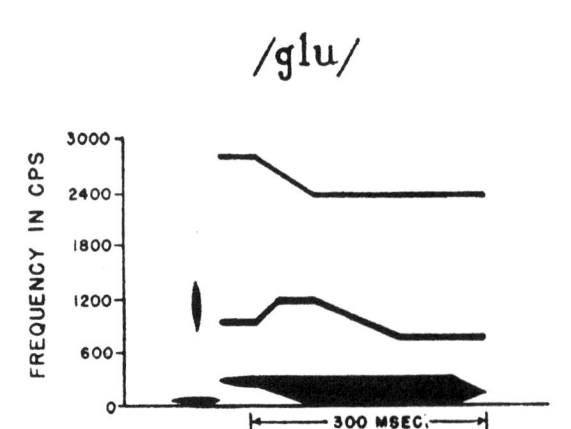

Figure 9.5
Pattern appropriate for the syllable /glu/.

In certain cases, however, it is not possible to derive a desired pattern entirely from the basic rules for the constituent phonemes, although we are never forced to the extreme of having to write an entirely new rule for such a case. Rather, we find that an appropriate pattern can be produced simply by applying a qualification or "position modifier" to the basic rule. An example of this is the pattern for the syllable /glu/ shown in figure 9.5. The basic rule for /g/ calls for an interval that is silent except for a voice bar, followed by a burst, and it further stipulates that adjacent formants have transitions which point to particular locus frequencies. The rule for /l/ calls for steady-state formants of a certain duration and specified intensities and frequencies, and it further requires that these /l/ formants be continuous with transitions to any adjacent formants. The rule for the vowel /u/ specifies the duration, intensity, and frequency of each of the three formants which are steady state, except as rules for neighboring phonemes prescribe transitions. Now a rigid application of the basic rule for the phonemes constituting the syllable /glu/ yields an ultimate acoustic output of less than tolerable intelligibility. A marked improvement is achieved if the basic rule for each phoneme is modified as follows: /g/ before /l/ requires only a burst of specified frequency; /l/ before /u/ has the frequency of its second formant lowered somewhat; /u/ following /l/ has a second formant which first rises from the second-formant frequency of /l/, and then, after a specified duration, shifts at a given rate to the normal steady-state frequency for /u/. At this point it should be remarked that these position modifiers operate on classes of phonemes; thus, the modification for /g/ applies also to the other stops, the modifier for /l/ applies also to /w,r,j/, and the modifier for /u/ applies also to /o/ and /ɔ/. In other words, the kind of economy gained by going from phoneme rules to subphonemic rules extends to the position modifiers as well.

Similar problems occur and similarly general solutions are found for other positional variations, as, for example, in the neighborhood of juncture.

Linguistic Digression

We should like to digress here to discuss briefly the implications of what has been said for the problem of how to define the phoneme. As you remember, we began by referring to a machine that would process a discrete phonemic input so as to produce a speech-like output. The phonemic input would be furnished by linguistic analysis. We might soon discover on consulting several equally competent linguists that they were of divided opinion on two subjects at least. First, they might have different ideas on the best way to define the phoneme; and second, they would not agree entirely on what the phonemes of a particular language are. Now the first point may be dismissed as a bit of academic quibbling, for we observe that two linguists with conflicting definitions of the phoneme can come out with phonemic analyses that are remarkably alike. It is of interest, nevertheless, that at least one linguist, Zellig Harris,[18] has proposed an operational definition of the phoneme which would require for its application that we synthesize speech from prerecorded utterances cut up into segments of phoneme length. For example, if the question were whether two sounds in different environments were or were not the same phoneme, one would interchange the appropriate snippets of tape, play back, and listen to determine whether the resulting utterance, as perceived, was reasonably satisfactory. Now we know that in many cases this operation cannot really be performed satisfactorily, and therefore has very little utility as a tool for phonemic analysis. However, the linguist may be able to do a roughly equivalent thing in terms of our rules and their modifiers. For the case of the sounds in different environments, the question would be whether one could satisfactorily synthesize them by using the same rule in both cases, provided only he applied the appropriate positional modifier.

The second point of dispute among the linguists is more important to us, since it actually affects what is to go into the input of the synthesizer. For example, one linguist will transcribe the vocalic part of the word *cake* with a single symbol where another will write it as a sequence of two. Then again, they may have differences of opinion about where to put the phonemes that sometimes mark boundaries between words. Instead of waiting for the linguists to resolve these conflicts among themselves, we might try each of the alternative analyses they provide, and then select that one which yields the most intelligible and natural-sounding speech output. Of course, if two alternatives yield the same kind of results by this test, then we may conclude that the problem is phonetically irrelevant and hand it back to the linguists.

Additional Rules for Stress and Syllabic Encoding

Before this digression into linguistics, we were considering the necessity of adding rules beyond the ideal minimum, and had discussed the matter of positional variations.

There remain two other types of complication that deserve mention. The first of these arises in connection with prosodic features, particularly stress.[19] We might have supposed that the basic rules, derived as they are largely from experiments with isolated syllables, would, if anything, yield connected speech that is "over-intelligible" to the point of sounding stilted. Now the speech we get certainly sounds stilted if differences in stress are provided for, but it is also often markedly less intelligible than would be predicted from the levels of intelligibility achieved for its constituent vowels and consonants when these are tested in nonsense syllables. The quality of the synthetic speech is improved, both in intelligibility and in naturalness, if at least two degrees of stress are provided for in the rules. The stress differences can be specified by one or more acoustic features, such as fundamental frequency, intensity,

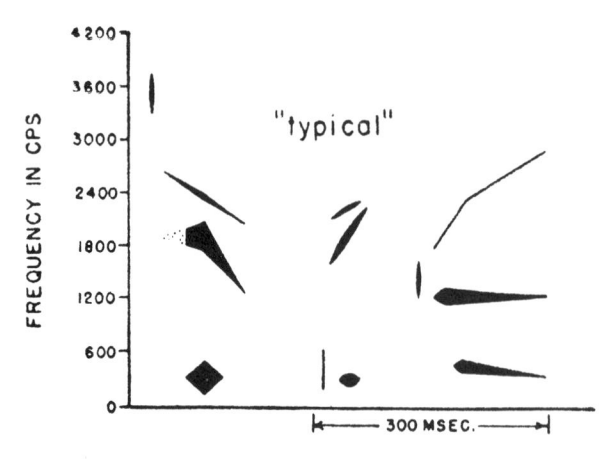

Figure 9.6
Pattern appropriate for the word "typical."

and duration. (Fundamental frequency is also, of course, the basis for variations in intonation, but no attempt has yet been made to include this feature in the rules.) At the present time only duration is actually being used in the rules for stress.

In order to achieve the greatest gain from adjusting vowel durations for two degrees of stress it is necessary to reduce the durations of some vowels, specifically those in medial unstressed syllables, to such an extent that no steady-state remains. By the rules for stressed syllables, a simple consonant-vowel-consonant pattern consists at the very least of initial transition, a steady-state segment, and a final transition. The steady-state segment has formant frequencies characteristic of the vowel alone; the transitions have durations and end points fixed according to the place and manner rules for the consonants. To convert such a syllable into a form appropriate for the unstressed condition, we must effectively omit the steady-state segment, as pointed out above. This means that the second and third formants are in fact drawn as straight lines connecting the end-point frequencies given by the place rules for the adjacent consonants. (It is necessary that the second formant pass through the 1000–2000 cps region. Where the straight line rule would violate this restriction—as, for example, in the case of a vowel between two labials—the second formant must be curved to bring it up or down into the required frequency range.) The configuration of the first formant will depend on whether the adjacent consonants are voiced or voiceless: if voiced, the first formant will move from its initial frequency to 500 cps and then to its final frequency; if voiceless, it will remain at a steady-state frequency of 500 cps. In figure 9.6 the pattern for the word "typical" shows an unstressed vowel between voiceless stops drawn according to this rule.

The other kind of complication is infrequent enough to be of no great practical consequence, perhaps, but is of some interest nevertheless. This difficulty arises because there is occasionally a rather complex relation between the phoneme as a perceptual unit and the sound that elicits it. An example is given in figure 9.7. Here we see a single locus for /g/ before the vowels /i,e,ɛ,a/, but between /a/ and /ɔ/ there is a large and sudden jump to a new locus. It is of more than passing interest that there is no corresponding break in the articulation of the consonant. Between /a/ and /ɔ/ there is a change from unrounded to rounded in the articulation of the vowel, and

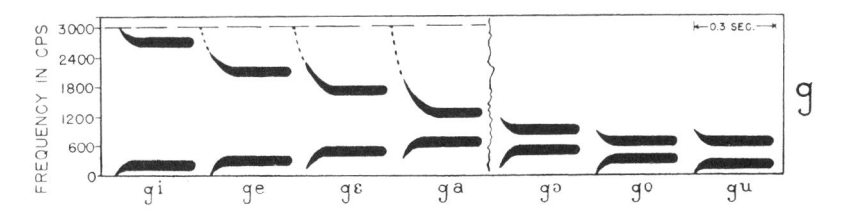

Figure 9.7
Patterns illustrating the second-formant transitions appropriate for /g/ before various vowels.

we may suppose that some rounding of the vowel concomitant with consonant articulation produces the sudden shift in consonant locus. It remains true, however, that so far as the consonant articulation itself is concerned, there is no discontinuity. This is to say, then, that the relation between articulation and phoneme is more nearly one-to-one than that between phoneme and sound. We have in other papers discussed the reason for and the possible significance of this fact.[20] Here we will simply note, first, that this requires an addition to the acoustic rules; second, that it must occasionally wreak havoc with attempts to work from prerecorded phonemic segments; and third, that this complication would not affect the rules of synthesis for an articulatory model. We should also stress the point, so clearly evident in this instance, that very often phonemes are laterally *encoded* into syllables at the acoustic level; in such cases the syllable becomes, in a very real sense, the irreducible acoustic unit.

Complexity versus Number of Rules; Resultant Intelligibility

We have so far talked about the number of rules required to do the job as if the matter of number were the only significant dimension of this problem. It is not. Obviously, we must consider not only the number of rules but also their simplicity. A rule, as we have been using the term, includes all the statements that must be made in order to specify a given unit of the system. Thus, at the subphonemic level, a rule includes all the specifications for a bilabial place of production, for example, or a stop consonant manner. A given rule may require many specifications or only a few. Simplicity or complexity is largely independent of the number of rules, and becomes, therefore, a separate consideration.

In the discussion so far we have also, perhaps, given the impression that there is a single, ideal, and final set of rules. It is, we suppose, obvious that beyond a certain point reduction in the number of rules, or an increase in their simplicity, will be accomplished only at the cost of naturalness and intelligibility. It remains to be determined just how and within what limits intelligibility and naturalness will vary as a function of the number of rules. In this paper we have more or less implicity assumed some particular and reasonable level of intelligibility, and have considered the *minimum* set of rules for that level. At present there are nine rules for place of consonant articulation, five for manner of consonant articulation, and three rules for voicing. For the vowels we have two manner and twelve place rules. In addition, we have one stress modifier and about twelve position modifiers. We should emphasize that there is nothing hard and fast about the numbers cited; they serve only to indicate roughly how large an inventory we are currently dealing with.

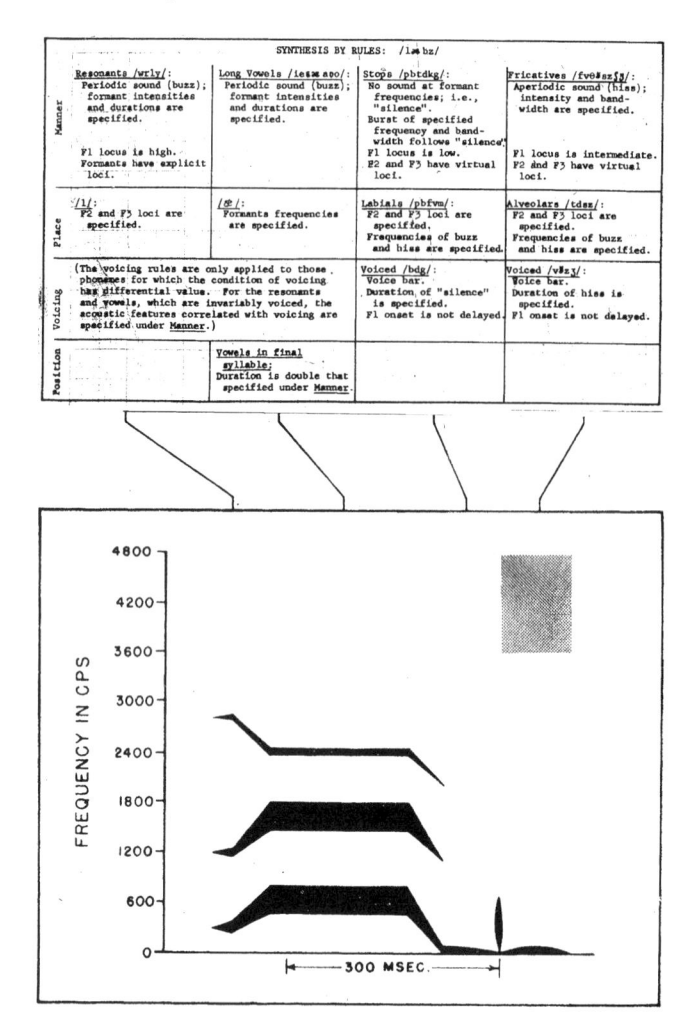

Figure 9.8
Table illustrating the rules for synthesizing the world /læbz/, and the pattern derived therefrom.

We have made no comprehensive attempt as yet to measure the intelligibility of the speech produced by such rules. This is not because we are uninterested in intelligibility, but rather because the rules have been changing rapidly, and the data on a really long test are likely to be out of data by the time they have been tabulated. We think it is safe to say that the intelligibility is of a fairly high order. In a few short and rather informal tests, sentence intelligibility has ranged between 60 percent and 100 percent depending on the nature of the sentences and the extent to which the listeners are accustomed to hearing this kind of synthetic speech.

Example of the Rules and Their Application

To illustrate just how the various categories of rules are combined to specify a pattern let us derive the pattern for the word "labs" as shown in figure 9.8. This word is represented in the input language by the sequence of phonemes: /læbz/.

/l/: The first phoneme is a member of the class of resonant consonants, that is, /w, r, l, j/. The *manner* rule for the resonants calls for three formants to be maintained (with specified intensities) at appropriate locus frequencies for 30 msec. The manner rule further specifies that adjacent formants shall have transitions of 75 msec drawn so as to be continuous with the locus formants. (This manner characteristic is referred to in the table of figure 9.8 as an "explicit locus.") The manner rule for the resonants also fixes the first-formant locus at 360 cps. Lastly, the resonant manner rule specifies a sound of the harmonic or "buzz" type. The *place* rule for /l/ specifies locus frequencies of 360, 1260, and 2880 cps.

/æ/: The next phoneme of the input is a member of the class of long vowels. The manner rule for this class calls for three formants of the buzz variety, having a duration of 150 msec. The place rule for /æ/ fixes formant frequencies at 750, 1650, and 2460 cps, and also specifies formant intensities.

/b/: The next phoneme shares its manner rule with all the other stops, /b, d, g, p, t, k/; this rule calls for an interval of "silence" (an interval devoid of acoustic energy at all frequencies above the fundamental of the buzz) followed by a burst, and further specifies that adjacent formants have 50-msec transitions pointing toward locus frequencies given by the place rule appropriate to the particular stop. ("Pointing to" means that the end-point frequencies of the actual transitions are midway between the locus frequencies and the formant frequencies of the next phoneme. This characteristic of the stop consonant manner is referred to in the table of figure 9.8 as a "virtual locus.") The manner rule also fixes the locus of the first formant at the frequency of the voice bar. The labial place rule, which serves equally for /b, p, m, f, v/, specifies that adjacent second- and third-formant transitions point to frequencies of 720 and 2100 cps, respectively. The *voicing* rule for stops (applicable equally to /b, d, g/) requires that the duration of the "silent" interval be 70 msec and that this interval be filled by a "voice bar," that is, acoustic energy at the buzz fundamental frequency.

/z/: For the final phoneme, the manner rule is that appropriate for the fricatives, /f, v, θ, ð, s, z, ʃ, ʒ/, and it calls for an interval of band-limited noise (that is, a "hiss" rather than a buzz sound). The fricative manner rule also specifies that adjacent formants have 50-msec transitions pointing toward virtual loci given by the place rule for the particular fricative; further by the manner rule, the first-formant locus is at 240 cps. The alveolar place rule for either /z/ or /s/ specifies that the noise (required by the fricative manner rule) have a lower cutoff frequency of 3600 cps, and that adjacent second- and third-formant transitions point to frequencies of 1800 and 2700 cps, respectively. The voicing rule states that the noise should be of low intensity, have a duration of 100 msec and be accompanied by a voice bar.

Finally, we apply a *position modifier* for syllables immediately before silence or juncture which doubles the duration of the vowel, making the overall duration of /æ/ 300 msec.

At this point we have completely specified a pattern that is directly convertible to an acoustic stimulus which the naive listener will readily identify as the word "labs."

Rules versus Prerecorded Elements: Further Discussion

Instead of trying now merely to summarize what has already been said, we would rather try to bring into the open a few considerations that have been only implicit in the discussion so far. In particular we should like to call attention to the fact that we have casually mixed two rather different aspects of the problem. The first has to do with the size of the unit in terms of which the rules are written, the second with the difference between assembling prerecorded elements on the one hand and the real honest-to-goodness fabrication of speech on the other. When we introduced the matter of prerecorded elements earlier, it was primarily to make a point about speech. This was somewhat unfair. Although the use of prerecorded elements is synthesis only in the most sweeping sense of the word,[21] it is sufficiently interesting both in practice and in principle that we ought to deal with it in its own right. The practical advantages of such a system are obvious enough. The difficulty, as we tried to point out earlier, is largely in the matter of linkage. As we have seen, linkage presents great difficulties at the level of phonemes. Indeed, the difficulties are likely to be so great that one will be driven to use elements which are of essentially syllabic dimensions, and even here problems will occur in the matter of joining the syllables. With units the size of words one will, of course, have much less difficulty about linkages, though he may not, even so, be completely out of the woods.

If we have seemed earlier in this discussion to be unenthusiastic about synthesis from prerecorded elements, we should say now that we have been sufficiently interested ourselves to have begun to explore the possibilities of such a system, at least at the level of words.[22] We have been particularly interested in trying to find the minimum number of versions of each word which will produce appropriate stresses and intonations when the words are arranged in various combinations. This has proved to be a challenging and interesting problem in the sense that its solution will either depend on the application of already known linguistic principles, or, alternatively, will provide information basic to the formulation of such principles.

To return to the point about linkages, the obvious generalization is that the problem grows less severe as the size of the prerecorded unit increases. There is, presumably, a function relating intelligibility or maximum speed of communication to size of the prerecorded units, and this function must certainly rise, though at an ever decreasing rate, as we go from smaller to larger units. At present, we know that with prerecorded phoneme units we are way down on the intelligibility or speed scale, if, indeed, we are on it at all. With prerecorded words we may be within shouting distance of the asymptote. We strongly suspect, without benefit of evidence, that syllables will be marginally useful if we want to communicate at normal speech rates.

It may well be that, for some purpose, prerecorded elements will turn out to be the method of choice. In principle, the system is interesting because when the units are of phonemic dimensions the difficulties one encounters illustrate some important truths about speech, and when the units are the size of words, we encounter some partially soluble and therefore challenging problems of stress and intonation—as well as of instrumentation.

We have already dealt at length with true synthesis as opposed to the use of prerecorded elements. With true synthesis the linkage problem is soluble at all levels, and has to a large extent been solved. The rules for synthesis can be written at various levels. Indeed, this system is inherently flexible in all respects. Its limits are set primarily by the limits of our knowledge about speech and, from a practical standpoint, by the difficulties of instrumenting true synthesis rather than random access.

We saw that with prerecorded elements the total inventory of segments (or rules) will likely approximate the number of syllables at the very least. By using true synthesis we can considerably reduce the number of rules by writing them either at the phoneme or subphoneme level. In either case some rules must be added to take care of positional variations, essential prosodic features, and the special cases in which the acoustic encoding of the phonemes into syllables makes it impossible to get along with only one rule for a single phoneme or subphonemic feature. When the rules are written at the phoneme level there must, of course, be provision for connecting the formant transitions or formants of successive phonemes, and at the subphonemic level additional arrangements must be made for simultaneous combination of the rules pertaining to the several features that constitute the phoneme.

Exactly how and where one might wish to make practical use of the rules for true synthesis depends on a large number of considerations that lie far outside the scope of this paper. In this account, we have been interested in such rules primarily because they constitute a description of the acoustic basis of speech perception. The kind of information contained in that description will, we think, prove useful for a variety of practical and theoretical purposes.

Notes

This paper was read by invitation before the Fifty-Sixth Meeting of the Acoustical Society of America in November 1958. The work described here was supported in part by the Carnegie Corporation of New York, in part by the Prosthetic and Sensory Aids Service of the Veterans Administration in connection with Contract No. V1005M1253, and in part by the Department of Defense in connection with Contract No. DA49-170-sc-2564.

1. For accounts of these research tools, see F. S. Cooper, J. Acoust. Soc. Am. 22, 761–762 (1950); Cooper, Liberman, and Borst, Proc. Natl. Acad. Sci. 37, 313–325 (1951); F. S. Cooper, Some instrumental aids to research on speech, in "Report of the fourth, annual round table meeting on linguistics and language teaching," pp. 46–56 (Washington, D.C., Institute of Languages and Linguistics, Georgetown University, 1953); J. M. Borst and F. S. Cooper, J. Acoust. Soc. Am. 29, 777 (A) (1957).
2. F. Ingemann, J. Acoust. Soc. Am. 29, 1255 (A) (1957).
3. For the purposes of this discussion it does not matter greatly whether the elements are pronounced and recorded in isolation or, alternatively, cut out of recordings of connected speech and then reassembled into new combinations. Some of the difficulties that arise in connection with the latter procedure are illustrated in Harris' account of his attempt to isolate the "building blocks of speech." See C. M. Harris, J. Acoust. Soc. Am. 25, 962–969 (1953).
4. Peterson, Wang, and Sivertsen, J. Acoust. Soc. Am. 30, 739–742 (1958).
5. We are here concerned only with those aspects of the acoustic pattern that carry the linguistic information.
6. A description of the acoustic basis of language in these terms is, of course, also incomplete unless the patterns present in each segment are fully described in acoustic terms.
7. As used in this paper a "rule" will refer to all the statements that must be made in order to specify whatever unit (e.g., phoneme, subphonemic feature, syllable) of the language is being used as a basis for synthesis.
8. Cooper, Delattre, Liberman, Borst, and Gerstman, J. Acoust. Soc. Am. 24, 597–606 (1952); Liberman, Delattre, Cooper, and Gerstman, Psychol. Monogr. 68, No. 8, 1–13 (1954); Liberman, Delattre, Gerstman, and Cooper, J. Exptl. Psychol. 52, 127–137 (1956); O'Connor, Gerstman, Liberman, Delattre, and Cooper, Word 13, 24–43 (1957).
9. It was found in an earlier study (see O'Connor et al., reference 8) that in the case of /w/ in initial position a brief steady-state segment at the onset helps to avoid a stop consonant effect, but it is not really essential. One must be careful, however, not to have the steady-state segment exceed about 30 msec, because at longer durations the listener hears a vowel preceding the /w/. It is not always clear in spectrograms of real speech whether or not there is an initial steady-state segment, and, if so, how long the segment is.
10. With the Pattern Playback it is possible to stop the pattern at any point and determine what that part of the pattern sounds like in steady state.

11. For the purposes of producing speech by recombining prerecorded phonemic segments, one might take advantage of this possibility with /w/ by isolating something approximating the initial steady state of /w/ which, when spliced in the proper temporal relationship to any of several vowels would, perhaps, produce a fair impression of /w/ plus vowel. This technique would almost certainly not work nearly so well with other consonants, and it will in any case probably be harder to do with real speech than with the idealized, schematized, hand-drawn patterns described in the text. In general, we should expect the application of this technique to be somewhat limited and to produce something less than ideal results, for at best it represents a way to force speech into a wholly unnatural mold.
12. See note 4.
13. For a detailed treatment of the "locus," see Delattre, Liberman, and Cooper, J. Acoust. Soc. Am. 27, 769–773 (1955); Harris, Hoffman, Liberman, Delattre, and Cooper, J. Acoust. Soc. Am. 30, 122–126 (1958). A rationalization in terms of articulatory-acoustic considerations is contained in a paper by Stevens and House [see K. N. Stevens and A. S. House, J. Acoust. Soc. Am. 28, 578–585 (1956)]. In certain ways the locus is similar to the "hub" [see Potter, Kopp, and Green, *Visible Speech* (D. Van Nostrand Company, Inc., New York, 1947)].
14. See Delattre et al., reference 13; O'Connor et al., reference 8.
15. Liberman, Delattre, and Cooper, Am. J. Psychol. 65, 497–516 (1952); C. Schatz, Language 30, 47–56 (1954); C. W. Hughes and M. Halle, J. Acoust. Soc. Am. 28, 303–310 (1956); Halle, Hughes, and Radley, J. Acoust. Soc. Am. 29, 107–116 (1957); K. S. Harris, Language and Speech, 1, 1–7 (1958).
16. Liberman et al., reference 8; O'Connor et al., reference 8.
17. L. Lisker, Word 13, 256–267 (1957); L. Lisker, Language 33, 42–49 (1957).
18. Z. S. Harris, *Methods in Structural Linguistics* (University of Chicago Press, Chicago, Illinois, 1951).
19. D. B. Fry, J. Acoust. Soc. Am. 27, 765–768 (1955); D. J., Bolinger and D. J. Gerstman, Word 13, 246–255 (1957); D. L. Bolinger, Lingua 7, 175–182 (1958); D. B. Fry, Language and Speech **1**, 126–152 (1958); D. L. Bolinger, Word 14, 109–149 (1958); L. Lisker, J. Acoust. Soc. Am. 30, 682 (A) (1958).
20. See Liberman, Delattre, and Cooper, reference 14; A. M. Liberman, J. Acoust. Soc. Am. 29, 117–123 (1957).
21. The speech sounds in the prerecorded elements are of course produced by human articulatory apparatus and recorded just as any other utterances can be. The synthetic aspect of this process consists only of entering these elements into combinations different from those in which they were originally recorded.
22. "Summary of fourth technical session on reading machines for the blind," Veterans Administration Washington, D.C., August 23–24, 1956; prepared by the Prosthetic and Sensory Aids Service, Veterans Administration, 252 Seventh Avenue, New York 1, New York.

PART III
Categorical Perception

Introduction to Part III

In chapter 1, I wrote at some length about our venture onto the stony ground of categorical perception, and what befell us there. Chapter 10 describes our initial foray. Chapter 11 is an early attempt to determine, with nonspeech controls, whether the discrimination peaks and troughs that reflect the perceived categories are examples of acquired distinctiveness, acquired similarity, or both. That question arose out of the assumption by the Early Motor Theory that categorical perception is the result of a learned association between an initial auditory representation and the sensory consequences of the same or different articulatory gestures required to match the acoustic signals. As I emphasized in chapter 1, I believe now that there is no initial auditory representation, only the unmediated perception of the gestural primitives. On that view, perception is as nearly categorical or continuous as the gestures it immediately represents; questions about acquired distinctiveness and acquired similarity become meaningless. It is still appropriate, however, to test the hypothesis that the discrimination peaks and troughs are specific to the phonetic process, not, as the horizontalists would have us believe, a characteristic of an initial auditory representation. For that purpose, the nonspeech controls are still relevant.

Chapter 10

The Discrimination of Speech Sounds within and across Phoneme Boundaries

In listening to speech, one typically reduces the number and variety of the many sounds with which he is bombarded by casting them into one or another of the phoneme[1] categories that his language allows. Thus, a listener will identify as *b*, for example, quite a large number of acoustically different sounds. Although these differences are likely to be many and various, some of them will occur along an acoustic continuum that contains cues for a different phoneme, such as *d*. This is important for the present study because it provides a basis for the question to be examined here: whether or not, with similar acoustic differences, a listener can better discriminate between sounds that lie on opposite sides of a phoneme boundary than he can between sounds that fall within the same phoneme category.

There are grounds for expecting an affirmative answer to this question. The most obvious, perhaps, are to be found in the common experience that in learning a new language one often has difficulty in making all the appropriate sound discriminations. The evidence for this is impressionistic in the extreme, and there is little information that would permit a definition of the more specific aspects of the difficulty. In whatever degree this difficulty exists, however, a reasonable assumption is that some part of it arises from the fact that a person who is newly exposed to the sounds of a strange language finds it necessary to categorize familiar acoustic continua in unfamiliar ways. If his discriminations have, by previous training, been sharpened and dulled according to the position of the phoneme boundaries of his native language, and if the acoustic continua of the old language are categorized differently by the new one, then the learner might be expected to have difficulty perceiving the sounds of the new language until he had mastered some new discriminations and, perhaps, unlearned some old ones.

In more explicit psychological terms, an affirmative answer is to be expected on the basis that the situations being considered here clearly meet the conditions for acquired similarity and acquired distinctiveness. If either or both of these processes do, in fact, occur, then two speech sounds which a listener normally lumps into the same phoneme class would come to be less discriminable than sounds to which he habitually attaches different phoneme labels. Indeed, one might conceivably find in language some very common and easily accessible cases in which the effects of such processes as acquired similarity and acquired distinctiveness are as great as many years of practice can make them.

The present experiment was designed to investigate the relation between phonemic labeling and discrimination in one language and within one group of phonemes. For this purpose a synthesizer was used to generate speech-like sounds and to vary

---

Originally published in *Journal of Experimental Psychology* 54, 5 (1957): 358–368, with Katherine Safford Harris, Howard S. Hoffman, and Belver C. Griffith. Reprinted with permission.

them in small steps along an acoustic continuum known to contain important cues for the perception of the voiced stops, *b*, *d*, and *g*. When listeners are asked to label these sounds as *b*, *d*, or *g*, they normally tend by their responses to divide the continuum into three sharply defined phoneme categories, the shifts from one response, or phoneme label, to another being very abrupt. It was the purpose of this experiment to determine how well these same sounds can be discriminated, and, in particular, to see whether the discrimination functions have sharp inflections that correspond in position to the abrupt shifts (i.e., phoneme boundaries) in the labeling responses. In addition, an attempt has been made to determine to what extent the relation between discrimination and labeling has here been reduced to its theoretical limit. For that purpose, the obtained discriminations have been compared with a function that is computed from the labeling data on the extreme assumption that the listener cannot hear any differences among these sounds beyond those that are revealed by this use of the phonemic labels.

Method

Apparatus
A special-purpose instrument, called a pattern playback, was used to generate the stimuli of this experiment. This instrument, which has been described in earlier papers (Cooper 1950, 1953; Cooper, Liberman, and Borst 1951), converts hand-painted spectrograms into sound, thus making it possible to synthesize speech-like auditory patterns and to control the various aspects of the pattern quite precisely.

Stimuli
Figure 10.1 illustrates the spectrograms used to produce the stimuli. The stimulus variable is the direction and extent of the second-formant transition, this variable having been found previously (Liberman et al. 1954) to be important for the perceived distinctions among *b*, *d*, and *g*. In the stimulus pattern at the extreme left of the top row of the figure, the second formant rises from a point 840 cps below its steady-state level, and in the pattern at the extreme right of the bottom row it falls from a point 720 cps above the steady state. Between these two extremes, the starting point of the transition varies in steps of 120 cps. For convenience these stimuli will be referred to by number, from 1 through 14, as indicated in figure 10.1.

The rising transition of the first formant had been found previously to be a marker for the class of voiced stops (Delattre, Liberman, and Cooper 1955) and, as can be seen in figure 10.1, this first-formant transition is constant in all the stimuli. In the steady-state part of the pattern the first formant centers at 360 cps and the second at 2160 cps. Formants at these frequencies produce a synthetic approximation to the vowel *e* (as in *gate*).

The spectrograms were converted into sound on the pattern playback and recorded on magnetic tape. By copying, cutting, and splicing the magnetic tape, all the stimulus arrangements described below were made.

Stimulus Presentation and Ss
The stimuli were presented to Ss in two ways; singly, to determine how Ss would label them as *b*, *d*, or *g*, and in an ABX arrangement to determine to what extent Ss could discriminate them on any basis at all.

Speech Sounds and Phoneme Boundaries 155

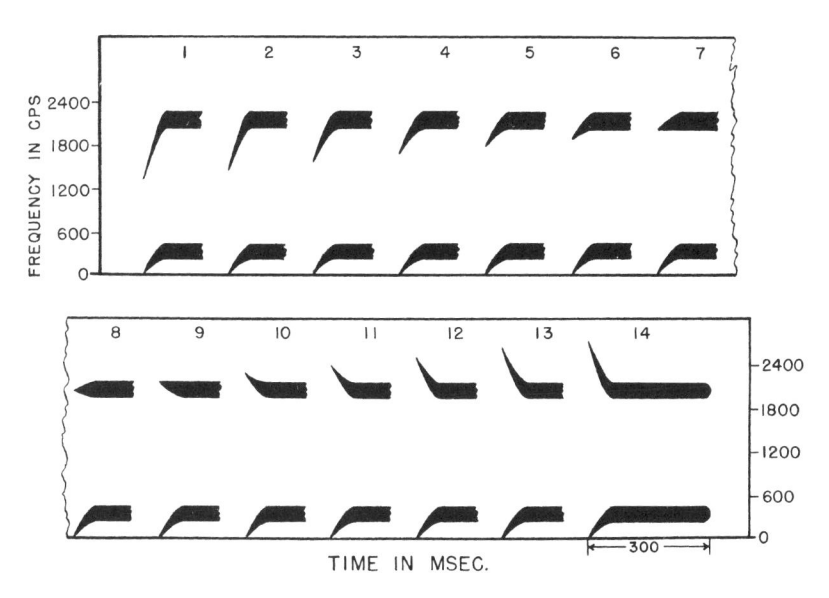

Figure 10.1
Illustrations of the spectrographic patterns from which the stimuli of the experiment were produced. Pattern 14, at the lower right, is complete in all respects.

For the labeling part of the experiment, six magnetic tapes were prepared, each of which contained a different randomization of the entire series of 14 stimuli. There was a 6-sec. interval between stimuli. These tapes were presented to Ss with instructions to judge each stimulus as *b*, *d*, or *g*.

To test discrimination by the ABX procedure, the stimuli were arranged in triads, each of which consisted of an A stimulus, a B stimulus, and a third stimulus, X, which was identical either to A or to B. The Ss were instructed to determine whether X was the same as A or the same as B. It was strongly emphasized to each S that he was to make his judgment on the basis of any cues he could hear. The measure of discriminability is, of course, the percentage of the time that the X stimulus is correctly matched to A or to B.

It was not the purpose of this experiment to obtain actual DL's, but only to measure relative discriminability at every step on the continuum. For that purpose, the A and B stimuli of the ABX triad were made up by pairing each stimulus with the stimulus one step, two steps, and three steps removed from it. Each stimulus was paired in this fashion with the stimuli lying to its right on the continuum shown in figure 10.1. Thus, Stimulus 1 was paired with Stimulus 2 to form the A and B stimuli, respectively, of one ABX triad. Stimulus 1 was paired with Stimulus 3 in another triad, and with Stimulus 4 in a third. Similarly, Stimulus 2 was paired with Stimulus 3, with Stimulus 4, and with Stimulus 5, and so on for the remaining stimuli on the continuum. There was no stimulus one step to the right of Stimulus 14, so 14 does not appear as an A stimulus in the one-step series. For analogous reasons, Stimuli 13 and 14 do not appear as A stimuli in the two-step series, and Stimuli 12, 13, and 14 are missing from the three-step series.

From the above discussion, it follows that the number of A and B combinations was 36. For each combination of A and B stimuli, there were two triads—one in which X was identical to A and one in which X was identical to B. The total number of triads was 72. These triads were arranged into six tapes of 12 triads each. Within each ABX triad, the stimuli were spaced at 1-sec. intervals; successive trials were separated by 10 sec.

There were two groups of Ss in the experiment. Since the procedures for the two groups were slightly different they will be described separately. Group I consisted of five paid volunteers, all undergraduate students at the University of Connecticut, who had never heard any synthetic speech prior to this experiment. For the first 17 sessions, Ss were given only the ABX discrimination task to do, without being told that these were synthetic speech sounds. Beginning with Session 18, they were informed that the sounds on the discrimination tapes were synthetic approximations to speech. At this point the labeling tapes were introduced, and for the next three sessions Ss were given four labeling tapes per session with instructions to identify each stimulus as a speech sound. During this period they were given no discrimination task. At Session 22 and thereafter Ss were asked to identify the stimuli on the labeling tapes as *b*, *d*, or *g*, and the discrimination task was resumed. In these sessions, the discrimination task was always undertaken after Ss had finished judging the stimuli on the labeling tapes.

For several reasons the discrimination data obtained before and after the introduction of the labeling tapes have been combined. First, an examination of the results showed that there was no obvious change in the discrimination judgments following the introduction of the labeling tapes and the instruction to judge the stimuli on those tapes as *b*, *d*, or *g*. Second, in the sessions in which the labeling tapes were first introduced, Ss reported that they had previously heard the sounds on the discrimination tapes as speech. Moreover, when they were asked to identify the speech sounds they heard, they responded mostly with *b*, *d*, and *g*.

When the discrimination data are combined, there are, for each S in Group I, a total of 21 judgments of each ABX triad. Since there were two triads for each combination of A and B stimuli, the total number of judgments of each A and B combination by each S was 42. For each of the stimuli on the labeling tapes there are, for each S, 32 judgments. All of the labeling judgments were obtained after Session 21—i.e., after Ss had been asked specifically to identify the stimuli on the labeling tapes as *b*, *d*, or *g*.

Two of the five Ss in Group I were eliminated because they failed to apply the phoneme labels consistently. Since these Ss did not clearly divide the stimulus continuum into phoneme categories, one cannot compare their discrimination of speech sounds within and across phoneme boundaries. It should be noted here that the stimuli of this experiment have previously been presented to large groups of listeners, and that it is quite unusual to find as many as two out of five who are as unreliable in their responses as the two Ss who were eliminated from this experiment.

Group II consisted of four workers at the Haskins Laboratories. These Ss had previously had extensive experience in listening to synthetic speech sounds. The procedure of Group II was like the procedure for Group I after Session 21. Thus, in each session, Ss identified the stimuli on one labeling tape, and then judged three of the discrimination tapes—a total of 36 ABX triads. (This plan could not be followed exactly in the last few sessions due to scheduling difficulties.) In all, each S identified each of the stimuli on the labeling tapes 25 times, and he judged each ABX triad a total of 13 times. Since there were two triads for each A and B combination, each S judged each A-B combination a total of 26 times.

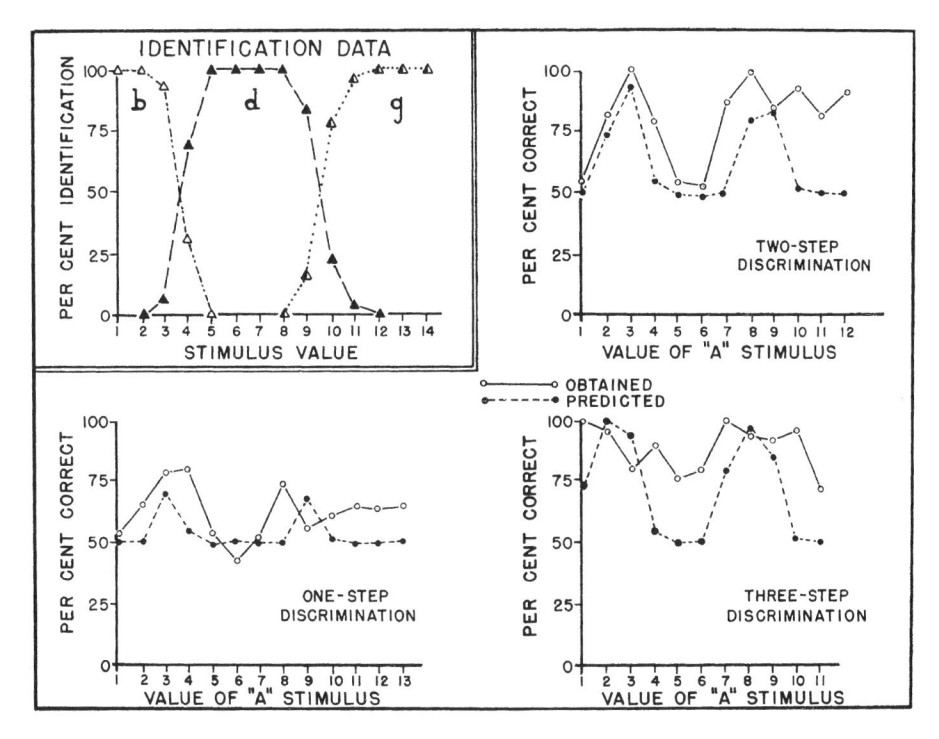

Figure 10.2
Labeling and discrimination data for a single S, CD. The values given on the ordinates in terms of percentages are based on 32 and 42 judgments for the labeling and discrimination data, respectively.

Of those Ss whose data will be shown individually in the following section on results, CD and RV are from Group I, while LG and KH are from Group II.

Results

In order to describe the method of presenting the data, and also to indicate in general terms the outcome of this study, the results that were obtained with one S, CD, will be presented first. At the upper left of figure 10.2 are plotted the labeling responses made by this S when the 14 stimuli were presented to him one at a time and in random order for judgment as *b*, *d*, or *g*. It can be seen that Stimuli 1, 2, and 3 were identified primarily as *b*, Stimuli 5, 6, 7, 8, and 9 as *d*, and Stimuli 11, 12, 13, and 14 as *g*. The shifts from one response to another are very abrupt, which is to say that the phoneme boundaries for this S are very sharp and stable.

The discrimination data obtained with the same S, CD, are also shown in figure 10.2. Only the "obtained" data points indicated by open circles and connected by solid lines will be considered at this time. Each point represents the percentage of correct responses for all ABX presentations (both ABA and ABB) when the A stimulus had the value shown on the abscissa and the B stimulus was one, two, or three steps removed (for the one-, two-; and three-step curves, respectively). Thus, for example, the first point on the one-step curve shows that this S correctly discriminated Stimulus 1 and Stimulus 2 (one step higher on our stimulus scale) 54 percent of the time.

A comparison of the discrimination functions with the labeling functions indicates that, other things equal, this S does, indeed, discriminate better between stimuli that lie on either side of a phoneme boundary than he does between stimuli that fall within the same phoneme category. For example, it can be seen from the labeling curves that Stimuli 1 and 3 were both identified as *b* almost all of the time, and the two-step discrimination curves show that this S correctly discriminated these stimuli only 55 percent of the time. Two steps beyond Stimulus 3, which was almost always identified as *b*, is Stimulus 5, which was always identified as *d*. The discrimination curves show that these two stimuli, consistently labeled as different phonemes, were correctly discriminated 100 percent of the time.

It must, of course, be supposed that if a listener can always identify two stimuli as different (as in the case of Stimulus 3 and Stimulus 5), he will surely be able to discriminate them. On the other hand, it does not necessarily follow from the fact that he identifies two stimuli as the same phoneme (as with Stimulus 1 and Stimulus 3) that he cannot discriminate them. One might think that he would hear *two* types of *b*—i.e., that he would hear what the linguist calls allophonic variations. In the example cited, S does not.

Clearly, the data obtained with this S are not all so neat and striking as the particular examples chosen, and some of the other Ss were more variable, especially in their responses to the discrimination task, than the one S, CD, whose responses have been shown in figure 10.2. It is, nevertheless, reasonably apparent from an inspection of the data of all Ss that the discriminations tend to be relatively more acute in the vicinity of phoneme boundaries than in the middle of phoneme categories. Before presenting these other data, however, it is desirable to provide a basis on which all the results can be evaluated. For that purpose the working hypothesis will be stretched to a theoretical limit and its quantitative implications will be developed.

Make the extreme assumption that S can discriminate the stimuli only to the extent that he can identify them as different phonemes. Then suppose that in the discrimination task—i.e., when S is presented with the stimuli in ABX fashion and asked to say whether X is like A or like B—he can only assign the phonemic labels *b*, *d*, and *g* to the individual stimuli, and that he has no other basis for discriminating among the stimulus members of the various ABX triads. One can, then, use S's responses in the phonemic labeling part of the experiment as a basis for calculating the frequency with which he will correctly discriminate in any given ABX arrangement of the stimuli. To do this, one must first refer to the labeling part of the experiment and take account of the relative frequency with which S identified each of the 14 stimuli as *b*, *d*, or *g*. It is, of course, possible to go from these data to calculations of the probabilities that a given ABX triad will be heard as any one of the possible sequences of the three phonemes. One then needs only to determine for each triad which of the possible phonemic sequences will lead to responses that would be counted as correct discriminations.

By reference to the phonemic labeling part of the experiment we first determine for each A and B stimulus of the various ABX triads the relative frequency with which it was identified as *b*, *d*, and as *g*. These relative frequencies will be used as estimates of the probabilities of hearing the various stimuli of the ABX triads as *b*, as *d*, and as *g*. Let us call the probabilities of hearing these phones p_b, p_d, and p_g in the case of an A stimulus and p'_b, p'_d, and p'_g in the case of a B stimulus. We assume next that the various stimuli within each triad are perceived independently of each other. It follows, then, that the probability (for a given ABA triad) of hearing a particular sequence, such as b, d, g, is $p_b p'_d p_g$. Since there are three alternative responses, there are $3 \times 3 \times 3$, or 27, such phoneme sequences possible.

For any triad the 27 possible phonemic sequences can be divided into three classes according to whether they lead S to make responses that would be counted as correct discriminations, as incorrect discriminations, or as discriminations that would on the average be correct half of the time and incorrect half of the time. In the case of any ABA type of triad, for example, S will be correct for any sequence in which the first and third stimulus members of the triad are heard as the same phoneme and the second member is heard as a different phoneme. He will be incorrect (again for the ABA type of triad) whenever the second and third members are heard as the same phoneme and the first is heard as a different phoneme. He will be correct half of the time and incorrect half of the time with two types of phoneme sequences: (a) all those in which he hears the first and second stimuli as the same phoneme and (b) those sequences in which he hears three different phonemes.[2]

These considerations can be expressed quantitatively in the following way. Let $PCorr_{(ABA)}$ be the proportion of the time that the listener is correct on a number of presentations of the same ABA sequence, P_R be the proportion of the time that the listener heard a sequence which would lead to correct discrimination, P_W be the proportion of the time that the listener heard a sequence which would lead to incorrect discrimination, and P_I be the proportion of the time that the listener heard a sequence which would, with equal likelihood, lead to correct and incorrect discriminations. Then

$$PCorr_{(ABA)} = 1P_R + 0P_W + .5P_I.$$

If the probabilities of the particular sequences described above are substituted appropriately for the general expressions P_R, P_W, and P_I, and if the resulting equation is then manipulated algebraically, we obtain

$$PCorr_{(ABA)} = .5 + \frac{(p_b^2 + p_d^2 + p_g^2 - p_b p'_b - p_d p'_d - p_g p'_g)}{2}.$$

So far, we have been concerned only with the case in which the presented sequence is ABA; analogous considerations lead to a similar equation for ABB, although the particular sequences which are correct and incorrect are different.

$$PCorr_{(ABB)} = .5 + \frac{(p'^2_b + p'^2_d + p'^2_g - p_b p'_b - p_d p'_d - p_g p'_g)}{2}.$$

The ABA and ABB sequences were presented equally often; therefore, an average $PCorr$ is given by

$$PCorr = .5 + \frac{(p_b - p'_b)^2 + (p_d - p'_d)^2 + (p_g - p'_g)^2}{4}.$$

The solid points connected by dashed lines in figure 10.2 represent the discrimination values derived from CD's labeling curves on the assumptions outlined above. It is seen in the case of this S that the predicted functions do indeed take care of some, although by no means all, of the variations in the obtained discriminations. The assumptions predict the points of high and low discrimination reasonably well, but they lead one to expect a general level of discrimination slightly lower than that obtained.

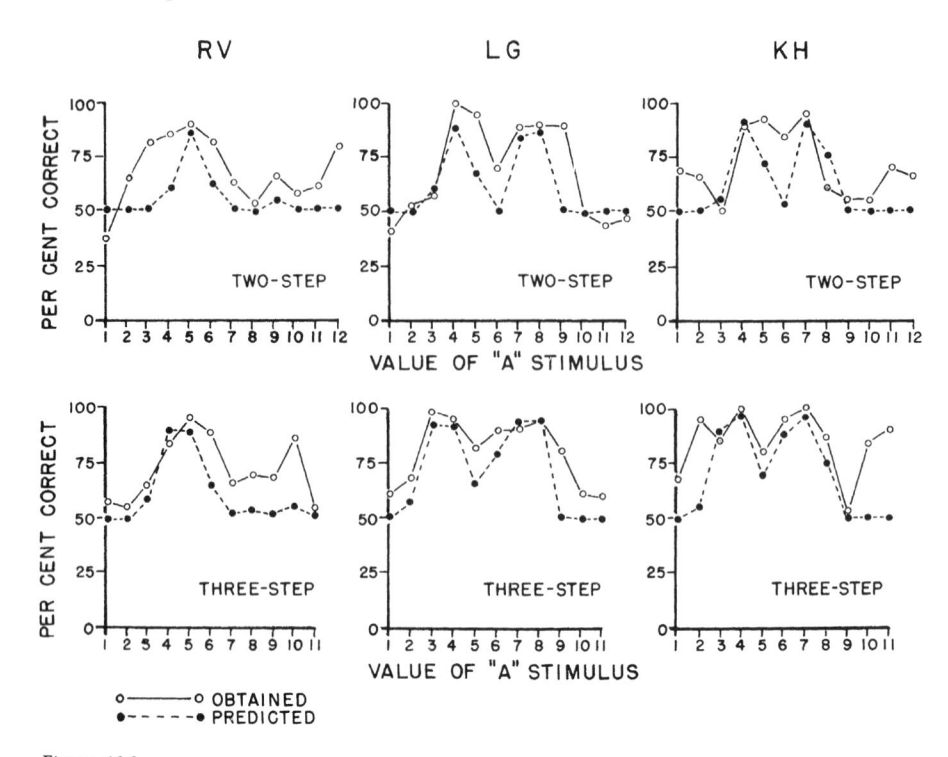

Figure 10.3
Predicted and obtained discrimination values at two and three steps for RV, LG, and KH. Each of the obtained values is based on 42 judgments in the case of RV, and on 26 judgments for LG and KH.

In figure 10.3 are data obtained with three other Ss. These data are not presented as a way of indicating the results for all Ss but only to show additional details of the results, including in particular a sample of the individual differences among Ss. It is seen that the position and number of the peaks in the predicted discrimination functions vary somewhat from one S to another, reflecting differences in the way Ss had assigned phoneme labels to the stimuli when they were presented for identification. It is also apparent that the obtained discriminations follow the inter-S differences in the predicted functions fairly well.

The simplest way to summarize the data for all Ss is to make a scatter plot of obtained values against predicted values. Such plots are shown in figures 10.4, 10.5, and 10.6 for one- two-, and three-step discriminations, respectively.[3] For the two- and three-step data, regression lines have been fitted by the method of least squares, and these are shown for each set of points. The regression for the one-step data has not been determined because so few predicted points lie above 50 percent that a meaningful fit cannot be obtained. The one-step data do not, therefore, provide a good test of our assumptions. For the two- and three-step data we should, of course, suppose that if the obtained data were essentially as predicted, give or take a little experimental error, the regression lines would be described by the equation "$x = y$."

The relationship between predicted and obtained values has been measured by computing tau,[4] a nonparametric measure of correlation. The correlations are $+.14$, $+.43$, and $+.43$ for the one-, two-, and three-step discriminations, respectively. Significance levels, in the same order, are $P = <.08$, $P = <.001$, and $P = <.001$. Thus, it

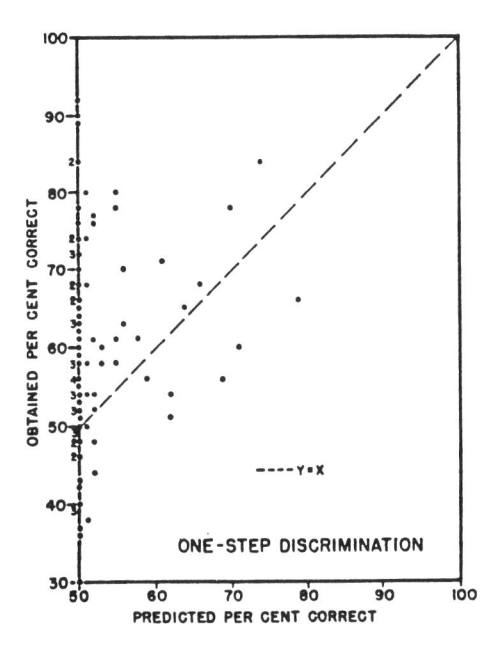

Figure 10.4
Scatter plot of predicted vs. obtained values on the one-step discrimination for all Ss. The small numerals have been placed on the graph to indicate, where necessary, the number of values that occupy the same position of the coordinates.

is seen that the correlations are highly significant for the two- and three-step discriminations, but in the case of the one-step discrimination the relationship could have arisen by chance. The failure to obtain significance for the one-step discrimination is out surprising since, as was pointed out earlier, most of the one-step points are predicted to lie at 50 percent.

Although there is a significant relationship between obtained and predicted points for the two- and three-step discrimination data, it is apparent in both cases that the lines of best fit are systematically displaced upward. This indicates that while the assumptions predict fairly well the occurrence and location of the inflections in the discrimination curves, they apparently lead to an under-estimation of the general level of discrimination. This was previously noted in the data of the individual Ss as shown in figures 10.2 and 10.3, where it was seen that the obtained discrimination functions tended to fit quite well with the predicted curves except that they were in general at a slightly higher level.

It is difficult on the basis of the data now available to make an unequivocal interpretation of the difference in level between obtained and predicted discrimination functions. One possibility, of course, is that this discrepancy represents a margin of "true" discrimination—i.e., an ability of S to distinguish the speech sounds, not solely on the basis of the phonemic labels, but also more directly by the essential acoustic differences among the patterns. A very different possibility is that the discrepancy between obtained and predicted is the result of certain detailed aspects of the experimental procedure. For example, irrelevant discriminable aspects of the stimuli,

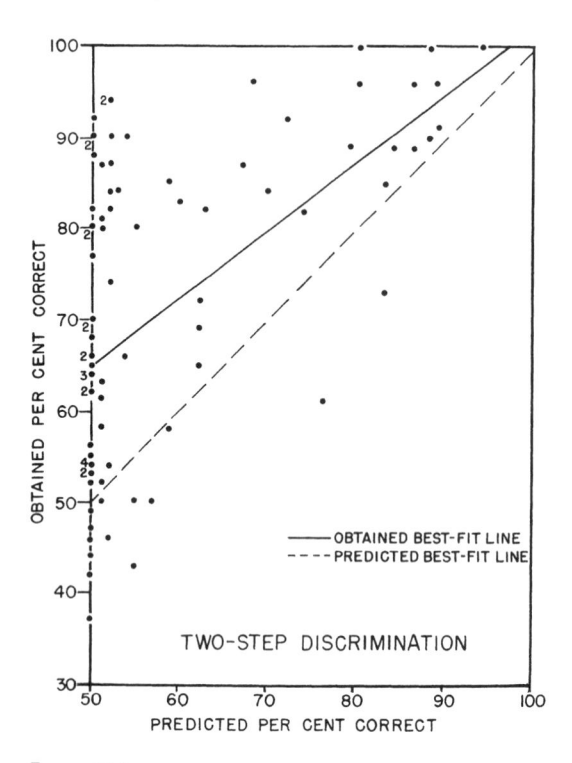

Figure 10.5
Scatter plot of predicted vs. obtained values on the two-step discrimination for all Ss. The small numerals have the same meaning as in figure 10.4.

such as accidental stray noise, could have provided Ss with an extraneous basis for deciding, in regard to the ABX triads, whether X was A or B. Such additional stimuli would, of course, have had no effect on Ss' responses in the phonemic labeling part of the experiment. The result would have been, then, to make the obtained discriminations somewhat better than one should have expected them to be. In general, the procedures of this experiment were not such as to control most effectively for these irrelevant discriminanda. It will be possible in future research to take greater precautions against their occurrence, and then to determine whether and to what extent the discrepancy between obtained and predicted is reduced.

Within the data of the present experiment, however, there is some evidence that the discrepancy between obtained and predicted discrimination functions is due, at least in part, to "true" discrimination. This evidence is to be found in the fact that the discrepancy would appear to be greater for the three-step than for the two-step function. One might expect to obtain this difference if S were truly discriminating the stimuli on the basis of their essential acoustic characteristics, since one would then presumably find as between the two- and three-step discriminations that the three-step discrimination was the easier. Other factors, such as the irrelevant discriminanda discussed in the preceding paragraph, would have affected the two- and three-step conditions equally, and would not have caused the departure from predicted values to be greater in the three- than in the two-step data.

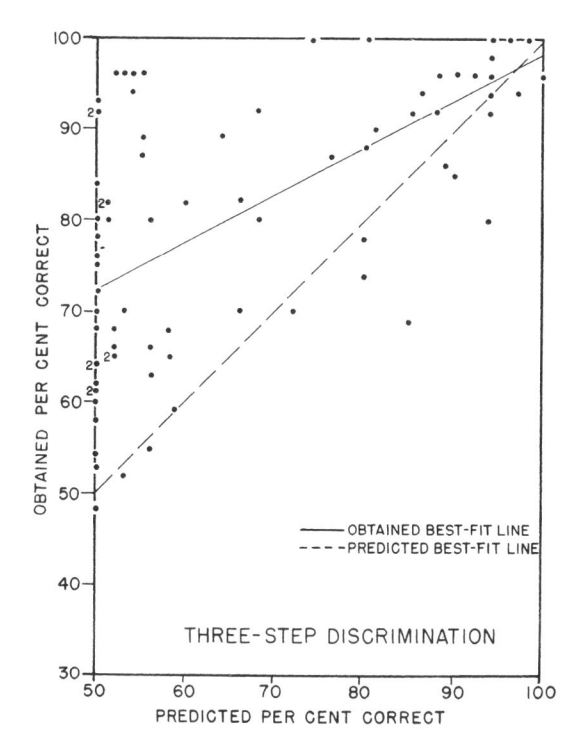

Figure 10.6
Scatter plot of predicted vs. obtained values on the three-step discrimination for all Ss. The small numerals have the same meaning as in figure 10.4.

Discussion

The results of this experiment cannot be assumed unequivocally to reflect the effects of learning on discrimination. There is, of course, the possibility that the inflections in the discrimination function are given innately, and that the phoneme boundaries have been placed so as to coincide with these discontinuities. This begins to seem unlikely when one considers that other languages have put phoneme boundaries at different places along the *b-d-g* continuum. In itself, this would appear to reduce the probability that the sharp inflections in the discrimination functions are innately given. One would have far more compelling evidence, however, if it were found that native speakers of such languages have their points of maximal and minimal differential sensitivity displaced along the continuum to correspond with the phoneme boundaries of their respective languages. Research to test this possibility is feasible.

In order to find out whether the effects here described represent acquired similarity, acquired distinctiveness, or a combination of both, it will, of course, be appropriate to obtain discrimination data on nonspeech stimuli that are otherwise identical with the synthetic approximations to speech. Complete identity is obviously impossible, unless one can get Ss to hear the same sounds sometimes as speech and sometimes not. One can, however, reasonably expect to make revealing comparisons between discrimination data obtained with speech and nonspeech stimuli that vary along the same, simple stimulus dimensions. Sheer temporal duration, for example, is sometimes a cue for distinguishing speech sounds. (Duration of transitions distinguishing stop consonant from semivowel; duration of fricative noise is a cue for distinguishing among the classes fricative, affricate, and stop.) It will be possible to obtain discrimination functions for variations in duration when those variations cue the perceived differences among phonemes, and to obtain comparable data for variations in duration of nonspeech sounds. We should suppose that a comparison of discrimination functions such as these would help greatly to determine whether the typical listener's long training in speech perception has served selectively to sharpen or to dull his discrimination of speech sounds, or whether, perhaps, it has done both.

Notes

This research was supported in part by the Carnegie Corporation of New York and in part by the Department of Defense in connection with Contract DA49-170-sc-1642.

1. The phoneme is most often taken to be the smallest unit of speech that can, by itself, distinguish one utterance from another as to meaning. Thus, the existence of the two words *bill* and *dill* makes it clear that *b* and *d* are different phonemes in English. It should be emphasized that the phoneme is not a single sound, but is, rather, a class which can and usually does include a great many sounds that differ from each other in various ways without causing any change in meaning.
2. When S hears a sequence of three different phonemes, he can be expected to make the correct discrimination half of the time only if we assume that he perceives each phoneme as equally like the other two. It is possible that the typical listener does not perceive *b*, *d*, and *g* in precisely this way. However, the labeling data of this experiment are such as to produce essentially zero probabilities of hearing such sequences in the ABX triads. We have, therefore, not yet attempted to determine how the similarities among *b*, *d*, and *g* are perceived, because a correction, no matter how large, would have negligible effect on the results being reported here.
3. It should be noted here that the reliabilities of all points in the scatter plots are not equal, since, as was pointed out under the section on procedure, the two groups of Ss made different numbers of judgments of the various ABX triads.
4. We have used a nonparametric measure because our data fail to meet the assumption of homoscedasticity. For a description of tau, see Kendall (1948).

References

Cooper, F. S. Spectrum analysis. *J. acoust. Soc. Amer.*, 1950, 22, 761–762.
Cooper, F. S. Some instrumental aids to research on speech. In *Report of the fourth annual round table meeting on linguistics and language teaching*. Washington, D.C.: Institute of Languages and Linguistics, Georgetown Univer., 1953. Pp. 46–53.
Cooper, F. S., Liberman, A. M., and Borst, J. M. The interconversion of audible and visible patterns as a basis for research in the perception of speech. *Proc. Nat. Acad. Sci.*, 1951, 37, 318–325.
Delattre, P. C., Liberman, A. M., and Cooper, F. S. Acoustic loci and transitional cues for consonants. *J. acoust. Soc. Amer.*, 1955, 27, 769–773.
Kendall, M. G. *Rank correlation methods*. London: C. Griffin, 1948.
Liberman, A. M., Delattre, P. C., Cooper, F. S., and Gerstman, L. J. The role of consonant-vowel transitions in the perception of the stop and nasal consonants. *Psychol. Monogr.*, 1954, 68, No. 8 (Whole No. 379).

Chapter 11

An Effect of Learning on Speech Perception: The Discrimination of Durations of Silence with and without Phonemic Significance

In studies of the perception of /b,d,g/, /d,t/, and /sl,spl/[1] (Liberman, Harris, Hoffman, and Griffith 1957; Griffith 1958; Bastian, Eimas, and Liberman 1961; Liberman, Harris, Kinney, and Lane 1961) we have found that discrimination of a given acoustic difference is considerably more acute across phoneme boundaries than in the middle of the phoneme categories. To make the appropriate measurements we had first to identify acoustic variables which are sufficient cues for the perceived phonemic distinctions. For that we were able to fall back on the results of earlier studies (Liberman, Delattre, Cooper, and Gerstman 1954; Delattre, Liberman, and Cooper 1955; Liberman, Delattre, and Cooper 1958; Harris, Hoffman, Liberman, Delattre and Cooper 1958; Bastian, Delattre, and Liberman 1959). Having thus selected for each phonemic distinction an appropriate acoustic cue, we prepared a series of synthetic patterns in which that cue was varied along a single continuum through a range large enough to encompass the phonemes being investigated. To measure discriminability, we arranged the patterns into ABX triads and asked the listeners to decide, on the basis of any similarities or differences they could hear, whether X was identical with A or with B. (A and B were, in fact, always different, and X was always identical with the one or the other.) To find the phoneme boundary, we presented the patterns with instructions to identify each one as /b/, /d/, or /g/ in the first experiment, as /d/ or /t/ in the second, and as /sl/ or /spl/ in the third.

Discrimination was so much better across the phoneme boundary than within the category as to suggest that the listeners could only hear these consonants categorically (i.e., as phonemes), and could discriminate no other differences among them. This suggestion was tested by finding the extent to which the discriminability of the patterns could be predicted from the way in which the listeners had assigned the stimuli to the various phoneme categories. Discrimination functions that were derived on this basis were found to fit rather closely those that had been obtained in the experiments.[2]

From a psychological point of view these results are quite unusual. With stimuli that vary along a single dimension (of frequency, intensity, or duration, for example) one typically finds that subjects discriminate many times more stimuli than they can identify absolutely (Pollack 1952, 1953; Garner 1953; Chapanis and Halsey 1956; Miller 1956). In everyday experience this is illustrated by the contrast between the ease with which we normally distinguish two tones as being of different pitch and, on the other hand, the great difficulty we have in absolutely specifying the pitch of either one. The very different result in the perception of /b,d,g/, /d,t/, and /sl, spl/ was

Originally published in *Language and Speech* 4 (October–December 1961, Part 4): 175–195, with Katherine Safford Harris, Peter Eimas, Leigh Lisker, and Jarvis Bastian. Reprinted with permission.

that discrimination was little better than absolute identification. It is as if our listeners were able to distinguish only as many pitches as they could correctly name.

Viewed from a linguistic standpoint, these results might not appear surprising. Apparently the linguist is prepared to find, with some phonemes at least, that variations in a speech sound will be heard by phonetically naive listeners only when these variations are phonemic. More generally, he might see the extent to which this happens as a precise expression of the degree to which linguistic categories are also categorical in perception.

Within either a psychological or linguistic framework, the peaks in discrimination should be of interest, we think, because their existence may be an important condition underlying the distinctiveness of speech sounds. Thus, an incoming stimulus which falls ever so slightly to one side of the peak becomes indistinguishable from, and no harder to identify than, a stimulus which lies in the precise centre of the phoneme region. The effect of this should be to reduce the area of uncertainty between phonemes, thereby increasing the accuracy and speed with which the listener sorts the various sounds of speech into the appropriate phoneme bins.

We should note that there appears to be considerable variation among phoneme classes in the size and sharpness of the discrimination peaks, and, correspondingly, in the extent to which the perception is categorical. For some phoneme distinctions there are no discrimination peaks at the phoneme boundaries, and the level of discrimination is far better than would be predicted from the extreme assumption that the listeners can hear the sounds only as phonemes. This kind of result has so far been found in the perception of vowels (Fry, Abramson, Eimas, and Liberman, in preparation), and of several prosodic features (tones and vowel duration) which are phonemic (Abramson 1961; Abramson and Bastian, in preparation).

To determine why the discrimination peaks develop at some phoneme boundaries and not at others, we should have to inquire quite deeply into the nature of the perceptual mechanism. For the purpose of this paper it is appropriate only to indicate the broad outline of our hypothesis. We believe that in the course of his long experience with language, a speaker (and listener) learns to connect speech sounds with their appropriate articulations. In time, these articulatory movements and their sensory feedback (or, more likely, the corresponding neurological processes) become part of the perceiving process, mediating between the acoustic stimulus and its ultimate perception. When significant acoustic cues that occupy different positions along a single continuum are produced by essentially discontinuous articulations (as, for example, in the case of second-formant transitions produced for /b/ by a movement of the lips and for /d/ by a movement of the tongue), the perception becomes discontinuous (i.e., categorical), and discrimination peaks develop at the phoneme boundary. When, on the other hand, acoustic cues are produced by movements that vary continuously from one articulatory position to another (as, for example, the frequency positions of first and second formants produced by various vowel articulations), perception tends to change continuously and there are no peaks at the phoneme boundaries. Various aspects of our view have been described elsewhere (Cooper, Delattre, Liberman, Borst, and Gerstman 1952; Liberman Delattre, and Cooper 1952; Liberman 1957; Cooper, Liberman, Harris, and Grubb 1961; Bastian, Eimas, and Liberman 1961; Harris, Bastian, and Liberman 1961), and it will be developed further in papers now in preparation. A theory which is in certain ways related to ours has been put forward in an interesting paper by Ladefoged (1959).

Basic to our speculation about the mechanism which accounts for the discrimination peaks is the simple assumption that they are learned. The primary purpose of the experiments to be reported here is to provide data relevant to that assumption. Whether the peaks are, in fact, acquired in experience, or whether they are somehow a part of our innately given sensitivity to the acoustic stimuli, is a question of broader scope than is a consideration of any particular mechanism as such.

We cannot dismiss, out of hand, the possibility that the discrimination peaks are innately given. If they are, we should suppose that the earliest speakers of the language wisely chose to locate the phoneme boundaries in the regions of highest discriminability. Assuming, alternatively, that the peaks reflect the learning that has occurred during each listener's long experience with the language, we must then answer a further question concerning the direction the learning has taken. Thus, it is possible that the peak is an increase in discrimination, acquired as a result of the listener's having had for many years to distinguish sounds that lie on opposite sides of the phoneme boundary. Such an effect might prove to be similar to what has been called "acquired distinctiveness"; for convenience, we will use that term to describe it. The contrary, and equally likely, possibility is that the peak is what remains after discrimination has been reduced by long training in responding identically to sounds that belong in the same phoneme class. This would likely be counted an example of "acquired similarity." It is also possible, of course, that the observed effect is the sum of both processes: acquired distinctiveness across the boundary and acquired similarity within the category.

As between these two assumptions—that the peaks are part of the listener's innately given sensory equipment, or, alternatively, that they are the result of learning—the latter interpretation is the more likely. One relevant consideration is that languages other than English have apparently located their phonemes differently on the acoustic continua with which we are here concerned. Although there are no data yet available to show that the inflections in the discrimination function are displaced to correspond with the different positions of the phoneme boundaries, the mere fact that the boundaries are differently located is, in itself, presumptive evidence that the highs and lows of the discrimination function are not innately given.

A learning interpretation is also favoured by the fact that the discriminations among synthetic /b,d,g/, /d,t/, and /sl,spl/ were so largely controlled and limited by the phoneme labels. As was pointed out above, this relatively close correspondence between differential sensitivity and absolute identification is in striking contrast to the usual psychophysical result. One may suspect that it has come about because the original or raw discriminations have been radically altered by long experience.

The experiment by Griffith (1958) on /b,d,g/, which we referred to earlier, has provided additional relevant evidence. Using essentially the same second-formant transitions employed by Liberman et al. (1957), he added one or another of two constant third-formant transitions which had the effect of changing the positions of the phoneme boundaries. The result was that the peaks and valleys of the discrimination functions shifted accordingly. Though not critical, this evidence strongly supports a learning interpretation.

The experiment with /d,t/ that was referred to earlier was also of a type designed to find out whether the observed peak in discrimination is a result of learning, and, if so, whether it is a case of acquired distinctiveness, acquired similarity, or both. The point of this kind of experiment is to measure the discriminability of an acoustic variable which cues a phonemic distinction, and then to measure the discriminability of essentially the same variable in a non-speech context. For /d,t/ the acoustic variable was the time of onset of the first formant relative to the second and third. It was found, as has already been pointed out, that discrimination of this variable was better across the phoneme boundary than within the phoneme category. To produce appropriate non-speech controls the experimenters simply inverted the speech patterns on the frequency scale, thus producing sounds which could not be perceived as speech while yet preserving quite exactly the acoustic variations that had, in the speech stimuli, cued the perceived linguistic distinction. In the discrimination of the control stimuli no peak in discrimination was found, either in the region corresponding to the location of the phoneme boundary or, indeed, in any other part of the stimulus continuum. This would indicate that the discrimination peak found with speech stimuli is to attributed to learning. It was apparent, further, that the discriminability of the non-speech controls was, at all points, below that of the speech. From this one would conclude that the learning effect consisted entirely of acquired distinctiveness.

The inverted patterns were not a perfect control. Nor was it possible that they could have been, since the ideal condition would have required that the controls be identical with the speech stimuli and yet not be perceived as speech. The control stimuli that were used in the experiment on /d,t/ had the salient shortcoming that the frequency of the formant whose time of onset varied was below the other two formant in the speech stimuli and above them in the controls. Since masking effects are greater from low frequencies to high, it is possible that the variations in onset were to some extent masked out in the control.

The specific purpose of the present experiments is to obtain data from an experiment analogous to the one just described, but with a more appropriate control. The linguistic distinction to be investigated is that between /b/ and /p/ in intervocalic position, specifically in the words *rabid* and *rapid*. In studying the perception of this distinction Lisker (1957, in preparation) has found that a sufficient cue—not the most important one, perhaps, but one that is nonetheless adequate—is the duration of the silent interval between the first and second syllables. When that interval is relatively short the listener hears *rabid*; increasing the interval causes the perception to change to *rapid*. The discriminability of such patterns, differing only in duration of the intervocalic silent interval, can, of course, be measured and then compared with the discriminability of the same durations of silence enclosed between two bursts of noise. These latter stimuli are particularly appropriate as non-speech controls, since they can be identical with the speech sounds, not only in the values of the stimulus variables (i.e., the duration of the silent interval), but also in regard to certain important constant aspects of the stimuli, such as the durations and amplitude envelopes of the sounds that bound the silent intervals. Comparing the discriminability of these speech and non-speech stimuli should help greatly to determine whether the discrimination of the speech sounds reflects the effects of learning, and, if so, to discover which direction the learning has taken.

Procedure

One set of stimuli was generated from a hand-painted spectrogram like that shown in figure 11.1. When converted to sound by the Pattern Playback, this spectrogram

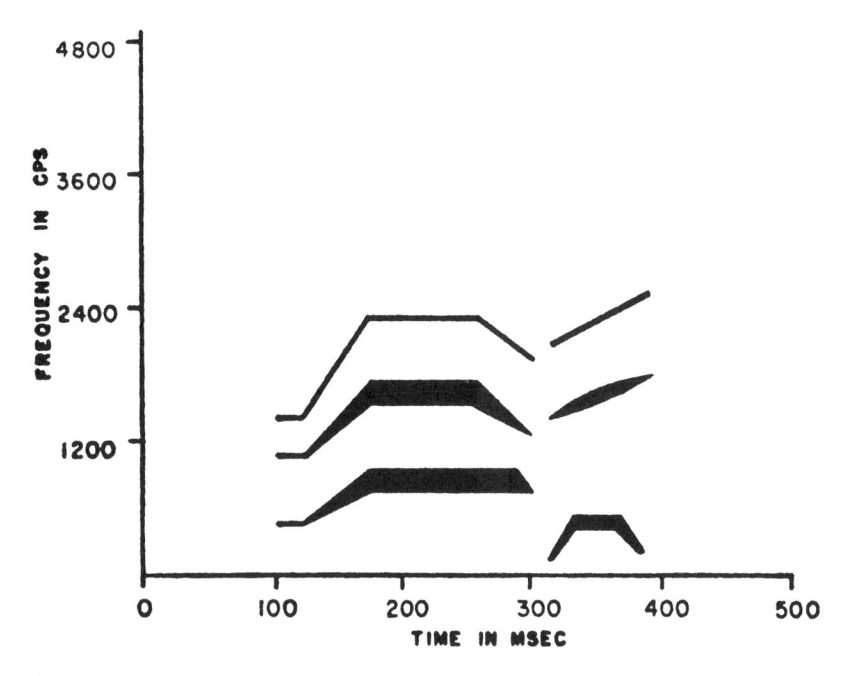

Figure 11.1
Hand-painted spectrogram from which the stimuli of the experiment were produced.

produces a reasonable approximation of the word *rabid*. From Lisker's research (in preparation), we know that if the interval of silence between first and second syllables is made longer than that shown, the listener will hear *rapid*. To vary duration of the silent interval and thus produce a series of sounds which would be perceived as *rabid* at one end and as *rapid* at the other, we made numerous magnetic tape recordings of the sound produced from the spectrogram shown in the figure, cut the magnetic tape in each case so as to separate the two syllables, and then inserted appropriate lengths of blank tape. In this way we created a series of 12 stimuli in which the silent interval varied between 20 and 130 msec. in steps of 10 msec. For convenience, we will refer to this set of sounds as the "speech stimuli" and designate each member of the set by the duration of the silent interval. Thus, Speech Stimulus 40 is that pattern which has 40 msec. of silent interval between the first and second syllables.

Our own listening convinced us that these particular stimuli did, indeed, sound like *rabid* or *rapid*, and that the shift from the one to the other occurred in the vicinity of 70 msec. Not unexpectedly, it appeared further that the longest silent intervals produced stimuli that would surely sound odd and unrealistic to speakers of English. We nevertheless included these extreme durations because we wanted to make certain that complete psychophysical functions would be obtained with the possibly less discriminable control stimuli to be described below.

It should be noted here that it is possible to begin with a recording of *rapid* as spoken by a human being and then, by reducing the duration of the interval between syllables, to convert it to *rabid*. The conversion is not wholly convincing, however, because there are several other cues to voicing besides the duration of the silent interval, and these are not changed as the interval is lengthened or shortened. Synthetic speech has the advantage here that it is possible to neutralize all the cues except the duration of the silent interval, and thus to produce a more satisfactory set of stimuli.

It was indicated in the introduction that we wanted as control stimuli a set of sounds as similar as possible to the speech series, and yet not perceivable as speech. To obtain such controls we used the speech stimuli to modulate noise signals and thus produce patterns consisting of noise-silent interval-noise in which the durations and rates of turn-on and turn-off would be the same as in the speech stimuli. The equipment and procedure for producing the control stimuli were as follow:[3]

The original speech stimuli were modulated by a 10 kc. carrier in a balanced modulator. The modulated signal was half-wave rectified, put through a low-pass filter (150 cps. cut-off), and this envelope waveform was then used to modulate a band-limited white noise (d.c. to 1500 cps.) in another balanced modulator. The circuit parameters were adjusted to give the possible match to the envelopes of the original set of speech stimuli.

The extent to which we succeeded in matching speech and control stimuli was measured in two ways. First, we made a detailed visual comparison of the oscillograms of several pairs of stimuli. The envelopes of the speech and control stimuli were found to be very similar. As a second check, we made spectrograms on a Kay Sonograph of 36 pairs of speech and control stimuli and measured the duration of each silent interval. The averages for the two kinds of stimuli proved to be almost exactly the same. The variability of the control stimuli was somewhat greater, as we might expect, but the difference was not significant by an F test.

Subjects

All subjects in the experiment were undergraduate or graduate students at the University of Connecticut. They were paid volunteers with no special training in phonetics, and they were naive with respect to the purposes of the experiment.

There were 12 subjects in all, chosen from a group of 31 on the basis of a pre-test. The purpose of the selection was to insure that all subjects ultimately serving in the experiment would have a sharp and clear phoneme boundary.[4] In the pre-test, the group of 31 subjects listened to the stimuli in various orders (approximately 28 presentations per stimulus) under instructions to identify each stimulus as *rabid* or *rapid*. On the basis of the data so obtained, we selected for service in the experiment the 12 subjects who had the sharpest phoneme boundaries. The results from this pre-test session were not otherwise used, and the data are not presented in the Results section. It should be noted, however, that all of the original group of 31 did reasonably well—so much so that the difference between the selected and rejected groups was very small.

Stimulus Presentation

As in the previous experiments in this series, the discriminability of both speech and control stimuli was measured by an ABX procedure—that is, the stimuli were presented in groups of three, and subjects were asked to determine, by whatever cues they could perceive, whether the third stimulus, X, was identical with the first stimulus, A, or the second stimulus, B. (In fact, X was always identical either with A or with B.) The measure of the discriminability of any pair of stimuli was, then, the proportion of the presentations on which the subject matched X correctly to A or B.

The A and B stimuli to be discriminated differed in silent interval by 20, 30, 40, 50, 60, 70, 80 and 90 msec. For example, Stimulus 20 was compared with Stimulus 40, 50, 60, 70, 80, 90, 100 and 110; Stimulus 30 was paired with Stimulus 50, 60, 70, 80, 90, 100, 110 and 120. The 10 stimulus comparisons in which pairs differ by 20 msec. will be called the 2-step series, the series of 9 pairs that differed by 30 msec. will be called the 3-step series, and so forth.

The total number of stimulus pairs is 52. Each stimulus comparison appeared in ABX triads of four forms—ABA, ABB, BAA, and BAB. For example, the four two-step comparisons for the 40-msec. stimulus were 40-60-40, 40-60-60, 60-40-40, and 60-40-60.

These triads were spliced together so as to form four test orders. Each stimulus comparison occurred once in each test order in one of its four forms. One second separated the members of a triad, while the triads were separated by four seconds. After the first four orders had been completed, a second set of four was made by shuffling each of the original orders. There were, then, eight test orders for the measurement of speech discrimination.

The non-speech stimuli were made into eight tapes in exactly the same fashion. That is, for each speech tape we made a control tape with a non-speech stimulus substituted for the speech having the same time separation between syllables.

The selected subjects listened to each of the eight speech and control tapes five times under discrimination instructions. Since a given stimulus comparisons is presented once on each tape, the measure of discriminability at any point on each stimulus continuum is based on 40 determinations for each subject.

The purposes of the experiment required a comparison of the speech stimuli within and across the *rabid-rapid* phoneme boundary. Accordingly, we needed an accurate determination of the location of the boundary for the 12 subjects of the experiment. To this end, the speech tapes were presented to each subject a total of 32 times with instructions to label each stimulus as *rapid* or *rabid*.

The whole experimental design, then, was set up so that each subject would perform three tasks: speech discrimination, noise discrimination, and phoneme labelling. A schedule was arranged for each subject such that the three tasks were distributed through all experimental sessions. Working in test sessions of about 20 minutes, each subject took about four months to complete the experiment.

Results

Phoneme Identification and the Location of the Boundary
Figure 11.2 shows how the listeners assigned the phoneme labels /b/ or /p/ to the various stimuli. These functions which represent the pooled responses of all subjects, indicate that the phoneme identifications were made with fair consistency, and that the boundary between /b/ and /p/ lay at about 70 msec. of silent interval. It is also apparent from these data that the phoneme boundary is reasonably sharp.

Discrimination of the Speech Stimuli
The solid lines of figure 11.3 connect points which represent the percent correct discrimination of various pairs of speech stimuli at all values of the stimulus variable. As in the labelling functions of figure 11.2, the data from all subjects have been pooled.

172 Chapter 11

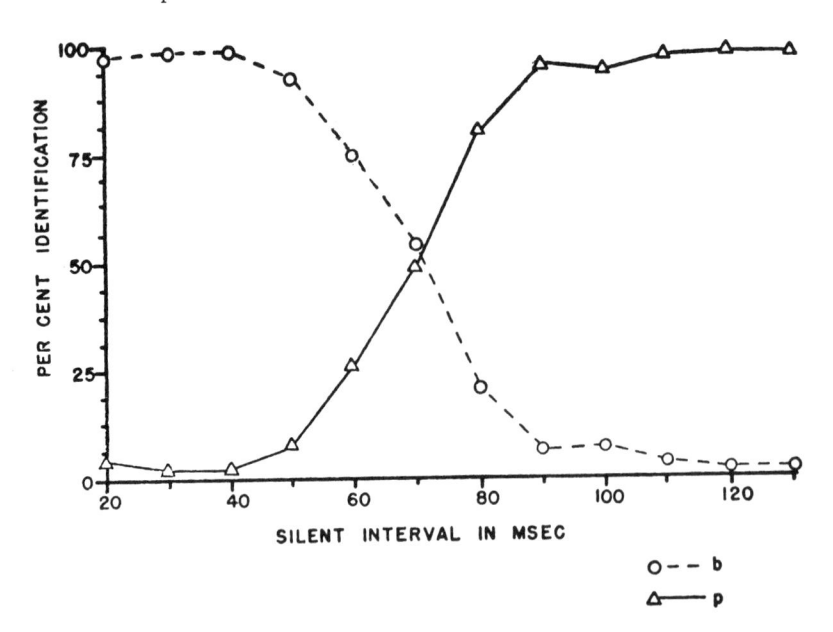

Figure 11.2
Identification of the synthetic speech stimuli as /b/ or /p/, plotted against the duration of the silent interval between first and second syllables. The data are from the pooled responses of all 12 subjects.

For greater ease in reading the data, the graphs have been separated according to the amount of difference in silent interval by which the two stimuli are separated. Thus, in the first graph at the upper left, labelled "2 step," the stimuli which were paired for discrimination (in ABX triads) always differed by 20 msec. (two steps on the stimulus, scale) of silent interval. The first point on this graph indicates, then, that the subjects discriminated with 53 percent accuracy when the stimuli in the ABX triads had 20 and 40 msec. of silent interval. The next point shows that discrimination rose to 61 percent for the stimuli with 30 and 50 msec. of silent interval. Data points on the graphs for the other stimulus comparisons, in which the differences between the stimuli ranged from three to nine steps, are to be read in similar fashion.

It is apparent, especially in the 2-, 3-, and 4-step graphs, that there are two peaks in the discrimination functions, a relatively large one near the centre of the stimulus continuum and a somewhat smaller one farther to the right. For the moment we will confine our attention to the larger peak.

Reference back to the phoneme identification data in figure 11.2 reminds us that the phoneme boundary is in the vicinity of 70 msec. and we see in figure 11.3 that the larger peak in the discrimination function occurs in the same region. This is to say, of course, that discrimination is better across the phoneme boundary than in the middle of the phoneme category. But instead of developing this comparison stimulus by stimulus, we will turn to a simple model developed in an earlier study (Liberman et al. 1957) of the same problem, and evaluate the data with regard to the extent to which they fit that model.

Make the extreme assumption that the listeners can only hear these stimuli phonemically—that is, as /b/ or /p/—and can detect no other differences among them. Using the phoneme labelling data as a basis, one then predicts the accuracy with

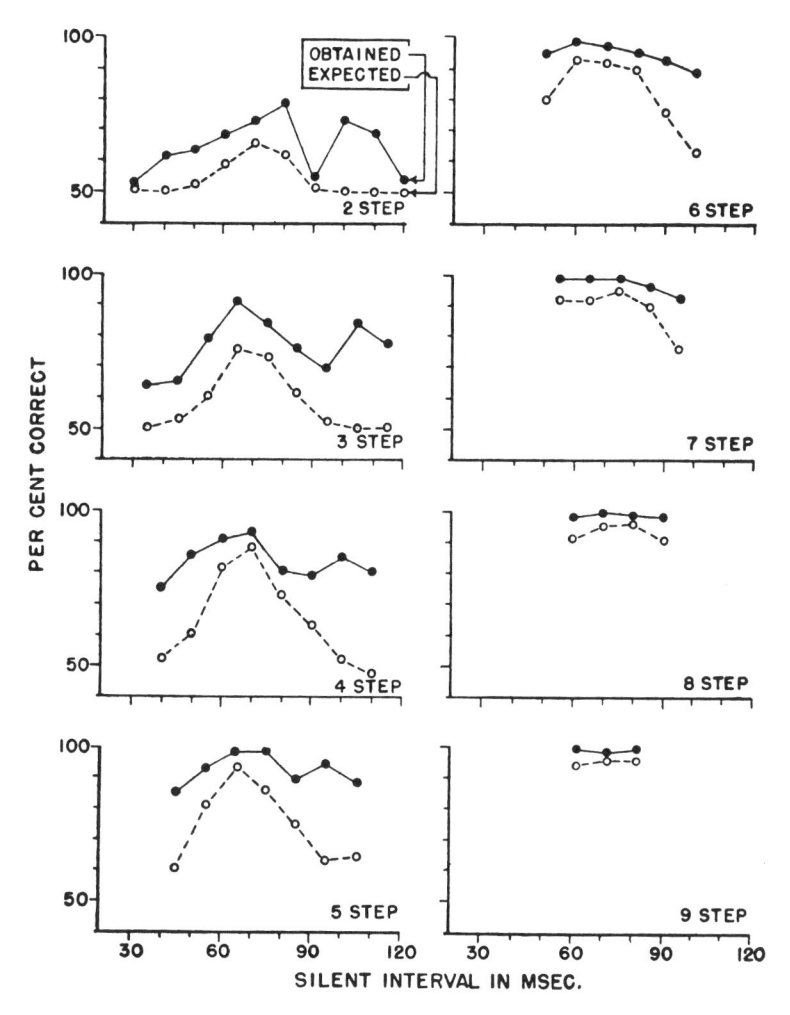

Figure 11.3
Obtained and expected discrimination for the 1- through 9-step differences among the synthetic speech stimuli. The data are from the pooled responses of all 12 subjects.

which the listener can be expected to discriminate all stimulus pairs. Thus, if the subject had always identified two stimuli as being members of the same phoneme class, he would be expected to discriminate the stimuli at a chance level. To the extent that he identifies two stimuli as belonging in different phoneme classes, he would, to precisely that extent, correctly discriminate them. In general, this assumption will predict peaks in the discrimination function wherever there are abrupt changes or inflections in the phoneme labelling curves, the height of the peak being a function of the abruptness and extent of the shift in phoneme labels. A more detailed description of the model and the derivation of the technique for predicting the discrimination functions are to be found in the earlier article (Liberman et al. 1957).[5]

The discrimination functions that are predicted from the assumption of categorical perception are shown in figure 11.3 as the dashed lines. A comparison of these "expected" curves with the discrimination data that were actually obtained, and described earlier, leads to several conclusions. First, it will be noted that the left-hand portions of the two curves are reasonably similar in shape. This means that the variations in discriminability follow the change in phoneme labels. More specifically, it means that a discrimination peak does, indeed, occur at the phoneme boundary. The second conclusion is that the obtained functions tend in general to lie above the expected functions. To that extent the listeners are able in discriminating these stimuli to extract some information in addition to that which is revealed by the way in which they label the stimuli as phonemes.

The Second Peak and a Third Category
Attention has been called to the fact that the obtained discrimination functions show a second peak at values of the stimulus variable greater than those at which the boundary between /b/ and /p/ is located. On the assumption that this might imply a third category, we listened again to the stimuli and found that we had, indeed, carried the values of the silent interval to such extreme lengths as to have created, perhaps, an additional class of sounds.[6] This was a strange and unnatural /p/ to American ears, but we thought that it might nevertheless be heard and articulated by our listeners almost as if it were a different speech entity. We therefore recalled as many of the subjects as were still available (the number was seven), discussed the stimuli with them, and discovered that they, too, thought that some of them belonged in a separate class. To obtain more information about this third category we presented the stimuli (in random order, as before) to these subjects with instructions to identify each one as /b/, /p/, or */p/, the last named being the designation we chose for what we, and our subjects, had heard as the unnatural /p/. That the third category, */p/, did exist for these subjects is indicated by the graphs of figure 11.4. A comparison of these graphs with those that describe the results of the two-category judgments (figure 11.2) indicates that the distinction between */p/ and /p/ is not so clear as that between /b/ and /p/ in the original judgments (for which the subjects were allowed only the /b/ and /p/ categories). This is to be inferred from the fact that the curves representing the /p/ and */p/ judgments (in figure 11.4) do not raise to 100 percent as the /b/ curve does, and as both the /b/ and /p/ curves do in the two-category situation (figure 11.2). Nevertheless, the labelling data show that a */p/ category does exist, and they provide a basis for predicting a new set of discrimination results from the assumption of categorical perception. These predictions are shown as the dotted lines in figure 11.5, together with the discrimination data that were actually obtained with the seven subjects who made the three-category judgments. There is a second peak in the expected discrimination function corresponding to the boundary between the second and third categories of figure 11.4. Moreover, this second peak fits moderately well the second peak in the obtained discrimination functions. Clearly, the expected and obtained functions now agree somewhat better than before, but there remains a constant difference between the functions in the direction of better discrimination than is to be expected on the extreme assumption of categorical perception. We will not try to specify the magnitude of the discrepancy in terms of some single meaningful quantity, because we are not prepared at this stage to decide which of several possible measures is best. We will only say that the discrepancy is somewhat greater here than it was in the studies of /b,d,g/, /d,t/, and /sl,spl/, where the perception was more nearly categorical; also, that it is less than in the vowels and

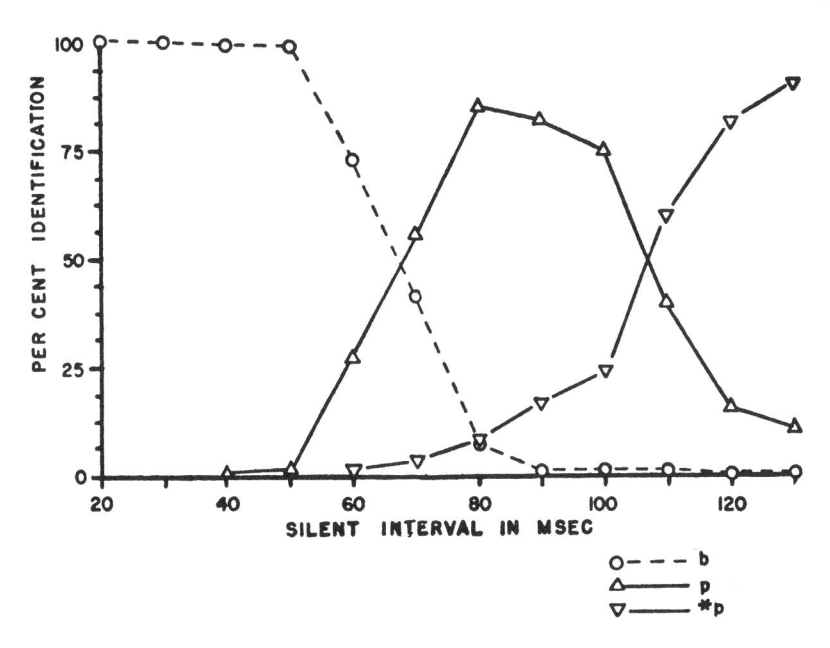

Figure 11.4
Identification of the synthetic speech stimuli as /b/, /p/, or */p/, plotted against the duration of the silent interval. The data were obtained from the pooled responses of the seven subjects who served in this part of the experiment.

prosodic features, where perception was essentially non-categorical, i.e., continuously changing with progressive changes in the stimulus.

In terms of the theory outlined in the introduction, perception of speech becomes linked to the feedback from the articulatory movements the listener makes in speaking. We should expect, then, that perception would be completely categorical (i.e., that the discrimination functions would show a peak at the phoneme boundary and be perfectly predictable from the phoneme labelling data) if the listener makes exactly the same articulatory response to the various stimuli to which he attaches the same phoneme label, and very different articulatory responses to sounds he calls by different phoneme names. At the other extreme, speech perception would be expected to be perfectly continuous (i.e., the discrimination function would show no peak at the phoneme boundary and might lie at a level far higher than that which is predicted from the phoneme labelling data) if the listener's mimicking articulations change in linear fashion with variations in the acoustic stimuli, both within and across phoneme boundaries.

One might expect something like the results we found in this experiment—perception which is almost categorical, but not quite—if it be the case that the articulatory response changes most rapidly at the phoneme boundary, but that there is, nevertheless, some small variation within the phoneme class. In an attempt to find out whether or not this was so, we had several of the listeners try to mimic the various stimuli, and then undertook to measure the duration of the silent interval between the two syllables. It proved to be difficult to obtain highly reliable measurements, chiefly because the subjects produced variations in other acoustic features, such as the first-formant transition and presence or absence of voicing, which are more important

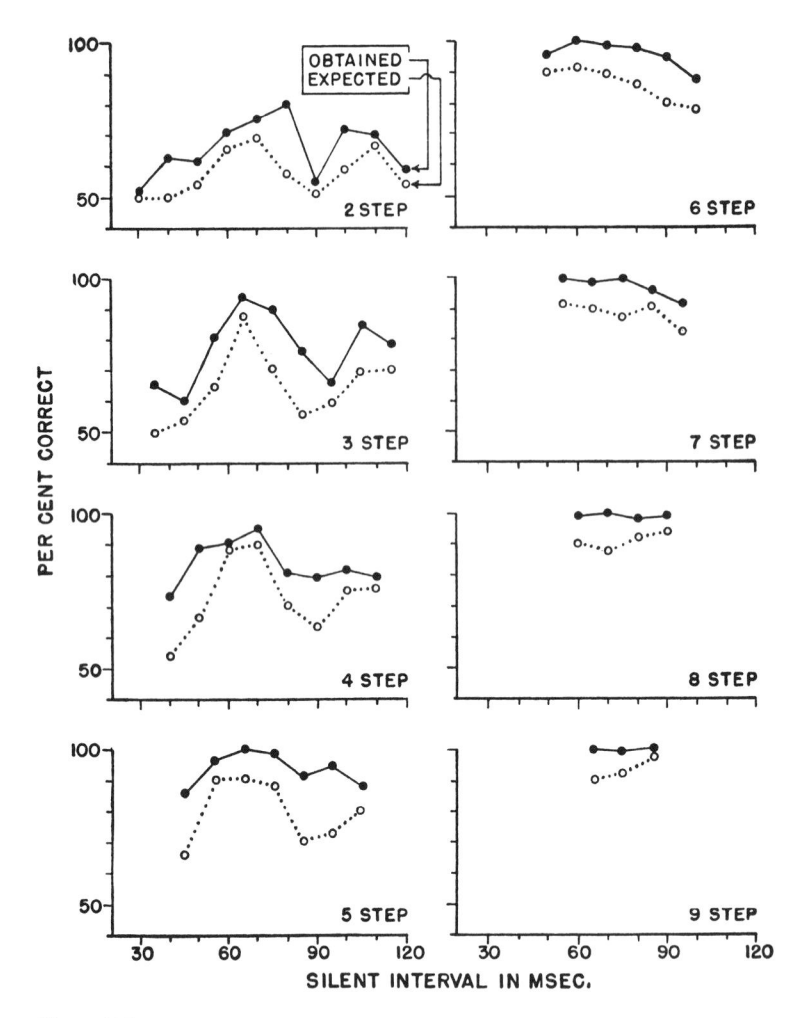

Figure 11.5
Expected discrimination functions corrected to take account of the subject's identification of the third category, */p/, together with the obtained discrimination functions. The data are from the pooled responses of the same seven subjects whose three-category identification functions are shown in figure 11.4.

than duration of silent interval as such, and which tended to obscure it. When, in the course of this work, it became apparent that we would be able to get far more precise mimicry data in the study of other phonemic distinctions,[7] we abandoned the attempt to measure the mimicry of *rabid-rapid*.

In some respects, then, this experiment yielded less than we might have wished. We should remember, however, that we undertook it because, being interested in the discrimination peaks which sometimes occur at phoneme boundaries, we wanted a fair comparison between the discrimination of an acoustic variable when it cues a phonemic contrast and when, in a non-speech context, it does not. Fortunately for that purpose, the discrimination of the speech stimuli does have a peak (or actually two) sufficiently high to make the comparison with the non-speech control an interesting one.

Effect of Learning on Speech Perception 177

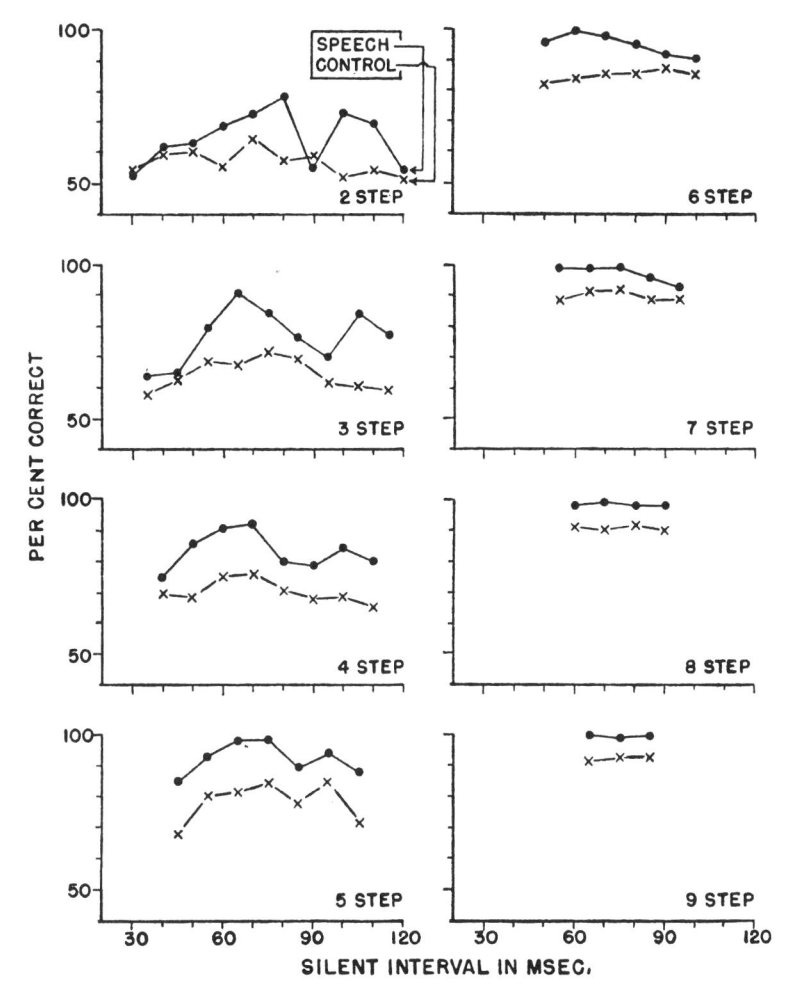

Figure 11.6
Discrimination functions for the 1- throught 9-step differences among the non-speech control stimuli. The obtained speech discrimination functions previously shown in figure 11.3 are reproduced here to facilitate comparison. For both sets of functions, the data are from the pooled responses of all 12 subjects.

Discrimination of Noise Control
In the stimuli used as controls, bursts of noise served to bound silent intervals that duplicated those of the speech stimuli. It is also relevant to recall that the noise bursts were matched with the speech syllables in regard to such constant features as amplitude envelope and duration.

The discrimination results obtained with the noise control are shown in figure 11.6. For comparison the results obtained with the speech stimuli and previously shown in figure 11.3 are also presented.

One sees immediately that the discrimination peaks of the speech stimuli are much higher and sharper than any peaks which appear in the control data. More generally it is clear that the discriminability of the speech sounds is considerably greater than the control at most points. At a few values of the stimulus variable the two are equal, or very nearly so. Out of a total of 52 points at which the two sets of curves can be compared there is only one at which the speech discrimination dips below the control. In this one case the difference is small, and probably not at all reliable. If the noise stimuli are truly an appropriate control—that is, if they fairly represent the discriminability of the speech stimuli prior to linguistic training—we may conclude that the results obtained with the speech stimuli reflect the effects of a very considerable amount of learning. It is clear, further, that the entire learning effect consists of a sharpening of discrimination in the vicinity of the phoneme boundary. There is no indication that discrimination of the speech has been reduced (below the control) within the phoneme category. In terms of the psychological processes discussed in the introduction, we should say that there is here a very considerable amount of acquired distinctiveness, but no acquired similarity.

Reference has been made to the earlier study of /d,t/, in which discrimination of variations in a cue for a phonemic distinction were compared with discrimination of the same variable in a non-speech context. It was pointed out that the acoustic variations might have been masked in the control stimuli, and the conclusion drawn from a comparison of speech and control discrimination was, therefore, thought to be open to question. We should note that the results of the present experiment, with its more adequate controls, agree with those of the earlier study in that there was evidence of a large amount of acquired distinctiveness and no acquired similarity.

We ought, perhaps, to remark on the fact that this experiment and the earlier one on /d,t/ differ somewhat in regard to the finding of no reduction in discrimination within the phoneme category (acquired similarity). In the earlier experiment the discriminability of the nonspeech stimuli was very poor, lying generally at or just slightly above chance. There was, then, no room for a process like acquired similarity to show itself, for no amount of training could possibly have reduced discrimination much further. In the present experiment the discrimination of the noise control stimuli rose to higher levels. To determine just how much room this provided for acquired similarity, we must compare the three discrimination functions previously presented: the obtained discrimination of the speech sounds, the expected discrimination of the speech sounds, and the obtained discrimination of the noise control. For that purpose the three functions are shown together in figure 11.7. (We here use the data for the seven subjects who made the three-category judgments, because these data most adequately depict the relationship between discrimination and phoneme labelling.)

Within the /b/ category—that is, on the left-hand side of the graphs—we see in the 2-, 3-, and 4-step data that the discriminability of the noise does lie somewhat above the predicted discriminability of the speech. This means that the original discriminability of speech may be presumed to have been greater than it needed to be to meet the requirements of the linguistic situation. It also means that if the listener makes the same articulatory response to these stimuli, we should expect, according to theory, that the discrimination of the speech would have been reduced below the noise control, down to the predicted level. We see that this has not happened, and we conclude that we have here a case in which acquired similarity did not occur, though there was room for it. Beyond the four-step comparisons practically all stimulus pairs fall across a phoneme boundary; discrimination is therefore predicted in general to be at fairly high levels, well above the noise control at all points, and we cannot make the kind of test we are here considering. Between the second and third categories (/p/ and */p/) the noise discrimination again lies above the expected values, and we find,

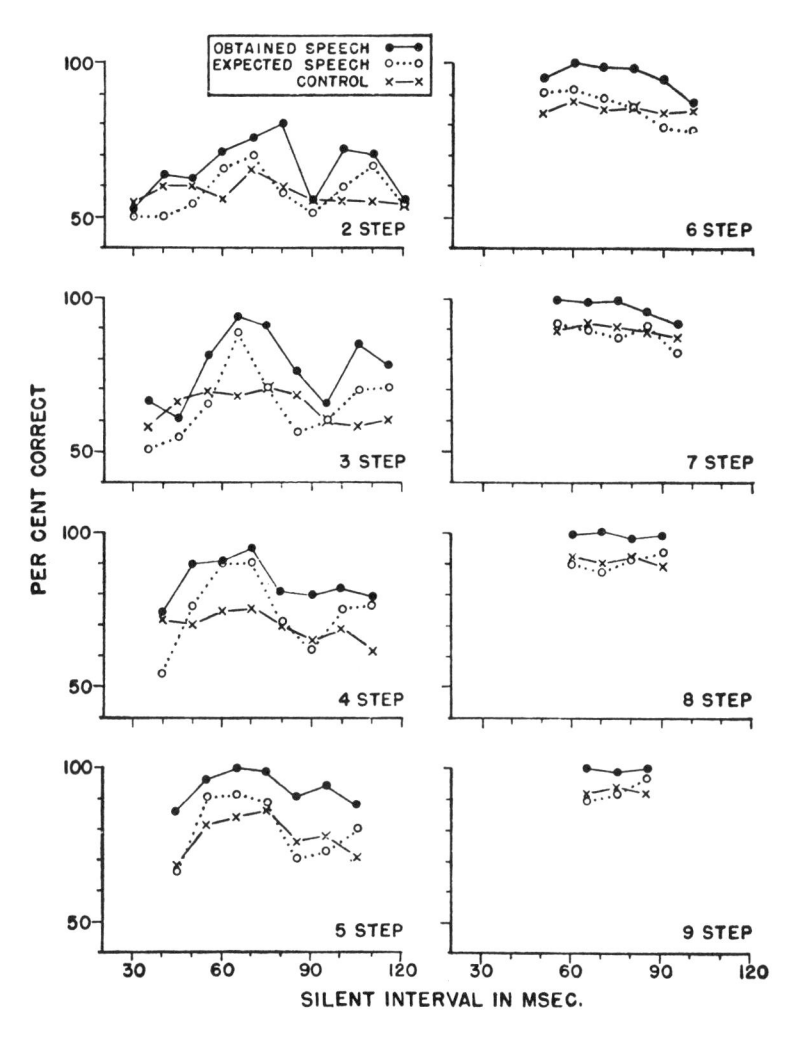

Figure 11.7
Obtained and expected speech discrimination functions, together with the discrimination functions for the non-speech control stimuli. The obtained and expected speech functions are the same as those shown in figure 11.5. All data are from the pooled responses of the seven subjects who provided the results shown in that figure.

as we did in the similar situation with the /b/ category, that the obtained speech discrimination has not been reduced to the expected level.

While the relevant data are not very clear or compelling, there is a certain amount of evidence that acquired similarity might have occurred but did not. Whether it *should* have occurred, according to theory, is a separate question, and one that is not readily answered because the critical mimicry data are missing. To see why these data are critical, let us imagine that reliable mimicry measurements have been obtained, and then consider the implications of different kinds of results. Suppose first, that the subjects are found to make the same articulatory response in mimicking the sounds within the phoneme category; the theory as it now stands demands that they be unable to discriminate these sounds. Given this outcome of the mimicry experiment, and given the fact that acquired similarity did not occur though there was room for it, we should have to modify the theory. It would appear then that while the articulatory responses become involved in the perception of speech, the listener still has some choice remaining to him: if falling back on the feedback from articulation serves to sharpen discrimination (as it apparently does at the phoneme boundary), the listener takes advantage of this possibility and discriminates better than he would otherwise have done; if the articulatory feedback has the effect of dulling discrimination, the listener effectively ignores it, responds directly to the acoustic stimulus, and suffers no loss in acuity. This would say, in general, that the acquired similarity paradigm describes an event which does not occur, at least not in speech perception; we should assume then that while we may, on occasion, find it necessary to disregard clearly perceptible differences, and for very practical reasons to call distinguishable stimuli by the same phoneme name, we do not as a consequence really lose our ability to discriminate.

The alternative result of the mimicry experiment would be to show that the listener can and does mimic some of the stimulus changes within the phoneme category—that while the articulatory response changes most rapidly at the phoneme boundary, there is nevertheless some variation in mimicking sounds the subject calls by the same phoneme name. In that case, we should not expect discrimination within the phoneme class to be reduced to chance, and, depending on the particular nature of the mimicry results, the theory in its present form might be rather precisely confirmed. We hope that more light will be shed on this question in research on other phoneme distinctions where mimicry can be more easily measured.

It will be recalled that the noise control stimuli were produced in such a way as to make their amplitude envelopes and durations approximate the speech signals as closely as possible. This is surely the most appropriate way to obtain control signals for use with the speech stimuli of this experiment, but it may raise a question about the extent to which the results represent what would be obtained with the simpler and more regular stimuli that are usual in psychophysical studies. To answer this question, we prepared a new set of control signals which had intervals of silence like those of the original controls, bounded by segments of noise which differed from the original in having abrupt onsets and offsets (produced by cutting the magnetic tape at a 90-degree angle) and in being of equal duration (300 msec.). On testing the discriminability of these stimuli with the same subjects who had served in the earlier parts of the experiment, we obtained results very similar to those found with the original set of controls.

As a further test of generality we undertook to obtain some indication of the effect, if any, of the particular psychophysical procedure (ABX) that had been used. For that purpose we measured the discriminability of the new noise stimuli by the ABX method and also by an adaptation of the forced-choice temporal interval method developed by Blackwell (1952) for measuring visual thresholds. In the latter procedure, as in ABX, the stimuli are presented in triads composed of two stimuli which are identical and one which is different, but the "different" stimulus can appear in any of the three positions (first, second, or third) of the triad, and the subject's task is to tell where, i.e., in which position, it is. When the data obtained by the two methods were adjusted to take account of the different levels of chance performance (50% in ABX and $33\frac{1}{3}$% in the new method), the levels of discrimination proved to be the same.

We feel reasonably certain that the original noise stimuli are appropriate controls. The two pulses of noise were carefully matched in envelope and duration with the two syllables of the speech stimuli, and the interval of silence, which was in both speech and control the variable part of the pattern, is out in the open, as it were, where it is not likely to be masked or otherwise interfered with. Moreover, as we have seen, the data obtained with these matched controls would appear to have some generality, since very similar results were found with more standard patterns and, indeed, with a different psychophysical method. We will assume, then, that the discrimination functions obtained with the noise controls approximate the discrimination of the speech patterns as they would have been without linguistic experience. The fact that the peaks of the speech discrimination functions rose above the control may then be taken to indicate a learned increase in discrimination across phoneme boundaries. The speech functions nowhere fell below the control, from which we conclude that there was, for whatever reason, no loss in discrimination within phoneme categories.

Notes

This research was supported by the Operational Applications Office of the Air Force Electronic Systems Division in connection with Contract AF 19(604)-2285.

1. These phonemes were presented in contexts as follows: /b,d,g/ were in absolute initial position before /a/; /d,t/ were in absolute initial position before /o/; /sl, spl/ were in the words slit and split.
2. In the case of /b,d,g/ the fit was better in the Griffith (1958) study than in the experiment by Liberman et al. (1957). This was attributed to the fact that Griffith's synthetic speech stimuli were more realistic, and to certain procedural improvements he was able to make.
3. We gratefully acknowledge our debt to Dr. Carl Brandauer for devising the method of generating the control stimuli.
4. Since the experiment was intended to yield information on the relative discriminability of sounds within and across phoneme boundaries, only subjects with sharp boundaries were suitable.
5. In the earlier experiment (Liberman et al. 1957) the labelling data were obtained by presenting the stimuli one at a time; in the present experiment the stimuli were presented for labelling intriads (see Procedure). Although the labelling functions were obtained by these different procedures, the calculation of the predicted discrimination values were made from the labelling data in exactly the same way in the two studies.
6. As was pointed out under Procedure, we were aware when we produced these speech sounds that curious effect could be heard at durations of silent interval greater than 100 msec., but we had decided to include these extreme stimulus values in order to be certain of obtaining complete psychophysical functions with the control stimuli.
7. One such study had been completed since this paper was written and has been published as an abstract, see Harris, Bastian, and Liberman (1961). It is now being prepared for regular publication.

References

Abramson, A. S. (1961). Identification and discrimination of phonemic tones. *J. acoust. Soc. Amer.*, 33, 842 (Abstract).

Abramson, A. S., Bastian, J. (in preparation). Identification and discrimination of phonemic vowel duration.

Bastian, J., Delattre, P., and Liberman, A. M. (1959). Silent interval as a cue for the distinction between stops and semivowels in medial position. *J. acoust. Soc. Amer.*, 31, 1568 (Abstract).

Bastian, J., Eimas, P. D., and Liberman, A. M. (1961). Identification and discrimination of a phonemic contrast induced by silent interval. *J. acoust. Soc. Amer.*, 33, 842 (Abstract).

Blackwell, H. R. (1952). Studies of psychophysical methods for measuring visual thresholds. *J. opt. Soc. Amer.*, 42, 606.

Chapanis, A. S., and Halsey, R. M. (1956). Absolute judgments of spectrum colours. *J. Psychol.*, 42, 99.

Cooper, F. S., Delattre, P. C., Liberman, A. M., Borst, J. M., and Gerstman, L. J. (1952). Some experiments on the perception of synthetic speech sounds. *J. acoust. Soc. Amer.*, 24, 597.

Cooper, F. S., Liberman, A. M., Harris, K. S., and Grubb, P. M. (1961). Some input-output relations observed in experiments on the perception of speech. *Proceedings of the Second International Congress on Cybernetics*. Namur, Belgium.

Delattre, P. C., Liberman, A. M., and Cooper, F. S. (1955). Acoustic loci and transitional cues for consonants. *J. acoust. Soc. Amer.*, 27, 769.

Fry, D. B., Abramson, A. S., Eimas, P. D., and Liberman, A. M. (in preparation). The identification and discrimination of synthetic vowels.

Garner, W. R. (1953). An informational analysis of absolute judgments of loudness. *J. exp. Psychol.*, 46, 373.

Griffith, B. C. (1958). A study of the relation between phoneme labelling and discriminability in the perception of synthetic stop consonants. *Unpublished Ph.D. dissertation, University of Connecticut*.

Harris, K. S., Bastian, J., and Liberman, A. M. (1961). Mimicry and the perception of a phonemic contrast induced by silent interval: electromyographic and acoustic measures. *J. acoust. Soc. Amer.*, 33, 842 (Abstract).

Harris, K. S., Hoffman, H. S., Liberman, A. M., Delattre, P. C., and Cooper, F. S. (1958). Effect of third-formant transitions on the perception of the voiced stop consonants. *J. acoust. Soc. Amer.*, 30, 122.

Ladefoged, P. (1959). The perception of speech. In *Mechanisation of Thought Processes*, Vol. I (London).

Liberman, A. M. (1957). Some results of research on speech perception. *J. acoust. Soc. Amer.*, 29, 117.

Liberman, A. M., Delattre, P. C., and Cooper, F. S. (1952). The role of selected stimulus variables in the perception of the unvoiced stop consonants. *Amer. J. Psychol.*, 65, 497.

Liberman, A. M., Delattre, P. C., and Cooper, F. S. (1958). Some cues for the distinction between voiced and voiceless stops in initial position. *Language and Speech*, 1, 153.

Liberman, A. M., Delattre, P. C., Cooper, F. S., and Gerstman, L. J. (1954). The role of consonant-vowel transitions in the perception of stop and nasal consonants. *Psychol. Monogr.*, 68, No. 8 (Whole No. 379).

Liberman, A. M., Harris, K. S., Hoffman, H. S., and Griffith, B. C. (1957). The discrimination of speech sounds within and across phoneme boundaries. *J. exp. Psychol.*, 54, 358.

Liberman, A. M., Harris, K. S., Kinney, J. A., and Lane, H. (1961). The discrimination of relative onset-time of the components of certain speech and non-speech patterns. *J. exp. Psychol.*, 61, 379.

Lisker, L. (1957). Closure duration and the inter-vocalic voiced-voiceless distinction in English. *Language*, 33, 42.

Lisker, L. (in preparation). On separating some acoustic cues to the voicing of intervocalic stops in English.

Miller, G. A. (1956). The magical number seven, plus or minus two: some limits on our capacity for processing information. *Psychol. Rev.* 63, 81.

Pollack, I. (1952). The information of elementary auditory displays. *J. acoust. Soc. Amer.*, 24, 745.

Pollack, I. (1953). The information of elementary auditory displays. II. *J. acoust. Soc. Amer.*, 25, 765.

PART IV
An Early Attempt to Put It All Together

Introduction to Part IV

Here is a summary of our results, together with my interpretations as of 1957. As an account of the results, the original article stands up quite well, I think, but the interpretations expose all the worst features of the Early Motor Theory and its associated behaviorist assumptions. (In that connection, I am especially embarrassed by the experiment I proposed at the very end of the article.) In addition, chapter 12 reflects throughout a preoccupation with perception so complete that all stimulus arrangements are taken to be accommodations to its needs, a view that still enjoys considerable currency in the speech-research community; the possibility that speech is as it is largely to suit the convenience of the vocal tract in meeting the rate requirement of phonological communication, which is what I now believe, is nowhere even hinted at.

Chapter 12
Some Results of Research on Speech Perception

I hope it is in keeping with the purpose of this conference for me to talk mostly about the work of my colleagues at the Haskins Laboratories. I hope, too, that it is appropriate not to be concerned with specific experiments and detailed results, but rather to speak in very general terms about some of our findings, and then to discuss a few interpretations that are currently much on our minds.

As some of your know, we of the Haskins group have been trying to learn something about the perception of speech, and to that end we have spent a rather large amount of our time searching for the acoustic cues on which that perception depends. We have, we think, been quite catholic in our choice and use of methods. In the main, however, we have relied on techniques which enable us to make controlled changes in various aspects of the acoustic pattern, and then to evaluate the effects of those changes on the sound as heard. For that rather general, and certainly not uncommon purpose, we have depended largely on the use of spectrographic displays as a basis for synthesizing and modifying the sounds of speech. The essential point of this synthesizing technique is that we paint our own spectrograms, using a highly simplified form which omits many of the constant accompaniments—I should like to say stigmata—of speech. It is very easy, then, to introduce a wide range of experimental changes in what we suspect are important parts of the spectrographic pattern. When we listen to these spectrograms—having first, of course, converted them to sound—we find out which of these changes are important, and which are not. The conversion from spectrogram to sound is accomplished by a machine, called a pattern playback, which has been described and demonstrated at previous M.I.T. speech conferences.[1,2]

This particular way of synthesizing speech has given us easy access to many of the significant parts of the acoustic pattern, and has proved in general to be remarkably convenient and flexible. On occasion, however, we have found it desirable to synthesize speech by other means. In our investigations of the fricatives,[3] for example, a synthesizer we call "Octopus"[4] proved to have certain advantages over the playback.

For some purposes we have used experimental techniques other than those of synthetic speech. Thus, like many other investigators, we have modified speech by cutting and rearranging sections of magnetic tape, or by putting speech through filters. And, of course, before beginning any experimental work we have always wanted to examine the complex sounds of speech to see what we might profitably experiment with. For that purpose we have found spectrograms indispensable, though we have even made oscillograms, and, in occasional desperate moments, studied them.

Originally published in *The Journal of the Acoustical Society of America* 29, 1 (January 1957): 117–123. Reprinted with permission.

By these means we have experimented with many aspects of the speech wave, and have succeeded, we think, in isolating some of the cues that carry the basic linguistic information. I will not attempt here to describe either the cues or their effects in detail. Much of this is to be found in papers that have already been published or that are about to be published, and we hope soon to undertake a comprehensive and detailed review of our findings. It will, however, be appropriate to the purposes of this paper to outline the types of acoustic cues—the acoustic stimulus dimensions, if you will—that we have so far found to be of some importance in the perception of the individual consonants of American English, and to offer a few examples of our results.

As a matter of convenience, I should like at the outset to divide the consonant cues into three classes, and to make this division according to where and how the sounds are produced. I am, of course, embarrassed to introduce a discussion of acoustic cues by classifying them on an articulatory basis. However, we find here, as we so often do, that it simplifies our data quite considerably to organize them by articulatory criteria. We certainly do not mean to imply by this that there are no acoustic differences among our classes, but only that it is hard to characterize these differences very simply in acoustic terms. For the purposes of this paper it would be footless to worry about this difficulty, so we will try, at least for now, simply to avoid the issue.

One class of consonant cues occurs in sounds that are produced at the consonant constriction. This class includes the frictions of the fricatives and affricates /f,θ,s,ʃ,tʃ,v,ð,z,ʒ,dʒ/ and the bursts of the stops /p,t,k,b,d,g/. It is a general characteristic of the constriction sounds that they are produced only during or just following the most nearly closed part of the consonant articulation. As the articulatory movement proceeds toward the more open position of the vowel, or, more generally, toward the next phone, the constriction sounds must quickly die away. Therefore, they would be expected to reflect little, if any, of the consonant movement, and in this respect the constriction sounds are to be contrasted with some other consonant cues that we will want to discuss shortly.

Among the constriction sounds we have found several types or dimensions of acoustic variation to be of importance for consonant perception. In one of our earliest experiments[5] we found that the frequency position of the burst enables listeners to distinguish among the voiceless stops /p,t,k/. More recently, it has been found that the frequency location of the friction noise, and in particular the lower frequency limit of this noise, is an overriding cue for distinguishing /s/ from /ʃ/, though this variable does not seem to contribute much to the perception of the other, less intense fricatives /f/ and /θ/.[6] In general it would appear that the frequencies of the constriction sounds provide the listener with significant information about the place of production of the stops and some of the fricatives.

Within this same group of constriction sounds, other dimensions of variation such as duration and the nature of the onset of the noise are proving to be of some importance, primarily as cues for various distinctions according to manner.[7] Even intensity appears to have some cue value in distinguishing /s,ʃ/ as a class from /f,θ/.[8] I say "even" intensity because we do not often find that intensity differences of any kind distinguish one consonant from another.

We should note, too, in any consideration of the constriction sounds as cues, that by their presence or absence they serve as important manner markers. Thus, a speech sound will not be heard as a member of the fricative class unless there is friction noise, or something that will pass for it: remove the friction from /ʃa/ and you will hear a perfectly satisfactory /ga/.

We come now to a second and very different class of consonant cues. These contrast with the constriction sounds in that the members of this second class result from, and can therefore provide information about, the movements of the articulators. It is characteristic of these sounds that they originate in the voice box, rather than at the point of consonant constriction, and that they must, therefore, travel through the entire vocal tract before issuing from the lips. Unlike the constriction sounds, then, these of the second class are affected by the articulatory movement that is made in going from the consonant to the next phone. Acoustically, they appear as the formant transitions, or frequency shifts, that we so commonly see in spectrograms. We know now that these transitions are not merely the incidental acoustic accompaniments of the movements that a speaker must make when he goes from "consonant" to "vowel." Rather, they are perceptual cues, and it is difficult to exaggerate their importance.

At an earlier Speech Conference here at M.I.T. we reported[2] the results of an experiment which indicated that the direction and extent of second-formant transitions is a potent cue for distinguishing within the classes of stop and nasal consonants. Since then we have found that this variable has a similar role with other consonant groups, such as /w,j,r,l/.[9] We also have evidence now that most of the distinctions that are cued by second-formant transitions are affected, though to a lesser extent, by transitions of the third formant. Our investigations into the effects of variations in direction and extent of first-formant transitions, which has so far been somewhat less systematic than our work on the second and third formants, indicates that these variations may help to distinguish among the classes: stops, nasals, liquids, and semivowels. These observations can, perhaps, be generalized by saying that variations in direction and extent of second- and third-formant transitions are cues for the perception of various consonants according to place of production, while comparable variations of the first formant are cues for manner.

We can generalize and simplify our description of these transition variations still further by assuming, as we have in an earlier publication,[10] that there are, for each consonant, characteristic frequency positions, or loci, at which the formant transitions begin, or to which they may be assumed to point. On this basis, the transitions may be regarded simply as movements of the formants from their respective loci to the frequency levels appropriate for the next phone, wherever those levels might be. The spectrographic patterns of figure 12.1 which produce /d/ before /i/, /a/, and /o/, show how this assumption suggests itself for the case of the second-formant transitions. We observe that all of these transitions seem to be pointing to a locus in the vicinity of 1800 cps. We should note, however, that the transitions only "point" to the locus; they do not originate there. Indeed, we find in the case of all the stop consonants—and we believe that this will be true of the nasal consonants too—that they can be successfully synthesized only if we introduce a silent interval between the locus and the start of the transition. This does not hold for such other consonants as /w,j,r,l/; here, as we will have occasion to point out later, the loci are the explicit starting points of the transitions.

We should note, too, that the locus concept is complicated somewhat by several special problems. One has to do with the velar consonants /k,g,ŋ/. Here we find a high-frequency locus at about 3000 cps, and this works rather well when the

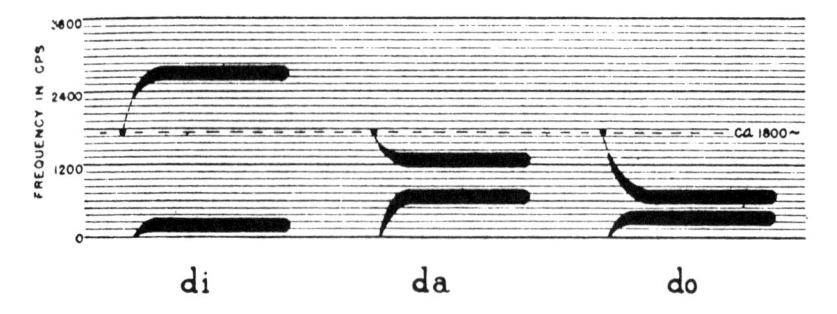

Figure 12.1
Spectrographic patterns that produce /di/, /da/, and /do/. The dashed lines are extrapolations to the /d/ locus at 1800 cps.

following vowel is in the range /i/ through /a/. Between the vowels /a/ and /ɔ/, however, there is a real discontinuity in the transition cue—and in the locus—and beginning with /ɔ/ we find that the /g/ locus is now very low in frequency and so vague that we have difficulty in specifying its precise position.

The second complication is that the locus tends to move, at least slightly, with the frequency level of the following vowel. In a very significant study Stevens and House[11] have presented some calculations which indicate that this should happen with two of the stops. Our own techniques are such that we could not expect to detect these movements in the case of the stops and the nasal consonants. The Stevens and House results prompted us to look more closely at some other consonants, however, and with /w,j,r,l/ we have, indeed, found direct evidence for such movement.[12]

Thus, the locus is somewhat more complicated than it might ideally be. However, the movement of the locus is much less than the range of frequencies through which the formants of the following vowels move, and there are, even for /g/, fewer loci than there are different transitions to various vowels, so the locus would still appear, on balance, to have considerable utility for simplifying the data of transition direction and extent.

Besides the direction and extent of the transitions, we have found another type of transition variation to be important for consonant perception. This consists of a pair of more or less correlated variables. One is transition duration, which we have found to be reasonably sufficient for distinguishing stop consonants from semivowels.[13] The other is the presence or absence of a silent interval between the locus and the start of the transition. We have already seen that the stop consonants, and probably the nasal consonants too, cannot be synthesized without such a silent interval. In the synthesis of the semivowels, on the other hand, it helps greatly to start the transitions right at their loci. The liquids, /r,l/ also require, even more than the semivowels, that there be no silent interval. Indeed, it is true of the liquids and the semivowels, but especially of the liquids, that they can be convincingly synthesized only if the transitions remain at their loci for 30 to 50 milliseconds.[14]

Thus, we have in regard to these two correlated transition cues at least two groups of sounds. There are in the one group the stop and, tentatively, the nasal consonants, of which we can say, first, that the total duration of the transition is quite short, and second, that there must be a silent interval between the locus and the start of the transition. In the second group are the semivowels and liquids, in which cases the total duration of transition is relatively long, and the transitions start at their loci.

We have so far covered two broad categories of consonant cues—constriction sounds and transitions—and between these two classes we have taken care of all but one of the cues that I want to include in this report. The remaining cue, which has got to be put into a separate class, results from the on-off action of a single fixed resonator, and, accordingly, this cue is either present or absent. The fixed resonator is in the nose, and the corresponding acoustic cue is an on-or-off nasal resonance that serves as an acoustic marker for the class of nasal consonants /m,n,ŋ/. This nasal cue does not, so far as we can tell, provide much of a basis for distinguishing the sounds within the class of nasal consonants. For that, the listener must rely on the transitions of the second and third formants.[15]

Having now come to the end of our discussion of these three types of cues, we ought to make some general observations concerning the number and variety of phones for which each type is important. We have already said that the constriction sounds occur in, and are important for, the fricatives, affricates, and stops, and that the nasal resonance is found only in the three nasal consonants /m,n,ŋ/, for which it serves in perception as a class marker. It has, perhaps, been only implicit in our discussion that all consonants produce transitions, and we have probably not made it sufficiently clear that for almost all the consonants the transitions have so far proved to be of considerable consequence as cues, either by themselves or together with the other cues we have been describing.

This is, perhaps, the point at which to say again that I have tried only to give examples of the kinds of cues we have found. Details and qualifications have been omitted virtually by the hundreds, and I have not gone out of my way to stake out the areas in which we are totally ignorant. It should be said, too, that the organization I have attempted to impose on our data is largely a matter of expository convenience. I hope nevertheless that this quick survey of our work has been sufficient at least to indicate the broader outlines of our results, and to provide a basis for the speculations about speech perception to which I should like now to turn.

In any search for the more general implications of what is known about the cues for speech perception, one can hardly avoid considering the fact that the data tend to arrange themselves in a very simple way. When we look, for example, at the transitions that are cues for the perception of the stop and nasal consonants, we find that they fall rather nicely into a three-by-three table such as we see in figure 12.2.

It is, of course, immediately obvious that this table parallels the well-known linguistic classification in terms of place and manner of articulation. And to the extent that there is a one-to-one correspondence between articulation and the acoustic result, the table seen in this figure is neither more nor less than we should expect. Though it is, perhaps, not surprising that the acoustic patterns should fall into place in this way, it is nonetheless marvelously convenient that they do. For this unearned increment of simplicity makes it possible for us to speak of an acoustic cue for an entire class of sounds. Thus, for a particular vowel, we can specify the second-formant transition that will produce an initial consonant having a bilabial place of production regardless of manner, and, similarly, we can describe the kind of first-formant transition that will serve as a manner marker for the class of voiced stops. Even more generally, of course, we can refer to the loci and avoid the necessity of specifying the associated vowel.

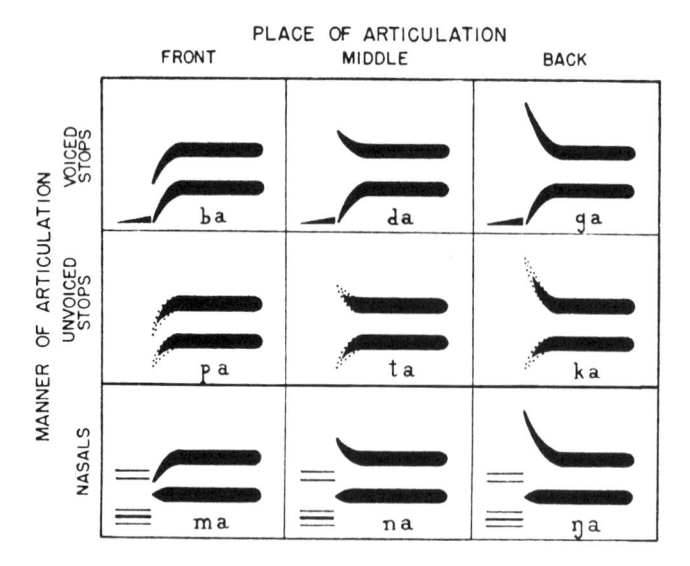

Figure 12.2
Spectrographic patterns that illustrate the transition cues for the stop and nasal consonants in initial position, with the vowel /a/. The dotted portions in the second row indicate the presence of noise (aspiration) in place of harmonics.

The table of figure 12.2 not only simplifies and generalizes some of our data, but, more importantly, it suggests a means by which distinctive stimuli are created. As we see from the figure, a limited number of cues on one dimension combine in all possible pairs with cues on each of several other dimensions to produce the sounds that we perceive as speech. Thus, we compound a rather large number of highly identifiable stimuli by freely combining a few values from each of several dimensions. As G. A. Miller has recently pointed out,[16] this possibility provides considerable solace to those of us psychologists who are currently much oppressed by the number seven. Lest the nonpsychologists in the audience think that we are now entering the field of numerology, I hasten to point out that, as Pollack[17,18] and others have found, seven is the upper limit on the number of simple stimuli—stimuli, that is, that vary on a single dimension—that a person can typically identify correctly. A basic problem in perception is to explain how, in the face of that limitation, we nevertheless identify as many stimuli as we do. The acoustic table of linguistic elements suggests that in the case of speech perception the problem has been solved by the use of stimuli that are simple mixtures of a relatively few stimulus values of cue elements from each of a number of different dimensions. In this way many distinctive stimuli are created without the perceiver being required to approach very close to the limit of seven. This general type of solution has for many years been at least implicit in the more familiar articulatory form of our table, and in the recent history of linguistic science it has become even more explicit in the work of Jakobson, Fant, and Halle.[19]

As a result of a very important experiment by Miller and Nicely,[20] we know now that the cue elements and dimensions are relatively independent of each other not only in the manner of their combination, but also in the way they are perceived. Some of the results of our own research point to essentially the same conclusion, but our evidence has been collected quite incidentally and is in general less systematic and less elegant than the Miller and Nicely data. I will not attempt to review any of this evidence here, but I would like to add a somewhat relevant observation that comes from experiments of a type made possible by our use of synthetic speech. Typically, as we have seen, we try to isolate the various cue elements, but often we put these elements together in various ways. We find in general that the individual cues retain their identities, so to speak, no matter how they are combined. Thus, if we add together two acoustic features that have been found in isolation to be cues for the same phone, the sound that results is always heard as that phone. New or different qualities never emerge, and, in general, we find essentially no interaction. In this same connection, we sometimes use our synthetic speech techniques to combine acoustic elements that are, in isolation, cues for different phones. These combinations, which one of my colleagues refers to as "unspeakable," are always perceived as if they were simple mixtures of essentially unchangeable elements.

We have so far been concerned with the possibility that relatively free combinations of independently perceived elements might be the basis for perception at the phonemic level, where we are dealing with the so-called empty symbols of language. We might note here that such a system would appear, within limits, to apply at the higher linguistic levels too, where meaning, for example, enters to complicate the psychological picture. Thus, we all know how morphemic elements are entered into various combinations to create a variety of words, each elements having a particular identity or meaning which it retains regardless of the combination in which it occurs. Indeed, we may suppose that combining independently variable stimulus elements is a workable basis for perception in the language area, and it is likely that this tells us something rather important about the human mind.

But whether we apply this perceptual scheme only to speech perception, or more broadly to language behavior in general, we will not be able to derive much satisfaction from our assumptions until two very pertinent questions have been answered. One of these asks whether any collection of dimensions and cue elements will do, or whether, alternatively, we must use only certain ones that have, perhaps, some special characteristics. It would take us far beyond the scope of this paper to discuss that issue. Besides, we have nothing to contribute at this point beyond an impression, based on our research experience, that some dimensions are going to work better than others. The second question takes into account the long experience that all listeners have had with the sounds of speech and asks then about the effects of learning on the distinctiveness of the cue elements and dimensions. We have some data and some speculations that bear on this point, and I will want to discuss them in a few minutes. But first I should like to return to the acoustic table of figure 12.2 and consider the possibility that proprioceptive, as well as acoustic, stimulus dimensions must be taken into account in any attempt to explain the perception of speech.

We said earlier that we should not be surprised to obtain this table of acoustic elements, given its familiar linguistic counterpart, and given, also, a one-to-one correspondence between articulation and sound. It cannot be too strongly emphasized that the correspondence between articulation and sound is not always one-to-one. Small difference in articulation sometimes cause very large differences at the acoustic level, and the converse is also true.

The occasional complexity of the relation between articulation and the resulting sound wave is, for the most part, a nuisance, but it does provide us with a rare opportunity to ask this interesting question: when articulation and sound wave go

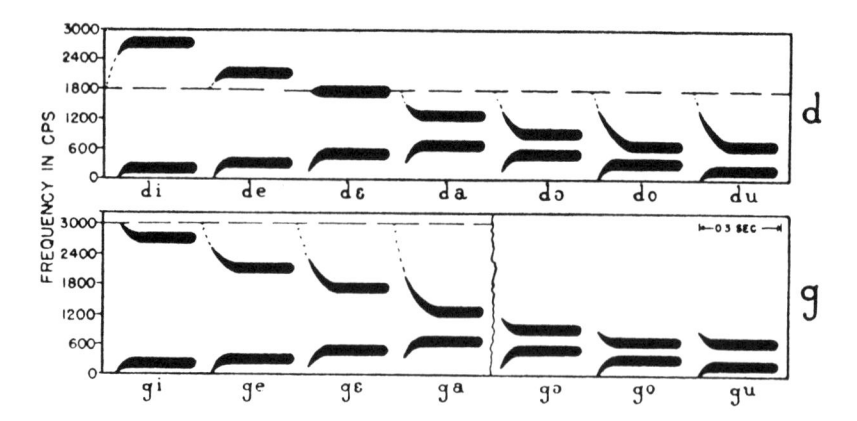

Figure 12.3
Spectrographic patterns that produce /d/ and /g/ before various vowels. The dashed lines are extrapolations to the /d/ and /g/ loci.

their separate ways, which way does the perception go? The answer so far is clear. The perception always goes with articulation.

We have found several extreme and, we think, striking examples of this in our research, and we have discussed one of them in a published paper.[21] It may nevertheless be appropriate to consider another example here.

Figure 12.3 shows the various transitions of the second formant that are required before each of several vowels to synthesize /d/ and /g/. We note in regard to /d/ that the direction and extent of its second-formant transition is different for different vowels. We also note that in all these cases—that is, with these various transitions—the perception of the consonant is always the same. One hears /d/ throughout.

In the simplest case, we should expect to explain the unchanging perception of /d/ by finding some aspect of the acoustic stimulus that does not change. As shown in figure 12.3, we do, in fact, find such an acoustic invariance in that the /d/ transitions for the various vowels seem to be coming from the same frequency position—namely, the /d/ locus at 1800 cps.

The situation is very different for the consonant /g/, however, as we noted earlier in this discussion, and as we can see in the bottom row of the figure. Here, the consonant takes a progressively bigger transition from the vowel /i/ through the vowel /a/, and we have evidence from our locus research that these transitions are all coming from around 3000 cps. Between /a/ and the next vowel /ɔ/, however, there is a large and sudden change. The best /g/ transition is now very small, and the locus, if indeed there is one, has shifted its position radically.

In this sudden shift between /ga/ and /gɔ/, we have a real discontinuity at the acoustic level. We have been able to find no acoustic invariant to correspond to—or, if you will, to explain—the unchanging perception of /g/ in this series, and there are reasonable grounds for supposing that none exists. The important thing, of course, is that this discontinuity at the acoustic level is not paralleled by any corresponding discontinuity in articulation or in perception. The /g/ articulation is essentially the same throughout, and so also is the perception.

If the perception depended most directly on the acoustic stimulus, then, in order to preserve the /g/ as perceived, we should have had to change the articulation radically so as to hold the acoustic pattern constant. The fact that we haven't done that, and that we nevertheless hear /g/ with all the vowels, would seem to argue that the perception is somehow more closely related to the articulation than to the acoustic stimulus.

All of this strongly suggests, as do other similar cases, that speech is perceived by reference to articulation—that is, that the articulatory movements and their sensory effects mediate between the acoustic stimulus and the event we call perception. In its extreme and old-fashioned form, this view says that we overtly mimic the incoming speech sounds and then respond to the proprioceptive and tactile stimuli that are produced by our own articulatory movements. For a variety of reasons such an extreme position is wholly untenable, and if we are to deal with perception in the adult, we must assume that the process is somehow short-circuited—that is, that the reference to articulatory movements and their sensory consequences must somehow occur in the brain without getting out into the periphery. I realize that this qualification tends to shield the theory from some of the revealing light of fact, but it does not render it wholly meaningless. The example we talked about a moment ago is still reasonably well explained by the assumption that the perception depends most directly on the sensory consequences of a mimicking articulation. On that basis we should expect that the very different acoustic stimuli for /g/ would come to sound exactly alike because they are produced by the same gross movement.

I should like to turn now to the results I spoke of a while back when I said that we had some data relating to the effects of learning on the distinctiveness of speech sounds. It is, I think, appropriate to have put off this discussion till now, because, as we will see, the results I want to describe appear to be somewhat easier to understand in the light of our assumptions concerning the importance of the sensory return from a mediating articulation.

The results have to do in general with the relation between a listener's phonemic identification of speech sounds and the extent to which he can discriminate these sounds as being different in any way. We find—and this will surely not surprise the linguist—that discrimination is better near the phoneme boundary than it is in the middle of the category.[22] For the particular experiments that we have so far carried out, we used a series of 14 synthetic speech patterns in which the extent of the second-formant transition was varied in small steps through a range sufficient to include /b/, /d/, and /g/. In one part of the experiment these stimuli were presented singly and in random order with instructions to identify them as /b/, /d/, or /g/, and to guess if necessary. As we had reason to anticipate on the basis of previous work with similar patterns, our listeners identified the stimuli in such a way as to divide the acoustic continuum up into three sharply defined phoneme categories, the shifts from one category to another being very abrupt. In another part of the experiment we arranged these same stimuli pairwise and determined by an ABX procedure how well these speech sounds could be discriminated as being different on any basis whatsoever. We found in general that discrimination was better near the phoneme boundaries than it was in the middle of the phoneme categories. This is to say that, with acoustic difference equal, our listeners more easily discriminated between sounds to which they habitually attach different phoneme labels than they did between sounds which they normally lump into the same phoneme class. Indeed, these effects were so great as to approximate rather closely to what we would expect to obtain on the basis of a most extreme assumption: namely, that the listener can discriminate these sounds only to the extent that he can identify them as different phonemes.

We will for the time being simply assume that we are here dealing with the effects of learning on discrimination—for we almost certainly are—and instead of asking whether this is learned, we will ask rather what is learned? It is tempting to speculate that what is learned is simply a connection between various acoustic stimuli and certain articulatory responses. Given that, and given the assumption that the articulation and its sensory consequences mediate between the acoustic stimulus and the perception, then the results we have been discussing follow.

One possibility, of course, is that in the raw these speech stimuli were all as highly discriminable as the most discriminable pair, and that the effect of our linguistic experience has been to dull our sensitivity to the differences within the phoneme category. This is called acquired similarity by one group of psychologists, and it can be made to fit our assumptions quite easily. In the case of that part of the acoustic continuum that runs from /b/ through /d/, for example, we may suppose that our naive American listener has only two possible responses available to him: the /b/ response with the lips and the /d/ response with the tongue. Intermediate articulations are not possible, and neither are intermediate perceptions. All the transition extents that get themselves attached to the /b/, or labial, response become indistinguishable because their perception comes to depend most directly on the sensory consequences of a single articulatory gesture.

The contrary possibility is that our stimuli were originally as little discriminable as the least discriminable pair, and that our discriminations have been selectively sharpened as a result of our long experience with the language. This effect, if it occurs, would be similar to what has been called acquired distinctiveness. Such a phenomenon probably has disturbing implications for some people in that it suggests the wrong kind of entropy and calls up visions of Maxwell's demon stationed at some strategic spot in the brain. If this were a problem, and I doubt that it would be in any case, we would want to dismiss it, because we have some direct, if very preliminary, evidence that in the case of some speech cues there does, in fact, appear to be a rather large amount of acquired distinctiveness.[23]

The mechanism to account for acquired distinctiveness is very easy to imagine in terms of the assumptions we have been making. We should suppose that the perceived difference between two relatively similar external stimuli could be increased if we could attach to those stimuli two very different mediating responses and hence gain the added distinctiveness of their very different proprioceptive returns.

The phenomenon of acquired distinctiveness has been investigated in various psychological laboratories. In setting up the conditions under which this distinctiveness is to be acquired, however, the investigators I know about have omitted one arrangement which is peculiar to, and possibly important for, linguistic perception. For in the perception of speech, the mediating articulation not only produces distinctive proprioceptive stimuli, but also external sounds which can be matched against the sounds being perceived. Or, perhaps, we should say that these sounds would be produced if the movements were overt, as they conceivably are in our early years. Considering our very great ability to discriminate two stimuli—that is, to tell whether they are the same or different—and considering also that the possibility of mimicking reduces the first step in the perception process to this very easy discrimination, we might suppose that the articulatory mediation would be of some help initially in getting some of the acoustic stimuli attached to the appropriate articulatory responses. To see this a bit more clearly, let us leave the field of speech perception and consider an example involving the identification of unidimensionally varying lights.

We would expect, on a basis which has already been mentioned, that a subject will be able to identify only about seven different brightnesses of light. These are brightnesses which are presented singly and in random order for absolute judgment. We know, too, that practice doesn't seem to help very much. Suppose now that we provide the subject with a second or comparison light, the brightness of which he can control with a series of levers. If he is permitted to match this comparison light with the standard stimulus, the number of brightnesses he can identify will obviously be increased very greatly. Given a sufficient number of distinctively different lever responses, his ability to identify the brightnesses is now limited only by his ability to discriminate them, and we know that the latter is normally very great.

In the beginning it would, of course, take our subject a long time to make each match. It is quite reasonable to suppose that practice would reduce the amount of trial and error, and that our subject would ultimately be able to make the matches much more quickly. The obviously critical question is this: what would happen, after a great deal of practice, if we removed the comparison light and then the levers, thus taking a step which might be analogous in the area of speech perception to putting an end to overt mimicry. If we knew the answer to that question we would, I think, be much closer to an understanding of how learning affects the perception of speech.

Notes

This paper was read, substantially as it is presented here, before the Conference on Speech Communication at the Massachusetts Institute of Technology on June 16, 1956. Apart from the particular form of the exposition—for which the author must bear sole responsibility—this paper should be regarded as a joint effort of the staff of Haskins Laboratories. The work of the Haskins Laboratories which is described in this paper has been supported in part by the Carnegie Corporation of New York and in part by the Department of Defense in connection with Contract DA49-170-sc-1642.

1. F. S. Cooper, J. Acoust. Soc. Am. 22, 761–762 (1950).
2. Cooper, Delattre, Liberman, Borst, and Gerstman, J. Acoust. Soc. Am. 24, 597–606 (1952).
3. K. S. Harris, J. Acoust. Soc. Am. 28, 160 (A) (1956).
4. Meeks, Borst, and Cooper, J. Acoust. Soc. Am. 26, 137 (A) (1954).
5. Liberman, Delattre, and Copper, Am. J. Psychol. 65, 497–516 (1952).
6. K. S. Harris, J. Acoust. Soc. Am. 26, 952 (A) (1954).
7. The work referred to, most of which is as yet unpublished, has been carried out at Haskins Laboratories by P. Delattre, H. Truby, and L. Gerstman. For one aspects of this research see L. J. Gerstman, J. Acoust. Soc. Am. 28, 160 (A) (1956).
8. See note 6.
9. O'Connor, Gerstman, Liberman, Delattre, and Cooper, "Acoustic cues for the perception of initial /w,j,r,l/, in English" (to be published).
10. Delattre, Liberman, and Cooper, J. Acoust. Soc. Am. 27, 769–773 (1955).
11. K. N. Stevens and A. S. House, J. Acoust. Soc. Am. 28, 578–585 (1956).
12. See note 9.
13. Liberman, Delattre, Gerstman, and Cooper, J. Exptl. Psychol. 52, 127–137 (1956).
14. See note 9.
15. Liberman, Delattre, Cooper, and Gerstman, Psychol. Monogr. 68, Whole No. 8, 1–13 (1954).
16. G. A. Miller, Psychol. Rev. 63, 81–97 (1956).
17. I. Pollack, J. Acoust. Soc. Am. 24, 745–749 (1952).
18. I. Pollack, J. Acoust. Soc. Am. 25, 765–769 (1953).
19. Jakobson, Fant, and Halle, Preliminaries to speech analysis (Acoustics Laboratory, Massachusetts Institute of Technology, Technical Report No. 13. Cambridge, Massachusetts, 1952).

20. G. A. Miller and P. E. Nicely, J. Acoust. Soc. Am. 27, 338–352 (1955).
21. See note 5.
22. Harris, Liberman, Hoffman, and Griffith, J. Acoust. Soc. Am. 28, 760 (A) (1956).
23. In an exploratory study at Haskins Laboratories Mr. Gerstman has dealt with classes of speech sounds (fricative, affricate, stop) that can be distinguished on the basis of duration. This makes it possible to compare discrimination data for durations of acoustic stimuli that are in the one case perceived as speech sounds and in another, only slightly different case, as sounds which are not speech. We should have evidence for acquired distinctiveness or acquired similarity if, with equal differences in duration, the speech stimuli should prove to be more (acquired distinctiveness) or less (acquired similarity) discriminable than the comparable nonspeech stimuli. The preliminary indications are that there is considerable acquired distinctiveness for the speech stimuli that lie near phoneme boundaries. There appears to be no acquired similarity for the stimuli in the middle of the phoneme categories.

PART V

A Mid-Course Correction

Introduction to Part V

The review that follows describes the relation between acoustic signal and phonetic message (the "speech code") as we saw it in 1967, and offers the theoretical notions we were entertaining at that time. Much of what we say about the speech code in chapter 13 we had said before, and there is undiminished emphasis on our old assumption that the objects of perception are the articulatory gestures. There are, however, important changes and additions. The most important by far is an abandonment of the horizontal aspects of the Early Motor Theory, with a compensatory shift toward a vertical orientation. According to the Early Motor Theory, as described in the chapters 1 and 12, there were two stages in the perceptual process: a perfectly general auditory process, followed by attachment to the sensory consequences of the gestures according to an equally general process of association learning. Accordingly, there was nothing biologically or psychologically distinct about speech perception; it just happened to offer an unexampled opportunity for two phonetically undistinguished processes to be conjoined. Now, in the 1967 review, we say not a word about two stages, but rather speak of "one process, with appropriate linkages between sensory and motor components," and of the "interdependence of perceptual and productive processes." We also assume explicitly that this interdependence occurs, not as an instance of some general process of action and perception, but in a distinct system we refer to as a speech "decoder," and in a correspondingly distinct perceptual register we call the "speech mode."

I find it hard now to understand why, in writing the original article, we did not even say, let alone emphasize, that the theory had taken a radical turn. It is likely that my coauthors had never taken the old version of the theory seriously. In my case, it might have been that the old theory had simply ceased to figure in my theoretical calculations; after all, ten years had elapsed since I promoted it explicitly in the 1957 paper (chapter 12 in this volume). But it might equally have been that I did not then appreciate how sharp a turn the theory had taken, for it was not until some time later that I began to think about the contrast between the horizontal and vertical positions, and to see that a move from the one to the other can hardly be gradual.

There is also, for the first time, an attempt to consider how the production of speech might be managed, but we stop short of claiming explicitly that its processes are a phonetically distinct set, and we loosen only slightly our hold on the mistaken idea that the invariant gestures are to be found at the level of the final common paths to the muscles.

In connection with our discussion of the complexities of the speech code, we note that alphabetic script is more simply related to phonological structure than are the sounds of speech, yet reading is biologically secondary, hence relatively difficult in contrast to perceiving speech, which is primary, hence easy. It was in response to this seeming paradox that I first became interested in the processes of writing and reading, and in trying to understand, from a biological point of view, how profoundly they differed from speech.

Of all the writing I have been associated with, chapter 13 has been, I think, the most frequently cited, but often, unfortunately, to the wrong effect and for the wrong reason. Thus, it has often been referenced as the source of a claim that we had taken categorical perception to be the primary (perhaps even the sole) support for a motor theory. Of course, categorical perception never occupied that place in our thinking, and chapter 13 gives the reader no reason to think it did.

Chapter 13
Perception of the Speech Code

Our aim is to identify some of the conditions that underlie the perception of speech. We will not consider the whole process, but only the part that lies between the acoustic stream and a level of perception corresponding roughly to the phoneme.[1] Even this, as we will try to show, presents an interesting challenge to the psychologist.

The point we want most to make is that the sounds of speech are a special and especially efficient code on the phonemic structure of language, not a cipher or alphabet. We use the term code,[2] in contrast to cipher or alphabet, to indicate that speech sounds represent a very considerable restructuring of the phonemic "message." The acoustic cues for successive phonemes are intermixed in the sound stream to such an extent that definable segments of sound do not correspond to segments at the phoneme level. Moreover, the same phoneme is most commonly represented in different phonemic environments by sounds that are vastly different. There is, in short, a marked lack of correspondence between sound and perceived phoneme. This is a central fact of speech perception. It is, we think, the result of a complex encoding that makes the sounds of speech especially efficient as vehicles for the transmission of phonemic information. But it also poses an important question: by what mechanism does the listener decode the sounds and recover the phonemes?

In this paper we will (a) ask whether speech could be well perceived if it were an alphabet or acoustic cipher, (b) say how we know that speech is, in fact, a complex code, (c) describe some properties of the perceptual mode that results when speech is decoded, (d) consider how the encoding and decoding might occur, and (e) show that the speech code is so well matched to man as to provide, despite its complexity, a uniquely effective basis for communication.

Could Speech Be Alphabetic?

There are reasons for supposing that phonemes could not be efficiently communicated by a sound alphabet—that is, by sounds that stand in one-to-one correspondence with the phonemes. Such reasons provide only indirect support for the conclusion that speech is a code rather than an alphabet. They are important, however, because they indicate that the encoded nature of speech may be a condition of its effectiveness in communication. More specifically, they tell us which aspects of the code are likely to be relevant to that effectiveness.

Originally published in *Psychological Review* 74, 6 (1967): 431–461, with F. S. Cooper, D. P. Shankweiler, and M. Studdert-Kennedy. Copyright 1967 by the American Psychological Association. Reprinted by permission of the publisher.

Phoneme Communication and the Properties of the Ear
Of the difficulties we might expect to have with a sound alphabet, the most obvious concerns rate. Speech can be followed, though with difficulty, at rates as high as 400 words per minute (Orr, Friedman, and Williams 1965). If we assume an average of four to five phonemes for each English word, this rate yields about 30 phonemes per second. But we know from auditory psychophysics (Miller and Taylor 1948) that 30 sounds per second would over-reach the temporal resolving power of the ear: discrete acoustic events at that rate would merge into an unanalyzable buzz; a listener might be able to tell from the pitch of the buzz how fast the speaker was talking, but he could hardly perceive what had been said. Even 15 phonemes per second, which is not unusual in conversation, would seem more than the ear could cope with if phonemes were a string of discrete acoustic events.

There is at least one other requirement of a sound alphabet that would be hard to satisfy: a sufficient number of identifiable sounds. The number of phonemes, and hence the number of acoustic shapes required, is in the dozens. In English there are about 40. We should, of course, be able to find 40 identifiable sounds if we could pattern the stimuli in time, as in the case of melodies. But if we are to communicate as rapidly as we do, the phoneme segments could last no longer than about 50 milliseconds on the average. Though it is not clear from research on auditory perception how many stimuli of such brief duration can be accurately identified, the available data suggest that the number is considerably less than 40 (Miller 1956a, 1956b; Nye 1962; Pollack 1952; Polack and Ficks 1954). We will be interested, therefore, to see whether any features of the encoding and decoding mechanisms are calculated to enhance the identifiability of the signals.

Results of Attempts to Communicate Phonemes by an Acoustic Alphabet
That these difficulties of rate and sound identification are real, we may see from the fact that it has not been possible to develop an efficient sound alphabet despite repeated and thoroughgoing attempts to do so. Thus, international Morse code (a cipher as we use the term here) works poorly in comparison with speech, even after years of practice. But Morse is surely not the best example: the signals are one-dimensional and therefore not ideal from a psychological standpoint. More interesting, if less well known, are the many sound alphabets that have been tested in the attempt to develop reading machines for the blind (Coffey 1963; Cooper 1950a; Freiberger and Murphy 1961; Nye 1964, 1965; Studdert-Kennedy and Copper 1966; Studdert-Kennedy and Liberman 1963). These devices convert print into sound, the conversion being made typically by encipherment of the optical alphabet into one that is acoustic. The worth of these devices has been limited, not by the difficulty of converting print to sound, but by the perceptual limitations of their human users. In the fifty-year history of this endeavor, a wide variety of sounds has been tried, including many that are multidimensional and otherwise appropriately designed, it would seem, to carry information efficiently. Subjects have practiced with these sounds for long periods of time, yet there has nowhere emerged any evidence that performance with these acoustic alphabets can be made to exceed performance with Morse, and that is little more than a tenth of what can be achieved with speech.

Reading and Listening
We hardly need say that language can be written and read by means of an alphabet, but we would emphasize how different are the problems of communicating phonemes

by eye and by ear, and how different their relevance to a psychology of language. In contrast to the ear, the eye should have no great difficulty in rapidly perceiving ordered strings of signals. Given the eye's ability to perceive in space, we should suppose that alphabetic segments set side by side could be perceived in clusters. Nor is there reason to expect that it might be difficult to find identifiable optical signals in sufficient number. Many shapes are available, and a number of different alphabets are, indeed, in use. Thus, written language has no apparent need for the special code that will be seen to characterize language in its acoustic form. In writing and reading it is possible to communicate phonemes by means of a cipher or alphabet; indeed, there appears to be no better way.

Spoken and written language differ, then, in that the former must be a complex code while the latter can be a simple cipher. Yet perception of speech is universal, though reading is not. In the history of the race, as in the development of the individual, speaking and listening come first; writing and reading come later, if at all. Moreover, the most efficient way of writing and reading—namely, by an alphabet—is nevertheless so unnatural that it has apparently been invented only once in all history (Gelb 1963). Perceiving the complex speech code is thus basic to language, and to man, in a way that reading an alphabet is not. Being concerned about language, we are therefore the more interested in the speech code. Why are speech sounds, alone among acoustic signals and in spite of the limitations of the ear, perceived so well?

Acoustic Cues: A Restructuring of Phonemes at the Level of Sound

To know in what sense speech sounds are a code on the phonemes, we must first discover which aspects of the complex acoustic signal underlie the perception of particular phonemes. For the most part, the relevant data are at hand. We can now identify acoustic features that are sufficient and important cues for the perception of almost all the segmental phonemes.[3] Much remains to be learned, but we know enough to see that the phonemic message is restructured in the sound stream and, from that knowledge, to make certain inferences about perception.

An Example of Restructuring
To illustrate the nature of the code, we will describe an important acoustic cue for the perception of the voiced stop /d/. This example is important in its own right and also broadly representative. The phoneme /d/, or something very much like it, occurs in all the languages of the world.[4] In English, and perhaps in other languages, too, it carries a heavy load of information, probably more than any other single phoneme (Denes 1963); and it is among the first of the phonemelike segments to appear in the vocalizations of the child (Whetnall and Fry 1964, p. 84). The acoustic cue we have chosen to examine—the second-formant transition[5]—is a major cue for all the consonants except, perhaps, the fricatives /s/ and /š/, and is probably the single most important carrier of linguistic information in the speech signal (Delattre 1958, 1962; Delattre, Liberman, and Cooper 1955, 1964; Harris 1958; Liberman 1957; Liberman, Delattre, Cooper, and Gerstman 1954; Liberman, Ingemann, Lisker, Delattre, and Cooper 1959; Lisker 1957; O'Connor, Gerstman, Liberman, Delattre, and Cooper 1957).

Context-Conditioned Variations in the Acoustic Cue Figure 13.1 displays two highly simplified spectrographic patterns that will, when converted into sound, be heard as

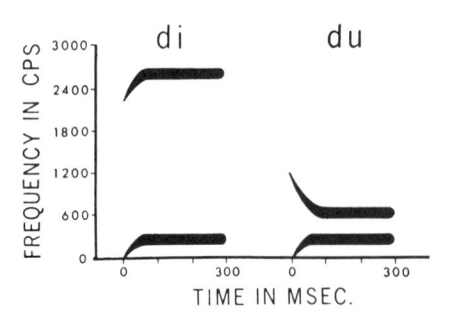

Figure 13.1
Spectrographic patterns sufficient for the synthesis of /d/ before /i/ and /u/.

the syllables /di/ and /du/ (Liberman, Delattre, Cooper, and Gerstman 1954). They exemplify the results of a search for the acoustic cues in which hand-drawn or "synthetic" spectrograms were used as a basis for experimenting with the complex acoustic signal (Cooper 1950, 1953; Cooper, Delattre, Liberman, Borst, and Gerstman 1952; Cooper, Liberman, and Borst 1951). The steady-state formants, comprising approximately the right-hand two-thirds of each pattern, are sufficient to produce the vowels /i/ and /u/ (Delattre, Liberman, and Cooper 1951; Delattre, Liberman, Cooper, and Gerstman 1952). At the left of each pattern are the relatively rapid changes in frequency of the formants—the formant transitions—that are, as we indicated, important acoustic cues for the perception of the consonants. The transition of the first, or lower, formant, rising from a very low frequency to the level appropriate for the vowel, is a cue for the class of voiced stops /b,d,g/ (Delattre, Liberman, and Cooper 1955; Liberman, Delattre, and Cooper 1958). It would be exactly the same for /bi, bu/ and /gi, gu/ as for /di, du/. Most generally, this transition is a cue for the perception of manner and voicing. The acoustic feature in which we are here interested is the transition of the second formant, which is, in the patterns of figure 13.1, a cue for distinguishing among the voiced stops, /b,d,g/; that is to say, the second-formant transition for /gi/ or /bi/, as well as /gu/ or /bu/, would be different from those for /di/ and /du/ (Liberman, Delattre, Cooper, and Gerstman 1954). In general, transitions of the second formant carry important information about the place of production of most consonants (Delattre 1958; Liberman 1957; Liberman, Delattre, Cooper, and Gerstman 1954).

It is, then, the second-formant transitions that are, in the patterns of figure 13.1, the acoustic cues for the perception of the /d/ segment of the syllables /di/ and /du/. We would first note that /d/ is the same perceptually in the two cases, and then see how different are the acoustic cues. In the case of /di/ the transition rises from approximately 2200 cps to 2600 cps; in /du/ it falls from about 1200 to 700 cps. In other words, what is perceived as the same phoneme is cued, in different contexts, by features that are vastly different in acoustic terms. How different these acoustic features are in nonspeech perception can be determined by removing them from the patterns of figure 13.1 and sounding them in isolation. When we do that, the transition isolated from the /di/ pattern sounds like a rapidly rising whistle or glissando on high pitches, the one from /du/ like a rapidly falling whistle on low pitches.[6] These signals could hardly sound more different from each other. Furthermore, neither of them sounds like /d/ nor like speech of any sort.

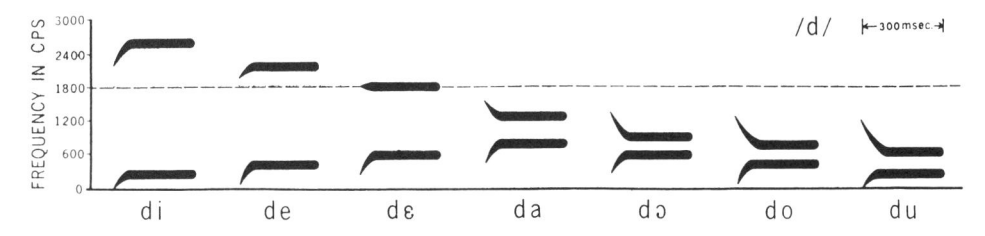

Figure 13.2
Spectrographic patterns sufficient for the synthesis of /d/ before vowels. (Dashed line at 1800 cps shows the "locus" for /d/.)

The Disappearance of Phoneme Boundaries: Parallel Transmission We turn now to another, related aspect of the code: the speech signal typically does not contain segments corresponding to the discrete and commutable phonemes. There is no way to cut the patterns of figure 13.1 so as to recover /d/ segments that can be substituted one for the other. Nor can we make the commutation simply by introducing a physical continuity between the cut ends, as we might, for example, if we were segmenting and recombining the alphabetic elements of cursive writing.

Indeed, if we could somehow separate commutability from segmentability, we should have to say that there is no /d/ segment at all, whether commutable or not. We cannot cut either the /di/ or the /du/ pattern in such a way as to obtain some piece that will produce /d/ alone. If we cut progressively into the syllable from the right-hand end, we hear /d/ plus a vowel, or a nonspeech sound; at no point will we hear only /d/. This is so because the formant transition is, at every instant, providing information about two phonemes, the consonant and the vowel—that is, the phonemes are being transmitted in parallel.

The Locus: An Acoustic Invariant?
The patterns of figure 13.2 produce /d/ in initial position with each of a variety of vowels, thus completing a series of which the patterns shown in figure 13.1 are the extremes. If one extrapolates the various second-formant transitions backward in time, he sees that they seem to have diverged from a single frequency. To find that frequency more exactly, and to determine whether it might in some sense be said to characterize /d/, we can, as in figure 13.3, pair each of a number of straight second formants with first formants that contain a rising transition sufficient to signal a voiced stop of some kind. On listening to such patterns, one hears an initial /d/ most strongly when the straight second formant is at 1800 cps. This has been called the /d/ "locus" (Delattre, Liberman, and Cooper 1955). There are, correspondingly, second-formant loci for other consonants, the frequency position of the locus being correlated with the place of production. In general, the locus moves somewhat as a function of the associated vowel, but, except for a discontinuity in the case of /k, g, ŋ/, the locus is more nearly invariant than the formant transition (Delattre, Liberman, and Cooper 1955; Ohman 1966; Stevens and House 1956).

Is there, then, an invariant acoustic cue for /d/? Consider the various second formants that all begin at the 1800-cycle locus and proceed from there to a number of different vowel positions, such as are shown in figure 13.4. We should note first that these transitions are not superimposable, so that if they are to be regarded as invariant acoustic cues, it could only be in the very special and limited sense that they start

Chapter 13

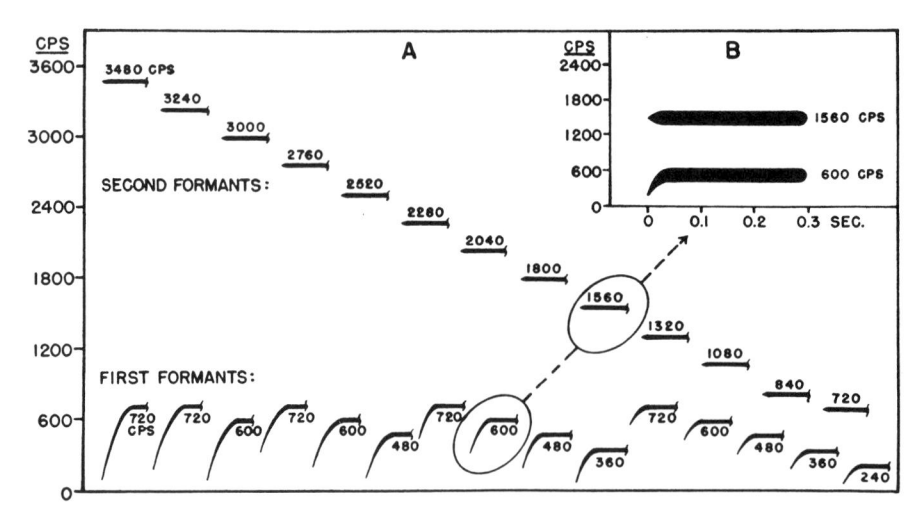

Figure 13.3
Schematic display of the stimuli used in finding the second-formant loci of /b/, /d/, and /g/. ((A) Frequency positions of the straight second formants and the various first formants with which each was paired. (B) A typical test pattern, made up of the first and second formants circled in A. The best pattern for /d/ was the one with the straight second formant at 1800 cps. Figure taken from Delattre, Liberman, and Cooper 1955.)

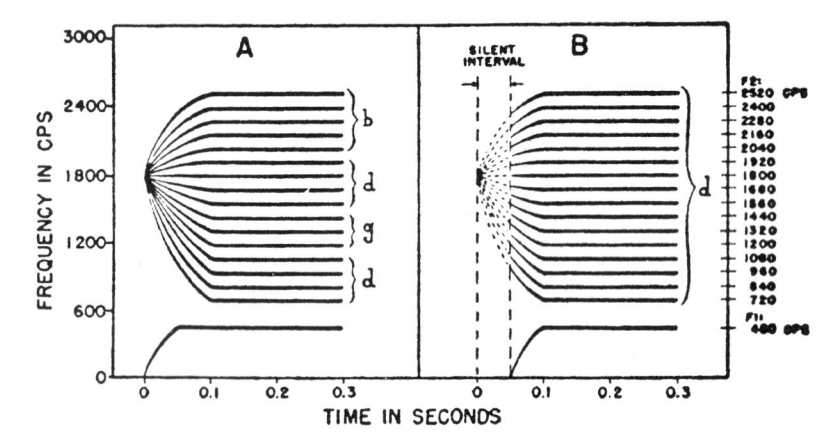

Figure 13.4
(A) Second-formant transitions that start at the /d/ locus, and (B) comparable transitions that merely "point" at it, as indicated by the dotted lines. (Those of (A) produce syllables beginning with /b/, /d/, or /g/, depending on the frequency-level of the formant; those of (B) produce only syllables beginning with /d/. Figure taken from Delattre, Liberman, and Cooper 1955.)

at the same point on the frequency scale. But even this very limited invariance is not to be had. If we convert the patterns of figure 13.4 to sound, having paired each of the second formants in turn with the single first formant shown at the bottom of the figure, we do not hear /d/ in every case. Taking the second formants in order, from the top down, we hear first /b/, then /d/, then /g/, then once again /d/, as shown in the figure. In order to hear /d/ in every case, we must erase the first part of the transition, as shown in figure 13.4B, so that it "points" at the locus but does not actually begin there. Thus, the 1800-cps locus for /d/ is not a part of the acoustic signal, nor can it be made part of that signal without grossly changing the perception (Delattre, Liberman, and Cooper 1955).

Though the locus can be defined in acoustic terms—that is, as a particular frequency—the concept is more articulatory than acoustic, as can be seen in the rationalization of the locus by Stevens and House (1956). What is common to /d/ before all the vowels is that the articulatory tract is closed at very much the same point. According to the calculations of Stevens and House, the resonant frequency of the cavity at the instant of closure is approximately 1800 cps, but since no sound emerges until some degree of opening has occurred, the locus frequency is not radiated as part of the acoustic signal. At all events it seems clear that, though the locus is more nearly invariant with the phoneme than is the transition itself, the invariance is a derived one, related more to articulation than to sound. As we will see later, however, the locus is only a step toward the invariance with phoneme perception that we must seek: better approximations to that invariance are probably to be had by going farther back in the chain of articulatory events, beyond the cavity shapes that underlie the locus, to the commands that produce the shapes.

How General Is the Restructuring?
Having dealt with the restructuring of only one phoneme and one acoustic cue, we should say now that, with several interesting exceptions yet to be noted, it is generally true of the segmental phonemes that they are drastically restructed at the level of sound.[7] We will briefly summarize what is known in this regard about the various types of cues and linguistic classes or dimensions.

Transitions of the Second Formant For the second-formant transition—the cue with which we have been concerned and the one that is, perhaps, the most important for the perception of consonants according to place of production—the kind of invariance lack we found with /d/ characterizes all the voiced stops, voiceless stops, and nasal consonants (Liberman, Delattre, Cooper, and Gerstman 1954; Malecot 1956). Indeed, the invariance problem is, if anything, further complicated in these other phonemes. In the case of /g, k, ŋ/, for example, there is a sudden and considerable shift in the locus as between the unrounded and rounded vowels, creating a severe lack of correspondence between acoustic signal and linguistic perception that we mentioned earlier in this paper and that we have dealt with in some detail elsewhere (Liberman 1957).

With the liquids and semivowels /r, l, w, j/ the second-formant transition originates at the locus—as it cannot in the case of the stop and nasal consonants—so the lack of correspondence between acoustic signal and phoneme is less striking, but even with these phonemes the transition cues are not superimposable for occurrences of the same consonant in different contexts (Lisker 1957; O'Connor, Gerstman, Liberman, Delattre, and Cooper 1957).

Transitions of the Third Formant What of third-formant transitions, which also contribute to consonant perception in terms of place of production? Though we know less about the third-formant transitions than about those of the second, such evidence as we have does not suggest that an invariant acoustic cue can be found here (Harris, Hoffman, Liberman, Delattre, and Cooper 1958; Lisker 1957b; O'Connor, Gerstman, Liberman, Delattre, and Cooper 1957). In fact, the invariance problem is further complicated in that the third-formant transition seems to be more or less important (relative to the second-formant transition, for example) depending on the phonemic context. In the case of our /di, du/ example (figure 13.1), we find that an appropriate transition of the third formant contributes considerably to the perception of /d/ in /di/ but not at all to /d/ in /du/. To produce equal—that is, equally convincing—/d/'s before both /i/ and /u/, we must use acoustic cues that are, if anything, even more different than the two second-formant transitions we described earlier in this section.

Constriction Noises The noises produced at the point of constriction—as in the fricatives and stops—are another set of cues for consonant perception according to place of production, the relevant physical variable being the frequency position of the band-limited noise. When these noises have considerable duration—as in the fricatives—the cue changes but little with context. Since the cue provided by these noises is of overriding importance in the perception of /s/ and /š/, we should say that these consonants show little or no restructuring in the sound stream (Harris 1958; Hughes and Halle 1956). (This may not be true when the speech is rapid.) They therefore constitute an exception to the usual strong dependence of the acoustic signal on its context—that is, to the effects of a syllabic coding operation.

On the other hand, the brief noise cues—the bursts, so called—of the stop consonants display as much restructing as do the transitions of the second formant (Liberman, Delattre, and Cooper 1952). Bursts of noise that produce the best /k/ or /g/ vary over a considerable frequency range depending on the following vowel. The range is so great that it extends over the domain of the /p, b/ burst, creating the curiosity of a single burst of noise at 1440 cps that is heard as /p/ before /i/ but as /k/ before /a/.[8] We should also note that the relative importance of the bursts, as of the transitions, varies greatly for the same stop in different contexts. For example, /g/ or /k/, which are powerfully cued by a second-formant transition before the vowel /æ/, will likely require a burst at an appropriate frequency if they are to be well perceived in front of /o/.[9] Thus, the same consonant is primarily cued in two different contexts by signals as physically different as a formant transition and a burst of noise.

Manner, Voicing, and Position In describing the complexities of the relation between acoustic cue and perceived phoneme, we have so far dealt only with cues for place of production and only with consonants in initial position in the syllable. A comparable lack of regularity is also found in the distinctions of manner and voicing and in the cues for consonants in different positions (Abramson and Lisker 1965; Delattre 1958; Delattre, Liberman, and Cooper 1955; Liberman 1957; Liberman, Delattre, and Cooper 1958; Liberman, Delattre, Cooper, and Gerstman 1954; Liberman, Delattre, Gerstman, and Cooper 1956; Lisker 1957a, 1957b; Lisker and Abramson 1964b; Ohman 1966). We will not consider these cues in detail since the problems they present are similar to those already encountered. Indeed, the cues we have discussed as examples of encoding are merely a subset of those that show extensive restructuring as a function of context: it is the usual case that the acoustic cues for a consonant are different when the consonant is paired with different vowels, when it is in different positions (initial, medial, or final) with respect to the same vowels, and for all types of cues (manner or voicing, as well as place). Thus, for example, the cues for manner, place, and voicing of /b/ in /ba/ are acoustically different from those of /b/ in /ab/, the transitional cues for place being almost mirror images; further, the preceding set of cues differs from corresponding sets for /b/ with each of the other vowels.

The Vowels We should remark, finally, on the acoustic cues for the vowels. For the steady-state vowels of figures 13.1 and 13.2, perception depends primarily on the frequency position of the formants (Delattre, Liberman, and Cooper 1951; Delattre, Liberman, Cooper, and Gerstman 1952). There is, for these vowels, no restructuring of the kind found to be so common among the consonant cues and, accordingly, no problem of invariance between acoustic signal and perception.[10]

However, vowels are rarely steady state in normal speech; most commonly these phonemes are articulated between consonants and at rather rapid rates. Under these conditions vowels also show substantial restructuring—that is, the acoustic signal at no point corresponds to the vowel alone, but rather shows, at any instant, the merged influences of the preceding or following consonant (Lindblom and Studdert-Kennedy, in press; Lisker 1958; Shearme and Holmes 1962; Stevens and House 1963).

In slow articulation, then, the acoustic cues for the vowels—and, as we saw earlier, the noise cues for fricatives—tend to be invariant. In this respect they differ from the cues for the other phonemes, which vary as a function of context at all rates of speaking. However, articulation slow enough to permit the vowels and fricatives to avoid being encoded is probably artificial and rare.

Phoneme Segmentation We return now to the related problem of segmentation, briefly discussed above for the /di, du/ example. We saw there that the acoustic signal is not segmented into phonemes. If one examines the acoustic cues more generally, he finds that successive phonemes are most commonly merged in the sound stream. This is, as we will see, a correlate of the parallel processing that characterizes the speech code and is an essential condition of its efficiency. One consequence is that the acoustic cues cannot be divided on the time axis into segments of phonemic size.[11]

The same general conclusion may be reached by more direct procedures. Working with recordings of real speech, Harris (1953) tried to arrive at "building blocks" by cutting tape recordings into segments of phoneme length and then recombining the segments to form new words. "Experiments indicated that speech based upon one building block for each vowel and consonant not only sounds unnatural but is mostly unintelligible ... [p. 962]." In a somewhat similar attempt to produce intelligible speech by the recombination of parts taken from previously recorded utterances, Peterson, Wang, and Sivertsen (1958) concluded that the smallest segments one can use are of roughly half-syllable length. Thus, it has not been possible, in general, to synthesize speech from prerecorded segments of phonemic dimensions. Nor can we cut the sound stream along the time dimension so as to recover segments that will be perceived as separate phonemes. Of course, there are exceptions. As we might expect, these are the steady-state vowels and the long-duration noises of certain fricatives in which, as we have seen, the sounds show minimal restructuring. Apart from these exceptions, however, segments corresponding to the phonemes are not found at the acoustic level.

We shall see later that the articulatory gestures corresponding to successive phonemes—or, more precisely, their subphonemic features—are overlapped, or shingled, one onto another. This parallel delivery of information produces at the acoustic level the merging of influences we have already referred to and yields irreducible acoustic segments of approximately syllabic dimensions. Thus, segmentation also exhibits a complex relation between linguistic structure or perception, on the one hand, and the sound stream on the other.

Perception of the Restructured Phonemes: The Speech Mode

If phonemes are encoded syllabically in the sound stream, they must be recovered in perception by an appropriate decoder. Perception of phonemes that have been so encoded might be expected to differ from the perception of those that have not and also, of course, from nonspeech. In this section we will suggest that such differences do, in fact, exist.

We have already seen one example of such a difference in the transition cues for /d/ in /di/ and /du/. Taken out of speech context, these transitions sound like whistles, the one rising through a range of high pitches and the other falling through low pitches: they do not sound like each other, nor even like speech. This example could be multiplied to include the transition cues for many other phonemes. With simplified speech of the kind already shown, the listener's perception is very different depending on whether he is, for whatever reason, in the speech mode or out of it (Brady, House, and Stevens 1961).

Even on the basis of what can be heard in real speech, one might have suspected that the perception of encoded and unencoded phonemes[12] is somehow different. One has only to listen carefully to some of the latter in order to make reasonably accurate guesses about the auditory and acoustic dimensions that are relevant to their perception. The fricatives /s/ and /š/, for example, obviously differ in manner from other phonemes in that there is noise of fairly long duration; moreover, one can judge by listening that they differ from each other in the "pitch" of the noise—that is, in the way the energy is distributed along the frequency scale. Consider, on the other hand, the encoded phonemes /b,d,g/. No amount of listening, no matter how careful, is likely to reveal that an important manner cue is a rapidly rising frequency at the low end of the frequency scale (first formant), or that these stops are distinguished from each of other primarily by the direction and extent of a rapid frequency glide in the upper frequency range (second and third formants).

These observations of perceptual differences between speech and nonspeech sounds, and even among classes of phonemes, do not stand alone. Controlled experiments can show more accurately, if sometimes less directly, the differences in perception. We will next consider some of these experiments.

Tendencies toward Categorical and Continuous Perception

Research with some of the encoded phonemes has shown that they are categorical, not only in the abstract linguistic sense, but as immediately given in perception. Consider, first, that in listening to continuous variations in acoustic signals, one ordinarily discriminates many more stimuli than he can absolutely identify. Thus, we discriminate about 1,200 different pitches, for example, though we can absolutely identify only about seven. Perception of the restructured phonemes is different in that listeners discriminate very little better than they identify absolutely; that is to say, they hear the phonemes but not the intraphonemic variations.

The effect becomes clear impressionistically if one listens to simplified, synthetic speech signals in which the second-formant transition is varied in relatively small, acoustically equal steps through a range sufficient to produce the three stops, /b/, /d/, and /g/. One does not hear steplike changes corresponding to the changes in the acoustic signal, but essentially quantal jumps from one perceptual category to another.

To evaluate this effect more exactly, various investigators have made quantitative comparisons of the subjects' ability to identify the stimuli absolutely and to discriminate them on any basis whatsoever. For certain consonant distinctions it has been found that the mode of perception is, in fact, nearly categorical: listeners can discriminate only slightly better than they can identify absolutely. In greater or lesser degree, this has been found for /b,d,g/ (Eimas 1963; Griffith 1958; Liberman, Harris, Hoffman, and Griffith 1957; Studdert-Kennedy, Liberman, and Stevens 1963, 1964); /d,t/ (Liberman, Harris, Kinney, and Lane, 1961);[13] /b,p/ in intervocalic position (Liberman, Harris, Eimas, Lisker, and Bastian 1961), and presence or absence of /p/ in *slit* vs. *split* (Bastian, Delattre, and Libermann 1959; Bastian, Eimas, and Liberman 1961; Harris, Bastian, and Liberman 1961).

The perception of unencoded steady-state vowels is quite different from the perception of stops.[14] To appreciate this difference one need only listen to synthetic vowels that vary, as in the example of the stops, in relatively small and acoustically equal steps through a range sufficient to produce three adjacent phonemes—say /i/, /I/, and /ɛ/. As heard, these vowels change step-by-step, much as the physical stimulus changes: the vowel /i/ shades into /I/, and /I/ into /ɛ/. Immediate perception is more nearly continuous than categorical and the listener hears many intraphonemic variations. More precise measures of vowel perception indicate that, in contrast to the stops, listeners can discriminate many more stimuli than they can identify absolutely (Fry, Abramson, Eimas, and Liberman 1962; Stevens, Ohman, and Liberman 1963; Stevens, Ohman, Studdert-Kennedy, and Liberman 1964). Similar studies of the perception of vowel duration (Bastian and Abramson 1962) and tones in Thai (Abramson 1961), both of which are phonemic in that language, have produced similar results. We should suppose that steady-state vowels, vowel duration, and the tones can be perceived in essentially the same manner as continuous variations in nonspeech signals. The results of a direct experimental comparison by Eimas (1963) suggest that this is so.

We emphasize that in speaking of vowels we have so far been concerned only with those that are isolated and steady state. These are, as we have said, unencoded and hence not necessarily perceived in the speech mode. But what of the more usual situation we described earlier, that of vowels between consonants and in rapid articulation? Stevens (1966) has supposed that the rapid changes in formant position characteristic of such vowels would tend to be referred in perception to the speech mode, and he has some evidence that this is so, having found that perception of certain vowels in proper dynamic context is more nearly categorical than that of steady-state vowels. Inasmuch as these rapidly articulated vowels are substantially restructured in the sound stream. Stevens' results may be assumed to reflect the operation of the speech decoder.

Lateral Differences in the Perception of Speech and Nonspeech
The conclusion that there is a speech mode, and that it is characterized by processes different from those underlying the perception of other sounds, is strengthened by recent indications that speech and nonspeech sounds are processed primarily in different hemispheres of the brain. Using Broadbent's (1954) method of delivering competing stimuli simultaneously to the two ears, investigators have found that speech stimuli presented to the right ear (hence, mainly to the left cerebral hemisphere) are better identified than those presented to the left ear (hence, mainly to the right cerebral hemisphere), and that the reverse is true for melodies and sonar signals (Broadbent and Gregory 1964; Bryden 1963; Chaney and Webster 1965; Kimura 1961, 1964, 1967). In the terminology of this paper, the encoded speech signals are more readily decoded in the left hemisphere than in the right. This suggests the existence of a special left-hemisphere mechanism different from the right-hemisphere mechanism for the perception of sounds not similarly encoded. It is of interest, then, to ask whether the encoded stops and the unencoded steady-state vowels are, perhaps, processed unequally by the two hemispheres. An experiment was carried out (Shankweiler and Studdert-Kennedy 1967b) designed to answer this question, using synthetic speech syllables that contrasted in just one phoneme. A significantly greater right-ear advantage was found for the encoded stops than for the unencoded steady-state vowels. The fact that the steady-state vowels are less strongly lateralized in the dominant (speech) hemisphere may be taken to mean that these sounds, being unencoded, can be, and presumably sometimes are, processed as if they were nonspeech. In another experiment (Shankweiler and Studdert-Kennedy 1967a), the consonant and vowel comparisons were made with real speech. Different combinations of the same set of consonant-vowel-consonant syllables were used for both tests. As before, a decisive right-ear advantage was found for contrasting stop consonants, and again there was no difference for vowels, even though these were articulated in dynamic context between consonants. We will be interested to determine what happens to lateral differences in vowel perception when the vowels are very rapidly articulated. Such vowels are, as has been said, necessarily restructured to some extent and may be correspondingly dependent on the speech decoder for their perception.

Perception of Speech by Machine and by Eye
If speech is, as we have suggested, a special code, its perception should be difficult in the absence of an appropriate decoder such as we presumably use in listening to speech sounds. It is relevant, therefore, to note how very difficult it is to read visual transforms of speech or to construct automatic speech recognizers.

Consider, first, a visual transform—for example, the spectrogram. As we have already seen, the spectrographic pattern for a particular phoneme typically looks very different in different contexts. Furthermore, visual inspection of a spectrogram does not reveal how a stretch of speech might be divided into segments corresponding to phonemes, or even how many phonemes it might contain: the eye sees the transformed acoustic signal in its undecoded form. We should not be surprised, then, to discover that spectrograms are, in fact, extremely difficult to read.

Some part of the difficulty may be attributed to inadequacies of the transform or to lack of training. But an improved transform, if one should be found, would not by itself suffice to make spectrograms readable, since it would not obviate the need to decode. Nor is training likely to overcome the difficulty. Many persons have had considerable experience with spectrograms, yet none has found it possible to read them well.[15] Ideally, training in "reading" spectrograms should cause the transitions for /d/ in /di/ and /du/ to look alike. The speech decoder, after all, makes them sound alike when speech is perceived by ear; moreover, it seems obvious that if the decoder did not do this, speech would be much more difficult to perceive. If, as we suspect, training alone cannot make the acoustic cues for the same phoneme *look* alike, then we should, perhaps, conclude that the speech decoder, which makes them *sound* alike, is biologically tied to an auditory input.

How, then, do machines fare in recognizing the encoded sounds of speech? If speech were a cipher, like print, it would be no more difficult to build a speech recognizer than a print reader. In fact, the speech recognizer has proved to be more difficult, and by a very wide margin, largely because it needs an appropriate decoder, as a print reader does not, and because the design of that decoder is not easily accomplished—a conclusion confirmed by two decades of intensive effort. We might repeat, in passing, that for human beings the difficulty is the other way around: perceiving speech is far easier than reading.

Encoding and Decoding: From Phoneme to Sound and Back

Conversions from Phoneme to Sound
Having considered the evidence that speech is a code on the phonemes, we must ask how the encoding might have come about. The schema in figure 13.5 represents the various conversions that presumably occur as speech proceeds from sentence, through the empty segments at the phoneme level, to the final acoustic signal. The topmost box, labeled Syntactic Rules, would, if properly developed, be further broken down into phrase-structure rules, transformation rules, morphophonemic rules, and the like. (See, for example, Chomsky 1964.) These processes would be of the greatest interest if we were dealing with speech perception in the broadest sense. Here, however, we may start with the message in the form of an ordered sequence of phonemes (or, as we will see, their constituent features) and follow it through the successive converters that yield, at the end, the acoustic waveform.

Subphonemic Features: Their Role in Production   First, we must take account of the fact that the phonemes are compounded of a smaller number of elements, and, indeed, shift the emphasis from the phoneme to these subphoneme features.[16] The total gesture in the articulation of /b/, for example, can be broken down into several distinctive elements: (a) closing and opening of the upper vocal tract in such a way as to produce the manner feature characteristic of the stop consonants; (b) closing and opening of the vocal tract specifically at the lips, thus producing the place feature termed bilability; (c) closing the velum to provide the feature of orality; and (d) starting vocal fold vibration simultaneously with the opening of the lips, appropriate to the feature of voicing. The phoneme /p/ presumably shares with /b/ features 1, 2, and 3, but differs as to feature 4, in that vocal fold vibration begins some 50 or 60 milliseconds after opening of the lips; /m/ has features 1, 2, and 4 in common with /b/, but differs in feature 3, since the velum hangs open to produce the feature of nasality; /d/ has features 1, 3, and 4 in common with /b/, but has a different place of articulation; and so on.

SCHEMA FOR PRODUCTION

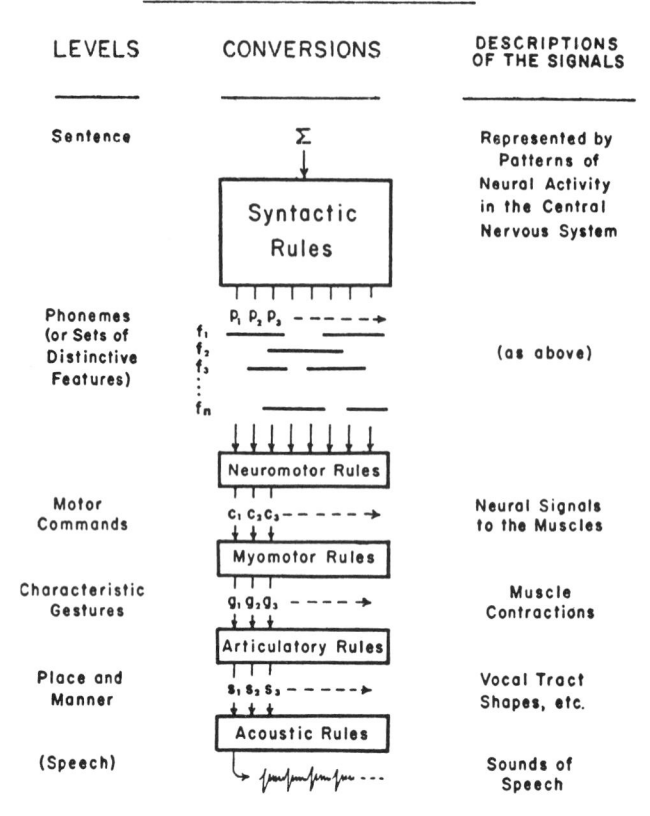

LEVELS	CONVERSIONS	DESCRIPTIONS OF THE SIGNALS
Sentence	Σ ↓ [Syntactic Rules]	Represented by Patterns of Neural Activity in the Central Nervous System
Phonemes (or Sets of Distinctive Features)	$P_1 P_2 P_3$ ----→ $f_1, f_2, f_3 ... f_n$ ↓↓↓↓↓↓↓ [Neuromotor Rules]	(as above)
Motor Commands	$C_1 C_2 C_3$ ----→ ↓↓↓ [Myomotor Rules]	Neural Signals to the Muscles
Characteristic Gestures	$g_1 g_2 g_3$ ----→ ↓↓↓ [Articulatory Rules]	Muscle Contractions
Place and Manner	$s_1 s_2 s_3$ ----→ ↓↓↓ [Acoustic Rules]	Vocal Tract Shapes, etc.
(Speech)	↳ 〰〰〰 ---	Sounds of Speech

Figure 13.5
Schematic representations of assumed stages in speech production.

That subphonemic features are present both in production and perception has by now been quite clearly established.[17] Later in this paper we will discuss some relevant data on production. Here we merely note that we must deal with the phonemes in terms of their constituent features because the existence of such features is essential to the speech code and to the efficient production and perception of language. We have earlier remarked that high rates of speech would overtax the temporal resolving power of the ear if the acoustic signal were merely a cipher on the phonemic structure of the language. Now we should note that *speaking* at rates of 10 to 15 phonemes per second would as surely be impossible if each phoneme required a separate and distinct oral gesture. Such rates can be achieved only if separate parts of the articulatory machinery—muscles of the lips, tongue, velum, etc.—can be separately controlled, and if the linguistic code is such that a change of state for any one of these articulatory entities, taken together with the current state of the others, is a change to another element of the code—that is, to another phoneme. Thus, dividing the load among the articulators allows each to operate at a reasonable pace, and tightening the code keeps the information rate high. It is this kind of parallel processing that makes it possible to get high-speed performance with low-speed machinery.

As we will see, it also accounts for the overlapping and intermixing of the acoustic signals for the phonemes that is characteristic of the speech code.

A Model for Production   The simplest possible model of the production process would, then, have the phonemes of utterance represented by sets of subphonemic features, and these in turn would be assumed to exist in the central nervous system as implicit instructions[18] to separate and independent parts of the motor machinery. The sequence of neural signals corresponding to this multidimensional string of control instructions may well require, for its actualization, some amplitude adjustments and temporal coordination, in the box labeled "Neuromotor Rules," in order to yield the neural impulses that go directly to the selected muscles of articulation and cause them to contract. If we are to continue to make the simplest possible assumption, however, we must suppose that reorganization of the instructions at this stage would be limited to such coordination and to providing supplementary neural signals to insure cooperative activity of the remainder of the articulatory apparatus; there would be no reorganization of the commands to the "primary" actuators for the selected features. In that case, the neural signals that emerge would bear still an essentially one-to-one correspondence with the several dimensions of the subphonemic structure. Indeed, this is a necessary condition for our model, since total reorganization at this stage would destroy the parallel processing, referred to earlier, on which high-speed reception depends, or else yield a syllabic language from which the phoneme strings could not be recovered.

The next conversion, from neural command (in the final common paths) to muscle contraction, takes place in the box labeled "Myomotor Rules." If muscles contract in accordance with the signals sent to them, then this conversion should be essentially trivial, and we should be able not only to observe the muscle contractions by looking at their EMG signals, but also to infer the neural signals at the preceding level.

It is at the next stage—the conversion from muscle contraction to vocal tract shapes by way of Articulatory Rules—that a very considerable amount of encoding or restructuring must surely occur. If we take into account the structure and function of the articulatory system, in particular the intricate linkages and the spatial overlap of the component parts, we must suppose that the relation between contraction and resulting shape is complex, though predictable. True encoding occurs as a consequence of two further aspects of this conversion; the fact that the subphonemic features can be, and are, put through in parallel means that each new set of contractions (a) starts from whatever configuration then exists (as the result of the preceding contractions) and (b) typically occurs before the last set has ended, with the result that the shape of the tract at any instant represents the merged effects of past and present instructions. Such merging is, in effect, an encoding operation according to our use of that term, since it involves an extensive restructuring of the output—in this case, the shape of the tract. The relation of message units to code becomes especially complex when temporal and spatial overlaps occur together. Thus, the conversion from muscle contraction to shape is, by itself, sufficient to produce the kinds of complex relation between phoneme and sound that we have found to exist in the overall process of speech production, that is, a loss of segmentability together with very large changes in the essential acoustic signals as a function of context. Given the structure of the articulatory apparatus, these complexities appear to be a necessary concomitant of the parallel processing that makes the speech code so efficient.

The final conversion, from shape to sound, proceeds by what we have in figure 13.5 called Acoustic Rules. These rules, which are now well understood,[19] are complex from a computational standpoint, but they operate on an instant-by-instant basis and yield (for the most part) one-to-one relations of shape to sound.

Does the Encoding Truly Occur in the Conversion from Command to Shape?
We have supposed that, of the four conversions between phoneme and sound, one at least—the conversion from contractions to tract shape—is calculated to produce an encoding of the kind we found when earlier we examined the acoustic cues for phoneme perception. But does it, in fact, produce that encoding, and if so, does it account for all of it? Downstream from this level there is only the conversion from shape to sound, and that, though complex, does not appear to involve encoding. But what of the upstream conversions, particularly the one that lies between the neural representations of the phonemes and the commands to the articulatory muscles? We cannot at the present time observe those processes, nor can we directly measure their output—that is, the commands to the muscles. We can, however, observe some aspects of the contractions—for example, the electromyographic correlates—and if we assume, as seems reasonable, that the conversion from command to contractions is straightforward, then we can quite safely infer the structure of the commands.[20] By determining to what extent those inferred commands (if not the electromyographic signals themselves) are invariant with the phoneme we can, then, discover how much of the encoding occurs in the conversion from contraction to shape (Articulatory Rules) and how much at higher levels.

Motor Commands as Presumed Invariants Before discussing the electromyographic evidence, we should say what kind of invariance with the subphonemic features (hence, with the phonemes) we might, at best, expect to find. It should be clear from many of the data presented in this paper that language is no more a left-to-right process at the acoustic level than it is syntactically. As we have seen, the acoustic representations of the successive phonemes are interlaced. Some control center must therefore "know" what the syllable is to be in order that its component subphonemic features may be appropriately combined and overlapped. There are other grounds than the data we have cited for inferring such syllabic organization. Temporal relations between syllables may be adjusted for slow or rapid speech and for changes in syllable duration such as Lindblom has reported for a given syllable placed in different polysyllabic contexts. But these changes in syllable duration do not affect all portions of the syllable equally: timing relations within the syllable are also adjusted according to context (Lindblom 1964), and this must entail variation in the relative timing of the component subphonemic features, as is suggested by Kozhevnikov and Chistovich's (1965) analysis of the articulatory structure of consonant clusters. Ohman (1964, 1966) has proposed a model for syllable articulation consistent with this analysis. Such contextual variations preclude the invariance of all the features that comprise a phoneme in a particular context. The most that we can expect is that some subset of these features, and so of the neural signals to the muscles (after operation of the Neuromotor Rules of figure 13.5), will be invariant with the phoneme; there will then be for each subphonemic feature characteristic neuromotor "markers," implicating only one or a few component parts of the system, perhaps only the contraction of a single specific muscle. These characteristic components of the total neural activity we will refer to as "motor commands."[21] We should also emphasize that we refer here to the phoneme as perceived, not as an abstract linguistic entity serving primarily a classificatory function.

Indications from Electromyography What, then, do we find when we look at the electromyographic (EMG) correlates of articulatory activity? Recent research in our laboratory and several others has been directed specifically to the questions raised in the preceding paragraphs, but the data are, as yet, quite limited. As we see these data, they do, however, permit some tentative conclusions.

When two adjacent phonemes are produced by spatially separate groups of muscles, there are essentially invariant EMG tracings from the characteristic gestures for each phoneme, regardless of the identity of the other.[22] This has been found for /f/, for example, followed by /s/, /t/, /ts/, /θ/, or /θs/ and preceded by /i/, /il/, or /im/ (MacNeilage 1963). Similarly, invariance has been found for /b/, /p/, and /m/ regardless of the following vowel (Fromkin 1966; Harris, Lysaught, and Schvey 1965). Here it is easy to associate the place and manner features with the contractions of specific muscles, and to equate the EMG signals for a specific feature wherever it occurs, at least within this limited set of phonemes. We should emphasize that corresponding invariance is not to be found in the acoustic signal: for /f/ the duration of the noise varies over a range of two to one in the contexts listed above: the vast differences in acoustic cue for /b/ or /p/ before various vowels were described in an earlier section.

When the temporally overlapping gestures for successive phonemes involve more or less adjacent muscles that control the same structures, it is of course more difficult to discover whether there is invariance or not.[22] This is the situation of the /di, du/ examples we used earlier. In our own studies of such cases we find essentially identical EMG signals from tongue-tip electrodes for the initial consonant; however, the signal for a following phoneme that also involves the tongue tip may show substantial changes from its characteristic form (Harris 1963; Harris, Huntington, and Sholes 1966). Such changes presumably reflect the execution of position-type commands (see notes 18 and 20) rather than reorganization at a higher level. True reorganization of the neural commands is not excluded by such data—indeed, we have some data that might be so interpreted (MacNeilage, DeClerk, and Silverman 1966)—but the evidence so far is predominantly on the side of invariance.

If the commands—or, indeed, signals of any kind—are to be invariant with the phonemes, they must reflect the segmentation that is so conspicuously absent at the acoustic level. Do we, then, find such segmentation in the EMG records? Before answering that question, we should remind ourselves that the activity of a single muscle or muscle group does not, in any case, reflect a phoneme but only a subphonemic feature, and that a change from one phoneme to another may require a change in command for only one of several features. We should not expect, therefore, that all the subphonemic features will start and stop at each phoneme boundary, and, in fact, they do not. We do find, however, in the onsets and offsets of EMG activity in various muscles a segmentation like that of the several dimensions that constitute the phoneme. One can see, then, where the phoneme boundaries must be.[23] This is in striking contrast to what is found at the acoustic level. There, as we have earlier pointed out, almost any segment we can isolate contains information about—and is a cue for—more than one phoneme. Thus in the matter of segmentation, too, the EMG potentials—and even more the motor commands inferred from them—bear a simpler relation to the perceived phonemes than does the acoustic signal.

In summary we should say that we do not yet know precisely to what extent motor commands are invariant with the phonemes. It seems reasonably clear, however, that they are more nearly invariant than are the acoustic signals, and we may conclude, therefore, that a substantial part of the restructuring occurs below the level of the commands. Whether some significant restructuring occurs also at higher levels can only be determined by further investigation.

Decoding: From Sound to Phoneme
If speech were a simple cipher one might suppose that phoneme perception could be explained by the ordinary principles of psychophysics and discrimination learning. On that view, which is probably not uncommon among psychologists, speech consists of sounds, much like any others, that happen to signal the phoneme units of the language. It is required of the listener only that he learn to connect each sound with the name of the appropriate phoneme. To be sure, the sounds must be discriminably different, but this is a standard problem of auditory psychophysics and poses no special difficulty for the psychologist. It would follow that perception of speech is not different in any fundamental way from perception of other sounds (assuming sufficient practice), and that, as Lane (1965) and Cross, Lane, and Sheppard (1965) suppose, no special perceptual mechanism is required.

The point of this paper has been, to the contrary, that speech is, for the most part, a special code that must often make use of a special perceptual mechanism to serve as its decoder.[24] On the evidence presented here we should conclude, at the least, that most phonemes cannot be perceived by a straightforward comparison of the incoming signal with a set of stored phonemic patterns or templates, even if one assumes mechanisms that can extract simple stimulus invariances such as, for example, constant ratios. To find acoustic segments that are in any reasonably simple sense invariant with linguistic (and perceptual) segments—that is, to perceive without decoding—one must go to the syllable level or higher. Now the number of syllables, reckoned simply as the number of permissible combinations and permutations of phonemes, is several thousand in English. But the number of acoustic patterns is far greater than that, since the acoustic signal varies considerably with the speaker and with the stress, intonation, and tempo of his speech (Cooper, Liberman, Lisker, and Gaitenby 1963; Liberman, Ingemann, Lisker, Delattre, and Cooper 1959; Lindblom 1963, Peterson and Sivertsen 1960; Peterson, Wang, and Sivertsen 1958; Sivertsen 1961). To perceive speech by matching the acoustic signal to so many patterns would appear, at best, uneconomical and inelegant. More important, it would surely be inadequate, since it must fail to account for the fact that we do perceive phonemes. No theory can safely ignore the fact that phonemes are psychologically real.

How, then, is the phoneme to be recovered? We can imagine, at least in general outline, two very different possibilities: one, a mechanism that operates on a purely auditory basis, the other, by reference to the processes of speech production.

The Case for an Auditory Decoder The relevant point about an auditory decoder is that it would process the signal in *auditory* terms—that is, without reference to the way in which it was produced—and successfully extract the phoneme string. On the basis of what we know of speech, and of the attempts to build an automatic phoneme recognizer, we must suppose such a device would have to be rather complex. There is, to be sure, some evidence for the existence of processing mechanisms in the auditory system that illustrate at a very simple level one kind of thing that an auditory decoder might have to do. Thus, Whitfield and Evans (1965) have found single cells in the auditory cortex of the cat that respond to frequency changes but not to steady tones. Some of these cells responded more to tones that are frequency modulated upward and others to tones modulated downward. Such specificity of response also exists at lower levels in the auditory nervous system (Nelson, Erulkar, and Bryant 1966). These findings are examples of a kind of auditory processing that might, perhaps, be part of a speech decoder, but one that would have to go beyond these processes—to more complex ones—if it were to deal successfully with the fact that very different transitions will, in different contexts, cue the same phoneme. But if this could be accomplished, and if it were done independently of motor parameters, we should have a purely auditory decoder.

The Case for Mediation by Production   Though we cannot exclude the possibility that a purely auditory decoder exists, we find it more plausible to assume that speech is perceived by processes that are also involved in its production. The most general and obvious motivation for such a view is that the perceiver is also a speaker and must be supposed, therefore, to possess all the mechanisms for putting language through the successive coding operations that result eventually in the acoustic signal.[25] It seems unparsimoniuos to assume that the speaker-listener employs two entirely separate processes of equal status, one for encoding language and the other for decoding it. A simpler assumption is that there is only one process, with appropriate linkages between sensory and motor components.[26]

Apart from parsimony, there are strong reasons for considering this latter view. Recall, for example, the case of /di, du/. There we saw that the acoustic patterns for /d/ were very different, though the perception of the consonantal segment was essentially the same. Since it appears that the /d/ gesture—or, at least, some important, "diagnostic" part of it—may also be essentially the same in the two cases, we are tempted to suppose that one hears the same /d/ because perception is mediated by the neuromotor correlates of gestures that are the same. This is basically the argument we used in one of our earliest papers (Liberman, Delattre, and Cooper 1952) to account for the fact that bursts of sound at very different frequencies are required to produce the perception of /k/ before different vowels. Extending the argument, we tried in that same paper to account also for the fact that the same burst of sound is heard as /p/ before /i/ but as /k/ before /a/, the point being that, because of temporal overlap (and consequent acoustic encoding), very different gestures happen to be necessary in these different vowel environments in order to produce the same acoustic effect (the consonant burst). The argument was applied yet again to account for a finding about second-formant transitions as cues: that the acoustic cues for /g/ can be radically different even when the consonant is paired with closely related vowels (i.e., in the syllables /ga/ and /gɔ/), yet the perception and the articulation are essentially the same (Liberman 1957). But these are merely striking examples of what must be seen now as a general rule: there is typically a lack of correspondence between acoustic cue and perceived phoneme, and in all these cases it appears that perception mirrors articulation more closely than sound.[27] If this were not so, then for a listener to hear the same phoneme in various environments, speakers would have to hold the acoustic signal constant, which would, in turn, require that they make drastic changes in articulation. Speakers need not do that—and in all probability they cannot—yet listeners nevertheless hear the same phoneme. This supports the assumption that the listener uses the inconstant sound as a basis for finding his way back to the articulatory gestures that produced it and thence, as it were, to the speaker's intent.

The categorical perception of stop consonants also supports this assumption.[28] As described earlier in this paper, perception of these sounds is categorical, or discontinuous, even when the acoustic signal is varied continuously. Quite obviously, the required articulations would also be discontinuous. With /b,d,g/, we can vary the acoustic cue along a continuum, which corresponds, in effect, to closing the vocal tract at various points along its length. But in actual speech the closing is accomplished by discontinuous or categorically different gestures: by the lips for /b/, the tip of the tongue for /d/, and the back of the tongue for /g/. Here, too, perception appears to be tied to articulation.

The view that speech is perceived by reference to production is receiving increased attention. Researchers at the Pavlov Institute in Leningrad have adduced various kinds of evidence to support a similar hypothesis (Chistovich 1960; Chistovich, Klaas, and Kuz'min 1962). Ladefoged (1959) has presented a motor-theoretical interpretation of some aspects of speech perception. More recently, Ladefoged and McKinney (1963) have found in studies of stress that perception is related more closely to certain low-level aspects of stress production than it is to the acoustic signal. And in a very recent study Lieberman (1967) has found interesting evidence for a somewhat similar conclusion in regard to the perception of some aspects of intonation.

The Role of Productive Processes in Models for Speech Perception In its most general form, the hypothesis being described here is not necessarily different in principle from a model for speech perception called "analysis-by-synthesis" that has been advanced by Stevens (1960) and by Halle and Stevens (1962; Stevens and Halle, in press) following a generalized model proposed by MacKay (1951). In contrast, perhaps, to the computer-based assumptions of analysis-by-synthesis, we would rather think in terms of overlapping activity of several neural networks—those that supply control signals to the articulators and those that process incoming neural patterns from the ear—and to suppose that information can be correlated by these networks and passed through them in either direction. Such a formulation, in rather general terms, has been presented elsewhere (Liberman, Cooper, Studdert-Kennedy, Harris, and Shankweiler, in press).

The most general form of the view that speech is perceived by reference to production does not specify the level at which the message units are recovered. The assumption is that at some level or levels of the production process there exist neural signals standing in one-to-one correspondence with the various segments of the language—phoneme, word, phrase, etc. Perception consists in somehow running the process backward, the neural signals corresponding to the various segments being found at their respective levels. In phoneme perception—our primary concern in this paper—the invariant is found far down in the neuromotor system, at the level of the commands to the muscles. Perception by morphophonemic, morphemic, and syntactic rules of the language would engage the encoding processes at higher levels. The level at which the encoding process is entered for the purposes of perceptual decoding may, furthermore, determine which shapes can and cannot be detected in raw perception. The invariant signal for the different acoustic shapes that are all heard as

/d/, for example, may be found at the level of motor commands. In consequence, the listener is unaware, even in the most careful listening, that the acoustic signals are, in fact, quite radically different. On the other hand, a listener can readily hear the difference between tokens of the morphophoneme {S} when it is realized as /s/ in cats and as /z/ in dogs, though he also "knows" that these two acoustic and phonetic shapes are in some sense the same. If the perception of that commonality is also by reference to production, the invariant is surely at a level considerably higher than the motor commands.

The Efficiency of the Speech Code

Speech can be produced rapidly because the phonemes are processed in parallel. They are taken apart into their constituent features, and the features belonging to successive phonemes are overlapped in time. Thus the load is divided among the many largely independent components of the articulatory system. Within the phonological constraints on combinations and sequences that can occur, a speaker produces phonemes at rates much higher than those at which any single articulatory component must change its state.[29]

In the conversion of these multidimensional and overlapping articulatory events into sound, a complex encoding occurs. The number of dimensions is necessarily reduced, but the parallel transmission of phonemic information is retained in that the cues for successive phonemes are imprinted on a single aspect of the acoustic signal. Thus, the movement of articulators as independent as the lips and the tongue both affect the second formant and its transitions: given an initial labile consonant overlapped with a tongue shape appropriate for the following vowel, one finds, as we have already shown, that the second-formant transition simultaneously carries information about both phonemic segments.[30]

If the listener possesses some device for recovering the articulatory events from their encoded traces in the sound stream, then he should perceive the phonemes well and, indeed, evade several limitations that would otherwise apply in auditory perception. As we pointed out early in this paper, the temporal resolving power of the ear sets a relatively low limit on the rate at which discrete acoustic segments can be perceived. To the extent that the code provides for parallel processing of successive phonemes, the listener can perceive strings of phonemes more rapidly than he could if the acoustic signals for them were arranged serially, as in an alphabet. Thus, the parallel processing of the phonemes is as important for efficient perception as for production.

We also referred earlier to the difficulty of finding a reasonable number of acoustic signals of short duration that can be readily and rapidly identified. This limitation is avoided if the decoding of the acoustic signal enables the listener to recover the articulatory events that produced it, since perception then becomes linked to a system of physiological coordinates more richly multidimensional—hence more distinctive—than the acoustic (and auditory) signal.

Having said of the speech code that it seems particularly well designed to circumvent the shortcomings of the ear, we should consider whether its accomplishments stop there. As we pointed out earlier, these shortcomings do not apply to the eye, for example, and we do indeed find that the best way to communicate language in the visual mode is by means of an alphabet or cipher, not a code. But we also noted that the acoustic code is more easily and naturally perceived than is the optical alphabet. Perhaps this is due primarily to the special speech decoder, whose existence we assumed for the conversion of sound to phoneme. We would suggest an additional possibility: the operations that occur in the speech decoder—including, in particular, the interdependence of perceptual and productive processes—may be in some sense similar to those that take place at other levels of grammar. If so, there would be a special compatibility between the perception of speech sounds and the comprehension of language at higher stages. This might help to explain why, so far from being merely one way of conveying language, the sounds of speech are, instead, its common and privileged carriers.

Notes

The research reported here was aided at its beginning, and for a considerable period afterward, by the Carnegie Corporation of New York. Funds have also come from the National Science Foundation and the Department of Defense. The work is currently supported by the National Institute of Child Health and Human Development, the National Institute of Dental Research, and the Office of Naval Research.

1. For our purposes the phoneme is the shortest segment that makes a significant difference between utterances. It lies in the lowest layer of language, has no meaning in itself, and is, within limits, commutable. There are, for example, three such segments in the word "bad—/b/,/æ/, and /d/—established by the contrasts with "dad," "bed," and "hat." As commonly defined, a phoneme is an abstract and general type of segment, represented in any specific utterance by concrete and specific tokens, called phones, that may vary noticeably as a function of context. The distinguishable variants so produced are referred to as allophones.

    We do not mean to imply that every phoneme is necessarily perceived as one listens to speech. Linguistic constraints of various kinds make it possible to correct or insert segments that are heard wrongly or not at all. Phonemes can be perceived, however, and some number of them must be perceived if the listener is to discover which constraints apply.

2. We borrow the terms cipher and code from cryptography. A cipher substitutes a symbol for each of the units (letters, usually) of the original message. In a code, on the other hand, the units of the original and encoded forms do not correspond in structure or number, the encoded message typically containing fewer units. Since these distinctions are relevant to our purpose here, we have adopted the terms cipher and code as a convenient way to refer to them. We should add, however, that the arbitrary relation between the original and encoded forms of a message, so usual in cryptography, is not a feature of the encoding of phonemes into syllables.

3. For the discussion that follows we shall rely most heavily on the results of experiments with synthetic speech carried out at Haskins Laboratories. The reader will understand that a review of the relevant literature would refer to many other studies, including, in particular, those that rest on analysis of real speech. For recent reviews and discussions, see Stevens and House, in press; Kozhevnikov and Chistovich 1965, chapter 6.

4. Some form of a voiceless unaspirated stop having a place of production in the alveolar-dental region is universal (Hockett 1955; Joseph Greenberg, personal communication, November 1966). The particular example, /d/, used here is a member of that class in almost all important respects. Even in regard to voicing, it is a better fit than might at first appear, since it shares with the voiceless, unaspirated stop of, say, French or Hungarian, the same position on the dimension of voice-onset-time, which is a most important variable for phonemic differences in voicing. (Lisker and Abramson 1964a, 1964b).

5. A formant is a concentration of acoustic energy within a restricted frequency region. Three or four formants are usually seen in spectrograms of speech. In the synthetic, hand-painted spectrograms of figures 13.1 and 13.2, only the lowest two are represented. Formants are referred to by number, the first being the lowest in frequency, the second, the next higher, and so on. A formant transition is a relatively rapid change in the position of the formant on the frequency scale.

6. This is true of the patterns shown in figure 13.1 as converted to sound by the Pattern Playback. When the formants correspond more closely in their various constant features to those produced by the human vocal apparatus, the musical qualities described above may be harder to hear or may disappear

altogether. So long as the second-format transitions of /di/ and /du/ are not heard as speech, however, they do not sound alike.
7. Somewhat similar complications arise in the suprasegmental domain. For data concerning the relation between the acoustic signal and the perception of intonation see Hadding-Koch and Studdert-Kennedy 1964a, 1964b.

   Lieberman (1967) has measured some of the relevant physiological variables and, on the basis of his findings, has devised a hypothesis to account for the perception of intonation, in particular the observations of Hadding-Koch and Studdert-Kennedy. Lieberman's account of perception in the suprasegmental domain fits well with our own views about the decoding of segmental phonemes, discussed later in this paper.
8. This result was obtained in the experiment (Liberman, Delattre, and Cooper 1952) with synthetic speech referenced above and verified for real speech in a tape-cutting experiment by Carol Schatz (1954).
9. This can be seen in the results of experiments on the bursts and transitions as cues for the stops (Liberman, Delattre, and Cooper 1952; Liberman, Delattre, Cooper, and Gerstman 1954). It is confirmed whenever one attempts, by using all possible cues, to synthesize the best stops.
10. The absolute formant frequencies of the same vowel are different for men, women, and children, and for different individuals, partly as a consequence of differences in the sizes of vocal tracts. This creates an invariance problem very different from the kind we have been discussing and more similar, perhaps, to the problems encountered in the perception of nonspeech sounds, such as the constant ratios of musical intervals.
11. This is not to say that the sound spectrogram fails to show discontinuities along the time axis. Fant (1962a, 1962b) discusses the interpretation to be given these abrupt changes and the temporal segments bounded by them. He warns: "Sound segment boundaries should not be confused with phoneme boundaries. Several adjacent sounds of connected speech may carry information on one and the same phoneme, and there is overlapping in so far as one and the same sound segment carries information on several adjacent phonemes [1962a, p. 9]."
12. There is a need, in much that follows, for a convenient way to refer to classes of phonemes that show much—or little—restructuring of their acoustic cues as a function of context. The former are, indeed, encoded. We shall refer to the latter as "unencoded phonemes," implying only that they are found at the other end of a continuum on degree of restructuring; we do not wish to imply differences in the processes affecting these phonemes, whether or not such differences can be inferred from their perceptual characteristics.
13. Studies of this distinction (and of the corresponding ones for the other stops) in 11 diverse languages indicate that it tends to be categorical also in production. (Abramson and Lisker 1965; Lisker and Abramson 1964a, 1964b.)
14. In experiments with mimicry, Ludmilla Chistovich and her colleagues have obtained differences between vowels and consonants that are consistent with the differing tendencies toward categorical and continuous perception described here. (Chistovich 1960; Chistovich, Klaas, and Kuz'min 1962; Galunov and Chistovich 1965; Kozhevnikov and Chistovich 1965.)
15. "As a matter of fact I have not met one single speech researcher who has claimed he could read speech spectrograms fluently, and I am no exception myself [Fant 1962a, p. 4]." Spectrograms are, even so, less difficult to read than oscillograms—whence their popular name, "visible speech," and much of the early enthusiasm for them (Potter, Kopp, and Green 1947).
16. The term "feature" has varied uses, even in this paper. Thus, in this paragraph, we describe a particular speech gesture in conventional phonetic terms, referring to how the articulators move and where the constrictions occur as the manner and place features that, taken together, characterize the gesture. Two paragraphs later, the description of a possible model for speech production identifies subphonemic features as implicit instructions to separate and independent parts of the motor machinery. Viewed in this way, the distinctive features of a phoneme are closely linked to specific muscles and the neural commands that actuate them.

    Distinctive features of this kind are clearly different from those so well known from the work of Jakobson and his colleagues. See Jakobson, Fant, and Halle (1952) and the various revisions proposed by the several authors (Fant 1967; Halle 1964; Jakobson and Halle 1956; Stevens and Halle, in press). We are, nevertheless, deeply indebted to them for essential points—in particular, that the phonemes can be characterized by sets of features which are few in number, limited to a very few states each, and maintained throughout several phonemes. Other important characteristics for an ideal system of dis-

tinctive features include mutual independence, clear correspondences with physiological—or acoustic—observables, and as much universality across languages as parsimony for a single language will allow.
17. For discussions of the psychological reality of phoneme segments and subphonemic features, see Kozhevnikov and Chistovich 1965; Stevens and House, in press; Wickelgren 1966.
18. These instructions might be of two types, "on-off" or "go to," even in a maximally simple model. In the one case, the affected muscle would contract or not with little regard for its current state (or the position of the articulator it moves); in the other, the instruction would operate via the γ-efferent system to determine the degree of contraction (hence, the final position of the articulator, whatever its initial position). Both types of instruction—appropriate, perhaps, to fast and slow gestures, respectively—may reasonably be included in the model.
19. The dependence of speech sound on vocal tract shape (and movement) has, of course, been studied by many workers and for many years. A landmark in this field, and justification for our statement, is the book by Fant (1960).
20. For commands of the on-off type (see note 18), we would expect muscle contractions—and EMG potentials—to be roughly proportional to the commands; hence, the commands will be mirrored directly by the EMG potentials when these can be measured unambiguously for the muscles of interest. All these conditions are realizable, at least approximately, for a number of phoneme combinations—for example, the bilabial stops and nasal consonants with unrounded vowels, as described in later paragraphs.

    Commands of the "go to" type, which may well be operative in gestures that are relatively slow and precise, would presumably operate via the γ-efferent system to produce only so much contraction of the muscle as is needed to achieve a target length. The contraction—and the resulting EMG signal—would then be different for different starting positions, that is, for the same phoneme in different contexts. Even so, the significant aspects of the command can be inferred, since presence versus absence and sequential position (if not the relative timing) of the EMG signal persist despite even large changes in its magnitude.

    For general discussions of the role of electromyography in research on speech, see the reviews by Cooper (1965) and Fromkin and Ladefoged (1966).
21. Thus, the motor commands are, in one sense, abstract "-eme" type entities, with invariance assumed and observation directed to their discovery and enumeration; in another sense, and to the degree that observation justifies the assumption about invariance, motor commands constitute the essential subset of real neural signals with which a general model of production and perception should be principally concerned.
22. It is not, of course, necessary that the EMG signals be precisely the same since invariance is expected only of the motor commands inferred from them. In the minimally complicated cases cited in this paragraph, the commands do transform into EMG potentials that are essentially the same (in different contexts), aside from some differences in magnitude.

    Magnitude differences do occur, however, variously for the individual and context, and may have linguistic significance attributed to them. Thus, Fromkin (1966) concludes, mainly from EMG data on the lip-closing gestures of her principal speaker:

    > The results of the present investigation do not support the hypothesis that a simple one-to-one correspondence exists between a phoneme and its motor commands. For the bilabial stops /b/ and /p/ different motor commands produce different muscular gestures for these consonants occurring in utterance initial and final positions [p. 195].

    Harris, Lysaught, and Schvey (1965) report, on the contrary, that differences in EMG signal for the lip-closing gesture did not reach statistical significance for two groups of five subjects each in two experiments, one of which overlapped Fromkin's study. They noted, though, that each of the subjects showed an individual pattern of small but consistent variations of EMG signal with context. (For a discussion of these differences in the interpretation of basically similar data, see Cooper 1966.)
22. A practical difficulty exists in allocating observed EMG potentials to specific muscles when more than one muscle is close to a surface electrode. Needle electrodes will often resolve such ambiguities, but they pose other problems of a practical nature.
23. In some cases the boundaries are sharply marked by a sudden onset of EMG signal for a particular muscle. Usually, though, the onsets are less abrupt and activity persists for a few hundred milliseconds. This might seem inadequate to provide segmentation markers for the rapid-fire phoneme sequences;

indeed, precise time relationships may be blurred in normal articulation, but without obscuring the sequential order of events and the separateness of the channels carrying information about the several features.

24. We referred earlier to perception in the speech mode and indicated that it was not operative—or, at least, not controlling—for some speech sounds as well as all nonspeech sounds. It need hardly be said, then, that the speech decoder provides only one pathway for perception; nonspeech sounds obviously require another pathway, which may serve adequately for the unencoded aspects of speech as well.

25. We have noted that training in reading speech spectrograms has so far not succeeded in developing in the trainee a visual decoder for speech comparable to the one that works from an auditory input. This may well reflect the existence of special mechanisms for the speech decoder that are lacking for its visual counterpart. In general, a theory about the nature of the speech decoder—and, in particular, a motor theory—must be concerned with the nature of the mechanism, though not necessarily with the question of how it was acquired in the history of the individual or the race. This is an interesting, but separate, question and is not considered here.

26. We should suppose that the links between perception and articulation exist at relatively high levels of the nervous system. For information about, or reference to, motor activity, the experienced organism need not rely—at least not very heavily and certainly not exclusively—on proprioceptive returns from the periphery, for example, from muscular contractions. (See von Holst and Mittelstadt 1950.)

27. For further discussion of this point, see Liberman 1957; Cooper, Liberman, Harris, and Grubb 1958; Lisker, Cooper, and Liberman 1962; Liberman, Cooper, Harris, MacNeilage, and Studdert-Kennedy, in press.

28. For further discussion of this point, see Liberman, Cooper, Harris, and MacNeilage 1962.

29. The phonological constraints may, in fact, play an essential part in making the decoding operation fast and relatively free of error. Since the set of phonemes and phoneme sequences that is used in any particular language is far smaller than the possible set of feature combinations—smaller even than the combinations that are physiologically realizable—information about the allowable combinations of features could be used in the decoding process to reestablish temporal relationships that may have been blurred in articulation (see note 23). Such a "recutting" operation would ease the requirements on precision of articulation and so allow faster communication; also, it would make unambiguous the segmentation into phonemes, thereby qualifying them as units of immediate perception. One may speculate, further, that the serial string of reconstituted phonemes is useful—perhaps essential—in the next operation of speech reception, namely, gaining immediate access to an inventory of thousands of syllable- or word-size units.

30. Fant (1962a, p. 5) makes essentially the same point:

> The rules relating speech waves to speech production are in general complex since one articulation parameter, e.g., tongue height, affects several of the parameters of the spectrogram. Conversely, each of the parameters of the spectrogram is generally influenced by several articulatory variables.

References

Abramson, A. S. Identification and discrimination of phonemic tones. *Journal of the Acoustical Society of America*, 1961, 33, 842. (Abstract)

Abramson, A. S., and Lasker, L. Voice onset time in stop consonants: Acoustic analysis and synthesis. *Reports of the Fifth International Congress on Acoustics*, 1965, Ia, Paper A51.

Bastian, J., and Abramson, A. S. Identification and discrimination of phonemic vowel duration. *Journal of the Acoustical Society of America*, 1962, 34, 743. (Abstract)

Bastian, J., Delattre, P. C., and Liberman, A. M. Silent interval as a cue for the distinction between stops and semivowels in medial position. *Journal of the Acoustical Society of America*, 1959, 31, 1568. (Abstract)

Bastian, J., Eimas, P. D., and Liberman, A. M. Identification and discrimination of a phonemic contrast induced by silent interval. *Journal of the Acoustical Society of America*, 1961, 33, 842. (Abstract)

Brady, P. T., House, A. S., and Stevens, K. N. Perception of sounds characterized by a rapidly changing resonant frequency. *Journal of the Acoustical Society of America*, 1961, 33, 1337–1362.

Broadbent, D. E. The role of auditory localization in attention and memory span. *Journal of Experimental Psychology*, 1954, 47, 191–196.

Broadbent, D. E., and Gregory, M. Accuracy of recognition for speech presented to the right and left ears. *Quarterly Journal of Experimental Psychology*, 1964, 16, 359–360.

Bryden, M. P. Ear preference in auditory perception. *Journal of Experimental Psychology*, 1963, 65, 103–105.
Chaney, R. B., and Webster, J. C. Information in certain multidimensional acoustic signals. Report No. 1339, 1965. United States Navy Electronics Laboratory Reports, San Diego, Calif.
Chistovich, L. A. Classification of rapidly repeated speech sounds. *Akusticheskii Zhurnal*, 1960, 6, 392–398. (Trans, in *Soviet Physics-Acoustics*, New York, 1961, 6, 393–398).
Chistovich, L. A., Klaas, Y. A., and Kuz'min, Y. I. The process of speech sound discrimination. *I'oprosy Psikhologii*, 1962, 8, 26–39. (Research Library, Air Force Cambridge Research Laboratories, Bedford, Mass. TT-64-13064 35-P)
Chomsky, N. Current issues in linguistic theory. In J. A. Fodor and J. J. Katz (Eds.), *The structure of language*. Englewood Cliffs, N. J.: Prentic Hall, 1964. Pp. 50–118.
Coffey, J. L. The development and evaluation of the Battelle Aural Reading Device. *Proceedings of the International Congress on Technology and Blindness I*. New York: American Foundation for the Blind, 1963. Pp. 343–360.
Cooper, F. S. Research on reading machines for the blind. In P. A. Zahl (Ed.), *Blindness: Modern approaches to the unseen environment*. Princeton, N. J.: Princeton University Press, 1950a. Pp. 512–543.
Cooper, F. S. Spectrum analysis. *Journal of the Acoustical Society of America*, 1950b, 22, 761–762.
Cooper, F. S. Some instrumental aids to research on speech. *Report on the Fourth Annual Round Table Meeting on Linguistics and Language Teaching*. Monograph Series No. 3. Washington: Georgetown University Press, 1953, Pp. 46–53.
Cooper, F. S. Research techniques and instrumentation: EMG. *American Speech and Hearing Association Reports*, 1965, 1, 153–158.
Cooper, F. S. Describing the speech process in motor command terms. *Journal of the Acoustical Society of America*, 1966, 39, 1221 (Abstract) (*Status Report of Speech Research, Haskins Laboratories, SR-5/6*, 1966, 2.1–2.27—text.)
Cooper, F. S. Delattre, P. C., Liberman, A. M., Borst, J., and Gestman, L. J. Some experiments on the perception of synthetic speech sounds. *Journal of the Acoustical Society of America*, 1952, 24 597–606.
Cooper, F. S. Liberman, A. M., and Borst, J. M. The interconversion of audible and visible patterns as a basis for research in the perception of speech. *Proceedings of the National Academy of Sciences*, 1951, 37, 318–325.
Cooper, F. S. Liberman, A. M., Harris, K. S., and Grubb, P. M. Some input-output relations observed in experiments on the perception of speech. *Proceedings of the Second International Congress of Cybernetics, 1958*. Namur, Belgium: Association Internationale de Cybernetique. Pp. 930–941.
Cooper, F. S., Liberman, A. M., Lisker, L., and Gaitenby, J. Speech synthesis by rules. *Proceedings of the Speech Communication Seminar*, Stockholm, 1962. Stockholm: Royal Institute of Technology, 1963. F2.
Cross, D. V., Lane, H. L., and Sheppard, W. C. Identification and discrimination functions for a visual continuum and their relation to the motor theory of speech perception. *Journal of Experimental Psychology*, 1965, 70, 63–74.
Delattre, P. C. Les indices acoustiques de la parole: Premier rapport. *Phonetica*, 1958, 2, 108–118, 226–251.
Delattre, P. C. Le jeu des transitions des formants et la perception des consonnes. *Proceedings of the Fourth International Congress of Phonetic Sciences, Helsinki, 1961*. 's-Gravenhage: Mouton, 1962. Pp. 407–417.
Delattre, P. C., Liberman, A. M., and Cooper, F. S. Voyelles synthétiques à deux formants et voyelles cardinales. *Le Maitre Phonétique*, 1951, 96, 30–37.
Delattre, P. C., Liberman, A. M., and Cooper, F. S. Acoustic loci and transitional cues for consonants. *Journal of the Acoustical Society of America*, 1955, 27, 769–773.
Delattre, P. C., Liberman, A. M., and Cooper, F. S. Format transitions and loci as acoustic correlates of place of articulation in American fricatives. *Studia Linguistica*, 1964, 18, 104–121.
Delattre, P. C., Liberman, A. M., Cooper, F. S., and Gestman, L. J. An experimental study of the acoustic determinants of vowel color: Observations on one- and two-formant vowels synthesized from spectrographic patterns. *Word*, 1952, 8, 195–210.
Denes, P. B. On the statistics of spoken English. *Journal of the Acoustical Society of America*, 1963, 35, 892–904.
Eimas, P. D. The relation between identification and discrimination along speech and non-speech continua. *Language and Speech*, 1963, 6, 206–217.
Fant, C. G. M. *Acoustic theory of speech production.* 's-Gravenhage: Mouton, 1960.
Fant, C. G. M. Descriptive analysis of the acoustic aspects of speech. *Logos*, 1962a, 5, 3–17.
Fant, C. G. M. Sound spectography. *Proceedings IV International Congress on Phonetic Sciences, Helsinki, 1961*. 's-Gravenhage: Mouton, 1962b. Pp. 14–33.

Fant, C. G. M. Theory of distinctive features. *Speech Transmission Laboratory Quarterly Progress and Status Report*, Royal Institute of Technology (KTH), Stockholm, January 15, 1967. Pp. 1–14.

Freiberger, J., and Murphy, E. F. Reading machines for the blind. *IRE Professional Group on Human Factors in Electronics*, 1961, H F E-2, 8–19.

Fromkin, V. A. Neuro-muscular specification of linguistic units. *Language and Speech*, 1966, 9, 170–199.

Fromkin, V. A., and Ladefoged, P. Electromyography in speech research. *Phonetica*, 1966, 15, 219–242.

Fry, D. B., Abramson, A. S., Eimas, P. D., and Liberman, A. M. The identification and discrimination of synthetic vowels. *Language and Speech*, 1962, 5, 171–189.

Galunov, V. I., and Chistovich, L. A. Relationship of motor theory to the general problem of speech recognition (review). *Akusticheskii Zhurnal*, 1965, 11, 417–426. (Trans, in *Soviet Physics-Acoustics*, New York, 1966, 11, 357–365.)

Gelb, I. J. *A study of writing*. Chicago: University of Chicago Press, 1963.

Griffith, B. C. A study of the relation between phoneme labeling and discriminability in the perception of synthetic stop consonants. Unpublished doctoral dissertation, University of Connecticut, 1958.

Hadding-Koch, K., and Studdert-Kennedy, M. An experimental study of some intonation contours. *Phonetica*, 1964a, 11, 175–185.

Hadding-Koch, K., and Studdert-Kennedy, M. Intonation contours evaluated by American and Swedish test subjects. *Proceedings of the Fifth International Congress of Phonetic Sciences*, Munster, August 1964b.

Halle, M. On the bases of phonology. In J. A. Foder and J. J. Katz (Eds.). *The structure of language*. Englewood Cliffs, N. J.: Prentice-Hall, 1964, Pp. 324–333.

Halle, M., and Stevens, K. N. Speech recognition: A model and a program for research. *IRE Transactions on Information Theory JT-8*, 1962, 2, 155–159.

Harris, C. M. A study of the building blocks in speech. *Journal of the Acoustical Society of America*, 1953, 25, 962–969.

Harris, K. S. Cues for the discrimination of American English fricatives in spoken syllables. *Language and Speech*, 1958, 1, 1–7.

Harris, K. S. Behavior of the tongue in the production of some alveolar consonants. *Journal of the Acoustical Society of America*, 1963, 35, 784. (Abstract)

Harris, K. S., Bastian, J., and Liberman, A. M. Mimicry and the perception of a phonemic contrast induced by silent interval: Electromyographic and acoustic measures. *Journal of the Acoustical Society of America*, 1961, 33, 842. (Abstract)

Harris, K. S., Hoffman, H. S. Liberman, A. M., Delattre, P. C., and Cooper, F. S. Effect of third-formant transitions on the perception of the voiced stop consonants. *Journal of the Acoustical Society of America*, 1958, 30, 122–126.

Harris, K. S., Huntington, D. A., and Sholes, G. N. Coarticulation of some disyllabic utterances measured by electromyographic techniques. *Journal of the Acoustical Society of America*, 1966, 39, 1219. (Abstract)

Harris, K. S., Lysaught, G., and Schvey, M. M. Some aspects of the production of oral and nasal labial stops. *Language and Speech*, 1965, 8, 135–147.

Hockett, C. F. *A manual of phonology*. Baltimore: Waverly Press, 1955.

Hughes, G. W., and Halle, M. Spectral properties of fricative consonants. *Journal of the Acoustical Society of America*, 1956, 28, 303-310.

Jakobson, R., Fant, G., and Halle, M. *Preliminaries to speech analysis. The distinctive features and their correlates*. Technical Report No. 13, 1952, Acoustics Laboratory, M.I.T. (Republished, Cambridge, Mass.: M.I.T. Press, 1963.)

Jakobson, R., and Halle, M. *Fundamentals of language*. 's-Gravenhage: Mouton, 1956.

Kimura, D. Cerebral dominance and perception of verbal stimuli. *Canadian Journal of Psychology*, 1961, 15, 166–171.

Kimura, D. Left-right differences in the perception of melodies. *Quarterly Journal of Experimental Psychology*, 1964, 16, 355–358.

Kimura, D. Functional asymmetry of the brain in dichotic listening. *Cortex*, 1967, 3, in press.

Kozhevnikov, V. A., and Chistovich, L. A. *Rech' Artikuliatsia i vospriiatic*. Moscow-Leningrad, 1965. (Trans, in *Speech: Articulation and perception*. Washington: Joint Publications Research Service, 1966, 30, 543.)

Ladefoged, P. The perception of speech. In *mechanization of thought processes*, 1959. London: H. M. Stationery Office. Pp. 397–409.

Ladefoged, P., and McKinney, N. P. Loudness, sound pressure, and sub-glottal pressure in speech. *Journal of the Acoustical Society of America*, 1963, 35, 454–460.

Lane, H. Motor theory of speech perception: A critical review. *Psychological Review*, 1965, 72, 275–309.

Liberman, A. M. Some results of research on speech perception. *Journal of the Acoustical Society of America*, 1957, 29, 117–123.

Liberman, A. M., Cooper, F. S., Harris, K. S., and MacNeilage, P. F. A motor theory of speech perception. *Proceedings of the Speech Communication Seminar*, Stockholm, 1962. Stockholm: Royal Institute of Technology, 1963, D3.

Liberman, A. M., Cooper, F. S., Harris, K. S., and MacNeilage, P. F., and Studdert-Kennedy, M. Some observations on a model for speech perception. *Proceedings of the AFCRL Symposium on Models for the Perception of Speech and Visual Form*, Boston, November 1964. Cambridge: Massachusetts Institute of Technology Press, in press.

Liberman, A. M., Cooper, F. S., Studdert-Kennedy, M., Harris, K. S., and Shankweiler, D. P. Some observations on the efficiency of speech sounds. Paper presented at the XVIII International Congress of Psychology, Moscow, August 1966. *Zeitschrift für Phonetik, Sprachwissenschaft und Kommunikationsforschung*, in press.

Liberman, A. M., Delattre, P. C., and Cooper, F. S. The role of selected stimulus variables in the perception of the unvoiced-stop consonants. *American Journal of Psychology*, 1952, 65, 497–516.

Liberman, A. M., Delattre, P. C., and Cooper, F. S. Some cues for the distinction between voiced and voiceless stops in initial position. *Language and Speech*, 1958, 1, 153–167.

Liberman, A. M., Delattre, P. C., and Cooper, F. S., and Gerstman, L. J. The role of consonant-vowel transitions in the perception of the stop and nasal consonants. *Psychological Monographs*, 1954, 68 (8, Whole No. 379).

Liberman, A. M., Delattre, P. C., Gerstman, L. J., and Cooper, F. S. Tempo of frequency change as a cue for distinguishing classes of speech sounds. *Journal of Experimental Psychology*, 1956, 52, 127–137.

Liberman, A. M., Harris, K. S., Eimas, P. D., Lisker, L., and Bastian, J. An effect of learning on speech perception: The discrimination of durations of silence with and without phonemic significance. *Language and Speech*, 1961, 4, 175–195.

Liberman, A. M., Harris, K. S., Hoffman, H. S., and Griffith, B. C. The discrimination of speech sounds within and across phoneme boundaries. *Journal of Experimental Psychology*, 1957, 54, 358–368.

Liberman, A. M., Harris, K. S., Kinney, J. A., and Lane, H. The discrimination of relative onset time of the components of certain speech and nonspeech patterns. *Journal of Experimental Psychology*, 1961, 61, 379–388.

Liberman, A. M., Ingemann, F., Lisker, L., Delattre, P. C., and Cooper, F. S. Minimal rules for synthesizing speech. *Journal of the Acoustical Society of America*, 1959, 31, 1490–1499.

Lieberman, P. *Intonation, perception and language.* Cambridge: Massachusetts Institute of Technology Press, 1967.

Lindblom, B. Spectrograph study of vowel reduction. *Journal of the Acoustical Society of America*, 1963, 35, 1773–1781.

Lindblom, B. Articulatory activity in vowels. *Journal of the Acoustical Society of America*, 1964, 36, 1038. (Abstract)

Lindblom, B., and Studdert-Kennedy, M. On the role of formant transitions in vowel recognition. *Speech transmission laboratory quarterly progress and status report*, Royal Institute of Technology (KTH), Stockholm, in press. (Also Status report of speech research. Haskins Laboratories, in press.)

Lisker, L. Closure duration and the voiced-voiceless distinction in English. *Language*, 1957a, 33, 42–49.

Lisker, L. Minimal cues for separating /w,r,l,j/ in introvocalic production. *Word*, 1957b, 13, 257–267.

Lisker, L. Anatomy of unstressed syllables. *Journal of the Acoustical Society of America*, 1958, 30, 682. (Abstract)

Lisker, L., and Abramson, A. S. A cross-language study of voicing in initial stops: Acoustical measurements. *Word*, 1964a, 20, 384–422.

Lisker, L., and Abramson, A. S. Stop categories and voice onset time. *Proceedings of the Fifth International Congress of Phonetic Sciences*, Munster, August, 1964b.

Lisker, L., Cooper, F. S., and Liberman, A. M. The uses of experiment in language description. *Word*, 1962, 18, 82–106.

MacKay, D. M. Mindlike behavior in artefacts. *British Journal for the Philosophy of Science*, 1951, 2, 105–121.

MacNeilage, P. F. Electromyographic and acoustic study of the production of certain final clusters. *Journal of the Acoustical Society of America*, 1963, 35, 461–463.

MacNeilage, P. F., DeClerk, J. L., and Silverman, S. I. Some relations between articulator movement and motor control in consonant-vowel-consonant monosyllables. *Journal of the Acoustical Society of America*, 1966, 40, 1272. (Abstract)

Malecot, A. Acoustic cues for nasal consonants. *Language*, 1956, 32, 274–284.

Miller, G. A. The magical number seven, plus or minus two, or, some limits on our capacity for processing information. *Psychological Review*, 1956a, 63, 81–96.

Miller, G. A. The perception of speech. In M. Halle (Ed.), *For Roman Jakobson*. 's-Gravenhage: Mouton, 1956b. Pp. 353–359.

Miller, G. A., and Taylor, W. G. The perception of repeated burst of noise. *Journal of the Acoustical Society of America*, 1948, 20, 171–182.

Nelson, P. G., Erulkar, S. D., and Bryan, S. S. Responses of units of the inferior-colliculus to time-varying acoustic stimuli. *Journal of Neurophysiology*, 1966, 29, 834–860.

Nye, P. W. Aural recognition time for multidimensional signals. *Nature*, 1962, 196, 1282–1283.

Nye, P. W. Reading aids for blind people—a survey of progress with the technological and human problems. *Medical Electronics and Biological Engineering*, 1964, 2, 247–264.

Nye, P. W. An investigation of audio outputs for a reading machine. February, 1965. Autonomics Division, National Physical Laboratory, Teddington, England.

O'Connor, J. D., Gerstman, L. J., Liberman, A. M., Delattre, P. C., and Cooper, F. S. Acoustic cues for the perception of initial /w,j,r,l/ in English. *Word*, 1957, 13, 25–43.

Ohman, S. E. G. Numerical model for coarticulation, using a computer-simulated vocal tract. *Journal of the Acoustical Society of America*, 1964, 36, 1038. (Abstract)

Ohman, S. E. G. Coarticulation in VCV utterances: Spectrographic measurements. *Journal of the Acoustical Society of America*, 1966, 39, 151–168.

Orr, D. B., Friedman, H. L., and Williams, J. C. C. Trainability of listening comprehension of speeded discourse. *Journal of Educational Psychology*, 1965, 56, 148–156.

Peterson, G. E., and Sivertsen, E. Objectives and techniques of speech synthesis. *Language and Speech*, 1960, 3, 84–95.

Peterson, G. E., and Wang, W. S.-Y., and Sivertsen E. Segmentation techniques in speech synthesis. *Journal of the Acoustical Society of America*, 1958, 30, 739–742.

Pollack, I. The information of elementary auditory displays. *Journal of the Acoustical Society of America*, 1952, 24, 745–749.

Pollack, I., and Ficks, I. Information of elementary multidimensional auditory displays. *Journal of the Acoustical Society of America*, 1954, 26, 155–158.

Potter, R. K., Kopp, G. A., and Green, H. C. *Visible speech*. New York: Van Nostrand, 1947.

Schatz, C. The role of context in the perception of stops. *Language*, 1954, 30, 47–56.

Shankweiler, D., and Studdert-Kennedy, M. An analysis of perceptual confusions in identification of dichotically presented CVC syllables. *Journal of the Acoustical Society of America*, 1967a, in press. (Abstract)

Shankweiler, D., and Studdert-Kennedy, M. Identification of consonants and vowels presented to left and right ears. *Quarterly Journal of Experimental Psychology*, 1967b, 19, 59–63.

Shearme, J. N., and Holmes, J. N. An experimental study of the classification of sounds in continuous speech according to their distribution in the formant 1-formant 2 plane. In *Proceedings of the Fourth International Congress of Phonetic Sciences*, Helsinki, 1961. 's-Gravenhage: Mouton, 1962. Pp. 234–240.

Sivertsen, E. Segment inventories for speech synthesis. *Language and Speech*, 1961, 4, 27–61.

Stevens, K. N. Toward a model for speech recognition. *Journal of the Acoustical Society of America*, 1960, 32, 47–55.

Stevens, K. N. On the relations between speech movements and speech perception. Paper presented at the meeting of the XVIII International Congress of Psychology, Moscow, August, 1966. (*Zeitschrift fur Phonetik, Sprachwissenschaft und Kommunikations-forschung*, in press.)

Stevens, K. N., and Halle, M. Remarks on analysis by synthesis and distinctive features. *Proceedings of the AFCRL Symposium on Models for the Perception of Speech and Visual Form*, Boston, November 1964. Cambridge: M.I.T. Press, in press.

Stevens, K. N., and House, A. S. Studies of formant transitions using a vocal tract analog. *Journal of the Acoustical Society of America*, 1956, 28, 578–585.

Stevens, K. N., and House, A. S. Perturbation of vowel articulations by consonantal context: An acoustical study. *Journal of Speech and Hearing Research*, 1963, 6, 111–128.

Stevens, K. N., and House, A. S. Speech perception. In J. Tobias and E. Schubert (Eds.), *Foundations of modern auditory theory*. New York: Academic Press, in press.

Stevens, K. N., Ohman, S. E. G., and Liberman, A. M. Identification and discrimination of rounded and unrounded vowels. *Journal of the Acoustical Society of America*, 1963, 35, 1900. (Abstract)

Stevens, K. N., Ohman, S. E. G., Studdert-Kennedy, M., and Liberman, A. M. Cross-linguistic study of vowel discrimination. *Journal of the Acoustical Society of America*, 1964, 36, 1989. (Abstract)

Studdert-Kennedy, M., and Cooper, F. S. High-performance reading machines for the blind; psychological problems, technological problems, and status. Paper presented at the meeting of St. Dunstan's International Conference on Sensory Devices for the Blind, London, June 1966.

Studdert-Kennedy, M., and Liberman, A. M. Psychological considerations in the design of auditory displays for reading machines. *Proceedings of the International Congress on Technology and Blindness*, 1963. Pp. 289–304.

Studdert-Kennedy, M., Liberman, A. M., and Stevens, K. N. Reaction time to synthetic stop consonants and vowels at phoneme centers and at phoneme boundaries. *Journal of the Acoustical Society of America*, 1963, 35, 1900. (Abstract)

Studdert-Kennedy, M., Liberman, A. M., and Stevens, K. N. Reaction time during the discrimination of synthetic stop consonants. *Journal of the Acoustical Society of America*, 1964, 36, 1989. (Abstract)

von Holst, E., and Mittelstadt, H. Das reafferenzprinzip. *Naturwissenschaft*, 1950, 37, 464–476.

Whetnall, E., and Fry, D. B. *The deaf child*. London: Heinemann, 1964.

Whitfield, I. C., and Evans, E. F. Responses of auditory cortical neurons to stimuli of changing frequency. *Journal of Neurophysiology*, 1965, 28, 655–672.

Wickelgren, W. A. Distinctive features and errors in short-term memory for English consonants. *Journal of the Acoustical Society of America*, 1966, 39, 388–398.

PART VI

The Revised Motor Theory

Introduction to Part VI

Here is the paper that brings the Motor Theory up to date. Now, ten years after its publication, there is but one point I wish we had not made. That is the claim that the phonetic module is unique in having to compete with other modules for the same stimulus variations. I do still believe that, in effect, the phonetic module does have to compete, as it were, but I also now believe, as chapter 1 makes clear, that the phonetic module is not unique in this respect.

Chapter 14
The Motor Theory of Speech Perception Revised

Together with some of our colleagues, we have long been identified with a view of speech perception that is often referred to as a "motor theory." Not *the* motor theory, to be sure, because there are other theories of perception that, like ours, assign an important role to movement or its sources. But the theory we are going to describe is only about speech perception, in contrast to some that deal with other perceptual processes (e.g., Berkeley 1709; Festinger, Burnham, Ono, and Bamber 1967) or, indeed, with all of them (e.g., Washburn 1926; Watson 1919). Moreover, our theory is motivated by considerations that do not necessarily apply outside the domain of speech. Yet even there we are not alone, for several theories of speech perception, being more or less "motor," resemble ours to varying degrees (e.g., Christovich 1960; Dudley 1940; Joos 1948; Ladefoged and McKinney 1963; Stetson 1951). However, it is not relevant to our purposes to compare these, so, for convenience, we will refer to *our* motor theory as *the* motor theory.

We were led to the motor theory by an early finding that the acoustic patterns of synthetic speech had to be modified if an invariant phonetic percept was to be produced across different contexts (Cooper, Delattre, Liberman, Borst, and Gerstman 1952; Liberman, Delattre, and Cooper 1952). Thus, it appeared that the objects of speech perception were not to be found at the acoustic surface. They might, however, be sought in the underlying motor processes, if it could be assumed that the acoustic variability required for an invariant percept resulted from the temporal overlap, in different contexts, of correspondingly invariant units of production. In its most general form, this aspect of the early theory survives, but there have been important revisions, including especially the one that makes perception of the motor invariant depend on a specialized phonetic mode (Liberman 1982; Liberman, Cooper, Shankweiler and Studdert-Kennedy 1967; Liberman and Studdert-Kennedy 1978; Mattingly and Liberman 1969). Our aim in this paper is to present further revisions, and so bring the theory up to date.

The Theory

The first claim of the motor theory, as revised, is that the objects of speech perception are the intended phonetic gestures of the speaker, represented in the brain as invariant motor commands that call for movements of the articulators through certain linguistically significant configurations. These gestural commands are the physical reality underlying the traditional phonetic notions—for example, "tongue backing,"

Originally published in *Cognition* 21 (1985): 1–36, with Ignatius G. Mattingly. Reprinted with permission.

"lip rounding," and "jaw raising"—that provide the basis for phonetic categories. They are the elementary events of speech production and perception. Phonetic segments are simply groups of one or more of these elementary events; thus [b] consists of a labial stop gesture and [m] of that same gesture combined with a velum-lowering gesture. Phonologically, of course, the gestures themselves must be viewed as groups of features, such as "labial," "stop," "nasal," but these features are attributes of the gestural events, not events as such. To perceive an utterance, then, is to perceive a specific pattern of intended gestures.

We have to say "intended gestures," because, for a number of reasons (coarticulation being merely the most obvious), the gestures are not directly manifested in the acoustic signal or in the observable articulatory movements. It is thus no simple matter (as we shall see in a later section) to define specific gestures rigorously or to relate them to their observable consequences. Yet, clearly, invariant gestures of some description there must be, for they are required, not merely for our particular theory of speech perception, but for *any* adequate theory of speech production.

The second claim of the theory is a corollary of the first: if speech perception and speech production share the same set of invariants, they must be intimately linked. This link, we argue, is not a learned association, a result of the fact that what people hear when they listen to speech is what they do when they speak. Rather, the link is innately specified, requiring only epigenetic development to bring it into play. On this claim, perception of the gestures occurs in a specialized mode, different in important ways from the auditory mode, responsible also for the production of phonetic structures, and part of the larger specialization for language. The adaptive function of the perceptual side of this mode, the side with which the motor theory is directly concerned, is to make the conversion from acoustic signal to gesture automatically, and so to let listeners perceive phonetic structures without mediation by (or translation from) the auditory appearances that the sounds might, on purely psychoacoustic grounds, be expected to have.

A critic might note that the gestures do produce acoustic signals, after all, and that surely it is these signals, not the gestures, which stimulate the listener's ear. What can it mean, then, to say it is the gestures, not the signals, that are perceived? Our critic might also be concerned that the theory seems at first blush to assign so special a place to speech as to make it hard to think about in normal biological terms. We should, therefore, try to forestall misunderstanding by showing that, wrong though it may be, the theory is neither logically meaningless nor biologically unthinkable.

An Issue that Any Theory of Speech Perception Must Meet
The motor theory would be meaningless if there were, as is sometimes supposed, a one-to-one relation between acoustic patterns and gestures, for in that circumstance it would matter little whether the listener was said to perceive the one or the other. Metaphysical considerations aside, the proximal acoustic patterns might as well be the perceived distal objects. But the relationship between gesture and signal is not straightforward. The reason is that the timing of the articulatory movements—the peripheral realizations of the gestures—is not simply related to the ordering of the gestures that is implied by the strings of symbols in phonetic transcriptions: the movements for gestures implied by a single symbol are typically not simultaneous, and the movements implied by successive symbols often overlap extensively. This coarticulation means that the changing shape of the vocal tract, and hence the result-

ing signal, is influenced by several gestures at the same time. Thus, the relation between gesture and signal, though certainly systematic, is systematic in a way that is peculiar to speech. In later sections of the paper we will consider how this circumstance bears on the perception of speech and its theoretical interpretation. For now, however, we wish only to justify consideration of the motor theory by identifying it as one of several choices that the complex relation between gesture and signal faces us with. For this purpose, we will describe just one aspect of the relation, that we may then use it as an example.

When coarticulation causes the signal to be influenced simultaneously by several gestures, a particular gesture will necessarily be represented by different sounds in different phonetic contexts. In a consonant–vowel syllable, for example, the acoustic pattern that contains information about the place of constriction of the consonantal gesture will vary depending on the following vowel. Such context-conditioned variation is most apparent, perhaps, in the transitions of the formants as the constriction is released. Thus, place information for a given consonant is carried by a rising transition in one vowel context and a falling transition in another (Liberman, Delattre, Cooper, and Gerstman 1954). In isolation, these transitions sound like two different glissandi or chirps, which is just what everything we know about auditory perception leads us to expect (Mattingly, Liberman, Syrdal, and Halwes 1971); they do not sound alike, and, just as important, neither sounds like speech. How is it, then, that, in context, they nevertheless yield the same consonant?

Auditory Theories and the Accounts They Provide The guiding assumption of one class of theories is that ordinary auditory processes are sufficient to explain the perception of speech; there is no need to invoke a further specialization for language, certainly not one that gives the listener access to gestures. The several members of this class differ in principle, though they are often combined in practice.

One member of the class counts two stages in the perceptual process: a first stage in which, according to principles that apply to the way we hear all sounds, the auditory appearances of the acoustic patterns are registered, followed by a second stage in which, by an act of sorting or matching to prototypes, phonetic labels are affixed (Crowder and Morton 1969; Fujisaki and Kawashima 1970; Oden and Massaro 1978; Pisoni 1973). Just why such different acoustic patterns as the rising and falling transitions of our example deserve the same label is not explicitly rationalized, it being accounted, presumably, a characteristic of the language that the processes of sorting or matching are able to manage. Nor does the theory deal with the fact that, in appropriate contexts, these transitions support phonetic percepts but do not also produce such auditory phenomena as chirps. To the contrary, indeed, it is sometimes made explicit that the auditory stage is actually available for use in discrimination. Such availability is not always apparent because the casual (or forgetful) listener is assumed to rely on the categorical labels, which persist in memory, rather than on the context-sensitive auditory impressions, which do not; but training or the use of more sensitive psychophysical methods is said to give better access to the auditory stage and thus to the stimulus variations—including, presumably, the differences in formant transition—that the labels ignore (Carney, Widin, and Viemeister 1977; Pisoni and Tash 1974; Samuel 1977).

Another member of the class of auditory theories avoids the problem of context-conditioned variation by denying its importance. According to this theory, speech perception relies on there being at least a brief period during each speech sound when its short-time spectrum is reliably distinct from those of other speech sounds. For an initial stop in a stressed syllable, for example, this period includes the burst and the first 10 ms. after the onset of voicing (Stevens and Blumstein 1978). That a listener is nevertheless able to identify speech sounds from which these invariant attributes have been removed is explained by the claim that, in natural speech, they are sometimes missing or distorted, so that the child must learn to make use of secondary, context-conditioned attributes, such as formant transitions, which ordinarily co-occur with the primary, invariant attributes (Cole and Scott 1974). Thus, presumably, the different-sounding chirps develop in perception to become the same-sounding (nonchirpy) phonetic element with which they have been associated.

The remaining member of this class of theories is the most thoroughly auditory of all. By its terms, the very processes of phonetic classification depend directly on properties of the auditory system, properties so independent of language as to be found, perhaps, in all mammals (Kuhl 1981; Miller 1977; Stevens 1975). As described most commonly in the literature, this version of the auditory theory takes the perceived boundary between one phonetic category and another to correspond to a naturally occurring discontinuity in perception of the relevant acoustic continuum. There is thus no first stage in which the (often) different auditory appearances are available, nor is there a process of learned equivalence. An example is the claim that the distinction between voiced and voiceless stops—normally cued by a complex of acoustic differences caused by differences in the phonetic variable known as voice-onset-time—depends on an auditory discontinuity in sensitivity to temporal relations among components of the signal (Kuhl and Miller 1975; Pisoni 1977). Another is the suggestion that the boundary between fricative and affricate on a rise-time continuum is the same as the rise-time boundary in the analogous nonspeech case—that is, the boundary that separates the nonspeech percepts "pluck" and "bow" (Cutting and Rosner 1974; but see Rosen and Howell 1981). To account for the fact that such discontinuities move as a function of phonetic context or rate of articulation, one can add the assumption that the several components of the acoustic signal give rise to interactions of a purely auditory sort (Hillenbrand 1984; but see Summerfield 1982). As for the rising and falling formant transitions of our earlier example, some such assumption of auditory interaction (between the transitions and the remainder of the acoustic pattern) would presumably be offered to account for the fact that they sound like two different glissandi in isolation, but as the same (non-glissando-like) consonant in the context of the acoustic syllable. The clear implication of this theory is that, for all phonetic contexts and for every one of the many acoustic cues that are known to be of consequence for each phonetic segment, the motivation for articulatory and coarticulatory maneuvers is to produce just those acoustic patterns that fit the language-independent characteristics of the auditory system. Thus, this last auditory theory is auditory in two ways: speech perception is governed by auditory principles, and so, too, is speech production.

The Account Provided by the Motor Theory The motor theory offers a view radically different from the auditory theories, most obviously in the claim that speech perception is not to be explained by principles that apply to perception of sounds in general, but must rather be seen as a specialization for phonetic gestures. Incorporating a biologically based link between perception and production, this specialization prevents listeners from hearing the signal as an ordinary sound, but enables them to use the systematic, yet special, relation between signal and gesture to perceive the gesture. The relation is systematic because it results from lawful dependencies among gestures, articulator movements, vocal-tract shapes, and signal. It is special because it occurs only in speech.

Applying the motor theory to our example, we suggest what has seemed obvious since the importance of the transitions was discovered: the listener uses the systematically varying transitions as information about the coarticulation of an invariant consonant gesture with various vowels, and so perceives this gesture. Perception requires no arbitrary association of signal with phonetic category, and no correspondingly arbitrary progression from an auditory stage (e.g., different sounding glissandi) to a superseding phonetic label. As Studdert-Kennedy (1976) has put it, the phonetic category "names itself."

By way of comparison with the last of the auditory theories we described, we note that, just as this theory is in two ways auditory, the motor theory is in two ways motor. First, because it takes the proper object of phonetic perception to be a motor event. And, second, because it assumes that adaptations of the motor system for controlling the organs of the vocal tract took precedence in the evolution of speech. These adaptations made it possible, not only to produce phonetic gestures, but also to coarticulate them so that they could be produced rapidly. A perceiving system, specialized to take account of the complex acoustic consequences, developed concomitantly. Accordingly, the theory is not indifferently perceptual *or* motor, implying simply that the basis of articulation and the object of perception are the same. Rather, the emphasis is quite one-sided; therefore, the theory fully deserves the epithet "motor."

How the Motor Theory Makes Speech Perception like Other Specialized Perceiving Systems
The specialized perceiving system that the motor theory assumes is not unique; it is, rather, one of a rather large class of special systems or "modules." Accordingly, one can think about it in familiar biological terms. Later, we will consider more specifically how the phonetic module fits the concept of modularity developed recently by Fodor (1983); our concern now is only to compare the phonetic module with others.

The modules we refer to have in common that they are special neural structures, designed to take advantage of a systematic but unique relation between a proximal display at the sense organ and some property of a distal object. A result in all cases is that there is not, first, a cognitive representation of the proximal pattern that is modality-general, followed by translation to a particular distal property; rather, perception of the distal property is immediate, which is to say that the module has done all the hard work. Consider auditory localization as an example. One of several cues is differences in time of arrival of particular frequency components of the signal at the two ears (see Hafter 1984, for a review). No one would claim that the use of this cue is part of the general auditory ability to perceive, as such, the size of the time interval that separates the onsets of two different signals. Certainly, this kind of general auditory ability does exist, but it is no part of auditory localization, either psychologically or physiologically. Animals perceive the location of sounding objects only by means of neural structures specialized to take advantage of the systematic but special relation between proximal stimulus and distal location (see, for example, Knudsen 1984). The relation is systematic for obvious reasons; it is special because it depends on the circumstance that the animal has two ears, and that the ears are set a certain distance apart. In the case of the human, the only species for which the appropriate test can be made, there is no translation from perceived disparity in time because there is no perceived disparity.

Compare this with the voicing distinction (e.g., [ba] vs. [pa]) referred to earlier, which is cued in part by a difference in time of onset of the several formants, and which has therefore been said by some to rest on a general auditory ability to perceive temporal disparity as such (Kuhl and Miller 1975; Pisoni 1977). We believe, to the contrary, that the temporal disparity is only the proximal occasion for the unmediated perception of voicing, a distal gesture represented at the level of articulation by the relative timing of vocal-tract opening and start of laryngeal vibration (Lisker and Abramson 1964). So we should expect perceptual judgments of differences in signal onset-time to have no more relevance to the voicing distinction than to auditory localization. In neither case do general auditory principles and procedures enlighten us. Nor does it help to invoke general principles of auditory interaction. The still more general principle that perception gives access to distal objects tells us only that auditory localization and speech perception work as they are supposed to; it does not tell us how. Surely the 'how' is to be found, not by studying perception, even auditory perception, in general, but only by studying auditory localization and speech perception in particular. Both are special systems; they are, therefore, to be understood only in their own terms.

Examples of such biologically specialized perceiving modules can be multiplied. Visual perception of depth by use of information about binocular disparity is a well-studied example that has the same general characteristics we have attributed to auditory localization and speech (Julesz 1960, 1971; Poggio 1984). And there is presumably much to be learned by comparison with such biologically coherent systems as those that underlie echolocation in bats (Suga 1984) or song in birds (Marler 1970; Thorpe 1958). But we will not elaborate, for the point to be made here is only that, from a biological point of view, the assumptions of the motor theory are not bizarre.

How the Motor Theory Makes Speech Perception Different from Other Specialized Perceiving Systems

Perceptual modules, by definition, differ from one another in the classes of distal events that form their domains and in the relation between these events and the proximal displays. But the phonetic module differs from others in at least two further respects.

Auditory and Phonetic Domains The first difference is in the locale of the distal events. In auditory localization, the distal event is "out there," and the relation between it and the proximal display at the two ears is completely determined by the principles of physical acoustics. Much the same can be said of those specialized modules that deal with the primitives of auditory quality, however they are to be characterized, and that come into play when people perceive, for example, whistles, horns, breaking glass, and barking dogs. Not so for the perception of phonetic structure. There, the distal object is a phonetic gesture or, more explicitly, an "upstream" neural command for the gesture from which the peripheral articulatory movements unfold. It follows that the relation between distal object and proximal stimulus will have the special feature that it is determined not just by acoustic principles but also by neuromuscular processes internal to the speaker. Of course, analogues of these processes are also available as part of the biological endowment of the listener. Hence, some kind of link between perception and production would seem to characterize the phonetic module, but not those modules that provide auditory localization or visual perception of depth. In a later section, we will have more to say about this link. Now we will only comment that it may conceivably resemble, in its most general characteristics, those links that have been identified in the communication modules of certain nonhuman creatures (Gerhardt and Rheinlaender 1982; Hoy, Hahn, and Paul 1977; Hoy and Paul 1973; Katz and Gurney 1981; Margoliash 1983; McCasland and Konishi 1983; Nottebohm, Stokes, and Leonard 1976; Williams 1984).

The motor theory aside, it is plain that speech somehow informs listeners about the phonetic intentions of the talker. The particular claim of the motor theory is that these intentions are represented in a specific form in the talker's brain, and that there is a perceiving module specialized to lead the listener effortlessly to that representation. Indeed, what is true of speech in this respect is true for all of language, except, of course, that the more distal object for language is some representation of linguistic structure, not merely of gesture, and that access to this object requires a module that is not merely phonetic, but phonological and syntactic as well.

Competition between Phonetic and Auditory Modes A second important difference between the phonetic module and the others has to do with the question: how does the module cooperate or compete with others that use stimuli of the same broadly defined physical form? For auditory localization, the key to the answer is the fact that the module is turned on by a specific and readily specifiable characteristic of the proximal stimulus: a particular range of differences in time of arrival at the two ears. Obviously, such differences have no other utility for the perceiver but to provide information about the distal property, location; there are no imaginable ecological circumstances in which a person could use this characteristic of the proximal stimuli to specify some other distal property. Thus, the proximal display and the distal property it specifies only complement the other aspects of what a listener hears; they never compete.

In phonetic perception, things are quite different because important acoustic cues are often similar to, even identical with, the stimuli that inform listeners about a variety of nonspeech events. We have already remarked that, in isolation, formant transitions sound like glissandi or chirps. Now surely we don't want to perceive these as glissandi or chirps when we are listening to speech, but we do want to perceive them so when we are listening to music or to birdsong. If this is true for all of the speech cues, as in some sense it presumably is, then it is hard to see how the module can be turned on by acoustic stigmata of any kind—that is, by some set of necessary cues defined in purely acoustic terms. We will consider this matter in some greater detail later. For now, however, the point is only that cues known to be of great importance for phonetic events may be cues for totally unrelated nonphonetic events, too. A consequence is that, in contrast to the generally complementary relation of the several modules that serve the same broadly defined modality (e.g., depth and color in vision), the phonetic and auditory modules are in direct competition. (For a discussion of how this competition might be resolved, see Mattingly and Liberman 1985.)

Experimental Evidence for the Theory

Having briefly described one motive for the motor theory—the context-conditioned variation in the acoustic cues for constant phonetic categories—we will now add others. We will limit ourselves to the so-called segmental aspects of phonetic structure, though the theory ought, in principle, to apply in the suprasegmental domain as well (cf. Fowler 1982).

The two parts of the theory—that gestures are the objects of perception and that perception of these gestures depends on a specialized module—might be taken to be independent, as they were in their historical development, but the relevant data are not. We therefore cannot rationally apportion the data between the parts, but must rather take them as they come.

A Result of Articulation: The Multiplicity, Variety, and Equivalence of Cues for Each Phonetic Percept

When speech synthesis began to be used as a tool to investigate speech perception, it was soon discovered that, in any specific context, a particular local property of the acoustic signal was sufficient for the perception of one phonetic category rather than another and, more generally, that the percept could be shifted along some phonetic dimension by varying the synthetic stimulus along a locally-definable acoustic dimension. For example, if the onset frequency of the transition of the second formant during a stop release is sufficiently low, relative to the frequency of the following steady state, the stop is perceived as labial; otherwise, as apical or dorsal (Liberman et at. 1954). A value along such an acoustic dimension that was optimal for a particular phonetic category, or, more loosely, the dimension itself, was termed an "acoustic cue."

Of course, the fact that particular acoustic cues can be isolated must, of itself, tell us something about speech perception, for it might have been otherwise. Thus, it is possible to imagine a speech-perception mechanism, equipped, perhaps, with auditory templates, that would break down if presented with anything other than a wholly natural and phonetically optimal stimulus. Listeners would either give conflicting and unreliable phonetic judgments or else not hear speech at all. Clearly, the actual mechanism is not of this kind, and the concept of cue accords with this fact.

Nevertheless, the emphasis on the cues has, perhaps, been unfortunate, for the term "cue" might seem to imply a claim about the elemental units of speech perception. But "cue" was simply a convenient bit of laboratory jargon referring to acoustic variables whose definition depended very much on the design features of the particular synthesizers that were used to study them. The cues, as such, have no role in a theory of speech perception; they only describe some of the facts on which a theory might be based (cf. Bailey and Summerfield 1980). There are, indeed, several generalizations about the cues—some only hinted at by the data now available, others quite well founded—that are relevant to such a theory.

One such generalization is that every "potential" cue—that is, each of the many acoustic events peculiar to a linguistically significant gesture—is an *actual* cue. (For example, every one of 18 potential cues to the voicing distinction in medial position has been shown to have some perceptual value; Lisker 1978). All possible cues have not been tested, and probably never will be, but no potential cue has yet been found that could not be shown to be an actual one.

A closely related generalization is that, while each cue is, by definition, more or less sufficient, none is truly necessary. The absence of any single cue, no matter how seemingly characteristic of the phonetic category, can be compensated for by others, not without some cost to naturalness or even intelligibility, perhaps, but still to such an extent that the intended category is, in fact, perceived. Thus, stops can be perceived without silent periods, fricatives without frication, vowels without formants, and tones without pitch (Abramson 1972; Inoue 1984; Remez and Rubin 1984; Repp 1984; Yeni-Komshian and Soli 1981).

Yet another generalization is that even when several cues are present, variations in one can, within limits, be compensated for by offsetting variations in another (Dorman, Studdert-Kennedy, and Raphael 1977; Dorman, Raphael, and Liberman 1979; Hoffman 1958; Howell and Rosen 1983; Lisker 1957; Summerfield and Haggard 1977). In the case of the contrast between fricative-vowel and fricative-stop-vowel (as in [sa] vs. [sta]), investigators have found that two important cues, silence and appropriate formant transitions, engage in just such a trading relation. That this bespeaks a true equivalence in perception was shown by experiments in which the effect of variation in one cue could, depending on its "direction," be made to "add to" or "cancel out" the effect of the other (Fitch, Halwes, Erickson, and Liberman 1980). Significantly, this effect can also be obtained with sine-wave analogues of speech, but only for subjects who perceive these signals as speech, not for those who perceive them as nonspeech tones (Best, Morrongiello, and Robson 1981).

Putting together all the generalizations about the multiplicity and variety of acoustic cues, we should conclude that there is simply no way to define a phonetic category in purely acoustic terms. A complete list of the cues—surely a cumbersome matter at best—is not feasible, for it would necessarily include all the acoustic effects of phonetically distinctive articulations. But even if it were possible to compile such a list, the result would not repay the effort, because none of the cues on the list could be deemed truly essential. As for those cues that might, for any reason, be finally included, none could be assigned a characteristic setting, since the effect of changing it could be offset by appropriate changes in one or more of the others. This surely tells us something about the design of the phonetic module. For if phonetic categories were acoustic patterns, and if, accordingly, phonetic perception were properly auditory, one should be able to describe quite straightforwardly the acoustic basis for the phonetic category and its associated percept. According to the motor theory, by contrast, one would expect the acoustic signal to serve only as a source of information about the gestures; hence the gestures would properly define the category. As for the perceptual equivalence among diverse cues that is shown by the trading relations, explaining that on auditory grounds requires ad hoc assumptions. But if, as the motor theory wold have it, the gesture is the distal object of perception, we should not wonder that the several sources of information about it are perceptually equivalent, for they are products of the same linguistically significant gesture.

A Result of Coarticulation: I. Segmentation in Sound and Percept
Traditional phonetic transcription represents utterances as single linear sequences of symbols, each of which stands for a phonetic category. It is an issue among phonologists whether such transcriptions are really theoretically adequate, and various alternative proposals have been made in an effort to provide a better account. This matter need not concern us here, however, since all proposals have in common that phonetic

units of some description are ordered from left to right. Some sort of segmentation is thus always implied, and what theory must take into account is that the perceived phonetic object is thus segmented.

Segmentation of the phonetic percept would be no problem for theory if the proximal sound were segmented correspondingly. But it is not, nor can it be, if speech is to be produced and perceived efficiently. To maintain a straightforward relation in segmentation between phonetic unit and signal would require that the sets of phonetic gestures corresponding to phonetic units be produced one at a time, each in its turn. The obvious consequence would be that each unit would become a syllable, in which case talkers could speak only as fast as they could spell. A function of coarticulation is to evade this limitation. There is an important consequence, however, which is that there is now no straightforward correspondence in segmentation between the phonetic and acoustic representations of the information (Fant 1962; Joos 1948). Thus, the acoustic information for any particular phonetic unit is typically overlapped, often quite thoroughly, with information for other units. Moreover, the span over which that information extends, the amount of overlap, and the number of units signalled within the overlapped portion all vary according to the phonetic context, the rate of articulation, and the language (Magen 1984; Manuel and Krakow 1984; Öhman 1966; Recasens 1984; Repp, Liberman, Eccardt, and Pesetsky 1978; Tuller, Harris, and Kelso 1982).

There are, perhaps, occasional stretches of the acoustic signal over which there is information about only one phonetic unit—for example, in the middle of the frication in a slowly articulated fricative-vowel syllable and in vowels that are sustained for articially long times. Such stretches do, of course, offer a relation between acoustic patterns and phonetic units that would be transparent if phonetic perception were merely auditory. But even in these cases, the listener automatically takes account of, not just the transparent part of the signal, but the regions of overlap as well (Mann and Repp 1980, 1981; Whalen 1981). Indeed, the general rule may be that the phonetic percept is normally made available to consciousness only after all the relevant acoustic information is in, even when earlier cues might have been sufficient (Martin and Bunnell 1981, 1982; Repp et al. 1978).

What wants explanation, then, is that the perception is segmented in a way that the signal is not, or, to put in another way, that the percept does not mirror the overlap of information in the sound (cf. Fowler 1984). The motor theory does not provide a complete explanation, certainly not in its present state, but it does head the theoretical enterprise in the right direction. At the very least, it turns the theorist away from the search for those unlikely processes that an auditory theory would have him seek: how listeners learn phonetic labels for what they hear and thus reinterpret perceived overlap as sequences of discrete units; or how discrete units emerge in perception from interactions of a purely auditory sort. The first process seems implausible on its face, the second because it presupposes that the function of the many kinds and degrees of coarticulation is to produce just those combinations of sounds that will interact in accordance with language-independent characteristics of the auditory system. In contrast, the motor theory begins with the assumption that coarticulation, and the resulting overlap of phonetic information in the acoustic pattern, is a consequence of the efficient processes by which discrete phonetic gestures are realized in the behavior of more or less independent articulators. The theory suggests, then, that an equally efficient perceptual process might use the resulting acoustic pattern to recover the discrete gestures.

A Result of Coarticulation: II. Different Sounds, Different Contexts, Same Percept
That the phonetic percept is invariant even when the relevant acoustic cue is not was the characteristic relation between percept and sound that we took as an example in the first section. There, we observed that variation in the acoustic pattern results from overlapping of putatively invariant gestures, an observation that, as we remarked, points to the gesture, rather than the acoustic pattern itself, as the object of perception. We now add that the articulatory variation due to context is pervasive: in the acoustic representation of every phonetic category yet studied there are context-conditioned portions that contribute to perception and that must, therefore, be taken into account by theory. Thus, for stops, nasals, fricatives, liquids, semivowels, and vowels, the always context-sensitive transitions are cues (Harris 1958; Jenkins, Strange, and Edman 1983; Liberman et al. 1954; O'Connor, Gerstman, Liberman, Delattre, and Cooper 1957; Strange, Jenkins, and Johnson 1983). For stops and fricatives, the noises that are produced at the point of constriction are also known to be cues, and, under some circumstances at least, these, too, vary with context (Dorman et al. 1977; Liberman et al. 1952; Whalen 1981).

An auditory theory that accounts for invariant perception in the face of so much variation in the signal would require a long list of apparently arbitrary assumptions. For a motor theory, on the other hand, systematic stimulus variation is not an obstacle to be circumvented or overcome in some arbitrary way; it is, rather, a source of information about articulation that provides important guidance to the perceptual process in determining a representation of the distal gesture.

A Result of Coarticulation: III. Same Sound, Different Contexts, Different Percepts
When phonetic categories share one feature but differ in another, the relation between acoustic pattern and percept speaks, again, to the motor theory and its alternatives. Consider, once more, the fricative [s] and the stop [t] in the syllables [sa] and [sta]. In synthesis, the second- and third-formant transitions can be the same for these two categories, since they have the same place of articulation; and the first-formant transition, normally a cue to manner, can be made ambiguous between them. For such stimuli, the perception of [sta] rather than [sa] depends on whether there is an interval of silence between the noise for the [s] and the onsets of the transitions.

Data relevant to an interpretation of the role of silence in thus producing different percepts from the same transition come from two kinds of experiments. First are those that demonstrate the effectiveness of the transitions as cues for the place feature of the fricative in fricative-vowel syllables (Harris 1958). The transitions are not, therefore, masked by the noise of the [s] frication, and thus the function of silence in a stop is not, as it might be in an auditory theory, to protect the transitions from such masking. The second kind of experiment deals with the possibility of a purely auditory interaction—in this case, between silence and the formant transitions. Among the findings that make such auditory interaction seem unlikely is that silence affects perception of the formant transitions differently in and out of speech context and, further, that the effectiveness of silence depends on such factors as continuity of talker and prosody (Dorman et al. 1979; Rakerd, Dechovitz, and Verbrugge 1982). But perhaps the most direct test for auditory interaction is provided by experiments in which such interaction is ruled out by holding the acoustic context constant. This can be done by exploiting "duplex perception," a phenomenon to be discussed in greater detail in the next section. Here it is appropriate to say only that duplex perception provides a way of presenting acoustic patterns so that, in a fixed context, listeners hear the same second- or third-formant transitions in two phenomenally different ways simultaneously: as nonspeech chirps and as cues for phonetic categories. The finding is that the presence or absence of silence determines whether formant transitions appropriate for [t] or for [p], for example, are integrated into percepts as different as stops and fricatives; but silence has no effect on the perception of the nonspeech chirps that these same transitions produce (Liberman, Isenberg, and Rakerd 1981). Since the latter result eliminates the possibility of auditory interaction, we are left with the account that the motor theory would suggest: that silence acts in the specialized phonetic mode to inform the listener that the talker completely closed his vocal tract to produce a stop consonant, rather than merely constricting it to produce a fricative. It follows, then, that silence will, by its presence or absence, determine whether identical transitions are cues in percepts that belong to the one manner or the other.

An Acoustic Signal Diverges to Phonetic and Auditory Modes
We noted earlier that a formant transition is perceptually very different depending on whether it is perceived in the auditory mode, where it sounds like a chirp, or in the phonetic mode, where it cues a "nonchirpy" consonant. Of course, the comparison is not entirely fair, since acoustic context is not controlled: the transition is presented in isolation in the one case, but as an element of a larger acoustic pattern in the other. We should, therefore, call attention to the fact that the same perceptual difference is obtained even when, by resort to a special procedure, acoustic context is held constant (Liberman 1979; Rand 1974). This procedure, which produces the duplex percept referred to earlier, goes as follows. All of an acoustic syllable except only the formant transition that decides between, for example, [da] and [ga] is presented to one ear. By itself, this pattern, called the "base," sounds like a stop-vowel syllable, ambiguous between [da] and [ga]. To the other ear is presented one or the other of the transitions appropriate for [d] or [g]. In isolation, these sound like different chirps. Yet, when base and transition are presented dichotically, and in the appropriate temporal relationship, they give rise to a duplex percept: [da] or [ga], depending on the transition, and, simultaneously, the appropriate chirp. (The fused syllable appears to be in the ear to which the base had been presented, the chirp in the other.)

Two related characteristics of duplex perception must be emphasized. One is that it is obtained only when the stimulus presented to one ear is, like the "chirpy" transition, of short duration and extremely unspeechlike in quality. If that condition is not met, as, for example, when the first two formants are presented to one ear and the entire third formant to the other, perception is not duplex. It is, on the contrary, simplex; one hears a coherent syllable in which the separate components cannot be apprehended. (A very different result is obtained when two components of a musical chord are presented to one ear, a third component to the other. In that case, listeners can respond to the third component by itself and also to that component combined with the first two (Pastore, Schmuckler, Rosenblum, and Szczesiul 1983).

The other, closely related characteristic of duplex perception is that it is precisely duplex, not triplex. That is, listeners perceive the nonspeech chirp and the fused syllable, but they do not also perceive the base—that is, the syllable, minus one of the formant transitions—that was presented to one ear (Repp, Milburn, and Ashkenas 1983). (In the experiment with musical chords by Pastore et al. 1983, referred to just above, there was no test for duplex, as distinguished from triplex, perception.)

The point is that duplex perception does not simply reflect the ability of the auditory system to fuse dichotically presented stimuli and also, as in the experiment with the chords, to keep them apart. Rather, the duplex percepts of speech comprise the only two ways in which the transition, for example, can be heard: as a cue for a phonetic gesture and as a nonspeech sound. These percepts are strikingly different, and, as we have already seen, they change in different, sometimes contrasting ways in response to variations in the acoustic signals—variations that must have been available to all structures in the brain that can process auditory information. A reasonable conclusion is that there must be two modules that can somehow use the same input to produce simultaneous representations of two distal objects. (For speculation about the mechanism that normally prevents perception of this ecologically impossible situation, and about the reason why that highly adaptive mechanism might be defeated by the procedures used to produce duplex perception, see Mattingly and Liberman 1985.)

Acoustic and Optical Signals Converge on the Phonetic Mode
In duplex perception, a single acoustic stimulus is processed simultaneously by the phonetic and auditory modules to produce perception of two distal objects: a phonetic gesture and a sound. In the phenomenon to which we turn now, something like the opposite occurs: two different stimuli—one acoustic, the other optical—are combined by the phonetic module to produce coherent perception of a single distal event. This phenomenon, discovered by McGurk and McDonald (1976), can be illustrated by this variant on their original demonstration. Subjects are presented acoustically with the syllables [ba], [ba], [ba] and optically with a face that, in approximate synchrony, silently articulates [bɛ], [vɛ], [ðɛ]. The resulting and compelling percept is [ba], [va], [ða], with no awareness that it is in any sense bimodal—that is, part auditory and part visual. According to the motor theory, this is to because the perceived event is neither; it is, rather, a gesture. The proximal acoustic signal and the proximal optical signal have in common, then, that they convey information about the same distal object. (Perhaps a similar convergence is implied by the finding that units in the optic tectum of the barn owl are bimodally sensitive to acoustic and optical cues for the same distal property, location in space; Knudsen 1982).

Even prelinguistic infants seem to have some appreciation of the relation between the acoustic and optical consequences of phonetic articulation. This is to be inferred from an experiment in which it was found that infants at four to five months of age preferred to look at a face that articulated the vowel they were hearing rather than at the same face articulating a different vowel (Kuhl and Meltzoff 1982). Significantly, this result was not obtained when the sounds were pure tones matched in amplitude and duration to the vowels. In a related study it was found that infants of a similar age looked longer at a face repeating the disyllable they were hearing than at the same face repeating another disyllable, though both disyllables were carefully synchronized with the visible articulation (MacKain, Studdert-Kennedy, Spieker, and Stern 1983). Like the results obtained with adults in the McGurk-MacDonald kind of experiment, these findings with infants imply a perception-production link and, accordingly, a common mode of perception for all proper information about the gesture.

The General Characteristics that Cause Acoustic Signals to Be Perceived as Speech
The point was made in an earlier section that acoustic definitions of phonetic contrasts are, in the end, unsatisfactory. Now we would suggest that acoustic definitions also fail for the purpose of distinguishing in general between acoustic patterns that convey phonetic structures and those that do not. Thus, speech cannot be distinguished from nonspeech by appeal to surface properties of the sound. Surely, natural speech does have certain characteristics of a general and superficial sort—for example, formants with characteristic bandwidths and relative intensities, stretches of waveform periodicities that typically mark the voiced portion of syllables, peaks of intensity corresponding approximately to syllabic rhythm, etc.—and these can be used by machines to detect speech. But research with synthesizers has shown that speech is perceived even when such general characteristics are absent. This was certainly true in the case of many of the acoustic patterns that were used in work with the Pattern Playback synthesizer, and more recently it has been shown to be true in the most extreme case of patterns consisting only of sine waves that follow natural formant trajectories (Remez, Rubin, Pisoni, and Carrell 1981). Significantly, the converse effect is also obtained. When reasonably normal formants are made to deviate into acoustically continuous but abnormal trajectories, the percept breaks into two categorically distinct parts: speech and a background of chirps, glissandi, and assorted noises (Liberman and Studdert-Kennedy 1978). Of course, the trajectories of the formants are determined by the movements of the articulators. Evidently, those trajectories that conform to possible articulations engage the phonetic module; all others fail.

We conclude that acoustic patterns are identified as speech by reference to deep properties of a linguistic sort: if a sound can be "interpreted" by the specialized phonetic module as the result of linguistically significant gestures, then it is speech; otherwise, not. (In much the same way, grammatical sentences can be distinguished from ungrammatical ones, not by lists of surface properties, but only by determining whether or not a grammatical derivation can be given.) Of course, the kind of mechanism such an "interpretation" requires is the kind of mechanism the motor theory presumes.

Phonetic and Auditory Responses to the Cues
Obviously, a module that acts on acoustic signals cannot respond beyond the physiological limits of those parts of the auditory system that transmit the signal to the module. Within those limits, however, different modules can be sensitive to the signals in different ways. Thus, the auditory-localization module enables listeners to perceive differences in the position of sounding objects given temporal disparity cues smaller by several orders of magnitude than those required to make the listener aware of temporal disparity as such (Brown and Deffenbacher 1979, chap. 7; Hirsh 1959). If there is, as the motor theory implies, a distinct phonetic module, then in like manner its sensitivities should not, except by accident, be the same as those that characterize the module that deals with the sounds of non-speech events.

In this connection, we noted in the first section of the paper that one form of auditory theory of speech perception points to auditory discontinuities in differential sensitivity (or in absolute identification), taking these to be the natural bases for the perceptual discontinuities that characterize the boundaries of phonetic categories. But several kinds of experiments strongly imply that this is not so.

One kind of experiment has provided evidence that the perceptual discontinuities at the boundaries of phonetic categories are not fixed; rather, they move in accordance with the acoustic consequences of articulatory adjustments associated with phonetic context, dialect, and rate of speech. (For a review, see Repp and Liberman, in press.) To account for such articulation-correlated changes in perceptual sensitivities by appeal to auditory processes requires, yet again, an ultimately countless set of ad hoc assumptions about auditory interactions, as well as the implausible assumption that the articulators are always able to behave so as to produce just those sounds that conform to the manifold and complex requirements that the auditory interactions impose. It seems hardly more plausible that, as has been suggested, the discontinuities in phonetic perception are really auditory discontinuities that were caused to move about in phylogenetic or ontogenetic development as a result of experience with speech (Aslin and Pisoni 1980). The difficulty with this assumption is that it presupposes the very canonical form of the cues that does not exist (see above) and, also, that it implies a contradiction in assuming, as it must, that the auditory sensitivities underwent changes in the development of speech, yet somehow also remained unchanged and nonetheless manifest in the adult's perception of nonspeech sounds.

Perhaps this is the place to remark about categorical perception that the issue is not, as is often supposed, whether nonspeech continua are categorically perceived, for surely some do show tendencies in that direction. The issue is whether, given the same (or similar) acoustic continua, the auditory and phonetic boundaries are in the same place. If there are, indeed, auditory boundaries, and if, further, these boundaries are replaced in phonetic perception by boundaries at different locations (as the experiments referred to above do indicate), then the separateness of phonetic and auditory perception is even more strongly argued for than if the phonetic boundaries had appeared on continua where auditory boundaries did not also exist.

Also relevant to comparison of sensitivity in phonetic and auditory modes are experiments on perception of acoustic variations when, in the one case, they are cues for phonetic distinctions, and when, in some other, they are perceived as nonspeech. One of the earliest of the experiments to provide data about the nonspeech side of this comparison dealt with perception of frequency-modulated tones—or "ramps" as they were called—that bear a close resemblance to the formant transitions. The finding was that listeners are considerably better at perceiving the pitch at the end of the ramp than at the beginning (Brady, House, and Stevens 1961). Yet, in the case of stop consonants that are cued by formant transitions, perception is better syllable-initially than syllable-finally, though in the former case it requires information about the beginning of the ramp, while in the latter it needs to know about the end. Thus, if one were predicting sensitivity to speech from sensitivity to the analogous nonspeech sounds, one would make exactly the wrong predictions. More recent studies have made more direct comparisons and found differences in discrimination functions when, in speech context, formant transitions cued place distinctions among stops and liquids, and when, in isolation, the same transitions were perceived as nonspeech sounds (Mattingly et al. 1971; Miyawaki, Strange, Verbrugge, Liberman, Jenkins, and Fujimura 1975).

More impressive, perhaps, is evidence that has come from experiments in which listeners are induced to perceive a constant stimulus in different ways. Here belong experiments in which sinewave analogues of speech, referred to earlier, are presented under conditions that cause some listeners to perceive them as speech and others not. The perceived discontinuities lie at different places (on the acoustic continuum) for the two groups (Best et al. 1981; Best and Studdert-Kennedy 1983; Studdert-Kennedy and Williams 1984; Williams, Verbrugge, and Studdert-Kennedy 1983). Here, too, belongs an experiment in which the formant-transitions appropriate to a place contrast between stop consonants are presented with the remainder of a syllable in such a way as to produce the duplex percept referred to earlier: the transitions cue a stop consonant and, simultaneously, nonspeech chirps. The result is that listeners yield quite different discrimination functions for exactly the same formant transitions in exactly the same acoustic context, depending on whether they are responding to the speech or nonspeech sides of the duplex percept; only on the speech side of the percept is there a peak in the discrimination function to mark a perceptual discontinuity at the phonetic boundary (Mann and Liberman 1983).

Finally, we note that, apart from differences in differential sensitivity to the transitions, there is also a difference in absolute-threshold sensitivity when, in the one case, these transitions support a phonetic percept, and when, in the other, they are perceived as nonspeech chirps. Exploiting, again, the phenomenon of duplex perception, investigators found that the transitions were effective (on the speech side of the percept) in cueing the contrast between stops at a level of intensity 18 db lower than that required for comparable discrimination of the chirps (Bentin and Mann 1983). At that level, indeed, listeners could not even hear the chirps, let alone discriminate them; yet they could still use the transitions to identify the several stops.

The Several Aspects of the Theory

For the purpose of evaluating the motor theory, it is important to separate it into its more or less independent parts. First, and fundamentally, there is the claim that phonetic perception is perception of gesture. As we have seen, this claim is based on evidence that the invariant source of the phonetic percept is somewhere in the processes by which the sounds of speech are produced. In the first part of this section we will consider where in those processes the invariant might be found.

The motor theory also implies a tight link between perception and production. In the second part of this section we will ask how that link came to be.

Where Is the Invariant Phonetic Gesture?
A phonetic gesture, as we have construed it, is a class of movements by one or more articulators that results in a particular, linguistically significant deformation, over time, of the vocal-tract configuration. The linguistic function of the gesture is clear enough: phonetic contrasts, which are of course the basis of phonological categories, depend on the choice of one particular gesture rather than another. What is not so clear is how the gesture relates to the actual physical movements of articulators and to the resulting vocal-tract configurations, observed, for example, in X-ray films.

In the early days of the motor theory, we made a simplifying assumption about this relation: that a gesture was effected by a single key articulator. On this assumption, the actual movement trajectory of the articulator might vary, but only because of aerodynamic factors and the physical linkage of this articulator with others, so the neural commands in the final common paths (observable with electromyographic techniques) would nevertheless be invariant across different contexts. This assumption was appropriate as an initial working hypothesis, if only because it was directly testable. In the event, there proved to be a considerable amount of variability which the hypothesis could not account for.

In formulating this initial hypothesis, we had overlooked several serious complications. One is that a particular gesture typically involves not just one articulator, but two or more; thus "lip rounding," for example, is a collaboration of lower lip, upper lip, and jaw. Another is that a single articulator may participate in the execution of two different gestures at the same time; thus, the lips may be simultaneously rounding and closing in the production of a labial stop followed by a rounded vowel, for example, [bu]. Prosody makes additional complicating demands, as when a greater displacement of some or all of the active articulators is required in producing a stressed syllable rather than an unstressed one; and linguistically irrelevant factors, notably speaking rate, affect the trajectory and phasing of the component movements.

These complications might suggest that there is little hope of providing a rigorous physical definition of a particular gesture, and that the gestures are hardly more satisfactory as perceptual primitives than are the acoustic cues. It might, indeed, be argued that there is an infinite number of possible articulatory movements, and that the basis for categorizing one group of such movements as "lip rounding" and another as "lip closure" is entirely a priori.

But the case for the gesture is by no means as weak as this. Though we have a great deal to learn before we can account for the variation in instances of the same gesture, it is nonetheless clear that, despite such variation, the gestures have a virtue that the acoustic cues lack: instances of a particular gesture always have certain topological properties not shared by any other gesture. That is, for any particular gesture, the same sort of distinctive deformation is imposed on the current vocal-tract configuration, whatever this "underlying" configuration happens to be. Thus, in lip rounding, the lips are always slowly protruded and approximated to some appreciable extent, so that the anterior end of the vocal tract is extended and narrowed, though the relative contributions of the tongue and lips, the actual degrees of protrusion and approximation, and the speed of articulatory movement vary according to context. Perhaps this example seems obvious because lip rounding involves a local deformation of the vocal-tract configuration, but the generalization also applies to more global gestures. Consider, for example, the gesture required to produce an "open" vowel. In this gesture, tongue, lips, jaw, and hyoid all participate to contextually varying degrees, and the actual distance between the two lips, as well as that between the tongue blade and body and the upper surfaces of the vocal tract, are variable; but the goal is always to give the tract a more open, horn-shaped configuration than it would otherwise have had.

We have pointed out repeatedly that, as a consequence of gestural overlapping, the invariant properties of a particular gesture are not manifest in the spectrum of the speech signal. We would now caution that a further consequence of this overlapping is that, because of their essentially topological character, the gestural invariants are usually not obvious from inspection of a single static vocal-tract configuration, either. They emerge only from consideration of the configuration as it changes over time, and from comparison with other configurations in which the same gesture occurs in different contexts, or different gestures in the same context.

We would argue, then, that the gestures do have characteristic invariant properties, as the motor theory requires, though these must be seen, not as peripheral movements, but as the more remote structures that control the movements. These structures correspond to the speaker's intentions. What is far from being understood is the nature of the system that computes the topologically appropriate version of a gesture in a particular context. But this problem is not peculiar to the motor theory; it is familiar to many who study the control and coordination of movement, for they, like us, must consider whether, given context-conditioned variability at the surface, motor acts are nevertheless governed by invariants of some sort (Browman and Goldstein 1985; Fowler, Rubin, Remez, and Turvey 1980; Tuller and Kelso 1984; Turvey 1977).

The Origin of the Perception–Production Link
In the earliest accounts of the motor theory, we put considerable emphasis on the fact that listeners not only perceive the speech signal but also produce it. This, together with doctrinal behaviorist considerations, led us to assume that the connection between perception and production was formed as a wholly learned association, and that perceiving the gesture was a matter of picking up the sensory consequences of covert mimicry. On this view of the genesis of the perception–production link, the distinguishing characteristic of speech is only that it provides the opportunity for the link to be established. Otherwise, ordinary principles of associative learning are adequate to the task; no specialization for language is required.

But then such phenomena as have been described in this paper were discovered, and it became apparent that they differed from anything that association learning could reasonably be expected to produce. Nor were these the only relevant considerations. Thus, we learned that people who have been pathologically incapable from birth of controlling their articulators are nonetheless able to perceive speech (MacNeilage, Rootes, and Chase 1967). From the research pioneered by Eimas, Siqueland, Jusczyk, and Vigorito (1971), we also learned that prelinguistic infants apparently categorize phonetic distinctions much as adults do. More recently, we have seen that even when the distinction is not functional in the native language of the subjects, and when, accordingly, adults have trouble perceiving it, infants nevertheless do quite well up to about one year of age, at which time they begin to perform as poorly as adults (Werker and Tees 1984). Perhaps, then, the sensitivity of infants to the acoustic consequences of linguistic gestures includes all those gestures that could be phonetically significant in any language, acquisition of one's native language being a process of losing sensitivity to gestures it does not use. Taking such further considerations as these into account, we have become even more strongly persuaded that the phonetic mode, and the perception–production link it incorporates, are innately specified.

Seen, then, as a view about the biology of language, rather than a comment on the coincidence of speaking and listening, the motor theory bears at several points on our thinking about the development of speech perception in the child. Consider, first, a linguistic ability that, though seldom noted (but see Mattingly 1976), must be taken as an important prerequisite to acquiring the phonology of a language. This is the ability to sort acoustic patterns into two classes: those that contain (candidate) phonetic structures and those that do not. (For evidence, however indirect, that infants do so sort, see Alegria and Noirot 1982; Best, Hoffman, and Glanville 1982; Entus 1977; Molfese, Freeman, and Palermo, 1975; Segalowitz and Chapman 1980;

Witelson 1977; but see Vargha-Khadem and Corballis 1979.) To appreciate the bearing of the motor theory on this matter, recall our claim, made in an earlier section, that phonetic objects cannot be perceived as a class by reference to acoustic stigmata, but only by a recognition that the sounds might have been produced by a vocal tract as it made linguistically significant gestures. If so, the perception–production link is a necessary condition for recognizing speech as speech. It would thus be a blow to the motor theory if it could be shown that infants must develop empirical criteria for this purpose. Fortunately for the theory, such criteria appear to be unnecessary.

Consider, too, how the child comes to know, not only that phonetic structures are present, but, more specifically, just what those phonetic structures are. In this connection, recall that information about the string of phonetic segments is overlapped in the sound, and that there are, accordingly, no acoustic boundaries. Until and unless the child (tacitly) appreciates the gestural source of the sounds, he can hardly be expected to perceive, or ever learn to perceive, a phonetic structure. Recall, too, that the acoustic cues for a phonetic category vary with phonetic factors such as context and with extraphonetic factors such as rate and vocal-tract size. This is to say, once again, that there is no canonical cue. What, then, is the child to learn? Association of some particular cue (or set of cues) with a phonetic category will work only for a particular circumstance. When circumstances change, the child's identification of the category will be wrong, sometimes grossly, and it is hard to see how he could readily make the appropriate correction. Perception of the phonetic categories can properly be generalized only if the acoustic patterns are taken for what they really are: information about the underlying gestures. No matter that the child sometimes mistakes the phonological significance of the gesture, so long as that which he perceives captures the systematic nature of its relation to the sound; the phonology will come in due course. To appreciate this relation is, once again, to make use of the link between perception and production.

How "Direct" Is Speech Perception?

Since we have been arguing that speech perception is accomplished without cognitive translation from a first-stage auditory register, our position might appear similar to the one Gibson (1966) has taken to regard to "direct perception." The similarity to Gibson's views may seem all the greater because, like him, we believe that the object of perception is motoric. But there are important differences, the bases for which are to be seen in the following passage (Gibson 1966, p. 94):

> An articulated utterance is a source of a vibratory field in the air. The source is biologically "physical" and the vibration is acoustically "physical." The vibration is a potential stimulus, becoming effective when a listener is within range of the vibratory field. The listener then *perceives* the articulation because the invariants of vibration correspond to those of articulation. In this theory of speech perception, the units and parts of speech are present both in the mouth of the speaker and in the air between the speaker and listener. Phonemes are in the air. They can be considered physically real if the higher-order invariants of sound waves are admitted to the realm of physics.

The first difference between Gibson's view and ours relates to the nature of the perceived events. For Gibson, these are actual movements of the articulators, while for us, they are the more remote gesturers that the speaker intended. The distinction would be trivial if an articulator were affected by only one gesture at a time, but, as we have several times remarked, an articulatory movement is usually the result of two or more overlapping gestures. The gestures are thus control structures for the observable movements.

The second difference is that, unlike Gibson, we do not think articulatory movements (let along phonetic structures) are given directly (that is, without computation) by "higher-order invariants" that would be plain if only we had a biologically appropriate science of physical acoustics. We would certainly welcome any demonstration that such invariants did exist, since, even though articulatory movement is not equivalent to phonetic structure, such a demonstration would permit a simpler account of how the phonetic module works. But no higher-order invariants have thus far been proposed, and we doubt that any will be forthcoming. We would be more optimistic on this score if it could be shown, at least, that articulatory movements can be recovered from the signal by computations that are purely analytic, if nevertheless complex. One might then hope to reformulate the relationship between movements and signal in a way that would make it possible to appeal to higher-order invariants and thus obviate the need for computation. But, given the many-to-one relation between vocal-tract configurations and acoustic signal, a purely analytic solution to the problem of recovering movements from the signal seems to be impossible unless one makes unrealistic assumptions about excitation, damping, and other physical variables (Sondhi 1979). We therefore remain skeptical about higher-order invariants.

The alternative to an analytic account of speech perception is, of course, a synthetic one, in which case the module compares some parametric description of the input signal with candidate signal descriptions. As with any form of "analysis-by-synthesis" (cf. Stevens and Halle 1967), such an account is plausible only if the number of candidates the module has to test can be kept within reasonable bounds. This requirement is met, however, if, as we suppose, the candidate signal descriptions are computed by an analogue of the production process—an internal, innately specified vocal-tract synthesizer, as it were (Liberman, Mattingly, and Turvey 1972; Mattingly and Liberman 1969)—that incorporates complete information about the anatomical and physiological characteristics of the vocal tract and also about the articulatory and acoustic consequences of linguistically significant gestures. Further constraints become available as experience with the phonology of a particular language reduces the inventory of possible gestures and provides information about the phonotactic and temporal restrictions on their occurrence. The module has then merely to determine which (if any) of the small number of gestures that might have been initiated at a particular instant could, in combination with gestures already in progress, account for the signal.

Thus, we would claim that the processes of speech perception are, like other linguistic processes, inherently computational and quite indirect. If perception seems nonetheless immediate, it is not because the process is in fact straightforward, but because the module is so well-adapted to its complex task.

The Motor Theory and Modularity

In attributing speech perception to a "module," we have in mind the notion of modularity proposed by Fodor (1983). A module, for Fodor, is a piece of neural architecture that performs the special computations required to provide central cognitive processes with representations of objects or events belonging to a natural class that is ecologically significant for the organism. This class, the "domain" of the module, is apt also to be "eccentric," for the domain would be otherwise merely a province of some more general domain, for which another module must be postulated anyway. Besides domain-specificity and specialized neural architecture, a module has other characteristic properties. Because the perceptual process it controls is not cognitive, there is little or no possibility of awareness of whatever computations are carried on within the module ("limited central access"). Because the module is specialized, it has a "shallow" output, consisting only of rigidly definable, domain-relevant representations; accordingly, it processes only the domain-relevant information in the input stimulus. Its computations are thus much faster than those of the less specialized processes of central cognition. Because of the ecological importance of its domain for the organism, the operation of the module is not a matter of choice, but "mandatory"; for the same reason, its computations are "informationally encapsulated," that is, protected from cognitive bias.

Most psychologists would agree that auditory localization, to return to an example we have mentioned several times, is controlled by specialized processes of some noncognitive kind. They might also agree that its properties are those that Fodor assigns to modules. At all events, they would set auditory localization apart from such obviously cognitive activities as playing chess, proving theorems, and recognizing a particular chair as a token of the type called "chair." As for perception of language, the consensus is that it qualifies as a cognitive process par excellence, modular only in that it is supported by the mechanisms of the auditory modality. But in this, we and Fodor would argue, the consensus is doubly mistaken; the perception of language is neither cognitive nor auditory. The events that constitute the domain of linguistic perception, however they may be defined, must certainly be an ecologically significant natural class, and it has been recognized since Broca that linguistic perception is associated with specialized neural architecture. Evidently, linguistic perception is fast and mandatory; arguably, it is informationally encapsulated—that is, its phonetic, morphological, and syntactic analyses are not biased by knowledge of the world—and its output is shallow—that is, it produces a linguistic description of the utterance, and only this. These and other considerations suggest that, like auditory localization, perception of language rests on a specialization of the kind that Fodor calls a module.

The data that have led us in the past to claim that "speech is special" and to postulate a "speech mode" of perception can now be seen to be consistent with Fodor's claims about modularity, and especially about the modularity of language. (What we have been calling a phonetic module is then more properly called a linguistic module.) Thus, as we have noted, speech perception uses all the information in the stimulus that is relevant to phonetic structures: every potential cue proves to be an actual cue. This holds true even across modalities: relevant optical information combines with relevant acoustic information to produce a coherent phonetic percept in which, as in the example described earlier, the bimodal nature of the stimulation is not detectable. In contrast, irrelevant information in the stimulus is *not* used: the acoustic properties that might cause the transitions to be heard as chirps are ignored—or perhaps we should say that the auditory consequences of those properties are suppressed—when the transitions are in context and the linguistic module is engaged.

The exclusion of the irrelevant extends, of course, to stimulus information about voice quality, which helps to identify the speaker (perhaps by virtue of some other module) but has no phonetic importance, and even to that extraphonetic information which might have been supposed to help the listener distinguish sounds that contain phonetic structures from those that do not. As we have seen, even when synthetic speech lacks the acoustic properties that would make it sound natural, it will be treated as speech if it contains sufficiently coherent phonetic information. Moreover, it makes no difference that the listener knows, or can determine on auditory grounds, that the stimulus was not humanly produced; because linguistic perception is informationally encapsulated and mandatory, he will hear synthetic speech as speech.

As might be expected, the linguistic module is also very good at excluding from consideration the acoustic effects of unrelated objects and events in the environment; the resistance of speech perception to noise and distortion is well known. These other objects and events are still perceived, because they are dealt with by other modules, but they do not, within surprisingly wide limits, interfere with speech perception (cf. Darwin 1984). On the other hand, the module is not necessarily prepared for nonecological conditions, as the phenomenon of duplex perception illustrates. Under the conditions of duplex perception the module makes a mistake it would never normally make: it treats the same acoustic information both as speech and as nonspeech. And, being an informationally encapsulated and mandatorily operating mechanism, it keeps on making the same mistake, whatever the knowledge or preference of the listener.

Our claim that the invariants of speech perception are phonetic gestures is much easier to reconcile with a modular account of linguistic perception than with a cognitive account. On the latter view, the gestures would have to be inferred from an auditory representation of the signal by some cognitive process, and this does not seem to be a task that would be particularly congenial to cognition. Parsing a sentence may seem to bear some distant resemblance to the proving of theorems, but disentangling the mutually confounding auditory effects of overlapping articulations surely does not. It is thus quite reasonable for proponents of a cognitive account to reject the possibility that the invariants are motoric and to insist that they are to be found at or near the auditory surface, heuristic matching of auditory tokens to auditory prototypes being perfectly plausible as a cognitive process.

Such difficulties do not arise for our claim on the modular account. If the invariants of speech are phonetic gestures, it merely makes the domain of linguistic perception more suitably eccentric; if the invariants were auditory, the case for a separate linguistic module would be the less compelling. Moreover, computing these invariants from the acoustic signal is a task for which there is no obvious parallel among cognitive processes. What is required for this task is not a heuristic process that draws on some general cognitive ability or on knowledge of the world, but a special-purpose computational device that relates gestural properties to the acoustic patterns.

It remains, then, to say how the set of possible gestures is specified for the perceiver. Does it depend on tacit knowledge of a kind similar, perhaps, to that which is postulated by Chomsky to explain the universal constraints on syntactic and phonological form? We think not, because knowledge of the acoustic-phonetic properties of the vocal tract, unlike other forms of tacit knowledge, seems to be totally inaccessible: no matter how hard they try, even post-perceptually, listeners cannot recover aspects of the process—for example, the acoustically different transitions—by which they might have arrived at the distal object. But, surely, this is just what one would expect if the specification of possible vocal-tract gestures is not tacit knowledge at all, but rather a direct consequence of the eccentric properties of the module itself. As already indicated, we have in earlier papers suggested that speech perception is accomplished by virtue of a model of the vocal tract that embodies the relation between gestural properties and acoustic information. Now we would add that this model must be part of the very structure of the language module. In that case, there would be, by Fodor's account, an analogy with all other linguistic universals.

Perception and Production: One Module or Two?

For want of a better word, we have spoken of the relation between speech perception and speech production as a "link," perhaps implying thereby that these two processes, though tightly bonded, are nevertheless distinct. Much the same implication is carried, more generally, by Fodor's account of modularity, if only because his attention is almost wholly on perception. We take pains, therefore, to disown the implication of distinctness that our own remarks may have conveyed, and to put explicitly in its place the claim that, for language, perception and production are only different sides of the same coin.

To make our intention clear, we should consider how language differs from those other modular arrangements in which, as with language, perception and action both figure in some functional unity: simple reflexes, for example; or the system that automatically adjusts the posture of a diving gannet in accordance with optical information that specifies the time of contact with the surface of the water (Lee and Reddish 1981). The point about such systems is that the stimuli do not resemble the responses, however intimate the connection between them. Hence, the detection of the stimulus and the initiation of the response must be managed by separate components of the module. Indeed, it would make no great difference if these cases were viewed as an input module hardwired to an output module.

Language is different: the neural representation of the utterance that determines the speaker's production is the distal object that the listener perceives; accordingly, speaking and listening are both regulated by the same structural constraints and the same grammar. If we were to assume two modules, one for speaking and one for listening, we should then have to explain how the same structures evolved for both, and how the representation of the grammar acquired by the listening module became available to the speaking module.

So, if it is reasonable to assume that there is such a thing as a language module, then it is even more reasonable to assume that there is only one. And if, within that module, there are subcomponents that correspond to the several levels of linguistic performance, then each of these subcomponents must deal both with perception and production. Thus, if sentence planning is the function of a particular subcomponent, then sentence parsing is a function of the same subcomponent, and similarly, mutatis mutandis, for speech production and speech perception. And, finally, if all this is true, then the corresponding input and output functions must themselves be as computationally similar as the inherent asymmetry between production and perception permits, just as they are in man-made communication devices.

These speculations do not, of course, reveal the nature of the computations that the language module carries out, but they do suggest a powerful constraint on our hypotheses about them, a constraint for which there is no parallel in the case of other module systems. Thus, they caution that, among all plausible accounts of language input, we should take seriously only those that are equally plausible as accounts of language output; if a hypothesis about parsing cannot be readily restated as a hypothesis about sentence-planning, for example, we should suppose that something is wrong with it.

Whatever the weaknesses of the motor theory, it clearly does conform to this constraint, since, by its terms, speech production and speech perception are both inherently motoric. On the one side of the module, the motor gestures are not the means to sounds designed to be congenial to the ear; rather, they are, in themselves, the essential phonetic units. On the other side, the sounds are not the true objects of perception, made available for linguistic purposes in some common auditory register; rather, they only supply the information for immediate perception of the gestures.

Note

The writing of this paper was supported by a grant to Haskins Laboratories (NIH-NICHD HD-01994). We owe a special debt to Harriet Magen for invaluable help with the relevant literature, and to Alice Dadourian for coping with an ever-changing manuscript. For their patient responses to our frequent requests for information and criticism, we thank Franklin Cooper, Jerry Foder, Carol Fowler, Scott Kelso, Charles Liberman, Robert Remez, Bruno Repp, Arthur Samuel, Michael Studdert-Kennedy, Michael Turvey, and Douglas Whalen. We also acknowledge the insightful comments of an anonymous reviewer.

References

Abramson, A. S. (1972) Tonal experiments with whispered Thai. In A. Valdman (Ed.), *Papers in Linguistics and Phonetics to the Memory of Pierre Delattre*, 31–44. The Hague: Mouton.

Alegria, J., and Noirot, E. (1982) Oriented mouthing activity in neonates: Early development of differences related to feeding experiences. In J. Mehler, S. Franck, E. C. T. Walker, and M. Garrett (Eds.), *Perspectives on Mental Representation.* Hillsdale, NJ: Erlbaum.

Aslin, R. N., and Pisoni, D. B. (1980) Some developmental processes in speech perception. In G. H. Yeni-Komshian, J. F. Kavanagh, and C. A. Ferguson (Eds.), *Child Phonology.* New York: Academic Press.

Bailey, P. J. and Summerfield, Q. (1980) Information in speech: Observations on the perception of [s]-stop cluster. *Journal of Experimental Psychology: Human Perception and Performance*, 6, 536–563.

Bentin, S., and Mann, V. A. (1983) Selective effects of masking on speech and nonspeech in the duplex perception paradigm. *Haskins Laboratories Status Report on Speech Research*, SR-76, 65–85.

Berkeley, G. (1709) *An essay towards a new theory of vision.* Dublin: Printed by Aaron Rhames for Jeremy Pepyal.

Best, C. T., Hoffman, H., and Gianville, B. B. (1982) Development of infant ear asymmetries for speech and music. *Perception and Psychophysics*, 31, 75–85.

Best, C. T., Morrongiello, B., and Robson, R. (1981) Perceptual equivalence of acoustic cues in speech and nonspeech perception. *Perception and Psychophysics*, 29, 191–211.

Best, C. T., and Studdert-Kennedy, M. (1983) Discovering phonetic coherence in acoustic patterns. In A. Cohen and M. P. R. van den Broecke (Eds.), *Abstracts of the Tenth International Congress of Phonetic Sciences.* Dordrecht, The Netherlands: Foris Publications.

Brady, P. T., House, A. S., and Stevens, K. N. (1961) Perception of sounds characterized by a rapidly changing resonant frequency. *Journal of the Acoustical Society of America*, 33, 1357–1362.

Browman, C. P., and Goldstein, L. M. (1985) Dynamic modeling of phonetic structure. In V. Fromkin (Ed.). *Phonetic Linguistics.* New York: Academic Press.

Brown E. L., and Deffenbacher, K. (1979) *Perception and the Senses.* New York: Oxford University Press.

Carney, A. E., Widin, G. P., and Viemeister, N. F. (1977) Noncategorical perception of stop consonants differing in VOT. *Journal of the Acoustical Society of America*, 62, 961–970.

Chistovich, L. A. (1960) Classification of rapidly repeated speech sounds. *Akustichneskii Zhurnal*, 6, 392–398. Trans, in *Soviet Physics-Acoustics*, 6, 393–398 (1961).

Cole, R. A., and Scott, B. (1974) Toward a theory of speech perception. *Psychological Review*, 81, 348–374.

Cooper, F. S., Delattre, P. C., Liberman, A. M., Borst, J. M., and Gerstman, L. J. (1952) Some experiments on the perception of synthetic speech sounds. *Journal of the Acoustical Society of America*, 24, 597–606.
Crowder, R. G., and Morton, J. (1969) Pre-categorical acoustic storage (PAS). *Perception and Psychophysics*, 5, 365–373.
Cutting, J. E., and Rosner, B. S. (1974) Categories and boundaries in speech and music. *Perception and Psychophysics*, 16, 564–570.
Darwin, C. J. (1984) Perceiving vowels in the presence of another sound: Constraints on formant perception. *Journal of the Acoustical Society of America*, 76, 1636–1647.
Dorman, M. F., Raphael, L. J., and Liberman, A. M. (1979) Some experiments on the sound of silence in phonetic perception. *Journal of the Acoustical Society of America*, 65, 1518–1532.
Dorman, M. F., Studdert-Kennedy, M., and Raphael, L. J. (1977) Stop consonant recognition: Release bursts and formant transitions as functionally equivalent, context-dependent cues. *Perception and Psychophysics*, 22, 109–122.
Dudley, H. (1940) The carrier nature of speech. *Bell Systems Technical Journal*, 19, 495–515.
Eimas, P., Siqueland, E. R., Jusczyk, P., and Vigorito, J. (1971) Speech perception in early infancy. *Science*, 171, 304–306.
Entus, A. K. (1977) Hemispheric asymmetry in processing dichotically presented speech and nonspeech stimuli by infants. In S. J. Segalowitz and F. A. Greber (Eds.), *Language Development and Neurological Theory*. New York: Academic Press.
Fant, C. G. M. (1962) Descriptive analysis of the acoustic aspects of speech. *Logos*, 5, 3–17.
Festinger, L., Burnham, C. A., Ono, H., and Bamber, D. (1967) Efference and the conscious experience of perception. *Journal of Experimental Psychology Monograph*, 74, (4, Pt. 2).
Fitch, H. L., Halwes, T., Erickson, D. M., and Liberman, A. M. (1980) Perceptual equivalence of two acoustic cues for stop consonant manner. *Perception and Psychophysics*, 27, 343–350.
Fodor, J. (1983) *The Modularity of Mind*. Cambridge, MA: MIT Press.
Fowler, C. A. (1982) Converging sources of evidence on spoken and perceived rhythms of speech: Cyclic production of vowels in monosyllabic stress feet. *Journal of Experimental Psychology: General*, 112, 386–412.
Fowler, C. A. (1984) Segmentation of coarticulated speech in perception. *Perception and Psychophysic*, 36, 359–368.
Flower, C. A., Rubin, P., Remez, R. E., and Turvey, M. T. (1980) Implications for speech production of a general theory of action. In B. Butterworth (Ed.), *Language Production*. New York: Academic Press.
Fujisaki, M., and Kawashima, T. (1970) Some experiments on speech perception and a model for the perceptual mechanism. *Annual Report of the Engineering Research Institute* (Faculty of Engineering, University of Tokyo), 29, 207–214.
Gerhart, H. C., and Rheinlaender, J. (1982) Localization of an elevated sound source by the green tree frog. *Science*, 217, 663–664.
Gibson, J. J. (1966) *The Senses Considered as Perceptual Systems*. Boston: Houghton Mifflin.
Hafter, E. R. (1984) Spatial hearing and the duplex theory: How viable is the model? In G. M. Edelman, W. E. Gall, and W. M. Cowan (Eds.), *Dynamic Aspects of Neocortical Function*. New York: Wiley.
Harris, K. S. (1958) Cues for the discrimination of American English fricatives in spoken syllables. *Language and Speech*, 1, 1–7.
Hillenbrand, J. (1984) Perception of sine-wave analogs of voice onset time stimuli. *Journal of the Acoustical Society of America*, 75, 231–240.
Hirsh, I. J. (1959) Auditory perception of temporal order. *Journal of the Acoustical Society of America*, 31, 759–767.
Hoffman, H. S. (1958) Study of some cues in the perception of the voiced stop consonants. *Journal of the Acoustical Society of America*, 30, 1035–1041.
Howell, P., and Rosen, S. (1983) Closure and friction measurements and perceptual integration of temporal cues for the voiceless affricate/fricative contrast. *Speech Hearing and Language Work in Progress*. University College London, Department of Phonetics and Linguistics.
Hoy, R., Hahn, J., and Paul, R. C. (1977) Hybrid cricket auditory behavior: Evidence for genetic coupling in animal communication. *Science*, 195, 82–83.
Hoy, R. and Paul, R. C. (1973) Genetic control of song specificity in crickets. *Science*, 180, 82–83.
Inoue, A. (1984) A perceptual study of Japanese voiceless vowels and its implications for the phonological analysis of voiceless consonants. Unpublished manuscript.

Jenkins, J. J., Strange, W., and Edman, T. R. (1983) Identification of vowels in 'voiceless' syllables. *Perception and Psychophysics*, 34, 441–450.

Joos, M. (1948) Acoustic phonetics. *Language Monograph* 23, Supplement to *Language*, 24.

Julesz, B. (1960) Binocular depth perception of computer-generated patterns. *Bell System Technical Journal* 39, 1125–1162.

Julesz, B. (1971) *Foundations of Cyclopean Perception*. Chicago: University of Chicago Press.

Katz, L. C., and Gurney, M. E. (1981) Auditory responses in the zebra finch's motor system for song. *Brain Research*, 221, 192–197.

Knudsen, E. I. (1982) Auditory and visual maps of space in the optic tectum of the owl. *Journal of Neuroscience*, 2, 1117–1194.

Knudesen, E. I. (1984) Synthesis of a neural map of auditory space in the owl. In G. M. Edelman, W. E. Gall, and W. M. Cowan, *Dynamic Aspects of Neocortical Function*. New York: Wiley.

Kuhl, P. K. (1981) Discrimination of speech by nonhuman animals: Basic auditory sensitivities conducive to the perception of speech-sound categories. *Journal of the Acoustical Society of America*, 70, 340–349.

Kuhl, P. K., and Meltzoff, A. N. (1982) The bimodal perception of speech in infancy. *Science*, 218, 1138–1144.

Kuhl, P. K., and Miller, J. D. (1975) Speech perception by the chinchilla: Voiced-voiceless distinction in alveolar plosive consonants. *Science*, 190, 69.

Ladefoged, P., and McKinney, N. (1963) Loudness, sound pressure, and subglottal pressure in speech. *Journal of the Acoustical Society of America*, 35, 454–460.

Lee, D. N., and Reddish, P. E. (1981) Plummeting gannets: A paradigm of ecological optics. *Nature*, 293, 293–294.

Liberman, A. M. (1979) Duplex perception and integration of cues: Evidence that speech is different from nonspeech and similar to language. In E. Fishcer-Jorgensen, J. Rischel, and N. Thorsen (Eds.), *Proceedings of the IXth International Congress of Phonetic Sciences*. Copenhagen: University of Copenhagen.

Liberman, A. M. (1982) On finding that speech is special. *American Psychologist*, 37, 148–167.

Liberman, A. M., Cooper, F. S., Shankweiler, D. P., and Studdert-Kennedy, M. (167) Perception of the speech code. *Psychological Review*, 74, 431–461.

Liberman, A. M., Delattre, P. C., and Cooper, F. S. (1952) The role of selected stimulus-variables in the perception of the unvoiced stop consonants. *American Journal of Psychology*, 65, 497–516.

Liberman, A. M., Delattre, P. C., Cooper, F. S., and Gerstman, L. J. (1954) The role of consonant-vowel transitions in the perception of the stop and nasal consonants. *Psychological Monographs*, 68, 1–13.

Liberman, A. M., Isenberg, D., and Rakerd, B. (1981) Duplex perception of cues for stop consonants: Evidence for a phonetic mode. *Perception and Psychophysics*, 30, 133–143.

Liberman, A. M., Mattingly, I. G., and Turvey, M. (1972) Language codes and memory codes. In A. W. Melton and E. Martin (Eds.), *Coding Processes and Human Memory*. Washington, DC: Winston.

Liberman, A. M., and Studdert-Kennedy, M. (1978) Phonetic perception. In R. Held, H. W. Leibownz, and H.-L. Teuber (Eds.), *Handbook of Sensory Physiology, Vol. VIII: Perception*. New York: Springer-Verlag.

Lisker, L. (1957) Closure duration, first-formant transitions, and the voiced-voiceless contrast of intervocalic stops. *Haskins Laboratories Quarterly Progress Report*, 23, Appendix 1.

Lisker, L. (1978) Rapid vs. rabid: A catalogue of acoustic features that may cue the distinction. *Haskins Laboratories Status Report on Speech Research*, SR-54, 127–132.

Lisker, L., and Abramson, A. (1964) A cross-language study of voicing in initial stops: Acoustical measurement. *Word*, 20, 384–422.

MacKain, K. S., Studdert-Kennedy, M., Spieker, S., and Stern, D. (1983) Infant intermodal speech perception is a left hemisphere function. *Science*, 219, 1347–1349.

MacNeilage, P. F., Rootes, T. P., and Chase, R. A. (1967) Speech production and perception is a patient with severe impairment of somaesthetic perception and motor control. *Journal of Speech and Hearing Research*, 10, 449–468.

Magen, H. (1984) Vowel-to-vowel coarticulation in English and Japanese. *Journal of the Acoustical Society of America*, 75, S41.

Mann, V. A., and Liberman, A. M. (183) Some differences between phonetic and auditory modes of perception. *Cognition*, 14, 211–235.

Mann, V. A., and Repp, B. H. (1980) Influence of vocalic context on the perception of [ʃ]-[s] distinction: I. Temporal factors. *Perception and Psychophysics*, 28, 213–228.

Mann, V. A., and Repp, B. H. (1981) Influence of preceding fricative on stop consonant perception. *Journal of the Acoustical Society of America*, 69, 548–558.

Manuel, S. Y., and Krakow, R. A. (1984) Universal and language particular aspects of vowel-to-vowel coarticulation. *Haskins Laboratories Status Report on Speech Research*, SR-77/78, 69–78.

Margolish, D. (1983) Acoustic parameters underlying the responses of song specific neurons in the white-crowned sparrow. *Journal of Neuroscience*, 3, 1039–1057.

Marler, P. (1970) Birdsong and speech development: Could there be parallels? *American Scientist*, 58, 669–673.

Martin, J. G., and Bunnel, H. T. (1981) Perception of anticipatory coarticulation effects in /stri, stru/ sequences. *Journal of the Acoustical Society of America*, 69, S92.

Martin, J. G., and Bunnel, H. T. (1982) Perception of anticipatory coarticulation effects in vowel-stop consonant-vowel sequences. *Journal of Experimental Psychology: Human Perception and Performance*, 8, 473–488.

Mattingly, I. G. (1976) Phonetic prerequisites for first-language acquisition. In W. Von Raffler-Engel, and Y. Lebrun (Eds.), *Baby Talk and Infant Speech*. Lisse, The Netherlands: Swets and Zeitlinger.

Mattingly, I. G., and Liberman, A. M. (1969) The speech code and the physiology of language. In K. N. Leibovic (Ed.), *Information Processing in the Nervous System*. New York: Springer-Verlag.

Mattingly, I. G., and Liberman, A. M. (1985) Verticality unparalleled. *The Behavioral and Brain Sciences*, 8, 24–26.

Mattingly, I. G., Liberman, A. M., Syrdal, A. M., and Halwes, T. (1971) Discrimination in speech and nonspeech modes. *Cognitive Psychology*, 2, 131–157.

McCasland, J. S., and Konishi, M. (1983) Interaction between auditory and motor activities in an avian song control nucleus. *Proceedings of the National Academy of Sciences*, 78, 7815–7819.

McGurk, H., and MacDonald, J. (1976) Hearing lips and seeing voices. *Nature*, 264, 746–748.

Miller, J. D. (1977) Perception of speech sounds in animals: Evidence for speech processing by mammalian auditory mechanisms. In T. H. Bullock (Ed.), *Recognition of Complex Acoustic Signals* (Life Sciences Research Report 5), p. 49. Berlin: Dahlem Konferenzen.

Miyawaki, K., Strange, W., Verbrugge, R., Liberman, A. M., Jenkins, J. J., and Fujimara, O. (1975) An effect of linguistic experience: the discrimination of [r] and [l] by native speakers of Japanese and English. *Perception and Psychophysics*, 18, 331–340.

Molfese, D. L., Freeman, R. B., and Palermo, D. S. (1975) The ontogeny of brain lateralization for speech and nonspeech stimuli. *Brain and Language*, 2, 356–368.

Nottbohm, F., Stokes, T. M., and Leonard, C. M. (1976) Central control of song in the canary. Serinus canarius. *Journal of Comparative Neurology*, 165, 457–486.

O'Connor, J. D., Gerstman, L. J., Liberman, A. M., Delattre, P. C., and Cooper, F. S. (1957) Acoustic cues for the perception of initial /w,r,l/ in English. *Word*, 13, 25–43.

Oden, G. C., and Massaro, D. W. (1978) Integration of featural information in speech perception. *Psychological Review*, 85, 172–191.

Ohman, S. E. G. (1966) Coarticulation in VCV utterances: Spectrographic measurements. *Journal of the Acoustical Society of America*, 39, 151–168.

Pastore, R. E., Schmuckler, M. A., Rosenblum, L., and Szczesiul, R. (1983) Duplex perception with musical stimuli. *Perception and Psychophysics*, 33, 469–474.

Pisoni, D. B. (1973) Auditory and phonetic memory codes in the discrimination of consonants and vowels. *Perception and Psychophysics*, 13, 253–260.

Pisoni, D. B. (1977) Identification and discrimination of the relative onset of two component tones: Implications for the perception of voicing in stops. *Journal of the Acoustical Society of America*, 61, 1352–1361.

Pisoni, D. B., and Tash, J. (1974) Reaction times to comparisons within and across phonetic categories. *Perception and Psychophysics*, 15, 285–290.

Poggio, G. F. (1984) Processing of stereoscopic information in primate visual cortex. In G. M. Edelman, W. E. Gall, and W. M. Cowan (Eds.), *Dynamic Aspects of Neocortical Function*. New York: Wiley.

Rakerd, B., Dechovitz, D. R., and Verbrugge, R. R. (1982) An effect of sentence finality on the phonetic significance of silence. *Language and Speech*, 25, 267–282.

Rand, T. C. (1974) Dichotic release from masking for speech. *Journal of the Acoustical Society of America*, 55, 678–680.

Recasens, D. (1984) Vowel-to-vowel coarticulation in Catalan VCV sequences. *Journal of the Acoustical Society of America*, 76, 1624–1635.

Remez, R. E., Rubin, P. E., Pisoni, D. B., and Carrell, T. D. (1981) Speech perception without traditional speech cues. *Science*, 212, 947–950.

Remez, R. E., and Rubin, P. E. (1984) On the perception of intonation from sinusoidal signals: Tone height and contour. *Journal of the Acoustical Society of America*, 75, S39.

Repp, B. H. (1984). The role of release bursts in the perception of [s]-stop clusters. *Journal of the Acoustical Society of America*, 75, 1219–1230.

Repp, B. H., and Liberman, A. M. (in press) Phonetic categories are flexible. In S. Harnad (Ed.), *Categorical Perception*. Cambridge: Cambridge University Press.

Repp, B. H., Liberman, A. M., Eccardt, T., and Pesetzky, D. (1978) Perceptual integration of acoustic cues for stop, fricative and affricate manner. *Journal of Experimental Psychology: Human Perception and Performance*, 4, 621–637.

Repp, B. H., Milburn, C., and Ashkenas, J. (1983) Duplex perception: Confirmation of fusion. *Perception and Psychophysics*, 33, 333–337.

Rosen, S. M., and Howell, P. (1981) Plucks and bows are not categorically perceived. *Perception and Psychophysics*, 30, 156–168.

Sondhi, M. M. (1979) Estimation of vocal-tract areas: the need for acoustical measurements. *IEEE Transactions on Acoustics, Speech and Signal Processing*, ASSP-27, 268–273.

Samuel, A. G. (1977) The effect of discrimination training on speech perception: Noncategorical perception. Perception and Psychophysics, 22, 321–330.

Segalowitz, S. J., and Chapman, J. S. (1980) Cerebral asymmetry for speech in neonates: A behavioral measure. *Brain and Language*, 9, 281–288.

Stetson, R. H. (1951) *Motor Phonetics: A Study of Speech Movements in Action*. Amsterdam: North-Holland.

Stevens, K. N. (1975) The potential role of property detectors in the perception of consonants. In G. Fant and M. A. Tatham (Eds.) *Auditory Analysis and Perception of Speech*. New York: Academic Press.

Stevens, K. N., and Halle, M. (1967) Remarks on analysis by synthesis and distinctive features. In W. Wathen-Dunn (Ed.). *Models for the Perception of Speech and Visual Form*. Cambridge, MA: MIT Press.

Stevens, K. N., and Blumstein, S. E. (1978) Invariant cues for place of articulation in stop consonants. *Journal of the Acoustical Society of America*, 64, 1358–1368.

Strange, W., Jenkins, J. J., and Johnson, T. L. (1983) Dynamic specification of coarticulated vowels. *Journal of the Acoustical Society of America*, 74, 695–705.

Studdert-Kennedy, M. (1976) Speech perception. In N. J. Lass (Ed.), *Contemporary Issues in Experimental Phonetics*. New York: Academic Press.

Studdert-Kennedy, M., and Williams, D. R. (1984) Range effects for speech and nonspeech judgments of sine wave stimuli. *Journal of the Acoustical Society of America*, 75, S64.

Suga, N. (1984) The extent to which bisonar information is represented in the auditory cortex. In G. M. Edelman, W. E. Gall, and W. M. Cowan (Eds.), *Dynamic Aspects of Neocortical Function*. New York: Wiley.

Summerfield, Q. (1982) Differences between spectral dependencies in auditory and phonetic temporal processing: Relevance to the perception of voicing in initial stops. *Journal of the Acoustical Society of America*, 72, 51–61.

Summerfield, Q., and Haggard, M. (1977) On the dissociation of spectral and temporal cues to the voicing distinction in initial stop consonants. *Journal of the Acoustical Society of America*, 62, 436–448.

Thorpe, W. H. (1958) The learning of song patterns by birds, with especial reference to the song of the chaffinch, Fringilla coelebs. *Ibis*, 100, 535–570.

Tuller, B., Harris, K., and Kelso, J. A. S. (1982) Stress and rate: Differential transformations of articulation. *Journal of the Acoustical Society of America*, 71, 1534–1543.

Tuller, B., and Kelso, J. A. S. (1984) The relative timing of articulatory gestures: Evidence for relational invariants. *Journal of the Acoustical Society of America*, 76, 1030–1036.

Turvey, M. (1977) Preliminaries to a theory of action with reference to vision. In R. Shaw and J. Bransford (Eds.), *Perceiving, Acting, and Knowing: Toward an Ecological Physiology*. Hillsdale, NJ: Erlbaum.

Vargha-Khadem, F., and Corballis, M. (1979) Cerebral asymmetry in infants. *Brain and Language*, 8, 1–9.

Washburn, M. F. (1926) Gestalt Psychology and Motor Psychology. *American Journal of Psychology*, 37, 516–520.

Watson, J. B. (1919) *Psychology from the Standpoint of a Behaviorist*. Philadelphia: J.B. Lippincott Co.

Werker, J. F., and Tees, R. C. (1984) Cross-language speech perception: Evidence for perceptual organization during the first year of life. *Infant Behavior and Development*, 7, 49–63.

Whalen, D. H. (1981) Effects of vocalic formant transition and vowel quality on the English [s]-[š] boundary. *Journal of the Acoustical Society of America*, 69, 275–282.

Williams, H. (1984) *A motor theory of bird song perception.* Unpublished doctoral dissertation. The Rockefeller University.

Williams, D. R., Verbrugge, R. R., and Studdert-Kennedy, M. (1983) Judging sine wave stimuli as speech and nonspeech. *Journal of the Acoustical Society of America*, 74, S66.

Witelson, S. (1977) Early hemispher specialization and interhemispheric plasticity: An empirical and theoretical review. In S. J. Segalowitz and F. A. Gruber (Eds.), *Language Development and Neurological Theory.* New York: Academic Press.

Yeni-Komshian, G. H. and Soli, S. D. (1981) Recognition of vowels from information in fricatives: Perceptual evidence of fricative-vowel coarticulation. *Journal of the Acoustical Society of America*, 70, 966–975.

PART VII

Some Properties of the Phonetic Module

Introduction to Part VII

In chapter 15, we considerably elaborate the notion, briefly alluded to in chapter 14, that the phonetic module has certain properties in common with other specializations for perception and, in the case of communication systems, for production as well.

Chapter 15

Specialized Perceiving Systems for Speech and Other Biologically Significant Sounds

Our aim is to promote the view that speech perception is to humans as sound localization is to barn owls. This is not merely to suggest that humans are preoccupied with listening to speech, much as owls are with homing in on the sound of prey. It is to offer a particular hypothesis: Like sound localization, speech perception is a coherent system in its own right, specifically adapted to a narrowly restricted class of ecologically important events. In this important respect, speech perception and sound localization are more similar to each other than is either to the processes that underlie the perception of such ecologically arbitrary events as squeaking doors, rattling chains, or whirring fans.

To develop the unconventional view, we contrast it with its more conventional opposite, say why the less conventional view is nevertheless the more plausible, and describe several properties of the speech-perceiving system that the unconventional view reveals. We compare speech perception with other specialized perceiving systems that also treat acoustic signals, including not only sound localization in the owl, but also song in the bird and echolocation in the bat. Where appropriate, we develop the neurobiological implications, but we do not try here to fit them to the vast and diverse literature that pertains to the human case.

Through most of this chapter we construe speech, in the narrow sense, as referring only to consonants and vowels. Then, at the end, we briefly say how our view of speech might nevertheless apply more broadly to sentences. Following the instructions of the editors, we discuss primarily issues and principles; however, we do offer the results of a few experiments, not so much to prove our argument as to illuminate it. [For full accounts of these experiments and the many others that support the claims we will be making below, see Liberman et al. (1967), Liberman and Mattingly (1986), and the studies referred to therein.]

Two Views of Speech Perception: Generally Auditory versus Specifically Phonetic

The conventional view derives from the common assumption that mental processes are not specific to the real-world events to which they are applied. Thus perception of speech is taken to be in no important way different from perception of other sounds. [Not surprisingly, there are a number of variations on the "conventional view"; they are discussed in Liberman and Mattingly (1986).] In all cases, it is as if the primitive auditory consequences of acoustic events were delivered to a common

Originally published in *Auditory Function*, ed. G. M. Edelman, W. E. Gail, and W. M. Cowan (John Wiley & Sons, 1988), 775–793, with Ignatius G. Mattingly. Reprinted with permission.

register (the primary auditory cortex?), from whence they would be taken for such cognitive treatment as might be necessary in order to categorize each ensemble of primitives as representative of squeaking doors, stop consonants, or some other class of acoustic events. On any view, there are, of course, specializations for each of the several auditory primitives that together make up the auditory modality, but there is surely no specialization for squeaking doors as such, and, on the conventional view, none for stop consonants either.

Our view is different on all counts. Seen our way, speech perception takes place in a specialized phonetic mode, different from the general auditory mode and served, accordingly, by a different neurobiology. Contrary to the conventional assumption, there is then a specialization for consonants and vowels as such. This specialization yields only phonetic structures; it does not deliver to a common auditory register those sensory primitives that might, in arbitrarily different combinations, be cognitively categorized as any of a wide variety of ordinary acoustic events. Thus specialization for perception of phonetic structures begins prior to such categorization and is independent of it.

The phonetic mode is not auditory, in our view, because the events it perceives are not acoustic. They are, rather, gestural. For example, the consonant [b] is a lip-closing gesture; [h] is a glottis-opening gesture. Combining lip-closing and glottis-opening yields [p]; combining lip-closing and velum-lowering yields [m], and so on. Despite their simplistic labels, the gestures are in fact quite complex: As we shall see, a gesture usually requires the movements of several articulators, and these movements are most often context-sensitive. A rigorous definition of a particular gesture has, therefore, to be fairly abstract. Nevertheless, it is the gestures that we take to be the primitives of speech perception, no less than of speech production. Phonetic structures are patterns of gestures, then, and it is just these that the speech system is specialized to perceive.

The Plausible Function of a Specifically Phonetic Mode

But why should consonants and vowels be gestures, not sounds, and why should it take a specialized system to perceive them? To answer these questions, it is helpful to imagine the several ways in which phonetic communication might have been engineered.

Accepting that Nature made a firm commitment to an acoustic medium, we can suppose that she might have defined the phonetic segments—consonants and vowels—in acoustic terms. This, surely, is what common sense suggests, and, indeed, what the conventional view assumes. The requirements that follow from this definition are simply that the acoustic signals be appropriate to the sensitivities of the ear, and that they provide the invariant basis for the correspondingly invariant auditory percept by which each phonetic segment is to be communicated. The first requirement is easy enough to satisfy, but the second is not. For if the sounds are to be produced by the organs of the vocal tract, then strings of acoustically defined segments require strings of discrete gestures. Such strings can be managed, of course, but only at unacceptably slow rates. Indeed, we know exactly how slow, because speaking so as to produce a segment of sound for each phonetic segment is what we do when we spell. Thus, to articulate the consonant-vowel syllables [di] and [du], for example, the speaker would have to say something like [də] [i] and [də] [u], converting each consonant and each vowel into a syllable. Listening to such spelled speech, letter by painful letter, is not only time-consuming but also maddeningly hard.

Nature might have thought to get around this difficulty by abandoning the vocal tract in favor of a to-be-developed set of sound-producing devices, specifically adapted for creating the drumfire that communication via acoustic segments would require if speakers were to achieve the rates that characterize speech as we know it, rates that run at eight to ten segments per second, on average, and at double that for short stretches. But this would have defeated the ear, severely straining its capacity to identify the separate segments and keep their order straight.

Our view is that Nature solved the problems of rate by avoiding the acoustic strategy that gives rise to them. The alternative was to define the phonetic segments as gestures, letting the sound go pretty much as it might, so long as the acoustic consequences of the different gestures were distinct. On its face, this seems at least a reasonable way to begin, for it takes into account that phonetic structures are not really objects of the acoustic world anyway; they belong, rather, to a domain that is internal to the speaker, and it is the objects of this domain that need to be communicated to the listener. But the decisive consideration in favor of the gestural strategy is surely that it offers critical advantages for rate of communication, both in production and in perception. These advantages were not to be had, however, simply by appropriating movements that were already available, for example, those of eating and breathing. Rather, the phonetic gestures and their underlying controls had to be developed, presumably as part of the evolution of language. Thus, as we will argue later, speech production is as much a specialization as speech perception; as we will also argue, it is indeed the same specialization.

In production, the advantage of the gestural strategy is that, given the relative independence of the muscles and organs of the vocal tract and the development of appropriately specialized controls, gestures belonging to successive segments in the phonetic string can be executed simultaneously or with considerable overlap. Thus the gesture for [d] is overlapped with component gestures for the following vowel, whether [i] or [u]. By just such coarticulation, speakers achieve the high rates at which phonetic structures are in fact transmitted, rates that would be impossible if the gestures had to be produced seriatim.

In perception, the advantage of the gestural strategy is that it provides the basis for evading the limit on rate that would otherwise have been set by the temporal resolving abilities of the auditory system. This, too, is a consequence of coarticulation. Information about several gestures is packed into a single segment of sound, thereby reducing the number of sound segments that must be dealt with per unit of time.

But the gain for perception is not without cost, for if information about several gestures is transmitted at the same time, the relation between these gestures and their acoustic vehicles cannot be straightforward. It is, to be sure, systematic, but only in a way that has two special and related consequences. First, there is no one-to-one correspondence in segmentation between phonetic structure and signal; information about the consonant and the vowel can extend from one end of the acoustic syllable to the other. Second, the shape of the acoustic signal for each particular phonetic gesture varies according to the nature of the concomitant gestures and the rate at which they are produced. Thus the cues on which the processes of speech perception must rely are context conditioned. For example, the perceptually significant second-formant transition for [d] begins high in the spectrum and rises for [di], but begins low in the spectrum and falls for [du].

How might the complications of this unique relation have been managed? Consider first the possibility that no further specialization is provided, the burden being put on the perceptual and cognitive equipment with which the listener is already endowed. By this strategy, the listener uses ordinary auditory processes to convert the acoustic signals of speech to ordinary auditory percepts. But then, having perceived the sound, the listener must puzzle out the combination of coarticulated gestures that might have produced it, or, failing that, learn ad hoc to connect each context-conditioned and eccentrically segmented token to its proper phonetic type. However, the puzzle is so thorny as to have proved so far to be beyond the capacity of scientists to solve; and given the large number of acoustic tokens for each phonetic type, ad hoc learning might well have been endless. Moreover, listening to speech would have been a disconcerting experience at best, for the listener would have been aware not only of phonetic structure but also of the auditory base from which phonetic structure would have had to be recovered. We gain some notion of what this experience would have been like when we hear, in isolation from their contexts, the second-formant transitions that cue [di] and [du]. As would be expected on psychoacoustic grounds, the transition for [di] sounds like a rising glissando on high pitches (or a high-pitched chirp); the transition for [du] like a falling glissando on low pitches (or a low-pitched chirp). If the second-formant transition is combined with the concomitant transitions of other formants, the percept becomes a "bleat" whose timbre depends on the nature of the component transitions. Fluent speech, should it be heard in this auditory way, would thus be a rapid sequence of qualitatively varying bleats. The plight of the listener who had to base a cognitive analysis of phonetic structure on such auditory percepts would have been like that of a radio operator trying to follow a rapid-fire sequence of Morse code dots and dashes, only worse, because, as we have seen, the "dots and dashes" of the speech code take as many different acoustic forms as there are variations in context and rate.

The other strategy for recovering phonetic structure from the sound—the one that must have prevailed—was to use an appropriate specialization. Happily, this specialization was already at hand in the form of those arrangements, previously referred to, that made it possible for speakers to articulate and coarticulate phonetic gestures. These must have incorporated in their architecture all the constraints of anatomy, physiology, and phonetics that organize the movements of the speech organs and govern their relation to the sound, so access to this architecture should have made it possible, in effect, to work the process in reverse—that is, to use the acoustic signal as a basis for computing the coarticulated gestures that caused it. It is just this kind of perception–production specialization that our view assumes. Recovering phonetic structure requires, then, no prodigies of conscious computation or arbitrary learning. To perceive speech, a person has only to listen, for the specialization yields the phonetic percept immediately. This is to say that there is no conscious mediation by an auditory base. The gestures for consonants and vowels, as perceived, are themselves the distal objects; they are not, like the dots and dashes of Morse code (or the squeak of the door), at one remove from it. But perception is immediate in this case (and in such similar cases as, for example, sound localization), not because the underlying processes are simple or direct, but only because they are well suited to their unique and complex task.

Some Properties of the Phonetic Mode Compared with Those of Other Perceptual Specializations

Every perceptual specialization must differ from every other in the nature of the distal events it is specialized for, as it must, too, in the relation between these events and the proximal stimuli that convey them. At some level of generality, however, there are properties of these specializations that invite comparison. Several of the properties that are common, perhaps, to all perceiving specializations—for example, "domain specificity," "mandatory operation," and "limited central access"—have been described by Fodor (1983) and claimed by us to be characteristic of the phonetic mode (Liberman and Mattingly 1986). We do not review these here, but choose to put our attention on four properties of the phonetic mode that are not so widely shared and that may, therefore, define several subclasses.

Heteromorphy
The phonetic mode, as we have conceived it, is "heteromorphic" in the sense that it is specialized to yield perceived objects whose dimensionalities are radically different from those of the proximal stimuli.[1] Thus the synthetic formant transitions that are perceived homomorphically in the auditory mode as continuous glissandi are perceived heteromorphically in the phonetic mode as consonant or vowel gestures that have no glissandolike auditory qualities at all. But is it not so in sound localization too? Surely, interaural disparities of time and intensity are perceived heteromorphically, as locations of sound sources, and not homomorphically, as disparities, unless the interaural differences are of such great magnitude that the sound-localizing specialization is not engaged. Thus the heteromorphic relation between distal object and the display at the sense organ is not unique to phonetic perception. Indeed, it characterizes not only sound localization but also echolocation in the bat, if we can assume that, as Suga's (1984) neurobiological results imply, the bat perceives not echo time as such but rather something more like the distance it measures. If we look to vision for an example, we find an obvious one in stereopsis, where perception is not of two-dimensionally disparate images but of third-dimensional depth.

To see more clearly what heteromorphy is, let us consider two striking and precisely opposite phenomena of speech perception together with such parallels as may be found in sound localization. In one of these phenomena, two stimuli of radically different dimensionalities converge on a single, coherent percept; in the other, stimuli lying on a single physical dimension diverge into two different percepts. In neither case can the contributions of the disparate or common elements be detected.

Convergence on a Single Percept: Equivalence of Acoustic and Optical Stimuli   The most extreme example of convergence in speech perception was discovered by McGurk and McDonald (1976). As slightly modified for our purpose, it takes the following form. Subjects are repeatedly presented with the acoustic syllable [ba] as they watch the optical syllables [bɛ], [vɛ], [ðɛ], and [dɛ] being silently articulated by a mouth shown on a video screen. (The acoustic and optical syllables are approximately coincident.) The compelling percepts that result are of the syllables [ba], [va], [ða], and

[da]. Thus the percepts combine acoustic information about the vowels with optical information about the consonants, yet subjects are not aware—indeed, they cannot become aware—of the bimodal nature of the percept.

This phenomenon is heteromorphy of the most profound kind, for if optical and acoustic contributions to the percept cannot be distinguished, then surely the percept belongs to neither of the modalities, visual or auditory, with which these classes of stimuli are normally associated. Recalling our claim that phonetic perception is not auditory, we add now that it is not visual, either. The phonetic mode accepts all information, acoustic or optical, that pertains in a natural way to the phonetic events it is specialized to perceive. Its processes are not bound to the modalities associated with the stimuli presented to the sense organs; rather, they are organized around the specific behavior they serve and thus to their own phonetic "modality."

An analogue to the convergence of acoustic and optical stimuli in phonetic perception is suggested by the finding of neural elements in the optic tectum of the barn owl that respond selectively, not only to sounds in different locations, but also to lights in those same locations (Knudsen 1984). Do we dare assume that the owl can't really tell whether it heard the mouse or saw it? Perhaps not, but in any case, we might suppose that, as in phonetic perception, the processes are specific to the biologically important behavior. If so, then perhaps we should speak of a mouse-catching "modality."

Putting our attention once more on phonetic perception, we ask: "Where does the convergence occur?" Conceivably, for the example we offered, "auditory" and "visual" processes succeed separately in extracting phonetic units. Thus the consonant might have been visual, the vowel auditory. These would then be combined at some later stage and perhaps in some more cognitive fashion. Of course, such a possibility is not wholly in keeping with our claim that speech perception is a heteromorphic specialization, nor, indeed, does it sit well with the facts now available. Evidence against a late-stage, cognitive interpretation is that the auditory and visual components cannot be distinguished phenomenally, and that convergence of the McGurk–McDonald type does not occur when printed letters, which are familiar but arbitrary indices of phonetic structure, are substituted for the naturally revealing movements of the silently articulating mouth. Additional and more direct evidence showing that the convergence occurs at an early stage, before phonetic percepts are formed, is available from a recent experiment by Green and Miller (1985; see also Summerfield 1979). The particular point of this experiment was to test whether optically presented information about rate of articulation affects placement on an acoustic continuum of a boundary known to be rate-sensitive, such as the one between [bi] and [pi]. Before the experiment proper, it was determined that viewers could estimate rate of articulation from the visual information alone, but could not tell which syllable, [bi] or [pi], had been produced; we may suppose, therefore, that there was no categorical phonetic information in the optical display. Nevertheless, in the main part of the experiment, the optical information about rate did affect the acoustic boundary for the phonetic contrast; moreover, the effect was consistent with what happens when the information about rate is entirely acoustic. We should conclude then that the visual and auditory information converged at some early stage of processing before anything like a phonetic category had been extracted. This is what we should expect of a thoroughly heteromorphic specialization to which acoustic and optical stimuli are both relevant, and it fits as well as may be with the discovery in the owl of bimodally sensitive elements in centers as low as the optic tectum.

Convergence on a Coherent Percept: Equivalence of Different Dimensions of Acoustic Stimulation Having seen that optical and acoustic information can be indistinguishable when, in the heteromorphic specialization, they specify the same distal object, we turn now to a less extreme and more common instance of convergence in speech perception: The convergence of the disparate acoustic consequences of the same phonetic gesture, measured most commonly by the extent to which these can be "traded," one for another, in evoking the phonetic percept for which they are all cues. If, as such trading relations suggest, the several cues are truly indistinguishable, and therefore perceptually equivalent, we should be hard put, given their acoustic diversity, to find an explanation in auditory perception. Rather, we should suppose that they are equivalent only because the speech perceiving system is specialized to recognize them as products of the same phonetic gesture.

A particularly thorough exploration of such equivalence was made with two cues for the stop consonant [p] in the word *split* (Fitch et al. 1980). To produce the stop and thus to distinguish *split* from *slit*, a speaker must close and then open his lips. The closure causes a period of silence between the noise of the [s] and the vocalic portion of the syllable; the opening produces particular formant transitions at the beginning of the vocalic portion. Each of these—the silence and the transition—is a sufficient cue for the perceived contrast between *split* and *slit*. Now the acid test of their equivalence would be to show that the *split-slit* contrast produced by the one cue cannot be distinguished from the contrast produced by the other. Unfortunately, to show this would be to prove the null hypothesis. So equivalence was tested, somewhat less directly, by assuming that truly equivalent cues would either cancel each other or summate, depending on how they were combined. The silence and transition cues for *split-slit* passed the test: Patterns that differed by two cues weighted in opposite phonetic directions (one biased *for* [p], the other against) were harder to discriminate than patterns that differed by the same two cues weighted in the same direction (both biased *for* [p]).

A similar experiment done subsequently on the contrast between *say* and *stay* (Best, Morrongiello, and Robson 1981) yielded similar results but with an important addition. In one part of this later experiment, the formants of the synthetic speech stimuli were replaced by sine waves made to follow the formant trajectories. As had been found previously, such sine wave analogues are perceived under some conditions as complex nonspeech sounds—chords, glissandi, and the like—but under others as speech (Remez et al. 1981). For those subjects who perceived the sine wave analogues as speech, the discrimination functions were much as they had been in both experiments with the full-formant stimuli. But for subjects who perceived the patterns as nonspeech, the results were different: Patterns that differed by two cues were about equally discriminable, regardless of the direction of a bias in the phonetic domain; these two-cue patterns were both more discriminable than those differing by only one. Thus the silence cue and the transition cue are equivalent only when they are perceived in the phonetic mode as cues for the same gesture.

If we seek parallels for such equivalences in the sound-locating faculty, we find one, perhaps, in data obtained with human beings. There, binaural differences in time and in intensity are both cues to location in azimuth, and there, also, it has been found that the two cues truly cancel each other, though not completely (Hafter 1984).

We consider equivalences among stimuli—whether between stimuli belonging to different modalities, as traditionally defined, or between stimuli that lie on different dimensions of the same modality—to be of particular interest, not only because they testify to the existence of a heteromorphic specialization, but also because they provide a way to define its boundaries.

Divergence into Two Percepts: Nonequivalence of the Same Dimension of Acoustic Stimulation in Two Modes We have remarked that a formant transition (taken as an example of a speech cue) can produce two radically different percepts: a glissando or chirp when the transition is perceived homomorphically in the auditory mode as an acoustic event, or a consonant, for example, when it is perceived heteromorphically in the phonetic mode as a gesture. But it will not have escaped notice that the acoustic context was different in the two cases—the chirp was produced by a transition in isolation, the consonant by the transition in a larger acoustic pattern—and the two percepts, of course, were not experienced at the same time. It would surely be a stronger argument for the existence of two neurobiologically distinct processes, and for the heteromorphic nature of one of them, if, with acoustic context held constant, a transition could be made to produce both percepts in the same brain and at the same time. Under normal conditions, such maladaptive "duplex" perception never occurs, presumably because the underlying phonetic and auditory processes are so connected as to prevent it. (In a later section, we will consider the form this connection might take.) By resort to a most unnatural procedure, however, experimenters have managed to undo the normal connection and so produce a truly duplex percept (Rand 1974; Liberman 1979). Into one ear—it does not matter critically which one—the experimenter puts one or another of the third-formant transitions (called the "isolated transition") that lead listeners to perceive two otherwise identical formant patterns as [da] or [ga]. By themselves, these isolated transitions sound like chirps, and listeners are at chance when required to label them as [d] or [g] (Repp, Milburn, and Ashkenas 1983). Into the other ear is put the remaining, constant portion of the pattern (called the "base"). By itself, the base sounds like a consonant–vowel syllable, ambiguous between [da] and [ga]. But if the two stimuli are presented dichotically and in approximately the proper temporal arrangement, then, in the ear stimulated by the base, listeners perceive [da] or [ga], depending on which isolated transition was presented, while in the other ear they perceive a chirp. The [da] or [ga] is not different from what is heard when the full pattern is presented binaurally, nor is the chirp different from what is heard when the transition is presented binaurally without the base.

It is, perhaps, not to be wondered at that the dichotically presented inputs fuse to form the "correct" consonant–vowel syllable, since there is a strong underlying coherence. What is remarkable is that the chirp continues to be perceived, though the ambiguous base syllable does not. This is to say that the percept is precisely duplex, not triplex. Listeners perceive in the only two modes available: the auditory mode, in which they perceive chirps, and the phonetic mode, in which they perceive consonant–vowel syllables.

The sensitivities of these two modes are very different, even when stimulus variation is the same. This was shown with a stimulus display, appropriate for a duplex percept, in which the third-formant transition was the chirp and also the cue for the perceived difference between [da] and [ga] (Mann and Liberman 1983). Putting their attention sometimes on the "speech" side and sometimes on the "chirp" side of the duplex percept, subjects discriminated various pairs of stimuli. The resulting discrimination functions were very different, though the transition cues had been presented in the same context, to the same brain, and at the same time: The function for the chirp side of the duplex percept was linear, implying a perceived continuum, while the function for the phonetic side rose to a high peak at the location of the phonetic boundary (as determined for binaurally presented syllables), implying a tendency to categorize the percepts as [da] or [ga].

These results with psychophysical measures of discriminability are of interest because they support our claim that hetoromorphic perception in the phonetic mode is not a late-occurring interpretation (or match-to-prototype) of auditory percepts that were available in a common register. Apparently, heteromorphic perception goes deep.

The facts about heteromorphy reinforce the view expressed earlier that the underlying specialization must become distinct from the specializations of the homomorphic auditory system at a relatively peripheral stage. In this respect, speech perception in the human is like echolocation in the bat. Both are relatively late developments in the evolution of human and bat, respectively, and both apparently begin their processing independently of the final output of auditory specializations that are older.

Generative Detection

Since there are many other environmental signals in the same frequency range to which the speech-perceiving system must be sensitive, we should wonder how speech signals as a class are detected, and what keeps this system from being jammed by nonspeech signals that are physically similar. One possibility is that somewhere in the human brain there is a preliminary sorting mechanism that directs speech signals to the heteromorphic speech-perceiving system and other signals to the collection of homomorphic systems that deal with environmental sounds in general. Such a sorting mechanism would necessarily rely not on the deep properties of the signal that are presumably used by the speech-perceiving system to determine phonetic structure but on superficial properties like those that man-made speech-detection devices exploit: quasi-periodicity, characteristic spectral structure, and syllabic rhythm, for example.

The idea of a sorting mechanism is appealing because it would explain not only why the speech perceiving system is not jammed but, in addition, why speech is not also perceived as nonspeech—a problem to which we have already referred and to which we will return. Unfortunately, this notion is not easy to reconcile with the fact that speech is perceived as speech even when its characteristic superficial properties are masked or destroyed. Thus speech can be high-pass filtered, low-pass filtered, infinitely clipped, spectrally inverted, or rate adjusted, and yet remain more or less intelligible. Even more remarkably, intelligible speech can be synthesized in very unnatural ways: for example, as already mentioned, with a set of frequency-modulated sinusoids whose trajectories follow those of the formants of some natural utterance. Evidently, information about all these signals reaches the speech perceiving system and is processed by it, even though they lack some or all of the characteristic superficial properties on which the sorting mechanism we have been considering would have to depend.

The only explanation consistent with these facts is that there *is* no preliminary sorting mechanism; it is, instead, the speech perceiving system itself that decides between speech and nonspeech, exploiting the phonetic properties that are intrinsic to the former and only fortuitously present in the latter. Presumably, distorted and unnatural signals like those we have referred to can be classified as speech because information about phonetic structure is spread redundantly across the speech spectrum and over time; thus much of it is present in these signals even though the superficial acoustic marks of speech may be absent. On the other hand, isolated formant transitions, which have the appropriate acoustic marks but, out of context, no definite phonetic structure, are, as we have said, classified as nonspeech. In short, the signal is speech if and only if the pattern of articulatory gestures that must have produced it can be reconstructed. We call this property "generative detection," having in mind the analogous situation in the domain of sentence processing. There superficial features cannot distinguish grammatical sentences from ungrammatical ones. The only way to determine the grammaticality of a sentence is to parse it—that is, to try to regenerate the syntactic structure intended by the speaker.

Is generative detection found in the specialized systems of other species? Consider first the mustached bat, whose echolocation system relies on biosonar signals (Suga 1984). The bat has to be able to distinguish its own echolocation signals from the similar signals of conspecifics. Otherwise, not only would the processing of its own signals be jammed, but many of the objects it located would be illusory, because it would have subjected the conspecific signals to the same heteromorphic treatment it gives its own. According to Suga, the bat probably solves the problem in the following way. The harmonics of all the biosonar signals reach the CF-CF and FM-FM neurons that determine the delay between harmonics F_2 and F_3 of the emitted signals and their respective echoes. But these neurons operate only if F_1 is also present. This harmonic is available to the cochlea of the emitting bat by bone conduction but is weak or absent in the radiated signal. Thus the output of the CF-CF and FM-FM neurons reflects only the individual's own signals and not those of conspecifics. The point is that, as in the case of human speech detection, there is no preliminary sorting of the two classes of signals. Detection of the required signal is not a separate stage but inherent in the signal analysis. However, the bat's method of signal detection cannot properly be called generative, because, unlike speech detection, it relies on a surface property of the input signal.

Generative detection is, perhaps, more likely to be found in the perception of song by birds. While, so far as we are aware, no one has suggested how song detection might work, it is known about the zebra finch that pure tones as well as actual song produce activity in the neurons of the song motor nucleus HVc (Williams 1984; Williams and Nottebohm 1985), a finding that argues against preliminary sorting and for detection in the course of signal analysis. Moreover, since the research just cited also provides evidence that the perception of song by the zebra finch is motoric, generative detection must be considered a possibility until and unless some superficial acoustic characteristic of a particular song is identified that would suffice to distinguish it from the songs of other avian species. Generative detection in birds seems the more likely, given that some species—the winter wren, for example—have hundreds of songs that a conspecific can apparently recognize correctly even if it has never heard them before (Konishi 1985). It is therefore tempting to speculate that the wren has a grammar that generates possible song patterns, and that the detection and parsing of conspecific songs are parts of the same perceptual process.

While generative detection may not be a very widespread property of specialized perceiving systems, what does seem to be generally true is that these systems do their own signal detection. Moreover, they do it by virtue of features that are also exploited in signal analysis, whether these features are simple superficial characteristics of the signal, as in the case of echolocation in the bat, or complex reflections of distal events, as in the case of speech perception. This more general property might be added to those that Fodor (1983) has identified as common to all perceptual modules.

Preemptiveness
As we have already hinted, our proposal that there are no preliminary sorting mechanisms leads to a difficulty, for without such a mechanism, we might expect that the general-purpose, homomorphic auditory systems, being sensitive to the same dimensions of an acoustic signal as a specialized system, would also process special signals. This would mean that the bat would not only use its own biosonar signals for echolocation, but would also hear them as it presumably must hear the similar biosonar signals of other bats; the zebra finch would perceive conspecific song not only as song but also as an ordinary environmental sound; and human beings would hear chirps and glissandi as well as speech. We cannot be sure with nonhuman animals that such double processing of special-purpose signals does not in fact occur, but certainly it does not for speech, except under the extraordinary and thoroughly unecological conditions, described earlier, that induce "duplex" perception. We should suppose, however, that except where complementary aspects of the same distal object or event are involved, as in the perception of color and shape, double processing would be maladaptive, for it would result in the perception of two distal events, one of which would be irrelevant or spurious. For example, almost any environmental sound may startle a bird, so if a conspecific song were perceived as if it were also something else, the listening bird might well be startled by it.

The general-purpose homomorphic systems themselves can have no way of defining the signals they should process in a way that excludes special signals, since the resulting set of signals would obviously not be a natural class. But suppose that the specialized systems are somehow able to preempt signal information relevant to the events that concern them, preventing it from reaching the general-purpose systems at all. The bat would then use its own biosonar signals to perceive the distal objects of its environment but would not also hear them as it does the signals of other bats; the zebra finch would hear song only as song; and human beings would hear speech as speech but not also as nonspeech.

An arrangement that would enable the preemptiveness of special-purpose systems is serial processing, with the specialized system preceding the general-purpose systems (Mattingly and Liberman 1985). The specialized system would not only detect and process the signal information it requires but would also provide an input to the general-purpose systems from which this information had been removed. In the case of the mustached bat, the mechanism proposed by Suga (1984) for the detection of the bat's own biosonar signals would also be sufficient to explain how the information in these signals, but not the similar information in the conspecific signals, could be kept from the general-purpose system. Though doubtless more complicated, the arrangements in humans for isolating phonetic information and passing on nonphonetic information would have the same basic organization. We suggest that the speech perceiving system not only recovers whatever phonetic structure it can but also filters out those features of the signal that result from phonetic structure, passing on to the general-purpose systems all of the phonetically irrelevant residue. If the input signal includes no speech, the residue will represent all of the input. If the input signal includes speech as well as nonspeech, the residue will represent all of the input that was not speech plus the laryngeal source signal (as modified by the effects of radiation from the head), the pattern of formant trajectories that results from the changing configuration of the vocal tract having been removed. Thus the perception not only of nonspeech environmental sounds but also of nonphonetic aspects of the speech signal, such as voice quality, is left to the general-purpose systems.

Serial processing appeals to us for three reasons. First, it is parsimonious. It accounts for the fact that speech is not also perceived as nonspeech, without assuming an additional mechanism and without complicating whatever account we may eventually be able to offer of speech perception itself. The same computations that are required to recover phonetic structure from the signal also suffice to remove all evidence of it from the signal information received by the general-purpose system.

Second, by placing the speech processing system ahead of the general-purpose systems, the hypothesis exploits the fact that while nonspeech signals have no specific defining properties at all, speech signals form a natural class, with specific, though deep, properties by virtue of which they can be reliably assigned to the class.

Third, serial processing permits us to understand how precedence can be guaranteed for a class of signals that has special biological significance. It is a matter of common experience that the sounds of bells, radiators, household appliances, and railroad trains can be mistaken for speech by the casual listener. On the other hand, mistaking a speech sound for speech sound for an ordinary environmental sound is comparatively rare. This is just what we should expect on ethological grounds, for, as with other biologically significant signals, it is adaptive that the organism should put up with occasional false alarms rather than risk missing a genuine message. Now if speech perception were simply one more cognitive operation on auditory primitives, or if perception of nonspeech preceded it, the organism would have to learn to favor speech, and the degree of precedence would depend very much on its experience with acoustic signals generally. But if, as we suggest, speech precedes the general-purpose system, the system for perceiving speech need only be reasonably permissive as to which signals it processes completely for the precedence of speech to be insured.

Commonality between the Specializations for Perception and Production
So far we have been concerned primarily with speech perception, and we have argued that it is controlled by a system specialized to perceive phonetic gestures. But what of the system that controls the gestures? Is it specialized, too, and how does the answer to that question bear on the relation between perception and production?

A preliminary observation is that there is no logical necessity for speech production to be specialized merely because speech perception appears to be. Indeed, our commitment to an account of speech perception in which the invariants are motoric deprives us of an obvious argument for the specialness of production. For if the perceptual invariants were taken to be generally auditory, it would be easy maintain that only a specialized motoric system could account for the ability of every normal human being to speak rapidly and yet to manipulate the articulators so as to produce just those acoustically invariant signals that the invariant auditory percepts would require. But if the invariants are motoric, as we claim, it could be that the articulators do not behave in speech production very differently from the way they do in their other functions. In that case, there would be nothing special about speech production, though a perceptual specialization might nevertheless have been necessary to deal with the complexity of the relation between articulatory configuration and acoustic signal. However, the perceptual system would then have been adapted very broadly to the acoustic consequences of the great variety of movements that are made in chewing, swallowing, moving food around in the mouth, whistling, licking the lips, and so on. There would have been few constraints to aid the perceptual system in recovering the gestures, and nothing to mark the result of its processing as belonging to an easily specifiable class of uniquely phonetic events. However, several facts about speech production strongly suggest that it is, instead, a specialized and highly constrained process.

It is relevant, first, that the inventory of gestures executed by a particular articulator in speech production is severely limited, both with respect to manner of articulation (i.e., the style of movement of the gesture) and place of articulation (i.e., the particular fixed surface of the vocal tract that is the apparent target of the gesture). Consider, for example, the tip of the tongue, which moves more or less independently of, but relative to, the tongue body. In nonphonetic movements of this articulator, there are wide variations in speed, style, and direction, variations that musicians, for example, learn to exploit. In speech, however, the gestures of the tongue tip, though it is perhaps the most phonetically versatile of the articulators, are restricted to a small number of manner categories: stops (e.g. [t] in *too*), flaps ([D] in *butter*), trills ([r] in Spanish *perro*), taps ([ɾ] in Spanish *pero*), fricatives ([θ] in *thigh*), median approximants ([ɹ] in *red*) and lateral approximants ([l] in *law*). Place of articulation for these gestures is also highly constrained, being limited to dental, alveolar, and immediately postalveolar surfaces (Ladefoged 1971; Catford 1977). These restricted movements of the tongue tip in speech are not, in general, similar to those it executes in nonphonetic functions (though perhaps one could argue for a similarity between the articulation of the interdental fricative and the tongue-tip movement required to expel a grape seed from the mouth. But, as Sapir (1925) observed about the similarity between an aspirated [w] and the blowing out of a candle, these are "norms or types of entirely distinct series of variants"). Speech movements are, for the most part, peculiar to speech; they have no obvious nonspeech functions.

The peculiarity of phonetic gestures is further demonstrated in consequence of the fact that, in most cases, a gesture involves more than one articulator. Thus the gestures we have just described, though nominally attributed to the tongue tip, actually require also the cooperation of the tongue body and the jaw to ensure that the tip will be within easy striking distance of its target surface (Lindblom 1983). The requirement arises because, owing to other demands on the tongue body and jaw, the tongue tip cannot be assumed to occupy a particular absolute rest position at the time a gesture is initiated. Cooperation between the articulators is also required in such nonphonetic gestures as swallowing, but the particular cooperative patterns of movement observed in speech are apparently unique, even though there may be nonspeech analogues for one or another of the components of such a pattern.

Observations analogous to those just made about the tongue tip could be made with respect to each of the other major articulators: the tongue body, the lips, the velum, and the larynx. That the phonetic gestures possible for each of these articulators form a very limited set that is drawn upon by all languages in the world has often been taken as evidence for a universal phonetics (e.g., Chomsky and Halle 1968). (Indeed, if the gestures were not thus limited, a general notation for phonetic transcription would hardly be possible.) That the gestures are eccentric when considered in comparison with what the articulators are generally capable of is evidence that speech production does not merely exploit general tendencies for articulator movement but depends, rather, on a system of controls specialized for language.

A further indication of the specialness of speech production is that certain of the limited and eccentric set of gestures executed by the tongue tip are paralleled by gestures executed by other major articulators. Thus stops and fricatives can be produced not only by the tongue tip but also by the tongue blade, the tongue body, the lips, and the larynx, even though these various articulators are anatomically and physiologically very different from one another. Nor, to forestall an obvious objection, are these manner categories mere artifacts of the phonetician's taxonomy. They are truly natural classes that play a central role in the phonologies of the world's languages. If these categories were unreal, we should not find that in language x vowels always lengthen before all fricatives, that in language y all stops are regularly deleted after fricatives, or that in all languages the constraints on the sequences of sounds in a syllable are most readily described according to manner of articulation (Jespersen 1920). And when the sound system of a language changes, the change is frequently a matter of systematically replacing sounds of one manner class by sounds of another manner class produced by the same articulators. Thus the Indo-European stops [p], [t], [k], [q] were replaced in Primitive Germanic by the corresponding fricatives [f], [θ], [x], [X] ("Grimm's law").

Our final argument for the specialness of speech production depends on the fact of gestural overlap. Thus in the syllable [du], the tongue-tip closure gesture for [d] overlaps the lip-rounding and tongue-body-backing gestures for [u]. Even more remarkably, two gestures made by the same articulator may overlap. Thus in the syllable [gi], the tongue-body-closure gesture for [g] overlaps the tongue-body-fronting gesture for [i], so that the [g] closure occurs at a more forward point on the palate than would be the case for [g] in [gu]. As we have already suggested, it is gestural overlap, making possible relatively high rates of information transmission, that gives speech its adaptive value as a communication system. But if the strategy of overlapping gestures to gain speed is not to defeat itself, the gestures can hardly be allowed to overlap haphazardly. If there were no constraints on how the overlap could occur, the acoustic consequences of one gesture could mask the consequences of another. In a word such as *twin*, for instance, the silence resulting from the closure for the stop [t] could obscure the sound of the approximant [w]. Such accidents do not ordinarily occur in speech, because the gestures are apparently phased so to provide the maximum amount of overlap consistent with preservation of the acoustic information that specifies either of the gestures (Mattingly 1981). This phasing is most strictly controlled at the beginnings and ends of syllables, where gestural overlap is greatest, and most variable in the center of the syllable, where less is going on (Tuller and Kelso 1984). Thus, to borrow Fujimura's (1981) metaphor, the gestural timing patterns of consonants and consonant clusters are icebergs floating on a vocalic sea. Like the individual gestures themselves, these complex temporal patterns are peculiar to speech and could serve no other ecological purpose.

We would conclude, then, that speech production is specialized, just as speech perception is. But if this is so, we would argue further that these two processes are not two systems, but, rather, modes of one and the same system. The premise of our argument is that because speech has a communicative function, what counts as phonetic structure for production must be the same as what counts as phonetic structure for perception. This truism holds regardless of what one takes phonetic structure to be, and any account of phonetic process has to be consistent with it. Thus, on the conventional account, it must be assumed that perception and production, being taken as distinct processes, are both guided by some cognitive representation of the structures that they deal with in common. On our account, however, no such cognitive representation can be assumed if the notion of a specialized system is not to be utterly trivialized. But if we are to do without cognitive mediation, what is to guarantee that at every stage of ontogenetic (and for that matter phylogenetic) development, the two systems will have identical definitions of phonetic structure? The only possibility is that they are directly linked. This, however, is tantamount to saying that they constitute a single system, in which we would expect representations and computational machinery not to be duplicated, but to coincide insofar as the asymmetry of the two modes permits.

To make this view more concrete, suppose, as we have elsewhere suggested (Mattingly and Liberman 1969; Liberman, Mattingly, and Turvey 1972; Liberman and Mattingly 1986), that the speech production–perception system is, in effect, an articulatory synthesizer. In the production mode, the input to the synthesizer is some particular, abstractly specified gestural pattern from which the synthesizer computes a representation of the contextually varying articulatory movements that will be required to realize the gestures, and from this articulatory representation, the muscle commands that will execute the actual movements, some form of "analysis by synthesis" being obviously required. In the perceptual mode, the input is the acoustic signal from which the synthesizer computes—again by analysis by synthesis—the articulatory movements that could have produced the signal, and from this articulatory representation, the intended gestural pattern. The computation of the muscle commands from articulatory movement is peculiar to production, and the computation of articulatory movement from the signal is peculiar to perception. What is common to the two modes, and carried out by the same computations, is the working out of the relation between abstract gestural pattern and the corresponding articulatory movements.

We earlier alluded to a commonality between modes of another sort when we referred to the finding that the barn owl's auditory orientation processes use the same neural map as its visual orientation processes do. Now we would remark the further finding that this arrangement is quite one-sided: The neural map is laid out optically, so that sounds from sources in the center of the owl's visual field are more precisely located and more extensively represented on the map than are sounds from sources at the edges (Knudsen 1984). This is of special relevance to our concerns, because, as we have several times implied, a similar one-sidedness seems to characterize the speech specialization: Its communal arrangements are organized primarily with reference to the processes of production. We assume the dominance of production over perception because it was the ability of appropriately coordinated gestures to convey phonetic structures efficiently that determined their use as the invariant elements of speech. Thus it must have been the gestures, and especially the processes associated with their expression, that shaped the development of a system specialized to perceive them.

More comparable, perhaps, to the commonality we see in the speech specialization are examples of commonality between perception and production in animal communication systems. Evidence for such commonality has been found for the tree frog (Gerhardt 1978); the cricket (Hoy and Paul 1973; Hoy, Hahn, and Paul 1977); the zebra finch (Williams 1984; Williams and Nottebohm 1985); the white-crowned sparrow (Margoliash 1983); and the canary (McCasland and Konish 1983). Even if there were no such evidence, however, few students of animal communication would regard as sufficiently parsimonious the only alternative to commonality: that perception and production are mediated by cognitive representations. But if we reject this alternative in explaining the natural modes of nonhuman communication, it behooves us to be equally conservative in our attempt to explain language, the natural mode of communication in human beings. Just because language is central to so much that is uniquely human, we should not therefore assume that its underlying processes are necessarily cognitive.

The Speech Specialization and the Sentence

As a coda, we here consider, though only briefly, how our observations about perception of phonetic structure might bear more broadly on perception of sentences. Recalling first the conventional view of speech perception—that it is accomplished by processes of a generally auditory sort—we find its extension to sentence perception in the assumption that coping with syntax depends on a general faculty too. Of course, this faculty is taken to be cognitive, not auditory, but like the auditory faculty, it is supposed to be broader than the behavior it serves. Thus it presumably underlies not just syntax but all the apparently smart things people do. For an empiricist, this general faculty is a powerful ability to learn, and so to discover the syntax by induction. For a nativist, it is an intelligence that knows what to look for because syntax is a reflection of how the mind works. For both, perceiving syntax has nothing in common with perception of speech, or, a fortiori, with perception of other sounds, whether biologically significant or not. It is as if language, in its development, had simply appropriated auditory and cognitive processes that are themselves quite independent of language and, indeed, of each other.

The parallel in syntax to our view of speech is the assumption that sentence structures, no less than speech, are dealt with by processes narrowly specialized for the purpose. On this assumption, syntactic and phonetic specializations are related to each other as two components of the larger specialization for language. We should suppose then that the syntactic specialization might have important properties in common, not only with the phonetic specialization but also with the specializations for biologically significant sounds.

Notes

The writing of this chapter was supported by a grant to Haskins Laboratories (NIH-NICHD-HD-01994). We are grateful to Harriet Magen and Nancy O'Brien for their help with references and to Alice Dadourian for invaluable editorial assistance and advice. We received shrewd comments and suggestions from Carol Fowler, Masakazu Konishi, Eric Knudsen, Daniel Margoliash, Bruno Repp, Michael Studdert-Kennedy,

Nobuo Suga, and Douglas Whalen. Some of these people have views very different from those expressed here, but we value their criticisms all the more for that.

1. Our notion of heteromorphy as a property of one kind of perceiving specialization seems consistent with comments about sound localization by Knudsen and Konishi (1978), who have observed that "[the barn owl's] map of auditory space is an emergent property of higher-order neurons, distinguishing it from all other sensory maps that are direct projections of the sensory surface ... these space-related response properties and functional organization must be specifically generated through neuronal integration in the central nervous system...." Much the same point has been made by Yin and Kuwada (1984), who say that "the cochlea is designed for frequency analysis and cannot encode the location of sound sources. Thus, the code for location of an auditory stimulus is not given by a 'labeled line' from the receptors, but must be the result of neural interactions within the central auditory system."

References

Best, C. T., B. Morrongiello, and R. Robson (1981) Perceptual equivalence of acoustic cues in speech and nonspeech perception. *Percept. Psychophys.* 29:191–211.

Catford, J. C. (1977) *Fundamental Problems in Phonetics,* Indiana Univ. Press, Bloomington.

Chomsky, N., and M. Halle (1968) *The Sound Pattern of English,* Harper and Row, New York.

Fitch, H. L., T. Halwes, D. M. Erickson, and A. M. Liberman (1980) Perceptual equivalence of two acoustic cues for stop consonant manner. *Percept. Psychophys.* 27:343–350.

Fodor, J. (1983) *The Modularity of Mind,* MIT Press, Cambridge, Massachusetts.

Fujimura, O. (1981) Temporal organization of speech as a multi-dimensional structure. *Phonetica* 38:66–83.

Gerhardt, H. C. (1978) Temperature coupling in the vocal communication system of the gray tree frog *Hyla versicolor. Science* 199:992–994.

Green, K. P., and J. L. Miller (1985) On the role of visual rate information in phonetic perception. *Percept. Psychophys.* 38:269–276.

Hafter, E. R. (1984) Spatial hearing and the duplex theory: How viable is the model? In *Dynamic Aspects of Necortical Function,* G. M. Edelman, W. E. Gall, and W. M. Cowan, eds., pp. 425–448, Wiley, New York.

Hoy, R., and R. C. Paul (1973) Genetic control of song specificity in crickets. *Science* 180:82–83.

Hoy, R., J. Hahn, and R. C. Paul (1977) Hybrid cricket auditory behavior: Evidence for genetic coupling in animal communication. *Science* 195:82–83.

Jespersen, O. (1920) *Lehrbuch der Phonetik,* Teubner, Leipzig.

Knudsen, E. I. (1984) Synthesis of a neural map of auditory space in the owl. In *Dynamic Aspects of Neocortical Function,* G. M. Edelman, W. E. Gall, and W. M. Cowan, eds., pp. 375–396, Wiley, New York.

Knudsen, E. I., and M. Konishi (1978) A neural map of auditory space in the owl. *Science* 200:795–797.

Konishi, M. (1985) Birdsong: From behavior to neuron. *Annu. Rev. Neurosci.* 8:125–170.

Ladefoged, P. (1971) *Preliminaries to Linguistic Phonetics,* Univ. Chicago Press, Chicago.

Liberman, A. M. (1979) Duplex perception and integration of cues: Evidence that speech is different from nonspeech and similar to language. In *Proceedings of the IXth International Congress of Phonetic Sciences,* Vol. 2, E. Fischer-Jorgensen, J. Rischel, and N. Thorsen, eds., pp. 468–473, Univ. Copenhagen, Copenhagen.

Liberman, A. M., and I. G. Mattingly (1986) The motor theory of speech perception revised. *Cognition* 21:1–36.

Liberman, A. M., and F. S. Cooper, D. P. Shankweiler, and M. Studdert-Kennedy (1967) Perception of the speech code. *Psychol. Rev.* 74:431–461.

Liberman, A. M., I. G. Mattingly, and M. Turvey (1972) Language codes and memory codes. In *Coding processes in Human Memory,* A. W. Melton and E. Martin, eds., pp. 307–334, Winston, Washington, D. C.

Lindblom, B. (1983) Economy of speech gestures. In *The Production of Speech,* P. MacNeilage, ed., pp. 217–245, Springer, New York.

Mann, V. A., and A. M. Liberman (1983) Some differences between phonetic and auditory modes of perception. *Cognition* 14:211–235.

Margoliash, D. (1983) Acoustic parameters underlying the responses of song-specific neurons in the white-crowned sparrow. *J. Neurosci.* 3:1039–1057.

Mattingly, I. G. (1981) Phonetic representation and speech synthesis by rule. In *The Cognitive Representation of Speech,* T. Myers, J. Laver, and J. Anderson, eds., pp. 415–420, North-Holland, Amsterdam.

Mattingly, I. G., and A. M. Liberman (1969) The speech code and the physiology of language. In *Information Processing in the Nervous System*, K. N. Leibovic, ed., pp. 97–117, Springer, New York.

Mattingly, I. G., and A. M. Liberman (1985) Verticality unparalleled. *Behav. Brain Sci.* 8:24–26.

McCasland, J. S., and M. Konishi (1983) Interaction between auditory and motor activities in an avian song control nucleus. *Proc. Natl. Acad. Sci. USA* 78:7815–7819.

McGurk, H., and J. MacDonald (1976) Hearing lips and seeing voices. *Nature* 264:746–748.

Rand, T. C. (1974) Dichotic release from masking for speech. *J. Acoust. Soc. Am.* 55:678–680.

Remez, R. E., P. E. Rubin, D. B. Pisoni, and T. D. Carrell (1981) Speech perception without traditional speech cues. *Science* 212:947–950.

Repp, B. H., C. Mulburn, and J. Ashkenas (1983) Duplex perception: Confirmation of fusion. *Percept. Psychophys.* 33:333–337.

Sapir, E. (1925) Sound patterns in language. *Language* 1:37–51. Reprinted in *Language, Culture and Personality: Selected Writings of Edward Sapir*, D. G. Mandelbaum, ed., pp. 33–45, Univ. California Press, Berkeley, 1963.

Suga, N. (1984) The extent to which bisonar information is represented in the bat auditory cortex. In *Dynamic Aspects of Neocortical Function*, G. M. Edelman, W. E. Gall, and W. M. Cowan, eds., pp. 315–373, Wiley, New York.

Summerfield, Q. (1979) Use of visual information for phonetic perception. *Phonetica* 36:314–331.

Tuller, B., and J. A. S. Kelso (1984) The relative timing of articulatory gestures: Evidence for relational invariants. *J. Acoust. Soc. Am.* 76:1030–1036.

Williams, H. (1984) *A Motor Theory of Bird Song Perception*, unpublished doctoral dissertation, Rockefeller University, New York.

Williams, H., and F. N. Nottebohm (1985) Auditory responses in avian vocal motor neurons: A motor theory for song perception in birds. *Science* 229:279–282.

Yin, T. C. T., and S. Kuwada (1984) Neuronal mechanisms and binaural interaction. In *Dynamic Aspects of Neocortical Function*, G. M. Edelman, W. E. Gall, and W. M. Cowan, eds., pp. 263–313, Wiley, New York.

PART VIII

More about the Function and Properties of the Phonetic Module

Introduction to Part VIII

Here we make more explicit the critical function of the phonetic module in phonological communication. We also develop the notion that the phonetic module belongs to one of two classes that can be defined by their common characteristics, and we consider the architectural arrangement of those modules that would permit them to represent a coherent percept.

Chapter 16
A Specialization for Speech Perception

Perceiving speech is generally assumed to be no different from perceiving sounds of other kinds.[1] All of auditory perception is supposed to depend on various specializations, each one adapted to analyze the acoustic signal in a distinct way and to produce for cognition a correspondingly distinct representation. One of these specializations, "auditory scene analysis,"[2] parses the signal, representing to cognition an array of localized sound sources; other specializations assign to each source appropriate values for such primitive auditory qualities as pitch, loudness, and timbre. The representations of, say, a squeaking door and a stop consonant differ only in the particular mix of values for these primitives. It is a later, cognitive stage that identifies the one mix as a squeaking door, the other as a stop consonant.

In the less conventional view that we mean to promote,[3] the specifically phonetic aspects of speech perception are the articulatory gestures of which all linguistic utterances are ultimately composed.[4,5] Recurrent and phonologically significant patterns of these gestures, misleadingly called "speech sounds" or "phonetic segments," are the basis for the consonant and vowel symbols of phonetic transcriptions. Accordingly, the gestures stand apart from the paraphonetic aspects of speech—for example, voice quality and affective tone—which are presumably like nonspeech sounds in the nature of their perceptual primitives and in the specialized processes that evoke them. Perception of the gestures is different, for it is controlled by a "phonetic module,"[6] a specialization for speech that has its own modes of signal analysis and its own primitives.[7] Thus, phonetic perception is immediate; no cognitive translation from patterns of pitch, loudness, and timbre is required.

Several kinds of evidence have been offered in support of the claim that such a phonetic module does exist.[4,5] Here, we will be concerned only with a kind that seems especially telling and exemplary. Then, taking a broader view of the claim, we will describe the function that the phonetic module serves, say how it compares to other modules of the auditory system, and speculate about where it fits in the architecture they form.

Evidence for a Phonetic Module: Duplex Perception

There is a species of psychoacoustic experiment that, in effect, dissects audition into its component processes, thus testing the hypothesis that the phonetic processes are distinct from the others. In this kind of experiment, two simultaneously presented

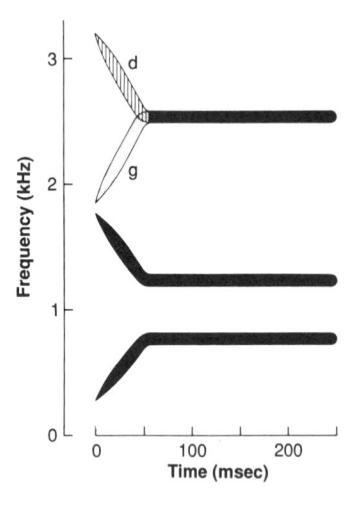

Figure 16.1
Patterns that show how the perceived difference between [da] and [ga] can be made to depend on the slope of the initial third-formant transition.

parts of a stimulus are made discordant, or in some other way acoustically inconsistent with one another, with the result that they are heard as separate sound sources; but the information required for the perception of a particular speech sound is divided between the parts. The consequence is that one source is perceived as a nonspeech sound that, not surprisingly, depends on information in one of the two parts, but the other is perceived as the particular speech sound that depends on information in both. Thus, one of the two parts contributes to both the speech and nonspeech percepts at the same time. This phenomenon is called "duplex perception."[8-14]

Appropriate raw materials for an experiment on duplex perception are the control patterns, shown in figure 16.1, for two synthetic consonant-vowel syllables. Acoustic waveforms computed from these patterns consistently yield percepts that may be phonetically transcribed as [da] and [ga]. The bars in the figure represent vocal-tract resonances, called "formants," which vary in center frequency as the articulators assume particular configurations. The sloping resonances at the beginning of the pattern ("transitions") reflect the movements of the articulators as consonant and vowel gestures combine to form syllables.

In natural speech, the acoustic information that cues a phonetic gesture is dispersed, both in time and frequency, and there are many perceptually significant differences between the patterns for [da] and [ga]. For our experimental purposes, however, we have omitted or neutralized all but the difference in the transitions of the third (highest) formant. Fixed parts of the pattern, including, in particular, the first- and second-formant transitions, indicate that a stop consonant is being produced, and exclude stops other than [d] or [g]. Thus, given the full syllabic pattern, the perceived difference between [d] and [g] depends entirely on the differing transitions of the third formant.[15] When presented in isolation, however, these transitions do not evoke speech percepts at all but, rather, nonspeech chirps of differing quality.[16] The point of the experiment is to test whether these two ways of perceiving

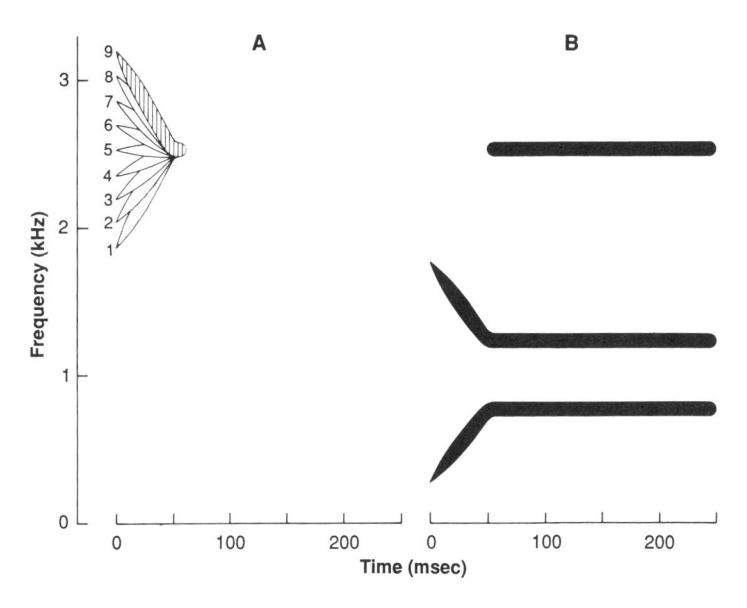

Figure 16.2
Dichotic stimuli yielding duplex perception, derived from the patterns of figure 16.1. (A) A series of third-formant transitions covering the range from [ga] to [da]. (B) The constant remainder of the syllable.

the same transition—as speech and as nonspeech—do, indeed, depend on different modules.

For the purposes of the experiment, each stimulus consists of two parts, as shown schematically in figure 16.2. One part, which is variable from presentation to presentation, is chosen from the series of third-formant transitions seen in figure 16.2A. These differ by equal steps in the frequencies at which they begin, covering a range that would, in full syllabic context, produce [ga] at the lower end of the scale and [da] at the higher, with a sharp break between the two at a point near the middle.[10,11] In isolation, each transition sounds, as we have said, like a nonspeech chirp, distinguishable from the others by its characteristic timbre. The other part of the stimulus, which is constant, is the remainder of the syllable, as shown in figure 16.2B. In isolation, this remainder sounds like a consonant-vowel syllable, but, lacking, the critical third-formant transition, it is ambiguous, being judged sometimes as [da], sometimes as [ga]. These two parts are presented dichotically, the transition at one ear, the remainder at the other. As a consequence, the third formant moves from one ear to the other at 50 milliseconds, producing a sharp discontinuity in interaural intensity.

The perceptual result accords with the general account of this kind of experiment that we have already offered. Listeners hear two sounds, one at each ear. At the ear receiving the transition, they hear a nonspeech chirp, just as they do when the transition is presented in isolation. At the ear receiving the remainder of the syllable, they hear [da] or [ga]. But, surprisingly, these latter percepts are not ambiguous, as they are when the remainder is presented in isolation; rather, they are unambiguously determined to be [da] or [ga] by the slope of the transition at the other ear, just as they are when an undivided syllable is presented in the normal way. Yet this percept required that information be combined across two parts of the stimulus that are heard as different sound sources, and one of these parts (the third-formant transition) evoked, simultaneously, the nonspeech chirp and the perceived difference between [da] and [ga].

But such duplex perception speaks to our claim about an independent phonetic module only if the two percepts—chirp and consonant—are wholly distinct representations. We must, therefore, eliminate the possibility that the timbre of the transition, though represented only once, is being cognitively interpreted in two different ways, as if listeners were simply following a rule that this representation is to be called a chirp when presented in isolation, but a stop consonant when in combination with the remainder of the acoustic pattern. Two facts satisfy any concern we might have on this score. One is that, in duplex perception, listeners do not hear the ambiguous syllable that is evoked when the remainder of the pattern is presented in isolation.[9-11] Thus, it cannot be that they are cognitively combining this percept with the chirp to get the unambiguous [da] or [ga]. The other relevant fact is that listeners are at chance when they try to match the isolated transitions to undivided [da]'s and [ga]'s; apparently they can neither hear [da] or [ga] in the chirps, nor chirps in the [da]'s and [ga]'s.[11,14]

We must, of course, also be sure that the two sides of the duplex percept are not merely two representations of the same kind, being composed of different combinations of the same primitives. They could be so interpreted if, as with the familiar visual examples, duplexity were the result of a shifting of attention between two representations of an ambiguous stimulus. But this interpretation is ruled out by the fact that the speech and nonspeech percepts are simultaneous and mandatory.

Additional evidence that the speech and nonspeech percepts are different kinds of representations comes from a further experiment on duplex perception, in which listeners were required to discriminate, on any basis, between two successive chirps heard at one ear, and, separately, between two successive speech sounds heard at the other, the two third-formant transitions in both cases being three steps apart on the series in figure 16.2A.[10] As shown in figure 16.3, the discrimination functions for

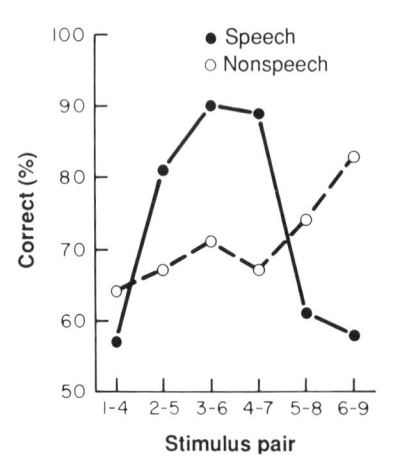

Figure 16.3
Discrimination functions for the speech and nonspeech sides of the duplex percept. The stimulus pairs are numbered to correspond to the formant transitions in figure 16.2. Chance performance is 50 percent correct.[10]

the nonspeech chirps and the speech are grossly different, though the stimuli that provided the only basis for the discrimination were identical. The function for the chirps is approximately linear, and conforms reasonably well to what is expected, given the results of psychoacoustic research on sloping resonances.[17] On the speech side, however, the function is sharply peaked, reflecting a strong tendency to hear the stimuli in the nearly categorical manner that has been found to characterize the perception of phonetic structures.[18]

Like the fact that transitions could not be matched to full syllables, this result of the discrimination test shows that listeners do not have access to any representation common to the speech and nonspeech aspects of the duplex percept. But it also strongly implies that the two representations they do have access to are of different kinds, being formed of different primitives—pitch and timbre in the one case, phonetic categories in other. For the stimuli that evoked the two percepts were identical pairs of transitions, they were presented in a perfectly constant context, and they were discriminated according to the same psychophysical procedure. Yet the resulting functions had markedly different shapes, each one appropriate, it would seem, to the kind of representation on which it was based.

Thus, duplex perception supports the claim that phonetic representations are formed by a distinct module, independently of the modules for pitch, loudness, and timbre. But it also shows that this phonetic module is independent of the module for scene analysis. For the [da] and [ga] percepts can only have been formed by combining information across two parts of a stimulus that are treated by scene analysis as separate sources at separate locations. This contrasts with the behavior of the modules for pitch, loudness, and timbre, since they did not combine information in this way, but rather attributed their auditory properties separately to each of the sources that scene analysis defined; hence the chirp-like character of one source and the voice-like character of the other. Thus, the phonetic module, but not the others, ignored what scene analysis had done, responding instead to a coherence that existed across both parts of the stimulus, though only in the phonetic domain, and that provided the only basis for assigning "da-ness" and "ga-ness" appropriately to the voice-like sources. The implication is that this module has its own, specifically phonetic criteria, different from those used by scene analysis, for determining what counts as one event and what counts as more than one. This seems the more remarkable when one takes into account how fundamental to auditory perception are the processes that assign sounds to localized sources. Apparently, the phonetic module is so independent that it somehow avoids those processes.

The Function of a Phonetic Module

Why should phonetic gestures be treated in a special way? Why should language, so often regarded as a cognitive capacity of the highest order, turn out to operate, like scene analysis or pitch perception, at a level that is clearly precognitive? The answer lies in the special means by which the phonetic gestures manage their communicative function. Although they are, to be sure, appropriate for producing audible sounds, they are also more specifically adapted to serve as the structural elements of phonology,[4,19] a part of natural human grammatical capacity that, together with syntax, distinguishes language from all other forms of communication. The specific function of phonology is to make possible a vocabulary comprising vastly more than the number of holistically different sounds that humans can efficiently produce and perceive. This it does by providing a system for combining and permuting a few dozen gestures, specifically phonetic objects that belong, thus, to a natural class. But the system works in practice only because there is a specialization for producing these phonetic objects, that is, for translating the abstract gestural structures we call words and sentences into neuromotor commands for the articulator movements of particular utterances.[4]

What is remarkable about this specialization is its capacity for parallel transmission of phonetic information. Such transmission is accomplished by coarticulation, that is, by overlapping the movements for gestures of different articulators and by merging into one continuous movement different gestures of the same articulator. The gestures that evolved for effective coarticulation are a distinct set, different, for the most part, from those people make when they lick their lips, chew, move food around the mouth, and so forth. These gestures are special, too, in the way that they are coordinated, both in space and in time. For the overlap and merging are thorough enough to permit the gestures to be produced at high rates, yet so controlled as to preserve information about their identities and their structural relation to one another.

While coarticulation greatly increases the rate at which phonetic information can be transmitted, it necessarily complicates the process of perception, because it precludes any simple correspondence between successive phonetic gestures and successive acoustic segments. Any particular stretch of a speech signal will commonly contain information about more than one gesture, and the acoustic information specifying a particular gesture will vary according to the phonetic context.[20]

One sees, now, the function of a specialization for speech perception. Adapted specifically to cope with the peculiar complications of speech, it processes the acoustic signal so as to recover the coarticulated gestures that produced it. These gestures are the primitives that the mechanisms of speech production translate into actual articulator movements, and they are also the primitives that the specialized mechanisms of speech perception recover from the signal. Indeed, there is but one specialization with two complementary processes, one for computing the articulator movements and one for dealing with the acoustic consequences.[4,5]

This aspect of the phonetic specialization is important for its relevance to a truism that applies to all communication systems: what counts as structure in production must count as structure in perception, else communication does not occur. If not by the kind of Janus-faced specialization we have described, how is this parity established and maintained as the system develops in the species and as it develops anew in each member? The question is the more worth asking, because the conventional view of speech implies an unparsimonious answer. For if, in speech, the auditory and motor representations are distinct from each other, having in common only that neither is specifically phonetic, then both must be translated into phonetic representations by matching them to phonetic prototypes or otherwise assigning them to appropriate phonetic categories, much as the conventional view assumes.[1] These prototypes and labels might have been established by agreement, as they obviously are in the case of invented communication systems like Morse code. Or, alternatively, they might have taken root as something like the "innate ideas" that some students of language invoke.[21] In either case, however, they are neither motoric nor perceptual; they are, rather, cognitive, and their role is just to relate nonphonetic modes of acting and perceiving to each other and to language. But if speech has anything like the characteristics we have attributed to it, then there is no need for agreements or innate ideas and the cognitive translations they participate in. At every stage of phylogenetic and ontogenetic development, the single precognitive specialization for production and perception provides a common currency of specifically phonetic primitives, hence a sufficient basis for the parity between sender and receiver that must exist.[4,5]

Experiments on the biology of parity in phonetic communication are, for obvious reasons, hard to carry out, but there is at least some direct evidence that production and perception do, indeed, have common and specific neural loci.[22] The biology of communication in nonhuman animals is, of course, more available to an experimenter, and, though such communication does not rest on a phonetic base, it is nonetheless subject to the requirement of parity. One is, therefore, not surprised to find, in the communication systems of a variety of species, that the biological bases of perception and production are associated in an especially intimate way.[23]

Speech and the Rest of the Auditory System: Open and Closed Modules

The modules of the auditory system (and, presumably, of other modalities as well) can be divided into two classes, which we have called "open" and "closed," according to the kind of representations that they characteristically produce and the way they respond to environmental influences. Among the open modules are those for pitch, loudness, and timbre. These are adapted for the perception of an indefinitely large number of acoustic events, including many that evolution could not have anticipated. Accordingly, each responds straightforwardly to the dimensions of the signal—pitch to frequency, loudness to intensity, and timbre to spectral shape—so the representations they produce deserve to be called "homomorphic." These modules correspond roughly to those aspects of perceptual systems that, in Konishi's neurobiological classification, produce "projectional maps"—that is, central neural maps that preserve the spatial relations of the responses at the sensory epithelium.[24]

Like all modules, those of the open class are influenced by environmental circumstances—witness the well-known effects of sensory deprivation—but such influences cannot be governed by acoustic events as such. Long experience with a variety of, say, squeaking doors must not make the open modules better adapted to that kind of event, lest they become that much less well adapted to other events that depend on a different mix of values of the same homomorphic primitives. Thus, such experience cannot change the internal working of the module, only the way its outputs are associated with the particular events that they come to signify.

The closed modules comprise a variety of specializations, including, for example, scene analysis, echo ranging, and phonetic perception. In Konishi's scheme, these belong to a class that requires "central synthesis" for formation of the appropriate neural map; direct projection will not suffice.[24] In our terms, the members of this class have in common that the percepts they produce are "heteromorphic": the dimensions of the percept do not correspond directly to dimensions of the signal; the signal dimensions are merely the data from which the very different, indeed incommensurate, dimensions of the percept are derived. The closed scene-analysis module, for instance, responds to the narrow range of interaural time disparities that is ecologically appropriate for a sounding object at different positions of azimuth.[25] What is perceived, however, is the location of the source, not temporal disparity as such. The bat's echo-ranging module measures the delay between the emitted cry and its reflection,[26] but what is perceived is presumably the distance of the reflecting object, not an echoing bat cry. Similarly, in our view, the phonetic module tracks the changing center frequencies of formants, but what is perceived is a sequence of phonetic events, not changing timbre or a medley of changing pitches.

As for environmental influences, the closed modules can respond, as the open modules cannot, by adapting their internal mechanisms, and hence their heteromorphic primitives, to just those events, or derived properties of events, they are concerned with; the homomorphic primitives that must be used for everything else are in no way affected. Consider, for example, how the sound-localization aspect of the scene-analysis module must adjust to changes in interaural time disparities as the head grows bigger. It can hardly be that the animal learns to translate old disparities into new locations, if only because its sound-localizing module never did perceive the disparities homomorphically as disparities. It must rather be that the module adjusts its internal processes, and hence its heteromorphic output (location of a source); thus, it is the module itself that learns. We should suppose that in the acquisition of any particular language, the phonetic module adjusts its internal processes and its heteromorphic representations in much the same epigenetic way. The child need never "translate" homomorphic auditory representations into the phonetic categories his language happens to represent.

Similar considerations apply, of course, to the development of phonetic perception in evolution. For the conventional assumption that speech and nonspeech share a common set of processes and primitives entails a constraint on evolutionary adaptation identical to the one that applies in ontogenesis: changes in the open modules that might be appropriate for speech sounds would be inappropriate for most others. But if, as we speculate, speech is managed by a closed module, its processes were free to go as evolution took them.

Architectural Relations between Open and Closed Modules

The homomorphic and heteromorphic representations that characterize open and closed modules are sometimes formed in response to signals in the same physical range. This is most obviously the case in speech, where, as we have seen in the phenomenon of duplex perception, exactly the same stimulus that causes the open module for timbre to represent homomorphic chirps causes the closed phonetic module to produce the difference between the heteromorphic representations [da] and [ga]. Why, then, are not all speech percepts duplex in this way? Why, when listeners hear [da] and [ga], do they not also hear chirps?

A similar question arises in the case of the bat. Given that the closed echo-ranging module represents the echoes of the bat's cries heteromorphically as objects at certain distances, why do the open modules not also represent them homomorphically as bat cries? Presumably the open modules do not, even though they respond to the physically similar cries of other bats.

Duplex perception would, of course, be prevented in such cases if the open modules had gates through which the unwanted signals could not pass, or inhibitory processes that would nullify whatever responses they might evoke. But there are no superficial properties of the signal that such gates or inhibitors could use. They would, therefore, need the same capacities to respond to underlying properties that the closed modules are specialized for—obviously, an unparsimonious arrangement.

A more parsimonious solution is an architecture that allows a closed module to preempt just the information that concerns it, thus preventing this information from reaching the open modules at all.[4,5] Indeed, precisely this kind of arrangement seems to characterize the relation between the closed scene-analysis module and the various open modules. For, as Bregman has made clear, scene analysis must segregate the acoustic information into separate streams according to source, if pitch, timbre, and loudness are to be properly assigned.[2] This is as much as to say that, with respect to the flow of information, this closed module is in series with, and precedes, each of the open modules. But scene analysis does not simply pass on all the information; rather, it preempts some of it in the very process of defining sound sources. Thus, a sufficiently great interaural disparity in time is taken to mean that the two signals correspond to two sources, regardless of their physical similarity, and the disparity is perceived as disparity. An appropriately small disparity, however, is used as evidence of the azimuth position of one source. Listeners hear this one source, but not the disparity, for that has been preempted in the process of localization. A similar architecture may define the relation of open and closed modules more generally and serve to resolve the competition between them.

In the case of the phonetic module, evidence for preemptiveness has been reported in an example of duplex perception somewhat different from the one described earlier.[14] The stimuli in this case are like those of the earlier example, except that the critical third-formant transitions are not resonances, but sinusoids that follow the center frequencies of the resonances. In isolation, these sinusoids sound like brief whistles, and, like the isolated resonances, they cannot be matched to [da] and [ga]. The point of the experiment was to see what happens as these sinusoids are increased in intensity from a level near zero, the sinusoids and resonances that form the remainder of the pattern being presented at both ears.

Within a certain range of intensities at the lower end of the scale, the sinusoids have an effect that is exclusively phonetic: listeners perceive [da] or [ga] appropriately; they do not also perceive whistles or any other kind of nonspeech that can be reliably associated with the sinusoids. In itself, this is of interest, since it offers further testimony to the ability of the phonetic module to respond to phonetic coherence, even though this may require ignoring a considerable discordance at the acoustic surface. Ignored in this case are the gross differences in fundamental frequency, spectrum, and harmonic structure between the sinusoids that critically distinguish [da] from [ga] and the resonances that form the remainder of the pattern.

With further increases in the intensity of the sinusoids, a point is reached at which they begin to serve a double purpose: listeners perceive [da] or [ga] appropriately, as before, but also one or another whistle, which they can reliably match to the whistles produced by the sinusoids in isolation. At first, this whistle is faint, but it grows steadily in loudness as the intensity of the sinusoid is further increased; meanwhile, perception of [da] and [ga] remains unchanged. As in the earlier example of duplex perception, the information in the transitions simultaneously produces speech and nonspeech percepts. In this case, however, it is apparent that the phonetic module is preemptive: it has first claim on the information in the sinusoids, allowing only the unwanted residue to evoke responses in the modules for pitch, loudness, and timbre.

The relation between the information the phonetic module receives and the information it passes on is not as yet clear. It certainly would not do to view the phonetic module as simply removing phonetically crucial portions of the represented signal (the formant transitions, for example), for the listener needs the paraphonetic information these portions also contain. Perhaps the action of the module is to be thought of as a kind of inverse filtering that undoes the effects of the resonant cavities of the vocal tract, leaving paraphonetic information about the excitation of the cavities as well as information about other ambient sounds. In the experiment just described, the residue for low intensities of the sinusoid is perceived just as laryngeal excitation, while at higher intensities a nonphonetic source, the whistle, also becomes obvious.

A Remaining Problem

According to our account of auditory architecture, the closed scene-analysis module represents an array of sources to cognition and segregates acoustic information according to source. Given these separate steams of information, open modules then attribute pitch, timbre, and loudness to each source. The phonetic module, independently of scene analysis, uses all the relevant information available to form phonetic percepts; information not so preempted becomes available to the open modules.

Thus, in the human case, the scene-analysis module precedes the open modules in series; so, too, does the phonetic module. But what is the architectural relation of the two closed modules themselves? A similar question arises for the bat. If the bat hears the echo-ranging cries of other bats, along with other ambient sounds, it must hear them as separate sources, and must, therefore, have its own scene-analysis module preceding the open modules. What, then, is the architectural relation of scene analysis and echo ranging?

A parallel arrangement of closed modules must, presumably, be ruled out in both cases, for such an arrangement would obviously defeat the preempting functions of these modules: acoustic information preempted by the phonetic module (or by the echo-ranging module) would reach the open modules through the scene-analysis module, and conversely. Thus, the closed modules must be in series, both in man and in bat; only the ordering within the series is in question.

In the bat, we suggest that echo ranging comes before scene analysis. Scene analysis has no concern with signals that originate in the bat itself; their preemption would simplify its task. Echo ranging has no need to know about the auditory scene: the emitted sonar signal and its echo are already defined sources, and the bat determines the position in azimuth of the reflecting object by pointing its head so as to minimize the interaural disparity of the echo signals.[27]

In man, we have conjectured that, in similar fashion, the closed phonetic module precedes the closed module for scene analysis.[12] In the examples of duplex perception offered here, the phonetic module makes no use of the separation of sources provided by scene analysis. If the phonetic module came after scene analysis, it would be reintegrating phonetically relevant signal information that had just been separated by source, yet still be obliged to pass along segregated streams of phonetically irrelevant information to the open modules. Such an arrangement is not very parsimonious. On the other hand, if scene analysis comes after the phonetic module, no similar difficulties arise. Scene analysis simply segregates the acoustic information that has not been preempted by the phonetic module, and the open modules operate on the resulting streams.

Unfortunately for such conjectures, it is the unparsimonious alternative that the evidence so far seems to favor. This evidence is owed to Darwin,[28,29] who has adduced a number of examples in which phonetic integration does not occur, although it might be expected to if the phonetic module precedes scene analysis in series. In one such example, a vowel is first synthesized without a particular harmonic it would naturally contain, with the result that it is perceived as different in quality from a synthetic vowel not thus depleted. If a tone equal in amplitude and frequency to the missing harmonic is added synchronously to the depleted vowel, the sum is of course perceived as the undepleted vowel, and the tone is not separately heard. But if the depleted vowel is short enough, and its onset follows that of the tone by some tens of milliseconds, the depleted vowel and, separately, the tone itself are heard.[28] It is as if scene analysis, preceding the phonetic module, had defined the asynchronous tone and vowel as separate events, which the phonetic module must then either use for their entire durations or not use at all. In light of effects such as this, it may be necessary to reconsider our simple account of the serial ordering of the two closed modules.

Broader Issues

Taken in their most general terms, the questions raised here are not necessarily limited to the phonetic domain; they can, rather, be extended in two directions. One looks toward the other aspects of language, where investigators have for some time been exploring the possibility that syntax, like phonetics, is part of a distinct, precognitive module, and not, as more commonly assumed, one among many expression of a general capacity for cognitive computation.[7] The other direction leads to any perceptual system that can be characterized as a group of modules; there it might prove rewarding to ask, further, how the modules can usefully be classified and what the architectural arrangements among them might be.[24,30]

Notes

Support from NIH grant H-01994 to Haskins Laboratories is gratefully acknowledged.

1. R. G. Crowder and J. Morton, *Percept. Psychophys.* 5, 365 (1969); K. N. Stevens, in *Auditory Analysis and Perception of Speech*, G. Fant and M. A. Tatham, Eds. (Academic Press, New York, 1975), pp. 303–330; J. D. Miller, in *Recognition of Complex Acoustic Signals*, T. H. Bullock, Ed. (Dahlem Konferenzen, Berlin, 1977), pp. 49–58; G. C. Oden and D. W. Massaro, *Psychol. Rev.* 85, 172 (1978); P. K. Kuhl, *J. Acoust. Soc. Am.* 70, 340 (1981).
2. A. S. Bregman, in *Attention and Performance*, J. Requin, Ed. (Erlbaum, Hillsdale, NJ, 1978), vol. 7, pp. 62–74.
3. See A. M. Liberman and I. G. Mattingly, "Signal and sense: Local and global order in perceptual maps," paper presented at the Fifth Annual Symposium of the Neurosciences Institute, Stockholm, Sweden, 31 May to 5 June 1987.
4. A. M. Liberman and I. G. Mattingly, *Cognition* 21, 1 (1985).
5. I. G. Mattingly and A. M. Liberman, in *Auditory Function: Neurobiological Bases of Hearing*, G. M. Edelman, W. E. Gall, W. M. Cowan, Eds. (Wiley, New York, 1988), pp. 775–793.
6. More properly, a *linguistic* module that not only perceives phonetic gestures, but also recognizes words and parses sentences. Our concerns, however, have been chiefly phonetic.
7. See J. Fodor, *The Modularity of Mind* (MIT Press, Cambridge, MA, 1983).

8. T. C. Rand, *J. Acoust. Soc. Am.* 55, 678 (1974); A. M. Liberman, in *Proceedings of the Ninth International Congress of Phonetic Science*, E. Fischer-Jorgensen, J. Rischel, N. Thorsen, Eds. (Univ. of Copenhagen Press, Copenhagen, 1979), vol. 2, pp. 468–473; J. E. Cutting, *Psychol. Rev.* 83, 114 (1976); B. Repp and S. Bentin, *Percept. Psychophys.* 36, 523 (1984).
9. A. M. Liberman, D. Isenberg, B. Rakerd, *Percept. Psychophys.* 30, 133 (1981).
10. V. A. Mann and A. M. Liberman, *Cognition* 14, 211 (1983).
11. B. Repp, C. Milburn, J. Askenas, *Percept. Psychophys.* 33, 333 (1983).
12. I. G. Mattingly, *J. Acoust. Soc. Am.* 82 (Suppl. 1), 120 (1987).
13. A. S. Bregman, in *The Psychophysics of Speech Perception*, M. E. H. Schouten, Ed. (Nijhoff, Dordrecht, 1987), pp. 95–111.
14. D. Whalen and A. M. Liberman, *Science* 237, 169 (1987).
15. K. S. Harris, H. S. Hoffman, A. M. Liberman, P. C. Delattre, F. S. Cooper, *J. Acoust. Soc. Am.* 30, 122 (1958).
16. I. G. Mattingly, A. M. Liberman, A. M. Syrdal, T. Halwes, *Cogn. Psychol.* 2, 131 (1971).
17. P. T. Brady, A. N. House, and K. N. Stevens, *J. Acoust. Soc. Am.* 33, 1357 (1961).
18. A. M. Liberman, K. S. Harris, H. S. Hoffman, B. C. Griffith, *J. Exp. Psychol.* 61, 379 (1961); A. M. Liberman, F. S. Cooper, D. P. Shankweiler, M. Studdert-Kennedy, *Psychol. Rev.* 74, 431 (1967); B. Repp and A. M. Liberman, in *Categorical Perception*, S. Harnad, Ed., (Cambridge Univ. Press, Cambridge, 1987), pp. 89–112.
19. C. P. Browman and L. Goldstein, *Phonol. Yearb.* 3, 219 (1986).
20. F. S. Cooper, P. C. Delattre, A. M. Liberman, J. Borst, L. Gerstman, *J. Acoust. Soc. Am.* 24, 597 (1952); G. Fant, *Logos* 5, 3 (1962).
21. N. Chomsky, *Cartesian Linguistics* (Harper & Row, New York, 1966).
22. G. Ojemann and C. Mateer, *Science* 205, 1401 (1979).
23. R. Hoy and R. C. Paul, ibid. 180, 82 (1973); R. Hoy, J. Hahn, R. C. Paul, ibid. 195, 82 (1977); H. C. Gerhardt, ibid. 199, 992 (1978); J. S. McCasland and M. Konishi, *Proc. Natl. Acad. Sci. U.S.A.* 78, 7815 (1983); D. Margoliash, *J. Neurosci.* 3, 1039 (1983); H. Williams and F. Nottebohm, *Science* 229, 279 (1985); M. J. Ryan and W. Wilczynski, *Science* 240, 1786 (1988).
24. M. Konishi, *Trends Neurosci.* 9, 163 (1986).
25. E. Hafter, in *Dynamic Aspects of Neocortical Function*, G. M. Edelman, W. E. Gall, W. M. Cowan, Eds. (Wiley, New York, 1984), pp. 425–448.
26. N. Suga, in ibid., pp.315–373.
27. J. Simmons, in *Directional Hearing*, W. A. Yost and G. Gourevitch, Eds. (Springer, New York, 1987), pp. 214–225.
28. C. J. Darwin, *J. Acoust. Soc. Am.* 76, 1636 (1984).
29. C. J. Darwin and N. S. Sutherland, *Q. J. Exp. Psychol.* 36A, 193 (1984).
30. M. Livingstone and D. Hubel, *Science* 240, 740 (1988); J. M. Wolfe, *Psychol. Rev.* 93, 269 (1986); R. Blake and R. P. O'Shea, ibid. 95, 151 (1988); J. M. Wolfe, ibid., p. 155.

PART IX

Auditory vs. Phonetic Modes

Introduction to Part IX

The chapters in this section are about a variety of experiments, having in common only that they bear more or less directly on the claim of the vertical view that there is a distinctly phonetic mode of perception, different in its primary perceptual representations from the auditory mode.

Chapter 17
An Effect of Linguistic Experience: The Discrimination of [r] and [l] by Native Speakers of Japanese and English

One way to examine the effect of linguistic experience on the perception of speech is to compare the discrimination of phonetic segments by two groups of speakers: one group speaks a language in which the segments under study are functionally distinctive, the other does not. In that circumstance, a difference in the ability to discriminate can be attributed to the linguistic use of the distinction in the one case and lack of such linguistic use in the other.

Two cross-language studies of the kind described above are relevant to the experiment reported in this paper. One study deals with vowels (Stevens, Liberman, Studdert-Kennedy, and Ohman 1969) and one deals with the voicing distinction in stops (Abramson and Lisker 1970). In the vowel study, linguistic experience appeared to have no effect. Discrimination of synthetic vowels was the same for Swedish and American listeners, though the vowels were phonemically distinct for the one group and not for the other. The voicing distinction in stops yielded an opposite result. More accurate discrimination was observed at those positions on the stimulus continuum that corresponded to the different positions of the voicing boundary for the language spoken by the subjects (Thai or English).

The difference in discriminability obtained with vowels and stops may be related to articulatory, acoustic, and perceptual differences between these two classes of sounds. For the stops, the articulatory gestures are relatively rapid movements to and from closures of the vocal tract. For the vowels, the movements are slower and the vocal tract is more nearly open. The acoustic cues for the stops are, correspondingly, characterized by rapid changes in amplitude and frequency within a relatively short interval (Delattre, Liberman, and Cooper 1955), while the cues for the vowels can be (and were in the experiment referred to above) associated with steady-state signals of longer durations (Fry, Abramson, Eimas, and Liberman 1962). It may also be relevant that the cues for the stops are complexly encoded in the sound stream in the sense that they are merged on the same acoustic parameter with cues for succeeding (or preceding) segments, while in the case of vowels there can be (and were in the experiment referred to above) stretches of sound that carry cues for only one (vowel) segment (Liberman, Cooper, Shankweiler, and Studdert-Kennedy 1967). In the perceptual domain, two differences between vowels and stops have been found. First, in the comparison with steady-state vowels, stops show a greater tendency toward categorical perception (Fry et al. 1962; Liberman, Harris, Hoffman, and Griffith 1957; Pisoni 1973, 1975; Stevens et al. 1969; Vinegrad 1972; Fujisaki and Kawashima 1969).

Originally published in *Perception & Psychophysics* 18, 5 (1975): 331–340, Kuniko Miyawaki, Winifred Strange, Robert Verbrugge, James J. Jenkins, and Osamu Fujimura. Reprinted with permission.

Second, stops yield a larger right-ear advantage in dichotic listening tests, presumably due to a greater reliance on the left-hemisphere processing (Shankweiler and Studdert-Kennedy 1967).

The experiment reported here is intended to investigate the effect of linguistic usage on the perception of yet another class of phones, the liquids [r] and [l]. There are several reasons why an investigation of these phones is of interest.

First, the perception of [r] and [l] is an obvious choice for a cross-language study of Japanese and English, since the distinction between these phones is phonemic in English but not in Japanese. In syllable-initial position, which is the only context we will be concerned with, [r] and [l] are in minimal contrast in English, as in "red" vs. "led." The articulation of these phones is hard to characterize because reasonably stable acoustic results can be achieved by a variety of articulatory strategies. Typically, however, the English [r] in syllable initial position is articulated with the tongue tip turned up against the post-alveolar region of the hard palate—the lateral palato-lingual contact spreading medially without forming a closure—while the medio-dorsum of the tongue maintains a concave shape (Miyawaki 1972). A syllable-initial [l], on the other hand, is articulated with the tongue tip in contact with only the medial portion of the alveolar ridge, forming no palato-lingual contact laterally. In both cases, the voicing continues throughout the articulation (Heffner 1952; Jones 1956). Acoustically, a sufficient and important cue for the distinction between [r] and [l] is the initial steady-state and transition of the third formant. For [r], the third formant originates just slightly above the starting frequency of the second-formant transition, while for [l], it starts from a much higher frequency, equal to or even higher than the steady-state frequency of the third formant of the adjoining vowel (O'Connor, Gerstman, Liberman, Delattre, and Cooper 1957).

In Japanese, [r] and [l] do not constitute a phonemic contrast. The phone that is referred to as a Japanese [r] is typically a loose alveolar stop in initial position or the so-called "flapped-r"—the tongue tip making a very brief contact with the alveolar ridge—in intervocalic position. To an American listener, the Japanese [r] often sounds like [d]. In some cases, the phone is produced with "lateral" articulation, usually with a tendency of retroflexing, and it might sound to an American like an [l] or an [r]. There is no apparent allophonic distribution of [r] and [l] in different contexts (Miyawaki 1973).

Acoustically, in contrast to the American liquids, the Japanese [r] tends to have little or no initial steady state. The starting point and the transition of the third formant seem to vary unsystematically over a range of values sufficient to distinguish the American [r] and [l], although it appears that in most cases F3 assumes relatively lower values more like the American [r] than [l]. It is important to note that both English [l] and English [r] are perceived by Japanese speakers as the same consonant, their /r/, and there is no other English consonant that shares this characteristic in word-initial position.

Second, a cross-language study of [r] and [l] is of interest because these phones form an articulatory manner class (liquids) that is not only different from the two classes previously studied (stops and vowels), but in some ways intermediate between them. Thus, the liquids are not articulated with the complete closure of the vocal tract that characterizes the stops, nor with the open vocal tract of the vowels. Also, their articulation is not so fast as that of the stops, nor so slow as the vowels. As for their acoustic characteristics, liquids in initial position typically have short steady-state portions with an appreciable amount of sound energy preceding the formant transitions, while stop consonants have only transitions with little or no sound energy preceding them and vowels can be produced entirely with steady-state formants.

From the standpoint of distribution, liquids in English are intermediate between vowels and stops in terms of their phonotactic property, viz, vowel affinity (Fujimura 1975). In Japanese /r/, the only liquid, behaves as a consonant from a functional point of view.

A third reason for a cross-language study of [r] and [l] is that it is quite easy to isolate the distinguishing acoustic cue for these phones. Thus, we can determine how the two language groups discriminate this cue, not only in a speech context, but also in isolation, when it is not perceived as speech. On this basis, we can judge whether the effect of linguistic experience, if any, is limited in the perceptual domain to speech or whether, alternatively, it extends to nonlinguistic auditory processes.

For these reasons, it is interesting to examine any difference between the Americans and the Japanese in the pattern of discrimination of this class of sounds. In addition, our study has a final point of interest in that it provides data relevant to some questions about tendencies toward continuous and categorical perception. So far, these questions have been asked about vowels and stops, but not about the liquids, the class of phones that we will study here.

Method

Stimulus Materials
A series of 15 three-formant speech patterns was generated with the parallel-resonance synthesizer at Haskins Laboratories. The structure of the third formant (F3) varied over a range sufficient to produce perception of the consonant-vowel syllables, [ra] and [la]. The stimuli consisted of three contiguous parts: an initial 50-msec steady-state portion, a 75-msec transition of the formant frequencies between the initial and final steady states, and a final steady-state vowel portion of 375 msec duration.

The 15 stimuli differed only in the frequency values of the third formant within the initial steady-state and transition portions. Initial steady-state values of F3 varied in 15 roughly equal steps from 1,362 to 3,698 Hz. Transitions of the formant frequency were linear functions of time from each initial steady-state value to the common steady-state value of 2,525 Hz for the vowel.

Frequency values of the first formant (F1) and second formant (F2) were identical for all 15 stimuli. F1 was set to a frequency of 311 Hz during the initial steady state, then was changed linearly during the transition to a frequency of 769 Hz for the vowel. F2 remained at a constant frequency of 1,232 Hz throughout the entire syllable.

Within the final 400 msec of each syllable, amplitudes of F2 and F3 were set to -3 and -15 dB relative to F1, respectively. The amplitude of F1 at its onset was -12 dB relative to its final value and increased as a decelerated function over the first 100 msec of the syllable. F2 amplitude over the first 100 msec was -3 dB relative to its final steady-state value. F3 amplitude remained constant throughout the syllable. Superimposed on these amplitude values was an overall amplitude contour on the first 50 msec of the syllable, which began 15 dB below its final value and rose linearly. The syllable had a gradually falling fundamental frequency contour from 114 to 96 Hz.

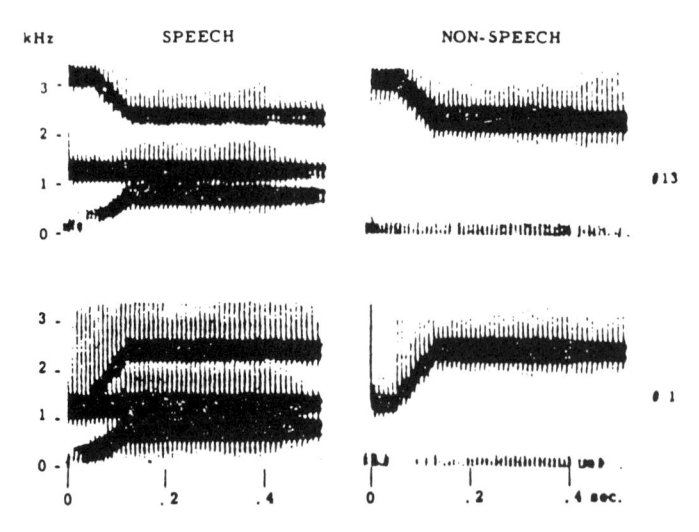

Figure 17.1
Spectrograms of speech and nonspeech stimuli—[la] upper and [ra] lower.

For comparison with the speech patterns, a set of nonspeech stimuli was generated which consisted of the 15 different F3 patterns in isolation. The stimuli were generated by setting the F1 and F2 amplitudes to zero throughout the syllable, so the resultant F3 patterns may be considered as acoustically identical to the F3 patterns *within* the speech stimuli. These stimuli did not sound like speech, but rather like high-pitched glissandos followed by a steady pitch. Figure 17.1 illustrates the two pairs of examples at nearly extreme F3 values. Stimuli are numbered consecutively with the lowest F3 initial value labeled "1."

Two types of tests were constructed from the speech stimulus set: an identification test and an oddity discrimination test. The former was constructed by recording the speech patterns one at a time in random order with a 1.5-sec interstimulus interval. Each stimulus appeared 10 times for a total of 150 trials. Trials occurred in blocks of 30 with a 5-sec interval between blocks. This test will be referred to as the identification test.

For oddity discrimination tests, Stimuli 14 and 15 were deleted.[1] Ten pairs of stimuli were selected such that each pair (AB) differed by three steps (i.e., 1–4, 2–5, ..., 10–13). For each pair, triads were constructed by duplicating one stimulus of the pair; all six permutations (AAB, ABA, BAA, ABB, BAB, BBA) were generated. Thus, the oddity test consisted of 60 triads, six permutations for each of 10 comparison pairs. The triads were recorded in random order with a 1-sec interstimulus interval and a 3-sec intertriad interval. Two such randomizations were recorded on audio tape for presentation to subjects. These will be referred to as Speech Tests 1 and 2, respectively.

Oddity discrimination tests of the nonspeech F3 patterns were constructed in the same way as the speech tests. This was accomplished by substituting the corresponding F3 stimulus for each speech stimulus. Thus, the pairing of stimuli and order of triads was the same as that in the speech tests. The two randomizations of 60 triads each will be referred to as Nonspeech Tests 1 and 2, respectively.

For purposes of familiarizing the subjects with the stimuli, two additional recordings were generated. The speech familiarization tape contained the following sequences: the speech stimulus set presented in succession from No. 1 to No. 15, the set repeated in reverse order, the patterns presented in random order with each stimulus occurring two times, and Stimuli 4 and 10 presented five times each. (The latter were judged to be the "best" tokens of [ra] and [la] by an experienced phonetician.) A nonspeech familiarization tape included a set of randomly presented F3 patterns, with each stimulus occurring twice and two nonspeech patterns, Stimuli 4 and 10, recorded five times each. All experimental materials were then rerecorded and the second-generation recordings used in the experiment.

Subjects
Subjects were 39 native speakers of American English and 21 native speakers of Japanese. The American subjects, undergraduate students at the University of Minnesota, were tested at different times and under somewhat different procedures. Nineteen of the American subjects were students in introductory psychology classes offered during the summer session; this group is referred to as Americans I. The remaining 20 subjects were students in introductory psychology classes during the regular fall quarter; they are referred to as Americans II. The students received monetary reimbursement and extra credit points toward their course grade. All subjects reported having normal hearing.

The Japanese subjects were students and staff at the University of Tokyo. Every member of the group had received at least 10 years of formal English language training. Two subjects had lived abroad from the age of 12 years to 16 years. K.M. attended English-speaking schools in Ceylon; S.A. attended school in Germany. Data obtained for these subjects are discussed separately in the results. (It should be understood that English teaching in Japan usually tends to stress reading and writing; conversational English is not emphasized.) Subjects were paid for their participation in the experiment. All subjects reported having normal hearing.

Procedure
The experimental procedures were basically the same for all three groups of subjects, Americans I and II and Japanese. This section describes the basic procedure; in appendix A, detailed procedural information for each group is given. The experiment consisted of three parts: familiarization, discrimination tests, and identification tests (for the Americans only).

Familiarization   The procedure for speech familiarization was as follows: Subjects listened to the ordered series without being told what speech sounds were represented. They were then informed that the stimuli were several instances of the English syllables [ra] and [la], and were presented the random series. Finally, they heard the five repetitions of Stimuli 4 and 10, which were described by the experimenter as the "best" instances of the two syllables.

For nonspeech familiarization, subjects were told that the stimuli were "related" to the speech sounds, but would probably not sound like speech. They heard the random series and were asked to describe them as best they could. They were then presented the repetitions of Stimuli 4 and 10 and asked if they could tell them apart easily.

Discrimination Subjects were told that they would hear triplets of sounds in which two were always identical and one different, and they were to indicate on printed score sheets whether the different one occurred first, second, or third in the triad. They were instructed to respond on every triad, even if they had to guess. They were told they could use any criterion to make the difference judgment.

All subjects completed two repetitions of Tests 1 and 2 (240 trials) for each stimulus set (speech and nonspeech) on the first day of testing. On Day 2, subjects were reminded of the procedure and again completed two repetitions of Tests 1 and 2 for each stimulus series. Thus, subjects completed a total of 480 trials, 48 judgments for each AB comparison pair, for both the speech stimuli and the nonspeech stimuli.

Identification (American subjects only) On the third day of testing, the American subjects were instructed to listen to each speech stimulus, and mark down on printed score sheets whether the syllable began with an "r" or an "l." They were told to identify every stimulus and were limited to the two response alternatives. They completed two repetitions of the identification test for a total of 300 trials, comprising 20 judgments for each of 15 stimuli.

Results

Comparison of American and Japanese Discrimination of the [r-l] Contrast
Most relevant to the purposes of this study are the data, shown in the lower half of figure 17.2, on the discrimination of [r-l] by the two language groups. But before comparing those data, we should note, in the upper half of the figure, the results of the identification test which was given only to the Americans. There, where the percent of "r" responses is plotted for each of the 13 stimuli[2] of the "speech" series, we see that the American subjects did, in fact, divide the stimuli rather neatly into the two phoneme categories that our synthetic patterns were designed to embrace and, further, that the boundary between the categories is in the neighborhood of Stimulus 7.

Looking now at the lower graph, where percent correct in the discrimination task is plotted against the stimulus pair being tested, we see immediately that the performance by the two groups was markedly different. The American subjects discriminated well between those stimuli that were drawn from different phoneme categories, that is, those that straddle or include the one (Stimulus 7) closest to the boundary between [r] and [l]. However, they discriminated rather poorly those that were given the same category assignment in the identification tests. The Japanese, on the other hand, showed no such increase in discrimination at the phoneme boundary; for the stimuli that lay within a phoneme class, their discrimination was close to that of the Americans.

Examination of the discrimination functions for individual subjects revealed that 34 of the 39 American subjects were highly accurate in discriminating pairs whose members were labeled as different phonemes (especially Pairs 5–8 and 6–9). Discrimination of pairs whose members were labeled as the same phoneme was considerably less accurate, although still above the 33 percent chance level. (A discussion of differences in discriminations data for the Americans I and Americans II groups is included in appendix A).

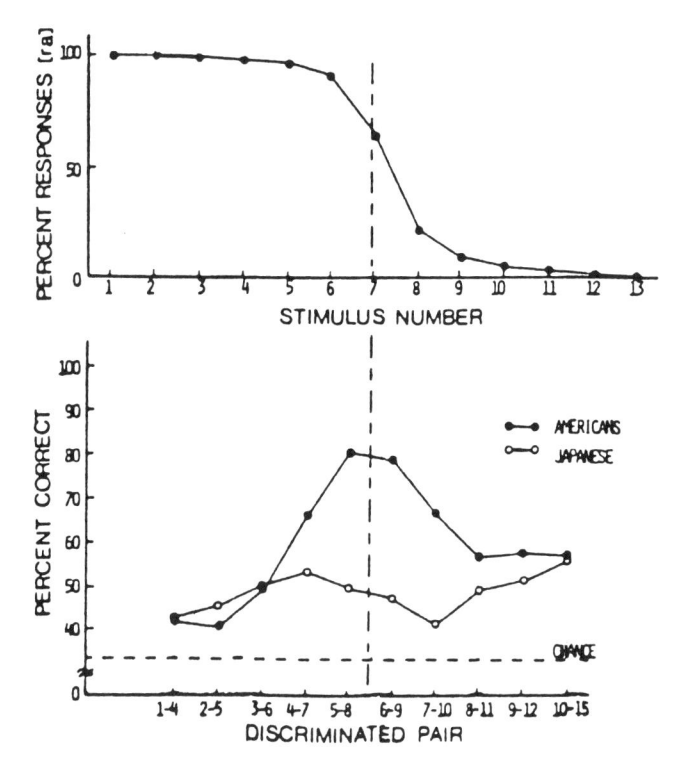

Figure 17.2
Upper graph: Pooled identification of speech stimuli by Americans. Lower graph: Pooled discrimination by Americans (closed circles) and Japanese (open circles).

Examination of the data for the Japanese subjects, however, found little evidence of such accurate discrimination. Only three subjects showed distinct peaks in discrimination in the vicinity of the phoneme boundary indicated in the American identification data. One of these subjects, S.A. (23 years) lived in Germany between the ages of 12 and 16 and is a fluent speaker of German. Subject K.M. (23 years) lived in Ceylon between the ages of 12 and 16 and is a fluent speaker of English. Subject M.S. (43 years) received regular English training in Japan with an emphasis on reading and writing, starting at the age of 12. (Discrimination data for each of these subjects and for the remainder of the sample are given in appendix B.)

Discrimination of the [r-l] Cue in Isolation [Nonspeech]—Americans and Japanese
As we pointed out in the introduction, it was possible in this experiment to compare the discrimination of the relevant acoustic cue (the F3 transition in this case) under two conditions: when it is the only basis for the perceived distinction (if any) between the speech sounds, and when it is presented in isolation and does not sound like speech at all. This comparison is of some interest even in the study of speech-sound discrimination that does not make a cross-language comparison. Thus, given an increase in the speech-sound discrimination at the phoneme boundary, as there was for the American subjects in our experiment, the nonspeech discrimination function helps us to know whether the discrimination peak is part of our general auditory

316 Chapter 17

perception or whether, alternatively, it is somehow peculiar to the speech context—that is, to perception in the speech mode. In the case of a cross-language comparison, the nonspeech discrimination data are potentially even more interesting. Having found a difference in speech-sound discrimination between the two language groups, as we did in our experiment, we can see in the nonspeech data where the difference might lie. If we assume, as we do, that the difference between the language groups reflects an effect of linguistic experience, then we can look to the nonspeech functions to help us decide whether that effect was at the auditory level or whether, alternatively, it was somehow specific to perception in the speech mode. If the effect were on auditory perception quite generally, we should expect the two groups to differ similarly on both the speech and nonspeech discrimination. Alternatively, if the effect is specific to the speech mode, we should expect the two groups to discriminate the nonspeech stimuli in similar fashion, however much they might differ in discrimination of the speech sounds. In all cases, a result that tends to put the effect in the speech mode could, of course, be interpreted alternatively as a purely auditory interaction between the cue and the constant acoustic context to which it is always added in the speech patterns. But such an interpretation is empty unless one can make sense of it in terms of what is known, on other grounds, about auditory perception.

In the case of cross-language comparisons, the results of the relevant nonspeech discrimination provide a useful check on the procedures as well. If there are no differences between groups for the nonspeech stimuli, we can be more confident that the differences in discrimination of the speech sounds were not due to some uncontrolled methodological factors in the conduct of the experiment.

The pooled data for discrimination of the F3 cue in isolation are shown in figure 17.3 for both the American and Japanese subjects. Looking first at the results for the American subjects, we see that the shape of the function is quite different from that obtained when the same acoustic variable was perceived in a speech context where it cued the distinction between [r] and [l]. The difference between speech and nonspeech discrimination functions is similar to the finding of an earlier experiment on place distinctions in voiced stops (Mattingly, Liberman, Syrdal, and Halwes 1971), where

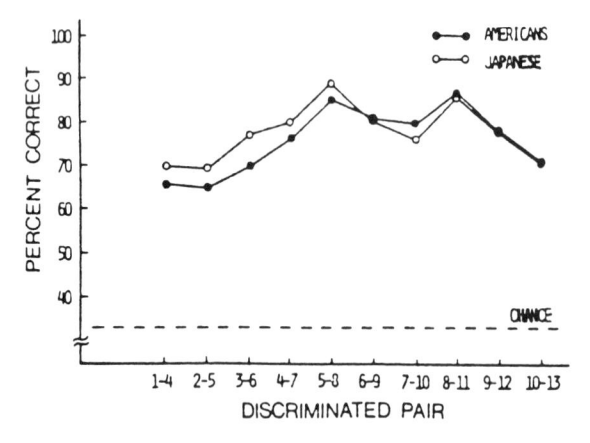

Figure 17.3
Pooled discrimination of nonspeech stimuli by Americans (closed circles) and Japanese (open circles).

the relevant cue was tested in and out of speech context. In both experiments, it is apparent that the discrimination peak obtained in the speech context is peculiar to that context and is not, more generally, characteristic of the way we perceive the relevant acoustic variable.

But it is the nonspeech discrimination function obtained with the Japanese subjects that is of particular interest. We see very clearly that the Japanese do not differ from the Americans on any of the comparison pairs. The nonspeech discrimination functions are virtually identical for the two groups of subjects. We conclude, then, that the differences between the groups on the speech stimuli are a function of processes specific to the perception of speech, or at least speech-like stimuli such as ours, as opposed to stimuli that cannot be identified as phonological units. Also, the results suggest that the procedures for testing the two groups were comparable, and that the differences on speech discrimination cannot be attributed to uncontrolled methodological factors.

It is interesting to note that, for both groups, discrimination for all nonspeech comparison pairs is quite accurate (ranging from 66% to 89%). That is, both Japanese and Americans were able to discriminate differences in F3 patterns when they were presented in isolation. This suggests that the poor discrimination by Japanese for all speech comparison pairs and by Americans for within-category pairs is not due to the acoustic differences per se being indiscriminable, but rather has something to do with the phonemic identity of the speech patterns which contain these F3 patterns. However, two factors may have contributed to the relatively better discrimination of the isolated formants: the F3 patterns were presented at a much higher amplitude than the F3 components within the speech patterns, and it is possible that the lower formants in the speech patterns masked the F3 component to some extent. More research that measures the effects of intensity and masking on the perception of nonspeech is needed to explore these factors.

In both the Japanese and American nonspeech functions, two comparison pairs appear to be discriminated slightly better than the others. It is interesting to note that each of these pairs contains Stimulus 8 (5–8 and 8–11). Stimulus 8 is unique in that its F3 does not contain a frequency transition. In other words, this pattern is a steady state in contrast to Stimuli 1 through 7, which contain rising transitions, and Stimuli 9 through 13, which have falling transitions. It appears that subjects were able to distinguish between "no transition" vs. "some transition" slightly better than between transitions with different slopes.

Categorical Perception of [r] and [l]
We may now turn to a consideration of the relation between the identification and discrimination functions obtained for the stimuli presented to the American subjects. A reexamination of figure 17.2 shows a striking correspondence between the sharp change in identification of the stimuli as [r] and [l] and the peak in the discrimination function. The close relation between identification and discrimination is similar to that found for stop consonants, and has been referred to as "categorical perception" (Liberman et al. 1957). In contrast, the correlation between identification and discrimination does not always hold for other speech sounds, such as steady-state vowels (Fry et al. 1962).

A strong test for the presence of categorical perception may be made by predicting the shape of the discrimination function. If one makes the extreme assumption that

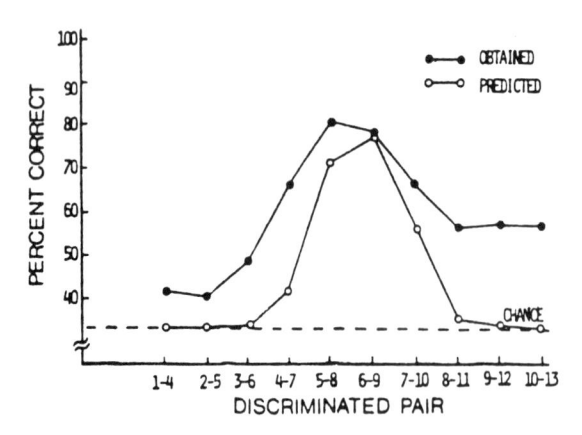

Figure 17.4
Obtained (closed circles) and predicted (open circles) functions for pooled discrimination by Americans. (See text for explanation of predicted function.)

subjects are able to discriminate speech stimuli only when they label them differently, it is possible to predict their discrimination functions from their identification performance. Each of the two stimuli in an oddity triad has a probability of being labeled as "r" or as "l," as determined in the identification test. From these data, it is possible to calculate the probability of the triad being heard as each of the possible sequences of the two phonemes. Only some of these perceived sequences will result in correct choices of the odd member, and those probabilities may be summed for each stimulus order. The probability of correct discrimination for a stimulus pair will be an average of the probabilities for the six possible orders. If Pr is the probability of one member being heard as "r" and Pr' is the probability of the other member being heard as "r," then the average probability of correct discrimination is found to be Pcorr = $[1 + 2(Pr - Pr')^2]/3$.

The predicted discrimination function for the pooled data is shown in figure 17.4. As is typical of such functions, the location and extent of the discrimination peak is fairly accurately predicted, while within-category discrimination is underestimated. This suggests that even though subjects labeled the stimuli as the same phoneme, they were able to discriminate intraphonemic variants to some extent. This point also conforms with the observation that the discrimination by Japanese subjects, even though poor, was better than chance.

Discussion

Returning now to the questions that prompted this study, we may conclude that rather clear answers have been obtained. We note, first, that familiarity with the [r-l] distinction obviously has a major impact on the ability to make correct discriminations in an oddity test. In this respect, the findings are overwhelming. American subjects show a peak of highly accurate discrimination at the point where stimuli from different phonetic classes are being contrasted. Japanese subjects show no such accurate discrimination at any point along the stimulus dimension. Moreover, the results are consistent for individuals, not merely characteristic of group averages. Of the 39 American subjects, 34 showed clear discrimination peaks in their individual protocols, while only 3 of the 21 Japanese subjects did. Furthermore, two of the three Japanese subjects who did show discrimination peaks learned languages with the relevant liquid contrast as early adolescents. It is reasonable to conclude, therefore, that considerable experience with the linguistic distinction is prerequisite to successful performance on the discrimination test with synthetic speech stimuli such as we have employed. Also, since all Japanese subjects had studied English extensively, it is tempting to hazard the hypothesis that discrimination requires effective *phonetic* experience at a relatively early age, say early adolescence.

The finding that Japanese subjects cannot for the most part discriminate [r] and [l] over this range of synthetic stimuli confirms the observation of Goto (1971) that native Japanese speakers who are highly fluent in English cannot perceive the distinction between [r] and [l] produced by other speakers (both Japanese and American). Even more interesting, Goto reports that his subjects cannot distinguish reliably *their own* tokens of [r] and [l], even when American speakers judge the tokens to be appropriate instances of the two phones. Thus, the lack of discrimination of synthetic stimuli covering a range of variation is in harmony with what is known about the properties of perception of real speech in normal contexts. This does not mean, however, that training after adolescence does not help at all. In fact, some of our Japanese subjects may not fail in discriminating natural utterances of [ra] and [la]. The stimuli compared on the discrimination test are undoubtedly much more similar to each other than optimal instances of the phonemes. Also, there may be other cues for the distinction in natural utterances which some Japanese subjects may depend on more heavily than do Americans.

Second, it is apparent that the difference in discrimination performance is limited to the speech-like condition. No difference appeared between the American and Japanese groups in the discrimination of the acoustic cue for [r] vs. [l] when it was presented in isolation. This finding is consistent with the argument that speech perception is a special mode of auditory perception that is accomplished in quite a different manner from general auditory perception. In all cases, such an argument must, as we said earlier, leave room for the fact that even though the acoustic cue being discriminated was always the only variable, it was presented by itself in the nonspeech case, while in the speech case, it was added to a fixed auditory pattern, thus creating the possibility of an auditory interaction. In this experiment, comparison of the speech and nonspeech discrimination functions must also take into account the differences in amplitude of the F3-transition cue in the two cases and the possibility that in the speech context the F3 cue was to some degree masked by the constant F1 and F2.

Finally, the study yielded results concerning the "categorical perception" of liquids in initial position in English. While American listeners make more correct discriminations of stimuli than would be predicted from a strict categorical perception hypothesis, the match between predicted and obtained discrimination functions resembles more closely that obtained for stop consonants than that obtained for vowels (Fry et al. 1962; Liberman et al. 1957).

Since the present study was performed, Eimas (in press) has studied how 2- and 3-month-old infants perceive the stimuli utilized in this study. Using a habituation paradigm, he tested the discrimination of speech stimuli both within and between the [l] and [r] categories. The infant discriminations were remarkably parallel to those we obtained with American adults. Infants who were habituated to stimuli from one side of the adult boundary and then switched to stimuli from the other side of the boundary showed impressive recovery from habituation. Within-class shifts of stimuli produced much less recovery. However, shifts within the [l] category produced greater recovery than shifts within the [r] category, reflecting the tendency shown by American subjects to discriminate within the [l] category better than within the [r] category. Infants tested with comparable shifts in the nonspeech stimuli (F3 alone) failed to show significantly different recovery from habituation in all conditions. Thus, the infant data are parallel in all respects to the American adult data that we have presented here. Obviously, it would be of great interest now to follow the course of habituation-discrimination in Japanese children.

Appendix A

Specific Procedures

Americans I Subjects were assigned to one of two counterbalanced conditions according to convenience in scheduling test sessions. Ten subjects were tested in the speech-first condition, nine subjects in the nonspeech-first condition. During an initial session, all subjects were given familiarization on both stimulus series. Discrimination testing began the following day, after subjects were again familiarized with the task by listening to 10 triads of the first test without responding. The procedures in speech-first and nonspeech-first conditions were identical except for the order of presentation of the stimulus series for discrimination. For the speech-first subjects, the order for the first day was as follows: Speech Tests 1 and 2, Nonspeech Tests 1 and 2, Speech Tests 1 and 2, Nonspeech Tests 1 and 2. For nonspeech-first subjects, the order was reversed, i.e., Nonspeech Tests 1 and 2, Speech Tests 1 and 2, etc. The order of presentation on the second day of discrimination testing was the same as for Day 1 for each group. Both groups completed identification tests on the third day.

Subjects were tested in small groups (from one to four) in sessions which lasted about 2 h. Testing was conducted in a quiet experimental room. Stimuli were reproduced on a Crown CS 822 tape recorder and presented to subjects binaurally over Koss Pro-600A earphones. Signal levels were monitored with a Heathkit IM21 AC VTVM at the output to the earphones. Both speech and nonspeech stimuli were presented at a sound level approximately 70 dB above threshold. The playback amplitude for the nonspeech stimuli was increased to make the isolated F3 patterns equal in peak amplitude to the three-formant speech patterns. Thus, the amplitude of the isolated F3 patterns was far greater than the amplitude of the comparable F3 components *within* the three-formant patterns. However, the *total* signal for each set of stimuli was equal in amplitude and duration.

Americans II The 20 subjects were divided into two groups of 10 each according to convenience in scheduling test sessions. The groups were tested in two counterbalanced conditions, speech first and nonspeech first, in a manner similar to the Americans I, except for the following. While the Americans I groups were presented Speech and Nonspeech Tests 1 and 2 alternately within a single session of discrimination testing, the Americans II groups completed two repetitions of Tests 1 and 2 for the first stimulus series before proceeding to the other stimulus series. Thus, on Day 1 the speech-first group completed *two* repetitions of Speech Tests 1 and 2, then completed two repetitions of Nonspeech Tests 1 and 2. The order on Day 2 was identical to that of Day 1 for each group.

Another difference in procedure from the Americans I was in familiarization. For the Americans II groups, familiarization took place for each stimulus series just prior to the first discrimination test in that series. After discrimination tests were completed for the first series (i.e., Tests 1, 2, 1, 2), subjects were given familiarization on the other stimulus series and then proceeded with the tests. No familiarization was given on Day 2; subjects were merely reminded of the test procedure and told what series they would be listening to first.

Subjects were tested in a sound-attenuated experimental room using the same equipment and procedures as for the Americans I. Speech stimuli were presented at a sound level about 70 dB above threshold. Nonspeech stimuli were presented at −5 dB relative to the speech. (The absolute amplitude of the isolated F3 patterns was still far above that of the F3 component within the speech patterns.)

Japanese All 21 subjects were tested using the Americans II nonspeech-first presentation order. That is, the order on Day 1 was: nonspeech familiarization, Nonspeech Tests 1, 2, 1, 2, speech familiarization, Speech Tests 1, 2, 1, 2. Day 2 was the same as Day 1, except that no familiarization was given.

Subjects were tested individually in a sound-attenuated experimental room. Stimuli were reproduced on a TEAC-type tape recorder and presented to subjects binaurally over Iwatsu DR-305 stereo earphones. Speech stimuli and nonspeech stimuli were output from the tape recorder at about 74 and 76 dB above threshold, respectively. However, each subject adjusted the signal level at his earphones by means of an Ando SAL-20 attenuator, which had a range of 20 dB in 2-dB steps. Attenuation levels that subjects selected as "most comfortable" varied from −2 to −16 dB. The average listening level for speech was approximately 68 dB above threshold; for the nonspeech stimuli, the average was approximately 70 dB above threshold. Thus, as was the case for the American subjects, the isolated F3 patterns were heard at a much higher absolute level than the F3 component within the speech patterns.

Comparison of Results for Speech-First and Nonspeech-First Groups
The upper panel of figure 17.5 presents the results of speech discrimination tests for the Americans I speech-first and nonspeech-first groups. The major difference between the groups is their discrimination of comparison pairs within the "l" category. The nonspeech-first subjects were able to discriminate these pairs as accurately as they did the between-category pairs. This could not be predicted from their identification performance, which was very similar to that of the speech-first subjects. An inspection of individual subjects' functions showed that six of the nine subjects produced functions with the elevated with-"l" discrimination. The other three subjects produced functions similar to the speech-first results.

The lower panel of figure 17.5 presents the comparable discrimination results for the Americans II speech-first and nonspeech groups. Again, the only difference between the groups is their performance on the within-"l" comparison pairs. However, the differences is much smaller than for the Americans I subjects. The Americans II nonspeech-first subjects showed more nearly "categorical" performance; i.e., in spite of better discrimination of the within-"l" pairs than the within-"r" pairs, performance within either category was still inferior to that for between-category pairs.

Two differences in procedure might have contributed to the difference results for Americans I and Americans II nonspeech groups. First, recall that for the Americans I group, familiarization took place in a separate session the day before discrimination

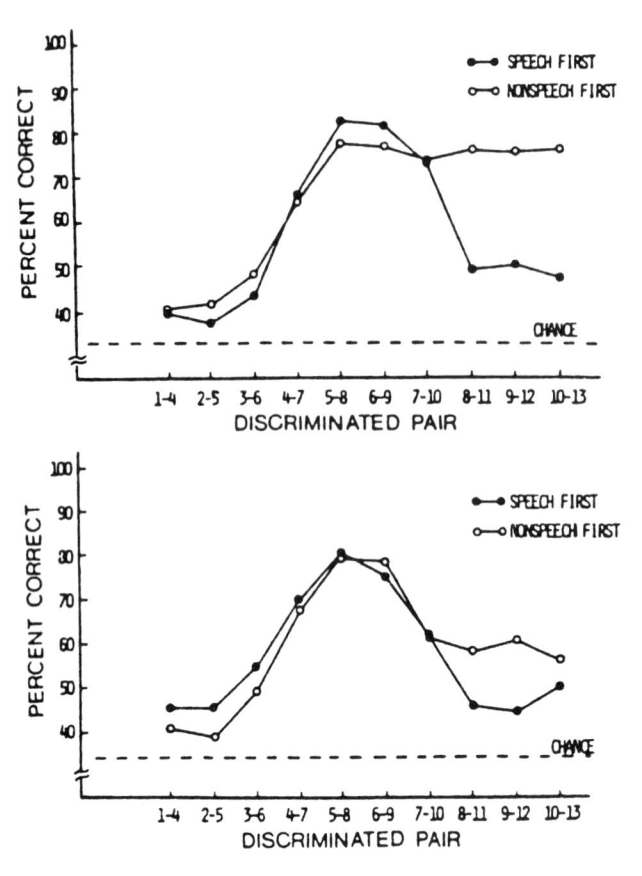

Figure 17.5
Pooled discrimination of speech stimuli for Americans I (upper graph) and Americans II (lower graph), speech-first and nonspeech-first conditions.

testing. Speech familiarization was always given before nonspeech familiarization. Thus, for these subjects, both nonspeech familiarization and testing (Tests 1 and 2) intervened between speech familiarization and the initial speech discrimination tests. In addition, both discrimination testing sessions began with the nonspeech stimuli. These factors apparently caused some "interference" in the speech discrimination task. Subjects may have adopted a "nonspeech" listening strategy, since they were told to use any criteria they could to discriminate the odd member of the triads. Once having established a strategy, the subjects seem to have maintained it throughout testing, since the data for the first and second halves of each day's testing, and the data for Day 1 and Day 2, are very consistent.

In contrast, the Americans II nonspeech-first group received their speech familiarization immediately prior to speech discrimination tests on the first day of testing. This might have helped to establish a "speech" listening strategy for these subjects. None of the 10 subjects produced speech functions like the Americans I nonspeech-group function, although most showed some elevation in discrimination of the within-"l" category pairs.

A second difference in procedure might have contributed in a related manner. The Americans I group switched from nonspeech to speech stimuli twice within a testing

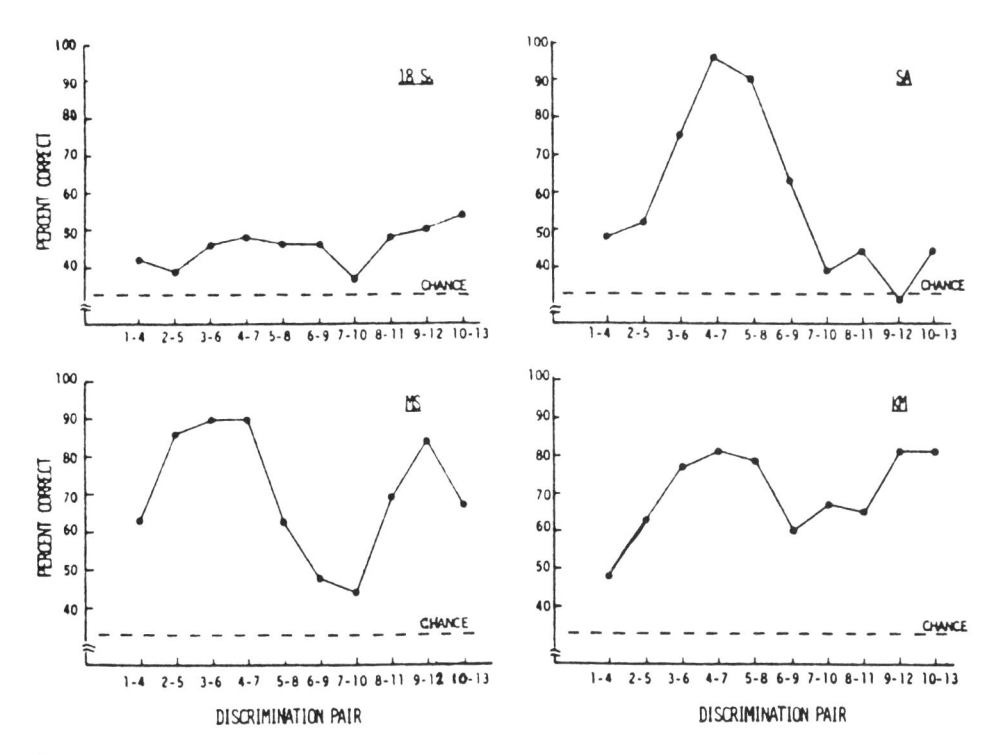

Figure 17.6
Pooled discrimination of speech stimuli by 18 Japanese subjects (upper left) and individual discrimination functions for three exceptional Japanese subjects. (See text for explanation of exceptional subjects.)

session, whereas the Americans II group completed all nonspeech tests before going on to speech tests. Again, the former procedure may have biased subjects toward a "nonspeech" listening strategy, whereas the latter procedure provided a clear distinction between the two series of stimuli. Additional support for the notion that the high discriminability of the within-"l" category pairs is a nonspeech phenomenon is given by the results of some of the Japanese subjects on the speech discrimination trials. The average curve for Japanese subjects climbs at the "l" end. (See figure 17.2.) Most of this is accounted for by five subjects whose individual discrimination functions showed relatively more accurate discrimination of Paris 8–11, 9–12, and 10–13.

The Japanese pooled data may be compared with the Americans II nonspeech-first group (compare figures 17.2 and 17.5), since the order of presentation is identical for the these groups. The difference in discrimination in the region of the Americans' category boundary is clearly present in this comparison.

Appendix B

The discrimination data for the three Japanese subjects who showed peaks of high discrimination are given in figure 17.6. As adolescents, K.M. and S.A. learned languages employing the phonemic distinction between [r] and [l]. M.S. did not. The upper left panel shows the pooled speech discrimination data for the remaining 18 Japanese subjects.

Notes

This research was supported by grants to the following: Haskins Laboratories, National Institute of Child Health and Human Development (HD-01994); the Center for Research in Human Learning, National Institute of Child Health and Human Development (HD-01136) and the National Science Foundation (GB 35703X); and James J. Jenkins, National Institute of Mental Health (MH-21153). Dr. Liberman received support from the Japan Society for the Promotion of Science for his contribution to this research. The authors wish to express their appreciation to Thomas Edman for testing the second group of American subjects and to Arthur Abramson and Leigh Lisker for their assistance in constructing the speech stimuli.

1. These two stimuli had such extreme values of F3 that some pilot subjects heard them as [ra], with a noisy glide superimposed on it.
2. Since Stimuli 14 and 15 were deleted from discrimination, the identification data for these stimuli were not included in the analysis.

References

Abramson, A. S., and Lisker, L. Discriminability along the voicing continuum: Cross-language tests. In *Proceedings of the 6th International Congress of Phonetic Sciences* (Prague, 1967). Prague: Academia, 1970. Pp. 569–573.

Delattre, P. C., Liberman, A. M., and Cooper, F. S. Acoustic loci and transitional cues for consonants. *Journal of the Acoustical Society of America*, 1955, 27, 769–773.

Eimas, P. D. Development aspects of speech perception. In R. Held, H. Leibowitz, and H. L. Teuber (Eds.), *Handbook of sensory physiology*. New York: Springer-Verlag, in press.

Fry, D. B., Abramson, A. S., Eimas, P. D., and Liberman, A. M. The identification and discrimination of synthetic vowels. *Language and Speech*, 1962, 5, 171–189.

Fujimura, O. Syllable as a unit of speech recognition. *IEEE Transactions on Acoustics, Speech, and Signal Processing*, 1975, 23, 82–87.

Fujisaki, H., and Kawashima, T. *On the modes and mechanisms of speech perception*. Research on Information Processing, Annual Report No. 2, University of Tokyo, Division of Electrical Engineering, Engineering Research Institute, 1969, 67–73.

Goto, H. Auditory perception by normal Japanese adults of the sounds "L" and "R." *Neuropsychologia*, 1971, 9, 317–323.

Heffener, R.-M. S. *General phonetics*. Madison: University of Wisconsin Press, 1952.

Jones, D. *An outline of English phonetics*. Cambridge Mass: Heffer, 1956.

Liberman, A. M., Cooper, F. S., Shankweiler, D. P., and Studdert-Kennedy, M. Perception of the speech code. *Psychological Review*, 1967, 74, 431–461.

Liberman, A. M., Harris, K. S., Hoffman, H. S., and Griffith, B. C. The discrimination of speech sounds within and across phoneme boundaries. *Journal of Experimental Psychology*, 1957, 54, 358–368.

Mattingly, I. G., Liberman, A. M., Syrdal, A. K., and Halwes, T. Discrimination in speech and nonspeech modes. *Cognitive Psychology*, 1971, 2, 131–157.

Miyawaki, K. *A preliminary study of American English /r/ by use of dynamic palatography*. Annual Bulletin, Research Institute of Logopedics and Phoniatrics, Faculty of Medicine, University of Tokyo, 1972, 6, 19–24.

Miyawaki, K. *A study of lingual articulation by use of dynamic palatography*. Masters thesis, Department of Linguistics, University of Tokyo, March 1973.

O'Connor, J. D., Gerstman, L. J., Liberman, A. M., Delattre, P. C., and Cooper, F. S. Acoustic cues for the perception of initial /w, j, r, l/ in English. *Word*, 1957, 13, 25–43.

Pisoni, D. B. Auditory and phonetic memory codes in the discrimination of consonants and vowels. *Perception & Psychophysics*, 1973, 13, 253–260.

Pisoni, D. B. Auditory short-term memory and vowel perception. *Memory & Cognition*, 1975, 3, 7–18.

Shankweiler, D. P., and Studdert-Kennedy, M. Identification of consonants and vowels presented to left and right ears. *Quarterly Journal of Experimental Psychology*, 1967, 19, 59–63.

Stevens, K. N., Liberman, A. M., Studdert-Kennedy, M., and Ohman, S. E. G. Cross-language study of vowel perception. *Language and Speech*, 1969, 12, 1–23.

Vinegrad, M. D. A direct magnitude scaling method to investigate categorical versus continuous modes of speech perception. *Language and Speech*, 1972, 15, 114–121.

Chapter 18
Some Experiments on the Sound of Silence in Phonetic Perception

Introduction

The several experiments to be reported here have in common a concern with silence as one of the cues for the perception of stop consonants. They were designed to illuminate further the processes by which that cue does its perceptual work.

That silence is important for the perception of stops has been established by several studies. Indeed, silence has been found to play a role in perceiving each of the three features—manner, voicing, and place—that a stop consonant comprises. Consider manner. By cutting and splicing magnetic tapes, Bastian, Eimas, and Liberman (1961) showed that the syllable "slit" is heard as "split" when a short interval of silence (about 40 ms) is introduced between the noise at the beginning of the syllable and the vocalic portion. As for voicing, Lisker (1957a) early found that intervocalic stops in trochees were perceived as voiced or voiceless (e.g., "rabid" or "rapid"), depending on the duration of silence between the syllables. Turning finally to place, we take account of the finding by Port (1976) that "rabid" is perceived as "ratted" when the duration of silence between the syllables is reduced.

Our experiments will deal only with the perception of stop-consonant manner. Taken together, and added (when appropriate) to the work of others, they are meant to bear on three related questions: (1) In what circumstances is silence a cue? (2) Does silence have its effect exclusively in the auditory domain, or also at some more abstract (phonetic) remove where perception is constrained as if by knowledge of what a vocal tract does when it makes linguistically significant gestures? (3) If the latter, then whose vocal tract provides the constraint?

Silence as a Necessary Condition before and after the Vowel; Perception of Transition Cues in Speech and Nonspeech Contexts

Evidence pointing to the importance of silence as a manner cue came first from experience with syllables in which a stop is (or is not) heard before the vocalic nucleus. Thus, in the early study by Bastian, Eimas, and Liberman (1961), the contrast was between "slit" and "split." Given similar phonetic contexts, the same effect is readily found, so readily indeed that it has become part of the lore of those who experiment with speech, and is taken into account in those formal rules that specify how speech is to be synthesized. In contrast, there is little information about the importance of

Originally published in *Journal of the Acoustical Society of America* 65, 6 (June 1979): 1518–1532, with Michael F. Dorman and Lawrence J. Raphael. Reprinted with permission.

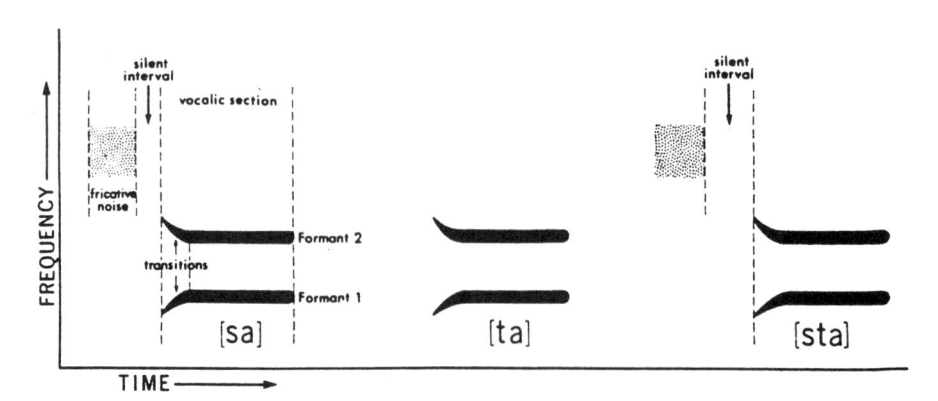

Figure 18.1
Schematic representation of stimulus patterns sufficient for the perception of [sa], [ta], and [sta]. Adapted from Liberman and Pisoni 1977.

silence as a manner cue for the perception of stops that follow the vocalic nucleus. We can infer, however, from an early observation by Lisker (1957a) and a more recent study by Abbs (1971) that a silent interval of some length must follow a vowel-stop syllable if the stop is to be perceived.

Our aim is to learn more about these phenomena. To that end, we will first assess the role of silence in the perception of stops (before the vowel) in the syllables [ʃpɛ] and [ʃkɛ] and (after the vowel) in the disyllables [bɛb dɛ], [bɛg dɛ] and [bɛd dɛ]. If, as we have reason to expect, silence proves to be important, we will use the results as a basis for further studies that might help us to understand why. Some of those will be reported in this section, others in the sections that follow.

To see what choices we face when we wonder why silence should be a cue for stops, we should first consider the perceptual consequences of altering the acoustic structure of the fricative-vowel syllable shown in figure 18.1: having recorded a naturally produced token of [sa], we find that removing the initial fricative noise will often leave a syllable that sounds like /da/ or [ta]; if we store the noise, but move it backward in time so as to leave a brief (say 50 ms) interval of silence between it and the vocalic portion of the syllable, we produce a syllable that sounds like [sta] (Bastian 1962). At one level of interpretation there is no mystery in this: the fricative [s] and the stop [t] have similar places of production, hence similar formant transitions. But it is not so clear why silence is necessary in order for the transition cues to give rise to the perception of a stop—that is, why a stop is not heard when fricative noise and formant transitions are separated by only a brief interval.

Broadly speaking, two interpretations are possible. The one we are inclined to favor is that the silence provides information to a (phonetic) perceiving device that is specialized to make appropriate use of it. To see why that is at least plausible, consider that a speaker cannot produce a stop without closing his vocal tract, and that he cannot close his vocal tract without producing a corresponding period of silence. When the listener hears an insufficiently long period of silence between the fricative noise and the vocalic section, it is, by this account, as if he "knew" that a stop should not be perceived because it was not produced.

An alternative interpretation puts the effect of the silence cue squarely in the auditory domain. Thus, we note about the example just offered, that it conforms to the paradigm for auditory forward masking. Conceivably, the fricative noise masks the transition cues that otherwise would be sufficient for the stops; in that case, the role of silence would be to provide time to evade masking. Or, keeping the interpretation still in the auditory domain, we might suppose that the silence collaborates in some kind of perceptual interaction with the transition cues, the result of the interaction being that experience we call a stop.

Some evidence relevant to these interpretations is already available. Harris (1958), for example, found recognition of [f]–[θ] contrast to be contingent primarily on the formant transitions that follow the fricative noise. This situation could only arise if the formant transitions had different effects in the auditory domain—that is, if they were not masked by the preceding noise. Evidence from dichotic listening supports this conclusion. Thus, Darwin (1971) found a larger right-ear advantage for fricatives synthesized with appropriate formant transitions following the fricative noise, than for fricatives synthesized without formant transitions. In this instance, too, the transitions must have had different auditory representations when they arrived at the central processing mechanisms responsible for the ear advantage.

Another pieces of relevant evidence comes from a study of selective adaption. Following a now standard adaptation procedure, Ganong (1975) first measured the displacement of [bɛ–dɛ] boundary caused by adaptation with [dɛ]. Fricative noise was then placed in front of the [dɛ], and the (perceived) [sɛ] that resulted was used as the adapting stimulus. The outcome was a shift in the [bɛ–dɛ] boundary as large as that found when the adapting stimulus was [dɛ]. Patterns that contained the noise, but not the formant transitions, did not produce so large a shift. This indicates not only that the transition cues were getting through, but that they were getting through in full strength.

Thus, we are led to believe that the transition cues make a significant perceptual contribution, whether or not they are preceded by a period of silence. On that view, silence is important, not because it provides time to evade masking, or because it collaborates in an auditory interaction, but because it provides information that is essential to determining how the transitions are to be interpreted in phonetic perception.

The experiments in this section are designed to get at that matter via a different—perhaps more direct—route by comparing the effect of the fricative noise on transition cues that are, in one case, in a speech context, and in the other, not. The results will bear, of course, on a masking interpretation, but also on the possibility of auditory interactions, since we will be able to determine whether or not there are qualitative changes in the perception of the nonspeech transition cues depending on the presence or absence of the silence.

Experiment 1
Our first experiment was designed (1) to assess the role of silence in the perception of stop manner prevocalically in the syllables [ʃpɛ] and [ʃkɛ], and (2) to determine whether the fricative noise of [ʃ] masks or interacts with information carried on the transition cues for the stops when those are isolated from the rest of the syllable and are heard as nonspeech.

Method Two sets of stimuli were made. Members of the one—to be referred to as the "speech" stimuli—were appropriate for determining the effect of silence on the perception of the stop consonants in [ʃpɛ] and [ʃkɛ]. They were made in the following way. First, syllables [ʃɛ], [gɛ], and [bɛ] were recorded by a male speaker, then

328   Chapter 18

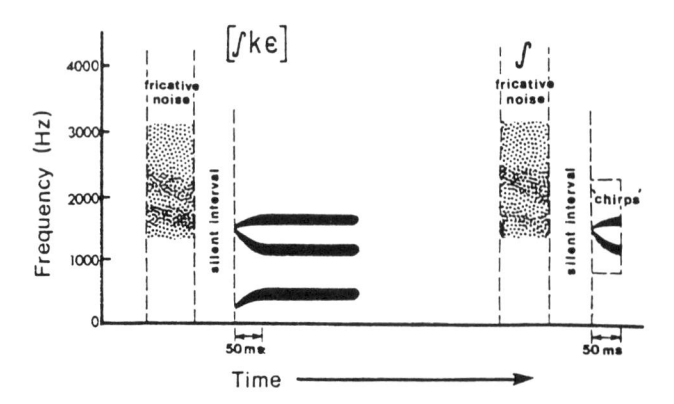

Figure 18.2
(a) Schematic representation of one of the speech patterns used in experiment 1. (b) Schematic representation of the corresponding nonspeech ("chirp") pattern.

digitized and stored, using the Pulse Code Modulation (PCM) system at Haskins Laboratories.[1] Working from high-resolution oscillograms, and taking advantage of computer control, we next separated the fricative noise of the [ʃ] from the vocalic portion of the syllable [ʃɛ], and removed the syllable-initial bursts from the [gɛ] and [bɛ]. To create the experimental stimuli, we prefixed the ʃ noise to what remained of the [bɛ] and [gɛ], leaving silent intervals of 0, 4, 8, 12, 16, 20, 40, 60, 80, and 100 ms between the offset of the fricative noise and the vocalic section appropriate for [gɛ] and [bɛ] [see figure 18.2(a) for a schematic representation of one of the ʃ noise plus [gɛ] stimuli]. Four tokens of each stimulus type were produced. These were randomized and recorded on magnetic tape with a 3-s interval between stimuli.

Members of the other set—to be referred to as the "nonspeech" stimuli—were intended to enable us to measure the extent to which the transition cues that distinguish the stops in [ʃpɛ] and [ʃkɛ] are themselves masked by the ʃ noise. These stimuli were made in the following way. First, the [bɛ] and [gɛ] patterns of the speech set were bandpass filtered between 0.9 and 3.5 kHz, and truncated so as to include only the first 50 ms of the signal. This procedure eliminated the first formant, producing signals that contained only the second- and third-formant transitions. (Listeners could hear these stimuli as "chirps," and we supposed that with only a few minutes of practice they would be able to identify them by pitch as "low" or "high.") Then, to create a test of the identifiability of these transitions for comparison with the condition in which they were the essential cues for place of articulation, we prefixed the ʃ noise, setting the same intervals of silence between it and the chirps that we had used in creating the "speech" stimuli. [See figure 18.2(b) for a schematic representation of the "chirp" stimulus derived from the "speech" stimulus shown in figure 18.2(a).] The resulting signals were randomized and recorded on magnetic tape with a 3-s interval between stimuli.

The subjects were nine volunteers, all undergraduates at Lehman College, who had not previously served in experiments on speech perception. Divided into groups of five and four, they listened in a sound-attenuated room, first to the speech stimuli, and then in a second session, to the "nonspeech" stimuli. In the speech condition, the listeners were told they would hear approximations of the syllables [ʃpɛ], [ʃkɛ], and

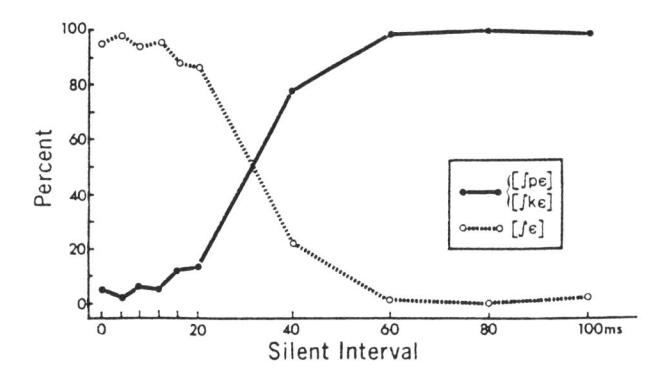

Figure 18.3
Silence as a necessary condition for stop manner; identification of stimulus patterns as [ʃpɛ] – [ʃkɛ] or [ʃɛ].

[ʃɛ], and were asked to indicate on a printed response sheet what they had heard. To provide some "practice," we presented twenty of the stimuli before the experiment proper began; no information was given about the "correctness" of the responses.

In the "nonspeech" condition, the subjects were told they would hear tokens of three stimulus types: ʃ noise alone, ʃ noise followed by a low-pitched chirp (which they were to call "low"), or ʃ noise followed by a high-pitched chirp (which they were to call "high"). They were asked to indicate on their response sheets what they had heard. In this condition, the "practice" consisted of presenting 50 of the stimuli. In order to make sure the subjects did, in fact, learn to identify the chirps, we provided knowledge of results. To preclude biasing the experimental outcome by experience during the practice sessions, we avoided all short silent intervals—in which the chirps might or might not be heard—presenting only those stimuli in which the noise preceded the chirps by 100 ms. During the experimental session, no information about "correct" responses was given.

In both "speech" and "nonspeech" conditions the stimuli were reproduced via a Revox 1240 tape recorder and AR-4x loudspeaker.

Results and Discussion The results for the speech condition are shown in figure 18.3. Since the identification functions for [ʃpɛ] and [ʃkɛ] were found on preliminary examination to have similar shapes, we have averaged them; this facilitates comparison with identification function for [ʃɛ]. We see that when the silent interval was less than 20 ms, listeners reported hearing [ʃɛ]—that is to say, they did not hear a stop. The stops were identified with 75 percent accuracy only when the silent interval exceeded about 40 ms. Thus, we find silence to be an important condition for the perception of stops in fricative-stop-vowel syllables.

The identification functions shown in figure 18.3 were derived from the responses of seven of the nine subjects. The two other subjects identified the ʃ noise plus [gɛ] stimuli in the same manner as the group of seven, but made a total of only one [ʃɛ] response to the ʃ noise plus [bɛ] stimuli. To account for that we should consider that in the case of [ʃpɛ] the places of articulation signaled by the fricative noise and the vocalic transitions were quite different, the former being palatal and the latter bilabial. In our own listening to these patterns, it seemed that when there was little silence between ʃ noise and [bɛ], we heard [ʃɛ], but with a nonspeech chirp—as if the transitions could not be integrated into the phonetic percept but were audible nevertheless.

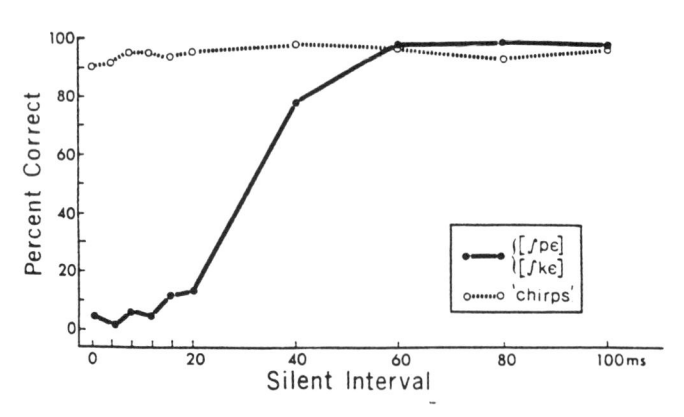

Figure 18.4
Percent correct identification of the transition cues in the speech ([ʃpɛ]–[ʃkɛ]) and nonspeech (chirps) contexts.

It is possible that our subjects, hearing the same chirp, elected to call these stimuli [ʃpɛ]. In the case of ʃ noise plus [gɛ] the disparity in place of articulation was not so great, and it is perhaps for that reason that when the ʃ noise was moved close to the [gɛ] we, and all our subjects, heard only [ʃɛ]. Indeed, the disparity in place of articulation can be reduced even further, as it is, for example, in the case of s-noise plus [ta] that we described in the introduction. There, the places of articulation for the fricative and stop are exactly the same, and the [sa] that results from putting the fricative noise close to the vocalic section is virtually indistinguishable from one that is produced by a human speaker who articulates in a perfectly normal way.

We should emphasize that the interval of silence necessary for stop perception in fricative-stop-vowel syllables is not invariant. Indeed, from the early work of Bastian (1962) and from recent work by Bailey, Summerfield, and Dorman (in preparation) and by Summerfield and Bailey (1977), we know that the interval varies according to how several other cues are set. These include, at the least, the duration of the fricative noise, the rate of fricative noise offset, the rise time of the amplitude envelope of the vocalic portion of the syllable, and the starting frequency of the first-formant transition. (We discuss the importance of such relations among cues more fully below.)

We should also emphasize that we do not mean to imply that listeners cannot discriminate between a naturally produced [ʃɛ] and one composed of ʃ noise followed at a brief interval by [gɛ] (or [bɛ]). As we pointed out above, in these cases a listener may hear a normal [ʃɛ] or [ʃɛ] with a nonspeech chirp in it. Now we should add that for some articulations of [gɛ] a fricative noise placed just in front will cause a listener to perceive [ʃjɛ] (Liberman and Pisoni 1977). The point we wish to make is that listeners do not in such cases commonly report a stop.

Redirecting our attention to experiment 1, we see in figure 18.4 that the results of the nonspeech condition are quite different from those of the speech condition. The isolated formant transitions taken from [bɛ] and [gɛ] were clearly audible—indeed, highly identifiable—as chirps at all intervals of silence, even zero. That outcome is wholly consistent with the evidence presented at the introduction to this section in that transition cues that follow fricative noise are nonetheless effective as auditory events, whether separated from the noise or not. As for the possibility that the transition cues somehow interact with silence, there had previously been no data that were directly relevant. Now we see in the results of our experiment a suggestion that such auditory interaction does not occur: Our subjects not only heard the nonspeech transitions (no matter how close they were to the fricative noise), but they correctly identified them as well; moreover, our own listening made it plain that, more generally, the fricative noise did not appreciably affect the perception of the nonspeech transitions in any qualitative way.

Experiments 2a and 2b
In the previous experiment we found silence to be a necessary condition for the perception of stops in prevocalic position. The experiments reported here were designed to find out if silence is also a necessary condition for the perception of stops in postvocalic position. There were two such experiments, divided according to purpose and the nature of the stimuli.

In one experiment (2a), the stimuli were the synthetic disyllables [bɛb dɛ] and [bɛg dɛ], so made as to provide variation in the interval of silence between the first and second syllables. Given the hypothesis that underlies all the experiments of this paper, we should expect that a relatively long silence would be essential if the listener is to perceive both the syllable-final [b] and [g] and the syllable-initial [d], since a speaker must close his vocal tract for a longer period to say [bɛb dɛ] or [bɛg dɛ] then to say [bɛ dɛ], [bɛ bɛ], or [bɛ gɛ]. Pilot work revealed that with reductions in the duration of the silent interval, it was the syllable-final stops [b] and [g] that disappeared; the syllable-initial [d] could be heard even at very short intervals of silence. This may be owing, in part, to the fact that, in production, the [d], and especially the flapped [d], requires very little closure (Port 1976), and in part, perhaps, to the fact that unreleased syllable-final stops tend to be relatively unintelligible at best. At all events, it is the syllable-final stops that are, in the kinds of patterns we used, the more sensitive to variations in the duration of intersyllablic silence.

As in the experiments with prevocalic stops, we though it useful to provide data relevant to the possibility that the outcome is to be accounted for in terms of masking—backward masking in the case of the postvocalic stops—or auditory interaction. To that end, we determined whether silence is also necessary for the perception of the formant transitions that are sufficient to distinguish the syllable-final stops when those transitions are presented in isolation, and sound like chirps.

In the other experiment (2b), the stimuli were natural speech, not synthetic, and they included not only [bɛb dɛ] and [bɛg dɛ] but also the geminate condition [bɛd dɛ].[2] The use of natural speech will permit a comparison with the results obtained when the stimuli were synthetic. The point of testing the geminate condition is that, in production, the articulatory closure for the geminate stops is longer than that for single stops, and a study by Pickett and Decker (1960) leads us to suspect that the amount of silence necessary for perception may also be longer. A comparison of the two cases of syllable-final stops seemed, therefore, to be in order.

Method To produce stimuli for experiment 2a—the one with synthetic stimuli—we used the Haskins Laboratories parallel-resonance synthesizer to generate two-formant patterns appropriate for the disyllables [bɛb dɛ] and [bɛg dɛ]. A schematic representation of [bɛb dɛ] is shown in figure 18.5. That disyllable differed from the other one [bɛg dɛ] in the second-formant transition, the sole cue in these patterns for the perceived distinction between the syllable-final stops: for [b] the transition is falling,

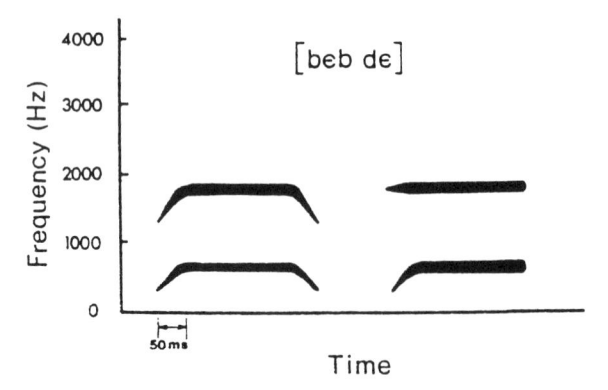

[Figure: Schematic spectrogram showing two formant patterns labeled [bɛb dɛ], with frequency (Hz) on y-axis from 0 to 4000, and time on x-axis with a 50 ms scale bar.]

Figure 18.5
Schematic representation of one of the stimulus patterns for experiment 2a.

as shown in the figure, while for [g] it is rising. We then introduced periods of silence between the second syllable [dɛ] and the first syllable [bɛb] or [bɛg]. These periods ranged from 0 to 150 ms in steps of 10 ms. Four tokens of each stimulus were generated. To produce a test sequence appropriate for presentation to our subjects, we put these stimuli into a random sequence with a 3-s interval between successive stimuli. That test sequence was used in what will be referred to as the "speech" condition.

To produce the corresponding stimuli for the "nonspeech" condition, we simply isolated the second-formant transitions that alone distinguished the [bɛb] and [bɛg] patterns of the "speech" stimuli (falling for [b], rising for [g]), and then produced stimuli that were otherwise identical with those of the "speech" condition—that is, we placed after the isolated transitions the same synthetic [dɛ] that had been used in the "speech" condition, and introduced between it and the transitions the same intervals of silence.

The subjects for experiment 2a were six undergraduates at Lehman College who had previously participated in experiments on speech perception. They were tested individually. Test order ("speech" versus "nonspeech") was counterbalanced across subjects. In the "speech" condition, the subjects were asked to respond [bɛb dɛ], [bɛg dɛ], or [bɛ dɛ], and to write their responses. To familiarize the subjects with the stimuli, we had them listen to twenty of the patterns before the experiment began. The stimuli were reproduced on a Revox 1240 tape recorder via TDH 39 headphones.

In the "nonspeech" condition, the subjects were told they would hear a high-pitched chirp followed by [dɛ], a low-pitched chirp followed by [dɛ], or [dɛ] alone. They were asked to respond accordingly. To teach the subjects to identify the chirps, and to make sure they could reliably do so, we first presented fifty [b] and [g] chirps in random order with feedback of results. Then we presented, also in random order, twenty-five [b] and [g] chirps followed in each case, after a 120 ms interval, by [dɛ]. Again, subjects were told the correct answers after they had made their responses. The point of using only the 120-ms interval was to avoid biasing the results by providing "correct" responses in those cases where the [dɛ] syllable was sufficiently close that "masking" might conceivably have occurred. Finally, the test proper was begun.

The procedures for experiment 2b—the one that included the geminate case and was done with natural speech—were as follows. Having recorded a male speaker

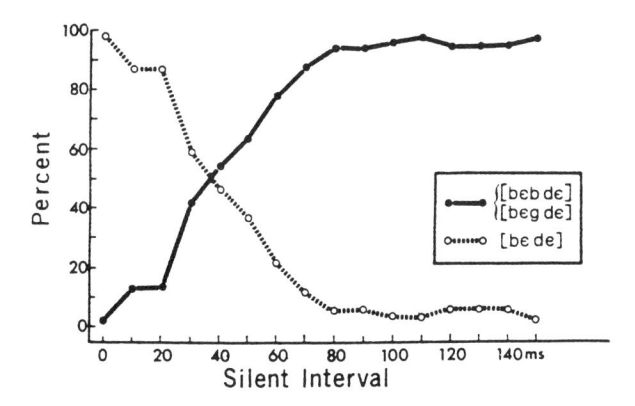

Figure 18.6
Silence as a necessary condition for stop manner; identification of stimulus patterns as [bɛb dɛ]–[bɛg dɛ], or [bɛ dɛ].

saying [bɛb], [bɛd], [bɛg], and [dɛ], we used the editing facilities provided by the Haskins Laboratories PCM systems to truncate closure voicing following the syllable-final transitions to 15 ms. To each of the syllables [bɛb], [bɛd] and [bɛg], we then appended the syllable [dɛ], separating it from [bɛb], [bɛd], or [bɛg] by periods of silence that ranged from 0 to 90 ms in steps of 10 ms. Three tokens of each stimulus were generated. These were randomized and recorded onto tape with 4-s interval between stimuli.

The subjects for this experiment were eight volunteers, all undergraduates at Lehman College who had not previously served in speech-perception studies. They were asked to identify each of the stimuli as [bɛb dɛ], [bɛb dɛ], [bɛd dɛ], or [bɛ dɛ] and, in writing their responses, to include the entire syllable. There was a preliminary "practice" session in which the subjects heard and identified twenty stimulus patterns. The signals were produced in the manner described in experiment 1.

Results and Discussion The effect of silence on the perception of syllable-final stops in synthetic [bɛb dɛ] and [bɛg dɛ] (experiment 2a) is shown in figure 18.6. There we have plotted the average [bɛb dɛ] and [bɛg dɛ] responses for comparison with the [bɛ dɛ] responses. (The identification functions for [bɛb dɛ] and [bɛg dɛ] were similar, so we have collapsed them into a single function.) One sees that, over the range 0 to about 30 ms of intersyllabic silence, the predominant response was [bɛ dɛ]—that is, our subjects did not report a syllable-final stop.[3] We should emphasize that, as in the experiment on prevocalic stops, it was not the case that a subject heard a stop but misidentified it; rather, he simply did not hear it. A silent interval of about 58 ms was necessary before the subjects identified the stops with 75 percent accuracy. Thus, for the perception of stops in postvocalic position, as for those that were prevocalic, silence is important.

It will be remembered that we were also concerned with how the isolated formant transitions of the syllable-final [b] and [g] (nonspeech condition) are affected when the stimulus patterns are otherwise exactly the same as in the speech condition just reported. The results of the nonspeech condition are shown in figure 18.7. We note, first, that no subject used the response "no chirp"—that is, no subject ever failed to hear a chirp, even when there was no silence between the chirp and the syllable. This

334 Chapter 18

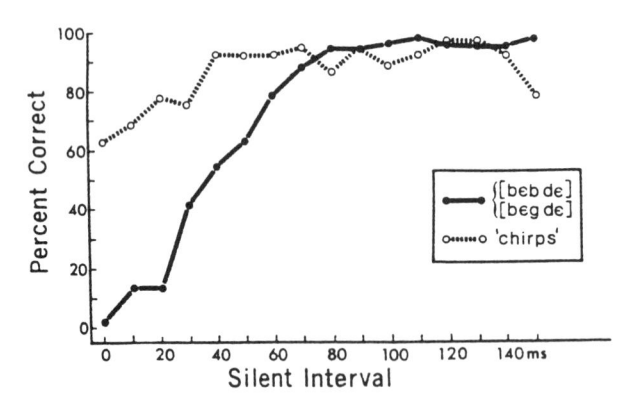

Figure 18.7
Percent correct identification of the transition cues in the speech [(bɛb dɛ]-[bɛg dɛ]) and nonspeech (chirps) contexts.

is dramatically different from the result obtained in the "speech" condition. There, given comparable conditions, our subjects did not hear the corresponding syllable-final stops at all. Looking at the percent correct identification of the chirps, we see that at the shortest intervals of silence identification is less accurate than at the longest intervals. Indeed, this difference in accuracy is significant ($F = 2.07$, $p < 0.05$). We should note, however, that even at the brief intervals our listeners averaged about 70 percent correct. Thus, it does not appear that backward masking can account for the complete absence of the stop percept at brief silent intervals.

We turn now to the results of experiment 2b. It will be recalled that this experiment differed from the previous one in that the geminate condition was included, and natural rather than synthetic speech was used. Let us first compare the results obtained with natural speech and with synthetic speech. For that purpose we will look only at the data pertaining to syllable-final [b] and [g], omitting the geminate condition. These are shown in figure 18.8, together with the comparable data (from figure 18.7) for synthetic speech. The results are quite similar—in both conditions some interval of silence is necessary for listeners to identify a stop. However, the duration of that interval does differ by about 15 ms between the two conditions. We should suppose that this difference is due to variation between the conditions in the "settings" of the cues (for stop manner) other than silence, e.g., formant transitions.

Turning now to the comparison between geminate and nongeminate stops, we see in figure 18.9 that subjects needed a longer silent interval to identify syllable-final [d] than [b] or [g];[4] even at the longest interval the identification of [d] reached only 38 percent correct. Further research by Repp (1976) suggests that an interval of approximately 200 ms is necessary for listeners to identify the syllable-final stop in a sequence of identical stops (see also Pickett and Decker 1960; Fujisaki, Nakamura, and Imoto 1975). This result is then another piece of evidence that speaks against an explanation of the perceptual disappearance of the syllable-final stops in terms of recognition masking, for one would be hard-pressed to explain why syllable-initial [d] should "backward-mask" syllable-final [d] over a period four times longer than it masks [b], or [g].

More direct evidence that syllable-final transitions are not "backward masked" is also to be found in studies by Repp (1976, 1976). Having presented to listeners

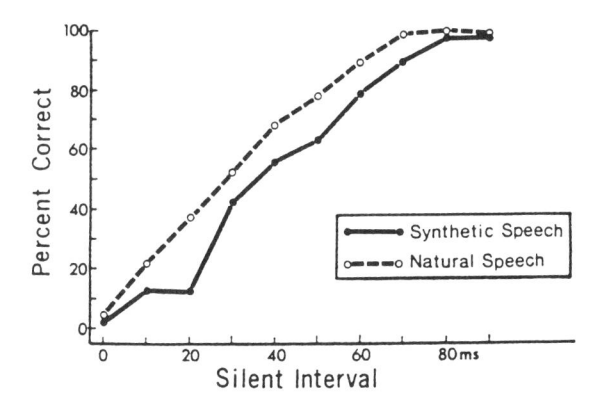

Figure 18.8
Identification functions for syllable-final stops in synthetic and natural speech.

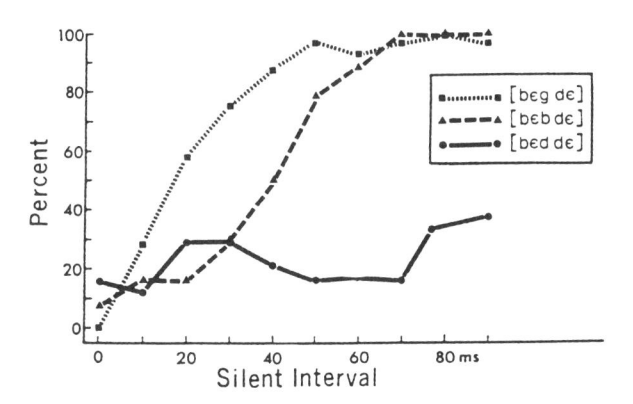

Figure 18.9
Identification of syllable-final stops in geminate ([bɛd dɛ]) and nongeminate ([bɛb dɛ] and [bɛg, dɛ]) conditions.

VCV's that had been synthesized with and without syllable-final transitions, he found, in the case of stimuli without syllable-final transitions, that the time required to identify the medial consonant increased as a function of the duration of the closure interval; in the case of stimuli with syllable-final transitions, however, the time required was more nearly constant (Repp 1976). Clearly, then, the syllable-final transitions had a perceptual effect even though they were not heard as discrete phonetic events. This same conclusion can be drawn from another experiment by Repp (1976). In that experiment the syllable [dɛ] was preceded, in the one case, by [ad], in the other case by [ab]. In both cases the listeners perceived [adɛ]. Nevertheless, they discriminated between the stimuli at a level slightly better than chance.

Returning now to our own results, we conclude from experiments 2a and 2b that, just as silence is important for the perception of stops in prevocalic position, so also is it important for the perception of stops in postvocalic position. Moreover, the results are consistent with the evidence presented in the Introduction—namely, that silence is important, not because it provides time to evade masking or because it enters into an auditory interaction, but rather because it provides information about the behavior of a vocal tract.

Silence as a Sufficient Condition before and after the Vowel; Perceptual Equivalence of Silence and Sound

In the studies so far described, stops were (or were not) perceived in patterns that contained transition cues appropriate for stop manner. Now we shall turn to cases in which the transition cues are absent, and it is left to the power of the silence cue itself to produce the effect of a stop. We should note that even in the early study by Bastian, Eimas, and Liberman (1961), silence might have borne the entire burden, but we cannot be sure because the procedures of cutting and splicing the magnetic tape may have introduced a transient, which of itself could contribute to the perception of a stop. We should also note that others (Summerfield and Bailey 1977), working independently of us, have recently demonstrated the power of silence to cue stop manner prevocalically in the context of fricative-vowel versus fricative-stop-vowel, e.g., [si] versus [ski], where the vocalic section alone is, by perceptual test, not sufficient to produce the stop. At all events, we, too, wish to test the silence cue in such circumstances, and to do it for several positions in the syllable: in prevocalic position ("slit" versus "split"); in intervocalic position ("say shop" versus "say chop," the affricate "ch" [tʃ] being taken here as a stop-initiated fricative); and in postvocalic position ("dish" versus "ditch"). The results may throw more light on the role of silence in the perception of stop manner, since in these instances there are no obvious transition cues to be masked. They will also provide the basis for further investigations into the reasons why silence should have a role in stop perception at all.

To see the point of one of these further investigations we should recall that, as we have supposed, the role of silence might be to tell the listener that the speaker either did or did not close his vocal tract appropriately for the production of a stop consonant. But to make that suggestion is to imply that our perception of speech is constrained to some degree by a device that acts as if it knew what vocal tracts can and cannot do when they make linguistically relevant gestures; or, more generally, that there is, in speech, a link between perception and production. Further evidence for such a link comes, for example, from studies that have established an equivalence in phonetic perception between cues that are very different from an acoustic (and presumably auditory) point of view, but which are the correlated results of the same articulatory gesture. One of the earliest of these is of special interest to us because it dealt with silence, albeit as a cue to voicing rather than manner (Lisker 1957b). The context was that of "rabid" versus "rapid." The results were (1) that variation in the duration of intersyllabic silence was sufficient to cue the voicing distinction between the two words, and (2) that the location of the voicing boundary on the continuum of intersyllabic silence varied as a function of whether the stimuli were synthesized, say, with or without a transition of the first formant at the end of the first syllable. Thus, cues with different acoustic properties were nevertheless found to be equivalent in phonetic perception: Just as stimuli characterized by the presence of a transition of the first formant and a relatively long silent interval were heard as "rapid," so also were stimuli characterized by the absence of a transition of the first formant and a shorter silent interval. We should ask now why silence should give rise to the same phonetic percept as the frequency modulation of the first-formant transition. The answer is surely hard to find so long as we think in terms of what we know, or can surmise, about auditory perception. But in articulation we find the tie that binds: These acoustically dissimilar events are both to be found among the many acoustic consequences of the gesture that converts "rabid" to "rapid." There are other, equally diverse acoustic consequences of the gesture, and these, too, according to the results of the early study and its current extensions (Lisker 1977) have an equivalence in phonetic perception.

Since articulatory gestures commonly have multiple and diverse acoustic consequences, we should expect to find many cases of such perceptual equivalence among acoustically dissimilar cues. To be sure, there is no problem in finding such cases; they abound, and have been studied for all three phonetic dimensions: manner, voicing, and place. (For a review, see Liberman and Studdert-Kennedy 1979). In the third experiment of this section we examine one additional case. Taking advantage of the fact that the stop gesture which differentiates fricative from affricate in "ditch" versus "dish" generates changes in both the duration of the silent closure interval and changes in the onset and duration of the fricative noise, we examine the perceptual equivalence between silence, on the one hand, and, on the other, the rise time of the friction and also its duration.

Experiment 3
Our third experiment was designed to determine whether the perception of "split" could be induced by inserting silence between the fricative noise of [s] and the syllable "lit." Is silence, in this sense, a sufficient condition for the perception of stop manner, and, if so, over what range of durations is silence effective? The second question is interesting because we know that neither a very brief nor a very long closure is appropriate for stop manner. A too-brief closure would presumably indicate that the speaker had not closed his vocal tract long enough to have said "split." A too-long closure, on the other hand, would suggest that he had produced the "s," then waited a while, and finally said "lit." That being so, we would suppose that only a limited range of silent intervals would signal the production of stop manner.

Method A male speaker's recordings of the fricative noise of [s] and the syllable "lit" were digitized and stored in computer memory. (Both segments were produced in isolation.) Having listened carefully to these segments, we judged that the noise of the [s] did not end with a stop, nor did the "lit" begin with a stop. Using the editing facilities provided by the Haskins Laboratories PCM system, we then appended the "s noise" to the "lit," separating these two segments by intervals of silence that ranged from 0 to 100 ms in steps of 15 ms, and from 100 to 650 ms in steps of 50 ms. Three tokens of each stimulus were generated. The resulting stimuli were randomized and recorded on audio tape with a 3-s interval between stimuli. The listeners were instructed to label the stimuli as "slit," "split," or "s" followed by "lit." (The last named category is not "slit," but rather "s" plus "lit," with a clearly perceptible period of silence in between.)

The subjects were ten volunteers, all undergraduates at Lehman College who had not previously served in experiments on speech perception. They were tested in two groups of five, each under conditions similar to those of experiment 1. To familiarize the listeners with the stimuli, we had them listen to the entire stimulus continuum before the test sequence began.

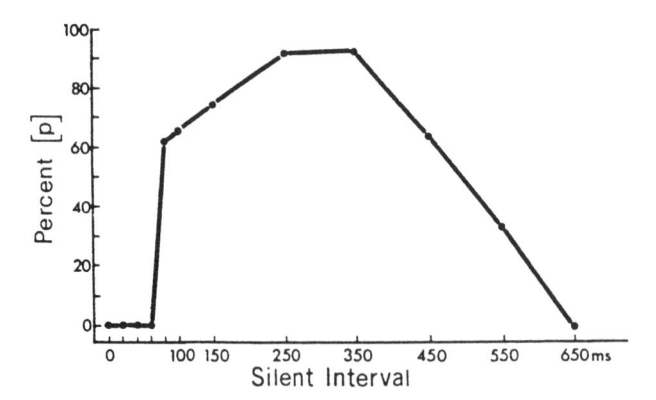

Figure 18.10
Silence as a sufficient condition of stop manner; identification of [p] in patterns composed of "s" followed by "lit."

Results and Discussion The effect of inserting intervals of silence between the "s-noise" and [lit] is shown in figure 18.10. There we see that at silent intervals of less than 60 ms listeners reported "slit," but at longer intervals—out to about 450 ms—they reported "split." In this case, then, silence is a sufficient condition for stop manner. Notice, however, that at the longest silent interval the stop was not heard; rather, the subjects reported "s-silence-lit." Thus, neither the very brief nor the very long silent intervals produced a stop percept. This outcome accords well with our earlier supposition that only a limited range of silent intervals should signal stop manner.

Experiment 4
To this point we have investigated silence as a condition for the perception of stop manner. Now we turn to silence as a condition for affricate manner. To see why, consider that just as a speaker must close his vocal tract to produce the stop that distinguishes, for example, [sta] from [sa], so also must he close his vocal tract to produce the stop-initiated fricative (i.e., affricate) that distinguishes, for example, the phrase "say chop" from "say shop." There is evidence, moreover, that the silence associated with vocal-tract closure is a cue for the affricate-fricative contrast in intervocalic position. This evidence comes from early experiments with synthetic speech (Kuypers 1955; Truby 1955). The purpose of the experiment to be described here is to replicate and expand these early findings. Specifically, we aim to determine whether silence can be a sufficient condition for the fricative-affricate contrast in the naturally produced utterances "say shop" and "say chop."

Method A male speaker's recording of "please say shop" was digitized and stored in computer memory. Using the editing facilities provided by the Haskins Laboratories PCM system, we removed the initial 15 ms of ʃ noise from "shop." The signal that remained still sounded to us like "shop."

We should note parenthetically that in situations of this kind, where there are presumably a number of different cues for the same distinction, it often happens that relatively extreme "settings" of one of the cues will cause the other cues to be "overridden" in perception. For example. in this case, we have reason to believe that the

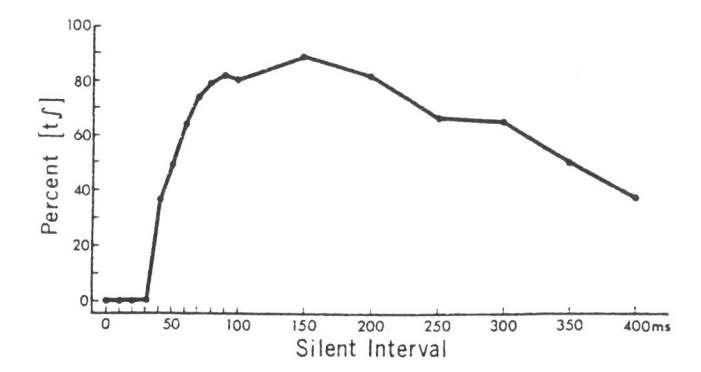

Figure 18.11
Silence as a sufficient condition for affricate manner; identification of [tʃ] in patterns composed of "please say" followed by "shop."

duration and onset of the fricative noise, as well as silence, are cues to the affricate-fricative distinction (see Gerstman 1957). Very long fricative noise, especially when combined with slow onset, may so bias perception toward the fricative that no amount of the silence cue can be effective.

To generate our experimental stimuli we inserted intervals of silence between the offset of "please say" and the onset of "shop." These intervals covered the range 0 to 400 ms. The steps were 10 ms each from 0 to 100 ms and 50 ms each from 100 to 400 ms. Four tokens of each stimulus were generated. The resulting stimuli were randomized and recorded on audio tape with a 4-s interval between stimuli.

The subjects were ten volunteers, all undergraduates at Lehman College who had not previously participated in experiments on speech perception. They were tested en masse under listening conditions similar to those of experiment 1. The subjects were told they would hear either "please say shop" or "please say chop," and were instructed to write either "shop" or "chop" on their response sheets. To familiarize them with the experimental stimuli, we played twenty of the stimuli before the test sequence began.

Results and Discussion   The effect of varying the duration of the silent interval between "please say" and "shop" is shown in figure 18.11. We see that "chop" responses begin to appear when the silent interval exceeds about 30 ms; by 70 ms they account for 75 percent of the responses. Thus, we conclude that silence can be a sufficient cue for distinguishing the affricate [tʃ] from the fricative [ʃ]. We should remark that, according to preliminary research we have done, the contrast between the voiced counterparts of those phones (i.e., [dʒ] and [ʒ]) can also be cued by silence.

Redirecting our attention to the data for the voiceless forms shown in figure 18.11, we see that at the very long intervals of silence there is a tendency for our listeners' perceptions to revert to the fricative [ʃ]. This tendency is similar to that we saw in the case of silence as a cue for stop manner in the contrast "split" versus "slit" (cf. figure 18.10), but it is not so marked. In that connection we note that the longest silent interval for the present experiment with "shop" and "chop" was 400 ms, whereas for the earlier experiment with "slit" and "split" it was 650 ms. When we examine the identification functions for "slit" versus "split," we see that at 400 ms our listeners' responses had only just begun to revert to "s-silence-lit." Presumably, then, in the present experiment, the "chop" responses would have reverted more nearly to "shop" had we carried the silent interval to greater lengths.

Having seen that we convert the utterance "please say shop" into "please say chop" by appropriately increasing the silent interval between "say" and "shop," we should wonder whether we can start with the utterance "please say chop" and convert it to "please say shop" by shortening the silence. The results from preliminary research suggests that this can, indeed, be done, though just how convincingly depends upon the "intensity" of the affricate articulation in "chop" (Raphael and Dorman 1977). Of course this is analogous to the results obtained in experiments 1 and 2, where too little silence caused stops not to be heard.

Experiment 5a and 5b
Having found silence to be sufficient for the perception of affricate manner in syllable-initial position ("shop" versus "chop"), we now wish to determine whether it can be sufficient in syllable-final position, as in "dish" versus "ditch." We also wish in these experiments to examine the effects of two other cues for affricate manner—namely, the duration and rise time of the fricative noise (see Gerstman 1957)—and to study such relations as there may be between these two cues, on the one hand, and silence on the other.

Method To provide a basis for the stimuli of experiments 5a and 5b, we twice recorded a male speaker saying "put it in the dish." These recordings were digitized and then stored in computer memory. To produce the experimental variation of primary interest we used the PCM editing system to introduce varying durations of silence between the end of voicing associated with the vowel [I] and the beginning of the noise of [ʃ]. These durations ranged from 20 to 150 ms in steps of 10 ms. To enable us to study the effects of the silence cue in combination with the cues of duration and rise time of the fricative noise, we introduced the silence cue into two series of stimuli. In one (experiment 5a) we combined the silence cue with each of two durations of fricative noise, 320 ms and 160 ms, using for this purpose one of the two recordings referred to above. We produced the two durations of noise in the following way. For one we simply used the noise of the original utterance, which was 320 ms in duration. To produce the other, which was 160 ms in duration, we removed 160 ms of noise from the center and then rejoined the cut ends. That operation obviously does not affect the onset or offset characteristics of the noise.

In the other series we combined the silence cue with each of two different conditions of noise rise time, using for this purpose the second of the recordings referred to above. We produced the two rise times in the following way. For one, we simply used the rise time of the original utterance, which was 35 ms. For the other, we reduced the rise time to 5 ms by removing the first 30 ms of the noise. To compensate in the simplest possible way for the resulting reduction in overall duration of the noise, we added 30 ms of noise to the center. (Given that the rise time was not instantaneous, this operation does not ensure that the durations of the stimuli with the two conditions of rise time were psychologically equal. We should note, however, that they were more nearly so than they would have been if the 30-ms insertion had not been made.)

The subjects for experiment 5a were ten undergraduate volunteers from Arizona State University who had not previously participated in research on speech percep-

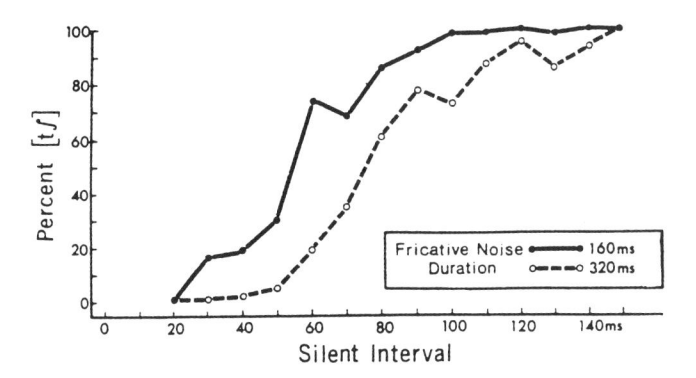

Figure 18.12
The relation between silence and sound; identification of [tʃ] for two conditions of fricative-noise duration.

tion. They were tested en masse in a large sound-attenuated room. The experimental stimuli were reproduced on a Magnecord 1032 tape recorder via a CEI 41-2 loudspeaker. The subjects for experiment 5b were 12 undergraduate volunteers from Lehman College who had not previously participated in research on speech perception. They were tested in groups of four under the conditions described for experiment 1. The subjects in both experiments were given the same instructions. They were told that they would hear either "put it in the dish" or "put it in the ditch" and were instructed to write either "sh" or "ch" on their response sheets. To familiarize the subjects with the experimental stimuli, we had them listen to twenty stimuli before we started the test sequence.

Results and Discussion We see the results of experiment 5a in figure 18.12. It is apparent that silence is sufficient in this case to cue the distinction between fricative and affricate postvocalically. At the short intervals of silence the stimuli in both conditions of fricative noise duration were heard as "dish," while at the longest intervals of silence they were heard as "ditch."

It is also apparent that there is a relation between the duration of silence and the duration of fricative noise. Thus, if we look at the silent interval necessary for 50 percent "ditch" responses, we see that it is approximately 75 ms when the noise is long (320 ms), but only 55 ms when the noise is short (160 ms). The difference in silent interval is significant ($T = 0$, $p < 0.005$). That is to say that 14 ms of silence (the difference between 89 and 75 ms) is equivalent in these phonetic perceptions to 160 ms of noise.

In figure 18.13 we see the results of experiment 5b. Since listeners report "dish" at the shortest intervals of silence and "ditch" at the longest intervals, we see, once again, that silence is sufficient to distinguish between fricative and affricate. And here, too, we see a relation between two acoustic cues to the same distinction: silence and rise time of the fricative noise. The boundary between fricative and affricate is at about 57 ms of silence when the rise time is slow (35 ms), but at 37 ms when the rise time is rapid (0 ms). This difference is significant ($T = 1$, $p < 0.005$).

We should note that relations of the kind described here can limit the effectiveness of silence as a cue. At one extreme we might have such a long duration of noise, and thus a strong bias toward a fricative, that no amount of silence would be sufficient to

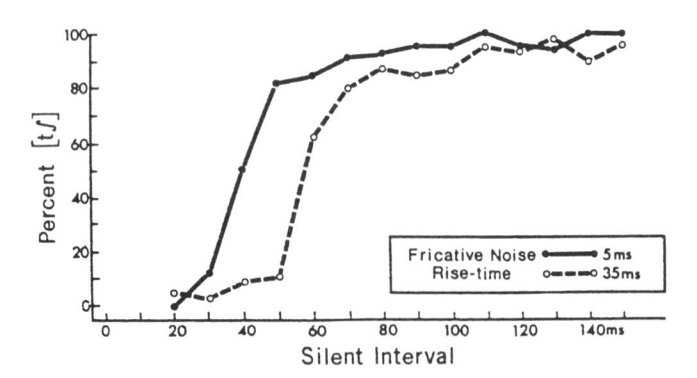

Figure 18.13
The relation between silence and sound; identification of [tʃ] for two conditions of fricative-noise rise time.

overcome it. At the other extreme we might have such a short duration and rise time of the noise, and thus so strong a bias toward the affricate, that even durations of silence near 0 ms would not alter the perception of the affricate. This is consistent with the caveat we mentioned in our earlier discussion. It would apply also in the case of "slit" and "split" to the trading relation between temporal (silence) and spectral cues that have been reported by other investigators (Erickson, Fitch, Halwes, and Liberman 1977; Liberman and Pisoni 1977).

Returning now to the main findings of our experiment, we should note that the relations among the effects of the several cues are, in principle, like those that have been reported for numerous others (for a review, see Liberman and Studdert-Kennedy 1979). In all cases, cues that are quite different from an acoustic point of view, nevertheless give rise to the same phonetic percept. It is consistent with our hypothesis to suppose that the perceptual equivalence of these cues is owning to the fact that they are the common products of the same linguistically significant gesture.

How the Effectiveness of Silence Depends on Whether It Comes from One Vocal Tract or Two: An Ecological Factor in Phonetic Perception

Having suggested that silence is important in stop perception because it provides information about the behavior of a vocal tract, we should now ask: whose vocal tract? We think it could hardly be that of the listener, nor of the speaker, nor, indeed, of any particular person. Rather, it must be some more abstract conception of the behavior of vocal tracts in general. At all events, it is possible to find out; we need only take advantage of certain facts about the ecology of speech.

Consider two of the examples we developed in the earlier parts of our paper. First there was the case of [bɛb dɛ] and [bɛg dɛ], where it was found that a syllable-final stop was not perceived when there was an insufficiently long period of silence between the syllables. We assumed that this was so because the relatively short silence informed the listener that the speaker must not have closed his vocal tract long enough to have produced a syllable-final stop. But what one speaker cannot do, two speakers can: Given collaboration between two speakers—or, indeed, given the accidents of speech when several are talking—the utterance [bɛb dɛ], for example, can be produced with no silence at all between the syllables. Therefore with two speakers (or more generally two sources of speech), the presence or absence of silence should have no phonetic significance.

Similar considerations apply to our finding that the phrase "please say shop" was heard as "please say chop" when silence was inserted between "say" and "shop." By our account, the silence told the listener that the speaker had closed his vocal tract in a manner appropriate to the production of an affricate; hence, the perception of an affricate. But here, too, the presence or absence of silence provides information only when there is but one speaker, for two can produce "please say" and "chop" with no silence at all between the words "say" and "chop."

Thus, silence does, or does not, provide useful phonetic information depending on whether (and how) the utterance was produced by one speaker or by two. The aim of the experiments to be reported here is to determine if listeners behave accordingly.

Experiment 6
The purpose of this experiment was to discover whether the effect of intersyllabic silence on the perception of syllable-final stops in the disyllables [bab da] and [bag da] is different when the syllables are produced by two speakers instead of one.

Method Except for the introduction of a "different voice" condition, the procedures of this experiment were similar to those of experiments 2a and 2b, where, as the reader may recall, we were concerned with the effect of intersyllable silence on the perception of syllable-final stops in [bɛb dɛ] and [bɛg dɛ]. First, we recorded a male saying [bab], [bag], and [da]. Those utterances were digitized and stored in computer memory. We then modified the [bab] and [bag] syllables by removing all but 15 ms of the voicing that followed the final formant transitions. To create the set of stimuli for the "same-talker" condition, we appended the syllable [da] to [bab] and [bag], so as to create intersyllabic intervals of silence from 0 to 90 ms in steps of 10 ms. Three tokens of each stimulus were generated. The entire sequence was then randomized and recorded on audio tape with a 3-s interval between stimuli. To generate stimuli for the "different-talker" condition, we followed exactly the same procedure, but substituted a female voice saying [da]. Thus, we produced disyllables in which the first syllable [(bab) or [bag]) was in a male voice and the second syllable [da] in a female voice.

The subjects were ten volunteers, all undergraduates at Lehman College who had previously participated in experiment 1. For the "same-talker" condition, the subjects were told that they would hear a male voice saying [bab da], [bag da], or [ba da]. For the different-talker condition, the subjects were told that they would hear a male voice saying [bab], [bag], or [ba] followed by a female voice saying [da]. In both conditions the subjects were asked to respond by writing on their response sheets the identity of the sound ([bab da], [bag da], or [ba_da]) at the end of the first (male produced syllable). The stimuli of the same- and different-talker conditions were presented in blocks. To control for practice effects, the order of the blocks was counterbalanced across the listeners. To familiarize the listeners with the stimuli, we presented 20 stimuli before each trial block.

Results and Discussion The results for the same- and different-talker conditions are shown in figure 18.14. Looking first at the same-talker condition, we see a result very similar to the one obtained in the analogous condition of one of our earlier experiments (experiment 2b): At short intervals of silence listeners did not hear syllable-

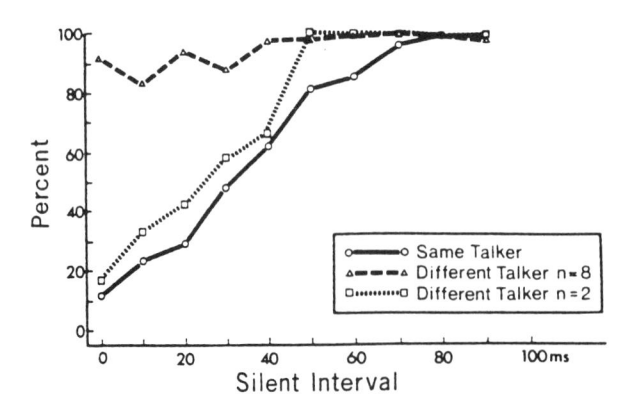

Figure 18.14
Silence as a condition for stop manner when it reflects the behavior of one vocal tract or two: identification of syllable-final stops in [bɛb dɛ] – [bɛg dɛ] in the same- and different-talker conditions.

final stops; these were heard with 75 percent accuracy only when the silence interval was about 45 ms in duration.

The result of the different-talker condition is quite different. Eight of the ten subjects identified syllable-final stops with near-perfect accuracy at every interval of silence, including even the very shortest. For these subjects, it is as if their perceptual machinery "knew" that, with two speakers, intersyllabic silence conveys no useful phonetic information. The remaining two subjects behaved in the different-talker condition almost exactly as they had when there was but a single talker. We cannot be sure why. We may note, however, that a single syllable by each talker provides very little information about the identity of the talker. Conceivably, therefore, the fact that the two syllables were produced by different talkers did not properly "register" with these two subjects. In that connection, it is relevant that one of these two subjects did remark at the end of the experiment, that she thought she had been listening to the same talker speaking on two different pitches. This suggests that the effect we obtained in the different-talker condition was not due solely to the acoustic differences between the voice as such, but rather to their role in informing the listeners that there were, indeed, two sources of speech.

Experiment 7
The purpose of this experiment was to determine if the effect of silence in converting "say shop" to "say chop" is different when the words on either side of the silence are produced by two talkers instead of one.

Method The stimuli for this experiment were produced in the same manner as those of experiment 4, except for the addition of a "different-voice" condition. First we digitized and stored in computer memory a male speaker's recording of "please say shop." To produce stimuli for the same-talker condition, we imposed intervals of silence between "please say" and "shop" in 10 ms steps over the range 0–100 ms. Three tokens of each stimulus were recorded. The entire sequence was then randomized and recorded with a 3-s interval between stimuli. To produce stimuli for the different-talker condition, we first digitized a female's recording of "please say shop." The phrase "please say" was excised from the recording and stored in computer

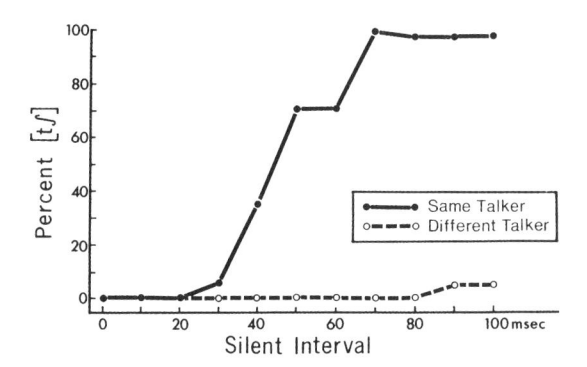

Figure 18.15
Silence as a condition for affricate manner when it reflects the behavior of one vocal tract or two: identification of [tʃ] in patterns composed of "please say" and "shop" in the same- and different-talker conditions.

memory. We then appended the male-produced "shop" to the female-produced "please say," leaving intervals of silence between "say" and "shop." These intervals ranged from 0 to 100 ms in steps of 10 ms. Three tokens of each stimulus were generated. The resulting stimuli were randomized and recorded on audio tape with a 3-s interval between stimuli.

The subjects were ten volunteers, all undergraduates at Lehman College who had not previously participated in research on speech perception. For the "same-talker" condition, the subjects were told that they would hear a male voice saying either "please say shop" or "please say chop." For the different-talker condition, the subjects were told that they would hear a female voice saying "please say" and a male voice saying either "shop" or "chop." In both conditions the subjects were asked to write either "sh" (for "shop") or "ch" (for "chop") on their response sheets. The subjects were tested in two groups of five under the listening conditions described in experiment 1. The stimuli of the same- and different-talker conditions were presented in blocks. The order of the blocks was counterbalanced across the two groups of subjects. To familiarize the subjects with the stimuli, we presented 20 stimuli before each trial block.

Results and Discussion The results of experiment 7 are shown in figure 18.15. One sees in the same-talker condition a result similar to that we obtained in the analogous condition of experiment 4: the fricative in the word "shop" was heard as the affricate in the word "chop" when the silent interval between it, and the immediately preceding word exceeded about 45 ms. In contrast, silence had no effect in the different-talker condition: increases in the silent interval did not convert "shop" to "chop."

We should note that the utterance "please say shop" used in this experiment should have provided more information about the identity of the talker (or talkers) than did the two syllables of the previous experiment. This may account for the fact that, in this experiment, though not in the other, the effect of the same- versus different-talker conditions was found in every subject. Perhaps, however, the effect would not have been so large had we used other settings of the cues for the fricative-affricate distinction. Obviously, further research is necessary to determine the limits over which the effect obtains. We should also wonder about the effect in connection with the trading relations among the fricative-affricate cues that we observed in our earlier experiments. Having found, for example in experiment 5, that duration of silence can be traded for friction duration, we might ask whether these cues also trade with the (perceived) magnitude of the difference between the voices.

We should emphasize that in both experiments the two talkers were male and female. Thus, the acoustic difference between the voices was relatively large. We are now conducting experiments contrived specifically for the purpose of helping us to determine whether the phenomenon we have here described depends critically on such an acoustic difference, or, alternatively, on an inference by the listener that he did or did not hear different sources of speech. At this point, we believe it is the latter.[5]

General Discussion

We should now assemble the results of our experiments in terms of their bearing on the three questions we raised at the very beginning. As for the first question—Is silence a cue to stop manner?—the answer is quite straightforward, and wholly in accord with the results of previous research. Silence is a cue, necessary in some cases, sufficient in others. Thus, given spectral cues appropriate for a stop in absolute initial position (e.g., [gɛ]), silence preceding those cues was found to be necessary if a stop was to be perceived as the second element of a fricative-stop-vowel syllable (e.g., [ʃkɛ]). Similarly, in the case of stops in syllable-final position (e.g., [bɛb]) silence following the spectral cues was necessary if they were to give rise to the perception of a stop when a second syllable was added (e.g., [bɛb dɛ]). More interesting, perhaps, is the finding that even in the absence of sufficient spectral cues, silence did, in some circumstances, produce the perception of a stop or affricate. Thus, prefixing the noise of [s] to the syllable "lit" produced "split" when the correct amount of silence was interposed; inserting silence between the words "say" and "shop" converted them to "say chop."

Our second question asked whether the effect of silence was exclusively auditory, or also phonetic. If auditory, we should expect to find explanations in terms of masking or any one of a variety of interactions. If phonetic, we should assume that silence informs the listener that the speaker did or did not make the closure that is the distinguishing characteristic of the stops, and further that the listener is sensitive to that information, just as he would be if his perception of speech were constrained by knowledge of what a vocal tract must (or must not) do when it makes a linguistically significant gesture. This question is, by its nature, more problematic than the first one, and the answer is correspondingly harder to find. We believe, however, that the pattern of results obtained in the experiments reported here lend support to the assumption that the effect of silence is, to a significant extent, phonetic. Having presented those data at various places in this paper, we should collect them here.

First, we should consider again the basic fact that silence was an important cue, and then note how difficult it is, given our results, to account for that solely in auditory terms. Thus, we found that the transition cues for the stops were neither appreciably masked nor altered by interaction when, having been isolated from the speech patterns, they were heard as nonspeech chirps. It is also relevant, of course, that, under some conditions, silence was a sufficient cue. There were, in those cases, no other sufficient cues to be masked. It is also telling that silence was effective as a cue only over a limited range, just as we should expect given the assumption that it provides information about a stop closure that lasts for a limited amount of time. Further evidence for a link between perception and production is provided by those of our experiments that showed an equivalence in phonetic perception between duration of silence and duration of friction (or between duration of silence and the rise time of the friction). That result—similar, as we have pointed out, to the results of other investigators—seems easiest to interpret on the assumption that the acoustically different cues give rise to the same phonetic percept because they are normally the correlated (but distributed) acoustic consequences of the same gesture.

Having said that the data of our experiments (and those of others) imply that perception of the silence cue is constrained as if by knowledge of what vocal tracts can do, we should offer a few parenthetical comments about what the data do not imply. First, they most certainly do not imply that a listener can hear only what a vocal tract can do. Indeed, it is for that reason that we have so often added the qualification "when the vocal tract makes linguistically significant gestures." For we know that synthetic speech can be readily perceived (as speech), though it departs, sometimes appreciably, from those acoustic patterns that real vocal tracts can produce. Thus, synthetic patterns sometimes contain only two formants, and the transitions are sometimes made to change direction instantaneously. But such departures, we should note, are not linguistically relevant. Languages cannot enforce a distinction between phones made with two formants and those made with the greater number of formants that real vocal tracts produce, nor can they contrast instantaneous changes in formant slope with those more gradual changes that must characterize the behavior of such real masses as the tongue. In cases like these, an experimenter can take all manner of liberties with the stimulus patterns without destroying or even distorting phonetic perception, provided he manages to include the acoustic information that enables the listener to hear the stimuli as speech. All this is to say that if the speech perceiving mechanism is "tuned" to a vocal tract, as we have implied it might be, then such "tuning" must hold only for those maneuvers that have linguistic significance.

Second, our assumption of a link between perception and production is not meant to imply anything about the nature of the mechanism that mediates the link, or about the relative contributions of nature and nurture to its formation. In regard to the nature of the mechanism, there are aspects of our results (and those of others) that speak against at least one very simple possibility: feature detectors that have evolved in such a way as to be "tuned" to respond to fixed acoustic consequences of articulatory gestures, and to be "sprung" when those consequences are present in the signal. In that connection, we note, first, that the relations among cues that we have found suggest that the setting of one detector (e.g., the silence detector) must be, in effect, variable and conditioned by the "value" of the other cues (e.g., duration of the noise). We should then note that, according to the results of the experiment on identification of syllable-final stops, a detector for the syllable-final transition cues could not respond directly upon sensing these cues, but would, instead, have to wait until it had information about the next syllable. At the least, it would have to know about that next syllable how far removed in time it was from the syllable containing the target phone and what kinds of phones it comprised. The consequence for a detector model is that it loses must of the appeal that it would otherwise have by virtue of its simplicity.

As for questions about the contributions of nature and nurture to the assumed link between perception and production, we should emphasize that such questions stand apart from those that pertain to the existence of such a link. Our experiments bear only on the latter.

We turn finally to the third question: Whose vocal tract is perception linked to? Given the results of our experiments with same and different talkers, we should suppose that the answer is quite clear: the relevant vocal tract is not that of the listener nor is it that of the speaker; it is rather some very abstract conception of vocal tracts in general. But those same results add support to the view that a link to some vocal tract, however abstract, does figure in the perception of speech.

Notes

This research was supported by a grant (HD-01994) from the National Institute of Child Health and Human Development to Haskins Laboratories. We wish to thank Bruno Repp for helpful comments on an earlier version of this paper. We also wish to thank Anthony Levas and Suzi Pollack for their assistance in collecting and tabulating portions of the data.

The results of experiments 1, 2a, 2b and 6 were described in a paper presented at the 89th Meeting of the Acoustical Society of America, Austin, Texas, 1975, and in the Haskins Laboratories (1975). Status Report on Speech Research, SR-42/43, 265–276; experiments 3, 4, and 7 at the 91st Meeting of Acoustical Society of America, Washington, DC, 1976, and (experiments 3 and 4 only) in the Haskins Laboratories (1976) Status Report on Speech Research SR-48, 199–208; and the results of experiments 5a and 5b at the 93rd Meeting of the Acoustical Society of America, State College, PA, 1977.

1. When native speakers of English produce [ʃpɛ] and [ʃkɛ], [p] and [k] are realized as voiceless inaspirates. It is for this reason that, when the fricative noise is removed from [ʃpɛ] and [ʃkɛ], listeners hear the stops that remain as voiced. In our experiment, it was necessary, therefore, to record [bɛ] and [gɛ] (rather than [pɛ] and [kɛ]), so that, when the fricative noise and vocalic segment were combined, the listeners would hear a normal sounding [ʃpɛ] and [ʃkɛ].
2. The term "geminate" is ordinarily used to refer to the doubling of a consonant within a word. Such doubling as we find in English occurs only across word boundaries. We nevertheless here use the term, though our subjects were native speakers of English and were accustomed to consonant doubling only at word boundaries.
3. Since writing this paper, a somewhat similar result by Rudnicky and Cole (1977) has come to our attention. Having recorded [ba ga] they found: (a) that after removing the [ga] their listeners heard [bag], (2) that after replacing the [ga] with [da] placed close in time to the first syllable, listeners heard [bai da], and (3) that when the second syllable was separated from the first syllable by a sufficient interval of silence, listeners heard [bag da]. This result is of particular interest from our point of view because, in the condition when the second syllable [da] was close to [ba] and the subjects heard [bai da], it is clear that the transition cues at the end of the first syllable were not being (backward) masked by the second syllable; they were being perceived, but as a glide to [i] rather than as a stop. That result is similar to the findings of Liberman and Pisoni (1977), referred to earlier in this paper, that ʃ noise placed close to [gɛ] causes listeners to perceive [ʃjɛ].
4. We have not commented on the difference between identification function for [b] and [g] because we have found that difference to change, even to be reversed, depending on the surrounding vocalic environment. We emphasize the geminate versus nongeminate contrast because it remains more nearly stable across vowel environments.
5. Using stimulus patterns and procedures very different from ours, Darwin and Bethell-Fox (1977) have, nevertheless, obtained results that are quite compatible. After synthesizing a pattern that was heard as an uninterrupted sequence of semivowels and vowels, they found that introducing changes in fundamental frequency at appropriate places in the pattern (without changing formant frequencies) caused the semivowels to be heard as stops. Their interpretation was that the rapid shifts in fundamental caused the sequence to "stream," thus permitting the listener to hear two voices; that, in turn, provided the silence necessary to convert semivowel to stop.

References

Abbs, M. (1971). "A study of cues for the identification of voiced stop consonants in intervocalic contexts," Doctoral dissertation, University of Wisconsin (unpublished).

Bailey, P., Summerfield, Q., and Dorman, M. "Friction duration and friction offset as cues to stop manner in fricative-stop-vowel sequences," (unpublished).

Bastian, J. (1962). "Silent intervals as closure cues in the perception of stops," Haskins Laboratories, Speech Res. Instrum. 9, Appendix F.

Bastian, J., Eimas, P., and Liberman, A. (1961). "Identification and discrimination of phonemic contrast induced by silent interval," J. Acoust. Soc. Am. 33, 842 (A).

Darwin, C. J. (1971), "Ear differences in the recall of fricatives and vowels," Q. J. Exp. Psychol. 23, 46–62.

Darwin, C. J., and Bethell-Fox, C. (1977). "Pitch continuity and speech source attribution," J. Exp. Psychol.; Hum. Perform. and Percept. 3, 665–672.

Erickson, D., Fitch, H., Halwes, T., and Liberman, A. (1977). "Trading relation in perception between silence and spectrum," J. Acoust. Soc. Am. 61, S46 (A).

Fujisaki, H., Nakamuro, K., and Imoto, T. (1975). "Auditory perception of duration of speech and nonspeech stimuli," *Auditory Analysis and the Perception of Speech*, edited by G. Fant and M. A. A. Tatham (Academic, London).

Ganong, W. (1975). "An experiment on 'phonetic adaptation,'" Research Laboratory of Electronics, MIT, Progress Report 116, 206–210.

Gerstman, L. J. (1957). "Perceptual dimensions for the friction portions of certain speech sounds," Doctoral dissertation, New York University (unpublished).

Harris, K. S. (1958). "Cues for the discrimination of American English fricatives in spoken syllables," Lang. Speech 1, 1–7.

Kuypers, A. (1955). "Affricates in intervocalic position," Haskins Laboratories, Q. Prog. Rep. 15, Appendix 6.

Liberman, A. M., and Pisoni, D. B. (1977). "Evidence in a special speech-processing subsystem in the human," *Recognition of Complex Acoustic Signals*, edited by T. H. Bullock (Dahlem Konfrerenzen, Berlin) Life Sciences Research Rep. 5.

Liberman, A. M., and Studdert-Kennedy, M. (1979). "Phonetic perception," in *Handbook of Sensory Physiology*, edited by R. Held, H. Leibowitz, and H. L. Teuber (Springer-Verlag, Heidelberg), Vol. VIII, "Perception".

Lisker, L. (1957a). "Closure duration and voiced-voiceless distinction in English," Language 33, 42–49.

Lisker, L. (1957b). "Closure duration, first-formant transitions and the voiced-voiceless contrast of intervocalic stops," Haskins Laboratories, Q. Prog. Rep. 23, Appendix 1.

Lisker, L. (1977). "Closure hiatus: cue to voicing, manner and place of consonant occlusion," J. Acoust. Soc. Am. 61, S48 (A).

Pickett, J. M., and Decker, L. (1960). "Time factors in perception of a double consonant," Lang. Speech 3, 11–17.

Port, R. (1976). "The influence of speaking tempo on the duration of stressed vowel and medial stop in English trochee words," Doctoral dissertation, University of Connecticut (unpublished).

Raphael, L. J., and Dorman, M. F. (1977). "Perceptual equivalence of cues for the fricative-affricate contrast," J. Acoust. Soc. Am. 61, S45 (A).

Repp, B. (1976). "Perception of implosive transitions in VCV utterances," Haskins Laboratories, Status Rep. Speech Res. SR-48, 209–234.

Repp, B. (1977). "Perceptual integration and selective attention in speech perception: further experiments on intervocalic stop consonants," Haskins Laboratories, Status Rep. Speech Res. SR-49, 37–70.

Rudnicky, A., and Cole, R. (1977). "Vowel identification and subsequent context," J. Acoust. Soc. Am. 61, S39 (A).

Summerfield, A. Q., and Bailey, P. (1977). "On the dissociation of spectral and temporal cues for stop consonant manner," J. Acoust. Soc. Am. 61, S46 (A).

Truby, H. (1955). "Affricates," Haskins Laboratories, Q. Prog. Rep. 11, 7–8.

Chapter 19
Perceptual Integration of Acoustic Cues for Stop, Fricative, and Affricate Manner

When a speaker makes an articulatory gesture appropriate for a phonetic segment, the acoustic consequences are typically numerous, diverse, and distributed over a relatively long span of the signal. In the articulation of an intervocalic stop consonant, for example, the characteristically rapid closing and opening of the vocal tract has acoustic consequences that include, among others, the following: various rising and falling transitions of the several formants; a period of significantly reduced sound intensity; and then a second, acoustically different set of formant transitions, plus (in the case of voiceless stops in iambic stress patterns) a transient burst of sound, a delayed onset of the first formant, and, for the duration of that delay, band-limited noise in place of periodic sound in the higher formants.

Despite their obvious diversity and their distribution over periods as long as 300 msec (Repp 1976), these acoustic features—usually referred to as "cues"—are nevertheless integrated into the unitary perception of a phonetic segment. In such cases of integration we find trading relations among the several cues that take part: Within limits, one cue can be exchanged for another without any change in the phonetic percept; in that sense, the cues are perceptually equivalent, though they may differ greatly in acoustic (and presumably auditory) terms and be quite far removed from each other in time.

To find the basis for the perceptual integration and for the perceptual equivalence it implies, we should first ask what it is that these diverse features have in common. As already implied, we have not far to look: Each is one of the normal products of the same linguistically significant act. Given that commonality, and given the convergence on a unitary phonetic percept, we find it most parsimonious to suppose that the acoustic cues are processed by a system specialized to perceive the phonetically significant act by which they were produced. On that assumption, the boundaries of the integration would be set not by the number, diversity, or temporal distribution of the cues but rather by a decision that they do (or do not) plausibly specify an articulatory act appropriate for the production of a single phonetic segment.

Just how the various cues contribute, separately and in various combinations, to the integrated phonetic percept has been the subject of the many experimental studies of speech perception carried out over the last 30 years. These have established the more or less important roles of the cues and, either directly or by implication, have outlined the trading relations—hence perceptual equivalences—among them. In one

Originally published in *Journal of Experimental Psychology: Human Perception and Performance* 4, 4 (1978): 621–637, with Bruno H. Repp, Thomas Eccardt, and David Pesetsky. Copyright 1978 by the American Psychological Association. Reprinted by permission of the publisher.

of the most recent of these studies, Summerfield and Haggard (1977) made explicit how a trading relation among the cues for the voicing distinction is to be understood by taking account of the fact that they are the common products of the same articulatory act. A more general discussion of this matter, with examples of the several classes of cues that engage in such trading relations, is to be found in Liberman and Studdert-Kennedy (in press).

In the experiments reported here, we put our attention on simple cues of a temporal sort: duration of silence and duration of fricative noise. We examined their integration in the perception of the distinction between fricative and affricate, and we also investigated the effect on that integration of a still more widely distributed temporal variable, namely, the rate at which the surrounding speech is articulated. In the second experiment, we studied the effects of those same temporal cues, but now in connection with the perception of juncture. That provided us with an opportunity to examine a case in which the integration occurs across syllable boundaries: A syllable-final stop is perceived or not, depending on a cue in the next syllable that simultaneously determines whether the initial segment in that syllable is taken to be a fricative or an affricate.

Experiment 1

In this experiment we selected two cues for study, both temporal in nature and both relevant to the fricative-affricate distinction. One of them is silence. A short period of silence (or near silence) in the acoustic signal tells the listener that the speaker has closed his vocal tract, a gesture characteristic of stop consonants and affricates. That silence is a powerful and often sufficient cue for the perception of stop or affricate manner can be experimentally demonstrated by inserting silence at the appropriate place in an utterance. So, for example, SLIT can be converted into a convincing SPLIT by inserting a sufficient amount of silence between the fricative noise and the vocalic (LIT) portion. That was done originally in tape-splicing experiments (Bastian, Eimas, and Liberman 1961; Bastian 1959, 1960). For the same phonetic contrast, investigators have more recently explored the range of effective silence durations (Dorman, Raphael, and Liberman 1976) and, in another study, revealed a trading relation between silence and a spectral cue (Erickson, Fitch, Halwes, and Liberman 1978). Other contrasts—similar in that they, too, are based on the presence or absence of stop or stoplike manner—have also been found to depend in important ways on the silence cue. Thus, with appropriate insertions of silence, SI can be made to sound like SKI, or SU like SPU (Bailey and Summerfield 1978). Silence can also be sufficient to cue the fricative-affricate contrast in, for example, SAY SHOP versus SAY CHOP (Dorman, Raphael, and Liberman 1976); it is this contrast that concerns us here.[1]

For the fricative-affricate contrast, there are, as always, other cues besides silence. The one we used in our experiment is duration of (fricative) noise, a cue shown originally by Gerstman (1957) to be important. Thus, we had two temporal cues, duration of silence and duration of noise, and we shall see how they are integrated to produce the perception of affricate manner. Then we shall examine the effect on that integration of a variable that is also temporal in nature: rate of articulation. Our interest in introducing that variable springs from several sources. We might expect, first of all, that the effect of articulatory rate would be especially apparent on cues that are themselves durational in nature. Several studies tend to confirm that expectation (e.g., Ainsworth 1974; Fujisaki, Nakamura, and Imoto 1975; Pickett and Decker 1960; Summerfield 1977). Indeed, one of these studies dealt with the same fricative-affricate contrast we studied, and it reported a seemingly paradoxical effect: Having determined that increasing the duration of silence between SAY and SHOP was sufficient to convert the utterance PLEASE SAY SHOP to PLEASE SAY CHOP, Dorman Raphael, and Liberman (1976) found that when the rate of the precursor PLEASE SAY was increased, more silence was needed to produce the affricate in CHOP. We wished to test for that effect at each of several durations of the fricative noise, and in a larger sentence context. The results may then bear on an interpretation of the paradoxical effect that is consistent with the hypothesis we have advanced to account for the integration of the segmental cues themselves—namely, that perception takes account of production.

To appreciate the point, we should take note of the claim by students of speech production (e.g., Kozhevnikov and Chistovich 1965) that changes in rate of articulation do not stretch or compress all portions of the speech signal proportionately. In that connection, the data most relevant to our purposes are owing to Gay (1978). He found that durations of silence associated with stop consonants change less with rate than do the durations of the surrounding vocalic portions. It is possible, then, that the somewhat corresponding cue elements of our experiment—duration of silence and duration of fricative noise—are, in like fashion, differentially affected by changes in speaking rate. If so, and if perception is indeed guided, as it were, by tacit knowledge of the consequences of articulation, then we should expect that the perceptual integration of the two cues would reflect such inequalities as the production may have caused.

Method

Subjects Seven paid volunteers (Yale University undergraduates) participated, as did three of the authors (Repp, Eccardt, and Pesetsky). All except Repp are native speakers of American English (he learned German as his first language). The results of all 10 subjects were combined since there were no substantial differences among them.

Stimuli A male talker recorded the sentence WHY DON'T WE SAY SHOP AGAIN at two different speaking rates, using a monotone voice and avoiding emphatic stress on any syllable. The fast sentence lasted 1.26 sec, and the slow sentence lasted 2.36 sec—a ratio of .53. The sentences were low-pass filtered at 4.9 kHz and digitized at a sampling rate of 10 kHz. This was done with the Haskins Laboratories Pulse Code Modulation (PCM) system. Monitoring the waveforms on high-resultion oscillograms, we excerpted the SH noise of the slow utterance (110 msec in duration) and substituted it for the SH noise in the fast utterance (originally 92 msec). Thus, the two utterances had identical noise portions.

Knowing that rate of onset of the fricative noise is an important cue for the fricative-affricate distinction (Cutting and Rosner 1974; Gerstman 1957), we were concerned that it be not too extreme. Preliminary observations suggested that the noise onset in our stimuli was so gradual as to bias the perception strongly toward fricative and even perhaps to override the effects of the two duration cues we wished to study. To remove, or at least reduce, that bias, we removed the initial 30 msec of the noise, leaving 80 msec. That maneuver had the effect of creating a more abrupt onset.[2]

We used the PCM system to vary the two temporal cues under study: noise duration and silence duration. Three different noise durations were created by either duplicating or removing 20 msec from the center of the 80-msec noise, leaving the onset and offset unchanged. Thus, the noise durations were 60, 80, and 100 msec in both sentence frames. In each of the resulting six sentences, varying amounts of silence were inserted before the fricative noise. Silence duration was varied from 0 to 100 msec in 10-msec steps. Eleven silence durations, three noise durations, and two speaking rates resulted in 66 sentences. These were recorded in five different randomizations, with 2 sec intervening between successive sentences.

To determine how the different noise durations were perceived outside the sentence context, we prepared a separate tape containing isolated SHOP (CHOP) words excerpted from the test sentences. (The stimuli consisted of the portion from the beginning of the fricative noise to the beginning of the P-closure.) Three different noise durations and two speaking rates yielded six stimuli; these were duplicated 10 times and recorded in a random sequence, separated by 3-sec intervals. The different speaking rates were reflected in the durations of the vocalic portions of the test words; they were 140 msec (slow) and 113 msec (fast).

Procedure The subjects listened in a quiet room over an Ampex Model 620 amplifier-speaker, as the tapes were played back on an Ampex Model AG-500 tape recorder. Intensity was set at a comfortable level. All subjects listened to the isolated words first, except for the three authors, who took this brief test at a later date. The task was to identify each word as either SHOP or CHOP, using the letters S and C for convenience in writing down the responses and guessing when uncertain. The same responses were required in the sentence test. The listeners were informed about the different speaking rates but not about the variations in noise and silence duration (obviously this does not apply to those authors who participated). After a pause, the sentence test was repeated, so that 10 responses per subject were obtained for each sentence.

Results

Consider first the results obtained for isolated words. Although the original utterance had contained SHOP, the isolated words were predominantly perceived as CHOP. Presumably, this was a consequence of our having cut back the original fricative noise and thus creating not only a shorter noise duration but also a more abrupt onset; both changes would be expected to bias perception toward affricate manner (Gerstman 1957). Despite the bias, there was a clear effect of the variations in noise duration: The percentages of CHOP responses to the three noise durations (60, 80, and 100 msec) were 99, 91, and 81 (slow rate) and 99, 90, and 73 (fast rate), respectively. Thus, as expected, the probability of hearing an affricate decreased as noise duration increased. In addition, there seemed to be a slight effect of vowel duration at the longest noise duration, again in the expected direction: When the vocalic portion was shorter—this being the only manifestation of the faster speaking rate in the isolated words—the probability of hearing CHOP was lower, which indicated that the noise duration was to some extent effectively longer at the fast speaking rate.

We turn now to the results of the main experiment. That silence was an effective cue for the fricative-affricate distinction in sentence context is shown in figure 19.1. There we see that the listeners heard SHOP or CHOP, depending on the duration of

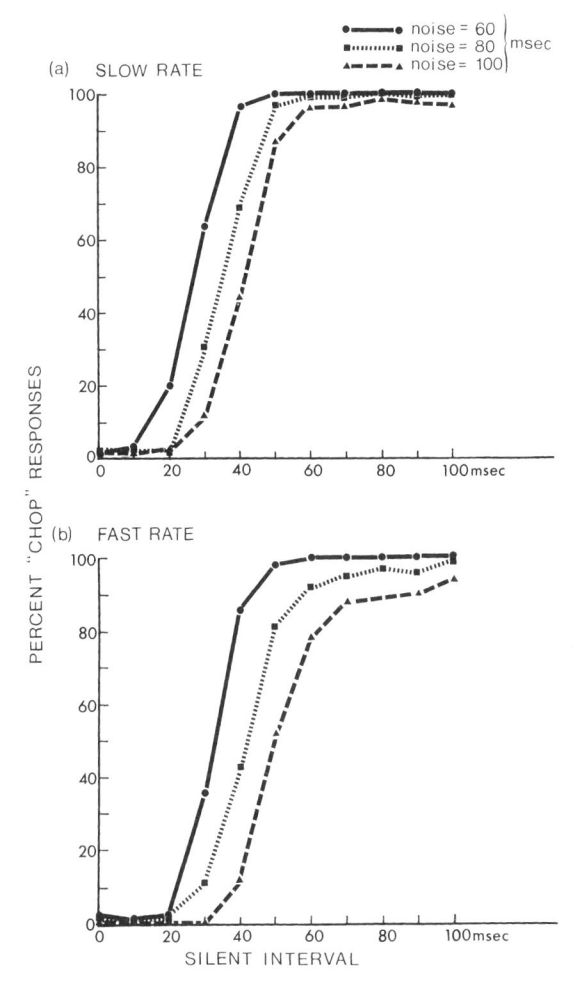

Figure 19.1
Effect of duration of silence and duration of fricative noise on the perceived distinction between fricative (SHOP) and affricate (CHOP). (This is shown for each of the two rates at which the sentence frame was articulated.)

the silence that separated the fricative noise from the syllable (SAY) immediately preceding it. This replicates earlier findings (Dorman, Raphael, and Liberman 1976). If, as is reasonable, we consider an affricate to be a stop-initiated fricative, then our result is also perfectly consistent with those of other investigators who have found silence to be important in the perception of stop-consonant manner.

We see, further, that duration of fricative noise had a systematic effect, as indicated by the horizontal displacement of the three functions in each panel of figure 19.1. The proportion of SHOP responses increased significantly with noise duration, $F(2, 18) = 32.36$, $p < .001$. That effect establishes a trading relation between silence and noise durations: As noise duration increases, more silence is needed to convert SHOP into CHOP.[3]

The effect of speaking rate can be seen by comparing the two panels of figure 19.1. We see that the paradoxical effect first discovered by Dorman, Raphael, and

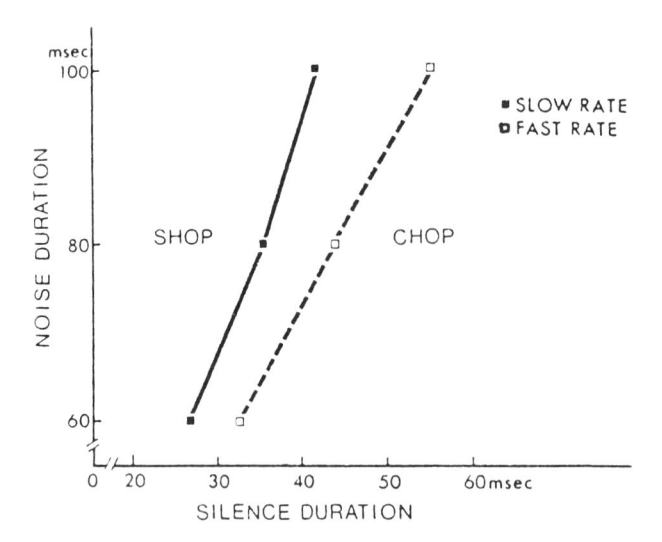

Figure 19.2
Boundaries between perceived fricative (SHOP) and affricate (CHOP) at each speaking rate as joint functions of the duration of silence and the duration of fricative noise.

Liberman (1976) was indeed replicated: For equivalent noise durations, more silence was needed in the fast sentence frame than in the slow sentence frame to convert the fricative into an affricate, $F(1, 9) = 16.35, p < .01$.

The foregoing results are represented more concisely in figure 19.2 where the data points are the SHOP–CHOP boundaries (i.e., the 50 percent crossover points of the six labeling functions) as estimated by the method of probits (Finney 1971). This procedure fits cumulative normal distribution functions to the data; it also yields estimates of standard deviations and standard errors of the boundaries.[4] To show the trading relation between the temporal cues more clearly, figure 19.2 plots the SHOP–CHOP boundaries (abscissa) as a function of noise duration (ordinate) and speaking rate (the two separate functions). Each function describes a trading relation between noise duration and silence duration by connecting all those combinations of silence and noise durations for which SHOP and CHOP responses are equiprobable. The joint dependence of perceptual judgments on both durational cues is indicated by the fact that the trading functions are neither perfectly vertical nor perfectly horizontal but have intermediate slopes. Both functions are strikingly linear.

Although an increase in speaking rate left the linear form of the trading relation unchanged, it shifted the function toward longer silence durations, simultaneously changing its slope and indicating that rate of articulation had a differential effect on the effective durations of silence and noise. In fact, the trading functions in figure 19.2 coincide well with straight lines through the origin of the coordinate system, which means that within each speaking-rate condition, the fricative-affricate boundary is associated with a constant ratio between silence and noise durations—approximately .44 at the slow rate and .55 at the fast rate. A separate analysis of variance of silence/noise ratios showed only a significant effect of speaking rate, $F(2, 18) = 14.60, p < .01$; the effect of noise duration and the interaction term were far from significance. Thus, the consequence of changing the rate of articulation was a change in the ratio of silence to noise required for the same phonetic perception.[5]

Discussion

It is not novel to find that variations in rate of articulation have an effect on the perception of temporal cues in speech. Nor is it entirely novel to find, as we have, that variations in rate have an unequal effect on the several temporal cues—duration of silence and duration of noise—that are effective in the perception of the fricative-affricate distinction; as we pointed out in the introduction, that conclusion was suggested by an experiment that is owing to Dorman, Raphael, and Liberman (1976). What we have done is to extend that finding. Having varied both the duration of silence and the duration of noise, we saw that the inequality is not peculiar to a particular duration of noise, and we saw, moreover, a trading relation between the two duration cues. That trading relation becomes now a component of one interpretation of the seemingly paradoxical rate effect.

To appreciate that interpretation in its broadest form, we should take note once again of the comments by several students of speech production that variations in rate of articulation do not affect all portions of the speech signal equally. To the extent that this is so, a listener cannot adjust for rate variations by applying a simple scale factor but must rather make a more complex correction, one that embodies a tacit knowledge, as it were, of the inequalities in the signal that rate variations generate. Perhaps the results of our experiment are an instance of that correction and that tacit knowledge. Suppose that in the case of utterances like those of our experiment, variations in rate of articulation cause the duration of the fricative noise to change more than the duration of the silence. If the listener's perception reflects an accurate understanding of that inequality, then he or she should expect that given an increase in rate, the noise would shorten more than the silence. But on hearing, as in some of the conditions of our experiment, that the noise duration remains constant when the rate increases, the listener would assign to the noise an effectively greater (relative) length. As we know, a longer noise duration biases the perception toward fricative, though, as shown by the trading relation in our results, that bias can be overcome by an increase in the duration of silence. A consequence of all that would be just the effect of rate we found in our experiment: When the rate was increased as the duration of noise was held constant, listeners required more silence to perceive an affricate.

The foregoing interpretation depends, among other considerations, on a determination that variations in rate do, in fact, produce the particular inequality we are here concerned with. As we pointed out earlier, Gay (1978) found in utterance types somewhat analogous to ours that rate variations produced smaller variations in the silence associated with stop consonants than in the durations of the surrounding vocalic portions. There are no data, unfortunately, on exactly those utterances we used in our experiment. We have made efforts in that direction, but the results so far are inconclusive. Until such time as we know more clearly just what happens in speech production, the interpretation we have offered here is, of course, quite tentative.

The interpretation must be tentative for yet another reason: It does not reckon with the possibility that certain other cues for the fricative-affricate distinction might have been at work in ways that we do not yet thoroughly understand. We have in mind, in particular, the rise time of the fricative noise. From the work of Gerstman (1957) and of Cutting and Rosner (1974), we know that it is a relevant cue. Dorman, Raphael, and Liberman (1978) recently varied noise rise time and silence duration to produce the distinction between DISH and DITCH, which is essentially similar to the SAY SHOP—SAY CHOP contrast investigated here, and showed that the two cues engage in an orderly trading relation, as we might have expected. However, we do not know how, or even whether, noise rise time varies with rate of articulation. Information on this matter might conceivably affect our interpretation of the present results.

Returning now to the most important results of our experiments, we should emphasize that there are two. The one has to do with the trading relation between duration of silence and duration of noise as joint cues for the fricative-affricate distinction. It is to us provocative that these cues, diverse and distributed as they seem, are nevertheless integrated into the unitary phonetic percept we call fricative or affricate. In our view, this integration occurs because cues such as these converge through a single decision process that takes account of their common origin: They are the consequences of the same articulatory act. The other result, which we have already discussed at some length, is that the two duration cues were affected unequally by a change in rate of articulation. We would now simply emphasize the inequality, which is a very reliable effect, for it does imply that perceptual correction for variations in rate is not made in this case by applying a simple scale factor but that it may rather require some more sophisticated computation that, like the integration of the duration cues, takes account of particular facts about speech production.

Experiment 2

While exploring the boundaries of the phenomenon reported in Experiment 1, we observed an effect that we have undertaken to investigate more systematically in Experiment 2. We reported in Experiment 1 that with increases in the duration of silence between SAY and SHOP, the fricative in SHOP changed to the affricate in CHOP. However, when the fricative noise was at its longest (100 msec), it occasionally seemed to us that CHOP changed back to SHOP and that the stoplike effect was displaced to the end of the preceding syllable, converting SAY to SAYT. If confirmed, that effect would be interesting from our point of view because it bespeaks an integration of perceptual cues across syllable (word) boundaries. It is also relevant to the problem of "juncture," so long a concern of linguists (see Lehiste 1960).

Our concern, then, is with the perceptual integration of the cues that affect perception and placement of stop-consonant manner, either as a final segment added to one syllable or as the conversion of the first segment of the next syllable from fricative to affricate. The cues we examined were the same as those of Experiment 1, duration of silence between the syllables and duration of the fricative noise at the beginning of the second syllable. However, there are two changes. To offer maximum opportunity for the stoplike effect to be transferred from the second syllable to the first, we included durations of fricative noise longer than those used in Experiment 1, thus providing a stronger bias against affricate percepts; and to make the alternative responses equally plausible to our subjects, we used a new sentence, DID ANYBODY SEE THE GRAY (GREAT) SHIP (CHIP). The sentence context was employed to make the test as natural as possible. (Rate of articulation was not a variable in this experiment.)

In a second part of the experiment (Experiment 2b), we assessed the effects of those spectral and durational cues that distinguish GRAY and GREAT. For that purpose,

Perceptual Integration of Acoustic Cues   359

we investigated how the results depend on whether, in the original recording, the word was pronounced as GRAY or as GREAT.

Method

Subjects   The subjects were the same as in Experiment 1.

Stimuli: Experiment 2a   The sentence DID ANYBODY SEE THE GRAY SHIP was produced by a male speaker in a monotone voice and recorded in digitized form. Using the editing facilities of Haskins Laboratories PCM System, we varied the duration of silence inserted before the word SHIP for 0 to 100 msec in steps of 10 msec. The duration of the fricative noise in SHIP was also varied. Starting with the duration of the noise as recorded, which was 122 msec, we excised or duplicated 20-msec portions from its center, thus shortening or lengthening it without changing the characteristics of its onset or offset. In this way we created four durations of noise—62, 102, 142, and 182 msec—for use in the experiment. Four noise durations and 11 silence durations led to 44 test utterances. These were recorded in five different randomizations, with intervals of 2 sec between sentences.

To see how the fricative-affricate distinction is affected by noise duration alone, we excised the word SHIP (CHIP) and varied the duration of the noise as described above, but in steps of 20 rather than 40 msec. These isolated words were recorded in a randomized sequence containing 10 repetitions of each stimulus. The interstimulus interval was 3 sec.

Stimuli: Experiment 2b   A second sentence, DID ANYBODY SEE THE GREAT SHIP, was recorded by the same speaker who had produced the sentence, DID ANYBODY SEE THE GRAY SHIP, of Experiment 2a. He attempted to imitate the intonation and speaking rate of the first-produced sentence. That he succeeded well was suggested by our own listening and by comparison of the waveforms. Using the PCM System, we excerpted the fricative noise from the SHIP of Experiment 2a and substituted it for the noise in the corresponding word of the new sentence. Thus, the two stimulus sentences had exactly the same fricative noise in the final word SHIP. Both sentences were used in Experiment 2b: the original sentence, DID ANYBODY SEE THE GRAY SHIP; and the new sentence, DID ANYBODY SEE THE GREAT SHIP; the important difference was simply in the opposition between the words GRAY and GREAT.

Inspection of waveforms and spectrograms revealed that there was only a slight difference in duration between the two utterances; this difference was almost entirely accounted for by the additional closure period between GREAT and SHIP in the second sentence. The final transitions of the second and third formants were, as expected, somewhat steeper in GREAT than in GRAY. Also, the GREAT syllable had a longer duration (210 msec, not including the following closure period) than GRAY (187 msec).[6] Their offset characteristics were similar.

Only two noise durations, 82 and 142 msec, were used, as against the four (62, 102, 142, and 182 msec) of Experiment 2a. There were more silence durations, on the other hand, covering the (wider) range from 0 to 150 msec in steps of 10 msec. Thus, with 2 noise durations, 16 silence durations, and 2 sentence frames, there were 64 test sentences in all. These were recorded in five randomized sequences.

Procedure   Experiments 2a and 2b were conducted in a single session of about 2-hours duration. The isolated word sequence was presented first (the response alternatives

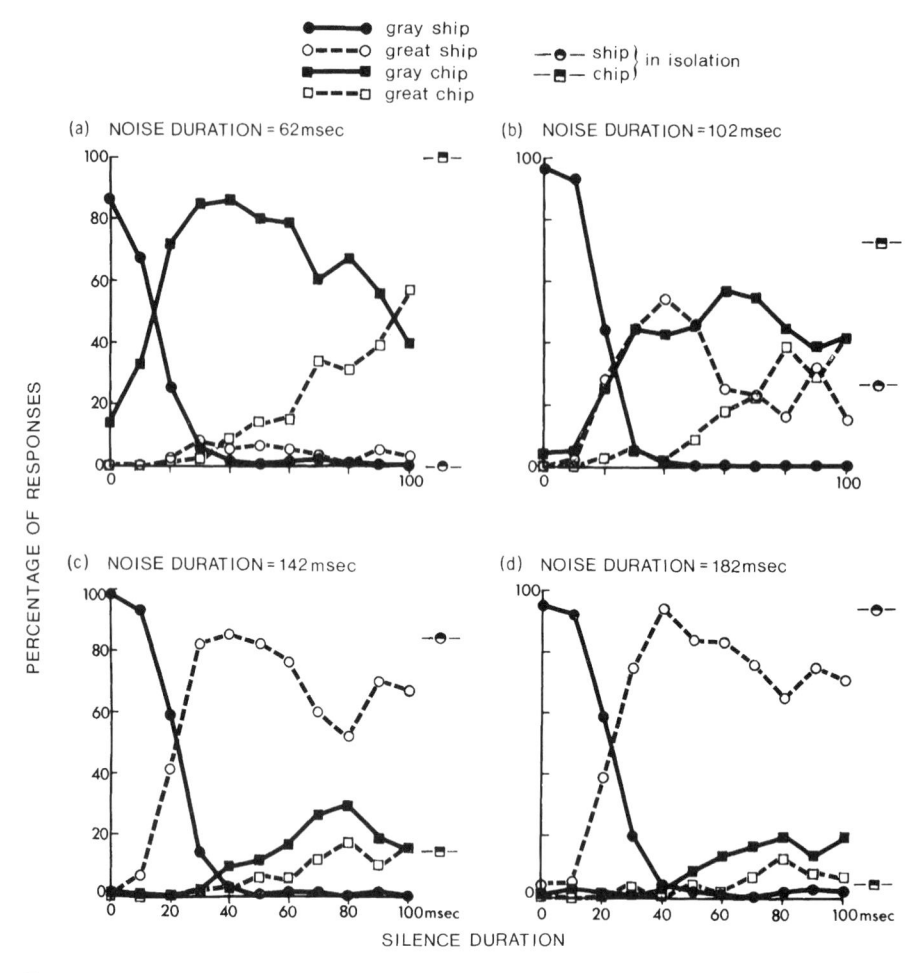

Figure 19.3
The effect of duration of silence, at each of four durations of fricative noise, on the perception and placement of stop (or affricate) manner.

being SHIP and CHIP), followed by the sentences of Experiments 2a and 2b, in that order. Each set of sentences was repeated once, so that each subject gave a total of 10 responses to each sentence. The subjects chose from four response alternatives, using letter codes in writing down their responses: A = GRAY SHIP, B = GREAT SHIP, C = GRAY CHIP, D = GREAT CHIP. No subject had any difficulties in using this system.

Results

Experiment 2a In figure 19.3 are shown the effects of the two cues, duration of silence and duration of fricative noise, on the perception of stop or stoplike manner in the utterance DID ANYBODY SEE THE GRAY (GREAT) SHIP (CHIP). Duration of silence is the independent variable; the four panels correspond to the durations of fricative noise. At the right of each panel, we also show the results obtained when the second of the key words, SHIP (CHIP), was presented in isolation.

Let us consider first the responses to the isolated word SHIP (CHIP). At noise durations of 62, 102, 142, and 182 msec—those used in the experiment—the percentages of CHIP responses were 100, 73, 16, and 6, respectively. Thus, as we had every reason to expect, duration of the noise is a powerful cue for the fricative-affricate distinction. The SHIP-CHIP boundary was estimated to be at 119 msec of noise duration. In contrast to the stimuli of Experiment 1, whose noise durations all fell below this boundary and therefore were predominantly heard as affricates, those of the present experiment spanned the entire range from affricate to fricative.

The more important results of the experiment are seen by examining the graphs that tell us how the stimuli were perceived in the sentence context. We note first that when the silence was of short duration (less than 20 msec), the subjects perceived primarily GRAY SHIP. At those very short durations of silence, no stoplike effect was evident, either as an affricate at the beginning of the second syllable (CHIP) or as a stop consonant at the end of the first syllable (GREAT). With increasing durations of silence, a stoplike effect emerged. As in Experiment 1, somewhat more silence was required at the longer noise durations for this stoplike effect to occur, $F(3, 27) = 6.93, p < .01$.

Perhaps the most interesting result was that once a stop was heard, its perceptual placement in the utterance depended crucially on the duration of the fricative noise: At short noise durations, the listeners reported predominantly GRAY CHIP; at longer noise durations, GREAT SHIP. This resulted in a significant response category by noise duration interaction, $F(9, 81) = 71.52, p < .001$.

We also see that the response percentages were in fair agreement with the results for isolated words. When the critical word was heard as CHIP in isolation, it was generally heard as (GRAY or GREAT) CHIP in sentence context, too—provided, of course, that it was preceded by at least 30 msec of silence—and words heard as SHIP in isolation were generally heard as (GREAT) SHIP. Responses in the GREAT CHIP category occurred at the longer silence durations when the noise was short, but even at the longest silence duration and shortest noise such responses reached only about 50 percent.

A more concise representation of the results, showing perceptual boundaries as determined by the probit method, is to be found in figure 19.4. There we see three functions, each of which links those combinations of silence duration and noise duration that are precisely balanced between certain response alternatives, as we specify below. The dashed horizontal line represents the SHIP-CHIP boundary for isolated words.

Consider first the nearly vertical function at the left (squares). This function characterizes the boundary between GRAY SHIP and all other responses. In other words, at each combination of silence and noise durations on this function, listeners were just as likely to hear a stoplike effect as they were to hear no stop at all. The lower part of this function, which represents the boundary between GRAY SHIP and GRAY CHIP, corresponds directly to the SAY SHOP—SAY CHOP boundary functions of Experiment 1 (cf. figure 19.2). As in Experiment 1, this part of the function is slanted and thus reflects a trading relation between silence and noise durations. Moreover, again in agreement with Experiment 1, the trading relation can be described as a constant ratio of silence to noise. However, this ratio (about .20) is considerably smaller than that obtained in Experiment 1 at a comparable speaking rate (.44). This is presumably due to the fact that in the present experiment less silence was needed to obtain a

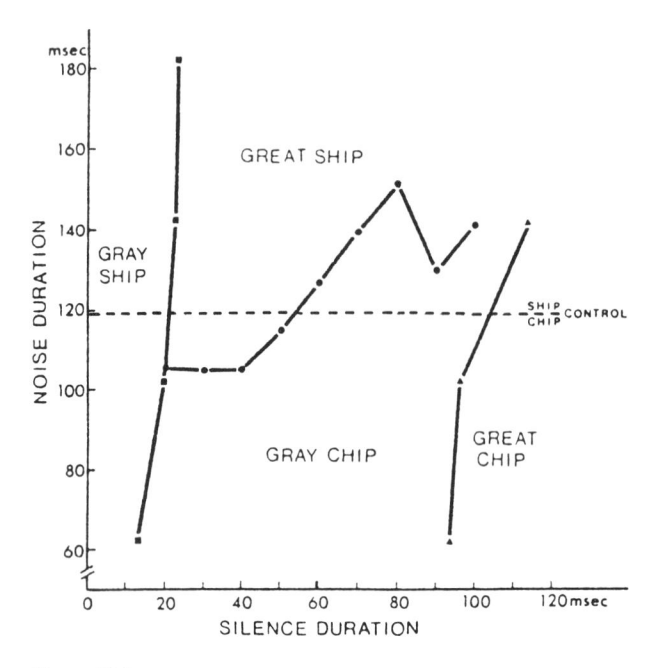

Figure 19.4
Boundaries that divide the several response categories, represented as joint functions of duration of silence and duration of fricative noise.

stoplike effect. The reason for that was suggested by listening to the words preceding the silence when taken out of context. The SAY of Experiment 1 actually sounded like SAY (not SAYT) in isolation, but the excised word GRAY of the present experiment, although correctly pronounced in the original sentence, sounded much more like GREAT. Thus, the vocalic portion preceding the silence contained stronger stop-manner cues in the present experiment than in Experiment 1, so that less silence was required to hear a stoplike effect. These observations provide indirect evidence for yet another trading relation between two cues for stop manner: the (spectral and temporal) characteristics of the vocalic portion preceding the silence, and silence duration itself.

Returning to the boundary function at the left of figure 19.4, we note that the function changes from slanted at short noise durations to completely vertical at longer noise durations. In other words, the trading relation between silence and noise durations which characterizes the GRAY SHIP versus GRAY CHIP distinction disappears as the distinction changes to GRAY SHIP versus GREAT SHIP. This phonetic contrast, located in the first syllable, is apparently not affected by further increases in noise duration in the second syllable but depends only on silence duration.

We turn now to the second function in figure 19.4, that connecting the circles. This function represents the boundaries between GREAT SHIP, on the one hand, and GRAY CHIP or GREAT CHIP on the other. (GRAY SHIP responses did not enter into the calculation of these boundaries.) Since GREAT CHIP responses occurred primarily at long silence durations, the major part of the boundary function represents the distinction between GREAT SHIP and GRAY CHIP, that is, the perceived location juncture. It is clear that noise duration was the major juncture cue, as we should have expected given earlier observations of Lehiste (1960) and Nakatani and Dukes (1977). Had it been the only cue, the boundary function would have been perfectly horizontal. As we see, however, the function shows a clear rise at intermediate silence durations (40–80 msec): GREAT SHIP responses were more frequent at short silence durations, and GRAY CHIP responses were more frequent at longer silence durations. Thus, silence duration was a secondary cue for the location of the word boundary (cf. Christie 1974, for a related result).

The third function in figure 19.4—that connecting the triangles—represents the boundary between GRAY CHIP and GREAT CHIP, excluding other responses. There was no obvious dependency of this boundary on noise duration; the uppermost data point, which may suggest such a dependency, was based on only a few observations, since at this noise duration (142 msec) GREAT SHIP responses predominated (cf. figure 19.3). We note that a fairly long period of silence (about 100 msec) was required to hear both a syllable-final stop and an affricate.

Experiment 2b By using the sentence containing the word GRAY as the "source" for half of the stimuli, Experiment 2b partially replicated Experiment 2a. There results are shown in the top panels of figure 19.5. They may be contrasted with the results obtained with the new GREAT source, shown in the bottom panels. For each source, the effects of noise and silence duration were similar to those observed in Experiment 2a; therefore, they need no further comment. The change in the response pattern as a function of noise duration was again highly significant, $F(3, 27) = 58.95, p < .001$.

The effect of primary interest was that of source. It can be seen that more GREAT (both GREAT SHIP and GREAT CHIP) responses occurred when the source was GREAT, as shown by a significant Source × Response Categories interaction, $F(3, 27) = 10.11$, $p < .01$. However, this effect did not substantially change the overall response pattern. At silence durations of less than 20 msec, the listeners still reported GRAY SHIP; at longer silence durations GRAY CHIP was heard when the noise was short, even though the original utterance had been GREAT. Thus, the cues for stop manner in the word GREAT were readily integrated with the initial consonant of the next word if the short noise biased perception toward hearing an affricate.

As in Experiment 2a, we calculated three kinds of perceptual boundaries (cf. figure 19.4).[7] These are shown in figure 19.6, where they are plotted, separately for each "source," as joint functions of silence duration and noise duration. We see that the boundary between GRAY SHIP and the other responses (squares) shifted significantly to the left as the source changed from GRAY to GREAT, $F(1, 9) = 33.66, p < .01$. In other words, less silence was needed to hear a stoplike effect (regardless of whether it was placed at the end of the first or at the beginning of the second syllable) when the original utterance had contained the word GREAT. Note that the stop-manner cues preceding a relatively short silence were readily integrated with those following the silence: Within the range of silence (and noise) durations in which the subjects' responses were either GRAY SHIP or CRAY CHIP, the frequency of GRAY CHIP responses actually was increased when the source was changed from GRAY to GREAT.

The second boundary function—that separating GREAT SHIP from GRAY CHIP and GREAT CHIP responses (circles)—also showed an interesting pattern of source effects. At shorter silence durations, in which the distinction was mainly between GREAT SHIP and GRAY CHIP, the change in source from GRAY to GREAT increased GREAT SHIP responses and decreased GRAY CHIP responses. This is reasonable, although it

364   Chapter 19

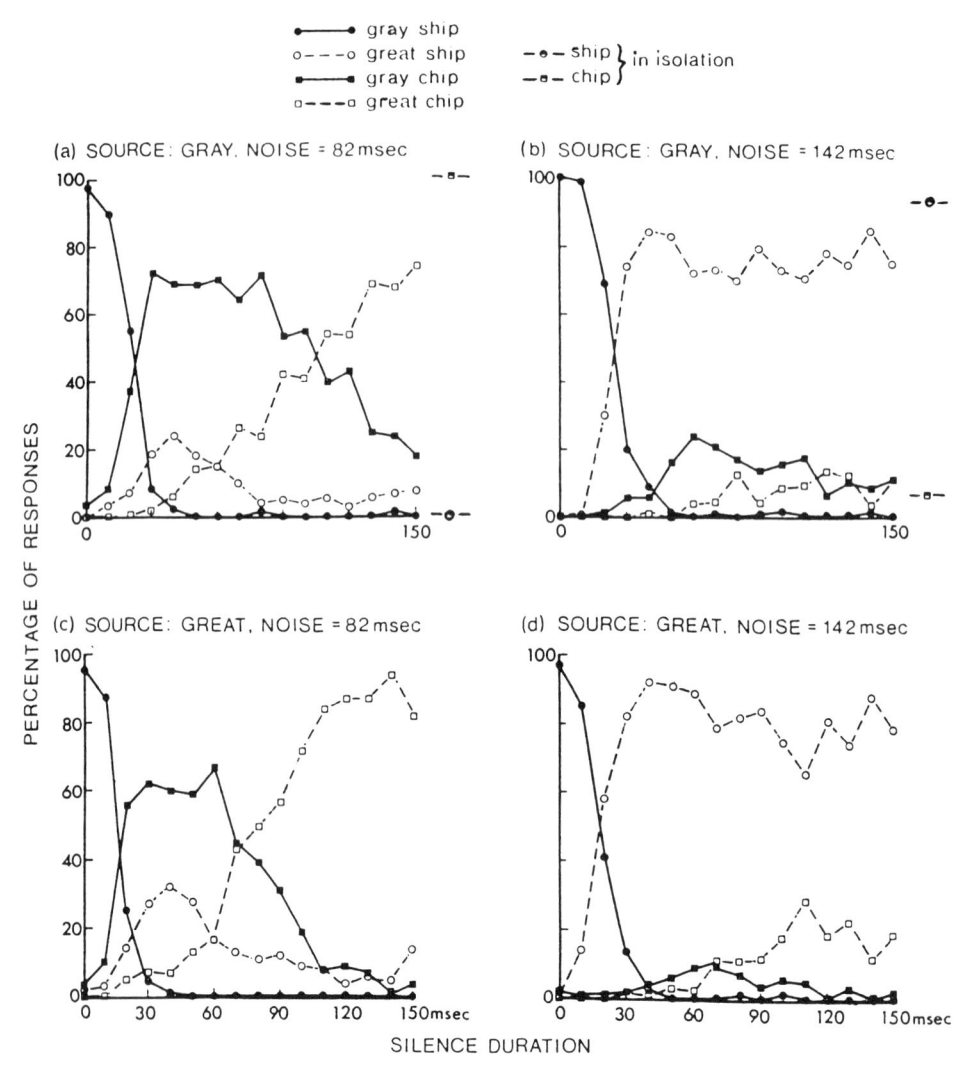

Figure 19.5
Effects of varying the "source" (original pronunciation as GRAY or GREAT) on the perception and placement of stop (or affricate) manner. (These are shown at each of two durations of noise and represented as the percentage of occurrence of the several responses plotted against the duration of silence.)

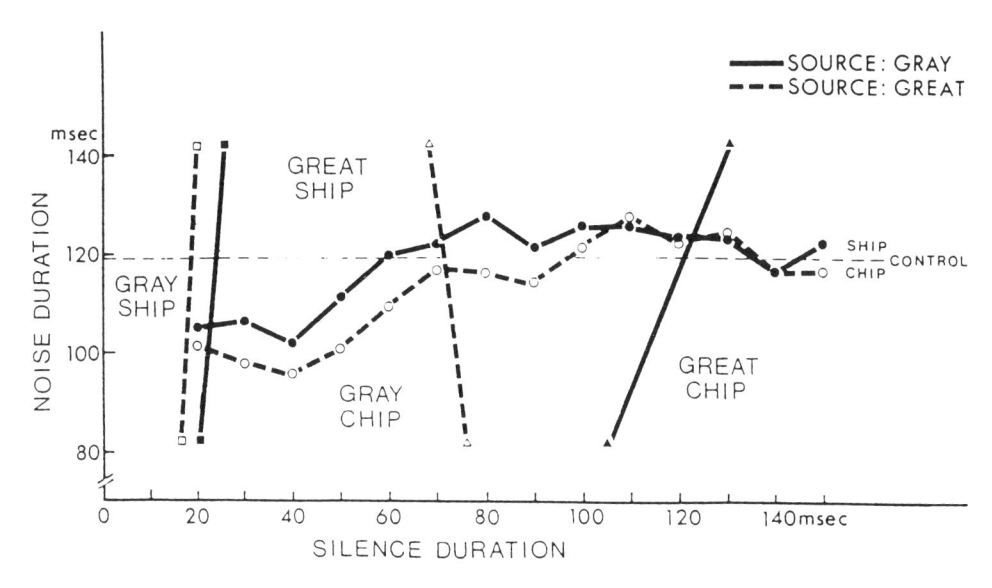

Figure 19.6
Effects of varying the "source" (original pronunciation as GRAY or GREAT) on the boundaries that divide the several response categories.

provides a counterexample to the recent conclusion by Nakatani and Dukes (1977) that cues in the first word have no effect on the perceived location of the word boundary. At long silence durations (beyond 100 msec), on the other hand, the phonetic distinction was primarily between GREAT SHIP and GREAT CHIP; there, source ceased to have any effect. Thus, when the silent interval exceeded about 100 msec, stop-manner cues preceding the silence were no longer integrated with those that followed it.

The third boundary, GRAY CHIP versus GREAT CHIP (triangles), showed by far the largest source effect. Since the phonetic contrast was located here in the word that was actually changed in pronunciation and since, because of the relatively long silence duration, the stop-manner cues preceding the silence were perceived independently of the cues following it, the large effect is readily understandable. On the other hand, the effect is not trivial, since, as we pointed out earlier, the word GRAY from the GRAY source actually sounded like GREAT in isolation. That the stimuli derived from the GRAY source received any GREAT CHIP responses at all was probably due to the presence of relatively strong stop-manner cues in the word GRAY.

General Discussion

The most interesting aspect of the data, in our view, is that whether a syllable-final stop consonant was perceived (GRAY vs. GREAT) depended on the duration of the noise following the silence—an acoustic event occurring much later in time. There are three questions we may ask about this temporal integration: Why does it occur? What are its limits? And when does the listener reach a decision about what he has heard? We consider these questions in turn.

Why does temporal integration occur? We have seen that cues as diverse and as widely distributed as (a) the spectral and temporal properties of the vocalic portion preceding the silence, (b) the silence duration itself, and (c) the spectral and temporal properties of the noise portion following the silence are all integrated into a unitary phonetic percept. Can we explain such integration on a purely auditory basis? Auditory integration does occur—for example, it is responsible for the perceptual coherence of homogeneous events such as the fricative noise—and surely we have much more to learn about such integration, especially in the case of complex acoustic signals. But it seems to us quite implausible to suppose that purely auditory principles could ever account for perceptual integration of acoustic cues as heterogeneous and temporally spread as those we have dealt with here.

We encounter similar problems when we seek to explain our results in terms of feature detectors as they have been postulated by several contemporary theorists (e.g., Blumstein, Stevens, and Nigro 1977; Eimas and Corbit 1973; Miller 1977). Consider again the case in which the perception of a syllable-final stop consonant (GREAT vs. GRAY) depends on whether the fricative noise following the silence extends beyond a certain duration. If a single phonetic feature detector were responsible for the syllable-final stop, then its integrative power and complexity would have to be so great as to remove from the concept of feature detector the simplicity that is its chief attraction. Alternatively, there might be many simple auditory feature detectors, each responsive to elementary properties of the signal, whose outputs are integrated by a higher level phonetic decision mechanism (cf. Massaro and Cohen 1977). But that view fails to provide any principled reason why the outputs of certain feature detectors feed into a single phonetic decision in the way they do. Without reference to the articulatory system that produced the speech signal, the rules by which the detector outputs might be integrated would seem entirely arbitrary.

One might suppose, of course, that the diverse cues have become integrated into a unitary percept as a result of learning. Surely, the cues have frequently been associated in the production and perception of speech. But would such association be sufficient to cause them eventually to sound alike, as the integration (and various trading relations) indicate that they do? Common experience and common sense suggest that it would not. Consider, for example, a listener who has for many years heard a bell and a buzzer, each of a particular kind, always sounded in close temporal and spatial contiguity. It is reasonable to expect that these very different stimuli (or rather their corresponding percepts) would become associated in his or her mind: On hearing one he or she would expect to hear the other, and either would presumably become a sufficient sign for whatever it was that the two, taken together, normally signified. But it seems implausible that they would ever be integrated into a unitary percept, the components of which are no longer readily available to introspection. Nor does it seem plausible that a change in, say, the duration of the buzz could be compensated for by a simultaneous change in the duration or frequency of the sound of the bell so as to produce exactly the same integrated percept. Yet that is exactly what is true of the diverse acoustic cues that converge on a unitary phonetic percept. At all events, we think it implausible to attribute the perceptual integration of the acoustic cues simply to learning by association.

As we pointed out in the introduction, we believe that the guiding principle of temporal integration in phonetic perception is to be found in the articulatory act that underlies the production of the relevant phonetic segment. By an *articulatory act* we mean not a particular articulatory gesture but all articulatory maneuvers that result from the speaker's "intention" to produce a given segment, for example, a stop consonant. Thus, our definition of the articulatory act is intimately tied to the hypothesis that units of phoneme size are physiologically real at some early level in speech production. At the later articulatory level, we can distinguish individual gestures (such as closing and opening the jaw, raising the tongue tip) that form the components of the articulatory act. It is, of course, these several gestures that produce the several (and sometimes even more numerous) acoustic cues. The perceptual process by which the acoustic cues are integrated into a unitary phonetic percept somehow recaptures the gestures and also mirrors the processes by which they unfolded from a unitary phonetic intention (or motor program). We find it plausible to suppose that speech perception, as a unique biological capacity, has in fact evolved to reflect the equally species-specific capacity for speech production. The consequence is that, in a very real sense, the listener perceives directly the speaker's "intent"—the phonetically significant articulatory act (for views related to ours in their emphasis on the perception of articulatory events but different from ours in other respects, see Fowler 1977; Bailey and Summerfield 1978; Summerfield 1977).

We turn now to our second question, that about the limits of temporal integration. From the data of our experiments, we obtain an estimate according to the following considerations. The boundary between GRAY CHIP and GREAT CHIP indicates the longest period of time over which the stop-manner cues preceding the silence are still integrated with the cues following the silence into a single stoplike percept (affricate). Although the exact temporal interval varied with the strength of the stop-manner cues preceding the silence (cf. figure 19.6), a silence duration of 100 msec is a reasonably typical value. To this must be added the approximate temporal extent of the relevant cues preceding and following the silence—at least 100 msec for the duration of both the vocalic portion and the fricative noise. We thus arrive at a temporal range of 300–350 msec for the integration of stop-manner cues. This estimate is in good agreement with results on the single-geminate distinction for intervocalic stop consonants (e.g., TOPIC vs. TOP PICK), since, as Pickett and Decker (1960) and Repp (1976) have shown, that boundary occurs around 200 msec of silence at normal rates of speech. Inasmuch as the manner cues following the closure interval (the formant transitions of the second vocalic portion) are shorter in this case (perhaps 50 msec), we arrive again at an integration period of about 350 msec. This coincidence is not surprising since the articulatory gesture underlying an intervocalic stop consonant is similar to that for a stop consonant embedded between a vowel and a fricative. In our view, the range of temporal integration in perception reflects not an auditory limitation—such as the duration of a preperceptual auditory store (Massaro 1975)—but the longest acceptable duration of the underlying articulatory act. Different articulatory acts may well be associated in perception with different ranges of temporal integration.

We thus arrive at our third question: When do the listeners decide what they have heard? Before we can answer that question, we must point out that there are two logically distinct decisions the listener must make: (a) *What* phoneme has occurred? (b) *Where* does it belong? Thus, in the case of the GREAT SHIP–GRAY CHIP distinction, the listener must decide first that a stop consonant has occurred and, then, whether it belongs with the first or the second syllable. We see three possibilities for the temporal organization of the listener's decisions: (a) Both the What and Where decisions occur after all relevant cues have been integrated; (b) the What decision occurs as soon as sufficient cues are available, but the Where decision is delayed until the end of the integration period; and (c) both a What decision and a Where (default) decision are made as soon as sufficient cues are available, but the Where decision may be revised in the light of later information. We discuss these hypotheses in turn.

The first hypothesis implies, in the case of GREAT SHIP, that listeners do not know whether they have heard a stop consonant until they have processed at least the first 120 msec of the fricative noise. This seems implausible on intuitive grounds. It is more likely that phonetic information accumulates continuously from the speech signal and that What decisions can be made, in principle at least, before all cues have been processed (cf. Remington 1977; Repp 1976). If this were not so, we should have to assume that the relevant cues are integrated at a prephonetic level and thus are held in a temporary auditory memory—precisely the argument we do not wish to make. On the other hand, if temporally separate cues (such as those preceding and following the silence in GRAY CHIP) are immediately translated into phonetic representations, temporal integration merely combines identical phonetic codes within a certain time span and thus is not dependent on auditory limitations. In terms of our experiment, this means that the listener already "knew" at the end of the vocalic portion of GRAY (which, as the reader may remember, contained sufficient stop-manner cues to be perceived as GREAT in isolation) that a stop had occurred; the silence duration cue (if less than about 100 msec) and the noise duration cue (if less than about 120 msec) merely confirmed this perceptual knowledge.

The remaining two hypotheses differ in their assumptions about when the Where decision occurs. According to one hypothesis, listeners do not know whether they have heard GRAY or GREAT until they have processed the fricative noise; in other words, the Where decision is postponed until all relevant cues have been integrated. The alternative hypothesis assumes that listeners group the stop consonant automatically with the preceding syllable until later information leads them to revise that decision. This leads to the paradoxical prediction that in an utterance heard as GRAY CHIP, listeners actually perceive GREAT for the brief moment that extends from the end of the vocalic portion to the end of the fricative noise, as they would have if CHIP had never occurred. We hope to conduct experiments in the future that will shed more light on these questions.

Notes

This research was supported by National Institute for Child Health and Human Development Grant HD01994 and by BRSG Grant RR05596. We would like to thank Georgann Witte for her help in data analysis. A short version of this paper was presented at the 94th meeting of the Acoustical Society of America in Miami Beach, Florida, December 1977.

1. It may be noted that the stop consonants (affricates) in the three examples given have different places of articulation. Perceptual information about place of articulation is provided by spectral cues preceding and following the silence (Bailey and Summerfield 1978). In our experiments we are concerned only with cues for stop manner and not with place distinctions. Therefore, we pass over the question why, in the last example, listeners hear SAY CHOP (SAY TSHOP) and not SAY PSHOP or SAY KSHOP.
2. This manipulation merely created a situation favorable for obtaining the desired effect and in no way affected the validity of the experiment. In fact, our cutting back the noise resulted in a moderate bias in the opposite direction, toward hearing an affricate (CHOP). It should be noted in this connection that not only does SAY SHOP turn into SAY CHOP when silence is inserted but that a natural SAY CHOP can also be turned into SAY SHOP by removing the silence that precedes the fricative noise. Both effects have limits, however: A noise with an extremely abrupt onset will not easily be heard as a fricative even in the

absence of silence, and a noise with an extremely gradual onset will not easily be heard as an affricate even if sufficient silence is present.
3. Strictly speaking, the term "trading relation" may not be appropriate for a positive relation between two cues, but for want of a better term, we use it. The positive covariation of the two perceptual cues is a direct consequence of their negative covariation in production: Fricatives have a long noise duration and no silence, whereas affricates have a shorter noise duration preceded by a closure interval. Genuine perceptual trading relations (negative covariation) are observed when two acoustic properties are positively correlated in production, such as, for example, silence and the extent of the first formant transition as cues for stop manner (Bailey and Summerfield 1978). In any case, a positive trading relation can be turned into a negative one by simply reversing the directionality of the scale on which one of the cues is measured.
4. The boundary estimates obtained from the average data of all subjects were virtually identical with the averages of the estimates for individual subjects, so the former have been plotted in figure 19.1. The response function for the longest noise seemed to reach asymptote below 100 percent CHOP responses, especially at the fast speaking rate. This caused the estimated boundaries to fall at somewhat longer silence durations than the 50 percent intercepts shown in figure 19.1.
5. It must be kept in mind that this description is true only within the limits of the present experiment. Had the noise duration been increased beyond 100 msec, a point would have been reached where no amount of silence would have led to a substantial percentage of CHOP responses (cf. Experiment 2).
6. Our intuition may tell us that GRAY should have been longer than GREAT. However, these intuitions are based on the pronunciation of these words in isolation, where word-final lengthening extends the vowel in GRAY. When followed by SHIP, on the other hand, the longer duration of GREAT is quite plausible. However, we do not know whether this observation has any generality.
7. The GREAT SHIP versus GRAY CHIP (+ GREAT CHIP) boundary estimates were based on only two data points (noise durations). To obtain probit estimates, we added two hypothetical anchor points: 22 msec (of noise) with 0 percent GREAT SHIP responses, and 202 msec (of noise) with 100 percent GREAT SHIP responses.

References

Ainsworth, W. A. The influence of precursive sequences on the perception of synthesized vowels. *Language and Speech*, 1974, 17, 103–109.

Bailey, P. J., and Summerfield, A. Q. *Some observations on the perception of [s] + stop clusters* (Status Report on Speech Research, SR-53, Vol. 2). New Haven, Conn.: Haskins Laboratories, 1978.

Bastian, J. *Silent intervals as closure cues in the perception of stop consonants.* (Quarterly Progress Report No.33, Appendix 1.) New Haven, Conn.: Haskins Laboratories, 1959.

Bastian, J. *Silent intervals and formant transitions as cues in the perception of stop phonemes.* (Quarterly Progress Report No.35, Appendix 2.) New Haven, Conn.: Haskins Laboratories, 1960.

Bastian, J., Eimas, P. D., and Liberman, A. M. Identification and discrimination of a phonemic contrast induced by silent interval. *Journal of Acoustical Society of America*, 1961, 33, 842. (Abstract)

Blumstein, S. E., Stevens, K. N., and Nigro, G. N. Property detectors for bursts and transitions in speech perception. *Journal of the Acoustical Society of America*, 1977, 61, 1301–1313.

Christie, W. M., Jr. Some cues for syllable juncture perception in English. *Journal of the Acoustical Society of America*, 1974, 55, 819–821.

Cutting, J. E., and Rosner, B. S. Categories and boundaries in speech and music. *Perception & Psychophysics*, 1974, 16, 564–570.

Dorman, M. F., Raphael, L. J., and Liberman, A. M. *Further observations on the role of silence in the perception of stop consonants* (Status Report on Speech Research, SR-48). New Haven, Conn.: Haskins Laboratories, 1976.

Dorman, M. F., Raphael, L. J., and Liberman, A. M. *Some experiments on the sound of silence in phonetic perception.* Unpublished manuscript, 1978.

Eimas, P. D., and Corbit, J. D. Selective adaptation of linguistic feature detectors. *Cognitive Psychology*, 1973, 4, 99–109.

Erickson, D., Fitch, H. L., Halwes, T. G, and Liberman, A. M. *A trading relation in perception between silence and spectrum.* Unpublished manuscript, 1978.

Finney, D. J. *Probit analysis* (3rd ed.). Cambridge, England: Cambridge University Press, 1971.

Fowler, C. A. *Timing control in speech production.* Unpublished doctoral dissertation, University of Connecticut, 1977.

Fujisaki, H., Nakamura, K., and Imoto, T. Auditory perception of duration of speech and non-speech stimuli. In G. Fant and M. A. A. Tatham (Eds.), *Auditory analysis and perception of speech*. London: Academic Press, 1975.

Gay, T. Effect of speaking rate on vowel formant movements. *Journal of the Acoustical Society of America*, 1978, 63, 223–230.

Gerstman, L. *Cues for distinguishing among fricatives, affricates, and stop consonants*. Unpublished doctoral dissertation, New York University, 1957.

Kozhevnikov, V. A., and Christovich, L. A. *Speech, articulation, and perception* (NTIS No. JPRS-305430) Washington, D.C.: U.S. Dept. of Commerce, 1965.

Lehiste, I. An acoustic-phonetic study of internal open juncture. *Phonetica Supplement*, 1960, 5, 1–54.

Liberman, A. M., and Studdert-Kennedy, M. Phonetic perception. In R. Held, H. Leibowitz, and H.-L. Teuber (Eds.), *Handbook of sensory physiology: Vol. 8. Perception*. Heidelberg: Springer-Verlag, in press.

Massaro, D. W. Preperceptual images, processing time, and perceptual units in speech perception. In D. W. Massaro (Ed.), *Understanding language: An information-processing analysis of speech perception, reading, and psycholinguistics*. New York: Academic Press, 1975.

Massaro, D. W., and Cohen, M. M. Voice onset time and fundamental frequency as cues to the /zi/–/si/ distinction. *Perception & Psychophysics*, 1977, 22, 373–382.

Miller, J. L. Properties of feature detectors for VOT: The voiceless channel of analysis. *Journal of the Acoustical Society of America*, 1977, 62, 641–648.

Nakatani, L. H. and Dukes, K. D. Locus of segmental cues for word juncture. *Journal of the Acoustical Society of America*, 1977, 62, 714–719.

Pickett, J. M., and Decker, L. R. Time factors in the perception of a double consonant. *Language and Speech*, 1960, 3, 11–17.

Remington, R. Processing of phonemes in speech: A speed-accuracy study. *Journal of the Acoustical Society of America*, 1977, 62, 1279–1290.

Repp. B. H. *Perception of implosive transitions in VCV utterances* (Status Report on Speech Research, SR-48). New Haven, Conn.: Haskins Laboratories, 1976.

Summerfield, A. Q. *On articulatory rate and perceptual constancy in phonetic perception*. Unpublished manuscript, 1977.

Summerfield, Q., and Haggard, M. On the dissociation of spectral and temporal cues to the voicing distinction in initial stop consonants. *Journal of the Acoustical Society of America*, 1977, 62, 435–448.

Chapter 20
Perceptual Equivalence of Two Acoustic Cues for Stop-Consonant Manner

In speech, the many-to-one relationship between stimulus and percept has two aspects: Several phonetic contrasts can be produced by the same acoustic cue; conversely, several acoustic cues can produce the same phonetic contrast. Examining the first aspect, one finds that the effect pervades all three phonetic dimensions. Thus, with all else constant, duration of (intersyllabic) silence, for example, can cue contrasts in manner (Haskins Laboratories 1954; Kuipers 1955), voicing (Lisker 1957a), and place (Port 1976). As for the other aspect, the various acoustic cues for a particular contrast can be radically different. For example, an intervocalic voicing contrast in disyllables with the trochaic stress (*rapid* vs. *rabid*) can be cued, all else constant, by the duration of the intersyllabic silence or, alternatively, by the formant transitions at the end of the first syllable and the beginning of the next (Lisker 1957b).

It is with the second aspect of the many-to-one relationship that this paper is concerned. Specifically, it examines two of the cues for the manner contrast exemplified by the words *slit* and *split*. One cue is temporal (the duration of silence between the noise associated with the initial [s] and the vocalic portion of the syllable); the other is spectral (the presence or absence of appropriate formant transitions at the onset of the vocalic portion of the syllable). Our aim is to see whether two such different acoustic cues engage in a trading relation, and also to discover how they might be combined so as to cause their effects to summate or to cancel each other. Taken together, the results may reflect an equivalence that implies phonetic (as distinct from auditory) perception.

Experiment 1

The importance of silence as a cue for the perception of stop-consonant manner was shown in early studies by Bastian, Delattre, and Liberman (1959) and Bastian (1959). Starting with magnetic-tape recordings of the real speech utterance *sag*, the former investigators inserted snippets of blank tape (hence silence) between the noise associated with the initial fricative and the vocalic portion of the syllable. Listeners perceived *sag* or *stag*, depending on the duration of the (intrasyllabic) silent interval.

More recent experiments on silence as a cue for manner have been designed to test the hypothesis that its effects in speech are instances of distinctively phonetic perception. In the phonetic domain, silence would lead to perception of a stop consonant, not only because the ear hears, but also, and crucially, because the silence

Originally published in *Perception & Psychophysics* 27, 4 (1980): 343–350, with Hollis L. Fitch, Terry Halwes, and Donna M. Erickson. Reprinted with permission.

specifies to an appropriately specialized perceptual system that the speaker closed his vocal tract, as he must when he produces a stop. Among the data relevant to that hypothesis are some that imply a trading relation—hence an equivalence in perception—between silence and various aspects of sound that are also related to the closing (and opening) gestures. An especially telling set of such data is owing to Bailey and Summerfield (1978). These investigators found that the amount of silence necessary to produce the stop consonant in fricative-stop-vowel syllables varied with another acoustic correlate of closure—namely, the onset frequency of the first formant. As the onset was lower, less silence was needed to hear the stop.

In the case just described—and in other cases that do not involve the silence cue—diverse acoustic events appear to sound alike. (For a review, see Liberman and Studdert-Kennedy 1977.) One asks why.

A purely auditory explanation of this equivalence would rely on a description of the way the auditory system processes sound, regardless of whether or not the sound is perceived as speech. One such auditory process is the kind of energy integration that leads to time-intensity tradeoffs in the perception of very brief tones and light flashes. In processes of this kind, a longer light flash of lower intensity, for example, is indistinguishable from a shorter light flash that has just the increment of intensity required to keep the total amount of energy constant. This energy integration is presumably due to limits on the resolving power of the peripheral sensory apparatus. It is unlikely, however, that such energy integration could account for the equivalence of two components of signal which, as in the cases of speech perception we are concerned with, are themselves separately resolvable.

Another auditory process that might explain the perceptual equivalence of two different acoustic dimensions would be some kind of functional interaction, presumably at "higher" levels of the system. To the extent that such interactions might apply to all patterns, and not just to those that can be perceived as speech, they would be of an auditory, not a phonetic, sort. However, nothing presently known about the auditory system provides a basis in principle for the many interactions that must be assumed if we are to account for the various trading relations among the speech cues. It would appear, then, that we could only multiply the assumed interactions ad hoc, with the result that we would, in the end, have as many assumed auditory interactions as there are trading relations.

An alternative view of the trading relations, which we find more appealing, differs from any auditory account in that it is not neutral with regard to the events by which the acoustic cues are produced. The advantage of this view is that it provides a principle that can be seen to underlie many different trading relations: Cues that are the common but distributed products of the same linguistically significant act will tend to trade. Consider again, for example, the equivalence between silence and the starting frequency of the first formant in the experiment by Bailey and Summerfield. As those investigators point out, the silence occurs as a consequence of the vocal-tract closure necessary for the stop, and the low-frequency onset of the first formant as a consequence of the subsequent opening. If we assume a perceiver sensitive to these cues as information about the source of phonetically significant acts, then silence and the starting frequency of the first formant might lead to the same percept because they specify the same phonetic act. On that interpretation, the trading relations we have described would hold only for sounds that were being processed as speech, and they would, accordingly, be reflections of phonetic perception.

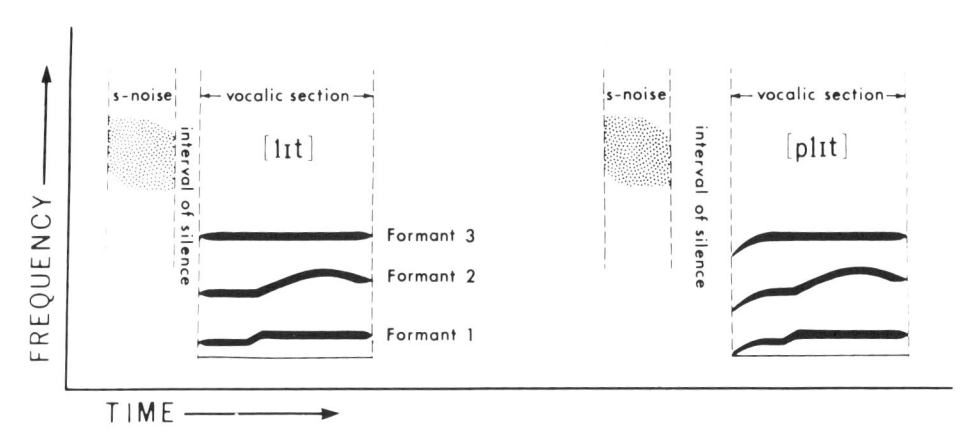

Figure 20.1
Schematic spectrograms of the stimulus patterns, showing two of the settings of the silent interval and both settings of the formant transition at the onset of the vocalic portion.

The first of the two experiments to be reported in this paper is similar to that of Bailey and Summerfield, already described, in that it will examine a trading relation between silence and spectrum in the perception of stop-consonant manner in an initial fricative-stop cluster. Our aim is to carry out a further study of this kind of trading relation, but also—indeed, especially—to provide a basis for a second experiment in which we will find the results of combining the two cues in different ways, and thus achieve a stricter test of the perceptual equivalence that the trading relation implies.

Method

Our aim in constructing the stimuli was to have two cues to the perceived contrast *slit* vs. *split*: temporal variation in silence and spectral variation in sound. To that end, we synthesized stimuli that consisted of an s-like noise, followed, after a variable amount of silence, by either of two vocalic syllables.

To synthesize the vocalic syllables, we first obtained approximate parameter values by making relevant measurements of the utterances [lit] and [plit] as spoken by a male. Using these to set the parameter values of a serial resonance synthesizer (OVE III), we synthesized the two different (vocalic) syllables. We then modified these syllables so as to meet the following requirements: that they be the same except at their onsets, where there would be a spectral difference (in formant transitions), and that the spectral difference not be so great so to override the effects of the variable silent interval in cuing *slit* vs. *split*. (It was also important, of course, that other cues to the contrast *slit* vs. *split*, such as amplitude rise-time, be effectively neutralized so as not to override the effects of the two cues, silence and spectrum, we wished to study.[1]) The syllables are shown in figure 20.1. One sees that the frequency contours of the formant onsets were relatively flat for one of the patterns and somewhat rising for the other. These shapes closely approximated the natural tokens of [lit] and [plit], respectively. Each vocalic section was 170 msec long.

To determine if the spectral difference alone would successfully bias those syllables towards [lit] and [plit], we tested them, without any preceding s-like noise, in forced-choice identification trials. Each of five subjects heard a randomized series containing

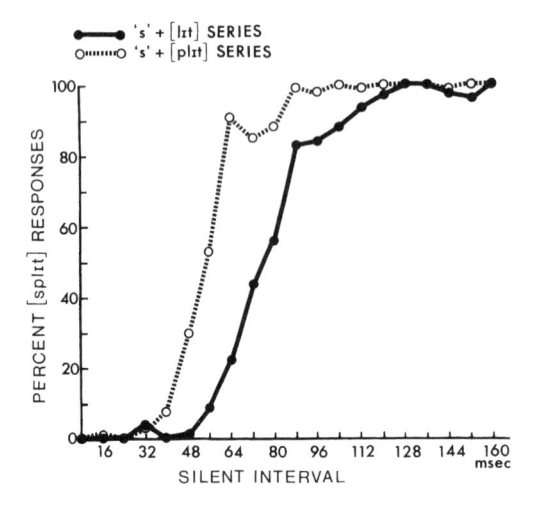

Figure 20.2
Effect of silent interval on the identification of the experimental syllables for each of the two stimulus series.

30 instances of each of the two syllables, labeling each token as [lit] or [plit]. The stimulus with the relatively flat formants was heard as [plit] 57 percent of the time; the stimulus with the rising formants was heard as [plit] 97 percent of the time. For convenience, we will call the former syllable [lit], the latter [plit].[2]

To produce the full stimulus patterns, we generated a 96-msec patch of band-limited noise appropriate for [s] (referred to hereafter as "s"), placed it in front of the [lit] and [plit] vocalic syllables and varied the interval of silence between the "s" and the vocalic portion from 8 to 160 msec in steps of 8 msec, making a total of 20 stimuli in each series.

To produce a set of test stimuli that would enable us to determine the location of the phonetic boundary in each series—and thus to see the trading relation, if any, between duration of silence and formant transitions as cues for the distinction between *slit* and *split*—we recorded the stimuli onto a tape appropriate for presentation to listeners. That tape contained six randomizations of the full set of 40 stimuli, 20 from the "s" + [lit] series and 20 from the "s" + [plit] series. There was a 3-sec pause between items and a 10-sec pause between randomizations.

The experimental tape was presented once to each subject, with instructions to identify each stimulus as "slit" or "split" and to guess if necessary. It was played over a loudspeaker at a comfortable listening level. The subjects were 12 college students. All were native American English speakers and claimed to have good hearing in both ears.

Results
The variation in silent duration was effective in producing a perceived contrast between [slit] and [split], as is apparent in figure 20.2. For both series ("s" + [lit] and "s" + [plit]), judgments shifted from [slit] to [split] as the silent interval increased.

More interesting is the displacement of the perceptual boundary between [slit] and [split] in the two series, for that reflects the trading relation between the temporal and the spectral cues that is the subject of this investigation. For the series "s" + [plit], the phonetic boundary (here defined as the point where the interpolated function crosses the 50% level) is at about 55 msec of silence, while for the series "s" + [lit] the boundary is at about 80 msec. Thus, it appears that about 25 msec less silence was required, on the average, to hear [split] when the formant transitions appropriate for [p] were present ("s" + [plit] series) than when they were absent ("s" + [lit] series). That finding defines a trading relation between the temporal cue and the spectral cue. Within the limits of that relation, these two very different acoustic cues appear to have equivalent effects in perception.

The results we have so far discussed were averaged across subjects. It is appropriate, therefore, to note that, although individual listeners differed in the absolute position of the phonetic boundary, every one of the 12 showed a boundary shift and in the same direction, though not necessarily by the same amount. The smallest shift shown by any subject was 8 msec; the largest was 40 msec.

We should note, further, that the magnitude of the phonetic boundary shift, whether for individuals or for the group, is presumably not fixed; settings of the formant transitions other than the two we selected would likely produce a smaller or larger shift, as would different settings of other relevant cues. These latter include, for example, the offset characteristics of the "s" (Bailey, Summerfield, and Dorman 1977). Moreover, as indicated in the method section, there are settings of the cues that cause one or more of them to override the others and thus preclude a trading relation. For our purposes, however, the important fact is that, within limits, the trading relation reported here does exist.

Experiment 2

The trading relation found in Experiment 1 implies a perceptual equivalence between two acoustic cues for the presence (or absence) of stop-consonant manner in the distinction between *slit* and *split*: One cue is silence, and its dimension of variation is temporal; the other is sound, and its dimension of variation is spectral. This perceptual equivalence is provocative, because the two cues that participate in it appear to have little in common from an acoustic or auditory point of view. As in the cases of equivalence referred to in the introduction to Experiment 1, however, they are the common products of the same phonetically significant gesture. Perhaps, then, the equivalence is owing to distinctively phonetic processes sensitive not to duration of silence or direction of formant excursions per se, but rather to these as information that reflects what the speaker did. If so, the equivalence might stand as an instance of phonetic perception.

Perhaps the simplest and most direct meaning of the perceptual equivalence we are now considering is that, as diagrammed in the top half of figure 20.3, the contrast between *slit* and *split* should sound the same whether it is made by the temporal cue (Pair 1) or the spectral cue (Pair 2). But there was, in Experiment 1, no provision for direct comparison of such pairs. Results from the phonetic labeling task alone do not preclude the possibility that the apparent equivalence is due to the fact that the listeners were limited to a forced choice between *slit* and *split*. A simple test of the discriminability of the two types of contrasts did not seem methodologically wise, however, because it would depend on producing an absolute negative result: inability to discriminate.

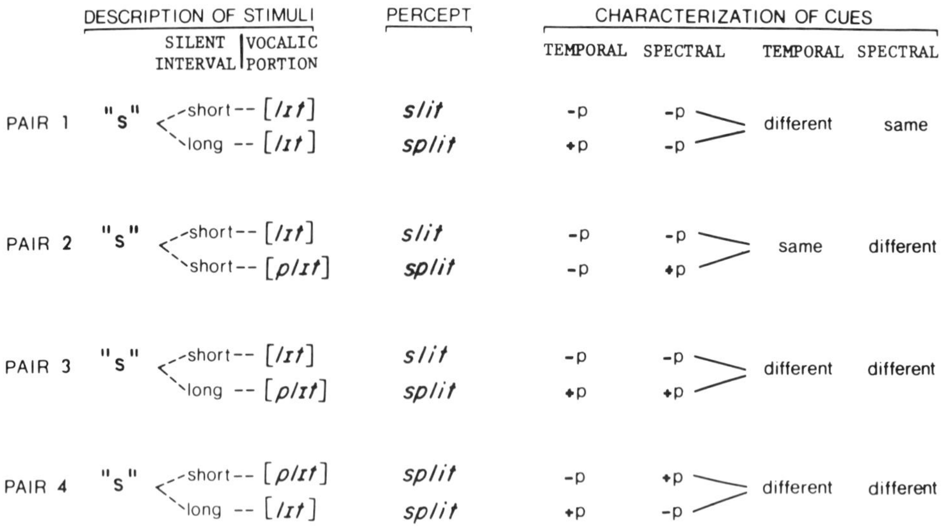

	DESCRIPTION OF STIMULI	PERCEPT	CHARACTERIZATION OF CUES
	SILENT INTERVAL | VOCALIC PORTION		TEMPORAL SPECTRAL TEMPORAL SPECTRAL

PAIR 1: "s" — short -- [ɪt] → *slit*; -p, -p → different, same
"s" — long -- [ɪt] → *split*; +p, -p

PAIR 2: "s" — short -- [ɪt] → *slit*; -p, -p → same, different
"s" — short -- [pɪt] → *split*; -p, +p

PAIR 3: "s" — short -- [ɪt] → *slit*; -p, -p → different, different
"s" — long -- [pɪt] → *split*; +p, +p

PAIR 4: "s" — short -- [pɪt] → *split*; -p, +p → different, different
"s" — long -- [ɪt] → *split*; +p, -p

Figure 20.3
Diagrams illustrating the phonetically equivalent effects of spectral and temporal cues and the phonetically different effects of combining these cues in two ways.

The second experiment, therefore, used a test of equivalence that not only provides for a reasonably direct assessment, as in the comparison just described, but also rests on an outcome that depends on differences in relative discriminability across several stimulus conditions rather than on utter indiscriminability in one. Basic to the development of such a test are the following considerations. If the silence cue and the spectral cue are truly equivalent in phonetic perception, then they should have their effects on the same (perceived) phonetic dimension. In that case, it should be possible to arrange the two cues so that, as in Pair 4 of figure 20.3, they effectively "neutralize" each other, producing two syllables that sound more alike than those that are produced, as in Pair 1 or Pair 2, by either cue alone. It should also be possible to arrange the same cues, as in Pair 3, so that they "cooperate," producing two syllables that are more discriminable than the syllables produced by either cue alone and, a fortiori, still more discriminable than the syllables produced when the cues are so arranged as to neutralize each other. Thus, the assumption of equivalence leads us to expect that the temporal and spectral cues can be added together so as to make pairs of stimuli that are either more or less discriminable than pairs that differ by one of the cues alone. The purpose of Experiment 2 is to provide a test of that expectation.

Method
Taking advantage of a particular procedure devised for us by Quentin Summerfield, we undertook to compare the discriminability of the stimuli of Experiment 1 in the three conditions of cue combination just described in the introduction. In one condition, the members of each pair of to-be-discriminated stimuli differed by only one of the two cues. We chose to make that the spectral cue. In the other two conditions, the members of each pair differed by both cues, temporal as well as spectral. For one of these latter conditions, the two cues were combined so as to "cooperate": One member of each pair had both cues biased toward *split*; the other had both cues

biased toward *slit*. The anticipated effect of such cooperating cues would be to place the percepts more clearly on opposite sides of the phonetic boundary and thus, given any region of uncertainty at that boundary, to increase discriminability by comparison with the pairs that differ by one cue alone. For the remaining condition in which the pairs differed by both cues, the arrangement of the cues was such as to put them in conflict: One member of each pair had one cue biased toward *split*, the other toward *slit*; in the other member of the pair, the cues (and their biases) were reversed. If these cues have their effect on the same perceived dimension, then this combination ought, by a kind of neutralization, to decrease discriminability by comparison with the condition in which the two cues cooperate, and even, indeed, by comparison with the condition in which the pairs differ by only one cue.

For the condition in which the pairs differed by only the spectral cue—let us call this the "one-cue condition"—the procedure was simple enough: The members of each pair had (of course) the same setting (duration) of the temporal cue, but the setting of that cue varied among the pairs. Thus, at one end of the range there was a pair comprising the stimuli (''s''–8 msec silence–[lit]) vs. (''s''–8 msec silence–[plit]); at the other end there was the pair (''s''–144 msec silence–[lit]) vs. (''s''–144 msec silence–[plit]). Between these two extremes were similar pairs for all intermediate settings of the temporal cue. (Since the stimuli with more than 144 msec of silence had all been perceive as *split*, they were, in the interest of economy, omitted.)

In both the other two conditions, where the members of each pair differed always by both cues, the procedure was somewhat more complex. Consider, first, the condition in which the cues were arranged so as to cooperate. Let us call this the "two-cooperating-cues condition." As in the one-cue condition, each pair had one member made from [lit] and one member made from [plit], but in the two-cooperating-cues condition the [plit] member of each pair had a silent interval 24 msec *longer* than the [lit] member. Thus, at the one end of the continuum of silent intervals, the stimulus (''s''–8 msec silence–[lit]) was paired with (''s''–32 msec silence–[plit]), and similar pairings were arranged through the entire range of silent intervals up to the pair (''s''–120 msec silence–[lit]) vs. (''s''–144 msec silence–[plit]).

Consider, finally, the other condition in which both cues differed, but now in such a way as to be in conflict. Let us call this the "two-conflicting-cues condition." Now the pairwise arrangement of the to-be-discriminated stimuli was here exactly the same as that for the two-cooperating-cues condition, except that, to produce the conflict, each [plit] member had 24 msec *less* silence than its [lit] companion. Thus, at the one end of the continuum of silent intervals, (''s''–32 msec silence–[lit]) was paired with (''s''–8 msec silence–[plit]), and similar pairings were made at all increasing values of the silent interval through the pair (''s''–144 msec silence–[lit]) vs. (''s''–120 msec silence–[plit]).

For the two-cooperating-cues and the two-conflicting-cues conditions, choosing the amount of silence by which the members of each pair differ is, of course, critical, if the experiment is to reveal most sensitively such differences in discriminability as there may be between the two conditions. That amount of silence would be equal to the amount by which the two perceptual identification functions—the one for stimuli made of [lit], the other for stimuli made of [plit]—are displaced (as in figure 20.2 of Experiment 1), since that is the amount of silence that, according to identification judgments, just compensates for bilabial transitions. Ideally, the amount of silence would be adjusted appropriately for each subject. For experimental convenience, we

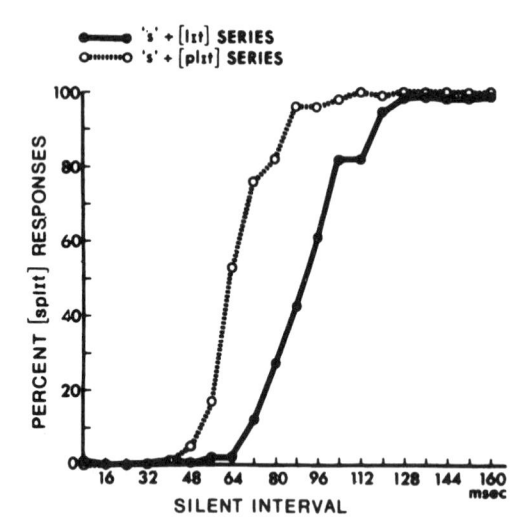

Figure 20.4
Effect of silent interval on the identification of the experimental syllables for each of the two stimulus series in Experiment 2.

did not make the adjustment for each subject, but rather used for all a single value, 24 msec, which is close to the average displacement obtained in Experiment 1.

An oddity test was used to measure discriminability of the members of these pairs. On each trial, one member of a pair was presented twice and the other member once. The listener was to determine which of the three stimuli was the odd one. For each pair of stimuli to be tested, six different oddity triplets—that is, all possible permutations—were generated. Each of these triplets occurred three times, yielding 24 presentations per pair for the subject to judge. There was 1 sec between successive syllables in a trial, and 4 sec between trials. The full test was a random ordering of all the triplets in the experiment. The discrimination test was administered in four 1-h sessions.

At each of these four discrimination-testing sessions, identification functions like those in Experiment 1 were obtained. The stimuli were presented one at a time and in random order for judgment as "slit" or "split," half at the beginning and half at the end of each session. The purpose of this part of the procedure was twofold: to see if the subjects in this experiment showed the same trading relation as found in Experiment 1, and to see if the trading relation was stable across the experimental sessions. The latter purpose was especially important, since it would not be proper to combine the discrimination data across the four experimental sessions if, for any reason, the trading relation that those data are supposed to test had itself undergone some change.

Five American-English-speaking college students with no known hearing deficit served as subjects.

Results

Part of this experiment—the identification of the stimuli as [slit] or [split]—was identical with Experiment 1, though with more repetitions and with different subjects. Figure 20.4 shows that the same result was obtained: Less silence was necessary to

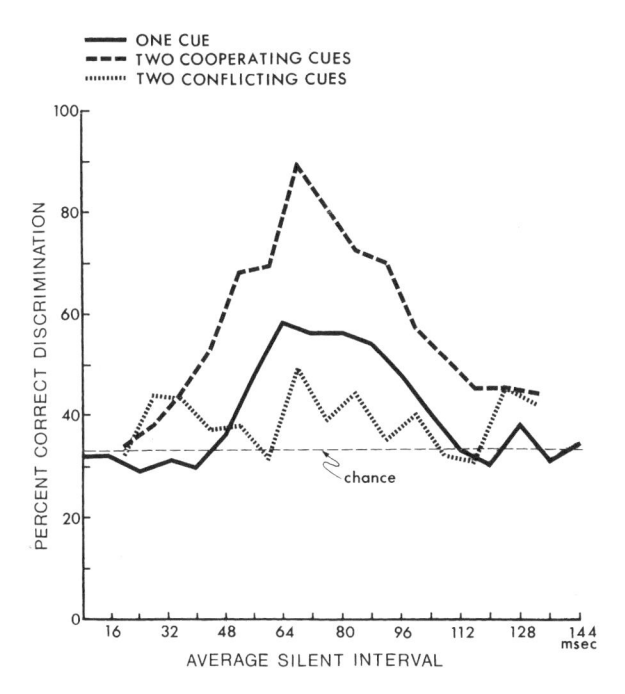

Figure 20.5
Percent correct discrimination for three types of stimulus pairs.

hear [split] when the transitions appropriate for [plit] were present. In the first experiment, the average difference was 25 msec; here it was 28 msec. As in Experiment 1, every subject showed a shift in the phoneme boundary and in the same direction. The smallest difference between "s" + [lit] and "s" + [plit] crossover points for any subject was 20 msec; the largest difference was 33 msec. No significant changes in the positions of these phonetic boundaries were noted across the four days of testing.

The results of the discrimination tests can be seen in figure 20.5. Consider first the one-cue condition—that is, the condition in which the pairs of stimuli to be discriminated differed only in the spectral cue at the beginning of the vocalic section. Examining the appropriate data, which are shown as the solid line, it can be seen that discrimination is relatively low at the extremes and relatively high in the region of the phonetic boundary. Given the outcome of the identification test, this is what would have been expected: At very short intervals of silence, patterns made of "s" plus either [lit] or [plit] should have sounded like [slit]; at long intervals of silence both should have sounded like [split]; and only in the region of the phonetic boundary should there have been a relatively high level of discrimination, for there the "s" plus [plit] would have begun to sound like [split], but the "s" plus [lit] would not.

Taking the one-cue condition as the baseline, consider next the results obtained in the two conditions in which the patterns to be discriminated differed by two cues. It will be remembered that in one of these two-cue conditions—the one called two cooperating cues—the spectral and temporal cues were so arranged that, based on the identification data of Experiments 1 and 2, it was expected that they would reinforce each other, resulting in enhanced discriminability by comparison with the one-cue condition.[3] The discriminability data of this two-cooperating-cues condition are

Table 20.1
Percent Correct Discrimination Averaged Over the Middle Third of the Stimulus Series for Each Subject

	Subject				
Condition	1	2	3	4	5
Two Cooperating Cues	.77	.75	.81	.77	.70
One Cue	.56	.55	.56	.50	.46
Two Conflicting Cues	.40	.43	.42	.34	.38

Note: Chance is 33%.

shown as the dashed line in figure 20.5. As in the one-cue condition, discrimination rises to a peak in the region of the phonetic boundary, but now the peak reaches a greater height. Thus, adding the temporal cue to the spectral cue in this condition made the paris easier to discriminate.

In the other two-cue condition—the one called two conflicting cues—the spectral and temporal cues were arranged so that, based on the identification data of Experiments 1 and 2, it was expected that they would neutralize each other and thus make discrimination difficult. The dotted line of figure 20.5, which represents the relevant data, indicates that discrimination was, in fact, difficult—more difficult, apparently, than in the one-cue condition, and more difficult by far than in the other two-cue condition.

Thus, taking as the base the condition in which the stimuli to be discriminated differ only by the spectral cue, we find that it is possible to add a fixed difference in the temporal cue so as to increase discriminability or to decrease it.

Having seen the average results for the group, examine now the relative discriminability of the pairs in the one-cue, two-operating-cues, and two-conflicting cues conditions for the individual subjects. Since the differences in these three conditions occurred primarily at the phoneme boundary (as we would expect), and since, although the position of the phoneme boundary varied slightly from subject to subject, it was always located near the middle of the range, the results from the middle third of the range are averaged. Those averages are presented in table 20.1. For every subject, the order of difficulty, from easiest discrimination to most difficult, is: (1) the condition with two cooperating cues, (2) the condition with one cue, and (3) the condition with two conflicting cues. Thus the group results, plotted in figure 20.5, accurately reflect the performance of each one of the subjects.

To compute the probability that this result could have been obtained by chance, we may take advantage of the fact that a particular ordering of the three conditions was expected. Since there are six possible orderings of three conditions, and only one of these was expected, then for any subject the exact likelihood of this particular ordering of results in the three conditions is one in six. The likelihood of obtaining this same ordering for each of five subjects is $(1/6)^5$, or once in 7,776 experiments.

Having seen the relative order of difficulty in discriminating the different types of syllable pairs, we should recall what this has to do with the claim that the spectral and temporal cues are equivalent when they converge on the perception of [p] in [split]. For that purpose, consider the two-conflicting-cues condition. If the two cues are truly equivalent in phonetic perception, then it should be possible to arrange them so that they effectively neutralize each other, producing two syllables—for example, [split] and [split]—that sound exactly alike. But while that should have been possible in principle, in practice it would have required that a precise adjustment of the cues be made separately for each subject to take account of the individual differences in the exact value of the tradeoff between the cues. (Moreover, it would have required that each subject be perfectly consistent in the value for the tradeoff.) That adjustment was not attempted. Rather, a setting of the cues was used that was appropriate only on average. A result is that the patterns could not be expected to be perfectly indiscriminable, only less or more discriminable, depending on the arrangement and number of the cues.

It is possible, even likely, that the absolute level of discrimination in the two-conflicting-cues condition could have been raised by using a different kind of discrimination test or more highly practiced subjects. However, there is reason to believe that changes in procedure would not have altered the *ordering* of discriminability among the conditions. Indeed, the same ordering of results has now been obtained in a study (Best 1979) similar to this one but using different syllables (*say* vs. *stay*) and a different kind of discrimination test (same-different). And it is this *relative ordering* among the conditions, rather than the absolute level of discriminability in any one condition, that is important to the inferences we would draw from our results.[4]

Discussion

As pointed out in earlier sections, the several cues for a phonetic contrast are typically found, in perceptual studies, to engage in a trading relation: Given a phonetic contrast for which each of two cues is relevant, the effects of varying one cue can, within limits, be compensated for by appropriate variations in the other. Such trading relations are of interest if only because they imply an equivalence among aspects of stimulation that are often quite different from an acoustic point of view. They are the more interesting if we are right in supposing that the equivalence reflects a sensitivity to the common origin in articulation of the different acoustic cues—that is, to processes that are distinctively phonetic.

The trading relation observed in Experiment 1 is novel only in that it is another token of a type. Surely, this token is a striking one, for the contrast between the cues that trade is very great indeed: One of them is silence, the other is sound. But even that contrast is not entirely new, as the reader can see in the paper by Bailey and Summerfield (1978), cited earlier. There one can find experiments on trading relations different from ours and also considerably more comprehensive. But we need note here only that, like us, Bailey and Summerfield studied the contrast between fricative-vowel and fricative-stop-vowel syllables; they employed temporal variations in silence and spectral variations in sound, just as we did; they found trading relations not different in principle from ours; and they offered an interpretation that is, in some important respects, similar to the one we favor.

But trading relations among acoustic cues, with the phonetic equivalence they imply, have been based on perceptual tests that only require a subject to attach phonetic labels. As mentioned in the introduction to Experiment 2, this leaves open the possibility that, for want of an alternative, subjects might sometimes have attached the same phonetic label to stimuli that were, in some peculiar way, as different as two stimuli to which they had found it possible to assign different labels. What is novel about this experiment is that we have subjected the claim of perceptual equivalence to a more rigorous test. The results of that test help to justify the inference about equivalence that had been made from the way the subjects assigned phonetic labels.

Now we would remark a possibly interesting by-product of Experiment 2: It may provide a test of phonetic perception that can be applied to nonhuman animals. Consider, again, the result with adult humans, which was that the two very different cues (silence and sound) could be so combined as to "neutralize" each other and thus produce pairs of syllables that are hard to discriminate—harder than pairs in which the same two cues are made to augment each other, and harder even than pairs that are distinguished by one of the two cues alone. That the cues have such effects can reasonably be taken to mean that, in the proper phonetic context, they are actually equivalent—that is, they do sound alike. But if we are right in supposing that the syllables with the different cues sound alike only to animals specialized to perceive their phonetic import, then to nonhuman animals they should sound quite different—as different, presumably, as they would to us when heard in a nonphonetic context. In that case, we should suppose that the two cues could not be made to neutralize each other. The result for the animals would then be that both of the pairs differing by the two cues would be easier than the pairs that differ by either cue alone. In any case, the outcome of the appropriate experiments could be straightforward and telling. What we should have to look for is only a difference in the order of discriminability. Moreover, the result to be expected is that the pair that is relatively the hardest for the human beings to discriminate would be one of the two easiest for the nonhuman animals. Such a result, if obtained, could not then be attributed to inattention or lack of motivation.

We realize that such an experiment might prove to be difficult in practice, if only because it requires a demonstration, before the critical test, that the animals are able to discriminate each of the two cues taken singly. Simpler syllables, such as the *say* vs. *stay* syllables used by Best (1979), may be easier than these to use with animals. In any case, all cues that engage in trading relations are candidates.

If, in the event, animals do show the different order of relative discriminability that we rather expect, then it would, of course, be of interest to apply the same test to human infants. Obviously, the considerations that make it a good test for animals would apply equally to human infants, though, just as obviously, it might be difficult with human infants to find cues that are discriminable yet appropriate. But if such cues can be found, then the kind of test we have proposed might provide a useful way to reveal (and study) an important biological predisposition to language.

At all events, the experiments reported here have isolated two very different acoustic cues that engage in a trading relation and are, in an important sense, perceptually equivalent. We have suggested that this equivalence is due to the fact that the cues are the common products of a single phonetically significant act, and are perceived by a system specialized to take account of that fact. If that is so, then a test for perceptual equivalence of two such different cues may provide an interesting basis for comparative studies among adult humans, preverbal infants, and nonhuman animals.

Notes

This work was supported by NICHD Grant HD01994. Special thanks are due to A. Quentin Summerfield for valuable suggestions, including especially one that led to the procedure used in Experiment 2. We also thank Bruno Repp and David Isenberg for helpful comments on an earlier draft of this paper. Some of the work reported here was presented at the Spring 1977 meeting of the Acoustical Society of America, Pennsylvania State University, University Park, Pennsylvania, June 6–10, 1977.

1. In addition to the intended difference in the frequency patterns of the formant transitions, there was a slight amplitude difference between the two syllables due to the particular characteristics of the OVE III synthesizer. The [plit] syllable was .8 dB less than the [lit] syllable on the first pitch pulse, and they were of equal amplitude from the second pitch pulse on. (If the difference in rise-time had an effect, it would be to bias the stimuli *against* the trading relation we expected to find.)
2. Although this experiment concerns cues for a manner contrast and not for place, one may nevertheless wonder why the listeners heard *split* rather than *sklit* or *stlit*. Perhaps the most important reason is that the acoustic cues in the vocalic section are reasonably appropriate for [p], even in the pattern that was minimally biased in that direction. Of course, we cannot exclude the possibility that listeners might also have been biased toward *split* because, unlike *stlit*, it is phonotactically regular and, unlike either *stlit* or *sklit*, it is a word.
3. On the assumption that perception of the speech patterns was categorical, or nearly so, one may ask how discriminability could be increased by adding another acoustic difference. The answer lies in the fact that the identification functions have sufficiently shallow slopes and are sufficiently close together that the members of the one-cue condition pairs never fail unambiguously on opposite sides of the phonetic boundary. Thus, as can be seen in figure 20.4, at 64 msec of silence the [lit] token is identified 100 percent of the time as [slit], but the [plit] token is identified as [split] only 62 percent of the time. Likewise, at 112 msec of silence, when the [plit] token has reached 100 percent identification as [split], the [lit] token is identified as [slit] only 19 percent of the time. It follows that, even if perception of the patterns were categorical, the one-cue condition would not be expected, for any of the pairs used in the experiment, to produce discrimination at the level of 100 percent. In the two-cooperating-cues condition, on the other hand, some of the pairs in the middle of the series comprised stimuli that the subject had consistently put into different phonetic categories; for such pairs, we should expect that discrimination would be enhanced.
4. There is also some evidence that the ordering of discriminability among the conditions *does* change, depending on whether the stimuli are heard as speech. In an experiment employing sinewave analogs to [sɛ] and [stɛ], listeners who, in fact, heard those syllables (whether spontaneously or through instruction) produced the "phonetic" ordering; listeners who heard the stimuli as nonspeech noises did not (Best 1979).

References

Bailey, P. J., and Summerfield, A. Q. *Some observations on the perception of [s] + stop clusters* (Haskins Laboratories Status Report on Speech Research, SR-53, 2, 25–60). New Haven: Haskins Laboratories, 1978.

Bailey, P. J., Summerfield, A. Q., and Dorman, M. F. Personal communication, 1977.

Bastian, J., Delattre, P., and Liberman, A. M. Silent interval as a cue for the distinction between stops and semi-vowels in medial position. *Journal of the Acoustical Society of America*, 1959, 31, 1568 (A).

Best, C. T. Personal communication, 1979.

Best, C. T., Morrongiello, B., and Robson, R. Perceptual equivalence of cues for a phonetic trading relation: Primacy of phonetic over psychoacoustic effects. *Journal of the Acoustical Society of America*, 1979, 66, S50 (A).

Haskins Laboratories. *Affricates: Duration cues for the perception of c in intervocalic position* (Quarterly Progress Report No. 12). New York: Haskins Laboratories, 1954.

[Kuipers, A.]. *Affricates in intervocalic position* (Quarterly Progress Report No. 15, Appendix 6). New York: Haskins Laboratories, 1955.

Liberman, A. M., and Studdert-Kennedy, M. Phonetic perception. In R. Held, H. Leibowitz, and H.-L. Teuber (Eds.), *Handbook of sensory physiology* (Vol. VIII). Heidelberg: Springer-Verlag, 1978.

Lisker, L. Closure duration and the intervocalic voiced-voiceless distinction in English. *Language*, 1957a, 33, 42–49.

Lisker, L. *Closure duration, first-formant transitions, and the voiced-voiceless contrast of intervocalic stops* (Quarterly Progress Report No. 23, Appendix 1). New York: Haskins Laboratories, 1957b.

Port, R. Influence of tempo on the closure interval cue to the voicing and place of intervocalic stops. *Journal of the Acoustical Society of America*, 1976, 59, S41–42 (A).

Chapter 21
Duplex Perception of Cues for Stop Consonants: Evidence for a Phonetic Mode

A biological specialization for language could become manifest in several ways. In the domain of speech perception, it might appear as a distinctive mode (or subsystem), different from the auditory mode(s), and comprising just those processes that come into play when, on being presented with the sounds of speech, a listener perceives consonants and vowels. That such a mode—let us call it "phonetic"—may, in fact, exist is implied by a variety of circumstantial evidence. (For reviews, see Darwin 1976; Liberman, Cooper, Shankweiler, and Studdert-Kennedy 1967; Liberman and Studdert-Kennedy 1978; Studdert-Kennedy 1976; but see Kuhl and Miller 1975; Miller 1977.) Our aim here is to offer evidence of a more direct sort. To that end, we take advantage of a procedure, contrived by Rand (1974), that produces an odd, and possibly unique, phenomenon: two quite different percepts arise simultaneously when the acoustic constituents of a (synthetic) syllable are separated and presented dichotically. One of these percepts is a coherent syllable that sounds just like the original, having been formed, evidently, by a fusion of the dichotically presented constituents. The other percept is a nonspeech "chirp" that contrasts strikingly with the syllable and corresponds closely to what one of the constituents sounds like in isolation. We take this duplex percept to be of interest, not only because it can demonstrate the simultaneous operation of phonetic and auditory modes, but, more particularly, because it can be used to determine why, in the perception of speech, certain aspects of the signal are effective cues. Here, we have used the duplexity to answer questions about silence as a cue for stop consonants. But we will defer those questions until we have seen more clearly just what duplex perception is and what it might represent.

An example of duplex perception, appropriate for purposes of explication, is found is a recent study of the perceived contrast between [ra] and [la] (Isenberg and Liberman 1978; Liberman 1979). The procedure for obtaining the phenomenon was like that of Rand, but duplexity was, perhaps, more thoroughly explored and more convincingly demonstrated. First, the syllables [ra] and [la], shown schematically in the top half of figure 21.1, were synthesized so as to make the perceived distinction depend entirely on the transition of the third formant. Then, as shown in the bottom half of the figure, these patterns were divided into two constituents. One constituent, labeled "base" and shown at the left, included all aspects of the pattern that were identical in the two syllables. When presented by itself, this common core was perceived as a syllable, almost always as [ra]. The other constituent, shown to the right, was one or the other of the third-formant transitions that, in the undivided syllable, critically distinguished [ra] from [la]. In isolation, these transitions were perceived

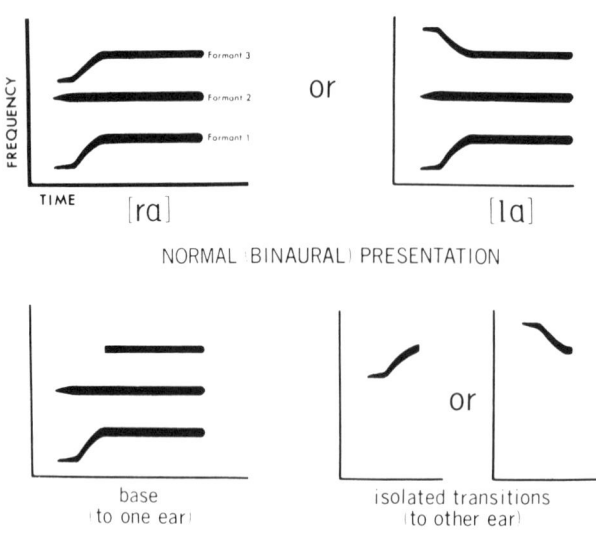

Figure 21.1
Schematic representations of patterns appropriate for duplex perception of [ra] and [la].

variously, but in no case did they sound the same as when, in the undivided patterns, they were essential to the difference between the syllables; by most listeners, indeed, they were thought to be not-very-speechlike, but discriminably different, "chirps." The last, and critical, step was to put the base into one ear and one or the other of the isolated transitions into the other, being careful, of course, to make the temporal relation between the dichotically presented constituents the same as it had been in the undivided patterns.

The result was a duplex percept. One component was a syllable that listeners "correctly" perceived as [ra] or [la] according to the nature of the third-formant transition. The other component, perceived at the same time as the syllable, was a not-very-speechlike chirp. This percept corresponded to the one that had been produced by the third-formant transition in isolation. The two percepts were not only phenomenally distinct but also dissociable, as could be inferred from the further finding that listeners were able to report changes in the loudness of the syllable or the chirp according as the intensity of the base or the third-formant transition was varied.

What interests us here is not so much that the dichotically presented constituents were fused in perception, but rather that one of them was also perceived as if it had not fused. This is the more interesting because the constituent that both fused and did not fuse is the one of the two that, in isolation, did not sound like speech. Thus, given the third-formant transition appropriate for [l] but perceived in isolation as a chirp, and given also the base that was perceived by itself as [ra], listeners did not perceive only the result of fusion: the syllable [la]. Had they perceived only [la], we should have supposed that they were experiencing an effect no different from the one that is obtained in ordinary dichotic fusion, as, for example, when all of the first and second formant is put into one ear and all of the third formant into the other (Broadbent 1955; Broadbent and Ladefoged 1957; Halwes 1969; Rand 1974; Tuerk,

Dorman, Franks, and Summerfield 1980; Darwin, Howell, and Brady 1976). Neither did the listeners perceive all possibilities: the "fused" [la], the "unfused" [ra], and the "unfused" chirp. Had they so perceived the dichotically presented stimuli, we might have supposed that there were, somehow, two consciously available stages (fused and unfused) of auditory processing, or, alternatively, an auditory stage (the two unfused percepts) followed by a phonetic stage (the fused percept). What the listeners did, in fact, perceive was the "fused" [la] and the "unfused" chirp. Thus, perception was not, as it might have been, either unitary or triplex. Quite remarkably, it was duplex, which is to say that it represented two ways of processing the stimuli: as speech and nonspeech. More to the point, the two ways of perceiving, and the duplex percept that resulted, turned on the [l] transition. On the "chirp" side of the percept, that transition was perceived in a way we will call "auditory," because the conscious impression was of sound but not speech; moreover, it had those characteristics that psychoacoustic considerations would have led us to expect. On the other side, the same transition was perceived as having the singularly different quality, hard to describe in auditory terms, that distinguishes [la] from [ra]. We take that different percept to result from correspondingly different processes; in our view, the mode which those processes serve deserves the name "phonetic," because its percepts have just those characteristics we can be aware of when we listen to consonants and vowels.

In the experiments to be reported in this paper, we have extended duplex perception to the case of fricative-stop-vowel syllables ([spa], [sta]) in which perception of the stop depends critically on an interval of silence positioned between the noise of the fricative and the (appropriate) vocalic transitions (Bailey and Summerfield 1980; Dorman, Raphael, and Liberman 1979; Bastian 1962). More particularly, we have exploited the auditory and phonetic sides of the duplex percept to determine why, in the perception of these stops, silence should be an important cue.

To understand the importance of silence as a cue for stop consonants, we might invoke either of two quite different accounts, one auditory and the other phonetic. An auditory account could have it, for example, that the silence enables the transition cues to evade (forward) auditory masking by the fricative noise. Failing that, it could fall back on the assumption that the silence and the transitions engage in an auditory interaction of some unspecified sort, from which emerges the percept we know as a stop consonant. But the particular nature of an auditory account need not concern us. For our purposes, the important characteristic of such a view is that the effect of silence would occur for all sounds that have certain attributes, and it would not matter that they were, or were not, perceived as speech.

Alternatively, the stop-producing effect of silence could reflect the operation of a distinctive phonetic process, specialized to perceive the silence in a linguistically appropriate way. Such a process would treat the presence or absence of silence as phonetically relevant information, revealing, for example, that the talker's vocal tract had closed, as it must to produce the stop consonant in [spa] or [sta], or that it had not, as it does not when the talker articulates the "stopless" [sa]. On this interpretation, silence would have its effect only when sounds were heard as speech.

The phonetic interpretation of the role of silence has found support in several recent experiments (Fitch, Halwes, Erickson, and Liberman 1980; Repp, Liberman, Eccardt, and Pesetsky 1978), including one (Dorman, Raphael, and Liberman 1979) that is most directly relevant to the current study. There, the investigators found that a preceding silent interval was, indeed, necessary if formant transitions were to function as cues for stop consonants, but that silence had little or no effect on the identification of those same transitions when, having been isolated from the rest of the pattern, they were perceived as nonspeech chirps. This result is, of course, open to the reservation that the transition cues were in different acoustic contexts in the two conditions of the experiment. The experiments reported here were designed to speak to that reservation. To that end, they first test for duplex perception with stimuli that comprise the appropriate cues of silence and transitions. That done, the duplexity is used to determine whether the silence affects the speech percept and the corresponding nonspeech differently, when, as in this case, the acoustic patterns that produce both percepts are exactly the same.

Experiment 1

The primary purpose of this experiment is to test for duplex perception in the case of the cues, silence and formant transitions, that produce the perceived distinctions among [spa], [sta], and [sa]. Secondarily, the experiment should provide evidence relevant to the hypothesis that the effectiveness of the silence cue is attributable to distinctively phonetic processes.

Given the transitions in one ear and the remainder of the pattern (the "base") in the other, we ask whether listeners perceive syllables appropriate to the fusion of the two while also perceiving a nonspeech chirp appropriate to the transition cues alone. In other words, do listeners achieve duplex perception? On the speech side of the duplex percept, the test will be to determine if the listeners "correctly" perceive [spa] and [sta] (depending on the nature of the transitions) when silence is present in the base, and [sa] (regardless of the transitions) when silence is not present. On the nonspeech side, the test must take into account that, unlike syllables, the chirps are not readily categorized; they are, however, discriminable. Accordingly, the test on the nonspeech side will be to see if listeners do, in fact, correctly discriminate the chirps (according to the nature of the transitions that evoke them) and, moreover, if they do this regardless of the presence or absence of silence in the base.

The results can establish the duplexity of the percept and the independence of its two sides. They can, in addition, speak to the possibility that the two perceptions of the transitions—as relevant to stop consonants and as chirps—are affected differently by silence, just as we should expect them to be if the effectiveness of the silence cue is an instance of phonetic perception. However, a further and arguably more severe test of this possibility, employing discrimination tests on both sides of the percept, must wait for Experiment 2.

Method

Stimuli In the top row of figure 21.2 are the synthetic syllables from which the stimuli of the experiment were derived. Shown there is the silent interval that serves in these patterns as a necessary condition for the perception of either of the stop consonants [p] or [t]. Shown also are the contrasting formant transitions that underlie the distinction between these stops.

In the bottom row, we see how the syllables were divided into constituents for dichotic (and duplex-producing) presentation. The constituent shown at the bottom right of the figure is simply the transitions of the second and third formants, the only

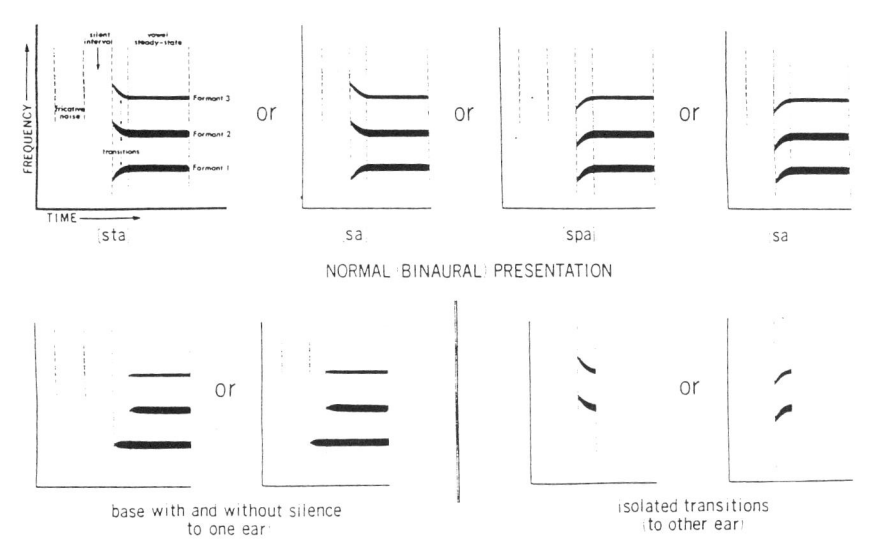

Figure 21.2
Schematic representation of patterns used as stimuli.

cues in these patterns that distinguish [spa] from [sta]. These formant transitions were produced on the parallel resonance synthesizer of the Haskins Laboratories. The [p] transitions started at 924 and 1,856 Hz and rose to 1,077 and 2,360 Hz; the [t] transitions started at 1,306 and 2,861 Hz and fell to 1,077 and 2,360 Hz. All transitions had a duration of 40 msec. When presented in isolation, they had 30 msec of steady-state formants appended to their trailing edges. The intensity of these appendages decreased gradually, complementing 30 msec of gradually increasing intensity in the corresponding formants of the "base"; though not essential to the duplex phenomenon, this manipulation of the intensity causes the transitions to "blend" more smoothly with the base. When the transitions were presented in isolation, they were perceived variously: some listeners identified them as speech-like sounds of some kind, but not as [p] or [t]; others heard them as musical glissandos; most listeners (all in this experiment) found "chirps" an acceptable characterization.

The second constituent is displayed at the lower left of figure 21.2 as the pattern labeled "base." This is what remains of the original syllables when the second- and third-formant transition cues have been removed and the transition of the first formant straightened. It consists of a patch of fricative noise, followed by a brief period of silence, and then by three steady-state formants. We straightened the first formant because, in the duplex percept, the rising transition seen in the pattern at the top of the figure is important but not absolutely necessary for the perception of a stop consonant. The result of this maneuver is to make the isolated second- and third-formant transitions carry, not only the distinction between [p] and [t], but also more of the information about stop-consonant manner.

The "fricative noise" of the base was produced from an s-like utterance (made by a human talker) in the following way. A 100-msec section of the noise was excerpted, low-passed at 5 kHz, and digitized. The amplitude envelope was tapered at either end, making the effective duration approximately 90 msec. There were energy peaks at about 3,500 and 4,500 Hz. The remainder of the base—the three formants—was produced on the Haskins parallel resonance synthesizer. The first formant centered at 637 Hz and had a duration of 256 msec. The second and third formants centered at 1,077 and 2,360 Hz, respectively. They began 40 msec after the first formant, with gradually rising intensity over the first 30 msec, and ended simultaneously with it. In the "silence" condition, the fricative noise was separated from the formants by 100 msec, during which there was little or no acoustic energy; in the "no-silence" condition, the corresponding interval was 20 msec.

To see how the base alone was perceived, we asked six members of the Speech Communication Group at M.I.T., none of whom had served in the main part of the experiment, to make phonetic identifications of the base pattern in both its silence and no-silence forms. (This was done as part of the larger task of identifying all of the speech stimuli that were used in this experiment.) Having been invited to use whatever phonetic categories they found most appropriate, these subjects identified the silence version as follows: 16 percent of the time as [s-a] (i.e., as [s], followed by silence, followed by [a]), 27 percent of the time as [s?a] (i.e., [s], followed by glottal stop, followed by [a]), 28 percent of the time as [sa], and 29 percent of the time as [sta]. They identified the no-silence version 10 percent of the time as [s-a], 13 percent of the time as [s?a], and 77 percent of the time as [sa]. The variability of these judgments was high, the standard error being about 15 percent.

Procedure The two constituents described above were always presented to a listener dichotically (base to the left ear, transitions to the right). They were timed to correspond to their occurrence in the normal (binaural) syllables. We will refer to each such dichotically presented pair as a "dichotic stimulus."

A single "experiment trial" consisted of two dichotic stimuli, presented sequentially, 420 msec apart. On each such trial, the base constituent of one of the dichotic stimuli had the silent interval appropriate for a stop consonant and the other did not. Both orders of presentation of the two conditions of the base (silence followed by no silence, no silence followed by silence) were used. The pairing of both conditions of the base (silence, no silence) with both conditions of the transitions ("p" transitions, "t" transitions) exhausted all possible combinations and yielded eight types of experimental trials. Thus, on any given experimental trial, a listener could not know which of the two base constituents would be in either dichotic stimulus or which of the two transitions would be paired with it.

The test tape was organized into 10 blocks of eight trials each. (Each block was a different permutation of the eight types of experimental trials.) The intertrial interval was 5 sec and the interblock interval was 8 sec. All subjects listened to the test tape three times.

On the first time through the test tape, the subjects were asked to attend to the speech side of the percept and, on each trial, to identify the pair as [spa]-[sa], [sta]-[sa], [sa]-[spa], or [sa]-[sta]. The point of this was to see whether they "correctly" fused the isolated transitions with the base, and also whether the silence cue affected the transitions when, having been fused with the base, those transitions were perceived as speech. Next, the subjects were instructed to attend to the nonspeech side of the percept, and, on each trial, to judge the chirps as "same" or "different." The point here was to make sure that the listeners did also perceive the transitions as nonspeech

Table 21.1
Individual Subject Performance on the Speech-Identification and (Nonspeech) Chirp-Discrimination Tasks

	Percentage of 'Correct' Judgments			
	Speech		Nonspeech	
Subject	S	B	N	B
1	88.8*	71.3*	98.8*	90.0*
2	100.0*	98.8*	78.8*	70.0*
3	98.8*	82.5*	92.5*	71.3*
4	88.8*	73.8*	65.0*	80.0*
5	100.0*	100.0*	88.8*	70.0*
6	93.8*	82.5*	72.5*	71.3*
7	97.5*	100.0*	50.0	57.5
8	93.8*	77.5*	50.0	62.5
9	90.0*	92.5*	90.0*	86.3*
10	91.3*	56.3*	93.8*	68.8*
Mean*	94.3	83.5*	78.0	72.8

Note: Asterisks indicate above chance performance ($p < .01$) by a binomial test. Chance was 25% on the speech task (four response alternatives) and 50% on the nonspeech task (two alternatives). S = reporting on speech percept only; B = reporting on both percepts; N = reporting on nonspeech percept only.

chirps and, additionally, to determine whether that perception was affected by the silence cue. Lastly, subjects were asked to attend, on each trial, to both sides of the duplex percept, and to respond as before. This tested the possibility that the responses given previously might have depended on the subjects' being able, by an effort of attention, to experience but one side of the percept at a time. Subjects responded by writing [spa], [sta], or [sa] in the speech task and "S" or "D" in the nonspeech task. For the condition in which both tasks were carried out on each trial, the subjects first wrote the speech response, then the nonspeech response.

Subjects The initial group of subjects comprised 14 college students. None was known to have any defect of hearing; all were native speakers of English; and, most important, all were naive with respect to the nature of the stimuli and the purpose of the experiment.

There was a screening procedure designed to eliminate any subjects who could not perceive the undivided syllables appropriately and also any who, upon being given trial dichotic presentations, did not report at least the impression of duplexity. As a result, 4 of the 14 subjects were excluded: two because they perceived some of the undivided syllables as containing [l] or [w] instead of [p] and [t], one because he apparently could not fuse the base and the isolated transition, and one because he did not hear the "chirp" as a clear and isolable percept.

Results and Discussion
The results of the tests for duplex perception are summarized in table 21.1. Looking first at the judgments made on the speech side of the percept, we see that all subjects fused the dichotically presented constituents, "correctly" identifying the syllable pairs with a frequency significantly above chance (p < .01, by a binomial test). That is,

they identified the syllables as [sa], [spa], or [sta] according to the presence or absence of silence in the base presented to one ear and the nature of the transitions presented to the other. This was so, not only when the subjects were attending exclusively to the speech percept, but also when they were attending to, and reporting on, both percepts. Plainly, the two kinds of isolated transitions did fuse with the base to produce the appropriate stop consonants. Just as plainly, the silence cue grossly affected the perception of the transitions when, on the speech side of the duplex percept, those transitions were serving as cues for stop consonants: given silence in the base, subjects correctly perceived [spa] or [sta] according to the nature of the transitions in the other ear; given no silence in the base, they perceived the "stopless" [sa], even though the transitions were present as before.

As this point, we should emphasize that perception of the syllables on the speech side of the duplex percept is, in a most important respect, like perception of those syllables when, as in the normal case, base and transitions are combined in a single stimulus pattern and presented to both ears. In neither case does a listener consciously perceive a chirp and then consciously decide to interpret it as one or another of the stop consonants. Rather, the listener perceives simply [sta], [spa], or [sa].

It should also be noted about the speech side of the duplex percept that the formant transitions apparently provided two kinds of information. The more obvious kind pertains to place of production: given that a stop is heard, the transitions are plainly critical in determining whether it is alveolar ([t]) or labial ([p]). Less obvious, perhaps, is the fact that these same transitions also played a role in determining perceived manner—that is, in determining that the consonant heard was, in fact, a stop of some kind. That this is so may be inferred from the way expert listeners had identified the base component in isolation when, in the pretest described under Procedure, they were invited to apply any phonetic categories they found appropriate. When the base contained the interval of silence, the experts reported a stop consonant of some kind 47 percent of the time; but, if we exclude glottal stop on the ground that it is different in manner from proper stops such as [p] and [t] (see, e.g., Ladefoged 1971), then stop manner was perceived only 27 percent of the time. That the subjects in the (duplex) experiment proper were perceiving stops with a greater frequency can be inferred from the data of table 21.1, where it is seen that overall correct syllable identification was 94.3 percent when listeners were reporting on the speech percept only and 83.5 percent when they were reporting on both percepts. Since the pretest and the experiment proper are not strictly comparable, the contrasting results do not permit a firm conclusion that the second- and third-formant transitions provided information about manner as well as place. However, they do suggest that this was so.

Finally, we should consider about the speech side of the percept whether the subjects heard not only the result of fusion, as demonstrated above, but also the unfused "base" constituent. For several reasons, we are confident that there was only the "fused" percept. First, of the several expert listeners who attended carefully to the duplex phenomenon, none ever reported hearing two syllables, one corresponding to the base and one to the result of fusion with the transitions. As for the naive listeners who served in the experiment, two observations are pertinent. One is that when, having been presented with a number of sample dichotic stimuli in the pretest (described in Procedure) and asked to identify the speech percept as [sa], [spa], or [sta], none ever reported having heard two syllables at once. The other observation pertains to the perception of [spa]. Recall, first, that the base alone was never perceived by the expert listeners (as described under Procedure) as [spa]. Now, if the listeners in the main part of the experiment had perceived (in the dichotically presented patterns) two syllables, one resulting from the base alone and one resulting from the fusion of base and transitions, then, assuming the choice of either percept was equally likely, they should have been correct with regard to [spa] no more than 50 percent of the time. That the listeners did considerably better than this in the (duplex) experiment proper can be inferred from the high accuracy of overall syllable identification, as seen in table 21.1 and noted in the previous paragraph. Taking all of these considerations into account, we conclude that, as in the [ra]-[la] experiment described in the introduction, the base constituent was absorbed, as it were, in the process of fusion.

Turning now to the nonspeech side of the duplex percept, we should comment first that listeners did hear the transitions as chirps; moreover, they heard them as such whether or not there was silence in the base. More significantly, we see in table 21.1 that most of the subjects judged accurately that the chirps were the same or different according as the transitions that gave rise to them were the same or different. When they had to judge only one of the two sides of the duplex percept, 7 of the 10 subjects performed at a level significantly above chance ($p < .01$). When both judgments were required on each trial, 8 of the 10 met the same criterion. (Performance for 7 of those 8 subjects was poorer when both judgments were made on each trial than when they were made on separate trials, although it was above chance on both. In any case, an exact comparison is difficult, because the difference between judgment conditions is confounded with the order of performance of tasks, and hence with practice.)

As for the three subjects who failed to discriminate the chirps accurately in the attend-chirps-only task, two were put through a further experiment to determine if they nevertheless could hear the chirps, especially when there was no silence in the base. This was done with stimuli in which the transitions and the base were sometimes presented dichotically, as in the experiment proper, and sometimes mixed electronically and presented to both ears. In the former case, the subjects did perceive chirps whether or not the silence was present; in the latter case, in which they would not have been expected to perceive chirps, they did not.

Finally, we should report that subjects were slightly more likely to judge "same" when the stimuli were different than they were to judge "different" when the stimuli were the same. If silence had affected perception of the chirps, we should expect the opposite bias, since, on each experimental trial, silence was always present in one of the dichotic stimuli but not the other.

The principal conclusion that can be drawn from all of these results is that duplex perception of the formant transitions did occur. On the speech side, the transitions were essential to the perceived distinction between [spa] and [sta], but only when there was an appropriate period of silence in the base constituent; without silence in the base, listeners perceived the "stopless" [sa], even though the same transitions had been presented. On the nonspeech side, the transitions were perceived as chirps. More importantly, these chirps were accurately discriminated as same or different according as the transitions that produced them were the same or different, and performance on this task was not measurably affected by the presence or absence of the silence cue in the base constituent presented to the other ear.

Second, these results provide some evidence relevant to the question: Does silence affect the transitions differently on the two sides of the duplex percept? An unequivocal answer is not to be had, if only because the perceptual tasks were different on the two sides of the percept, as, indeed, they had to be in order to test the duplexity. Still, it is surely worth noting that silence did have a gross effect on the transitions when they were being processed as speech, in which case they were critical to the perceived distinction between [spa] and [sta], although the same silence had no measurable influence on those same transitions when, simultaneously, they were being discriminated as nonspeech chirps.

Experiment 2

The primary result of Experiment 1 was that formant transitions were found to be perceived simultaneously in two phenomenally different ways: as speech, in that they provided information for perception of the stops in [spa] and [sta], and as nonspeech chirps. A further result was that a short interval of silence, known to be a cue for stop consonants, affected the speech but not the nonspeech. The interpretation of that further result was not straightforward, however, because the two sides of the duplex percept were measured in different ways: by identification on the speech side (because only identification could establish that the stimuli were, in fact, heard as speech) and by discrimination on the nonspeech side (because identification of the chirps is rather difficult and also not necessary for the purpose of proving that the subjects did, in fact, perceive the nonspeech appropriately). There was, then, no comparison of the effect of silence on speech and nonspeech percepts when the subjects had to perform the same task in response to both. The purpose of this second experiment is to repair that omission. Accordingly, the subjects will be required to discriminate not only the chirps, but also the speech. Given that duplex perception of the transitions was demonstrated in Experiment 1, these discrimination measures should provide a further test of the hypothesis that in the perception of these stops the effect of silence is phonetic rather than auditory.

Method

Stimuli The stimuli of this experiment were identical to those of Experiment 1.

Procedure As in the first experiment, a single experimental trial consisted of the presentation of one dichotic stimulus followed, after 420 msec, by presentation of another. In other respects, however, the procedure of this second experiment differed from that of the first. Most importantly, it differed in the task set for the subjects and in the combinations of dichotic stimuli that were used in the various experimental trials.

Consider, first, the subjects' task. It was, on both sides of the percept, to try to discriminate the successively presented stimuli of each trial. Subjects were asked to listen for a difference in these stimuli and then to report how confident they were that a difference had been detected. In rating confidence, they were instructed to use the following scale: "1" if "not confident" that a difference had been detected, "5" if "completely confident," and "2," "3," or "4" for intermediate degrees of confidence. It was strongly emphasized to all subjects that they were to base their ratings on any difference they could detect. Indeed, subjects were given explicitly to understand that even though two dichotic stimuli might appear to them as tokens of the same type (for example, as tokens of [sa]), they were nevertheless to listen carefully for any difference they might hear and, if confident a difference (of any kind) had been detected, to assign an appropriately high confidence rating.

As for the combinations of dichotic stimuli in the experimental trials, they were so composed as to exhaust all possible pairings of silence/no silence and "p"/"t" transitions. Thus, a single experimental trial had in its two base constituents one of the following three combinations: silence in both, silence in neither, or silence in one but not the other. As for the combinations of transitions, they were, on each experimental trial, either the same (both "p" or both "t") or different (one "p" and the other "t"). There were, then, three combinations of the base times two combinations of the transitions, making a total of six combinations overall. These six are the fundamental conditions of this experiment and will hereafter be so called.

For each of the conditions described above, we made several types of experimental trials. This was done in order to take into account that there were two ways in which the transitions could be the same (both could be "p" or both could be "t"), and also to counterbalance for order whenever the two dichotic stimuli of a trial were different (silence vs. no silence in the base constituents, or "p" vs. "t" in the transition constituents). The result was a total of 16 types of experimental trials. These were recorded onto a test tape in four different randomizations. With this procedure, the experimental conditions with silence in both base constituents were represented on the tape eight times each, as were those with silence in neither base. As a result of counterbalancing, the conditions with silence in one base constituent but not the other were represented 16 times each.

Having satisfied ourselves in Experiment 1 that subjects could, on each experimental trial, judge both sides of the duplex percept, we decided in this experiment to set them the simpler task of judging but one side of the percept at a time. The tape was presented four times. On two of those presentations, subjects were asked to judge the speech side of the percept; on the remaining two, they judged the nonspeech side, the order of speech and nonspeech judgements having been counterbalanced. There were, then, 16 speech and 16 nonspeech judgments made in each experimental condition that had silence in both base constituents or in neither; in the conditions with silence in one base constituent but not the other, 32 speech and 32 nonspeech judgment was made. The dichotic arrangement of the stimuli—the pairing of constituent (base or transitions) with ear (right or left)—was half the time one way and half the other. The order of these arrangements was counterbalanced.

Subjects Ten college students were in the initial pool of subjects. As in Experiment 1, all were native speakers of English, none had any known hearing loss, and all were naive with respect to the nature of the stimuli and the purpose of the experiment.

The screening procedure employed in this experiment differed from that of Experiment 1. Here, there were two tests: Having been presented (binaurally) with the electronically fused constituents, the subjects were first asked to identify the resulting stimuli as [spa], [sta], or [sa]; then, having been presented (binaurally) with the isolated transitions, they were asked to identify them as patterns, that "glided up" or "glided down." On the basis of these tests, 2 of the 10 subjects were eliminated: one because she could not identify the syllables and the other because she could not identify the chirps.

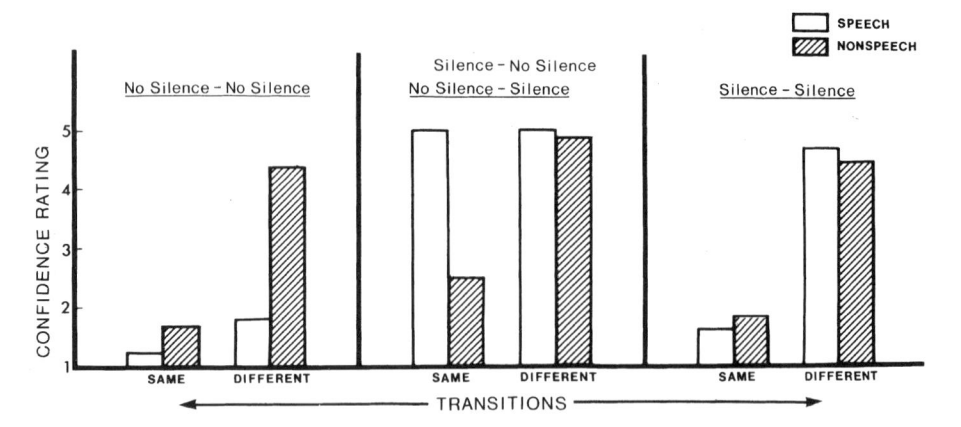

Figure 21.3
Mean ratings assigned in the conditions of the experiment. Ratings were assigned by the eight subjects to reflect their confidence that the two stimuli of each experimental trial were different.

There was also a brief training session, aimed at getting the subjects accustomed to the dichotically presented pairs and to perceiving the two sides of the duplex percept. In this session, the patterns were presented dichotically, and the subjects, having been asked to attend to the speech on some trials and to the nonspeech on others, identified the stimuli as in the screening test. All subjects performed well with the speech stimuli, but two of the eight managed to perform only slightly above chance with the nonspeech chirps. Nevertheless, these two subjects were not eliminated from the experiment.

Results and Discussion
The aim of this experiment, it will be remembered, was to determine whether the silence cue has a different effect on the discriminability of the formant transitions when, on the one side of the duplex percept, they are critical for the perception of stop consonants and when, on the other, they are perceived as nonspeech chirps. In figure 21.3, we see the mean confidence ratings that constitute the results of the experiment. These ratings reflect the subjects' confidence that they detected differences in the pairs of dichotic stimuli presented on each experimental trial. (The scale on which those ratings were ordered ranged from 1 to 5.) Plainly, there is a difference in the mean ratings, depending on whether the subjects were judging the speech or the nonspeech sides of the percept.

Consider, first, the leftmost panel of the figure, which displays the results for the condition in which there was no silence in either of the base constituents. Though such a combination was never presented as such in Experiment 1, we should infer from the results obtained there that the speech side of the duplex percept would have sounded more or less like [sa], regardless of the transitions. Accordingly, we should expect that the transitions would be relatively hard to discriminate when perceived as part of the speech pattern. On the nonspeech side, however, we should suppose that, as in Experiment 1, discriminability would be relatively little affected by the absence of silence. The results of this second experiment confirm these expectations. Given no silence in either base constituent, the speech percepts were not well discriminated, though the ratings were somewhat higher, when the transitions were, in fact, different.[1] On the nonspeech side, the results stand in contrast. There, the transitions were relatively well discriminated when they were, in fact, different, although not, of course, when they were the same. A two-way analysis of variance (with the factors speech-nonspeech and same-different transitions) confirmed that silence did, indeed, affect the discriminability of the transitions differently on the speech and nonspeech sides of the percept [$F(1, 7) = 26.17$, $p < .01$].

Consider, next, the center panel, where we see the results for the condition in which there was silence in one of the base constituents but not in the other. This is the same as the condition that was used throughout Experiment 1, where subjects identified the pattern with silence as [spa] or [sta] (depending on the nature of the transitions in the other ear), while identifying the pattern without silence as [sa] (regardless of the transitions). We are not surprised, therefore, to see, in Experiment 2, that when subjects discriminated the speech percepts they confidently perceived a difference between the "silence" and "no-silence" dichotic stimuli, and they did so whether the transitions were the same or different. (Presumably, they perceived a stop in the one case but not in the other.) The result on the nonspeech side is different. There, the stimuli were readily discriminated when the transitions were different but not when they were the same, notwithstanding the fact that silence was always present in one of the dichotic stimuli but not in the other. That silence affected the discriminability of the transitions differently for speech and nonspeech in this condition is confirmed by analysis of variance [$F(1, 7) = 40.93$, $p < .01$].

Finally, there is the condition in which there was silence in both base constituents. Although this condition was not presented as such in Experiment 1, we can infer from the results obtained there that all stimuli would have been perceived, on the speech side, as containing stops. What is more, stops would have been perceived to be the same or different depending on whether the transitions were the same or different. Not surprisingly, we see this inference supported in the results of Experiment 2: subjects discriminated the speech percepts as different when the transitions were different, but not when the transitions were the same. On the nonspeech side, we should expect the same result, and we see that it was, in fact, obtained. That discriminability of the transitions was not significantly different on the speech and nonspeech sides of the percept was confirmed by analysis of variance [$F(1, 7) = .68$].

To see how fairly the group data, as shown in figure 21.3 and discussed above, represent the performance of individual subjects, we should examine table 21.2. There, we see that seven of the eight subjects conformed quite well to the group result. The single exception (Subject 8) is one of the two subjects who, as noted under Method, performed poorly with the chirps during the training session that preceded the experiment proper.

The results can be summarized quite simply: The silence cue had a different effect on discrimination of the formant transitions depending on whether they supported the perception of stop consonants or whether, alternatively, they were perceived as nonspeech chirps.

Summary and Conclusions

The first conclusion, established by the results of Experiment 1, is that the formant transitions simultaneously supported speech and nonspeech percepts. This duplex

Table 21.2
Confidence Ratings Assigned by the Individual Subjects

	Transitions			
	Same		Different	
Subjects	Speech	Non-Speech	Speech	Non-Speech
No Silence/No Silence* Experimental Condition				
1	1.00	2.00	1.00	4.50
2	1.51	1.57	1.57	4.69
3	1.38	1.44	1.51	4.44
4	1.32	1.07	3.32	4.75
5	1.00	1.88	1.00	4.63
6	1.26	1.00	1.75	4.94
7	1.25	2.25	3.00	4.32
8	1.25	2.13	1.25	2.63
Mean	1.25	1.67	1.80	4.36
Silence/No Silence and No Silence/Silence** Experimental Condition				
1	5.00	2.88	5.00	4.97
2	5.00	2.04	5.00	4.85
3	5.00	2.69	5.00	4.69
4	5.00	1.23	5.00	5.00
5	5.00	2.72	5.00	4.91
6	4.63	1.00	5.00	4.94
7	5.00	3.91	5.00	5.00
8	5.00	3.38	5.00	4.38
Mean	4.95	2.48	5.00	4.84
Silence/Silence* Experimental Condition				
1	1.50	2.13	4.94	4.94
2	1.82	1.57	4.38	4.63
3	1.75	1.69	4.82	4.44
4	1.63	1.00	4.75	5.00
5	1.38	2.94	5.00	4.75
6	1.83	1.00	3.88	4.94
7	1.50	2.25	4.75	4.32
8	1.57	2.13	5.00	2.63
Mean	1.62	1.84	5.69	4.46

* Each of these scores is the mean of 16 judgments.
** Each of these scores is the mean of 32 judgments.

perception was obtained by presenting a base constituent to one ear and, at the same time, particular formant transitions to the other. The base constituent consisted of a patch of fricative noise appropriate for [s], followed by a vocalic segment appropriate for [a]. These acoustic elements were sometimes separated by a brief period of silence and sometimes not. The formant transitions, presented to the other ear, were appropriate for the stop consonants [p] and [t]. By itself, the base constituent was perceived as a syllable, but never as [spa] and rarely as [sta]; the transitions were perceived in isolation as not-very-speechlike chirps. Given dichotic presentation of the two constituents, there were three consequences in perception: (1) the two constituents (base and transitions) fused to produce the same syllable—[spa], [sta], or [sa]—that would have been perceived had the components been electronically mixed and presented in normal fashion; (2) the transitions that, in isolation, produced nonspeech chirps continued to do so; and (3) the base constituent that, in isolation, produced a syllable different from the "correct" fused syllable was not perceived as such, having been absorbed, as it were, in the process of fusion. What the listeners heard, then, was precisely duplex: a syllable in which the transition cues were interpreted in linguistically normal fashion, and a nonspeech chirp that resembled the percept produced when the transitions were presented alone. Evidently, the subjects simultaneously perceived the transitions in two ways. We have termed the one way "auditory," because the percept (the chirp) resembles that produced by sounds other than speech. We have termed the other way "phonetic," because its percept has those characteristics we ordinarily associate with consonants and vowels—that is, it has those characteristics that are manifest when patterns of sound are being perceived as speech.

The second conclusion pertains to the effect of the silence cue on the perception of the transitions, and thus to the role of silence in the perception of the transitions, and thus to the role of silence in the perception of stops. In the results of Experiment 1, we saw a large effect of silence on the speech side of the percept: when paired with a base constituent that contained the silence cue, the formant transitions led to the perception of the appropriate stop consonants; when paired with a base that lacked the silence cue, they did not. On the nonspeech side, where the transitions were perceived as chirps, silence had no measured effect: although silence was paired with one transition and not with the other, most subjects correctly perceived that the corresponding chirps were the same when the transitions that produced them were the same and different when the transitions were different. The implication of those results was supported by the outcome of Experiment 2, in which the subjects were required, on both sides of the percept, to discriminate the dichotic stimuli of each experimental trial on the basis of any differences they could detect. There it was found that the effect of silence on discrimination of the transitions was significantly different when, in the one case, those transitions were supplying information critical for the perception of stop consonants, and when, in the other, they were being perceived as nonspeech chirps. Putting these results together, we conclude that the importance of silence in the perception of stop consonants is owing to specifically phonetic (as distinguished from generally auditory) processes, and that effect of silence in such cases is an instance of perception in a distinctively phonetic mode.

Notes

This research was supported by the following grants from the National Institutes of Health: HD01994 (National Institute of Child Health and Human Development); RR05596 (Biomedical Research Support,

Division of Research Resources); NS05493 and NS07040 (National Institute of Neurological and Communicative Disorders and Stroke). We thank Terry Halwes for his help in the preparation of the stimuli, and we thank Michael Studdert-Kennedy, Bruno Repp, and Dennis Klatt for their many useful comments.

1. Just how discriminable patterns of this sort will be depends, in our experience, on several factors. When silence is removed from a pattern containing a "t" transition, the resulting percept is not likely to be very different from a perfectly normal [sa], if only because the places of production (hence, the second- and third-formant transitions) for "t" and "s" are virtually the same (alveolar). The "p" transitions, on the other hand, are appropriate to a different place of production (bilabial); hence, they are not so readily "absorbed" into the fricative percept when, in the absence of silence, perception of the stop vanishes. If the "p" transitions are of very low intensity, it is possible that the listener will simply perceive [sa]. But, if perception is affected by the "p" transitions, then we can expect any one of the following consequences: (1) The perceived fricative takes on the place of production of the "p" transitions, in which case the percept becomes [fa]; (2) a semivowel appropriate to the place of the "p" transitions is introduced, in which case the percept becomes [swa]; or (3) the transitions are rejected as speech yet remain audible, in which case the listener is aware of a nonspeech "chirp" or "thump." At all events, we do not expect—at least not in all cases—that the "t" and "p" transitions will be perfectly indiscriminable when they are heard as speech in the no-silence condition.

References

Bailey, P., and Summerfield, A. Q. Information for speech: Observations on the perception of [s]-stop clusters. *Journal of Experiment Psychology: Human Perception and Performance*, 1980, 6, 536–563.

Bastian, J. *Silent intervals as closure cues in the perception of stops* (Speech Research Instrumentation, 9, Appendix F). New Haven, Conn: Haskins Laboratories, 1962.

Broadbent, D. E. A note on binaural fusion. *Quarterly Journal Experimental Psychology*, 1955, 7, 46–47.

Broadbent, D. E. and Ladefoged, P. On the fusion of sounds reaching different sense organs. *Journal of the Acoustical Society of America*, 1957, 29, 708–710.

Darwin, C. J. The perception of speech. In E. Carterette and M. Friedman (Eds.), *Handbook of perception* (Vol. 7). New York: Academic Press, 1976.

Darwin, C. J., Howell, P., and Brady, S. A. *Laterality and localization: A right ear advantage for speech heard on the left* (Status Report on Speech Research, SR-48, 257–277). New Haven, Conn: Haskins Laboratories, 1976.

Dorman, M. F., Raphael, L. J., Liberman, A. M. Some experiments on the sound of silence in phonetic perception. *Journal of the Acoustical Society of America*, 1979, 65, 1518–1532.

Fitch, H. L. Halwes, T., Erickson, D. M., and Liberman, A. M. Perceptual equivalence of two acoustic cues for stop-consonant manner. *Perception & Psychophysics*, 1980, 27, 343–350.

Halwes, T. G. *Effects of dichotic fusion on the perception of speech.* Unpublished doctoral dissertation, University of Minnesota, 1969. (Issued as Supplement to Haskins Laboratories Status Report on Speech Research, September 1969).

Isenberg, D. S., and Liberman, A. M. Speech and nonspeech percepts from the same sound. *Journal of the Acoustical Society of America*, 1978, 64(S1), S20. (Abstract)

Kuhl, D. S., and Miller, J. D. Speech perception by the chinchilla: Voiced-voiceless distinction in alveolar plosive consonants. *Science*, 1975, 190, 69–72.

Ladefoged, P. *Preliminaries to a linguistic phonetics.* Chicago: University of Chicago Press, 1971.

Liberman, A. M. Duplex perception and integration cues: Evidence that speech is different form nonspeech and similar to language. In E. Fisher-Jorgensen, J. Rishel, and N. Thorsen (Eds.), *Proceedings of the IXth International Congress of Phonetic Sciences* (Vol. 2). Copenhagen: University of Copenhagen Press, 1979.

Liberman, A. M., Cooper, F. S., Shankweiler, D. S., and Studdert-Kennedy, M. Perception of the speech code. *Psychological Review*, 1967, 74, 431–461.

Liberman, A.M., and Studdert-Kennedy, M. Phonetic perception. In R. Held, H. Leibowitz, and H.-L. Teuber (Eds.), *Handbook of sensory physiology* (Vol. 8) *Perception.* Heidelberg: Springer-Verlag, 1978.

Miller, J. D. Perception of speech sounds in animals: Evidence for speech processing by mammalian auditory systems. In T. H. Bullock (Ed.), *Recognition of complex acoustic signals.* Berlin: Dahlem Konferenzen, 1977.

Rand, T. C. Dichotic release from masking for speech. *Journal of the Acoustical Society of America*, 1974, 55, 678–680.

Repp, B. H., Liberman, A. M., Eccardt, T., and Pesetsky, D. Perceptual integration of acoustic cues for stop, fricative, and affricate manner. *Journal of Experimental Psychology: Human Perception and Performance,* 1978, 4, 621–637.

Studdert-Kennedy, M. Speech perception. In N. J. Lass (Ed.), *Contemporary issues in experimental phonetics.* New York: Academic Press, 1976.

Turek, S. V., Dorman, M. F., Franks, J. R., and Summerfield. Q. Identification of synthetic /bdg/ by hearing-impaired listeners under monotonic and dichotic formant presentation. *Journal of the Acoustical Society of America,* 1980, 67, 1031–1040.

Chapter 22
Some Differences between Phonetic and Auditory Modes of Perception

In the phonetic domain, the relation between acoustic cue and percept has several characteristics that have been taken to imply a special mode of processing (for recent reviews, see: Liberman 1982; Liberman and Studdert-Kennedy 1978; Repp 1982; Studdert-Kennedy 1980); but see, for example: Kuhl 1981, Kuhl and Miller 1975; Miller 1977. One such characteristic is that frequency-modulated acoustic cues are integrated with other cues into unitary percepts that seemingly lack the qualities we might have been led, on purely psychoacoustic grounds, to expect. A case in point, and the one with which we will be concerned, is in the perception of the stop consonants [d] and [g]. As has long been known, sufficient cues for the perceived distinction between these phones are transitions—that is, frequency modulations—of the second or third formant. Thus, when appropriate transitions of the third formant—the cue that will be the subject of our investigation—are presented in an otherwise fixed acoustic context, listeners perceive a syllable consisting of [d] or [g], followed by a vowel. Of special interest to us is that one hears in these percepts none of the time-varying quality, a "chirpiness," for example, or a glissando, that might be thought to correspond to the time-varying nature of the frequency-modulated signal. Indeed, one finds it difficult to characterize the [d] and [g] percepts, and especially the differences between them, in auditory terms of any kind. It is as if the percepts were as abstract as the phonetic segments they represent.

We might nevertheless account for the percepts without reference to specialized processes of a phonetic sort. Thus we might assume, most simply, a low-level process of sensory integration, similar, perhaps, to the integration of intensity and time into the perception of loudness. But such an assumption is ruled out by the finding that listeners do, in fact, hear the to-be-expected chirps and glissandi when the transition cues are removed from the larger context and sounded alone (Mattingly et al. 1971). Still, we might save an auditory account by noting that the transitions are normally presented in a larger acoustic context, and that they are, therefore, subject to the effects of a purely auditory interaction with the remainder of the pattern. On that account, the peculiarly abstract character of the percept would be thought to emerge from the interaction. Nothing we know about auditory perception suggests the existence of such an interaction, but the possibility is not precluded.

There is, in any case, another characteristic of the way formant transitions function when they cue stop consonants: the phonetic percepts they support are appropriate to their role in language, not only in their abstractness, but also in the extent to which they are categorical. Given transitions that change in relatively small physical

Originally published in *Cognition* 14 (1983): 211–235, with Virginia A. Mann. Reprinted with permission.

steps, from one appropriate for [d] to one appropriate for [g], the percept changes, not in correspondingly small steps, but suddenly (Liberman et al. 1957; Mattingly et al. 1971; Repp, in press; Studdert-Kennedy et al. 1970). This nearly categorical shift marks a sharp boundary between the two phones [d] and [g]; it is commonly reflected and measured as a relative increase in discriminability of the stimuli at the category boundary. But such tendencies toward categorical perception do occur in nonspeech perception as well (see, for example: Burns and Ward 1978; Locke and Kellar 1973; Miller et al. 1976; Parks et al. 1969; Siegel and Siegel 1977), so the question is not whether it is unique to the perception of stop consonants (and other phonetic segments), but, more properly, whether the categorical boundary between the phonetic segments is of an auditory sort. We have reason to believe it is not, for when the same formant transitions are presented in isolation (and perceived as nonspeech chirps), the obtained discrimination function is continuous—that is, it does not display the abrupt peaks and troughs that typify categorical perception. This result has been obtained in adults (Mattingly et al. 1971) and in infants (Eimas 1974). It follows, then, that if the categorical effect in the full speech context is to be assigned a purely auditory cause, then, as in the previously noted case, it must be referred, ad hoc, to some assumed auditory interaction between the transitions and the remainder of the acoustic pattern.

A quite different characteristic of the way formant transitions cue [d] and [g] is that their effects are subject to the influences of phonetic context. Thus, given abutting vowels, the transition must, of course, move into or out of the vocalic nucleus; hence, the boundary between [d] and [g] will occur in transitions that are at different positions on the spectrum for different vocalic contexts (Delattre, Liberman, and Cooper 1955; Liberman et al. 1954). More relevant to our concern here, however, is the fact that, given a fixed continuum of formant transitions, a shift in the [d-g] boundary can be produced by neighbouring consonants. Such effects have been found with preposed fricatives (Mann and Repp 1981; Repp and Mann 1981) and across a syllable boundary with preposed [al] or [ar] (Mann 1980). In both cases, the shift in the position of the boundary was found to be consistent with the way the formant transitions for [d] and [g] are affected in normal speech by coarticulation with fricatives or with liquids. Therefore, the movement of the category boundary is most plausibly to be understood as a perceptual compensation for the effects of coarticulation. As such, it would presumably reflect a phonetic rather than an auditory process. To appeal, instead, to an auditory interaction would require not only that we set aside the coarticulatory facts, together with the reasonable interpretation based on them, but also that we make a seemingly unreasonable assumption about why speech perception finds parallels in speech production—to wit, that speakers adjust the behavior of their articulatory organs so as to produce in every context just those acoustic effects that will fit boundary shifts caused by pre-existing auditory interactions. Such an interpretation becomes, in the end, hopelessly ad hoc and, given what we know of constraints on articulation, quite implausible. But, again, it cannot, in principle, be ruled out.

To control for auditory interaction, we should contrive acoustic patterns that can, depending on specifiable circumstances, be perceived either as speech or as nonspeech. Two techniques are available for this purpose, and both have been used in other studies to gain the control we seek. One employs stripped-down versions of synthetic speech that can be heard as speech or nonspeech, depending on the natural proclivities of the listeners, how long they have been listening, and just what has or has not been suggested to them (Best, Morrongiello, and Robson 1981; Remez et al. 1981). The other method, and the one we will use, takes advantage of a phenomenon in which, with auditory input held constant, the acoustic cue of interest is perceived *simultaneously* as a nonspeech chirp and as critical support for a phonetic segment. This phenomenon, called "duplex perception," was first reported by Rand (1974). Recently, it has been further studied in an investigation of the cues for the liquids [l] and [r] (Isenberg and Liberman 1978), and it has been used to control for auditory interaction in a study of silence as a cue for stop consonants (Liberman, Isenberg, and Rakerd 1981). Here, we will exploit it to provide an appropriate control for auditory interaction in investigations of the third-formant transition as a cue for the perceived distinction between [d] and [g]. In the first of these, we will be concerned to find out whether the integration of such transitions into unitary phonetic categories is to be attributed to processes of a generally auditory sort, or whether it is the result of process that are distinctively phonetic. The second part of our study is designed to determine if context-conditioned movement of the boundary between the [d] and [g] categories is also to be regarded as a special attribute of phonetic perception.

Experiment I

Our aim in the first experiment was to measure discriminability of third-formant transitions on both sides of a duplex percept—that is, when, on the "speech" side, the transitions provided crucial support for the perceived difference between [da] and [ga], and when, on the "nonspeech" side, they are heard as unspeechlike "chirps." The stimulus patterns were three-formant synthetic syllables in which the third formant varied in nine steps, from a setting appropriate for [da] to one appropriate for [ga].

To produce duplex perception of these third-formant transitions, we separated them from the (fixed) remainder of the pattern—which we will, for convenience, call the "base"—and presented the separated constituents dichotically. Thus, the transitions, which in isolation sound like chirps, and the base, which in isolation sounds like a syllable (most commonly, [da]), are free to mix and hence to interact in the listener's nervous system. The usual result is two percepts, present simultaneously. On one side of this duplexity is a syllable, [da] or [ga], which is perceptibly different from the base but very similar, perhaps identical, to what is heard when the two constituents (transition and base) are mixed electronically and presented in the normal manner (Liberman, Isenberg, and Rakerd 1981; Repp 1982). On the other side is a nonspeech "chirp" that seems identical to what is heard when the transition is presented in isolation.

Given systematic variation in the formant transitions, we can measure discriminability, hence tendencies toward categoricalness, of the resulting speech and nonspeech components of the duplex percept. To the extent that there is categorical discrimination of the formant transitions heard on the speech side of the duplex percent, the discrimination function should have marked peaks and troughs which accord with predictions derived from phonetic labeling responses (Liberman et al. 1957). To the extent that the phonetic categories themselves have a purely auditory basis, the discrimination function for the same formant transitions when heard on the nonspeech side of the duplex percept should also have marked peaks and troughs and,

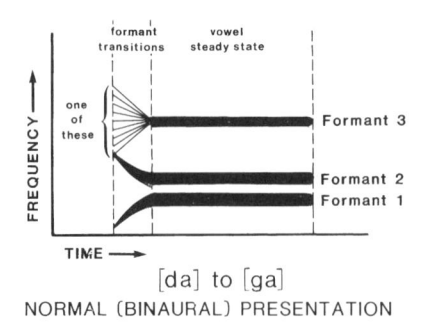

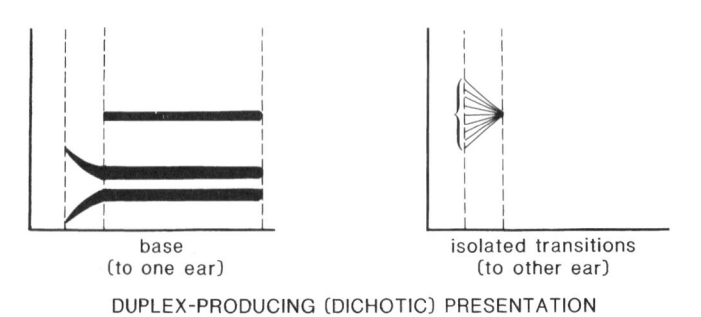

Figure 22.1
Schematic representation of the patterns used to produce the duplex percepts, including the constant base portion and the continuum of nine formant transitions.

like the function for discrimination of speech percepts, should meet with predictions derived from phonetic labeling.

Method

Materials

Stimulus Continuum At the top of figure 22.1 is a schematic representation of the stimulus patterns. These patterns, very similar to those used by Mann (1980) in the study referred to in the Introduction, were designed to be synthetic approximations to the syllables [da] and [ga]. They were produced on the parallel resonance synthesizer at Haskins Laboratories. The lower half of figure 22.1 shows how the stimuli were divided into the two constituents—the fixed "base" and the variable "isolated transitions"—that will, when presented dichotically, produce the duplex percept. The base is 250 msec in total duration, with a 50-msec ramp in overall intensity at onset and offset, and a fundamental frequency that falls linearly from 110 to 80 Hz. The first- and second-formant transitions are 50 msec in duration and step-wise linear in 5-msec steps; they begin at 279 and 1764 Hz, arriving finally at steady-state values of 765 and 1230 Hz, with bandwidths of 60 and 80 Hz, respectively. The third formant of the base begins 50 msec later than the others and maintains a steady state at 2527 Hz with a bandwidth of 120 Hz. In accordance with natural speech, this third formant is slightly less intense that the other two.

The continuum of nine formant transitions was synthesized separately from the base. Each transition is 50 msec in duration and step-wise linear in 5-msec steps; fundamental frequency and amplitude contour are as in the first 50 msec of the base stimulus, the offset frequency is the steady-state third-formant frequency of the base, and the bandwidth is 120 Hz. Onset frequency systematically varies across the continuum in eight equal steps, from 3196 Hz in Stimulus 1 to 1853 Hz in Stimulus 9. As can be seen in figure 22.1, the first four transitions have falling slopes, the fifth is flat, and the final four are rising. The slopes of the four rising transitions are equal in value to the slopes of the transitions that fall. For convenience, we will refer to the transitions hereafter by number, as shown in figure 22.1, from most falling to most rising.

Test Tapes The base stimulus and the continuum of transitions were digitized at 10,000 Hz prior to begin recorded onto magnetic tape for the purpose of testing. As was appropriate for dichotic presentation (and duplex perception), the base was recorded onto one track, the isolated transitions onto the other.

A (duplex perception) labeling tape was constructed for use in the initial screening of subjects and for determining how the subjects identified the stimuli. This tape comprised a practice sequence consisting of four repetitions of the base in conjunction with each of the two endpoint transitions, followed by a test sequence with four sets of 27 stimuli each. Across these sets, the nine transitions occurred twelve times each in a randomized order. The inter-stimulus interval was 3 sec; the inter-set interval was 6 sec.

Our measure of discrimination performance was obtained by the method known as AXB. (A and B are two stimuli to be discriminated; X is one or the other. The subject's task is to decide if X is less like A or less like B.) We chose to present stimuli at three-step intervals along the continuum of formant transitions, because pilot work (Mann et al. 1981) had suggested that for most subjects a separation of that size puts discrimination of the chirps and the speech in a sensitive region—that is, it keeps discrimination from falling to the floor or rising to the ceiling. This step size also provided a sensitive measure of the context-induced shifts in phonetic category boundary which were to be the concern of our second experiment.

The duplex-perception discrimination tape consisted, then, of sets of stimulus triads, one practice set and six test sets. Each such set contained randomized sequences of the six possible three-step combinations of stimuli along the continuum (i.e., by stimulus number; 1 *versus* 4, 2 *versus* 5, 3 *versus* 6, 4 *versus* 7, 5 *versus* 8, and 6 *versus* 9), occurring once each in AAB, ABB, BAA, and BBA triads. Thus, over the course of the test sets, listeners responded to a total of 24 triads for each pair. Within triads, the inter-stimulus interval was 500 msec, the inter-triad interval was 3 sec, and the inter-set interval was 6 sec.

An additional AXB discrimination tape was constructed to be used in pretest screening of the subjects, since pilot work (Mann et al. 1981) had suggested that some subjects encounter specific difficulty in discriminating isolated chirps at three-step intervals along the continuum, and that such subjects also fail to discriminate chirp components of the duplex percept. This same tape served the further purpose of providing a basis for comparison with the nonspeech side of the duplex percept. The stimulus arrangement was analogous to that of the duplex-perception discrimination tape, save that there was no base stimulus for presentation to the other ear, and different randomizations determined the order of triads within each set.

Procedure

Subjects in an initial pool of 14 were pretested in groups of three or four while seated in a quiet room as the stimuli were played over earphones. For convenience, the third-formant transitions were always presented to the right ear and the base stimulus to the left. The purpose of the first pretest was to see if the subjects could discriminate the transitions when they are presented in isolation. To that end, subjects listened to the discrimination tape that contained the isolated transitions and were instructed to respond "A" or "B" according to whether the first or the third stimulus of each triad was less like the other two. Completion of the practice and test sets of item triads was followed by a second pretest. This served two purposes. First, it was a screening device by which we could determine whether subjects were consistent in their labeling of the endpoint stimuli of the duplex [da]-[ga] continuum. While the vast majority of subjects give consistent responses to the end points of our continuum when the base and third-formant stimuli are electronically fused, some subjects tend to give inconsistent responses when base and transition are dichotically presented, and we wished to exclude such subjects from our study. The second purpose served by the pretest was to provide a full identification function by which to determine, for those subjects in the main experiment, the extent to which discrimination on the speech side of the duplex percept is categorical. Both purposes of the second pretest were accomplished by having the subjects listen to the practice and test sequences of the duplex labeling tape and respond "d" or "g" as appropriate.

The subjects who survived the pretest participated in experiments that provided the results we will present. These experiments were divided into two sessions, one week apart and counterbalanced in order across subjects. In the test sessions, as in the pretest, the third-formant transitions were always presented to the right ear and the base stimulus to the left. In one session, subjects were instructed that the goal was to determine how well speech sounds could be discriminated in the face of some nonspeech distractors. They then listened to the practice and test sets of the duplex-perception AXB discrimination tape, responding on the basis of the perceived similarity in the speech percepts of each stimulus triad. In the other session, the subjects were instructed that the goal was to determine how well nonspeech sounds could be discriminated in the face of speech sounds as distractors. At this time, they also listened to the practice and test sets of the duplex AXB discrimination tape, but responded on the basis of the perceived similarity among chirp percepts. Subjects listened to the same tape in the two sessions, but were kept in ignorance of this fact. They were instructed to listen to the target speech sounds or chirps, according to the session, and to ignore the "distractor" on the ground that attention to it could only impair their performance on the assigned task.

Subjects

The subjects were paid student volunteers recruited from an introductory psychology course. All were female, and none had extensive experience in listening to synthetic speech. Of an initial pool of fourteen, six subjects were judged on the basis of the pretests to be insufficiently consistent in their responses and were therefore excluded from the experiment proper, two for having been unable to discriminate the isolated transitions at a level above chance, and four for having been inconsistent in the way they labeled the endpoints of the duplex continuum as "d" (stimulus one) and "g" (stimulus nine). Thus the final subject group included a total of eight subjects who participated in each of two sessions.

Results

We should first report the phenomenological results of the experiment, which were clear. Given the variable third-formant transitions in one ear and the remaining, fixed part of the acoustic pattern (the base) in the other, the subjects did report duplex percepts: a syllable, [da] or [ga], depending on the transition, and a nonspeech "chirp." The chirps on the nonspeech side of the duplexity had a time-varying quality corresponding, apparently, to the time-varying nature of the formant transitions. This is to say, they were not noticeably different from what the subjects perceived when the transitions were presented in isolation. On the speech side, the syllable [da] or [ga] lacked the "chirpiness" that characterized perception on the nonspeech side, and they were not different from what listeners perceive when transitions and base are mixed electronically and presented in the normal manner. The base, which sounded like [da], was *not* perceived. That is, when the transition was appropriate for [ga], listeners typically perceived [ga], not [ga] and also (or half the time) [da]. Thus, perception was *duplex* not triplex: listeners perceived only speech (the fusion of base and transitions) and nonspeech (the transitions as if in isolation).

Beyond these observations, the data (averaged across the eight subjects) consist of discrimination functions for the speech and chirp components of the duplex percept (figure 22.2); a labeling function for the speech component of the duplex percept

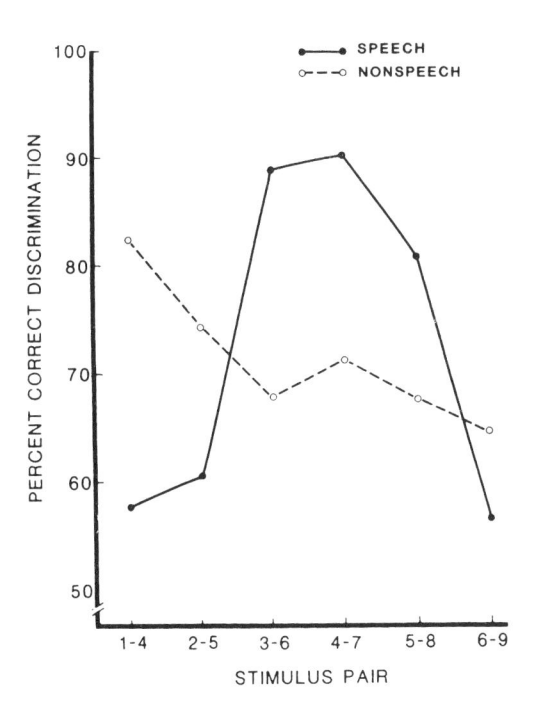

Figure 22.2
Discrimination of the third-formant transitions on the speech and nonspeech sides of the duplex percept.

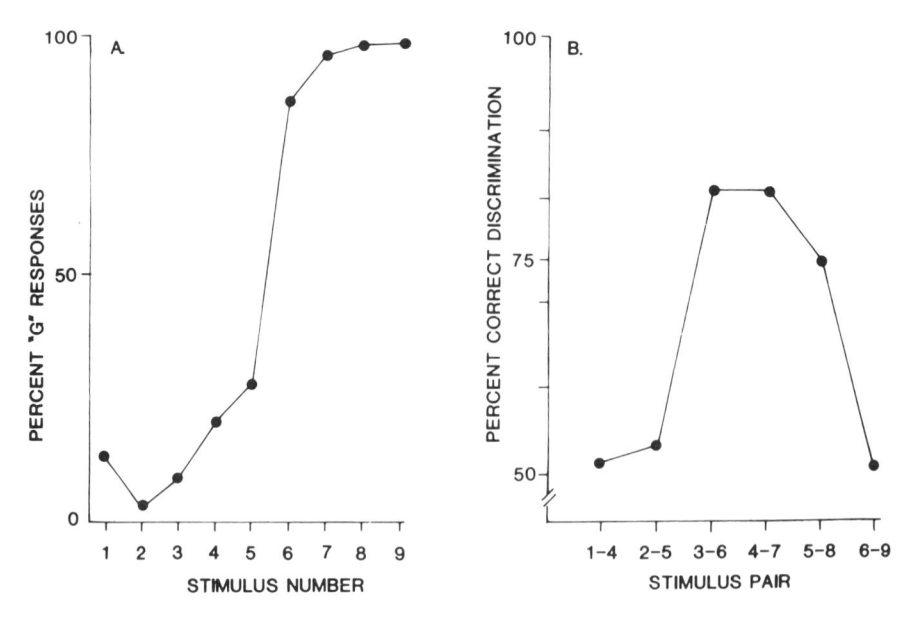

Figure 22.3
(A) Labeling of speech percepts as [d] or [g]. (B) Discrimination function predicted from labeling responses, given the assumption of categorical perception.

(figure 22.3A), together with the discrimination function (figure 22.3B) that is predicted from it on the assumption of categorical perception (Liberman et al. 1957); and a discriminating function for chirps presented in isolation (figure 22.4). Consider, first, figure 22.2, which compares discrimination of the duplex percepts under instructions to concentrate on speech (solid line) with that under instructions to concentrate on chirps (dashed line). Note that, while the overall level of performance on the two tasks is roughly comparable, the shapes of the two functions differ markedly. This is verified statistically by a significant interaction between the nature of the attended percept and the stimulus pair being discriminated: $F(5, 35) = 13.9$, $p < 0.001$.

The overall shape of the speech function—its marked peaks and troughs—is consistent with categorical perception. To see how consistent, however, we must compare the speech-discrimination function that was obtained with the one that is predicted on the assumption of perfectly categorical perception. Plainly, the predicted discrimination function, which is in figure 22.3B, is quite similar to the one we obtained. We conclude, therefore, that when the third-formant transitions were integrated into a phonetic percept, where they provided critical support for the distinction between [da] and [ga], they were perceived quite categorically.

In contrast to the way the transitions were discriminated on the speech side of the duplex percept is the discrimination function obtained with the same transitions on the nonspeech side, where they were perceived as chirps. As shown in figure 22.2, the "chirp" function has no marked peaks or troughs and is similar in shape to the function obtained with isolated transitions in figure 22.4, although the absolute level is lower: $F(1, 7) = 7.3$, $p < 0.05$. The initial pair of rising chirps (Pair 1-4) is significantly more discriminable than the final pair of falling chirps (Pair 6-9), both for

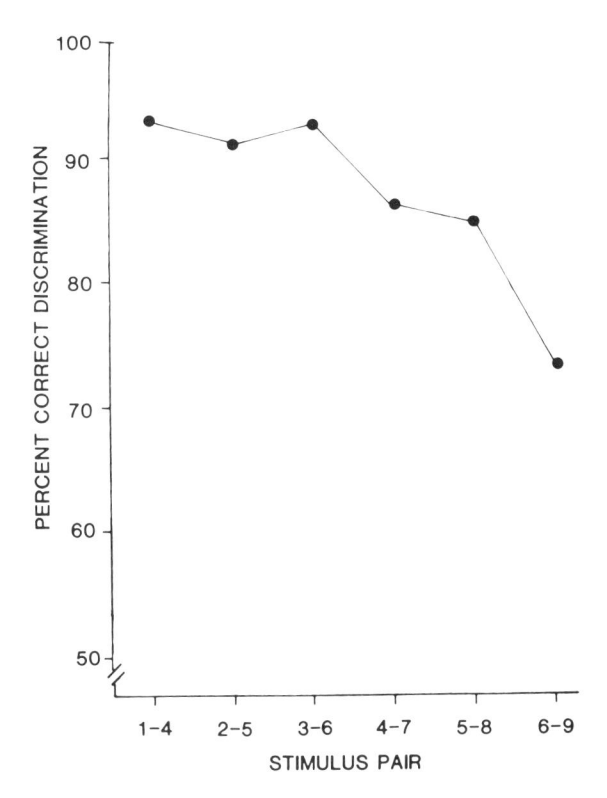

Figure 22.4
Discrimination of isolated third-formant transitions.

isolated chirps, $t(14) = 4,37$, $p < 0.005$ and for the chirp components of the duplex percent, $t(14) = 2.6$, $p < 0.02$.

As noted by Mattingly et al. (1971), there are at least two strategies that listeners might use in discriminating the isolated transitions: they could, in effect, judge their slopes or, alternatively, their most apparent pitches. If our subjects had opted for the first strategy, as the subjects in the Mattingly et al. study appear to have done, then discrimination would have been best for the transitions that straddle the horizontal transition (Transition 5). But that was not the result. Rather, discrimination became poorer as the transitions changed progressively from most falling to most rising. That result leads us to take into account an observation by Brady, House, and Stevens (1961), who noted that the most apparent pitch of frequency ramps, which resemble isolated transitions, is closer to the frequency of their offsets than their onsets. They also observed, however, that this effect is stronger for rising ramps than for falling ones. Since our transitions have variable onset frequencies but the same offset, we should suppose that if, as in the study by Brady, House, and Stevens, the tendency to judge pitch by the offset increased as the transitions changed from falling to rising, then we should have obtained the decrease in discrimination that our results do, in fact, show. We are inclined to conclude, therefore, that our subjects were, to a considerable extent, discriminating the transitions on the basis of their most apparent pitches.

Though the overall level of discrimination for the two sides of the duplex percept was roughly equal, as noted earlier, discrimination of the transitions on the speech side was, in its most sensitive region, better than discrimination of the transitions on the nonspeech side. But, surely, we do not therefore conclude that speech discrimination exceeds the resolving power of the system, only that we have no idea how the resolving power is to be measured. Beyond this truism, two observations are pertinent. One is that, as can be seen by comparing figures 22.2 and 22.4, the general level of nonspeech discrimination obtained when the transitions were presented outside the duplex context was somewhat higher than when they were perceived inside it. Perhaps this should be attributed to distractions provided by the circumstance that, in the duplex case, the two percepts, speech and nonspeech, were present at the same time. The other observation is that we should not, in any case, rule out the possibility that the human listener is, in fact, more sensitive to the formant transitions when they support a phonetic percept than when they do not. Indeed, Bentin and Mann (in press) have evidence that, in the matter of absolute threshold sensitivity, the speech context does provide the more sensitive measure—that is, the closer approximation to the physiological limit—and for interesting reasons.

In summary, the difference between the two sides of the duplex percept is very great indeed. On the nonspeech side, the formant transitions evoke a percept that has the time-varying, chirpy quality that psychoacoustic considerations should have led us to expect, and the discrimination function is continuous. On the speech side, where the same formant transitions provide critical support for the stops in the syllables [da] and [ga], there is no apparent chirpiness in the percepts, and discrimination is nearly categorical.

Experiment II

The second experiment draws on the fact, noted in the Introduction, that the category boundary along a synthetic [da]–[ga] continuum in which the third-formant onset provides the sufficient cue, can be systematically shifted by the presence of a preposed [al] or [ar] (Mann 1980). For stimuli preceded by [al], the category boundary shifts towards a higher third-formant onset (more "g" responses), whereas a preceding [ar] causes a shift in the opposite direction. Both perceptual shifts are consistent with observations about the acoustic consequences of articulatory accommodation to the new contexts: stop consonants that are coarticulated with a preceding liquid apparently assimilate toward the place of liquid articulation. That is, stops preceded by [al] tend to contain a higher third-formant onset frequency than those preceded by [ar], suggesting that they receive a more forward place of articulation. On that basis, Mann (1980) supposed that the perceptual context effect of the (preposed) liquids reflects the application to perception of some tacit knowledge about speech production. This in turn implies the existence of some specialized phonetic process.

But, as we pointed out in the introduction, the possibility of auditory interaction exists, at least in principle. To control for such interaction, we will again take advantage of duplex perception. That will be done by putting the syllables [al] and [ar] in front of the "base" of the dichotically presented (and duplexly perceived) [da]-[ga] stimuli of Experiment I. We can find out then whether the preposed [al] and [ar] affect perception of the formant transitions on both sides of the duplex percept or, as we suspect, only when they are perceived as speech.

Method

Materials

Stimulus Continua   Two continua of disyllables were constructed by putting in front of the synthetic stimuli of Experiment I naturally produced syllables whose fundamental frequency and formant structure approximated those of the synthetic stimuli and thus permitted the disyllable to be perceived as a coherent utterance produced by one and the same vocal tract. An [al-da] to [al-ga] continuum was formed in this way, using the base stimulus from Experiment I and a token of [al] that had been excised from an utterance of [al-da] produced by a male native speaker of English. An [ar-da] to [ar-ga] continuum was constructed by putting in front of the base a token of [ar] excised from an utterance of [ar-da] produced by the same speaker. In each case, a 100-msec silent gap separated the offset of the natural syllable from the onset of the synthetic one. The continuum of formant transitions that cued the [d]-[g] distinction was as in Experiment I.

Test Tapes   All stimuli were digitized at 10,000 Hz prior to being recorded onto magnetic tape for the purpose of testing. The arrangements of the stimuli on the magnetic tape was as in Experiment I, except, of course, that the "base" was preceded by [al] or [ar].

To determine how the subjects would identify the stimuli, and thus provide a basis for predicting what perfectly categorical discrimination functions should look like, we made a dichotic "labeling" tape, appropriate for duplex perception. It consisted of a practice sequence containing four repetitions of each endpoint transition paired with [al] plus base, and four repetitions of each endpoint transition paired with [ar] plus base, followed by a test sequence containing eight sets of 27 stimuli each. Over the test sets, each of the nine transitions occurred, in random order, a total of twelve times in conjunction with each preposed syllable.

To test discrimination by the method of AXB, another dichotic tape was prepared in which the stimuli were recorded in triads, exactly as in Experiment I, except that the base stimulus in half the triads was preceded by [al] and in half by [ar]. Which syllable ([al] or [ar]) preceded the base was randomized from trial to trial. For both [al] and [ar] conditions, the six pairs of to-be-discriminated transitions were equally represented across the triads, as were the various orders of transitions within each pair. As in Experiment I, listeners gave a total of 24 responses to each pair of transitions as preceded by each of the two syllables.

Procedure

Experiment II was run in two experimental sessions that also included Experiment I. Thus, in one session—the session in which the instruction was to attend to speech percepts—the subjects first heard the labeling tape and then the discrimination tapes for the two experiments. Order was counterbalanced. In the other session, where the instruction was to attend to chirp percepts, they also listened to the two discrimination tapes. Here, too, order was counterbalanced.

Subjects

The subjects were the same eight young women who participated in Experiment I.

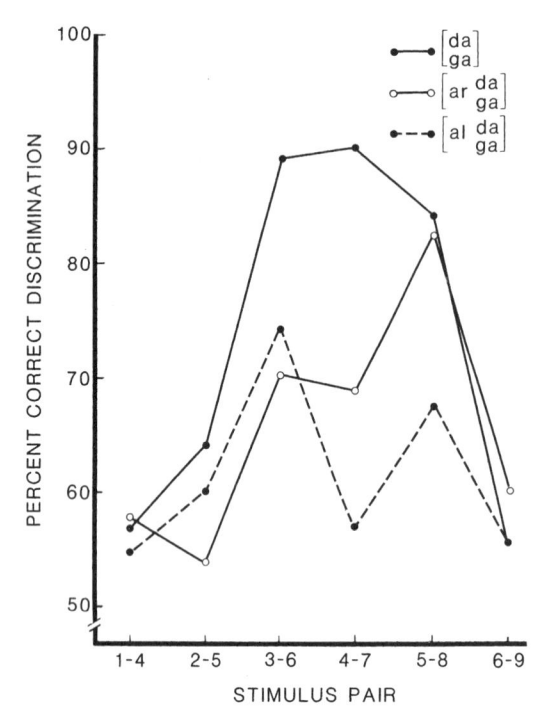

Figure 22.5
The influence of preposed syllables, [al] and [ar], on discrimination of the transitions on the speech side of the duplex percept. The analogous function obtained without preposed syllables (Experiment I) is reproduced for purposes of comparison.

Results

The point of this experiment, it will be remembered, was to test the effects of a preposed [al] or [ar] on the perception of third-formant transitions when, in the one case, they are integrated into a speech percept and when, in the other, they are perceived as nonspeech chirps. To display those effects, we have, in figures 22.5 and 22.6, combined the results of Experiments I and II. Discrimination functions for the speech side of the duplex percepts are in figure 22.5 and those for the nonspeech side in figure 22.6. A glance at these two figures reveals our main finding: context had a strong effect on discrimination of the transitions on the speech side of the percept but not on the nonspeech side. Looking more closely at the speech side in figure 22.5, we see that the peak in the function for [da]-[ga] syllables preceded by [ar] (solid lines and open circles) is shifted to the right of that obtained in Experiment I, where there was no preposed [ar] (solid lines, closed circles). On the assumption that the location of the discrimination peak reflects the location of the phonetic boundary, an assumption we will justify later, the direction of the shift in the peak is consistent with the earlier results of Mann (1980). Those same earlier results led us to expect a shift in the opposite direction when [al] is preposed. As can be seen in the function described by the dashed lines (filled circles), the nature of the shift due to [al] is somewhat less clear. Possible reasons for this will be discussed later. For the moment, however, the

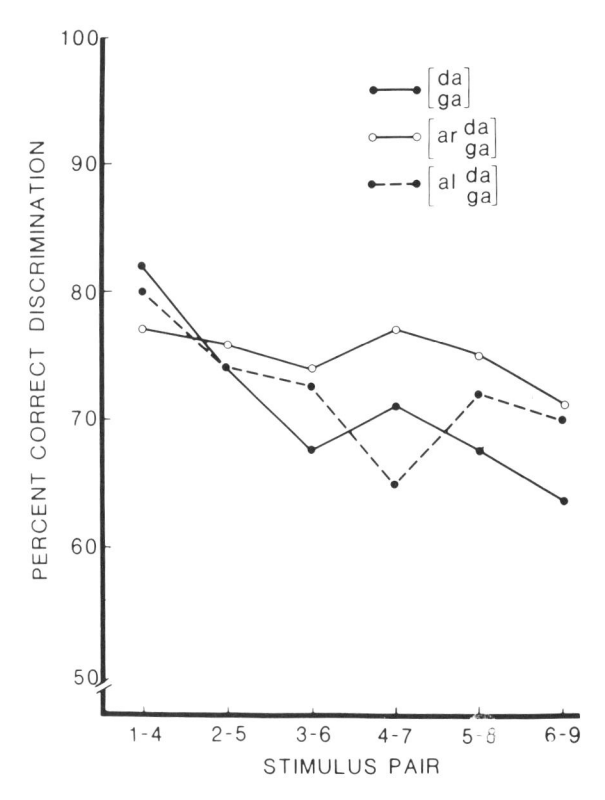

Figure 22.6
The influence of preposed syllables, [al] and [ar], on discrimination of the transitions on the nonspeech side of the duplex percept. The analogous function obtained without preposed syllables (Experiment I) is reproduced for purposes of comparison.

point to be made is that the speech function obtained in this context is, in any case, different from both of the other two.

In contrast to the results obtained on the speech side, the functions of figure 22.6 indicate that preposed [al] and [ar] had no effect on discrimination of the transitions when they were perceived, on the nonspeech side, as chirps.

To support the assertions of the preceding paragraphs, we offer the results of a three-way analysis of variance, conducted with the following factors: attended percept (speech or chirps); context (isolated duplex stimuli, stimuli preceded by [al], or stimuli preceded by [ar]); and stimulus pair. Although there was no significant effect of attended percept, suggesting that the average level of performance in our experiments was equivalent for speech and chirps, there was an effect of context: $F(2, 14) = 5.38$, $p < 0.025$, and an effect of stimulus pair: $F(5, 35) = 5.83$, $p < 0.001$. Most important to our observations about the special influence of context on speech perception are the interactions among the three main factors. First, there was an interaction between attended percept and stimulus pair, revealing that the relative difficulty of discriminating individual pairs depended on whether the instruction was to attend to speech or to the chirps: $F(5, 35) = 13.18$, $p < 0.001$. Second, there was an interaction between attended percept and context, revealing that the effect of context was

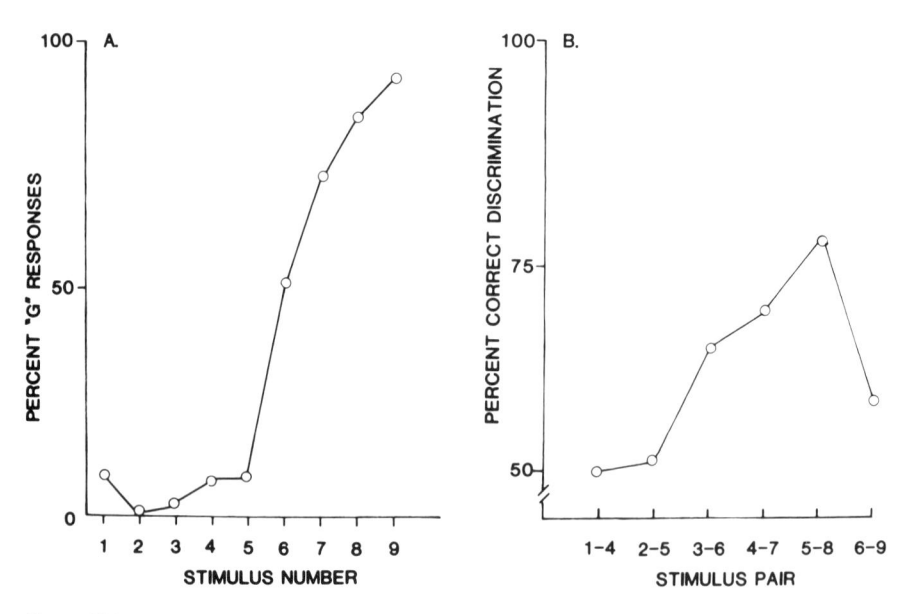

Figure 22.7
(A) The influence of a preposed [ar] on labeling of speech percepts as [d] or [g]. (B) Corresponding predicted discrimination function, given the assumption of categorical perception.

greater for speech percepts than for the chirps: $F(2, 14) = 11.59$, $p < 0.001$. Finally, there was an interaction of context and stimulus pair: $F(10, 70) = 2.46$, $p < 0.025$, and a three-way interaction: $F(10, 70) = 2.00$, $p < 0.05$. Separate analyses of variance for the two percepts reveal that, in the case of the speech percepts, the preceding syllables influenced both the level: $(F(2, 14) = 12.35, p < 0.001)$, and also the pattern of speech discrimination across stimulus pairs: $(F(10, 70) = 3, 17, p < 0.005)$. For the nonspeech chirps, on the other hand, an analysis of variance indicates that the preposed syllables had no significant effect on either the level or the pattern of performance.

Having seen that the discrimination functions reflect an effect of context on the speech side of the duplex percept, we should now consider the extent to which those functions are predicted from the phonetic labeling results, given the assumption of categorical perception. Consider, first, the results obtained for stimuli preceded by [ar], as shown in figure 22.7A. We see that the [da]-[ga] boundary occurs somewhere between Stimulus 5 and Stimulus 6. Comparison with the boundary obtained for the isolated [da]-[ga] stimuli of Experiment I (figure 22.3) shows that, as in the earlier experiment by Mann (1980), the [ar] context moved the boundary toward the [ga] end of the stimulus continuum, thus increasing the number of [da] responses. On the assumption of completely categorical perception (Liberman et al. 1957), we should have expected to obtain the discrimination function shown in figure 22.7B. In fact, the discrimination function we did obtain (solid lines and open circles of figure 22.5) is quite similar to the expected one. Certainly, the peak is in the right place and only slightly higher (as it so often is in such situations) than it should have been. Thus, the obtained discrimination function does reflect the phonetic boundary; moreover, it can be seen, by comparison with the result for the isolated syllables, to reflect the context-conditioned shift in that boundary caused by the preposed [ar].

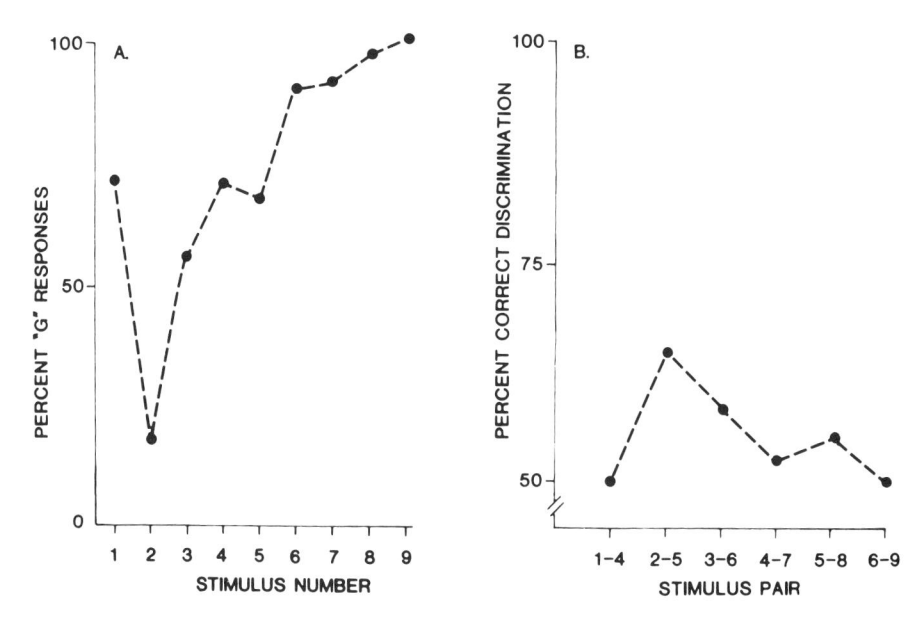

Figure 22.8
(A) The influence of a preposed [al] on labeling of speech percepts as [d] or [g]. (B) Corresponding predicted discrimination function, given the assumption of categorical perception.

As for the labeling function obtained with the preposed [al], seen in figure 22.8A, we note, first, a large inversion in the responses to Stimulus 1. Putting that aside for the moment, we see that, by comparison with the labeling data for the isolated syllables (figure 22.3), the [da]-[ga] boundary with preposed [al] is shifted strongly toward [da], producing, thus, an increase in the number of [ga] responses. This, too, is consistent with the earlier finding by Mann. However, the most extreme falling transition of her earlier study did not evoke the large number of [ga] responses that its counterpart (Stimulus 1) did in the present one. Of course, the conditions of the two experiments were not identical. In the present experiment, but not in the earlier one, the judgments were made on the speech side of a duplex percept. Another difference between the experiments, and a second likely cause of the difference in result, is that the stimuli were not exactly the same. Perhaps, then, the most extreme falling transition of this experiment went beyond the limit for [da]. At all events, we should note that in the other two labeling functions obtained in this experiment ([da]-[ga] in isolation, as in figure 22.3, and [da]-[ga] with [ar] preposed, as in figure 22.7) there is also a tendency for the responses to the extreme falling transition of Stimulus 1 to show some inversion toward [ga]. Perhaps the inversion in the [al] context is simply an exaggeration of that tendency, and, as such, a further reflection of the strong bias toward [ga] produced by the preposed [al].

In any case, the labeling results for the [al] context yield the predicted discrimination function seen in figure 22.8B. There is only a low peak, but its position reflects a shift in the phonetic boundary opposite to that which was produced by the preposed [ar]. Looking now at the obtained discrimination function in figure 22.5, we see a moderately good fit to the one that was predicted. We conclude, then, that in the [al] context, as in the [ar] context, the discrimination function reasonably reflects the phonetic boundary and the effect that context has on it.

In striking contrast to the effects of phonetic context on the speech side of the duplex percept is the absence of such effects on the nonspeech side. As shown in figure 22.6, and as previously noted, the discrimination functions for the transitions perceived as chirps are much the same when [ar] or [al] is preposed as when, in Experiment I, they were not. Moreover, the shape of the functions reflects perception that is more nearly continuous than categorical. The slopes indicate that, as in the case of the isolated patterns of Experiment I, discrimination of falling transitions *versus* less falling ones was, other things equal, better than rising *versus* less rising: $t(14) = 2.75$, $p < 0.02$ for stimuli preceded by [al], and $t(14) = 2.7$, $p < 0.02$ for those preceded by [ar].

Discussion

Our concern has been to account for two effects previously observed in the perception of formant transitions as cues for stop consonants: tendencies toward categorical perception and shifts in the positions of category boundaries with phonetic context. Categorical perception, which we will consider first, has two manifestations, at least in the case of speech perception. The one, and the one to which attention has hitherto been directed almost exclusively, is the discontinuity in perception that defines a boundary on some physical continuum. The other is in the phenomenal nature of the perceived category, which is more appropriate to a linguistic object than to an auditory one (Liberman 1982). In speech perception, these two manifestations presumably reflect the same underlying process, but they are separable, at least in principle, and we should take a moment to say how.

Given that the formant transitions are modulations in frequency, they might be perceived, correspondingly, as modulations in pitch. If so, perception could be nonetheless categorical. Thus, given a continuum of transitions, the listener might perceive them discontinuously—for example, as rising or falling pitches. Such automatic sorting of auditory percepts would, of course, be of use to listeners since it would relieve them of having deliberately to make the categorical assignments that the phonetic and phonological structure of the language require. But if, as in this example, perception of the transition cues, and all the other cues for the same phone, retained their auditory character, then perception of speech would be like perception of Morse code or some other arbitrary acoustic cipher. In that case, a listener would perceive rising or falling pitches, together with the auditory correlates of the many other acoustic cues, and have then to "interpret" the resulting melange as a unitary phone. Presumably, the process of interpretation would, in time, become automatic, as, indeed, it does with people skilled at Morse, but the purely auditory character of the percept would continue to intrude. This would be the more distressing because the auditory percept has little or nothing to do with the linguistic function of the phonetic unit it conveys.

To draw an analogy from visual perception of depth, consider how confusing it would be if, in the use of the retinal disparity cue, we were aware, not just of the distal depth, but also of the proximal disparity (doubling of images) which provided the relevant information. Fortunately, processing is accomplished in this case by a specialized module that uses the proximal disparity to yield, in consciousness, only perception of the distal depth relationships among visual surfaces.

We would argue, then, that a similar module operates in speech perception to yield, in consciousness, only the distal phonetic object, free of the chirps or glissandos we would otherwise hear. This would, as we have indicated, be especially appropriate for the purposes of language, given that everything that we need to know about a stop consonant, for example, has been provided when any particular token has been identified as this stop consonant and not that one. In that sense, a stop consonant represents nothing but the categorical and abstract segment the speaker intended. Hence, awareness of the auditory attributes of its various acoustic cues would, like awareness of proximal retinal disparity, be irrelevant at best, and, at worst, seriously distracting.

As pointed out in the Introduction, listeners are, indeed, quite aware of the auditory attributes of the transitions when they are presented in isolation, in which case they sound like chirps, but not when, as part of a larger acoustic pattern, they support perception of stop consonants. This difference, as was also pointed out, occurs in conjunction with a difference in categorical perception in the more usual sense: discrimination of the transitions is continuous or categorical, depending on whether they are perceived in isolation, as chirps, or, together with the rest of the acoustic pattern, as stop-vowel syllables. As we have indicated, we find it plausible to suppose that incorporation of the transitions into stop percepts, and, in particular, the contrast this presents to their perception as chirps, reflects a specialized phonetic process, well-adapted to providing just the abstract categories the larger language system uses. But it is at least conceivable, if implausible, that ordinary auditory perception is at work—that in this, and in all the many similar cases where there exist parallels between speech perception and speech production, the articulators are so controlled as to produce exactly those combinations of cues that fit into independently existing interactions of an auditory sort.

The second effect that concerns us, namely, that the positions of the category boundaries shift with phonetic context, has been taken as a reflection of the context-conditioned variation in the acoustic signal that results from the way it is produced. Specifically, the variations in the signal are the consequence of the coarticulatory arrangements that make it possible for speakers to fold phonetic segments into larger units—syllables, for example—and thus produce the segments much faster than they otherwise could. (To do otherwise, in this case, would entail making each segment a syllable—that is, to spell.) But listening to speech would be awkward if all the auditory consequences of these context-conditioned variations were prominent in consciousness. Given, in the cases we are concerned with, that the perceptual compensation is made automatically—that is, that the category boundaries shift appropriately—we assume that in this instance, too, we are seeing the effect of a highly adaptive and distinctively phonetic process. But, again, one might suppose, however implausibly, that the effect is simply auditory—that in this, and in every other such case, coarticulation occurs, not to make it easier to speak, but only to accommodate the sounds of speech to the characteristics of the auditory system, and especially to auditory interactions.

The purpose of the experiments reported here was to exploit the phenomenon of duplex perception to provide data relevant to deciding between these phonetic and auditory interpretations of stop consonant categories and their movement with context. The results were quite clear. Given an isolated third-formant transition appropriate for the stop in [da] or [ga] to one ear, and the remainder of the acoustic syllable to the other, listeners perceived the transitions in two phenomenally different ways: as nonspeech chirps, just like those they perceived when the transitions were presented in isolation, and as critical support for the stops in syllables [da] and [ga], in which case the percept was just like the one that was evoked when the transitions were electronically fixed with the rest of the acoustic pattern and presented in the normal manner. The remainder of the acoustic syllable, which in isolation sounds like speech, was not also perceived, which is to say that the percept was duplex, not triplex. On the nonspeech side of the duplexity, the chirp percept conformed reasonably to what psychoacoustic considerations might have led us to expect. Moreover, perception of these chirps was continuous, and there was no measurable effect of phonetic context. On the speech side, there was a phonetic percept—a stop consonant—not readily describable in auditory terms. In addition, perception was strongly categorical and the category boundary moved in expected ways as a function of phonetic context.

We should emphasize that the two classes of percept were evoked by transitions that were always paired, albeit in the other ear, with the remainder of the acoustic syllable. Thus, the two constituents of the dichotically presented pair, having been mixed in the nervous system, were free to interact or not. If, in that circumstance, we were to attribute the results on the speech side of the percept to interactions of an auditory kind, what would we say then about the results on the other side? How would we, on such an auditory account, explain why the dichotic constituents interact to produce a normal [da] or [ga], but also fail to interact, not for both constituents, but only for one—the isolated transitions? Why, that is, was there perception of the isolated transition as such, but no comparable "isolated" perception of the stimulus to the other ear, the 'base' that, by itself, sounds like speech? To account for the fact that the percept was, in this way, only duplex, we should suppose that there are two modes of processing at work in the perception of the transitions, and that, happily from our point of view, the peculiar conditions of the dichotic presentation make the results of both modes available to consciousness. In the one mode, which is auditory, are the processes that underlie perception of the transitions as nonspeech chirps. In the other, which is phonetic, the transitions are incorporated into the speechlike pattern that was presented to the other ear, where they serve the singularly linguistic purpose of distinguishing the abstract categories [da] and [ga].

Note

The research described in this paper was supported by NICHD Grant HD-01994 and BRS Grant RR-05596 to Haskins Laboratories and by Bryn Mawr College. We wish to thank J. Michael Russell and James Madden for their assistance in scoring the data for this experiment and for their participation in pilot studies.

References

Bentin. S., and Mann, V. A. (in press). Speech and nonspeech perception in duplex: Prevalence of the phonetic mode. Manuscript in preparation.

Best, C. T., Morrongiello, B., and Robson, R. (1981). Perceptual equivalence of acoustic cues in speech and nonspeech perception. *Percep. Psychophys.*, 29, 191–211.

Brady, P. T., House, A. S., and Stevens, K. N. (1961). Perception of sounds characterized by a rapidly changing resonant frequency, *J. acoust. Soc. Amer.*, 33, 1357–1362.

Burns, E. M., and Ward. W. D. (1978). Categorical perception—phenomenon or epiphenomenon: Evidence from experiments in the perception of melodic musical intervals. *J. acoust. Soc. Amer.*, 63, 456–468.

Delattre, P. C., Liberman, A. M., and Copper, F. S. (1955). Acoustic loci and transitional cues for consonants. *J. acoust. Soc. Amer.*, 27, 769–773.

Eimas, P. D. (1974). Auditory and linguistic processing of cues for place of articulation by infants. *Percep. Psychophys.*, 16, 513–521.

Isenberg, D., and Liberman, A. M. (1978). Speech and non-speech percepts from the same sound. *J. acoust. Soc. Amer.*, 64, Suppl. No. 1. S20 (Abstract)

Kuhl, P. K. (1981). Discrimination of speech by nonhuman animals: Basic auditory sensitivities conductive to the perception of speech-sound categories. *J. acoust. Soc. Amer.*, 70, 340–349.

Kuhl, P. K., and Miller, J. D. (1975). Speech perception by the chinchilla: Voiced-voiceless distinction in alveolar plosive consonants. *Sci.* 190, 69–72.

Liberman, A. M. (1982). On finding that speech is special. *Amer. Psychol.* 37, 148–167.

Liberman, A. M., Delattre, P. C., Copper, F. S., and Gerstman, L. J. (1954). The role of consonant-vowel transitions in the perception of the stop and nasal consonants. *Psychol. Mono.* 68, 1–13.

Liberman, A. M., Harris, K. S., Hoffman, H. S., and Griffith, B. C. (1957). The discrimination of speech sounds within and across phoneme boundaries. *J. Exper. Psychol.* 53, 358–368.

Liberman, A. M., Isenberg, D., and Rakerd, B. (1981). Duplex perception of cues for stop consonants: Evidence for a phonetic mode. *Percep. Psychophys.* 30, 133–143.

Liberman, A. M., and Studdert-Kennedy, M. (1978). Phonetic perception. In R. Held, H. W. Leibowitz, and H.-L. Teuber (Eds.), *Handbook of Sensory Physiology, Vol. VIII: Perception.* New York, Springer-Verlag, 143–178.

Locke, S., and Kellar, L. (1973). Categorical perception in a non-linguistic mode. *Cortex*, 9, 353–367.

Mann, V. A. (1980). Influence of preceding liquid on stop-consonant perception. *Percep. Psychophys.* 28, 407–412.

Mann, V. A., Madden, J., Russell, J. M., and Liberman, A. M. (1981). Further investigation into the influence of preceding liquids on stop consonant perception, *J. acoust. Soc. Ameri.*, 69, S91. (Abstract)

Mann, V. A., and Repp, B. H. (1981). Influence of preceding fricative on stop consonant perception. *J. acoust. Soc. Amer.*, 69, 548–558.

Mattingly, I. G., Liberman, A. M., Syrdal, A. M., and Halwes, T. (1971). Discrimination in speech and non-speech modes. *Cog. Psychol.* 2, 131–157.

Miller, J. D. (1977). Perception of speech sounds in animals: Evidence for speech processing by mammalian auditory mechanisms. In T. H. Bullock (Ed.), *Recognition of Complex Acoustic Signals.* Berlin, Abakon Verlagsgesellschaft.

Miller, J. D., Wier, C. C., Pastore, R., Kelly, W. J., and Dooling R. J. (1976). Discrimination and labeling of noise-buzz sequences with varying noise-lead times: An example of categorical perception. *J. acoust. Soc. Amer.*, 60, 410–417.

Parks, T., Wall. C., and Bastian, J. (1969). Category and intracategory discrimination for one visual continuum. *J. exper. Psychol.*, 31, 241–245.

Rand, T. C. (1974). Dichotic release from masking for speech. *J. acoust. Soc. Amer.*, 55, 678–680.

Remez, R. E., Rubin, P. E., Pisoni, D. B., and Carrell, T. D. (1981). Speech perception without traditional speech cues. *Sci.*, 212, 947–950.

Repp, B. H. (1982). Phonetic trading relationships and context effects: New experimental evidence for a speech mode of perception. *Psychol. Bull.*, 92, 81–110.

Repp, B. H. (in press). Categorical perception: Issues, methods, findings. In N. J. Lass (Ed.), *Speech and language: Advances in basic research and practice* (Vol. 9). New York, Academic Press.

Repp, B. H., and Mann, V. A. (1981). Perceptual assessment of fricative-stop coarticulations. *J. acoust. Soc. Amer.*, 69, 1154–1163.

Repp, B. H., Milburn, C., and Ashkenas, J. (1983). Duplex perception: Confirmation of fusion. *Percep. Psychophys.*, 33, 333–337.

Siegel, J. A., and Siegel, W. (1977). Categorical perception of tonal intervals: Musicians can't tell *sharp* from *flat*, *Percep. Psychophys.*, 21, 399–407.

Studdert-Kennedy, M. (1980). Speech perception. *Lang. Sp.*, 23, 45–66.

Studdert-Kennedy, M., Liberman, A. M., Harris, K. S., and Cooper, F. S. (1970). Motor theory of speech perception: A reply to Lane's critical review. *Psychol. Rev.*, 77, 234–249.

Chapter 23

Speech Perception Takes Precedence over Nonspeech Perception

One theory of speech perception holds that there is a biologically distinct system, or module, specialized for extracting phonetic elements (especially consonants and vowels) from the sounds that convey them.[1] The percepts produced by this module are immediately phonetic in character; accordingly, they stand apart from auditory percepts that are composed of standard dimensions such as pitch, loudness, and timbre. There is, then, no first-stage auditory percept, as most other theories of speech suppose,[2] and hence no need for a subsequent stage in which the auditory tokens are matched to phonetic prototypes and thereby made appropriate for further processing as language. Indeed, as the experiments reported here show, it is the phonetic module that has priority, as if its processes occurred before, not after, those that yield the standard dimensions of auditory perception.

Consistent with the existence of a distinct phonetic mode is the observation that a particular piece of sound can evoke radically different percepts, depending on whether or not it engages the phonetic module. Consider, for example, acoustic patterns sufficient for synthesizing on a computer the syllables "da" and "ga" (figure 23.1, top). The three formants represent resonances of the vocal tract and have, at their onsets, frequency sweeps called transitions. These transitions last approximately 50 msec and reflect the way in which the resonances change as the tongue and jaw move from the consonant to the vowel. Normally, the perceived distinction between "da" and "ga" depends on many acoustic variables; as seen in figure 23.1, however, it can be made to depend only on differences in the transition of the third formant. Thus, in the context of the syllable, these transitions become crucial to the phonetic percept. In isolation (figure 23.1, bottom right), however, they are heard as the glissandi or differently pitched "chirps" that would be expected on the basis of psychoacoustic considerations. These two ways of perceiving the formant transitions—one phonetic, the other auditory—are strikingly different: there is no hint of chirpiness in the "da" or "ga," and no "da"-ness or "ga"-ness in the chirps. Moreover, the transitions are discriminated differently depending on the mode in which they are perceived.[3]

Under special circumstances, the transitions can simultaneously evoke the phonetic and auditory percepts. This effect, called duplex perception, occurs when the third-formant transition is presented by itself to one ear, while the remainder of the pattern, called the base (figure 23.1, bottom left), is presented to the other. Listeners then simultaneously hear a chirp (in the ear to which the transition is presented) and the

Originally published in *Science* 237 (10 July 1987): 169–171, with D. H. Whalen. Reprinted with permission.

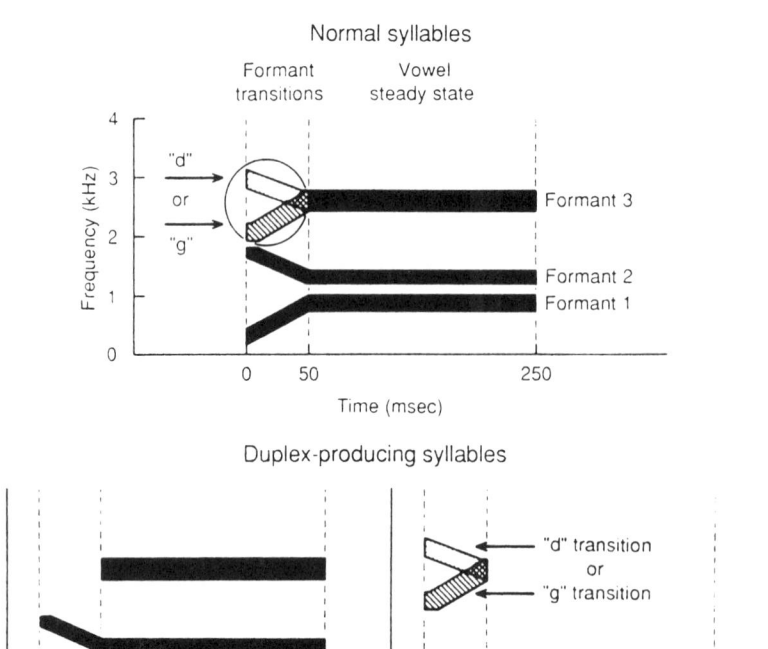

Figure 23.1
Schematic representation of the syllables "da" and "ga."

syllable "da" or "ga" (in the other ear), as determined by the transition. These simultaneous percepts, and the different discrimination functions they yield, are nearly the same as those produced separately by the isolated transitions and the whole syllable.[4]

Since duplex perception occurs in response to a fixed acoustic pattern and results in two simultaneous percepts, it cannot be attributed to auditory interactions arising from changes in acoustic context or to a shifting of attention between two forms of an ambiguous stimulus. Further, that the "da" or "ga" is perceived to be entirely in one ear, even though the critical transition is presented only to the other, indicates that the incorporation of the transition into the base is an integration at the perceptual level, not a "cognitive" afterthought that deliberately combines what had initially been perceived as separate. Thus the phenomenon of duplex perception provides support for the view that there are distinct phonetic and auditory ways of perceiving the same (speech) signal. At the same time, however, it raises the question of why, in the normal case, the components of speech are not perceived in a duplex fashion; that is, why is the "da" or "ga" not normally accompanied by the chirp?

Relying on considerations of plausibility and simplicity, Mattingly and Liberman[5] proposed that the phonetic module preempts the phonetically relevant parts of the signal before making the remainder available to auditory processing. This proposal seemed plausible because, in contrast to the indefinitely large set of acoustic events that occur, phonetic events form a natural class that is defined by its correspondence to the acoustic results of specialized movements of the articulatory organs. The proposal was simple because the very processes of phonetic perception remove from the signal all evidence of those phonetic events and thus preclude such (parallel) processing as would cause them to be perceived yet again as chirps. This preemptiveness is similar to the precedence described above, which we have here demonstrated directly with a new and somewhat simpler version of a duplex phenomenon.[6]

Our procedure differs from that used previously in that the two parts of the signal are not divided between the ears but are presented equally to both. Duplexity is produced (in both ears at once) by changing the intensity of the transition relative to the base. At relatively low intensities, the transitions serve only their expected phonetic function. At higher intensities, however, the transitions continue to make their phonetic contribution but simultaneously evoke nonspeech chirps. On the basis of these observations, which we made initially in pilot experiments, we tested the following generalizations.

1. In isolation, neither transition sounds like "da" or "ga."
2. In syllabic context, the transitions will, at some intensity, evoke nonspeech chirps, establishing a duplexity threshold.
3. Above the duplexity threshold, the chirps can be matched to those evoked by the transitions in isolation.
4. Both below and above the duplexity threshold, the transitions appropriately determine whether the syllable is heard as "da" or "ga."

The stimuli were the same as those represented in figure 23.1, except that the third-formant transitions were not frequency bands excited by a fundamental (as were the formants of the base) but rather time-varying sinusoids that follow the center frequencies. Such sinusoidal transitions combine with the formant-synthesized base to make coherent phonetic percepts, in this case "da" and "ga." The sinusoids have the advantage, for our purposes, that in isolation they produce whistles, which were more easily discriminated than the chirps and also less speechlike.

The base syllable was created with a software formant synthesizer; the sinusoids were created with another software synthesizer designed for the generation of pure tones. From a set of input parameter values representing frequencies and amplitudes, each synthesizer calculated a digital waveform that was then turned into sound through a digital-to-analog converter. The base was synthesized in one computer file and the two sinusoidal transitions (one modeled after "d" and one after "g") in two other files. The base and one transition could then be output through synchronized digital-to-analog channels, separately attenuated, and electronically combined for presentation through headphones as a single sound to subjects. The base was presented at a fixed intensity of 72-dB sound-pressure level.

Eleven young adult speakers of English (six female and five male) with no reported hearing problems were tested in separate sessions. None knew anything about the composition of the stimuli or the purpose of the experiment. One subject did not perceive in a duplex fashion at the intensity levels available and therefore was excluded from all analyses.

Initially, subjects were asked to identify the sinusoidal transitions as "da" or "ga." Twenty repetitions of each were presented in random order. The subjects' responses are shown in table 23.1, task 1. (For all tests, there was no significant difference between the responses to the "d" and "g" stimuli, so that only the combined percentages are reported.) Most subjects identified one whistle or the other as "da" and held

Table 23.1
Correct performance (in percent) on the four main tasks (results from 40 trials per subject). Task 1, identification of isolated sinusoids as "d" or "g"; task 2, match of duplex to isolated sinusoids; task 3, identification of syllables as "da" or "ga" below duplexity threshold; task 4, identification of syllables as "da" or "ga" above duplexity threshold.

Subject	Task 1	Task 2	Task 3	Task 4
1	72.5	92.5	100.0	100.0
2	100.0	65.0	100.0	97.5
3	15.0	97.5	100.0	100.0
4	95.0	97.5	100.0	100.0
5	30.0	85.0	97.5	100.0
6	95.0	72.5	92.5	85.0
7	100.0	87.5	82.5	97.5
8	0.0	95.0	52.5	100.0
9	50.0	47.5	100.0	97.5
10	90.0	65.0	100.0	100.0
Mean	64.8	79.5	92.5	97.8
SEM	±12.1	±5.4	±4.8	±1.5

to that consistently. Some happened to identify the correct one; others were just as consistently wrong. One (subject 9) simply called all the whistles "da." Overall, identification accuracy did not differ significantly from chance [$t(9) = 1.22$].

To find the intensity at which the sinusoids in syllabic context evoked nonspeech whistles in addition to "da" or "ga" (the duplexity threshold), we had the subjects adjust the attenuator that controlled the intensity of the sinusoid until the whistle was just audible. This was done three times for each sinusoid. The mean duplexity thresholds for all subjects, expressed in relation to the steady state of the third formant, were −6.4 dB (SD, 5.0 dB) for the "da" sinusoid and 0.0 dB (SD, 4.9 dB) for the "ga" sinusoid. This difference in duplexity thresholds, which was found for all ten subjects, is consistent with the fact that, in isolation, the "da" sinusoid (the one with the lower duplexity threshold) was the louder of the two.

To ensure that the whistle component of the duplex percept was comparable to the whistle of the sinusoid in isolation, we performed a matching test. On each trial, three stimuli were presented: first one sinusoid in isolation, then either of the two sinusoids in syllabic context, and finally the other sinusoid in isolation. Each sinusoid occurred with the syllable 20 times, matching the first sinusoid or the last an equal number of times. The sinusoid in the syllable was presented at 6 dB above the duplexity threshold for "ga." Subjects judged whether the duplexly perceived whistle was more like the isolated whistle that preceded or followed it. Subjects were able to make this judgment accurately well above the level of change [$t(9) = 5.50$, $P < 0.001$; table 23.1, task 2].[7]

To test whether the sinusoids reliably determined how the syllable was perceived below the duplexity threshold, we set them 4 dB below the "da" duplexity threshold and presented 20 repetitions of each in random order. Subjects were to identify the consonant as "d" or "g." Again, they did so at a level well above chance [$t(9) = 8.88$, $P < 0.001$; table 23.1, task 3].

It remained, then, to determine whether the sinusoids continue to provide phonetic information even when they also evoke whistles. For that purpose, we set the sinusoids at 6 dB above the higher ("ga") duplexity threshold and performed another identification test. Subjects' identifications were no less accurate above the duplexity threshold than below it [$t(9) = 32.60$, $P < 0.001$; table 23.1, task 4].

Thus, at lower levels of intensity, the sinusoids provide the basis for the perceived distinction between "da" and "ga"; at higher levels, they serve this same phonetic purposes but also evoked nonspeech whistles. As we found from our own listening, the phonetic information is provided over a range of approximately 20 dB below the duplexity threshold;[8] the whistles, which are of course barely audible at the duplexity threshold, become louder as the intensity of the sinusoid is increased. These results show that processing of the sinusoid as speech has priority, thereby defining what we mean by precedence of the phonetic module.

Unlike the earlier version of a duplex phenomenon,[9] which required that the transitions and the remainder of the pattern be presented to different ears, the one reported here puts all parts of the pattern equally into both ears. It thereby avoids such complications of interpretation as may arise with dichotic stimulation and so makes more straightforward the inference that duplex perception reflects distinct auditory and phonetic ways of perceiving the same stimulus. Beyond that, the results obtained with the new form of the duplex phenomenon support the hypothesis that the phonetic mode takes precedence in processing the transitions, using them for its special linguistic purposes until, having appropriated its share, it passes on the remainder to be perceived by the nonspeech system as auditory whistles. Such precedence reflects the profound biological significance of speech.

Notes

Supported by National Institute of Child Health and Human Development grant HD-01994 to Haskins Laboratories. We thank C. A. Fowler, I. Mattingly, B. Repp, L. Rosenblum, P. Rubin, and M. Studdert-Kennedy for helpful comments.

1. A. M. Liberman and I. G. Mattingly, *Cognition* 21, 1 (1985).
2. R. A. Cole and B. Scott. *Psychol. Rev.* 81, 348 (1974); G. C. Oden and D. W. Massaro, ibid. 85, 172 (1978); K. N. Stevens, in *Auditory Analysis and Perception of Speech,* G. Fant and M. A. Tatham, Eds. (Academic Press, New York, 1975), pp. 303–330.
3. I. G. Mattingly, A. M. Liberman, A. K. Syrdal, T. Halwes, *Cogn. Psychol.* 2, 131 (1971).
4. V. A. Mann and A. M. Liberman, *Cognition* 14, 211 (1983).
5. I. G. Mattingly and A. M. Liberman, in *Functions of the Auditory System,* G. M. Edelman, W. E. Gall, W. M. Cowan, Eds. (Wiley, New York, in press).
6. See page 206 of C. S. Darwin and N. S. Sutherland [*Q. J. Exp. Psychol.* 36A, 194 (1984)] for a related observation.
7. Below the duplexity threshold, such matching would presumably be at the level of chance. It is possible, however, that forced matching is a more sensitive measure than the one we used to obtain the threshold itself. We therefore applied the matching procedure at 4 dB below the lower ("d") threshold, using eight highly practiced subjects. As expected, the responses [45.3 percent correct, $t(7) = -1.28$, $P > 0.2$] were at the level of chance.
8. S. Bentin and V. A Mann [*Haskins Laboratories Status Report on Speech Research SR-76* (1983)] found a similar range in a dichotic task, although they interpreted it as a difference in sensitivity, not as preemption.
9. See note 5.

PART X

Reading/Writing Are Hard Just Because Speaking/Listening Are Easy

Introduction to Part X

From a biological point of view, there is a vast difference between the production and perception of speech, on the one hand, and writing/reading, on the other. Surely, a proper appreciation of this difference is prerequisite to an understanding of the reading process, yet a reasoned account of it does not commonly figure in discussion and debate about reading. Perhaps this is because the difference simply cannot be seen on the horizontal view of speech that most students of reading (and speech) take more or less for granted. The vertical view nicely exposes the difference, and thus provides an answer to the question that must set the aim of reading instruction: what is it that would-be readers must know that mastery of speech will not have taught them?

Chapter 24
The Relation of Speech to Reading and Writing

Theories of reading/writing and theories of speech typically have in common that neither takes proper account of an obvious fact about language that must, in any reckoning, be critically relevant to both: there is a vast difference in naturalness (hence ease of use) between its spoken and written forms. In my view, a theory of reading should begin with this fact, but only after a theory of speech has explained it.

My aim, then, is to say how well the difference in naturalness is illuminated by each of two theories of speech—one conventional, the other less so—and then, in that light, to weigh the contribution that each of these can make to an understanding of reading and writing and the difficulties that attend them. More broadly, I aim to promote the notion that a theory of speech and a theory of reading/writing are inseparable, and that the validity of the one is measured, in no small part, by its fit to the other.

What Does It Mean to Say That Speech Is More Natural?

The difference in naturalness between the spoken and written forms of language is patent, so I run the risk of being tedious if I elaborate it here. Still, it is important for the argument I mean to make that we have explicitly in mind how variously the difference manifests itself. Let me, therefore, count the ways.

1. Speech is universal. Every community of human beings has a fully developed spoken language. Reading and writing, on the other hand, are relatively rare. Many, perhaps most, languages do not even have a written form, and when, as in modern times, a writing system is devised—usually by missionaries—it does not readily come into common use.

2. Speech is older in the history of our species. Indeed, it is presumably as old as we are, having emerged with us as perhaps the most important of our species-typical characteristics. Writing systems, on the other hand, are developments of the last few thousand years.

3. Speech is earlier in the history of the individual; reading/writing come later, if at all.

4. Speech must, of course, be learned, but it need not be taught. For learning to speak, the necessary and sufficient conditions are but two: membership in the human race and exposure to a mother tongue. Indeed, given that these two conditions are met, there is scarcely any way that the development of speech can be prevented.

Originally published in *Orthography, Phonology, Morphology, and Meaning*, ed. R. Frost and L. Katz (Elsevier Science Publishers B.V., 1992), 167–178. Reprinted with permission.

Thus, learning to speak is a precognitive process, much like learning to perceive visual depth and distance or the location of sound. In contrast, reading and writing require to be taught, though, given the right ability, motivation, and opportunity, some will infer the relation of script to language and thus teach themselves. But, however learned, reading/writing is an intellectual achievement in a way that learning to speak is not.

5. There are brain mechanisms that evolved with language and that are, accordingly, largely dedicated to its processes. Reading and writing presumably engage at least some of these mechanisms, but they must also exploit others that evolved to serve nonlinguistic functions. There is no specialization for reading/writing as such.

6. Spoken language has the critically important property of "openness," unlike nonhuman systems of communication, speech is capable of expressing and conveying an indefinitely numerous variety of messages. A script can share this property, but only to the extent that it somehow transcribes its spoken-language base. Having no independent existence, a proper (open) script is narrowly constrained by the nature of its spoken-language roots and by the mental resources on which they draw. Still, within these constraints, scripts are more variable than speech.

One dimension of variation is the level at which the message is represented, though the range of that variation is, in fact, much narrower than the variety of possible written forms would suggest. Thus, as DeFrancis (1991) convincingly argues, any script that communicates meanings or ideas directly, as in ideograms, for example, is doomed to arrive at a dead end. Ideographic scripts cannot be open—that is, they cannot generate novel messages—and the number of messages they can convey is never more than the inventory of one-to-one associations between (holistically different) signals and distinctly different meanings that human beings can master. Indeed, it is a distinguishing characteristic of language, and a necessary condition of its openness, that it communicates meanings indirectly, via specifically linguistic structures and processes, including, nontrivially, those of the phonological component. Not surprisingly, scripts must follow suit; in the matter of language, as with so many other natural processes, it is hard to improve on nature.

Constraints of a different kind apply at the lower levels. Thus, the acoustic signal, as represented visually by a spectrogram, for example, cannot serve as a basis for a script; while spectrograms can be puzzled out by experts, they, along with other visual representations, cannot be read fluently. The reason is not primarily that the relevant parts of the signal are insufficiently visible; it is, rather, that, owing to the nature of speech, and especially to the coarticulation that is central to it, the relation between acoustic signal and message is complex in ways that defeat whatever cognitive processes the "reader" brings to bear. Narrow phonetic transcriptions are easier to read, but there is still more context-, rate-, and speaker-conditioned variation than the eye is comfortable with. In any case, no extant script offers language at a narrow phonetic level. To be usable, scripts must, apparently, be pitched at the more abstract phonological and morphophonological levels. That being so, and given that reading-writing require conscious awareness of the units represented by the script, we can infer that people can become conscious of phonemes and morphophonemes. We can also infer about these units that, standing above so much of the acoustic and phonetic variability, they correspond approximately to the invariant forms in which words are presumably stored in the speaker's lexicon. A script that captures this invariance is surely off to a good start. At all events, some scripts (e.g., Finnish, Serbo-Croatian) do approximate to purely phonological renditions of the language, while others depart from a phonological base in the direction of morphology. Thus, English script is rather highly morphophonological, Chinese even more so. But, as DeFrancis (1991; see also Wang 1981) makes abundantly clear, all these scripts, including even the Chinese, are significantly phonological, and, in his view, they would fail if they were not; the variation is simply in the degree to which some of the morphology is also represented.

Scripts also vary somewhat, as speech does not, in the size of the linguistic segments they take as their elements, but here, too, the choice is quite constrained. Surely, it would not do to make a unit of the script equal to a phoneme and a half, a third of a syllable, or some arbitrary stretch—say 100 milliseconds—of the speech stream. Still, scripts can and do take as their irreducible units either phonemes or syllables, so in this respect, too, they are more diverse than speech.

7. All of the foregoing differences are, of course, merely reflections of one underlying circumstance—namely, that speech is a product of biological evolution, while writing systems are artifacts. Indeed, an alphabet—the writing system that is of most immediate concern to us—is a triumph of applied biology, part discovery, part invention. The discovery—surely one of the most momentous of all time—was that words do not differ from each other holistically, but rather by the particular arrangement of a small inventory of the meaningless units they comprise. The invention was simply the notion that if each of these units were to be represented by a distinctive optical shape, then everyone could read and write, provided he knew the language and was conscious of the internal phonological structure of its words.

How Is the Difference in Naturalness to Be Understood?

Having seen in how far speech is more natural than reading/writing, we should look first for a simple explanation, one that is to be seen in the surface appearance of the two processes. But when we search there, we are led to conclude, in defiance of the most obvious facts, that the advantage must lie with reading/writing, not with speech. Thus, it is the eye, not the ear, that is the better receptor; the hand, not the tongue, that is the more versatile effector; the print, not the sound, that offers the better signal-to-noise ratio; and the discrete alphabetic characters, not the nearly continuous and elaborately context-conditioned acoustic signal, that offers the more straightforward relation to the language. To resolve this seeming paradox and understand the issue more clearly, we shall have to look more deeply into the biology of speech. To that end, I turn to two views of speech to see what each has to offer.

The Conventional View of Speech as a Basis for Understanding the Difference in Naturalness

The first assumption of the conventional view is so much taken for granted that it is rarely made explicit. It is, very simply, that the phonetic elements are defined as sounds. This is not merely to say the obvious, which is that speech is conveyed by an acoustic medium, but rather to suppose, in a phrase made famous by Marshall McLuhan, that the medium *is* the message.

The second assumption, which concerns the production of these sounds, is also usually unspoken, not just because it is taken for granted, though it surely is, but also because it is apparently not thought by conventional theorists to be even relevant. But, whatever the reason, one finds among the conventional claims none which implies the existence of a phonetic mode of action—that is, a mode adapted to phonetic purposes and no other. One therefore infers that the conventional view must hold (by default, as it were) that no such mode exists. Put affirmatively, the conventional assumption is that speech is produced by motor processes and movements that are independent of language.

The third assumption concerns the perception of speech sounds, and, unlike the first two, is made explicitly and at great length (Cole and Scott 1974; Crowder and Morton 1969; Diehl and Kluender 1989; Fujisaki and Kawashima 1970; Kuhl 1981; Miller 1977; Oden and Massaro 1978; Stevens 1975). In its simplest form, it is that perception of speech is not different from perception of other sounds; all are governed by the same general processes of the auditory system. Thus, language simply accepts representations made available to it by perceptual processes that are generally auditory, not specifically linguistic. So, just as language presumably recruits ordinary motor processes for its own purposes, so, too, does it recruit the ordinary processes of auditory perception; at the level of perception, as well as action, there is, on the conventional view, no specialization for language.

The fourth assumption is required by the second and third. For if the acts and percepts of speech are not, by their nature, specifically phonetic, they must necessarily be made so, and that can be done only by a process of cognitive translation. Presumably, that is why conventional theorists say about speech perception that after the listener has apprehended the auditory representation he must elevate it to linguistic status by attaching a phonetic label (Crowder and Morton 1969; Fujisaki and Kawashima 1970; Pisoni 1973), fitting it to a phonetic prototype (Massaro 1987; Oden and Massaro 1978), or associating it with some other linguistically significant entity, such as a "distinctive feature" (Stevens 1975).

I note, parenthetically, that this conventional way of thinking about speech is heir to two related traditions in the psychology of perception. One, which traces its origins to Aristotle's enumeration of the five senses, requires of a perceptual mode that it have an end organ specifically devoted to its interests. Thus, ears yield an auditory mode; eyes, a visual mode; the nose, an olfactory mode; and so on. Lacking an end organ of its very own, speech cannot, therefore, be a mode. In that case, phonetic percepts cannot be the immediate objects of perception; they can only be perceived secondarily, as the result of a cognitive association between a primary auditory representation appropriate to the acoustic stimulus that excites the ear (and hence the auditory mode) and, on the other hand, some cognitive form of a linguistic unit. Such an assumption is, of course, perfectly consistent with another tradition in psychology, one that goes back at least to the beginning of the eighteenth century, where it is claimed in Berkeley's "New Theory of Vision" (1709) that depth (which cannot be projected directly onto a two-dimensional retina) is perceived by associating sensations of muscular strain (caused by the convergence of the eyes as they fixate objects at various distances) with the experience of distance. In the conventional view of speech, as in Berkeley's assumption about visual depth, apprehending the event or property is a matter of perceiving one thing and calling it something else.

Some of my colleagues and I have long argued that the conventional assumptions fail to account for the important facts about speech. Here, however, my concern is only with the extent to which they enlighten us about the relation of spoken language to is written derivative. That the conventional view enlightens us not at all becomes apparent when one sees that, in contradiction of all the differences I earlier enumerated, it leads to the conclusion that speech and reading/writing must be equally natural. To see how comfortably the conventional view sits with an (erroneous) assumption that speech and reading/writing are psychologically equivalent, one need only reconsider the four assumptions of that view, substituting, where appropriate, "optical" for "acoustic" or "visual" for "auditory."

One sees then, that, just as the phonetic elements of speech are, by the first of the conventional assumptions, defined as sounds, the elements of a writing system can only be defined as optical shapes. As for the second assumption—viz., that speech production is managed by motor processes of the most general sort—we must suppose that this is exactly true for writing; by no stretch of the imagination can it be supposed that the writer's movements are the output of an action mode that is specifically linguistic. The third assumption of the conventional view of speech also finds its parallel in reading/writing, for, surely, the percepts evoked by the optical characters are ordinarily visual in the same way that the percepts evoked by the sounds of speech are supposed to be ordinarily auditory. Thus, at the level of action and perception, there is in reading/writing, as there is assumed to be in speech, no specifically linguistic mode. For speech, that is only an assumption—and, as I think, a very wrong one—but for reading/writing it is an incontrovertible fact; the acts and percepts of reading/writing did not evolve as part of the specialization for language, hence they cannot belong to a natural linguistic mode.

The consequence of all this is that the fourth of the conventional assumptions about speech is, in fact, necessary for reading/writing and applies perfectly to it: like the ordinary, nonlinguistic auditory and motor representations according to the conventional view of speech, the correspondingly ordinary visual and motor representations of reading/writing must somehow be made relevant to language, and that can only be done by a cognitive process; the reader/writer simply has to learn that certain shapes refer to units of the language and that others do not.

It is this last assumption that most clearly reveals the flaw that makes the conventional view useless as a basis for understanding the most important difference between speech and reading/writing—namely, that the evolution of the one is biological, the other cultural. To appreciate the nature of this shortcoming, we must first consider how either mode of language transmission meets a requirement that is imposed on every communication system, whatever its nature and the course of its development. This requirement, which is commonly ignored in arguments about the nature of speech, is that the parties to the message exchange must be bound by a common understanding about which signals, or which aspects of which signals, have communicative significance; only then can communication succeed. Mattingly and I have called this the requirement for "parity" (Liberman and Mattingly 1985; Liberman and Mattingly 1989; Mattingly and Liberman 1988). One asks, then, what is entailed by parity as the system develops in the species and as it is realized in the normal communicative act.

In the development of writing systems, the answer is simple and beyond dispute: parity was established by agreement. Thus, all who use an alphabet are parties to a compact that prescribes just which optical shapes are to be taken as symbols for which phonological units, the association of the one with the other having been determined arbitrarily. Indeed, this is what it means to say that writing systems are artifacts, and that the child's learning the linguistic significance of the characters of the script is a cognitive activity.

Unfortunately for the validity of the conventional assumptions, they require that the same story be told about the development of parity in speech. For if the acts and percepts of speech are, as the conventional assumption would have it, ordinarily motor and ordinarily auditory, one must ask how, why, when, and by whom they were invested with linguistic significance. Where is it written that the gesture and percept we know as [b] should count for language, but that a clapping of the hands should not? Is there somewhere a commandment that says. Thou shalt not commit [b] except when it is thy clear intention to communicate? Or are we to assume, just as absurdly, that [b] was incorporated into the language by agreement? It is hard to see how the conventional view of speech can be made to provide a basis for understanding the all-important difference in evolutionary status between speech and reading/writing.

The problem is the worse confounded when we take account of both sides of the normal communicative act. For, on the conventional view the speaker deals in representations of a generally motor sort and the listener in representations of a generally auditory sort. What is it, then, that these two representations have in common, except that neither has anything to do with language? One must thus suppose for speech, as for writing and reading, that there is something like a phonetic idea—a cognitive representation of some kind—to connect these representations to each other and to language, and so to make communication possible.

Thus it is that at every biological or psychological turn the conventional view of speech make reading and writing the equivalents of speech perception and production. Since these processes are plainly not equivalent, the conventional view of speech can hardly be the starting point for an account of reading and writing.

The Unconventional View of Speech as a Basis for Understanding the Difference in Naturalness

The first assumption of the unconventional view is that the units of speech are defined as gestures, not as the sounds that those gestures produce. (For recent accounts of the unconventional view, see Liberman and Mattingly 1985, 1989; Mattingly and Liberman 1988, 1990). The rationale for this assumption is to be understood by taking account of the function of the phonological component of the grammar and of the requirements it imposes. As for the function of phonology, it is, of course, to form words by combining and permuting a few dozen meaningless segments, and so to make possible a lexicon tens of thousands of times larger than could ever have been achieved if, as in all natural but nonhuman communication systems, each "word" were conveyed by a signal that was holistically different from all others. But phonology can serve this critically important function only if its elements are commutable; and if they are to be commutable, they must be discrete and invariant.

A related requirement has to do with rate, for if all utterances are to be formed by variously stringing together an exiguous set of signal elements, then, inevitably, the strings must run to great lengths. It is essential, therefore, if these strings are to be organized into words and sentences, that they be produced and perceived at reasonable speed. But if the auditory percepts of the conventional view are to be discrete and invariant, the sounds and gestures must be discrete and invariant, too. Such sounds and gestures are possible, of course, but only at the expense of rate. Thus one could not, on the conventional view, say "bag," but only [b] [a] [g], and to say [b] [a] [g] is not to speak but to spell. Of course, if speech were like that, then everyone who could speak or perceive a word would know exactly how to write and read it, provided only that he had managed the trivial task of memorizing the letter-to-sound correspondences. The problem is that there would be no language worth writing or reading.

There seems, indeed, no way to solve the rate problem and still somehow preserve the acoustic-auditory strategy of the conventional view. It would not have helped, for example, if Nature had abandoned the vocal tract and equipped her human creatures with acoustic devices adapted to producing a rapid sequence of sounds—a drumfire or tattoo—for that strategy would have defeated the ear. The point is that speech proceeds at rates that transmit up to 15 or even 20 phonemes per second, but if each phoneme were represented by a discrete sound, then rates that high would seriously strain and sometimes overreach the ability of the ear to resolve the individual sounds and to divine their order.

According to the unconventional view, Nature solved the problem by avoiding the acoustic-auditory strategy that would have created it. The alternative she chose was to define the phonetic elements as gestures, as the first assumption of the unconventional view proposes. Thus, [b] is a closing at the lips, [h] an opening at the glottis, [p] a combination of lip closing and glottis opening, and so forth. In fact, the gestures are far more complex than this, for a gesture usually comprises movements of several articulators, and these movements are exquisitely context-conditioned. Given such complications, I must wait on others to discover how best to characterize these gestures and how to derive the articulatory movements from them. But while I'm waiting, I can be reasonably sure that the unconventional view heads the theoretical enterprise in the right direction, for it permits coarticulation. That is, it permits the speaker to overlap gestures that are produced by different organs—for example, the lips and the tongue in [ba]—and to merge gestures that are produced by different parts of the same organ—for example, the tip and body of the tongue, as in [da]—and so to achieve the high rates that are common.

But the gestures that are coarticulated, and the means for controlling them, were not lying conveniently to hand, just waiting to be appropriated by language, which brings us to the second assumption of the unconventional view: the gestures of speech and their controls are specifically phonetic, having been adapted for language and for nothing else. As for the gestures themselves, they are distinct as a class from those movements of the same organs that are used for such nonlinguistic purposes as swallowing, moving food around in the mouth, licking the lips, and so on. Presumably, they were selected in the evolution of speech in large part because of the ease with which they lent themselves to being coarticulated. But the control and coordination of these gestures is specific to speech, too. For coarticulation must walk a fine line, being constrained on either side by the special demands of phonological communication. Thus, coarticulation must produce enough overlap and merging to permit the high rates of phonetic segment production that do, in fact, occur, while yet preserving the details of phonetic structure.

The third assumption of the unconventional view is that, just as there is a specialization for the production of phonetic structures, so, too, is there a specialization for their perception. Indeed, the two are but complementary aspects of the same specialization, one for deriving the articulatory movements from the (abstract) specification of the gestures, the other for processing the acoustic signals so as to recover the coarticulated gestures that are its distal cause. The rationale for this assumption about perception arises out of the consequences of the fact that coarticulation folds information about several gestures into a single piece of sound, thereby conveying the information in parallel. This is of critical importance for language because it relaxes by a large factor the constraint on rate of phonetic-segment perception that is set by the temporal resolving power of the ear. But this gain has a price, for coarticulation produces a complex and singularly linguistic relation between acoustic signal and the phonetic message it conveys. As is well known, the signal for each particular phonetic element is vastly different in different contexts, and there is no direct correspondence in segmentation between signal and phonetic structure. It is to manage this language-specific relation between signal and appropriate percept that the specialization for speech perception is adapted. Support for the hypothesis that there is such a specialized speech mode of perception is to be found elsewhere. (See references given at the beginning of this section.) What is important for our present purposes is only that, according to this hypothesis, the percepts evoked by the sounds of speech are immediately and specifically phonetic. There is no need, as there is on the conventional view, for a cognitive translation from an initial representation, simply because there is no initial auditory representation.

Now one can see plainly the difference between speech and reading/writing. In reading, to take the one case, the primary perceptual representations are, as we have seen, inherently visual, not linguistic. Thus, these representations are, at best, arbitrary symbols for the natural units of language, hence unsuited to any natural language process until and unless they have been translated into linguistic form. On the other hand, the representations that are evoked by the sounds of speech are immediately linguistic in kind, having been made so by the automatic processes of the phonetic module. Accordingly, they are, by their very nature, perfectly suited for the further automatic and natural processing that the larger specialization for language provides.

As for parity and its development in evolution and in the child, it is, on the unconventional view, built into the very bones of the system. For what evolved, on this view, was a specifically phonetic process, together with representations that were thus categorically set apart from all others and reserved for language. The unconventional view also allows us to see, as the link between sender and receiver, the specifically phonetic gestures that serve as the common coin for the conduct of their linguistic business. There is no need to establish parity by means of (innate) phonetic ideas—e.g., labels, prototypes, distinctive features—to which the several nonlinguistic representations must be cognitively associated.

How Can Reading/Writing Be Made to Exploit the More Natural Processes of Speech?

The conventional view of speech provides no basis for asking this question, since there exists, on this view, no difference in naturalness. It is perhaps for this reason that the (probably) most widely held theory of reading in the United States explicitly takes as its premise that reading and writing are, or at least can be, as natural and easy as speech (Goodman and Goodman 1979). According to this theory, called "whole language," reading and writing prove to be difficult only because teachers burden children with what the theorists call "bite-size abstract chunks of language such as words, syllables, and phonemes" (Goodman 1986). If teachers were to teach children to read and write the way they were (presumably) taught to speak, then there would be no problem. Other theorists simply ignore the primacy of speech as they describe a reading process in which purely visual representations are sufficient to take the reader from print to meaning, thus implying a "visual" language that is somehow parallel to a language best described as "auditory."

On the unconventional view, however, language is neither auditory nor visual. If it seems to be auditory, that is only because the appropriate stimulus is commonly acoustic (pace Aristotle). But optical stimuli will, under some conditions, evoke equally convincing phonetic percepts, provided (and this is a critical proviso) they specify the same articulatory movements (hence, phonetic gestures) that the sounds of speech evoke. This so-called McGurk effect works powerfully when the stimuli are the natural movements of the articulatory apparatus, but not when they are the arbitrary letters of the alphabet. Thus, language is a mode, largely independent of end organs, that comprises structures and processes specifically adapted to language, hence easy to use for linguistic purposes. Therefore, the seemingly sensible strategy for the reader is to get into that mode, for once there, he is home free; everything else that needs to be done by way of linguistic processing is done for him automatically by virtue of his natural language capacity. As for where the reader should enter the language mode, one supposes that earlier is better, and that the phonological component of the mode is early enough. Certainly, making contact with the phonology has several important advantages: it makes available to the reader a generative scheme that comprehends all the words of the language, those that died yesterday, those that live today, and those that will be born tomorrow; it also establishes clear and stable representations in a semantic world full of vague and labile meanings; and, not least, it provides the natural grist for the syntactic mill—that is, the phonological representations that are used by the working memory as it organizes words into sentences.

The thoroughly visual way to read, described earlier, is the obvious alternative, doing everything that natural language does without ever touching its structures and processes. But surely that must be a hard way to read, if, indeed, it is even possible, since it requires the reader to invent new and cognitively taxing processes just in order to deal with representations that are not specialized for language and for which he has no natural bent.

What Obstacle Blocks the Natural Path?

As we have seen, the conventional view allows two equivalent representations of language—one auditory, the other visual—hence two equally natural paths that language processes might follow. In that case, such obstacles as there might be could be no greater for the visual mode; indeed, accepting the considerations I mentioned earlier, we should have to suppose that visual representations would offer the easier route.

The unconventional view, on the other hand, permits one to see just what it is that the would-be reader and writer (but not the speaker/listener) must learn, and why the learning might be at least a little difficult. The point is that, given the specialization for speech, anyone who wants to speak a word is not required to know how it is spelled; indeed, he does not even have to know that it has a spelling. He has only to think of the word: the speech specialization spells it for him, automatically selecting and coordinating the appropriate gestures. In an analogous way, the listener need not consciously parse the sound so as to identify its constituent phonological elements. Again, he relies on the phonetic specialization to do all the hard work; he has only to listen. Because the speech specialization is a module, its processes are automatic and insulated from consciousness. There are, therefore, no cognitively formed associations that would make one aware of the units being associated. Of course, the phonological representations, as distinguished from the processes, are not so insulated; they are available to consciousness—indeed, if they were not, alphabetic scripts would not work—but there is nothing in the ordinary use of language that requires the speaker/listener to put his attention on them. The consequence is that experience with speech is normally not sufficient to make one consciously aware of the phonological structure of its words, yet it is exactly this awareness that is required of all who would enjoy the advantages of an alphabetic scheme for reading and writing.

Developing an awareness of phonological structure, and hence an understanding of the alphabetic principle, is made the more difficult by the coarticulation that is central to the function of the phonetic specialization. Though such coarticulation has the crucial advantage of allowing speech production and perception to proceed at reasonable rates, it has the disadvantage from the would-be reader/writer's point of view that it destroys any simple correspondence between the acoustic segments and the phonological segments they convey. Thus, in a word like "bag," coarticulation folds three phonological segments into one seamless stretch of sound in which information about the several phonological segment is thoroughly overlapped. Accordingly, it avails the reader little to be able to identify the letters, or even to know their sounds. What he must know, if the script is to make sense, is that a word like "bag" has three pieces of phonology even though it has only one piece of sound. There is now much evidence (1) that preliterate and illiterate people (large and small) lack such phonological awareness; (2) that the amount of awareness they do have predicts their success in learning to read, and (3) that teaching phonological awareness makes success in reading more likely. (For a summary, see, for example, Liberman and Liberman 1990).

Why Should the Obstacle Loom Especially Large for Some?

Taking the conventional view of speech seriously makes it hard to avoid the assumption that the trouble with the dyslexic must be in the visual system. It is, therefore, not in the least surprising to find that by far the largest number of theories about dyslexia do, in fact, put the problem there. Thus, some believe that the trouble with dyslexics is that they cannot control their eye movements (Pavlides 1981), or that they have problems with vergence (Stein, Riddell, and Fowler 1988) or that they see letters upside down or wrong side to (Orton 1937), or that their peripheral vision is better than it should be (Geiger and Lettvin 1988), and so on.

The unconventional view of speech directs one's attention, not to the visual system and the various problems that might afflict it, but rather to the specialization for language and the reasons why the alphabetic principle is not self-evident. As we have seen, this view suggests that phonological awareness, which is necessary for application of the alphabetic principle, does not come for free with mastery of the language.

As for dyslexics—that is, those who find it particularly hard to achieve that awareness—the unconventional view of speech suggests that the problem might well arise out of a malfunction of the phonological specialization, a malfunction sufficient to cause the phonological representations to be less robust than normal. Such representations would presumably be just that much harder to become aware of. While it is difficult to test that hypothesis directly, it is possible to look for support in the other consequences that a weak phonological faculty should have. Thus, one would expect that dyslexics would show such other symptoms as greater-than-normal difficulty in holding and manipulating verbal (but not nonverbal) materials in working memory, in naming objects (that is, in finding the proper phonological representation), in perceiving speech (but not nonspeech) in noise, and in managing difficult articulations. There is some evidence that dyslexics do show such symptoms. (For a summary, see Liberman, Shankweiler, and A. Liberman 1989.)

What Are the Implications for a Theory of Speech?

Those who investigate the perception and production of speech have been little concerned to explain how these processes differ so fundamentally in naturalness from those of reading and writing. Perhaps this is because the difference is so obvious as to be taken for granted and so to escape scientific examination. Or perhaps the speech researchers believe that explaining the difference is the business of those who study reading and writing. In any case, neglect of the difference might be justifiable if it were possible for a theory of speech to have no relevant implications. But a theory of speech does inevitably have such implications, and, as has been shown, the implications of the conventional theory run counter to the obvious facts. My concern in this paper has been to show that, as a consequence, the conventional theory is of little help to those who would understand reading and writing. Now I would suggest that, for exactly the same reason, the theory offers little help to those who would understand speech, for if the theory fails to offer a reasonable account of a most fundamental fact about language, then we should conclude that there is something profoundly wrong with it.

The unconventional theory of speech described in this paper was developed to account for speech, not for the difference between its processes and those of reading and writing. That it nevertheless shows promise of also serving the latter purpose may well be taken as one more reason for believing it.

Summary

The difference in naturalness between speech and reading/writing is an important fact for the psychology of language and the obvious point of departure for understanding the processes of literacy, yet it cannot be accounted for by the conventional theory of speech. Because this theory allows no linguistic specialization at the level of perception and action, it necessarily implies that the primary representations of speech are just like those of reading/writing: neither is specifically linguistic, hence both must first be translated into linguistic form if they are to serve a linguistic function. Thus, the effect of the conventional theory is to put speech and reading/writing at the same cognitive remove from language and so make them equally unnatural.

A less conventional view shows the primary motor and perceptual representations of speech to be specifically phonetic, the automatic results of a precognitive specialization for phonological communication. Accordingly, these representations are naturally appropriate for language, requiring no cognitive translation to make them so; in this important respect they differ from the representations of reading/writing. Understanding the source of this difference helps us to see what must be done if readers and writers are to exploit their natural language faculty; why reading and writing should be at least a little difficult for all; and why they might be very difficult for some.

Note

This work was supported by NIH grant HD-01994 to Haskins Laboratories. This paper was presented at a conference on "Language and Literacy: Comparative Approaches" in Bellagio, Como, Italy in March 1991. The conference was organized by Beatrice de Gelder and José Morais.

References

Berkeley, G. (1709). *An essay towards a new theory of vision.* Dublin: Printed by Aaron Rhames for Jeremy Pepyal.

Cole, R. A., and Scott, B. (1974). Toward a theory of speech perception. *Psychological Review*, 81, 348–374.

Crowder, R. G., and Morton J. (1969). Pre-categorical acoustic storage (PAS). *Perception & Psychophysics*, 5, 365–373.

DeFrancis, J. (1991). *Visible speech: The diverse oneness of writing systems.* Honolulu: University of Hawaii Press.

Diehl, R., and Kluender, K. (1989). On the objects of speech perception. *Ecological Psychology*, 1, 121–144.

Fujisaki, M., and Kawashima, T. (1970). Some experiments on speech perception and a model for the perceptual mechanism. *Annual Report of the Engineering Research Institute* (Faculty of Engineering, University of Tokyo), 29, 207–214.

Geiger, G., and Lettvin, J. Y. (1988). Dyslexia and reading as examples of alternative visual strategies. In C. von Euler, I. Lundberg, and G. Lennerstrand (Eds.), *Wenner-Gren Symposium Series 54, Brian and Reading.* London: The Macmillan Press Ltd.

Goodman, K. S. (1976). Reading: A psycholinguistic guessing game. In H. Singer and R. B. Ruddell (Eds.), *Theoretical models and processes of reading.* Newark, DE: International Reading Association.

Goodman, K. S. (1986). *What's whole in whole language: A parent-teacher guide.* Portsmouth, NH: Heinemann.

Goodman, K. S. and Goodman, Y. M. (1979). Learning to read is natural. In L. B. Resnick and P. A. Weaver (Eds.), *Theory and practice of early reading*, Vol. 1. Hillsdale, NJ: Erlbaum.

Kuhl, P. K. (1981). Discrimination of speech by nonhuman animals: Basic auditory sensitivities conducive to the perception of speech-sound categories. *Journal of the Acoustical Society of America*, 70, 340–349.

Kuhl, P. K., and Miller, J. D. (1975). Speech perception by the chinchilla: Voiced-voiceless distinction in alveolar plosive consonants. *Science*, 190, 69.

Liberman, A. M. and Mattingly, I. G. (1985). The motor theory of speech perception revised. *Cognition*, 21, 1–36.

Liberman, A. M. and Mattingly, I. G. (1989). A specialization for speech perception. *Science*, 243, 489–494.

Liberman, I. Y., and Liberman, A. M. (1990). Whole language vs. code emphasis: Underlying assumptions and their implications for reading instruction. *Annals of Dyslexia*, 40.

Liberman, I. Y., Shankweiler, D., and Liberman, A. M. (1989). The alphabetic principle and learning to read. In D. Shankweiler and I. Y. Liberman (Eds.), *Phonology and reading disability: Solving the reading puzzle.* Research Monograph Series. Ann Arbor: University of Michigan Press.

Mattingly, I. G., and A. M. Liberman (1988). Specialized perceiving systems for speech and other biologically significant sounds. In G. M. Edelman, W. E. Gall, and W. M. Cowan (Eds.), *Functions of the auditory system* (pp. 775–793). New York: Wiley.

Mattingly, I. G. and A. M. Liberman (1990). Speech and other auditory modules. In G. M. Edelman, W. E. Gall and W. M. Cowan (Eds.), *Signal and sense: Local and global order in perceptual maps.* New York: Wiley.

Miller, J. D. (1977). Perception of speech sounds in animals: Evidence for speech processing by mammalian auditory mechanisms. In T. H. Bullock (Ed.), *Recognition of complex acoustic signals*. (Life Sciences Research Report 5). Berlin: Dahlem Konferenzen.

Oden, G. C., and D. W. Massaro (1978). Integration of featural information in speech perception. *Psychological Review*, 85, 172–191.

Orton, S. J. (1937). *Reading, writing and speech problems in children*. New York: W. W. Norton & Co.

Pavlides, G. T. (1985). Eye movement differences between dyslexics, normal and retarded readers while sequentially fixating digits. *American Journal of Opto and Physiological Optics*, 62, 820–832.

Pisoni, D. B. (1973). Auditory and phonetic memory codes in the discrimination of consonants and vowels. *Perception and Psychophysics*, 13, 253–260.

Stein, J., Riddell, P., and Fowler, S. (1988). Disordered right hemisphere function in developmental dyslexia. In C. von Euler, I. Lundberg, and G. Lennerstrand (Eds.), *Brain and Reading*. England: The Macmillan Press Ltd.

Stevens, K. N. (1975). The potential role of property detectors in the perception of consonants. In G. Fant and M. A. Tatham (Eds.), *Auditory analysis and perception of speech*. New York: Academic Press.

Wang, W. S-Y. (1981). Language structure and optimal orthography. In O. J. L. Tzeng and H. Singer (Eds.), *Perception of print: Reading research in experimental psychology*. Hillsdale, NJ: Lawrence Erlbaum Associates.

Index

Abramson, Arthur, 23–24
ABX method, 19, 20, 154–155, 170, 181. *See also* AXB method
Acoustic alphabet, 4, 7, 204
Acoustic code, 224
Acoustic cue(s), 22, 57, 187–188, 191–193, 244–245
  articulatory gestures in, 193–195, 196–197
  for /b/, 136
  for consonants, 99–100, 136, 138, 188–192
  and context, 13, 16
  integration of, 35–36
    experiments on, 40, 351–368
    influence of results on, 28
  multiplicity of, 34–35
  and parallel transmission, 223 (*see also* Parallel processing or transmission)
  vs. percept, 221, 403, 419
  perceptual equivalence of (temporal and spectral), 371–382
  vs. phonetic gestures, 253
  for stop-consonant manner, 371
  for /w/, 136, 147n.9, 148n.11
Acoustic-cue discriminability, 19. *See also* Discrimination
Acoustic information, integration of, 36–37
Acoustic locus. *See* Locus(i)
Acoustic-phonetic boundaries. *See* Boundary(ies); Phoneme boundaries
Acoustic signals
  and articulatory gestures, 238–239
  and auditory interaction, 404–405
  and auditory patterning, 7
  context-conditioned variation in, 419
  and cue-phoneme relation, 221
  and parallel transmission, 223
  perception of, 38
  phonetic vs. non-phonetic sorting of, 254–255
  and phonetic percept, 237
  and script, 434
  in search for acoustic cues, 187, 191
  and speech quality, 14
Acoustic stimulus, for unvoiced stop consonants, 59, 61–74. *See also* Acoustic cue(s)

Acoustic substitutes for speech, 43
Acquired distinctiveness, 18–19, 151, 153, 163, 167, 168, 178, 196
Acquired similarity, 18–19, 151, 153, 163, 167, 178, 180, 196
[æ]
  in "labs," 144, 145
  sample pattern for, 113
Affricates. *See also* Fricative-affricate distinction
  in consonant classification, 188
  and silence, 338–342, 345
Age differences, in formant frequencies, 225n.10
Allophones, 224n.1
Allophonic variations, 134, 158
Alphabet, 205, 223, 224, 435, 442
Analogy of light brightness, 197
Analysis-by-synthesis model, 222, 256, 285
Animals, nonhuman
  and auditory boundaries, 34, 35
  communication systems of
    non-cognitive specialization in, 32
    perception-production commonality in, 286
  and perceptual equivalence experiment, 382
Aristotle, 436, 441
Articulatory gestures, 201, 252–254, 273–275, 293. *See also* Speech production
  acoustic consequences of, 351
  acoustic plus optical signals of, 36–37, 249–250, 257, 275–277, 441
  analysis of /b/, 215
  vs. articulatory act, 366–367
  constriction sounds in, 188, 210
  as criteria for consonant cue classification, 188
  and cue integration, 358
  and cue trading relations, 352
  and "direct perception," 255–256
  electromyographic correlates of, 218–219
  in encoding, 217–220
  and formant transitions, 16, 75
  and locus, 209
  and motor theory, 30–31, 34, 237–239, 245, 247, 255–256 (*see also* Motor Theory, Revised)

Articulatory gestures (cont.)
  overlapping of, 253, 284
  and perceptual equivalence, 372, 375
  and phonetic boundaries, 251
  and phonetic categories, 255
  and phonetic module (mode), 29–30, 256, 272
  and rate of communication, 273
  for [r] and [l], 310
  and speech perception, 13, 72, 193–195, 196–197, 221–222
    discrimination in, 166, 175, 180
    as distal object, 27, 242–243
    and initial auditory percept, 14
    and silence, 336–337
  and speech production as specialized, 282–286
  and stimulus information, 34
  in unconventional view of speech, 438, 439
  and voice-onset-time, 24
Articulatory place of production. See Place of articulation
Articulatory synthesis, 25
Articulatory synthesizer, 285
Artificial language, and reading machine, 5
Aspiration, 121
Auditory decoder, 220–221
Auditory discriminability, 3–7
Auditory integration, 366, 412
Auditory interaction, 247–248, 404–405, 420, 424
Auditory (sound) localization, module for, 241–242, 257
  and phonetic module, 39, 242–243, 250
Auditory (sound) localization, and speech perception, 271
  and heteromorphy, 275
Auditory mode or module, 243, 248–249, 275, 278, 299
Auditory patterning, 7–8
Auditory percept, 18, 27, 418, 423
Auditory perception, and spectrogram, 49
Auditory scene analysis, 293, 297, 299–300, 302
Auditory theory, 239–240, 250–251
  and context-conditioned variation, 247
  and duplex perception, 420
  and evidence about perception of phonetic segments, 34–37
  vs. gestural strategy, 274
  of perceptual equivalence, 372
  and silence in stop consonants, 387
  unlikely processes, 246, 247
Automatic speech recognizers, 214
AXB method, 407, 413. See also ABX method

Back vowels, 67
  and [k], 68–69

and second-formant transition, 90
"Base," 40, 248, 278, 385, 386, 388, 389, 420
Bats. See Echolocation
Behaviorist stimulus-response tradition, 2, 18
Bell Telephone laboratories, 9–10
Berkeley, George, 436
Binary decisions, 16–17, 22
Biology. See also Evolution
  and motor theory, 254
  and parity, 299
  and speech vs. reading/writing, 437
  and vertical vs. horizontal view, 26
Birds, generative detection in, 280
Blachman, Benita, 27
Blind persons, reading machine for. See Reading machine for the blind
Boundary(ies). See also Phoneme boundaries
  multiplicity of, 34–35
  shift in, 117–119
Brady, Susan, 27
Brain
  lateral processing of speech vs. nonspeech sounds in, 214
  lateral processing of stops in, 310
  and phonological communication, 29
Broca, Paul, 257
Browman, Cathe, 31

Carnegie Corporation of New York, 9
Categorical perception, 18–22, 151, 201, 212–213, 317, 418
  auditory and phonetic boundaries in, 251
  and discrimination experiments, 19–20, 153–164, 165–168
  with silent interval, 168–181
  of [r] and [l] (Japanese-American experiment), 311, 317–318, 319
  and stop consonants, 222, 403–404
  in duplex-perception experiment, 410, 419
Children, preliterate, 42. See also Infants
Chimpanzees, 30
Chomsky, Noam, 258
Cipher, 224n.2
Coarticulation, 33–34, 238–239, 440
  and acoustic signal, 13
  and context-conditioned variation, 247
  and cue integration, 36
  gestures for, 298
  and phonological awareness, 442
  and phonological communication, 30
  and rate of speech, 273
  and reading of speech, 47
  and segmentation, 246–247
  and shift in [d-g] boundary, 404
  and signal variations, 419
  and transitions, 241
  in unconventional view of speech, 439

Code, 203, 224n.2. *See also* Morse code; Speech code
Cognitive process
  and humans vs. animals, 32
  and speech perception, 257, 258, 286, 424, 436, 438, 440, 444
Communication
  and parity, 31–32
  phonological
    vs. nonhuman, 32
    requirements of, 32–34
Consonant(s), 110n.3. *See also* Liquids; Nasal consonants; Semivowels; Stop consonants
  cue classification for, 99–100, 188–192
  and cue-phoneme relation, 210
  loci of, 17, 112, 137, 189, 207–209 (*see also* Locus(i))
  perception of
    as categorical, 21 (*see also* Categorical perception)
    third-formant transitions in, 210
    of unvoiced stop consonants, 59, 61–73
  transitions for, 137
    second-formant, 99, 189, 205, 206, 209 (*see also* under Second-formant transition)
    vs. steady state, 136
Constriction sounds, 188, 210
Context, and transitions, 138
Context-conditioned variations, 12–13, 15–16, 239, 244
  in acoustic cue, 16, 205–206, 419
  and auditory theories, 239–240
  and coarticulation, 247
  and coordinative structures, 27
  and Early Motor Theory, 13, 33
  and motor acts, 254
  and stop consonants, 404
  and "virtual" acoustic invariant, 17
Convergence in speech perception, 275–278. *See also* McGurk effect
Conversion, intersensory pattern, 49–54
Cooper, Frank, 2, 4, 6, 7, 9, 10, 12, 25, 43
Coordinative structures, 27, 30. *See also* Articulatory gestures
Cross-language studies
  on [r-l] discrimination (Japanese-Americans), 310–323
  on voicing distinction in stops, 309
  on vowels, 309
Cue addition, and third-formant transitions, 117–119
Cues. *See* Acoustic cue(s)
Cursive writing, 33
Cutback, first-formant, 121, 122–127, 128, 129–131

Deaf persons, and reading of spectrograms, 47

Decoder, auditory, 220–221
Decoder, speech, 201, 214, 224, 227n.25
Decoding, 220–223
  and identifiability, 204
  and perception by eye, 215
  and rapidly articulated vowels, 213
Delattre, Pierre, 11–12, 23, 24
Depth, visual perception of, 242, 418, 436
Detector model, 347, 366
Direct perception, of speech, 255–256
Direct translators, 3–4
Discrimination, 3–7, 19–20, 153–164, 165–168, 195, 212
  and duplex perception, 278–279, 296–297
  and third-formant transitions (experiment), 405–418
  of liquids [r-l] by Japanese and Americans, 310–323
  of nonspeech chirps, 404
  of paired cues (perceptual equivalence experiment), 376–381
  in silent interval experiment, 168–180
  true, 161–162
  of voicing in stops (Thai and English listeners), 309
  of vowels (Swedish and American listeners), 309
Distinctiveness, acquired, 18–19, 151, 153, 163, 167, 168, 178, 196
Divergence in speech peception, 248–249, 278
Domain specificity, 257, 275
Duplex perception, 40, 248–249, 252, 278–279, 293–297, 300–301, 385–387, 405, 423–425
  "da"-"ga" experiment on, 425–427
  equal-presentation procedure in, 425, 427
  and phonetic module or mode, 248–249, 258, 278–279, 293–297, 301, 385, 420
  and preemptiveness, 281
  and scene analysis/phonetic module, 302–303
  of stop consonants (experiment), 387–399
  for third-formant transitions (stop consonants experiment), 405–418, 419–420
Duration
  and acquired distinctiveness or similarity, 198n.23
  as cue, 163–164
  of fricative noise, 352–365
  of vowels, 142
Duration of silence. *See* Silent interval
Duration of transition
  and stop consonants, 78, 88n.7, 94
  and stop-semivowel distinction, 18, 164, 190
  and tempo, 103, 104, 105, 106, 107–109
Dyads, 135
Dyslexia, 442–443

Early Motor Theory. *See* Motor Theory, Early
Echolocation, 26
  and generative detection, 280, 281
  and heteromorphic representation, 39, 275, 279, 300
  and modularity, 242
  and scene analysis, 302
Electromyographic (EMG) correlates of articulatory activity, 218–219
Empty symbols of language, 193
Encoding, 210
  and identifiability, 204
  and speech production, 215–220
Energy integration, 372
Equivalences, perceptual, 36, 351–352, 372, 375. *See also* Trading relations
Ethology, 26
Eve (subject in reading-machine experiment), 6
Evolution
  and motor theory, 241
  phonetic perception in, 300
  and speech, 1, 28–31, 47, 435

Fant, Gunnar, 23
Feature detectors, 347, 366
First formant
  and nasals, 16
  onset time and frequency of, 23, 372
First-formant cutback, 121, 122–127, 128, 129–131
First-formant locus, 90, 95–96, 112
First-formant transition, 15–16
  and tempo, 100–104, 107–109
  and third formant, 112
  for voiced stops, 16, 78, 80, 92, 113, 206
  and voicing, 78–79, 80, 121–127, 128
Flynn, John, 6
FM (frequency-modulation) reading machine, 4–6
Fodor, J., 28, 38, 256–257, 259, 281
Forced-choice temporal interval method, 181
Formant(s), 74n.7, 87n.1, 294, 423. *See also* First formant; Second formant
Formant frequencies, invariance problem with, 225n.10
Formant transitions, 15–16, 99, 111, 136–137, 189–191, 294, 423. *See also* First-formant transition; Second-formant transition; Third-formant transition
  and acoustic loci, 17
  in auditory vs. phonetic mode, 239, 240, 248
  and auditory theories, 240
  and binary decisions, 17
  and categorical perception, 418
  and coarticulation, 241
  for consonants, 137, 191–192

and context-conditioned variability, 206, 239
context-sensitive, 247
as cues, 191
for [d], 274
in duplex perception, 392, 393, 394, 396–399
and duration, 18
falling, 91
frequency specification of difficult, 24
and fricatives, 247
isolated, 278, 280
and loci, 189
and nasal consonants, 16, 76, 84–87, 89
parallel transmission through, 207
and "ramps," 251
and silence, 247
 in stop-consonant perception, 327
speech and nonspeech percepts from, 239, 240, 248, 278
and stop consonants, 16, 75–76, 77–83, 100–104, 403–404, 418
Fowler, Anne, 27
Fowler, Carol, 27
Frequency shifts. *See* Formant transitions
Fricative-affricate distinction
  and auditory theory, 240
  in integration experiments, 352–365
  and silence, 338–339, 341–342, 345
  stop gesture in, 337
Fricatives
  in consonant classification, 188
  constriction noises in, 210
  context-sensitive transitions as cues for, 247
  and dynamic shaping, 15
  noise cues for, 210, 211, 247
  and "Octopus" synthesizer, 187
  production of, 283, 284
  and second-formant transition, 205
  and silent interval, 326–327, 329, 336, 337
  and synthesizer, 22–23
  and transitions, 247
Front vowels, 67
  and [k], 68–69
  and second-formant locus, 90

"gas," spectrogram of, 8
Geminate condition, 331, 348n.2
Gender differences, in formant frequencies, 225n.10
Generality, and speech perception as special, 37–38
Generative detection, 279–281
Gestures. *See* Articulatory gestures
"glu" syllable, pattern for, 140
Goldstein, Louis, 31
Grammar, speech as analogous to, 250, 280. *See also* Syntax

Griffith, Belver, 19
Grimm's law, 284

Harris, Katherine, 20, 27
Harris, Zellig, 141
Haskins Laboratories, 1, 9, 133, 156, 187, 197n, 311
  parallel-resonance synthesizer of, 331, 389, 390
  Pulse Code Modulation system at, 328, 353, 359
  resonance synthesizer at, 406
Heteromorphy (heteromorphic representation), 39, 275–279, 299, 300
Homomorphic representations, 39, 41, 300
Horizontal view of speech, 2–3, 26
  and acoustic substitutes for speech, 43
  and boundaries, 35
  and categorical perception, 151
  and Early Motor Theory, 13–14
  and evolution, 28, 29
  and human vs. nonhuman communication, 32
  and integration of acoustic with optical information, 37
  and parity, 31
  and pattern-perception experiment, 11
  and psycholinguistics, 20
  and reading/writing vs. speaking/listening, 431
  and requirements for phonological communication, 32–33
  shortcomings of, 27, 28
  and speech perception as special, 37–38
  and stimulus information, 34
  vs. vertical, 201
  and writing/reading vs. speech, 41–42
Hub, of stop consonants, 97n.6

Individual differences, in formant frequencies, 225n.10
Infants
  discrimination experiment for, 382
  [l-r] discriminations of, 319–320
  prelinguistic
    and McGurk effect, 37, 249
    phonetic-perception capacity of, 27, 254
Ingemann, Frances, 24, 133
Innate ideas, 298
Innate specification of phonetic mode, 254. See also Module, phonetic
Integration
  of acoustical and optical information, 36–37
  of acoustic cues, 28, 35–36, 40, 351–368
  auditory, 366, 412
  energy, 372
  of phonemes, 7
  and phonetic module, 38

Intensity, as cue, 188
Intersensory pattern conversion, 49–54
Interval of silence. See Silent interval
Invariance problem, 225n.10
  and second-formant transition, 209
Invariant phonetic structures. See Articulatory gestures
Inverted-pattern experiment, 168
Isolated transition, 278, 280

Japanese speakers, and [r-l] distinction (cross-language study), 310–323
Jaw raising, 238
Jones, Daniel, 12
Juncture, in integration experiment, 352, 358–365

"kill," and perception of phones, 12
Konishi, Mark, 26, 299

Labeling
  and phoneme discrimination (experiments), 154–164, 171–180, 195–197
  and perceptual equivalence, 381–382
"labs," as synthesis example, 144–145
Language
  acquisition of, 254–255
  module for, 257, 258, 259–260, 303n.6
  perception of, 257
  and speech, 2, 224
  spoken vs. written, 205, 433 (see also Writing)
Lateral processing in brain
  of speech vs. nonspeech sounds, 214
  of stops, 310
Learning (training). See also Acquired distinctiveness; Acquired similarity
  and acoustic cues through sight vs. hearing, 215
  and articulatory-gesture establishment, 14
  and categorical perception (Early Motor Theory), 151
  and discrimination, 163, 193, 195–197
  and perception-production link, 254
  and perceptual integration, 366
    McGurk effect, 36–37, 249–250, 257, 275–277, 441
  of phoneme discrimination, 167
  experiment on, 168–181
Liberman, Isabelle, 27, 42
Limited central access, 275
Linguistic experience, cross-language studies on, 309
  discrimination of [l] and [r], 310
  discrimination of voiced/voiceless stops, 309
  discrimination of vowels, 309
Linkage, as problem, 146
Lip rounding, 238

Liquids, 310–311
  context-sensitive transitions as cues for, 247
  cross-language discrimination study on, 310–323
  and duplex perception, 405
  perceptual context effect of, 412–418
  and second-formant transitions, 209
  and silent interval, 190–191
Lisker, Leigh, 23–24
Listening, vs. reading, 41–43, 204–205, 442. *See also* Speech perception
Localization, auditory. *See* Auditory (sound) localization
Locus(i), 17–18, 89, 97n.3, 112, 137, 189, 207–209. *See also* First-formant locus; Second-formant locus(i); Third-formant locus
  and classification, 191
  complications of, 189–190
  for /d/, 207

MacNeilage, Peter, 27
Malecot, Andre, 23
Mandatory operation, 275
Mann, Virginia, 27
Manner of production (articulation)
  and consonant categorization, 110n.3, 191–192
  and cue-phoneme relation, 210
  and first-formant locus, 96
  and first-formant transition, 138, 189, 206
  and formant transitions, 392
  perceptual equivalence of (stop consonants), 371–382
  as restricted, 283
  and silence in stop-consonant perception (experiments), 325–348, 371–382
  for stop and nasal consonants, 100, 109–110n.2
Markers, 80–81, 86–87
  nasal, 84
  neuromotor, 218
Marler, Peter, 26
Mattingly, Ignatius, 25, 26, 27, 30, 31, 38, 40, 42
McGurk, Harry, 36
McGurk effect, 36–37, 249–250, 257, 275–277, 441
McLuhan, Marshall, 435
Meaning, 193
Mid-vowel, 90
Mimicry
  in discrimination experiment, 175–176, 180
  and Early Motor Theory, 254
  and speech perception, 195, 196, 197
Modularity of Mind, The (Fodor), 28
Module, 256–257, 259
  auditory, 243, 248–249, 275, 278, 299

auditory (sound) localization, 39, 242–243, 250
  classification of as issue, 303
  closed, 39, 41, 299–301, 302
  in duplex perception, 249
  and generative detection, 281
  language, 257, 258, 259–260, 303n.6
  open, 38–39, 41, 299, 300–301, 302
  phonological and syntactic, 243
  scene-analysis, 299–300, 301, 302
  as specialized perception examples, 242
  for visual depth perception, 418
Module, phonetic (phonetic mode), 29–31, 241–242, 293, 419, 423, 442
  and acoustic-optic convergence, 249–250, 257
  and articulatory gestures, 29–30, 256, 272
  and auditory module, 243
  as closed, 39, 40
  and conventional view, 436
  and duplex perception, 248–249, 258, 278–279, 293–297, 301, 385, 420
  and evolution, 29–30, 47
  and formant trajectories, 38
  function of, 297–299
  and gestural strategy, 273–275
  as heteromorphic, 275–279
  as linguistic module, 257, 258, 259–260, 303n.6
  and motor theory, 35, 235, 237, 238, 241–242
  and non-speech module, 250
  and perception-production link, 243
  precedence of, 423, 427
  as preemptive, 301–302, 424–425 (*see also* Preemptiveness)
  and scene analysis, 302–303
  and silence in perception of stop consonants, 399
  vs. speech as spelling, 272–273
  and speech/writing difference, 440
  in vertical view, 42
  and vocal-tract synthesizer, 256
Morse code, 204, 274, 298, 418
Motor commands, 218–219
Motor invariants, 27, 30. *See also* Articulatory gestures
Motor theory(ies), 237
Motor Theory, Early, 13–14, 18, 30, 185
  and categorical perception, 19, 21, 151
  and context-conditioned variability, 33
  and perception-production link, 254
  and prelinguistic infants, 27
  and revised theory, 237
  and speech-code article, 201
Motor Theory, Revised, 30–31, 237–238, 240–241
  and articulatory gesture, 34

vs. auditory theories, 239–240
and coarticulation, 238–239
and "direct perception," 255–256
experimental evidence for, 244–252
and invariant phonetic gesture, 252–254
and motor invariants, 30–31
parts of, 244
and perception-production link, 254–255, 259–260
and phonetic module, 35, 235, 237, 238, 241–242 (*see also* Module, phonetic)
and modularity, 256–259
and specialized nature of speech perception, 241–243
and stimulus equivalence, 36
and variability, 33
and vertical view, 26
and voicing distinction, 23

Nasal consonants. *See also* Consonant(s)
acoustic cues for, 99, 100, 138
context-sensitive transitions as cues for, 247
and formant transitions, 16, 76, 84–87, 89, 189, 191, 192, 209
and locus, 137
and place of articulation, 86
and resonance, 191
and silent interval, 190–191
Nasality, and Delattre, 11–12
Naval Medical Research Laboratory, 6
Noise control, discrimination of, 177–180, 181
Noise cues, 210, 211, 247
Nonspeech perception, acoustic features in, 206
Nonspeech sounds
and categorical perception, 404
and duplex perception, 248–249, 252, 294–297, 385–387, 390, 405 (*see also* Duplex perception)
and phoneme discrimination experiments, 164, 168
in reading-machine test, 5
in [r-l] discrimination study, 312, 315–317, 319, 321–323
and sensitivity to speech, 251–252
and silence in stop-consonant perception (experiment), 328, 329–331, 332, 333–334
vs. speech, 250, 254–255, 257–258, 279–280, 281–282
Nottebohm, Fernando, 26
Nye, Patrick, 25

"Octopus" synthesizer, 187
Oddity test, 378
Optical information, integrated with phonetic percept. *See* McGurk effect

Optophone, 4, 5
Oscillogram, 52, 187
Owl
bimodal sensitivity of, 249
and sound location, 271, 276

Parallel processing or transmission, 207, 216–217, 223, 298
Parity, 31–32, 298–299, 437, 440
Parsimony, and speech perception as special, 37
Pattern conversion, intersensory, 49–54
Patterning, auditory, 7–8
Pattern perception, 11, 47
and spectrogram, 47
Pattern playback, 2, 8–11, 49–54, 59, 62–63, 74n.8, 77, 101
and Delattre, 12
as experimental tool, 57
and phonetic structure, 38
spectrogram from, 50, 51, 59, 60, 77, 91, 101
in transition-tempo experiment, 187
vs. Voback, 128, 130
and voicing distinction, 22–23
PCM (Pulse Code Modulation) system, 327–328, 353, 359
Perceiving modules, biologically specialized, 242
Perception
categorical, 18–22
preoccupation with, 185
Perception of speech. *See* Speech perception
Perceptual equivalence, 36, 351–352, 372. *See also* Trading relations
Perceptual integration. *See* Integration
Phi phenomenon, 11
Phoneme(s), 164n.1, 224n.1
and acoustic unit, 13
and categorization, 153
communication of through speech vs. writing, 204–205
and consonant cues, 191
definition of, 140–141
in dyads, 135
experimental separation of, 15
parallel processing of, 223 (*see also* Parallel processing or transmission)
perception of, 12–13, 212–215, 220–223
and phonetic pronunciation, 135
prerecorded, 7
and segmentation problem, 134, 203
vs. sound, 203
and sound alphabet, 204
and transition, 136
unencoded, 212, 213, 225n.12
Phoneme boundaries, 118, 134
and articulatory adjustments, 251

Phoneme boundaries (cont.)
  and auditory theory, 240
  in cross-language [r-l] study, 314–315
  disappearance of, 207
  discrimination across, 153–164, 165–168, 195, 212 (see also Discrimination)
  in silent interval experiment, 168–180
  in perceptual-equivalence experiment, 379, 380
  and subphonemic features, 219
Phoneme segmentation, 207, 211. See also Segmentation
Phonetic gesture. See Articulatory gestures
Phonetic module or mode. See Module, phonetic
Phonetic perception or percept
  vs. acoustic patterns, 237
  and horizontal assumption, 20
  and speech quality, 14
Phonetic rules, synthesis by, 135–138
Phonetics, universal, 284
Phonetic specialization, 32
Phonetic structure
  integration into, 38
  precognitive apprehension of, 20
  for production and perception, 285, 298
  segmentation of, 15
Phonetic transcription, 245
Phonological awareness, 42, 442
Phonological communication, 185
  development of, 28–31, 47
Phonological specialization, and dyslexics, 443
Phonology
  function of, 297–298
  requirements of, 32–34
Physiology, and vertical vs. horizontal view, 26
Place of articulation (production)
  and consonant categorization, 86, 100, 109–110n.2, 110n.3, 191–192
  and duration of silence, 371
  and formant transitions, 392
    second-formant transition, 15–16, 138, 189, 206
    third-formant transition, 189, 210
  as restricted, 283
  and second-formant locus, 89–90, 94
  and silence in consonant-stop perception, 325
Place error, 124
Place rule, 145
Playback. See Pattern playback
Positional variations, and synthesis by rule, 139–140
Position modifier, 145
Preemptiveness, 281–282, 301, 424–425
Preliterate children, 42. See also Infants
Prerecorded elements, synthesis from, 134–135, 145–146

Projectional maps, 299
Proprioceptive return, and speech perception, 72
Proprioceptive stimuli, 193, 196
Psycholinguistics, 20
  and categorical perception, 21
Pulse Code Modulation (PCM) system, 328, 353, 359

Rabid-rapid distinction, in silent-interval experiment, 168–176
"Ramps," 251, 411
Rate of articulation
  and boundaries, 34–35
  and coarticulation, 246
  in integration experiment, 352–365
  and optical information, 276
  and second-formant transition, 94
Rate of production, as communication requirement, 32–33
Rate of speech
  and phoneme distinctiveness, 216
  and sound alphabet, 204
  and speech perception, 273
  and unconventional view, 438–439
Reading, vs. listening (speech perception), 41–43, 201, 204–205, 431, 433–435, 437–438, 440, 442, 443–444
Reading disability. See Dyslexia
Reading instruction, 431, 441
  whole-language theory of, 440–441
Reading machine for the blind, 2, 8, 25–26, 47
  and auditory discriminability, 3–7
  and auditory patterning, 7–8
  and context-conditioned variability, 13
  and horizontal view of speech, 3, 43
  sound alphabets for, 204
  as synthesized-speech application, 134
Reading rate, and learnability of nonspeech signals, 5–6
Recognition machines, 3–4
Reflection spectrograms, 50, 51
Resolving power of ear, 6–7, 204, 216, 223, 439, 440
Revised Motor Theory. See Motor Theory, Revised
Rubin, Hyla, 27
Rubin, Philip, 31

Saltzman, Elliot, 31
Scene analysis, auditory, 293, 297, 299–300, 302
Script, 434–435
  alphabetic, 42, 201
Second formant, and context experiment, 12–13
Second-formant locus(i), 82, 89–90, 112, 207–209

of /b/, /d/, and /g/, 208
of voiced stop consonants, 91–95
Second-formant transition, 15, 16, 75, 89–90, 205
  and acoustic locus, 89–90, 93–95
  and consonants, 99, 189, 205, 206, 209
    b and *d*, 137
    d and *g*, 194
    d locus, 208
    nasals, 16, 76, 84–87, 89, 189, 191, 209
    stops, 75–76, 77–83, 189, 209, 244, 403
    voiced stops, 78, 79, 89–90, 112, 113–118, 206
  and discriminability, 19, 154
  for liquids, 209
  and parallel processing, 223
  for semivowels, 96, 209
  and tempo, 100–104, 105–106, 107–109
  and third formant, 111, 112, 113–114
Segmentation, 33, 245–247
  of acoustic vs. phonetic structure, 15
  of EMG records, 219
  and phonetic structure vs. signal, 273
  problem of, 134, 207, 211
Semivowels
  context-sensitive transitions as cues for, 247
  and second-formant transition, 96, 209
  vs. stop, 18
  and transition tempo, 100–104
Sentence, and speech specialization, 286
Serial processing, 281–282
Shankweiler, Donald, 27, 42
Silent interval, 96, 145, 352
  and auditory interaction, 247–248
  in consonant perception, 190
  as discrimination cue (experiment), 168–180
  in integration experiment, 352–365
  and manner of production, 325–348, 371–382
  and [sta] vs. [sa], 247
  and stop consonants, 190, 325, 346–348, 371–382
    and duplex perception, 385, 387–399, 405
    as necessary condition, 325–336
    and one vocal tract vs. two, 342–346, 348
    in perception of [d], 93–94
    as sufficient condition, 336–342, 346
  and voicing, 371
Similarity, acquired, 18–19, 151, 153, 163, 167, 178, 180, 196
Sinusoids, 38, 40, 279, 301, 425–427
Slow articulation, 211
Sound alphabet, 203–204
Sound localization. *See* Auditory (sound) localization
Sound spectrograph, 8–9, 49, 54. *See also* Spectrograms

Spectral cues, temporal cues as equivalent to, 373–382
Spectrograms, 8–9, 10, 11, 47, 187
  and aspiration, 121
  and /d/, 190, 206
  as difficult to read, 47, 214–215, 225n.15, 434
  and pattern playback, 49–54, 59, 60, 77, 91, 101 (*see also* Pattern playback)
  reflection spectrograms, 50, 51
  of speech and nonspeech stimuli, 312
  of stop consonants plus vowels, 75, 76
  of synthesized speech, 133
  transmission spectrograms, 50, 51
  of unvoiced stop consonants, 61
  and vocal cord vibration, 121
Speech
  acoustic substitutes for, 43
  and evolution, 1, 28–31, 47, 435
  and language, 2
  and phonological communication, 185
  and psycholinguistics, 20
  vs. reading/writing, 41–43, 201, 204–205, 431, 433–435, 437–438, 440, 442, 443–444
  views of
    conventional, 435–438, 440, 441, 442, 443
    horizontal, 2–3, 26 (*see also* Horizontal view of speech)
    unconventional, 438–440, 441–443
    vertical, 2–3, 26–28 (*see also* Vertical view of speech)
Speech code, 201, 203
  and alphabet, 203–205
  and cue-phoneme restructuring, 205–212
  decoding, 220–223
  encoding in production, 215–220
  and perception of restructured phonemes, 212–215
Speech decoder, 201, 214, 224, 227n.25
Speech mode, 201, 213–214, 257
  and cross-language [r-l] study, 316
Speech perception
  and acoustic cues, 187–193 (*see also* Acoustic cue(s))
  and articulatory movements, 193–197
  isolation of, 244
  plus optical signals, 36–37, 249–250, 257, 275–277, 441
  and acoustic surface, 237
  and articulated utterance, 255 (*see also* Articulatory gestures)
  auditory theories of, 239–240, 250–251 (*see also* Auditory theory)
  categorical perception in, 18–22, 151, 201, 212–213, 317, 418 (*see also* Categorical perception)

Speech perception (cont.)
  of consonants, 110n.3, 188–191 (see also Consonant(s))
    affricates, 188 (see also Affricates)
    fricatives, 188–189, 247 (see also Fricatives)
    liquids, 190–191, 311–323 (see also Liquids; individual consonants)
    nasals, 76, 84–87, 190 (see also Nasal consonants; individual consonants)
    stops, 59, 61–74, 75, 77–83, 188–190, 213, 325, 403–404 (see also Stop consonants; Voiced stops; Voiceless (unvoiced) stops; individual consonants)
  conventional view on, 436
  as decoding, 204, 213, 215, 220–223
  duplex perception in, 423–425 (see also Duplex perception)
  Early Motor Theory on, 201 (see also Motor Theory, Early)
  efficiency of, 223–224
  as interpretation of acoustic signal, 250
  listener decision making in, 367–368
  by machine and by eye, 214–215
  and motor theory, 241–243, 259 (see also Motor Theory, Revised)
  as nonspecific (conventional view), 271–272
  and nonspeech noise, 250, 254–255, 257–258, 279–280, 281–282 (see also Nonspeech sounds)
  as proprioceptive return, 70
  psychologists' view of, 220
  and question of whose vocal tract, 342, 348
  and sound vs. perceived phoneme, 203
  as specialized system, 37–41, 241–243, 271, 272, 439–440
    and generative detection, 279–281
    and gestural strategy, 273–275
    and heteromorphy, 275–279
    and perception-production commonality, 273, 282–286
    and phonetic module (mode), 29–31, 241–242, 293, 297–299, 419, 423, 442 (see also Module, phonetic)
    and preemptiveness, 281–282, 301, 424–425
    and speech-as-spelling alternative, 272–273
    and syntax, 286
  and speech production, 221–223, 282–286
    and articulatory gestures, 336
    and auditory view, 404
    and integration experiment, 353
    and motor theory, 238
    origin of link, 254–255, 347–348
    and phonetic module, 243, 259–260, 298
    and speaker intent, 367
    and specialization, 273, 282–286

Speech production. See also Articulatory gestures
  and Early Motor Theory, 14, 201
  model for, 217–218
  rate of, 32–33 (see also Rate of speech)
  as specialized, 273
  and speech perception, 221–223, 282–286 (see also Speech perception)
  stages in, 216
  subphoneme elements in, 215–217
  and theoretical reconsiderations, 201
  vs. writing, 41–43, 201, 205, 431
Speech quality, and phonetic information, 14
Speech signal, dynamic aspects of, 15–16
Speech synthesis, 244. See also Synthesis of speech by rule; Synthetic speech
Spelling, and speech, 272–273
Standard feature dimensions, independence in perception of, 15
Stereopsis, comparison with phonetic module, 40–41, 275
Stimulus equivalence, 36
Stimulus-response tradition, 2, 18
Stop consonants. See also Consonant(s)
  coarticulated with preceding liquid, 412
  in consonant classification, 188
  in cross-language study, 309
  cues for
    context-sensitive transitions as, 247
    noises as, 210, 247
    perceptual equivalence of, 371–382
  duplex perceptions of, 387–399
  formant transitions for, 16, 75–76, 77–83, 403–404, 418
  and transition tempo, 100–104
  hub of, 97n.6
  and left-hemisphere processing, 310
  and locus, 137
  perception of, 59, 61–74, 75, 77–83, 188–190, 213, 325, 403–404
  production of, 283, 284
  and "ramps," 251
  and second-formant transitions, 75–76, 77–83, 189, 209, 244, 403
  vs. semivowels, 18
  and silence, 325, 346–348
    and duplex perception, 399
    as necessary condition, 325–336
    and one vocal tract vs. two, 342–346, 348
    as sufficient condition, 336–342, 346
  third-formant locus for, 96
  and third-formant transitions, 403
    duplex perception experiment on, 405–418, 419–420
  voiced and voiceless, 22–23 (see also Voiced-voiceless (voicing) distinction)
"Streaming," 11

Stress
  and speech perception, 222
  and synthesis by rule, 141–142
Studdert-Kennedy, Michael, 26
Subphonemic features, 215–216
  and phoneme boundary, 219
Subphonemic rules, synthesis by, 138–139, 143
Suga, Nobuo, 26
Summerfield, Quentin, 376
Syllabic encoding, and synthesis by rule, 142–143
Syllabic organization, 218
Syllable(s)
  and acoustic patterns, 220
  as acoustic unit, 13
  and loci (first-, second- and third-formant), 137
Syntax
  and acoustic signals, 38
  module for, 303
  and phonetic representations, 30
  and speech perception, 286
Synthesis of speech by rule, 24–25, 133–134, 146–147
  and complexity vs. number of rules, 143–144
  example of ("labs"), 144–145
  and phoneme disagreements, 140–141
  by phonemic rules, 135–138
  and positional variations, 139–140
  from prerecorded elements, 134–135, 145–146
  and silence, 325
  and stress, 141–142
  by subphonic rule, 138–139, 143
  and syllabic encoding, 142–143
Synthesizer, speech production-perception system as, 285
Synthetic speech, 258, 279
  cue-element combination in, 193
  and experiment on silence and stop consonants, 331, 334, 335
  perception of as speech, 347
  and phonetic structure, 38
  in transition-tempo experiment, 103

Tempo of frequency change. See Transition tempo
Temporal cues, spectral cues as equivalent to, 373–382
Temporal integration, of cues, 365–368. See also Integration
Temporal resolving power, of ear, 6–7, 204, 216, 223, 439, 440
Third-formant locus, 96–97, 117
Third-formant transition, 83, 96, 111, 210
  and consonant distinctions, 189

in duplex-perception experiments, 385–387
  on stop consonants, 405–418, 419–420
  "isolated," 278
  and nasal consonants, 191
  problems in experimenting with, 111–112
  and [r] vs. [l], 310, 385–386
  and stop consonants, 403, 405–418, 419–420
  and voiced stops, 22, 111, 112–119
Tongue backing, 237
Tongue tip, articulatory gestures of, 283, 284, 310
Trading relations, 15, 351–352, 356, 357, 358, 362, 369n.3
  influence of results on, 28
  and learning, 366
  and perceptual equivalence experiment, 371, 372, 373, 374–375, 378, 381, 382
Transcription, phonetic, 245
Transition tempo
  and distinction between *b* and *w*, 104–109
  and distinctions among stop consonants, semivowels, and vowels of changing color, 100–104
Transitions. See Formant transitions
Transmission spectrograms, 50, 51
Tuning, of speech perceiving mechanism, 347
Turvey, Michael, 27
"typical," pattern appropriate for, 142

Unit, acoustic, as syllable vs. phone, 13
Universal phonetics, 284
Unvoiced stop consonants. See Voiceless (unvoiced) stops

Variability (variation), context-conditioned. See Context-conditioned variations
Velar consonants, 189
Vertical view of speech, 2–3
  and evolution, 28, 29–30
  and experiments, 307
  vs. horizontal, 201
  and human vs. nonhuman communication, 32
  and integration of acoustic with optical information, 37
  modality assumption of, 14
  movement toward, 26–28
  and parity, 31–32
  and rate of production, 33
  and reading/writing vs. speaking/listening, 431
  and speech perception as special, 38
  and stimulus information, 34
  and writing/reading vs. speech, 42–43
Virtual locus, 145
Visual transforms of speech, 214
Voback, 23, 128, 130

Vocal cord vibration, 121, 132n.1
Vocal-tract synthesizer, 256
Voice bar, 80–81, 86–87, 99, 121
  and voiced-voiceless distinction, 121, 123, 124
Voiced stops. *See also* Stop consonants
  acoustic cues for, 99, 100, 138
  first-formant loci of, 92, 95–96
  first-formant transitions of, 16, 78, 80, 92, 113, 206
  and place of articulation, 86
  production of, 61
  second-formant loci of, 91–95
  second-formant transitions for, 78, 79, 89–90, 112, 113–118, 206
  and third-formant transitions, 22, 111, 112–119
Voiced-voiceless (voicing) distinction, 22–24
  acoustic cues for, 99
  auditory theory on, 240
  cross-language study on, 309
  and cue-phoneme relation, 210
  and duration of silence, 371
  and first-formant cutback, 121–127, 128, 129–131
  and first-formant onset, 23
  and motor theory, 242
  and noise in transitions, 121, 123, 127–131
  and silence in consonant-stop perception, 325, 336
  and vocal cord vibration, 121, 132n.1
Voiceless (unvoiced) stops. *See also* Stop consonants
  acoustic cues for, 99, 100, 138
  experiment on, 12
  perception of, 59, 61–74
    and bursts of noise, 75, 188
    first-formant transitions in, 16, 80
    second-formant transitions in, 77, 78, 79, 89
  and place of articulation, 86
  production of, 61
  and synthesizer, 23
  types of confusion over, 67
Voice-onset-time (VOT), 24, 248
Voicing, and transitions, 16
Voicing distinction. *See* Voiced-voiceless (voicing) distinction
Voicing rule, 145
Vowel color, and second-formant loci, 90
Vowels
  acoustic cues for, 211
  back, 67, 68, 69, 90
  of changing color (and transition tempo), 100–104
  context-sensitive transitions as cues for, 247
  in cross-language study, 309
  front, 67, 68, 69, 90
  mid-vowels, 90
  rapidly articulated, 213, 214
  and steady state, 136, 213, 214
  in transition experiments, 77, 78, 82
  in unvoiced-stop-consonant study, 63–64, 66, 74n.14

Whole language theory, 440–441
Writing
  alphabetic, 41
  cursive, 33
  vs. speech, 41–43, 201, 205, 431, 433–435, 437–438, 440, 442, 443–444
"Wuhzi" (language), 5